The Cambridge Companion to the United States Constitution

This Companion provides a broad, historically informed introduction to the study of the U.S. constitutional system. In place of the usual laundry list of constitutional clauses and doctrines, it presents a picture of the constitutional system in action, with separate sections devoted to constitutional principles, organizational structures, and the various legal and extra-legal "actions" through which litigators and average citizens have attempted to bring about constitutional change. Finally, the volume covers a number of subjects that are rarely discussed in works aimed at a general audience, but which are critical to ensuring that constitutional rights are honored in the day-to-day lives of citizens. These include standing and causes of action, suits against officeholders, and the inner workings of the Foreign Intelligence Surveillance Court (FISC). This Companion places present-day constitutional controversies in historical context, and offers insights from a range of disciplines, including history, political science, and law.

Karen Orren is Distinguished Professor of Political Science at UCLA. Her previous books with Cambridge University Press include *Belated Feudalism* and *The Search for American Political Development*, with Stephen Skowronek. Her most recent book, also with Stephen Skowronek, is *The Policy State*.

John W. Compton is Associate Professor of Political Science at Chapman University. He is the author of *The Evangelical Origins of the Living Constitution*.

The Cambridge Companion to the United States Constitution

Edited by

KAREN ORREN
University of California Los Angeles

JOHN W. COMPTON
Chapman University, Orange California

CAMBRIDGE
UNIVERSITY PRESS

CAMBRIDGE
UNIVERSITY PRESS

University Printing House, Cambridge CB2 8BS, United Kingdom

One Liberty Plaza, 20th Floor, New York, NY 10006, USA

477 Williamstown Road, Port Melbourne, VIC 3207, Australia

314-321, 3rd Floor, Plot 3, Splendor Forum, Jasola District Centre, New Delhi - 110025, India

79 Anson Road, #06-04/06, Singapore 079906

Cambridge University Press is part of the University of Cambridge.

It furthers the University's mission by disseminating knowledge in the pursuit of education, learning and research at the highest international levels of excellence.

www.cambridge.org
Information on this title: www.cambridge.org/9781107094666
DOI: 10.1017/9781316148488

© Cambridge University Press 2018

First published 2018

A catalogue record for this publication is available from the British Library

Library of Congress Cataloging in Publication data
NAMES: Orren, Karen, editor. | Compton, John W., 1977- editor.
TITLE: The Cambridge companion to the United States Constitution / edited by Karen Orren, University of California, Los Angeles; John Compton, Chapman University, Orange California.
DESCRIPTION: Cambridge [UK] ; New York : Cambridge University Press, [2017] | Includes bibliographical references and index.
IDENTIFIERS: LCCN 2017030492 | ISBN 9781107094666 (alk. paper)
SUBJECTS: LCSH: Constitutional law – United States. | United States. Constitution.
CLASSIFICATION: LCC KF4550 .C36 2017 | DDC 342.7302–dc23
LC record available at https://lccn.loc.gov/2017030492

ISBN 978-1-107-09466-6 Hardback
ISBN 978-1-107-47662-2 Paperback

Contents

Contributors

Tomiko Brown-Nagin is Daniel P. S. Paul Professor of Constitutional Law and Professor of History at Harvard University.

Michael G. Collins is Joseph M. Hartfield Professor of Law at the University of Virginia School of Law.

John W. Compton is Associate Professor of Political Science at Chapman University.

Barry Cushman is John P. Murphy Foundation Professor of Law at the University of Notre Dame Law School.

Donald A. Dripps is Warren Distinguished Professor of Law at the University of San Diego School of Law.

Mark A. Graber is University System of Maryland Regents Professor at the University of Maryland Francis King Carey School of Law.

John I. Hanley is Lecturer in Political Science at the University of Central Florida.

Gary Jeffrey Jacobsohn is H. Malcolm Macdonald Professor in Constitutional and Comparative Law at the University of Texas at Austin.

Andrew Kent is Professor of Law at Fordham University School of Law.

Orin S. Kerr is Fred C. Stevenson Research Professor of Law at George Washington University Law School.

Ken I. Kersch is Professor of Political Science at Boston College.

Julian Davis Mortenson is Professor of Law at the University of Michigan Law School.

Karen Orren is Distinguished Professor of Political Science at the University of California, Los Angeles.

James E. Pfander is Owen L. Coon Professor of Law at Northwestern University Pitzker School of Law.

Andrew Rehfeld is Associate Professor of Political Science at Washington University in St. Louis.

Edward L. Rubin is University Professor of Law and Political Science at Vanderbilt University.

Howard Schweber is Professor of Political Science at the University of Wisconsin.

Gordon Silverstein is Assistant Dean for Graduate Programs at Yale Law School.

Amanda L. Tyler is Professor of Law at Berkeley School of Law, University of California.

Ann Woolhandler is William Minor Lile Professor of Law at the University of Virginia School of Law.

Acknowledgments

The editors thank Robert Dreesen of Cambridge University Press for initiating this project, and Dean Patrick Fuery of Chapman University and the UCLA Academic Senate for funding its preparation. A slightly different version of Professor Orin Kerr's essay, "Balancing Privacy and National Security: A Rule of Lenity for National Security Surveillance Law," appeared in *Virginia Law Review* 100 (2014).

Introduction

Karen Orren and John W. Compton

The essays that comprise this volume are written at a time when respected commentators across the ideological spectrum depict the condition of the US Constitution in terms of opprobrium falling somewhere between deviant and dysfunctional.[1] Ours is a period of political and institutional unease, when rules and rights long taken for granted are in fierce dispute, often under constitutional auspices, and when the accustomed means of resolution are themselves under serious questioning. Any reader's companion to the Constitution today should take these circumstances into account. Accordingly, in these introductory remarks we will stifle all impulses toward reassurance and instead offer a guide for situating the insights of the essays within what we perceive to have been an essential and ongoing problematic of American constitutionalism over time.

Our approach to understanding the Constitution normalizes today's constitutional disputes within a pattern of incongruent elements that has characterized American fundamental law from its beginnings. The approach consists of two essential steps. The first is to conceive of the Constitution's original character as a historical halfway station: halfway between monarchy and democracy, halfway between judicial sovereignty and legislative sovereignty, halfway between prescribed rights and "natural" rights, halfway between jurisprudence and politics, halfway in other respects that we will discuss as we proceed. Variously, over several constitutional crises in American history, one of the halves mentioned can be seen to push and pull against its opposite. These oppositions complicate the project inherent in all constitutions, which is adaptation to changing circumstances. To the degree that words written down more than two centuries ago serve as constant reference and touchstone

---

[1] In a growing literature see, on "deviant," Philip Hamburger, *Is Administrative Law Unlawful?* (Chicago: University of Chicago Press, 2014); and on "dysfunctional," Sanford Levinson, *Framed: America's Fifty-One Constitutions and the Crisis of Governance* (New York: Oxford University Press, 2012).

for every move on every side, they carry this deep unsettlement forward into the present.

The second step in our approach involves taking into account certain implications of the precise moment in English history when the Constitution was framed. This goes beyond the truism that every enterprise, constitutional or otherwise, is limited by the vistas imaginable by its creators. In the case at hand, the effects are concretely lodged in the massive historical fact that every American state in the original republic formally received into its own law the common law and statutes of England as of some specified date, usually the time of the colony's settlement, as its own; only provisions considered on their face to be "repugnant" in this country – for instance, those on the royal succession or on the Anglican church – were excluded from this reception. Except for Louisiana, all subsequent states and territories followed suit, expressly, through constitutions or in legislation; likewise, after initial controversy, so did the federal government.[2] By this means, the new American governments grafted onto themselves the fruits of English political history, including both national rules and individual rights that were established to that point.

Notice that we are not talking here about influences but about *legal provision*, already up and running or soon to be implemented. The founders themselves accomplished their handiwork atop an immense grid of prior institutional experience, one that would serve to demarcate channels of future discord. From then forward, American judges would argue whether a given right had "vested" with ratification of the Constitution or if a particular substantive or procedural question was the subject of Parliamentary legislation at the date of reception specified and therefore did or did not qualify as a legitimate – that is to say constitutional – subject for American legislation, state or federal. To recognize this inheritance is in no way to discount the spirit of genius and creativity that permeated events in Philadelphia in 1787. Nor does it lessen the significance of the momentous proposals and compromises fashioned there. But it does help explain certain otherwise quizzical features: how, for instance, the constitutional text could be so short and how it could have been expected that such diverse states would fit smoothly into a single union.

Following its own civil war and revolution, English government was by the eighteenth century partly, but by no means completely, extricated from its premodern past. The authority of the King was greatly diminished and the prerogative courts through which he had governed all but destroyed. Religious and commercial affairs, as well as ultimate control of governmental

---

[2] Elizabeth Gaspar Brown, *British Statutes in American Law, 1887–1836* (Ann Arbor, MI: University of Michigan Law School, 1964). Eleven states had provisions at the time of the framing. Rhode Island followed in 1798, Connecticut in 1818. On the federal law, see Morris L. Cohen, "The Common Law in the American Legal System, the Challenge of Conceptual Research," *Law Library Journal* 81 (1989): 13.

offices, had passed into the jurisdiction of Parliament, to be ruled from now on by statutes. Individual protections like freedom from censorship and search and seizure without warrant had been added to rights claimed by ancient patrimony. The totality was administered by the several courts of common law, in which, after the Act of Settlement of 1701, judges could for the first time make their decisions independently of the crown's will. At this same juncture, common law in the colonies became, if anything, an even more central institution than in Great Britain. At American independence, common law courts would constitute the most important local institutions of colonial government.[3]

From their disparate beginnings, the colonies' legal systems converged to rely on English rules, English lawbooks, and English-trained judges, both to punish crimes and to regulate civil matters ranging from land sales to education. An ocean away, and therefore untainted by memories of intrigue and bloody reprisals associated with their English counterparts, common law courts enjoyed great respect and incurred none of the hostility visited on the Admiralty courts from the middle of the eighteenth century, though both systems were staffed by Americans. Moreover, common law proceedings included the jury trial, widely regarded by contemporaries as the quintessence of colonial democracy. Importantly, this broad development appears not to have been imposed by English governors but to have proceeded indigenously.[4] Lawyers were in the forefront of the revolutionary struggle. All of these circumstances supported the significant role eventually assigned the judicial branch of government under the Constitution.

As we will see, the inheritance of English law has anchored, defined, and motivated American constitutional law throughout its history. The procedural provisions received then continue to guide in important ways virtually every decision issued by an American court. The substantive provisions, on the other hand, have had the greatest bearing on constitutional change. It has become something of a commonplace today that the participants at Philadelphia were all white men and that the Constitution they wrote would require amending before their exclusive position in public affairs would be successfully challenged. What is perhaps less understood is how their superior status was hardwired into the Constitution by way of Article III. William Blackstone described the "private relations" of English law as master and servant, husband and wife, parent and child, guardian and ward; in the United States, James Kent would add the variation of domestic slavery. The eradication of these relations, both the rules they countenanced and the hierarchies they expressed, would become the central challenge of constitutional politics for the next two hundred years. It continues into our own time.

---

[3] William E. Nelson, *The Common Law in Colonial America*, Vol. III, The Chesapeake and New England, 1660–1750 (Oxford: Oxford University Press, 2016), 132–33.

[4] William B. Stoebuck, "The Reception of English Common Law in the American Colonies," *William and Mary Law Review* 10 (1968): 393.

The essays in this volume employ no single chronological grid. Yet those that make demarcations in time repeatedly show them in correspondence to this historical project. Diverse conflicts and disruptions cause constitutional strain, including, as we will see, in foreign affairs. Still, it is striking how on every plane – principles, structures, actions – major turning points referenced are the removal of slavery at the end of the civil war; the battle to end master-and-servant law in the "Lochner era" and the coming of the New Deal; the ongoing offensive against the effects of Jim Crow, starting with the Warren Court. Today's openly politicized judiciary features at center stage the demise of traditional family relations and, with this step, unprecedented discord among jurists and scholars over what a Constitution "is" and what its existing words might legitimately command.

The progression to constitutional free fall, that is, to a politically chosen realm without firm rules rooted in the past, exhibits two genealogies. Each stems from the Constitution's "halfway" beginnings. Both of them are typified in the canonical writings of William Blackstone. Blackstone famously depicted English law as a feudal castle, but he set it down in a landscape of natural rights. All evidence indicates that the framers lived comfortably in both places. In Jefferson's correspondence we read how, for instance, when the author of "life, liberty, and the pursuit of happiness" was tasked with the job of purging English residues from the laws of his own state, he backed off, doing no more than "omitting the expired, the repealed and the obsolete." To act otherwise, he thought, would, "from the imperfection of human language and its inability to express distinctly every shade of idea ... involve us for ages in litigation and render property uncertain ...."[5] English common law and statutes prior to 1607 and all English law in colonial usage were retained by the Virginia legislature.

Jefferson's ease in such matters was impossible for his successors, many of whom found elements of the English inheritance intolerable. Their eventual dissolution by events caused a continuing division in constitutional thought that persists until today. On the one side are what we might call the "Extra-foundationists." These anticipate what will be discarded with interpretive add-ons: in the 1850s, "higher law"; in the 1930s, "legal realism"; in the 1950s, "evolving standards of decency"; in the 1970s, "representational reinforcement"; in the 2000s, "popular constitutionalism."[6] On the other side, those we might

---

[5] Paul Lester Ford, ed. *Autobiography of Thomas Jefferson 1740–1793, Together with a Summary of the Chief Events in Jefferson's Life* (New York: G. P. Putnam & Sons, 1914), 66–67.

[6] A few illustrative Extra-foundationist works are Robert M. Cover, *Justice Accused: Antislavery and the Judicial Process* (New Haven: Yale University Press, 1975); Morton J. Horowitz, *The Transformation of American Law, 1870–1960: The Crisis of Legal Orthodoxy* (New York: Oxford University Press, 1992); Alexander M. Bickel, *The Least Dangerous Branch: The Supreme Court at the Bar of Politics* (Indianapolis: Bobbs-Merrill, 1962); John Hart Ely, *Democracy and Distrust: A Theory of Judicial Review* (Cambridge, MA: Harvard University Press, 1980); Larry M. Kramer, *The People Themselves: Popular Constitutionalism and Judicial Review* (New York: Oxford University Press, 2004).

deem "Foundationists" cleave to the original constitutional package. The common lawyers and formalists of history, when what remains of the past is largely the document itself, they become advocates for the constitutional text; after decades of staring into the abyss – *Brown* v. *Board, Engel* v. *Vitale, Roe* v. *Wade* – they become "originalists," in the difficult position of proceeding as if momentous social transformations never happened or did not touch on the framers' core assumptions.[7]

The following essays take no side in this debate. Written independently of these introductory remarks, each offers its own analysis and evaluation of the constitutional topics it surveys. What we propose in light of the foregoing is to convey beforehand how their subjects operate and change together in response to a common set of historical tensions. The essays are arranged in three categories: principles, structures, and actions. We will discuss each in turn, elaborating as we go the historical perspective of a Constitution "halfway."

---

[7] Illustrative works in the Foundationist vein include Robert Bork, *The Tempting of America: The Political Seduction of the Law* (New York: Free Press, 1990); Antonin Scalia, *A Matter of Interpretation: Federal Courts and the Law* (Princeton: Princeton University Press, 1998); Michael W. McConnell, "Originalism and the Desegregation Decisions," *Virginia Law Review* 81 (1995): 947–1140; Randy E. Barnett, *Restoring the Lost Constitution: The Presumption of Liberty* (Princeton: Princeton University Press, 2004).

PART I

PRINCIPLES

The US Constitution was drafted at a time when the conceptual architecture of what is today called liberal constitutionalism was largely in place. Still, institutions inherited from the premodern past retained considerable authority, both morally and legally. The ideas that dominated public discourse in this period were, likewise, awash in tensions. Their unsettled nature is evident in the writings of the political theorists believed to have had the greatest influence on the framers. Montesquieu, for example, was largely responsible for popularizing the emblematic liberal idea that constitutional design, the particular arrangement of governing institutions, was critical to the preservation of liberty. Yet he was equally committed to the classical conviction that no republic, no matter how well designed, was likely to survive the absence of a virtuous citizenry. Those who shaped the founding era's understanding of rights were similarly caught between two worlds. John Locke, Frances Hutcheson, and Thomas Reid all embedded their political ideas within broader religious or natural law frameworks that softened their radical implications. Locke made the case for human government by consent; yet he also "encumbered the freedom of individuals at every turn" with moral obligations derived from natural law.[1] Similarly, Hutcheson, Reid, and the Scottish common sense realists appealed to an inborn sense of right and wrong as consolation to those who, even at this early date, perceived in the argument for human equality a threat to the social fabric.

Taking account of this wider intellectual milieu, it is not surprising that prominent members of the founding generation saw no contradiction in combining expansive statements of principle with textual provisions supporting inherited and illiberal authority. Consider, for example, the principle expressed in the famous opening section of the Declaration of Independence: "[A]ll men are created equal." Although the word "equality" does not appear in the original text of the Constitution, writers of the era never tired of describing the United States as

---

[1] James T. Kloppenberg, "The Virtues of Liberalism: Christianity, Republicanism, and Ethics in Early American Political Discourse," *The Journal of American History* 74 (1987): 9–33, 16.

the only nation on earth where no man held social or political superiority over his neighbors. And not without justification: by the 1780s, Americans had abolished primogeniture, forbidden titles of nobility, and extended the suffrage far beyond the mother country. Yet in countless ways, American society remained rigidly hierarchical. Over a half-million persons in the labor force were African slaves. The suffrage, though broad relatively speaking, excluded slaves, women, "servants, apprentices, short-term tenants, minors, and sons over twenty-one still living at home with their parents."[2] The reception of English common law, discussed previously, ensured that most Americans for the foreseeable future would remain locked in legal relations of subordination, reinforced in important ways by the new Constitution.[3]

Similar contradictions adhered to the principle of popular sovereignty. That the framers believed that legitimate political authority derived from the people themselves is suggested not only by their placing "We the people" in the Constitution's Preamble but also by their reliance on popularly elected conventions to ratify the document. Fulfilling Madison's promise that American government would answer not to "the rich, more than the poor; ... the learned, more than the ignorant; ... the haughty heirs of distinguished names, more than the humble sons of obscurity and unpropitious fortune," the new national legislature was made more popularly accountable than Parliament.[4] To ensure against England's "rotten boroughs," the convention mandated that congressmen reside in the districts they represented, with seats reapportioned every ten years. Yet the framers also believed that the popular will required "refining" before it could provide a suitable basis for lawmaking. This distrust was registered in the creation of a Senate whose members were chosen by state legislatures and a President elected through an elaborate process in which the people played only an indirect role.

Also in an ambivalent state were ideas concerning individual liberties. Although several framers felt a list of constitutionally guaranteed civil liberties was unnecessary, the ten amendments eventually submitted to the Congress and the states for approval in 1789 endorsed all those achieved by the English to that point. But here again timing was important. In England, freedom of speech meant the absence of censorship, not freedom from arrest for publishing matters considered offensive after the fact. In America, words against the Christian religion or established social mores were punished with particular severity.[5] And although the First Amendment barred Congress from establishing a

---

[2] Gordon S. Wood, *The Radicalism of the American Revolution* (New York: Vintage, 2011), 56.
[3] The fugitive slave clause, for example, authorized the forced recapture of individuals "bound to service" in another state, and Article I left the authority to define the extent of the suffrage almost entirely in the hands of the states where, in many cases, strict property qualifications remained firmly in place.
[4] James Madison, *Federalist* 57. http://avalon.law.yale.edu/18th_century/fed57.asp.
[5] See John Compton's chapter ("Civil Liberties and the Dual Legacy of the Founding") in this volume.

national church, it left the states free to follow the English model in matters of religion; at the time the Amendment was ratified, five of the thirteen had religious establishments.

It perhaps goes without saying that ideas in the young nation were anything but static. Through a series of profound social and political changes, many of the inherited institutions described came to appear glaringly out of place with principles that had launched the nation's constitutional experiment. By the 1830s, the advent of universal white male suffrage, coupled with mass-based parties and a partisan press, threatened to transform the framers' elite-led republicanism into something resembling Madison's prediction. By the 1840s, significant numbers of Americans had concluded that slavery – or its expansion beyond its original boundaries – was incompatible with the nation's founding commitment to natural equality. As the path of social development diverged increasingly from what the framers envisioned, Americans, perhaps uniquely, were forced at every major turn of events to consider which principles were so fundamental as to bind the present generation.

One prominent constitutional interpreter who wrestled repeatedly with these questions was Abraham Lincoln. In his most original meditation on the subject, penned in the tumultuous weeks before his first inauguration, Lincoln drew on the biblical Book of Proverbs. The Constitution and its principles, he said, were like a "picture of silver," whose purpose was to "frame" or "preserve" a still deeper principle, the "apple of gold," namely, the equality proclaimed in the Declaration. It was in the name of equal liberty for all persons that "our fathers" began the Revolution, Lincoln wrote, and it was with the aim of institutionalizing this principle that they authored the Constitution. If Americans remained loyal to the Constitution in the present, it was because they sensed that "in back of" the formal trappings, "entwining ... closely about the human heart," lay that which gave "hope to all." A sectional compromise that renounced equality would amount to a renunciation of the Constitution itself. "The *picture* was made *for* the apple – *not* the apple for the picture."[6]

Lincoln never incorporated the passage into a public address or other published work. That he chose to abandon this line of reasoning – or at least this way of presenting his argument – may be because the metaphor tended to highlight the very problem he was trying to resolve. To suggest that the Constitution was designed to "preserve" the principle of equality was to draw attention to a "frame" that, if not entirely comfortable with slavery, could at least include its perpetuation as an acceptable price to pay for the blessings of Union. As the essays in this section make clear, a similarly divided position shapes American constitutional thinking in the present. Agreeing that legitimacy rests on principles in "back of" the formal document – equality, individual liberty, popular sovereignty, the rule of

---

[6] Abraham Lincoln, "Fragment on the Constitution and the Union," in Roy P. Basler, ed., *The Collected Works of Abraham Lincoln*, Vol. 4 (New Brunswick, NJ: Rutgers University Press, 1953), 168–69.

law – judges, elected officials, and commentators alike have increasingly come to interpret them in ways more aligned with contemporary conceptions than those of the late eighteenth century. Yet the original "picture," far from fading, remains remarkably vibrant, limiting avenues of reform and providing high ground to defenders of the status quo. The difficulty of reconciling new doctrines with governing structures inherited from a very different epoch has meant that even the most celebrated reforms remain surprisingly precarious.

In his essay "A Lighter Touch: American Constitutional Principles in Comparative Perspective," Gary Jacobsohn suggests another way of underscoring the "half-way" position of the Constitution's principles, namely, to consider the extent to which the course of constitutional development in the United States has diverged from that of other liberal democracies. Jacobsohn observes that among the many nations that have equality as a core constitutional principle, the commitment of the USA seems strikingly half-hearted. German and Indian courts, for example, have ruled that constitutional guarantees concerning equality are effectively unamendable, thereby establishing their supremacy among protected values. American courts, in contrast, have often limited the penetration of equality into the polity in the name of preserving other Founding-era principles like federalism, liberty, and the sanctity of the private sphere. The irony here, Jacobsohn argues, is that the ideals that gave rise to the American constitutional system have had their greatest impact in countries where constitutional designers have felt free to build on the American model while simultaneously severing it from its original social moorings.

Other essays in this section examine the evolution of constitutional principles over time, paying particular attention to the relationship between specific ideals and the "picture" in which they are embedded. In "Due Process: A Unified Understanding," Donald Dripps explores the contentious history of "due process of law." Originating in Magna Carta and incorporated into the US Constitution with the Fifth (and later Fourteenth) Amendment, due process arrived freighted with the legal baggage of five and half centuries, effectively freezing in place the rights and legal procedures of English law to that point. At the same time, the principle of due process has given American constitutionalism an abstract "higher law" standard for the evaluation of specific legislative acts. From its common law beginnings due process was understood, for instance, to prohibit laws that worked a naked transfer of property from A to B and made a man judge in his own case. The end result, as Dripps shows, has been a principled constitutional provision that over the course of American history has proven equally useful to radical reformers and defenders of the status quo. Depending on the relative weight afforded precedent versus higher law, this protean idea has been authoritatively interpreted as prohibiting and protecting institutions from slavery and coverture to abortion and same-sex marriage.

In contrast to due process, civil liberties guarantees generated relatively little controversy until the twentieth century. As John Compton points out in "Civil Liberties and the Dual Legacy of the Founding," this was because most nineteenth-century judges and commentators agreed these provisions were not to be interpreted in ways that conflicted with Protestant beliefs or inherited common law prerogatives. This consensus lasted exactly as long as the personal relations it presupposed. As these gave way, interpreters repeatedly felt the strain between, on the one hand, expansively worded guarantees and, on the other, entrenched forms of illiberal authority. At the most abstract level, Compton argues, the response of the Supreme Court was to subordinate the latter to the former, treating civil liberties as the "fixed star" around which constitutional system as a whole revolves. Yet agreement on normative foundations capable of filling the void left by the collapse of the common law framework has proved elusive. Detached from their original moorings, civil liberties have become, in Compton's words, ideological weapons, "capable of challeng[ing] or buttress[ing] almost any form of authority, whether public or private, national or local, old or new."

In "Political Representation and the US Constitution," Andrew Rehfeld shifts the focus to popular sovereignty and democratic representation, principles that were clearly incorporated into the original structure, albeit in an ethically compromised manner. Rehfeld observes that one of the Convention's most radical innovations was a lower house in which the object of representation would be "the people" themselves as opposed to political subunits like states, counties, and towns. And yet, for reasons both principled and pragmatic, the framers sharply limited the people's influence over their own specially designated chamber. To guard against the influence of faction, they authorized unusually large legislative districts, thus ruling out the possibility of meaningful contact between representatives and average voters; to appease Southern states, they counted three-fifths of the slave population for the purpose of allocating House seats. Finally, they left the critical matters of defining the electorate and drawing legislative districts almost entirely in the hands of the state legislatures. The resulting ungainly system bequeathed to future generations a host of internal tensions that have only become more pronounced over time.

Finally, Ken Kersch returns the focus to the "golden apple" of equality, if only to reject the whiggish view that constitutional development in this area has consisted of the slow but inexorable advance of a single, true conception. Rather, in his reading, the principle of equality has been continuously refined to accommodate pressures on entrenched patterns of authority. Here Kersch emphasizes that the American polity will, at any given moment, consist of "a multiplicity of equality configurations," with authority in different sectors organized along different – but always professedly principled – lines. The story of constitutional development with respect to equality, then, becomes the story of how particular time- and space-bound meanings are constructed, legitimated, dismantled, and reconstructed, always in the name of the nation's "bedrock, creedal commitment to liberty, equality, and justice under law."

nineteenth-century judges and commentators agreed that these prohibitions were not to be interpreted in ways that conflicted with the certain beliefs ... imported common law for the ... province. This conception lasted security as long as the personal character ... presupposes ... these gave way, interpreters at least with the small ... on the one hand, expansively wielded guarantees and, on the other, ... terms of difficult ... at ... most abstract level. Governors ... the re-issue of the Supreme Court was to subordinate the laws ... to the formal mechanisms it liberated as the "fixed ones" around which the constitutional system as a whole revolves. The approach ... an ... rative foundations capable of lifting the total left to the surface of the common law framework has acquired. Detached from ... of legal meanings, civil liberties have become in Company's words, individual weapons, "capable of challenging or defeat ... almost ... nature ... whether public or private, national or local...."

In ... "Political Rights, structure, and the US Constitution," "Amar or Refilled ... live the frenzy in popular sovereignty and democratic ... conversation, principles that were to be impervious ... can the natural structure came, albeit in ... ethically comprehensible channel, ... all otherwise, that some of the Convention's pen ... what innovation was a ... recorded in ... that the object of representation was ... to "the people" themselves as opposed to political abstracts like states, counties, and towns. And yet, for reasons both principled and pragmatic, the framers should imbue the people's citizens over their own specific designated character. To guard against the influence of faction they ... authorized, federally, large legislative districts ... that minimal coercive, resulting of meaningful contact between representatives and ... over-the-counter to impress Southern states, they counted three-fifths of the slave population for the purpose of allocating ... seats. Finally, they left the critical matters of defining the electorate ... determining legislative districts almost entirely in the hands of the state legislatures. The resulting ... makeup text ... that its future an exclusive ... not of ... natural resources that have only become these pronounced ... time.

Finally, Ken Karst ... mines the recent ... the "judicial appeal" of equality, "a value to date ... the whole ... constitutional development in this area has operated of the only ... the reasonable power of a simple, clear conception. Karst in his reading the principle of equality has been continuously relied to accommodate pressures on ... of authority. Here Karst emphasizes that American polity with an eye toward ... it consists of "a multiplicity of equality ... configurations," with authority in different sectors organized along different ... but bluntly, professedly pluralist views. The sum of constitutional ... development lends respect to equality ... then becomes the source of ... there passes at times ... space bound measures are constructed, regulated, dismantled, ... reconstructed, always in the name of the nation's ... character, a creedal commitment to liberty, equality, and ... under law."...

I

A Lighter Touch: American Constitutional Principles in Comparative Perspective

Gary Jeffrey Jacobsohn

The United States is perhaps the most frequently cited example of a nation constituted by its constitution. "The U.S. Constitution functions as something more than a binding legal instrument. As often observed, it has taken on over time something of the character of a civic religion – in the sense that commitment to the Constitution is a central, indeed constitutive, element of national identity."[1] For many of those embracing this commonly held view the Constitution's centrality in the development of American national identity is predicated on its incorporation of foundational political principles whose scope transcends the boundaries of time and place. "[M]ore than most people," wrote Martin Diamond, "we tend to consider the relationship between ethics and politics in universal terms."[2] This relationship received its most eloquent articulation in the person of Abraham Lincoln, who famously maintained that "I have never had a feeling politically that did not spring from the sentiments embodied in the Declaration of Independence."[3] These words were spoken just prior to Lincoln's ascendance to the presidency and at the place where the Constitution had been composed. What followed, of course, was the tragic and climactic testament to the fact that many people did not share in those sentiments. Or to the extent that they did, they were understood so divergently that the directive force of these principles on subsequent constitutional development was only lightly felt.[4]

---

[1] Vicki C. Jackson, *Constitutional Engagement in a Transnational Era* (New York: Oxford University Press, 2010), 104. Or as Bruce Ackerman has written, "[O]ur constitutional narrative constitutes us as a people." Bruce Ackerman, *We the People: Foundations* (Cambridge, MA: Harvard University Press, 1991), 36.

[2] Martin Diamond, "Ethics and Politics: The American Way," in Robert H. Horwitz, ed., *The Moral Foundations of the American Republic* (Charlottesville: University of Virginia Press, 1977), 39.

[3] Roy Basler, ed., *The Collected Works of Abraham Lincoln*, Vol. 4 (New Brunswick, NJ: Rutgers University Press, 1953), 240.

[4] Applicable here is Rogers Smith's "multiple traditions" thesis, which holds that "American political actors have always promoted civic ideologies that blend liberal, democratic republican,

In this essay I conclude that a comparative national assessment of constitutional principles reveals a less decisive constitutive significance in the American case than is widely assumed. Consistent with this assumption one might think, for example, that the following declaration comes from the pages of the *U.S. Reports*, but the source is a landmark German Constitutional Court decision, often referred to as that nation's *Marbury* v. *Madison*. "There are constitutional principles that are so fundamental and to such an extent an expression of a law that precedes even the constitution that they also bind the framers of the constitution."[5] The comparison with *Marbury* is apt inasmuch as the Federal Constitutional Court (FCC) for the first time in its history exercised its power of judicial review to invalidate a law of the national legislature, but it went considerably beyond what its American counterpart had done by claiming the additional authority to invalidate a constitutional amendment on substantive grounds. In itself this greater willingness to assert judicial dominance over the higher lawmaking power may not be an indication of substantial national differences in the role played by principles in constitutional practice; thus to this day the FCC has not struck down a constitutional revision, even as it has continued to maintain that the "core of the Basic Law is exempt from amendment."[6] Elsewhere – India is the main additional example I will discuss – constitutional amendments *have* been invalidated; while very significant this too does not independently signal a contrast of comparative consequence. Still, what I will argue is that the jurisprudential underpinnings of the commitment to exercise judicial power in this way present us with an important starting point for a comparative depiction of constitutional principles as playing a less prominent role in American political life than its familiar depiction in the "Constitution as constitutive of the nation" story.

The argument proceeds as follows. I use the German and Indian cases in the first section briefly to contrast the increasingly widespread practice of judicial invocation of implicit and explicit substantive limits to formal constitutional change with its absence in the American constitutional experience. The German and Indian examples are themselves distinguishable from each other, in that the constitution of the former, like that of the United States, contains certain entrenched provisions that are designated unamendable, whereas in India the substantive constraints on the amendment process are only those that emerge from the activity of judicial interpretation. Yet it is the willingness of the courts in these two foreign polities to defend identity-defining principles against the higher lawmaking power of the state that sets them apart from the American

---

and inegalitarian ascriptive elements in various combinations designed to be politically popular." Rogers Smith, *Civic Ideals: Conflicting Visions of Citizenship in U.S. History* (New Haven: Yale University Press, 1997), 6.

[5] *Southwest Case*, 1BVerfGE14 (1951), S4c. D, par. 2 (quoting from the statement of the Bavarian Supreme Court).

[6] *Maastricht Treaty Case*, 89 BVerfGE 155 (1993), Sec. B, par. 5.

aversion to do the same. Again, this contrast can readily be understood in a way that does not implicate the constitutive role of principles; for example, as an expression of the relative difficulty of amending the document in the United States as compared to these other places. Nothing in such an explanation, however, requires that we abandon a supplementary account in which both the relatively equivocal commitment to foundational principles – as well as the nature of those principles – possesses explanatory value in illuminating the American case.

As with so much in the unfolding drama of constitutionalism in the United States, the omnipresence of the slavery issue is hugely significant. In this connection I argue that the compromised circumstance of the American constitutional launching is critical for assessing the character and subsequent application of principles. Here it is noteworthy that one of the two unamendable provisions in the American document concerns the slave trade and the other involves Senate representation, which, if it did not originate as a concession to slave interests, in time came to serve them.[7] The contrast with the objects that are protected against amendment in Germany and India could not be more striking, much of the substance of which concerns constitutional commitments to human dignity and freedom. Whether textually provided as in Germany or judicially constructed as in India, they betray a more acquiescent jurisprudential orientation than is evident in the United States toward the invocation of defining principles of constitutional identity.

The essay's second section explores the comparative timidity of constitutional actors in deploying political principles to defend the idea of republican governance. The early landmark Supreme Court case of *Luther* v. *Borden*, which had no direct connection to the slavery issue, is illustrative of a phenomenon that represents a recurring theme in the essay. There are instances, such as in *Luther* and *Barron* v. *Baltimore* (to be discussed in the following section) where critical decisions are made that have the effect of setting limits on the potential scope and impact of constitutional principles while ostensibly advancing basic regime features such as liberalism and federalism. Although these decisions are about other things, a full account of them cannot avoid their significance for the tortured subject of race. Accordingly, a major theme in this essay is that comparative reflection on the expressive importance of American constitutional principles must consider the ways in which the founding contradictions concerning that subject, in tandem with broader commitments to liberalism and federalism, have functioned to resist the imposition of what in Germany has come to be known as "an objective order of values" and in India as a mandated set of constitutional essentials grouped under the rubric of "basic structure."

---

[7] As Vicki C. Jackson points out, "The fact that the constitutional rule for the Senate reflected a compromise meant that it did not stand for a broader constitutional principle." Jackson, *Constitutional Engagement in a Transnational Era*, 228.

The relative pervasiveness of constitutional principles is specifically taken up in the third section. The question of whether the rights and principles embedded in the Bill of Rights are applicable to the states was first resolved in 1833 by Chief Justice John Marshall and later restored for vigorous debate by the ambiguous terms of the Fourteenth Amendment. There are arguments on both sides of the debate that appeal to eminently reasonable principles that are commonly associated with constitutional democracy. Some say that if rights are important enough to bind the national government, then there is no good reason to accept their limited applicability to other levels of government. If in one nation constitutional rights are applied uniformly and in another they are incompletely enforced, then it is logical to conclude that the principles have more constitutive weight in the first polity than in the second. To this it might be said that the willingness to embrace more diversity within the different parts of the system actually reveals a strong commitment to principles of federalism that advance the end of democratic politics and innovation. In this account limiting the reach of certain principles does not in itself diminish the power of principles in providing definitional meaning to the nation. But what if the deference to locality is historically associated with deference to the unprincipled politics of racial discrimination?

While the incorporation controversy is a uniquely American debate, the other contestable uniformity/consistency issue emerging from the adoption of the post-War amendments is ubiquitous in comparative constitutional experience. Does the reach of constitutional principles extend beyond the public domain to order relationships and conduct in the strictly private sphere? Here again the issue of race in the United States looms large in assessing the constitutive significance of a reserved application of principles. Consider that the only explicit mention of slavery in the American Constitution appears in the amendment that makes its continued practice illegal. The Thirteenth Amendment, however, has another feature that sets it apart from other provisions, in particular the two that follow it: the wrong that is affirmed in its language must be terminated regardless of the source of the targeted injustice. Slavery "shall [not] exist within the United States" reads very differently than do the amendments that make the denial of equality, due process, and the franchise constitutional encroachments only when the state is responsible for violating a person's rights. A comparative perspective on the limited reach of the American Constitution – its "vertical" as opposed to "horizontal" application – enables us to appreciate this characteristic liberal feature of American constitutionalism as more than a choice of one theory of government over another but as a further manifestation of the less conspicuous way in which, relative to some other places, constitutional principles function in the United States. The German model is in this regard most strikingly different, as the "radiating" effect of certain "objective values" indirectly governs the arena of private-law disputes, with results similar to their direct application to the domain of state action.

Nothing in what follows is meant to suggest that we should begin anew the account of constitutional principles as critical to an understanding of American self-understanding. Rather, my aim is to gain some comparative perspective on the role such principles play in this process, thus providing a more tempered and realistic assessment. If indeed my consideration of unamendable amendments, republican guarantees, and limits on the reach of judicially enforceable entitlements suggests a lighter touch in the constitutive meaning of American constitutional principles, the most we can say is that the validity of such a finding is established only within the framework of a very limited comparison of specifically selected regimes. This may be sufficient to conclude that the United States is not the paradigmatic case of a nation constituted by its constitution; it is certainly insufficient to conclude that its constitution is unimportant in that regard or that it does not in this connection outrank most constitutions.

OBJECTIVE AND SUBJECTIVE COHERENCE

In 1776 two new state constitutions – New Jersey's and Delaware's – included provisions explicitly limiting the amendment power. These constitutions prohibited amendments involving important matters: for example, in New Jersey, the non-establishment of churches and the provision for trial by jury; in Delaware, the bans on slave importation and the establishment of a specific religious sect.[8] No new ground was broken, therefore, when eleven years later the document framed in Philadelphia also included two provisions that were textually designated immune from subsequent constitutional revision. Yet it is fair to say that what was prohibited in Article V from being amended – abolition of the slave trade until 1808 and equal suffrage in the Senate – were more the result of practical compromise than of a determination to entrench core principles of constitutional identity.[9]

That there are such core principles is commonly viewed as certain, although the early lack of agreement on what they were makes their absence as entrenched principles in the Constitution unsurprising. While the Supreme Court has not embraced the idea of implicit substantive limits, others with allegiance to principles that they comprehend as so vital to American national identity as to require their enforced immutability have argued for the Court's authority to declare

---

[8] Yaniv Roznai, "Unconstitutional Constitutional Amendments – The Migration and Success of a Constitutional Idea," *The American Journal of Comparative Law* 61 (2013): 657, 662.

[9] Or as Melissa Schwartzberg has argued, "This was [done] not on the grounds of moral or rational certainty, but on the grounds that without these self-interested provisions, the entire constitutional project would fail." Melissa Schwartzberg, *Democracy and Legal Change* (Cambridge: Cambridge University Press, 2007), 151. Schwartzberg, however, is skeptical that failure would have resulted from the noninclusion of the entrenched provisions. Her skepticism supports her general opposition to constitutional entrenchment of any kind. "In disabling amendment we may protect the reprehensible, instead of simply securing the precious." Ibid.

a constitutional amendment unconstitutional. John Rawls, for example, believed that adopting a principle-repudiating amendment – one, say, reversing the First Amendment – would be tantamount to "constitutional breakdown, or revolution in the proper sense, and not a valid amendment of the Constitution."[10] What is more, "The successful practice of its ideas and principles over two centuries places restrictions on what can now count as an amendment, whatever was true at the beginning."[11] In this he was following in the tradition of Lincoln, who famously said in his First Inaugural: "This country belongs to the people who inhabit it. Whenever they should grow weary of the existing government, they can exercise their CONSTITUTIONAL right of amending it, or their REVOLUTIONARY right to dismember or overthrow it."[12]

Tellingly, however, Lincoln's comment appears in the same paragraph as his mention of having no objection to the adoption of the so-called Corwin Amendment, which would have prohibited any amendment extending to Congress the power to abolish or interfere with slavery within any state.[13] In light of how events unfolded we can only speculate whether, had it been ratified, this extraordinary concession to slave interests would have led to a serious effort to establish its unconstitutionality; thus one can imagine an argument predicated on Lincoln's own logic, according to which the pro-slavery thrust of the amendment was so palpably offensive to the Constitution's underlying commitment to human freedom that it constituted a revolutionary act rather than one suitable for the amendment process. For someone like Lincoln, whose sentiments about the Constitution's meaning sprung from ideas "embodied in the Declaration of Independence," such reasoning hardly seems strained.[14] On the other hand, as noted by Mark Brandon, it is by no means clear that the amendment was indeed revolutionary. "[I]n order for an amendment to render the text incoherent, it would have to be a stark departure from a widely accepted meaning of the text to which it is attached. The Corwin Amendment was not such a radical departure."[15]

---

[10] John Rawls, *Political Liberalism* (New York: Columbia University Press, 1993), 239.
[11] Ibid.   [12] Abraham Lincoln, *First Inaugural Address*.
[13] As Mark Brandon has noted, "Lincoln may have understood the amendment to protect slavery only where it then existed, but the amendment's plain words do not suggest such a limitation." Mark Brandon, "The 'Original' Thirteenth Amendment and the Limits to Formal Constitutional Change," in Sanford Levinson, ed., *Responding to Imperfection: The Theory and Practice of Constitutional Amendment* (Princeton: Princeton University Press, 1995), 219.
[14] As Don E. Fehrenbacher has written, "Mainstream abolitionists were ... disposed to consider the Constitution proslavery in certain details but antislavery in underlying purpose and ultimate potential." Don E. Fehrenbacher, "Slavery, the Framers, and the Living Constitution," in Robert A. Goldwin and Art Kaufman, eds., *Slavery and Its Consequences* (Washington: AEI Press, 1988), 5. Assuming Lincoln to have been of this mindset, the Corwin Amendment could not easily have been reconciled with such purpose and potential.
[15] Brandon, "The 'Original' Thirteenth Amendment and the Limits to Formal Constitutional Change," 235. Consider in this regard Luther Martin's reflections in 1787 on the Declaration and the Constitution. "That *slavery* is *inconsistent* with the *genius of republicanism, and has a*

Lincoln of course was concerned with heading off the revolutionary act of secession, but to appreciate the vexed nature of constitutional principles in the American experience with substantive limits to constitutional change, consider these views of one whose understanding of those principles was decidedly different from Lincoln's. In his *Discourse on the Constitution and Government of the United States*, John C. Calhoun wrote: "[I]f it transcends the limits of the amending power, – be inconsistent with the character of the Constitution and the ends for which it was established, – or with the nature of the system ... [i]n such case, the State is not bound to acquiesce. It may choose whether it will, or whether it will not secede from the Union ...."[16] Calhoun does not detail what the Supreme Court would be authorized to do "if a power should be inserted by the amending power, which would radically change the character of the Constitution,"[17] but given the legitimacy that such a development would confer upon the much more extreme act of secession, one can easily imagine that while remaining wary of an extraordinary exercise of national power, for him the lesser act would also be justified.

A radical change in "the character of the Constitution" presumes that such a character exists, in which case, as Rawls suggested, a transgressive amendment could portend "constitutional breakdown" or "revolution in the proper sense." This might be the only point of agreement between Rawls and Calhoun, both of whom subjectively ascribe to the Constitution a coherent meaning or identity whose violation could validly trigger a response that embodies the derivative presumption that this sort of challenge to constitutional particularity is illegitimate. If these bedfellows are not strange enough, we might add both the abolitionists like Lysander Spooner, who subscribed to *The Unconstitutionality of Slavery*,[18] and their Garrisonian adversaries who saw the Constitution as an unambiguously hellish pro-slavery document. The first, as will be discussed in the next section, advocated for the Guarantee Clause as a club to be used against states whose slavery institutions were a glaring repudiation of the Constitution's commitment to republican principles; and the second advanced its own version of secession under the banner of "No Union With Slaveholders." What all of these examples have in common is a rendering of the Constitution as the embodiment of a unified vision, the supreme importance of which justifies an extraordinary response to actions that would, for better or worse, effectively render that vision incoherent. Calhoun and Spooner (and more famously

---

tendency to destroy those *principles* on which it is *supported*, as it *lessons the sense* of the *equal rights of mankind*, and habituates us to *tyranny* and *oppression*." Luther Martin, "The Constitution and Slavery," in Justin Buckley Dyer, ed., *American Soul: The Contested Legacy of the Declaration of Independence* (Lanham: Rowman & Littlefield, 2012), 47.

[16] John C. Calhoun, *Disquisition on Government: And, a Discourse on the Constitution and Government of the United States* (Ithaca: Cornell University Press, 2009), 300.

[17] Ibid., 301.

[18] Lysander Spooner, *The Unconstitutionality of Slavery* (Portland: Gregorivs Publishing, 2010).

Frederick Douglass[19]) as well as Garrison (Rawls is a more complicated case) saw in the exercise of constituent power that formed the Constitution the instantiation of a principled commitment to pursue noble ends (Calhoun, Spooner, Douglass) or evil ones (Garrison). Their particular and very subjective perspectives on these principles dictated whether they were prepared to attribute sacrosanct status to this original expression of constituent power. However divergently they viewed this expression, their general level of agreement that a discernible and clear constitutional identity was manifest in the document embodying it, led each to accept the conceptual possibility that has never been embraced by the Supreme Court, that there could be an unconstitutional constitutional amendment.

The approach of the Court's German counterpart is revealingly different. Thus there is no comparable statement in American constitutional jurisprudence to this assertion by the FCC: "Article 79, para. 3 of the GG [Grundgesetz] links the development of the State in Germany to that core of the constitutional order which it itself describes, and thus seeks to secure the prevailing constitution against any development which endeavors to establish a new constitution ...."[20] While the United States is often cited as the paradigmatic instance of a nation constituted by its constitution, it is the German document that is arguably the better example of this phenomenon.[21] To be sure, national identity is not necessarily coterminous with constitutional identity. So where a constitution is designed to function in effect as a subversive instrument seeking transformation of an entrenched social order central to the nation's identity, care must be taken not to mistake one identity for the other. India and South Africa are examples of transformative constitutions whose success or failure can be measured by their ability to facilitate the restructuring of their respective societies. Hence progress in these places is marked by the degree of achieved

[19] "In that instrument [the Constitution] I hold there is neither warrant, license, nor sanction of the hateful thing [slavery]; but interpreted, as it ought to be interpreted, the Constitution is a GLORIOUS LIBERTY DOCUMENT ... [T]ake the Constitution according to its plain reading, and I defy the presentation of a single pro-slavery clause in it. On the other hand, it will be found to contain principles and purposes, entirely hostile to the existence of slavery." Frederick Douglass, "Fourth of July Oration," in Herbert J. Storing, ed., *What Country Have I?* (New York: St. Martin's Press, 1970), 37, 38.

[20] *Maastricht Treaty Case*, at Sec. B, par. 5.

[21] Not everyone would agree. Michel Rosenfeld is correct to see in the German model of constitutional identity a strong negation of the past and a commitment to endow the constitutional order with a new content. But I disagree with him in saying: "Constitutional identity ... is much more central to national identity in the United States model than in the ... German model. In short, in the German model, the constitution is supposed to provide the means for giving expression to an existing national identity ...." As much as the new German constitutional order seeks to establish an "ethnocentric democracy," to see this effort as affirming an existing national identity may obscure its more radical intent. Michel Rosenfeld, "The European Treaty-Constitution and Constitutional Identity: A View from America," *International Journal of Constitutional Law* 3 (2005): 316, 323.

convergence between national and constitutional identities; in theory maximum success would mean they had become indistinguishable. There is a transformative aspect to the German constitution as well, but it is the specific document itself that embodies the requisite change, in the sense that its creation signals the moment when Germany acquired its new identity.[22] "To a great extent," according to Juliane Kokott, "the national identity of post-war Germany is founded on and shaped by the Constitution ... [R]espect for the Constitution is indispensable and has to be ensured to prevent even the appearance of a relapse to the past."[23]

As astutely expressed by another German constitutional theorist, Ulrich Preuss, this indispensability illuminates the unconstitutional amendment issue. "[N]o constitution can contain rules which allow its abolishment altogether; this would permit revolution, whereas it is the very meaning of constitutions to avoid revolutions; and to make them dispensable."[24] But if constitutions do not explicitly contain rules for their own eradication, most do not provide insurance against the possibility of this happening. Germany is the most notable exception; its eternity clauses are, in Preuss's terms, intended to render revolutions dispensable. Its document is structured to prevent a transformation of such principled magnitude that its constitutional identity would become something very different from what it is. Or as Kokott's formulation would have it, an arrangement of this type is essential in order to preclude any possibility that the substance of German national identity would be permitted to look anything like it did before the constitutional revolution that culminated in the Basic Law.

Ironically, it is the constitutional theorist most prominently linked to the earlier discredited totalitarian regime who developed the ideas deemed essential for preventing this catastrophic reversion to the past. On the occasions when the FCC has declared its rationale for holding amendments subject to substantive limitations in the existing document, its reasoning is clearly traceable to the theorizing of Carl Schmitt, who insisted on the distinction between "constitutional change" and "constitutional annihilation."[25] "The boundaries of the authority

---

[22] Fritz Stern's illuminating memoir, *Five Germanys I Have Known* (New York: Farrar, Straus & Giroux, 2006), is a wonderful meditation on the identity transitions in German history, poignantly capturing the significance of the post-War constitutional moment.

[23] Juliane Kokott, "Report on Germany," in Anne-Marie Slaughter, Alec Stone Sweet and J. H. H. Weiler, eds., *The European Court and National Courts – Doctrine and Jurisprudence: Legal Change in its Social Context* (Oxford: Hart, 1998), 77–131, 111.

[24] Ulrich K. Preuss, "Constitutional Powermaking for the New Polity: Some Deliberations on the Relations between Constituent Power and the New Constitution," in Michel Rosenfeld, ed., *Constitution, Identity, Difference, and Legitimacy* (Durham, NC: Duke University Press, 2004), 157.

[25] Carl Schmitt, *Constitutional Theory* (Durham, NC: Duke University Press, 2008), 151. As Ulrich Preuss points out, "Carl Schmitt was the pioneer of the intellectual movement that aimed to limit the power of the *Reichstag* ... Article 79, sec. 3 incorporated Schmitt's idea that certain core elements of the constitution should remain unamendable, even by super majorities in

for constitutional amendments result from the properly understood concept of constitutional change. The authority to 'amend the constitution' [must proceed] under the presupposition that the identity and continuity of the constitution as an entirety is preserved."[26] Elsewhere he contended that an amendment process functioning in total indifference to itself and its own system of legality was a testament to the blind subordination of substance to form that was the basis of modern constitutionalism, of which, of course, Weimar was exhibit A. In such a system, Schmitt wrote, "A purely formal concept of law, independent of all content, is conceivable and tolerable."[27] Echoes of Schmitt's boundary setting reverberate in the *Southwest Case* in the early days of the post-War constitutional regime: "A constitution has an inner unity, and the meaning of any one part is linked to that of other provisions. Taken as a unit, a constitution reflects certain overarching principles and fundamental decisions to which individual provisions of the Basic Law are subordinate."[28] As the Court elaborated nearly twenty years later, "even basic constitutional principles" may be modified by constitutional amendment, as long as this occurs in a "system-immanent manner."[29]

With this in mind we might speculate that had Calhoun's argument about "transcend[ing] the limits of the amending power" and not "radically chang[ing] the character of the Constitution" connected with an American analogue to what in Germany is held to be "an objective ordering of values," he might have enjoyed the same ultimate jurisprudential prominence as Schmitt. "[R]ather than being shattered by the Third Reich, the German belief in law over politics motivated a return to law as it originally and naturally was – a legal renaissance as a natural law renaissance."[30] But unlike the constitutional project of reconstructed Germany, no comparable development has occurred in the United States that extends to American constitutional principles an arrangement for their objective

---

both houses." Preuss, "Constitutional Powermaking for the New Polity," 438–39. Melissa Schwartzberg agrees that Schmitt could legitimately claim to be the father of entrenchment in Germany, but "less plausible" is that he was the source for making unamendable the clause on human dignity. Schwartzberg, *Democracy and Legal Change*, 173.

[26] Schmitt, *Constitutional Theory*, 150.

[27] Carl Schmitt, *Legality and Legitimacy* (Durham, NC: Duke University Press, 2004), 20.

[28] 1 BVerfGE 14, 32 (1951). Consider Justice Dieter Grimm's comment on the substance of these principles, around which there has developed a consensus as to their foundational value: "human dignity and the commitment to republicanism, democracy, rule of law, and the social state." Dieter Grimm, "The Basic Law at 60 – Identity and Change," *German Law Journal* 11 (2010): 33.

[29] 30 BVerfGE 1 (1970).

[30] Bernhard Schlink, "German Constitutional Culture in Transition," in Michel Rosenfeld, ed., *Constitutionalism, Identity, Difference, and Legitimacy: Theoretical Perspectives* (Durham, NC: Duke University Press, 1994), 210. According to Schlink, the framers of the Basic Law "considered fundamental rights as necessary, but not sufficient, conditions for a satisfactory ordering of social relations." Ibid., 211. Beyond such [subjective] rights there were "'objective principles,' [according to which] social relationships, as well as the relationship between state and society, are to be ordered." Ibid., 203. The comparative implications of this orientation will be pursued more fully in the third section.

ordering within a "system-immanent" document.[31] Calhoun of course believed in the fundamentality of the rights he held sacrosanct – of slaveholders, of states – yet given the objective constitutional incoherence that resulted from the tragic compromises of the founding, his commitments were of no enduring consequence and most assuredly not amenable to constitutional or judicial entrenchment. His views on the unconstitutional amendment are of only antiquarian interest, whereas Schmitt's similar views have survived the taint of their author's place in history to greatly influence the contours of modern German constitutionalism.

Indeed their influence extends well beyond Germany. Thus in two tumultuous decades in India – the sixties and seventies – Schmitt's understanding of immutable principles and the amendment process was refined by a German South Asia scholar, Dietrich Conrad, and injected into the local constitutional discourse, ultimately to shape the most distinctive feature of Indian constitutionalism.[32] This became evident in the 1973 case *Kesavananda Bharati v. State of Kerala*,[33] arguably India's most important constitutional decision. At the core of *Kesavananda* is the "basic structure" doctrine, according to which specific features of the Constitution are deemed sufficiently fundamental to the integrity of the constitutional project to warrant immunity from drastic alteration. Under the theory that *constitutional* change must not destroy what it modifies, the Court affirmed its institutional authority to invalidate any amendment whose adoption would, in its judgment, result in radical transformation of regime essentials. A subsequent judicial declaration made clear the underlying logic: "The Constitution is a precious heritage; therefore you cannot destroy its identity."[34]

The political and jurisprudential implications of this unenumerated power were substantial, easily making the counter-majoritarian difficulties of conventional judicial review pale in comparison. Armed with this doctrine, the contents of which would be determined over time, the Court in effect designated itself enforcer of constitutional entrenchment at its deepest level,

---

[31] Another way of putting this has been suggested by Ken Kersch, who, following Arendt Lijphart, conceptualizes the United States at the founding as a classic consociational order. Thus the initial bargain, in which there was a bracketing of deep moral disagreement, sacrificed a shared commitment to substantive principles as a price worth paying in the interest of stability. In a sense, then, the lack of principled coherence was a matter of constitutional design. Ken I. Kersch, "He'll Take His Stand," (review essay of Mark A. Graber, *Dred Scott and the Problem of Constitutional Evil*) *Constitutional Commentary* 24 (2007): 773, 777.

[32] Conrad, who chaired the law department of the South Asia Institute of the University of Heidelberg in Germany, visited India in 1965 to deliver a lecture on "Implied Limitations of the Amending Power." This work and additional articles written over the next decade were cited in the important Supreme Court cases affirming the authority of that Court to declare a constitutional amendment unconstitutional. See also Dietrich Conrad, "Constituent Power, Amendment and Basic Structure of the Constitution: A Critical Reconsideration," *Delhi Law Review* (1977–78).

[33] Kesavananda Bharati v. State of Kerala, A SC 1461 (FB) (1973).

[34] Minerva Mills, Ltd. v. Union of India, AIR 1980 SC 1789 (1980), 1798.

able henceforth to nullify the results of legislative rule-making even when such action expressed itself in the exalted form of the constituent power. Underlying the Court's theory is the presumption that Parliament's amending power is subordinate to the creative authority that first established the Constitution's basic features and structure. Simply put, the implicit substantive limits to the amending power are inscribed in constitutional provisions in whose contents are to be found an articulation of a discernible constitutional identity. As Bhikhu Parekh has observed, "There was an extensive debate ... in the Constituent Assembly, resulting in the Indian Constitution, which provides the clearest statement of the country's self-given identity."[35]

The same can be said about the debates in the Constitutional Convention of 1787. Indeed, imagining an indigenously generated identity that assumes lasting constitutive significance has a distinctly American ring to it, as when in a Fourth of July oration John Quincy Adams proclaimed, "A nation was born in a day."[36] America, he said, "spoke herself into existence as a nation,"[37] which for Adams, a stalwart abolitionist of the Constitution-as-antislavery school, doubtless meant that this document signified the *legal codification* into existence of the nation. What differentiates the work of the two exercises of constituent power, both of which – Indian and American – represent a principled break with British imperial power, is the former's more coherent post-independence ideational line of march. That Adams and Calhoun, for example, could have such different readings of the policy trajectory and implications of their Constitution's identity-instantiating principles is importantly revealing in this regard. It is also not surprising. As Rogers Smith notes, "[T]he framers sought compromise via silence and ambiguity. The Constitution could be interpreted as ... either sanctioning slavery in perpetuity or contemplating its eventual abolition, with equal citizenship for free blacks."[38]

To be sure, India is no exception to the disharmony that is ubiquitous in constitutional framing and practice. As I have argued elsewhere, conflicting and enduring understandings of the constitutional self in India have played off against one another since the time of the Constitution's adoption.[39] The tension between the ameliorative and communal strands within the constitutional filament has provided an element of ambiguity to the nation's constitutional identity. Still, the transformational ethos of Indian constitutionalism, embodied in its most visible textual expression – the Directive Principles of State Policy – is, quite literally, a principled constitutional directive quite unlike anything in the American

---

[35] Bhikhu Parekh, "The Constitution as a Statement of Indian Identity," in Rajeev Bhargava, ed., *Politics and Ethics of the Indian Constitution* (New Delhi: Oxford University Press, 2008), 46.

[36] John Quincy Adams, "American Principles," in Justin Buckley Dyer, ed., *American Soul: The Contested Legacy of the Declaration of Independence*, 31.

[37] Ibid., 32.   [38] Smith, *Civic Ideals*, 133.

[39] Gary Jeffrey Jacobsohn, *Constitutional Identity* (Cambridge, MA: Harvard University Press, 2010), 125–32.

experience. The provisions contained in this section are not enforceable by the judiciary, but as stated in Article 37, "the principles therein laid down are nevertheless fundamental in the governance of the country and it shall be the duty of the State to apply these principles in making laws." As has been noted with only slight exaggeration, these principles "constitute the soul, the very spirit of ... the Constitution. [They] are the epitomes of social policy whereupon the State has been enjoined to embark on the goals of distributive justice."[40] At best this clear injunction has been incompletely respected; yet as will be discussed in the next section, it has, in contrast with the United States, provided a severely principled constitutional foundation for the defense of republicanism.

CALHOUN'S REVENGE: DEFENDING REPUBLICAN PRINCIPLES

Unlike the constitutions of some countries – Germany among them – India's constitution does not identify republicanism as a regime principle to be sheltered from the prospect of being amended away.[41] It does, however, include a provision expressly modeled after the Guarantee Clause in the American Constitution, which is Article 356, establishing President's Rule. The language is not the same, but it incorporates a similar idea as Article IV's mandated assurance by the federal government of a republican form of government in the states, as is clear from what B. R. Ambedkar, the James Madison of India, said at the Indian Constituent Assembly: "When we say that the Constitution must be maintained in accordance with the provisions in the Constitution we mean what the American Constitution means, namely that the [republican] form of the constitution prescribed in this Constitution must be maintained."[42] And so, according to this emergency provision, the President of India is empowered to assume the functions of any state that has not been governed "in accordance with the provisions of [the] Constitution." Thus if there is a "failure of constitutional machinery," the central government may

---

[40] Sudesh Kumar Sharma, *Directive Principles and Fundamental Rights: Relationship and Policy Perspectives* (New Delhi: Deep & Deep Publications, 1990), 5. That the attainment of a democratic revolution was a major component in the vision animating many of the framers of the Constitution is undeniable and abundantly manifest in some key provisions in the document they cobbled together. Even as an unfulfilled aspiration it must be considered highly germane to any assessment of Indian constitutional identity; its fulfillment would remove any tentativeness from an assessment of its relevance. This is consistent with Pratap Bhanu Mehta's contention that "the constitution was a radical idea, without itself containing guarantees that the social transformation it promised would come about ...." Pratap Bhanu Mehta, *The Burden of Democracy* (New Delhi: Penguin Books, 2003), 56.

[41] For example, Article 139 of the Italian Constitution mandates: "The republican form of the State cannot be the subject of constitutional amendment."

[42] Constituent Assembly Debates 1949, 175. In the preceding sentence Ambedkar said: "I would like to draw ... attention to the article in the American Constitution, where the duty of the United States is definitely expressed to be to maintain the republican form of the Constitution."

dismiss an elected state government and rule in its place for a specified period of time.

This indeed is what famously happened after the most horrific episode of bloodletting in India since Partition.[43] Three state governments were dismissed for their role in the 1992 destruction of a mosque in northern India and the ugly communal violence that it precipitated. The Supreme Court's landmark ruling in the wake of the debacle and subsequent dismissals was framed within an explicitly articulated commitment to the protection of certain substantive principles – specifically concerning secularism – against assaults that threatened to undermine their privileged status within the constitutional order. What is more, the decision in *S. R. Bommai* v. *Union of India*, affirming principle-based state removals, was directly related to the politics of constitutional entrenchment. By linking the *basic structure* argument of *Kesavananda* to Article 356's requirement that the states adhere to republican principles, the Court effectively upheld the designation of threshold constitutional essentials as the predicate for their uniform compliance within a federal system. "We do not know how the Constitution can be amended so as to remove secularism from the basic structure of the Constitution. Nor do we know how the present Constitution can be replaced by another; it is enough for us to know that the Constitution does not provide for such a course – that it does not provide for its own demise."[44]

The Court's linkage of basic structure limitations on the amending process with Article 356 responses to failures of constitutional compliance in the states cast the Central Government as a proactive player in the explication and enforcement of the constitutional essentials of the Indian republic. The contrast between the American and Indian approaches in these matters is instructive in seeing how constitutional principles have left their political imprint within the two systems. In the face of substantive challenges to their legitimacy, elected governments in the United States are accorded substantially more deference than they receive in India. The very different histories of the two "guarantee" clauses arguably has much to do with the presence within their respective polities of alternative theories of Center–State relations, but the contrasting experience also mirrors crucial conceptual differences in the role of a constitution in establishing political and social priorities within the larger society. And once again the issue of slavery is critical to assessing the disparity.

In this regard, the leading student of the American clause concluded that Chief Justice Taney's opinion in *Luther* v. *Borden*, although pregnant with implications for the slavery issue, was surprisingly uninfluenced by considerations connected

---

[43] A Hindu mob's destruction of the Babri Masjid mosque in Ayodha was "the site of the most piercing assault ever faced by the Indian state, one that shook its basic political identity." Sunil Khilnani, *The Idea of India* (New York: Farrar Straus Giroux, 1997), 151.

[44] S. R. Bommai v. Union of India, 3 SC 1 (1994), 237.

to that subject.[45] On the other hand, it will come as no surprise that John C. Calhoun "perceived more clearly than most the threat posed to slavery as a system of race control by the constitutional issues raised in the Rhode Island controversy."[46] The enunciation of the "political question" doctrine in this case accomplished what pointedly was rejected by the Indian Supreme Court a century and a half later in *Bommai*, namely detaching the nation's highest tribunal from any role in providing meaning to the object – republicanism – of the Constitution's guarantee.[47] This did not prevent Calhoun, true to his views on fundamental rights, from arguing that republicanism meant something very specific; as Wiecek noted, "[A] republican form of government is one in which the people govern themselves, in the limited sense that some part of the State's residents exercise some choice in deciding who the elected officials of government shall be."[48] This was the same argument that the losing states in India argued in opposition to the Article 356 dismissals of the central government. They, like Calhoun, contended that "the President would be obliged to support any extant legitimate regime."[49] Self-government for the American states, free from federal interference, would allow them to protect the primary right of the slaveholder to his constitutionally guaranteed property entitlement. "Give to the Federal Government the right to establish its own abstract standard of what constitutes a republican form of government ... and it would be made the absolute master of the States."[50] Calhoun was not deterred by the perverse irony of his position; for him the enslavement of one people by another could not become the excuse for the enslavement of one government by another.

As later events were to demonstrate, Calhoun's worries about the potential use by the national government of the power to impose upon the slaveholding states an "abstract standard" of republicanism were not unfounded. Nothing was clearer to such passionate antislavery advocates as Charles Sumner and William Goodell than the incompatibility of slavery with the principles of the Declaration of Independence, principles that formed the core and essence of republican government. Just as these principles provided limits for the amending process, they established for the elected branches of the national

---

[45] William M. Wiecek, *The Guarantee Clause of the U.S. Constitution* (Ithaca: Cornell University Clause, 1972), 133.

[46] Ibid.

[47] In this connection one should consider the constitutional debate concerning the reapportionment question in the next century. Justice Frankfurter always insisted that the equal protection claims for invalidating malapportioned legislatures were disguised Guarantee Clause arguments that in effect "asked of the Court ... to choose among ... competing theories of political philosophy in order to frame an appropriate frame of government ... for all the States of the Union." Baker v. Carr, 369 U.S. 186, 300 (1962). Had Frankfurter used the language of the Guarantee Clause he would have said that the Court has no business imposing its preferred understanding of republicanism on the states.

[48] Wiecek, *The Guarantee Clause of the U.S. Constitution*, 135.   [49] Ibid.

[50] Richard K. Cralle, ed., *The Works of John C. Calhoun*, Vol. 6 (New York: D. Appleton, 1855), 221.

government republican standards by which to implement the Article IV mandate. For those abolitionists who believed the Constitution incorporated these principles, the duty of the federal government was clear – enforce the guarantee of republican government on those states not acting (in the words of the Indian document) "in accordance with the provisions of the Constitution."

Yet in a sense it was these very provisions that ensured that "the theorists who placed their chief hopes on the Guarantee Clause as a way of destroying slavery in the states were complete failures."[51] As Calhoun insisted, "[I]f not rigidly restricted to the objects intended by the Constitution, [the Guarantee Clause] is destined to be a pretext to interfere with our political affairs and domestic institutions in a manner infinitely more dangerous than any other power which has ever been exercised in the part of the General government."[52] On both sides of the slavery issue the case could be made that "the objects intended by the Constitution" were consistent with a fervently held set of logically coherent political ideas. But as we saw with the amendment question, logic and coherence are less perceptible constitutional attributes when viewed from a more objective external perspective, which is the vantage point from which actual constitutional politics takes its bearings. We might agree with the late Walter Murphy's defense of substantive limits on the amendment process and still conclude that his sentiments are readily adaptable to an understanding of why that argument has gotten so little traction in the United States and also why the related issue of republican guarantee enforcement has been largely irrelevant to the American experience. "One might," wrote Murphy, "logically infer that, insofar as American tradition implants the nation's founding document, the Declaration of Independence, into the larger Constitution, natural rights imposes binding standards on public officials."[53] The logical inference is correct, which provides some insight into why, comparatively speaking, American public officials have not for the most part been so bound.

A recognition of the binding power of constitutional principles in American constitutional development should not therefore obscure acknowledgment of a comparatively "lighter touch" in their application. We might attribute the difference to a less ardent commitment in the United States than elsewhere to substantive as opposed to procedural concerns, even as later the adoption of the post-War amendments sought to reconfigure the balance between the two. Calhoun's root concerns were of course substance based; in the presence of entrenched disharmony, however, the incentives for expressing them in the language of process – respect for the choices made through the electoral process – often present themselves in politically and constitutionally attractive

---

[51] Wiecek, *The Guarantee Clause of the U.S. Constitution*, 165.   [52] Quoted in ibid., 136.

[53] Walter F. Murphy, "Merlin's Memory: The Past and Future Imperfect of the Once and Future Polity," in Sanford Levinson, ed., *Responding to Imperfection: The Theory and Practice of Constitutional Amendment* (Princeton: Princeton University Press, 1995), 180.

ways. To be sure, within the realm of political discourse bold assertions of substantive principles are a common occurrence, but to the extent that these assertions speak to the existence of baseline constitutional ambivalences or tensions, their translation into decisive principled outcomes is much less evident.

The "Calhoun position" lost in India because the Supreme Court found in the Constitution's commitment to secularism a powerful "directive" aggressively to defend this basic feature against a threat to its long-term sustainability. The same commitment has led the Court to uphold efforts to protect the secular identity of the state from the dangers of religiously inspired electoral participation.[54] As Jan-Werner Müller has noted, "[T]here is one ... area of highly contentious contemporary politics where militant democracy has ... been invoked more frequently in recent years: challenges to secularism."[55] Such invocations are applied with especially vigorous heavy handedness where, more so than in India, a nation's constitutional identity is bound up with republican ideals entailing the confinement of religion to the nonpublic sphere. The prime examples are Turkey and France, both of whom have attracted much attention through their efforts at relegating religious symbolism to the realm of the private. In Turkey, for example, two constitutional amendments that explicitly provided for the right to wear headscarves were invalidated for subverting the very foundations of the secular state. These secular foundations were "irrevocable" under the Constitution, which meant that any effort to amend them would have to be deemed illegitimate.[56] Translation: the essentials of Turkish constitutional identity are unalterable.

The unalterability of these essentials seems less secure since those decisions were rendered; indeed, soon thereafter the Constitutional Court narrowly rejected the option of banning the political party responsible for encroaching on the secular domain. That such an option – exclusion from democratic politics of those blatantly opposed to the Constitution's principles – is available in republican polities is most commonly associated with the "militant democracy" strand in German constitutional law.[57] Also referred to as "defensive democracy," it

---

[54] Prabhoo v. Kunte, 1 Sup Ct 130 (1996).

[55] Jan-Werner Müller, "Militant Democracy," in Michel Rosenfeld and Andras Sajo, eds., *The Oxford Handbook of Comparative Constitutional Law* (Oxford: Oxford University Press, 2012), 1256.

[56] To that end, Article IV states: "The provisions of Article 1 of the Constitution establishing the form of the state as a Republic [a democratic, secular and social state governed by the rule of law] ... shall not be amended, nor shall their amendment be proposed."

[57] Nancy Rosenblum points out, however, that "identity need not be constitutionally defined as it was in Germany after the Second World War when the country set out political principles that could not be altered and amended." Nancy Rosenblum, *On the Side of Angels: An Appreciation of Parties and Partisanship* (Princeton: Princeton University Press, 2008), 439. Her discussion of "existential danger" (i.e., the threat to a state's identity) as one of the bases for invoking militant democracy focuses on the justifications advanced in a number of countries – Turkey, Israel, India – for banning political parties that use the electoral process to transform political identity.

supports the various preemptive measures used to "prevent those aiming at subverting democracy with democratic means from destroying the democratic regime."[58] The risk of course is that the application of undemocratic measures to safeguard democracy will end up undermining the very thing needing protection. For the Germans, however, it is all about defending constitutional principles. "To the extent that a constitutional democracy dynamically embodies the freedom of a people to govern itself and participate in the formation of laws governing its future, self-determination provides a measure of normative legitimacy to at least some forms of state action designed to combat threats to democracy itself."[59]

Whatever, therefore, may be the illiberal implications of such policies, the FCC has held them to be consistent with a Constitution that embraces an understanding of republican principles that are more substantive than formal in their essence. "Recalling the conditions that led to the Hitler state, the founders resolved that the Federal Republic could never be neutral in the face of its mortal enemies."[60] The resulting "militant democracy" (*streitbare Demokratie*) is manifest in several key provisions, all designed to preserve the polity's constitutional essentials in perpetuity. Article 21 of the Basic Law in particular could not be any clearer: "Parties which, by reason of their aims or the behavior of their adherents, seek to impair or destroy the free democratic basic order or to endanger the existence of the Federal Republic of Germany shall be unconstitutional."[61]

Significantly, the jurisprudential assumptions underlying both constitutional entrenchment and the commitment to militant democracy are similar to those invoked by the FCC in connection with the complex set of issues related to European integration. They both assume the existence and importance of a constitutional identity whose protection is a principal responsibility of the Court. In its controversial *Lisbon* decision upholding the latest and most comprehensive collective provision for EU governance, the Court cited German constitutional identity nearly forty times to affirm an impregnable barrier against European encroachment based upon the same objective order

---

Her assessment of these arguments leaves her unpersuaded: "Defining the identity of the state against parties that would alter it is an invitation to discrimination and exclusion." Ibid., 440.

[58] Müller, "Militant Democracy," 1253.

[59] Patrick Macklem, "Militant Democracy, Legal Pluralism, and the Paradox of Self-Determination," *International Journal of Constitutional Law* 4 (2006): 505.

[60] Donald Kommers, *The Constitutional Jurisprudence of the Federal Republic of Germany*, 2nd ed. (Durham, NC: Duke University Press, 1997), 218.

[61] The FCC in a 1956 case explained the rationale of the constitutional commitment. "The Basic Law represents a conscious effort to achieve a synthesis between the principle of tolerance with respect to all political ideas and certain inalienable values of the political system. Article 21 (2) does not contradict any basic principle of the Constitution; it expresses the conviction of the [founding fathers], based on their concrete historical experience, that the state could no longer afford to maintain an attitude of neutrality toward political parties. The [Basic Law] has in this sense created a 'militant democracy,' a constitutional [value] decision that is binding on the Federal Constitutional Court." *Communist Party Case*, BVerfGE85, 139 (1956).

of values that defined the Constitution's eternity clauses and the larger commitment to militant democracy. That there has never been a comparable citation exercise in the American judicial experience can be at least partially explained by the absence in the United States of an external political entity presenting itself as an existential threat to the Constitution's distinctive identity. In the years leading up to the Lisbon Treaty, a period that included the failure to adopt a constitution for Europe, constitutional identity was at the center of continental debate and discussion. The contestation focused not only on how extra-national precepts and principles could be integrated into the jurisprudence of nations possessing unique histories and ways of doing things but how – or whether – the distinctive political and legal cultures of a diverse group of nations could be incorporated within an overarching framework of international governance so as to create a constitutional identity for the new entity as a whole.[62] Much like the adoption of a federal state in 1787 presented political units at the local level with challenging questions about their identities in relation to the larger American whole – what is it that makes Virginia what it is? – the prospect of a European federal state inevitably fueled concerns in Germany and other countries about the status of their own self-understandings, particularly if, as was widely believed, "constitutional identity is an inalienable element to the democratic self-determination of a people."[63]

In truth, of course, there has been an external existential threat to American constitutional identity. It came from those political entities whose secession from the Union ensured that the post-War re-entry of these units into the American state would precipitate a crisis of identity, specifically one that implicated "the self-determination of a people." In no small measure the struggle over Reconstruction was a replay of the debate over slavery and republicanism, in which the admission of the former states of the Confederacy hinged on the outcome of a contest over the status of the newly emancipated class of people. In Bruce Ackerman's telling, "[T]here was nothing to stop the Republicans from attempting a revolutionary reinterpretation of the Guaranty Clause – one that went beyond antebellum abolitionism in insisting that 'republican' government required not merely that blacks be free but that they be enfranchised."[64] Ackerman then proceeds to explain some of the factors that did stop them, including the politically awkward reality of pervasive Northern exclusion of blacks from the franchise. More to the point of this essay's argument was the continuing vitality of Calhoun's antebellum view of the nature of the Constitution's republican guarantee, that as Wiecek has noted,

---

[62] See, for example, the entries in the special edition on the proposed European Constitution published in the *International Journal of Constitutional Law* in May 2005.

[63] Pola Cebulak, "European Constitutional Identity 'Inside Out': Bringing European Jurisdiction under One Roof," Paper presented at the Advanced Issues of European Law Conference, Dubrovnik, Croatia, April 22–28, 2012, 22.

[64] Bruce Ackerman, *We the People: Transformations* (Cambridge, MA: Harvard University Press, 1998), 106.

"[I]t was a conservative rather than an innovative promise." As such, to "deprive the southern polities of self-government" in pursuit of a radically inclusive vision of republican governance was destined to culminate in disappointment, highlighting "an astonishing disavowal of principle."[65]

Still, divesting the former slaveholding states of self-governing authority is the spine of the Reconstruction storyline, even if in the end the Guaranty Clause does not figure prominently in the narrative. The multi-faceted settlement imposed by congressional Republicans on the South remains a source of intense scholarly disputation.[66] One account in particular directly implicates our comparative concerns, concluding, "Reconstruction is a paradigmatic case of militant democracy."[67] Thus by conditioning full incorporation into the federal constitutional structure upon acceptance of democratic practices of self-governance, congressional Republicans essentially implemented an aggressive program in defense of "a free democratic basic order" long before the Germans settled on the constitutionally sanctioned policies that have provided the nomenclature for the relevant underlying theory. Radical, moderate, and conservative Republicans were distinguishable by how aggressive they were in the demands they made of the South; what motivated all of the factions was a vision of American constitutional identity to which the formerly rebellious states would be required to adhere.

Yet if Reconstruction was "a dramatic test for a theory of militant democracy,"[68] it is not clear how one should grade the results. The lack of enforcement of Section 2 of the Fourteenth Amendment (requiring state forfeiture of representation for any denial of voting rights) meant that the politically dominant actors of the Old South were able to maintain control over the meaning of constitutional identity at the local level at odds with the national definition inscribed in the amendment's first section, to say nothing of the Declaration's first paragraph.[69] Much more, however, warrants consideration.

---

[65] Wiecek, *The Guarantee Clause of the U.S. Constitution*, 172, 208.

[66] It is hard to ignore the conclusion of a leading chronicler of the period: "The general verdict of historians is that Republicans failed to achieve their goals in Reconstruction." Michael Les Benedict, *Preserving the Constitution: Essays on Politics and the Constitution in the Reconstruction Era* (New York: Fordham University Press, 2006), 168. That conclusion seems sensible given the sorry state of racial justice in 1877, yet a longer view, emphasizing "the enduring changes in the laws and Constitution that fundamentally altered federal-state relations and redefined the meaning of American citizenship," leads one to the safer assessment that "historians have yet to produce a coherent account of [Reconstruction] ...." Eric Foner, *Reconstruction: America's Unfinished Revolution, 1863–1877* (New York: Harper Perennial, 2014), x.

[67] Alexander S. Kirshner, *A Theory of Militant Democracy: The Ethics of Combating Political Extremism* (New Haven: Yale University Press, 2014), 144.

[68] Ibid., 143.

[69] As Richard Valelly has pointed out, this nonenforcement meant that Southern Democrats received twenty-five additional seats in Congress for each decade between 1903 and 1953. "[W]hite supremacist interests were not only entrenched but overrepresented." Richard M.

Bruce Ackerman, for example, sees the election of 1866 as raising a basic constitutive question: was racial or political identity more fundamental to the American Union?[70] That he finds in the results a decisive victory for the latter cannot obscure the fact that the abandonment shortly thereafter of any militancy in the pursuit of full democratic participation – a retreat mirrored in the decisions of the Supreme Court – "[left] the task of securing racial justice to later generations of Americans."[71] We were reminded of this – as well as the Court's earlier obstructionist history – in Justice Ruth Ginsberg's dissent in *Shelby County* v. *Holder*: "[The Voting Rights Act] is extraordinary because Congress embarked on a mission long delayed and of extraordinary importance: to realize the purpose and promise of the Fifteenth Amendment."[72] Indeed, the preclearance requirements of the 1965 Voting Rights Act of 1965 – centerpiece of the "second reconstruction" – possessed an unmistakable likeness to the "militant" efforts of the previous century that were instituted to achieve a more inclusive democracy.

Nearly fifty years after the law's enactment the states that had felt the heavy hand of national enforcement of voting rights saw a lifting of that weight by a Supreme Court decision premised on a judicially derived theory of "equal state sovereignty."[73] That outcome, widely interpreted as a major setback for a principled implementation of constitutionally mandated equality, arguably conforms to a narrative about the nation's historic ambivalence about race – an argument that need not be resolved here. Regardless of its resolution, the ruling's lighter touch, particularly when viewed comparatively, displays an equivocal attitude about the reach of constitutional principles, a cautious deportment in embracing the logic of full extension. Do the principles stop at state boundaries? And of similar importance (although not at stake in the voting rights case), are they experienced differently in the public and private arenas? The next section addresses these questions.

THE REACH OF THE CONSTITUTION

Constitutional principles come in different types. There are principles that embody precepts of political morality rooted in a nation's past, whose meaning derives from experience within a specific political and cultural context – national or subnational – and whose reach may not extend beyond the relevant local context. Other principles make a claim of universality, such that the moral truths they are said to embody are precisely the ones whose

---

Valelly, *The Two Reconstructions: The Struggle for Black Enfranchisement* (Chicago: University of Chicago Press, 2004), 8.

[70] Ackerman, *We the People: Transformations*, 181.

[71] Michael Les Benedict, *The Blessings of Liberty* (Boston: Wadsworth, 2006), 187.

[72] Shelby County v. Holder, 570 U.S. ___, slip opinion 36 (2013).

[73] Shelby County v. Holder, at slip opinion 1. The equal sovereignty argument was based on Coyle v. Smith, 221 U.S. 559 (1911), a case involving the admission of states into the Union.

recognition is required for a constitution to exist in more than name only. Of these latter it might be said that the strength of a nation's commitment to the enforcement of constitutional principle correlates positively with a felt need for consistent application across all sectors of the constitutional order.

Or does it? After all, a liberal constitutional order is arguably premised on principles that favor segmented enforcement, most conspicuously in its protection of a private sphere within which legal obligations that are binding for public actors do not extend. Additionally, if this constitutional order happens also to be federal in structure, it cannot in principle be the case that principles are of little importance if rights are applied one way at the center and differently at the periphery. Federalism, after all, makes a virtue out of diversity. Both of these departures from an expectation of equivalence present us with a challenging question: if the limited reach of principles, even ones deemed essential to justice, is dictated by other principles – specifically of a kind connected to regime characteristics – is there any justification for assuming the existence of a less prominent role for constitutional principles than in polities where such principles are given full extension?

So for example: with regard to rights inscribed in their constitutions, people in India and Germany need not inquire as to whether their entitlements must be similarly guaranteed at all levels of government. If in those countries there is a right that has been so codified, they will not find their enjoyment of it limited in such a manner as was once upheld by Chief Justice John Marshall: "[T]he fifth amendment must be understood as restraining the power of the general government, not ... the states."[74] And in Germany they will not read anything comparable to what a later Chief Justice said of that same provision: "Its purpose was to protect the people from the State, not to ensure that the State protected them from each other."[75]

The constitutional doctrines incorporated in these quotes – "Bill of Rights protection against federal infringement only" and "state action" – are the most obvious manifestations of the limited reach of American constitutional principles. Although both are defensible as principle-based expressions of larger regime commitments, with regard to the specific matters subject to boundary restrictions they can be criticized as insufficiently protective. In 1992 the Supreme Court of the Czech Republic insisted, "A democratic State has not only the right, but also the duty to assert and protect the principles on which it is based."[76] If, say, free speech is vitally important to the health of a constitutional democracy, then, in the spirit of the Czech opinion, should it not be defended against violations by local authorities and powerful private

---

[74] Barron v. Baltimore, 32 U.S. 243, 247 (1833).
[75] DeShaney v. Winnebago County Department of Social Services, 489 U.S. 189, 196 (1989).
[76] Quoted in Samuel Issacharoff, "Fragile Democracies," *Harvard Law Review* 120 (2007): 1405, 1430.

actors?[77] What is more, if the abstract arguments invoked to defend constrained application of constitutional principles are historically associated with the taint of moral compromise, can we still say there is a strong case available for the constitutive significance of those principles?

I   Bill of Rights Incorporation

Much like *Luther v. Borden*, a case with no direct connection to slavery but having profound implications for that problem, the importance of *Barron v. Baltimore* extends in similar ways far beyond the specific issues in the case. As Michael Kent Curtis has argued, "The decision in *Barron* never mentioned slavery, but it seems unlikely that the issue can have been far from the minds of the Justices."[78] This was John Marshall's states' rights opinion, with results very different from those that accompanied his famous nationalist rulings. It "left southern states free to suppress speech and press on the question of slavery and left them free to deny procedural and substantive rights to blacks. That the decision may be the most reasonable reading of the constitutional text is, of course, only part of the explanation for it."[79] Just as Calhoun was able to discern the larger implications of *Luther's* relegating of the Constitution's republican guarantee provision to political question status, so too was it evident that *Barron's* pronouncement that the Bill of Rights applied only to the national government would have a profound effect on the institution of slavery, to say nothing of its subsequent legacy.

All of this is manifest in the constitutional politics of Reconstruction. *Barron* to the contrary notwithstanding, some abolitionists had all along maintained that the Bill of Rights applied to the states, thus providing historians with many opportunities for scholarly disputation. Much of it has focused on the question of whether the Fourteenth Amendment was adopted in part to reverse *Barron*; the high-stakes debate between Charles Fairman and William Crosskey is exhibit A. Crosskey, whose controversial two-volume 1953 study of the Constitution as a decidedly nationalist document provided the argumentation

---

[77] Hadley Arkes points out that the Jeffersonians resisted the Sedition Act as an unconstitutional exercise of federal power but were not inhibited at all in using sedition statutes in the states to prosecute their most intemperate critics. Hadley Arkes, *Beyond the Constitution* (Princeton: Princeton University Press, 1990), 157. One might very well ask, what's wrong with this picture?

[78] Michael Kent Curtis, *No State Shall Abridge: The Fourteenth Amendment and the Bill of Rights* (Durham, NC: Duke University Press, 1984), 23. Surely they had in mind the nullification crisis of one year earlier.

[79] Ibid. William W. Crosskey's judgment that *Barron* was "incorrectly decided" is not the favored view among most scholars who have examined the question. William W. Crosskey, *Politics and the Constitution in the History of the United States* (Chicago: University of Chicago Press, 1953), 1056. As far as the text is concerned, William M. Wiecek concedes that it left "open the syntactical possibility that [Amendments Two through Ten] were universally applicable." William M. Wiecek, *The Sources of Antislavery Constitutionalism in the America, 1760–1848)* (Ithaca: Cornell University Press, 1977), 267.

for the more radical view, maintained that it had been the framers' intent to hold the states to the same rights' standards as applied to the federal government.[80] The Fourteenth Amendment, then, corrected the massive interpretive error of the past. Fairman's conclusion that reversal of *Barron* had not been a motivation for the authors of the Fourteenth Amendment, seems to have won over the most important audience, namely, the justices of the Supreme Court (with the notable exception of Justice Hugo Black); perhaps more significant for my argument is Pamela Brandwein's insightful rendering of the debate, which places the argument concerning the Amendment's reach within two contrasting interpretive matrixes. Of particular relevance is her finding that Fairman's account was "like the Northern Democrats, rooted [in] a collective national identity in the tradition of decentralized politics."[81] It was an account that slighted important features of slavery politics – especially brutal state policies – and drew attention to "James Madison's argument that states could repress individual liberty no less than the federal government."[82]

If, then, contrary to Crosskey, one were to ascribe to both the framers of the 1787 document and the amenders of 1868 an intention to exclude the states from Bill of Rights obligations, and if in addition such exemption represented good faith efforts to comply with the requirements of broader regime political principles, it would still be true that the entwinement of this compliance with the tragic subject of slavery and its legacy leaves a lighter principled impression on the landscape of American constitutional development than would otherwise be the case. A principle, Ronald Dworkin explained, is "a standard that is to be observed, not because it will advance or secure an economic, political, or social situation deemed desirable, but because it is a requirement of justice or fairness or some other dimension of morality."[83] Consistent with such an understanding we might say that while limiting the reach of the moral principle embodied in, say, the First Amendment is, in the abstract, compatible with the moral commitments that extend from fidelity to the constitutional ethos of liberalism and federalism, the lamentable fact that these principled commitments are historically aligned with policies of racial superiority is not without significance to the issue at hand.

The dispute over the nature of Bill of Rights incorporation was famously featured in *Adamson* v. *California*, with Justices Black and Frankfurter judicially reenacting the Crosskey/Fairman debate. Adopting the Fairman view, Frankfurter prevailed in the case, at one point citing such luminaries as

---

[80] William W. Crosskey, *Politics and the Constitution* (Chicago: University of Chicago Press, 1953), 2 volumes.

[81] Pamela Brandwein, *Reconstructing Reconstruction: The Supreme Court and the Production of Historical Truth* (Durham, NC: Duke University Press, 1999), 135.

[82] Ibid. See James Madison's speech introducing the Bill of Rights into the First Congress on June 8, 1789.

[83] Ronald Dworkin, *Taking Rights Seriously* (Cambridge, MA: Harvard University Press, 1977), 22.

Holmes, Brandeis, and Cardozo as justices who both agreed with him on the constitutional question and were known for their alertness to the interests of liberty and human dignity. "[T]hey were also judges mindful of the relation of our federal system to a progressively democratic society and therefore duly regardful of the scope of authority that was left to the States even after the Civil War."[84] Thus, in this account, their position on the Fourteenth Amendment was appropriately informed by regime principles; what is more, they, like Frankfurter, would not embrace a view that would "tear up by the roots much of the fabric of law in the several States, and would deprive the States of opportunity for reforms in legal process designed for extending the area of freedom."[85] To be sure, pursuing "a progressively democratic society" and "extending the area of freedom" are, in theory, distinct possibilities when contemplating jurisdictional limits on the applicability of constitutional rights; yet the failure to mention the actual alternative reality that had been experienced within the narrowed "scope of authority" is also suggestive of other possibilities – at least for any final assessment of the constitutive role of principles.

That assessment must come to terms with this presumption: "To the extent that the Bill of Rights leads us back to real principles of law ... then those principles must, perforce, be binding on the states as well as on the national government."[86] It is an insight that correctly leads Hadley Arkes to argue against the reasoning in *Barron* v. *Baltimore*. It does not, however, require adoption of the Crosskey/Black position on total incorporation, since the principles critical for the administration of justice, while they must apply at all levels of government, are synonymous not with the text of the Bill of Rights but only to the parts of it that are logically necessary for fulfilling the promise of such principles. On this account the Fairman/Frankfurter incorporation position is preferable to the alternative, in that its philosophically informed application would mean a rejection of a "mindless literalism" in favor of an approach that "would enforce upon the states only the real principles of law that can be found in the Bill of Rights."[87]

The problem, however, is that this way of thinking about rights and principles is not a comfortable fit within the American judicial experience. More typical is what we find in Justice Frankfurter's actual incorporation regimen, in which, following Justice Benjamin Cardozo, the critical question was whether "a principle of justice [is] so rooted in the traditions of our people as to be ranked as fundamental."[88] Thus when judges affirm or reject the existence of rights on the basis of their appearance or absence as protected interests in the tradition of the society, they are in effect declaring that constitutional recognition and legitimation are to be exclusively extended to

---

[84] Adamson v. California, 332 U.S. 46, 62 (1947).   [85] Ibid.
[86] Hadley Arkes, *Beyond the Constitution*, 167.   [87] Ibid.
[88] Palko v. Connecticut, 302 U.S. 319 (1937), 325.

claims whose normative standing is a function of their historic validation. As noted earlier, that tradition emerges from the compromised condition of the American founding, from, that is, a conflicted tradition that has produced diverse moral resources from which public and private actors have drawn to direct the flow of constitutional development. Whether, therefore, selective incorporation succeeds in contributing to and consolidating a principled basis for American national identity is dependent on its practitioners' success in establishing a normative consensus on the superiority of one specific aspirational strand in the nation's conflicted political tradition.

2   State Action

One route to the establishment of an identity-affirming normative consensus is through recognition of the constitution as the quintessence of an objective hierarchy of values. In what is arguably Germany's most important constitutional decision, the FCC supplied such an acknowledgment in very direct language:

[T]he Basic Law is not a value-neutral document. Its section in basic rights establishes an objective order of values and this order strongly reinforces the effective power of basic rights. This value system, which centers upon the dignity of the human personality developing freely within the social community, must be looked upon as a fundamental constitutional decision affecting all spheres of law, both public and private ... Every provision of private law must be compatible with this system of values, and every such provision must be interpreted in its spirit.[89]

By insisting that objective norms inform the substance of private law the German Court created an option for addressing the reach of constitutional principles that did not conform to the stark choice between exclusively vertical enforcement of rights – regulating interactions between the individual and the state – and an application that would also extend obligations in a horizontal direction to relations between private parties. It was a momentous decision; by one estimation, a "juridical coup d'etat."[90] Without declaring that the Basic Law's explicit provision for defensive rights against the state applied in equally direct fashion to interactions among private actors, it introduced the idea of indirect effect, or, as the Court formulated it in the *Luth Case*, the "radiating effect" of basic rights for the content of private law. Thus private actors will henceforth find themselves bound by constitutionally derived rights even if those explicitly enunciated rights are not the direct source for the regulative activity. Additionally, as pointed out by the German constitutional theorist Mattias Kumm, "The idea that constitutional principles radiate to affect the rights and duties of all actors within the jurisdiction is the basis not

---

[89] *Luth Case*, 7BVerfGE 198 (1958).
[90] Alec Stone Sweet, "The Juridical Coup d'Etat and the Problem of Authority," *German Law Journal* 10 (2007): 915, 920.

just for an expansion of the Court's rights jurisprudence to private law cases. It is also the basis for establishing individual rights to positive actions by the state."[91]

Kumm's larger point speaks directly to the argument of this essay. He argues that through the jurisprudence of the FCC – with *Luth* at its core – the German Basic Law has become a "total constitution," by which he means that all political questions are subject to constitutionally compelled substantive constraints. Protection of an "objective order of values" requires that legislatures and courts take this prioritizing into account when legislating and adjudicating relationships between private individuals. In light of the totalitarian background to this innovative jurisprudence, one needs to distinguish the total constitution from the total state, the latter conceiving law as "the continuation of politics by other means," the former conceiving politics as "the continuation of law by other means."[92] Where the total state politicizes the relationship between private individuals, the more recent construction constitutionalizes it. The arrangement thus functions as a "[a] kind of juridical genome that contains the DNA for the development of the whole legal system."[93] With the objective ordering of values as the wellspring for the normative choices that are to govern public interventions in the affairs of individuals, the total constitution's reach is in principle unlimited and in practice restrained by the moderate dictates of dignitarian jurisprudence.[94]

The same assumptions underlying the strikingly original doctrine of indirect effects support the constitutive weight of the earlier examples of the distinctively German commitment to deeply etched legal/philosophical principles. Indeed, the idea of the total constitution is as relevant to the unconstitutional constitutional amendment story as it is to the effective deconstruction of the legal partition of public and private. "Taken as whole," the Court said in the *Southwest Case*, "a constitution reflects certain overarching principles . . . ."[95]

---

[91] Mattias Kumm, "Who Is Afraid of the Total Constitution? Constitutional Rights and the Constitutionalization of Private Law," *German Law Journal* 7 (2006): 341, 350.

[92] Ibid., 343. Or as another German constitutional theorist puts it, "In the Weimar Republic, the demand that the legislature change the social order in accordance with fundamental rights stood in opposition to the demand that it leave a society already secured by fundamental rights alone – an objective principle conception of rights opposing a subjective rights conception." Schlink, "German Constitutional Culture in Transition," 209. Thus subjective rights are specifically conceived as rights of citizens against the state, whereas objective rights govern the entire legal order.

[93] Kumm, "Who Is Afraid of the Total Constitution?," 344.

[94] To the objection that constraining the behavior of individuals in a way that ignores the public/private distinction of conventional liberal political theory renders the total constitution no different from the total constitution, Kumm argues that under the former there exists an obligation to "take into consideration the principle of private autonomy as a countervailing concern." Ibid., 362. Jurisprudentially this occurs through a contextually sensitive application of proportionality analysis.

[95] *Southwest State Case*, 1 BVerfGE 14 (1951), Sec. D, par. 2.

Accordingly, what admits of a distinct possibility, that "a constitutional provision may itself be null and void," is predicated on the same conviction that led the Court in the *Luth Case* to align itself with an equally "un-American" approach to state action, namely the belief in a coherent corpus of all-embracing principles whose objective standing requires nothing short of totality in relation to their enforcement. In similar fashion, the practice of militant democracy incorporates a confidently held and assertively pursued substantive vision that leads to an uncompromising stance of political nullification toward threats to that vision. More portentously it challenges the Court to provide reassurance that the conceptual wall separating the total constitution from the total state is one that is destined to remain impermeable.

No such reassurance is required in the American rights regime, where the absence of horizontal effects – direct or indirect – may be understood to reflect a cardinal principle of constitutional liberalism that finds in the potential abuses of state power a basis for denying that very power the authority to extend its reach into places where individuals are abused by other individuals.[96] In this account a "partial constitution" is no less principled than its totalistic counterpart; limiting its reach actually manifests a stronger commitment to democratic constitutionalism. As Chief Justice Rehnquist argued in *DeShaney* about the due process clause of the Fourteenth Amendment, "Its purpose was to protect the people from the State, not to ensure that the State protected them from each other. The Framers were content to leave the extent of governmental obligation in the latter area to the democratic political processes."[97] Such is the dominance of this view in the American constitutional world that when the holding in a state action case is disputed, the dissenter – Justice Brennan in this case – does not contest the sanctity of the doctrine but instead chooses to interpret relevant facts so as to conform to conventional wisdom's restrictive conditions.[98]

Of course in the early days of state action instantiation and development its core liberal message was, as we have seen in connection with republican government and Bill of Rights guarantees, obscured by and embroiled in the American struggle over racial justice. In his dissenting opinion in the *Civil Rights Cases* Justice John Marshall Harlan asked, "If ... exemption from

---

[96] It may also reflect another hallmark of American constitutional jurisprudence, the resistance to the migration of ideas, most notably from foreign and international sources. As Mayo Moran points out, "[T]he U.S. context reveals the unwillingness to allow that constitutional values migrate, even into the domain of private law." Mayo Moran, "Inimical to Constitutional Values: Complex Migrations of Constitutional Rights," in Sudit Choudhry, ed., *The Migration of Constitutional Ideas* (Cambridge: Cambridge University Press, 2006), 249.

[97] DeShaney v. Winnebago County Department of Social Services, at 196.

[98] In *DeShaney* Justice Brennan found that the Wisconsin officials who had failed to respond appropriately to gross domestic abuse perpetrated by a parent on his child were guilty of unconstitutional state action because their indefensible inaction in the case could be construed as a form of state action.

discrimination in respect of civil rights is a new constitutional right, secured by the grant of State citizenship to colored citizens of the United States, why may not the nation, by means of its own legislation of a primary direct character, guard, protect, and enforce that right?"[99] Justice Joseph Bradley's response for the majority makes no mention of race. "The wrongful act of an individual . . . is simply a private wrong, or a crime of that individual; an invasion of the rights of the injured party, it is true, whether they effect his person, his property, or his reputation; but if not sanctioned in some way by the State, or done under State authority, his rights remain in full force, and may presumably be vindicated by the laws of the State for redress . . . ."[100] In following this constitutional logic a century later, Chief Justice Rehnquist cannot be criticized for his own silence about race, and not only because *DeShaney* was a case without any explicit connection to the issue. While the origins of the doctrine he invoked may have been enmeshed in the ugly politics of racial discrimination, its philosophical affinities to respectable theories of liberalism and federalism were by then substantially cleansed of their original taint.

It has, however, been forcefully argued that the outcome in *The Civil Rights Cases* has been widely misconstrued, that the Bradley opinion was in fact an exercise in racial moderation consistent with a sincere commitment to core civil rights.[101] According to Pamela Brandwein, failure to grasp the Court's embrace of politically centrist principles has led scholars mistakenly to see the ruling as part of the "abandonment narrative" in which the fortunes of blacks were essentially left to the malign state-controlled hands of their former masters.[102] If correct, the finding would surely go a long way to restoring the reputation of the Waite Court, yet it would do little to efface the sad fact that for much of its history the state action doctrine sanctioned, if it did not encourage, "an enormous network of racial exclusion and humiliation, characterizing both North and South."[103] Thus whatever may or may not have been the benign motives behind the crafting of the landmark decision overturning the Civil Rights Act of 1875, a by now painfully familiar question remains: if the limited reach of constitutional principles – those embodied in the Bill of Rights and the Reconstruction Amendments – is an artifact of good faith regime principles whose historically forceful implementation has nevertheless been strongly associated with a discriminatory racial purpose and agenda, then does not the very existence of a restricted enforcement scope bespeak a less prominent constitutive role for principles in the shaping of national identity – at

---

[99] *The Civil Rights Cases*, 109 U.S. 3 (1883).   [100] Ibid., at 17.

[101] Pamela Brandwein, "The Civil Rights Cases and the Lost Language of State Neglect," in Ronald Kahn and Ken I. Kersch, eds., *The Supreme Court and American Political Development* (Lawrence, KS: University Press of Kansas, 2006).

[102] Ibid., 304.

[103] Charles L. Black, "State Action," in Kenneth L. Karst, ed., *Civil Rights and Equality* (New York: Macmillan Publishing Co., 1989), 47.

least when contrasted with constitutional polities where such constraints do not apply?

CONCLUSION

Somewhat less clear is the status of the state action doctrine in India. On the question of direct effects the Supreme Court has held, with several notable exceptions, that the Constitution's section on rights applies only against the government, not to private individuals.[104] Similarly, with respect to indirect effects, the Court has only weakly asserted a requirement that constitutional principles provide radiating power over the purely private affairs of individuals.[105] Still, as one Indian scholar has argued, "The proposition of enforceability of Fundamental Rights only against the State finds no explicit mention in the Constitution. The Courts have been applying rights horizontally without explicitly acknowledging them and are steadily moving ... towards enforcing rights against private bodies."[106] What is more, with the loosening of standing rules and substantive legal requirements under the Court's expansive public interest litigation regime and with its capacious rendering of Article 21's human dignity provision in light of the Directive Principles of State Policy, a jurisprudential path has been established for a potentially ambitious adjudication of social rights with important implications for the private sector.

---

[104] Stephen Gardbaum, "Horizontal Effect," in Sujit Choudhry, Madhav Khosla, and Pratap Bhanu Mehta, eds., *Oxford Handbook to the Indian Constitution* (New Delhi: Oxford University Press, 2016). Those exceptions, however, are potentially important. For example, in Indian Medical Association v. Union of India, 7 SCC 179 (2011), the Supreme Court held that under Article 15(2) private schools were subject to the same standards of nondiscrimination as public educational institutions. Notable is the Court's reference to the fact that "the doctrine of basic structure has emanated from the German Constitution ...." (par. 87) The doctrine led the Court to conclude: "[T]he State was given the responsibility to balance the exigencies of the needs, between social justice and formal equality, between a command and control economy to the private sector ...." (par. 101). And so: "[W]e cannot in the same breath then turn around and say the same concerns, of national purpose, goals and objectives that inform the constitutional identity miraculously disappear in the context of the private sector" (par. 108).

[105] A *Luth* jurisprudential opening has, however, been clearly established. See in particular R. Rajagopal v. State of Tamil Nadu, 6 SCC 632 (1994), which, as in the German case, addressed questions of defamation and privacy that had previously fallen exclusively under the rubric of common law torts.

[106] Karishma D. Dodeja, "Indian Medical Association v. Union of India: The Tablet of Aspir(in)ation," *Indian Journal of Constitutional Law* 5 (2011): 215. In his classic book on the framing of the Indian Constitution, Granville Austin does find in the text of the document several explicit articles "designed to protect the individual against the action of other private citizens." Among these is Article 17, which, like the Thirteenth Amendment of the American Constitution abolishing slavery, abolishes untouchability. More contestable is Austin's conclusion that "[a]ll citizens were to be equally free from coercion or restriction by the state, or by society privately ...." Granville Austin, *The Indian Constitution: Cornerstone of a Nation* (New Delhi: Oxford University Press, 1966), 51.

Regardless of the ultimate impact of these Directive Principles as an instrument for societal transformation, they are worth considering for their comparative implications. In an insightful study of the Declaration of Independence, the philosopher Morton White noted that in the document's rough draft, just after listing the trio of unalienable rights, Thomas Jefferson wrote "that to secure these *ends* [emphasis added] governments are instituted among men, deriving their just powers from the consent of the governed," whereas in the final version the word "ends" is replaced by "rights."[107] White argued that the replacement of "ends" with "rights" required the obligation to guard rights already enjoyed by the people rather than a responsibility to attain ends not yet in their possession.[108] This textual alteration changes the sense of the word "secure" from its original meaning, *attain*, to a linguistically more plausible final meaning, to *make secure*. Very different from how we are invited to think about the Indian Constitution's Directive Principles, this signifies a "dilut[ion] in the purpose of government" – from an instrument for the attainment of mandated ends as yet unrealized to an instrument for the protection of rights already in existence.[109]

As to which rights were thus implicated, we are brought back to the conflicted visions of the founding and the contrasting sets of rights traditions that emerged from them. Herbert Storing's provocative claim in an important essay on slavery and the moral foundations of the American republic was that "slavery . . . can be seen as a radicalization of the principle of individual liberty on which the American polity was founded."[110] Defying conventional wisdom, he focused on the substance of the liberty principle rather than on the failure of the founders for having betrayed that principle. The "underlying tension" illuminated by the institution of slavery was that the idea of individual rights might clash with "the necessary moral ground of any government instituted to secure those rights."[111] Hence the terrible irony was that, however wrong or debased the abolitionist might have thought him to be, the slave holder could have seen in the compromises of the Constitution a commitment to secure his

---

[107] Morton White, *The Philosophy of the American Revolution* (New York: Oxford University Press, 1978), 245.

[108] With respect to the lighter touch in the application of constitutional principles, the fact that the framers backed away from the frequent early state practice of beginning with commitments to secure rights is not without comparative significance. Recent constitutions, including those of Germany and India, signal a heavier commitment to securing rights for all by positioning this aspiration earlier in the document. Of course there is no guarantee that these aspirations will be vigorously pursued, but the deliberate choice of the framers of the American Constitution not to follow the well-known state practice tends to reinforce White's argument concerning a more modest role for the Constitution in the realm of rights enforcement.

[109] White, *The Philosophy of the American Revolution*, 251.

[110] Herbert J. Storing, "Slavery and the Moral Foundations of the American Republic," in Robert A. Goldwin and Art Kaufman, eds., *Slavery and Its Consequences* (Washington, DC: AEI, 1988), 56.

[111] Ibid., 57.

rights precisely in the sense depicted in White's account of the Declaration's verbal evolution. After all, did not Calhoun view the Constitution as a document that, correctly interpreted, made secure the right to own property in slaves? However disturbing to modern sensibilities (and to opponents of slavery at the time), Storing's account would at least suggest a plausible basis for such a view.

So, finally, what are we to make of the familiar narrative of a constituted American nation, as expressed, for example, in this straightforward way? "America has to be constituted in terms of its basic principles."[112] Or as Jack Balkin has argued, "The Declaration is our constitution. It is our constitution because it constitutes us as a people 'conceived in liberty and dedicated to a proposition.'"[113] Especially as its "prophecy of redemption" may very well have been largely fulfilled, and much more so in the spirit of Frederick Douglass than John C. Calhoun, does not the assertion bespeak a fundamental truth about the constitutive role of American constitutional principles? To this one might confidently answer in the affirmative, but without further elaboration there remains the challenge of determining the precise nature of that truth. The burden of this essay has been to provide some comparative context for addressing that challenge. Thus in considering the claim of the Constitution's centrality for American national identity we would do well to observe closely how that claim plays out in other national settings. We have seen in Germany and India more resolute and less equivocal reliance upon constitutional principles to establish and defend an idea of nationhood. To the extent that these comparative examples have left us with the impression of a lighter touch in the United States with respect to the application of such principles, we might wish to moderate the volume with which the familiar narrative is proclaimed. If doing so focuses more attention on the reasons for the differences, our efforts will have been more than justified.

---

[112] Comment by Ralph Lerner for a Jack Miller Center sponsored event, "The Declaration in a House Divided," www.youtube.com/watch?v=2410IpZAOBY.

[113] Jack M. Balkin, *Constitutional Redemption: Political Faith in an Unjust World* (Cambridge, MA: Harvard University Press, 2011), 19.

Due Process: A Unified Understanding

Donald A. Dripps

A recent term of the US Supreme Court provides a characteristic assortment of due process decisions. The Court relied on the denial of due process in one case to invalidate state statutes that precluded same-sex marriage; in another, to hold void for vagueness a clause in the federal Armed Career Criminal Act. In still another, the justices ruled that that the Sixth Amendment's confrontation clause did not bar the use as evidence of a hearsay declaration from a child too young to be a competent witness in court. Apart from the fact that due process figured into each decision, the three seem utterly disparate. How is same-sex marriage connected to whether a federal criminal statute is clear enough to count as law or to a defense attorney's inability to cross-examine a child witness? In this essay, I will explain that these instances appear as unlike each other as they do because each illustrates a distinctive component of the due process guarantee.

The distinction between "procedural" and "substantive" due process, which may be familiar from other essays in this volume, forms only a subset within the first component of the unified definition offered here. That is, every due process claim begins with a *deprivation*, specified in the Fifth and Fourteenth Amendments to be a deprivation of "life, liberty, or property." Second, to constitute due process, the deprivation must have been, prospectively, *authorized by valid law*. And third, due process requires that the deprivation be accomplished along with a *fair hearing* about whether the law, though valid, also applies to the case at hand. At the risk of asserting a negative, I know of no American judge who does not accept this basic description of due process.

Typically, the plaintiff claiming a constitutional violation will insist that there has been a deprivation, but components two and three have not been complied with. The government, on the other hand, will deny the existence of a deprivation altogether, or, if it admits one occurred, it will argue that the second two components were present. The constitutional text, coupled with the practice of judicial review, means that to the extent that ordinary statutes were the instruments of denial they may be declared void. The canonical examples are a statute purporting to transfer the estate of one private person to another and a statute assigning one party in a lawsuit to be judge in her own case. In short, "life, liberty, and property," legality, and procedural fairness are not whatever it is that the legislature decrees.

The following discussion proceeds in four stages. First, we consider the origins and analytical structure of the Fifth Amendment Due Process Clause. Second, we trace the evolution of its constituent concepts in antebellum America. Third, we consider how the Fourteenth Amendment altered the legal and institutional ecology of constitutional interpretation in the years between the Civil War and the Second World War. Fourth, we explicate how the Supreme Court, in the second half of the twentieth century, invoked due process to expand and unify the scope of individual rights against both federal and state abridgement.

We close by returning to the cases referred to at the outset, which we will identify as *Obergefell, Johnson,* and *Clark.* At issue in *Obergefell* was the nature of "liberty." The sole issue in *Johnson* was the nature of valid "law." In *Clark* the issue concerned the meaning of fair "process." Each decision may one day be reversed; there were dissents in *Obergefell*, and both *Johnson* and *Clark* reversed the decision immediately below. Judicial error, it must be emphasized, differs categorically from judicial usurpation. The courts have always denied that liberty, property, legality, and fairness mean whatever legislatures say they mean. Given the soundness of that premise, what divides justices (and their critics) is precisely how to formulate such capacious concepts as due process more precisely, not whether to do so is the courts' constitutional duty.

"DUE PROCESS": THE TEXT

One must read through several other provisions of the Fifth Amendment before encountering the phrase "due process":

No person shall be held to answer for a capital, or otherwise infamous crime, unless on a presentment or indictment of a grand jury, except in cases arising in the land or naval forces, or in the militia, when in actual service in time of war or public danger; nor shall any person be subject for the same offense to be twice put in jeopardy of life or limb; nor shall be compelled in any criminal case to be a witness against himself, nor be deprived of life, liberty, or property, without due process of law; nor shall private property be taken for public use, without just compensation.

The seemingly incongruous commingling of the fundamental rule-of-law guarantee with technical rules of criminal procedure and the prohibition on confiscations can be understood at one level by taking into account the circumstances facing the First Congress. It is hardly surprising that federal lawmakers would give priority to establishing operational necessities like the executive departments and the federal courts over meticulous drafting of a Bill of Rights only reluctantly agreed to as a condition of ratification.

Looking deeper into English constitutional history offers addition clarification, based on the origin of the phrase "due process" and the associations it likely invoked in the minds of the framers. The concept itself first arose in Magna Carta's famous Chapter 39, in which King John pledged not to kill, imprison, fine, or dispossess any free man except "per legale judicium parium suorum vel per legem terrae." There is some slight disagreement about the precise translation, but "by a lawful judgment of peers or the law of the land" was (and still is) widely accepted. English kings periodically reissued the Great Charter in somewhat amended form, and it was also periodically confirmed by Parliament as that institution emerged as a lawmaking body.[1] The first known use of the phrase "due process of law" appears in one of these early statutes, adopted during the reign of Edward III in 1354.[2]

In *Federalist* 84, Alexander Hamilton had argued that English declarations of rights – Magna Carta, the Petition of Right, and so on – being concessions by kings, were poor models for the new republic. But the framers' own rhetoric belied his viewpoint. In 1761, James Otis relied on Parliament's acts confirming Magna Carta the Charter to challenge the writs of assistance, general warrants provided to tax collectors, authorizing search of any property without probable cause, for goods smuggled in to avoid payment of import duties.[3] Representing the colonies in the British House of Commons in 1766, Benjamin Franklin had invoked Magna Carta and the Petition of Right to deny the power of Parliament to tax unrepresented constituents.[4] The constitutions of the new American states typically included a clause incorporating Magna Carta's Chapter 39, with Massachusetts, Virginia, Pennsylvania, and the Carolinas adopting the words "law of the land." Paul Revere's 1775 state seal for Massachusetts featured a patriot soldier with a sword in one hand and Magna Carta in the other.[5]

To the extent that Americans reflexively lumped together offenses by both the law courts and the legislature under the heading of "due process," they carried on a venerable tradition. The abuse condemned by Chapter 39 and the Petition of Right was capital punishment followed by a trial. Charles I broadened the pattern, incarcerating subjects who refused his forced loans, indefinitely and with no trial at all.[6] The New York ratifying convention, no doubt well aware of this history, called for an amendment declaring that "no

---

[1] J. C. Holt, *Magna Carta*, 3rd ed. (Cambridge: Cambridge University Press, 2015), 39–40.
[2] 28 Edw. III 3 (1354).
[3] John Adams, *The Works of John Adams*, Volume II (Boston: Little Brown, 1850), 519–20 (reporting Otis's argument).
[4] *The Examination of Dr. Franklin before an August Assembly Relating to the Repeal of the Stamp Act* (Boston, anonymous, 1866), 21–22, available online at www.masshist.org/revolution/doc-viewer.php?old=1&mode=nav&item_id=282.
[5] Massachusetts Secretary of State, *The History of the Arms and Great Seal of the Commonwealth of Massachusetts*, available online at www.sec.state.ma.us/pre/presea/sealhis.htm.
[6] *See* Darnell's Case, 3 How. St. Tr. 1 (K.B. 1627) (holding royal prerogative a good return to a writ of habeas corpus). The Petition of Right did not prevent Charles I from charging parliamentary opponents for sedition, an accusation that could be filed by information rather than indictment, was not automatically bailable, and could be tried without a jury in the common law courts where the judges served at the king's pleasure. Rex v. Eliot, 3 How. St. Tr. 294 (1629).

person ought to be taken, imprisoned, or disseized of his freehold, or be exiled, or deprived of his privileges, franchise, life, liberty, or property, but by due process of law." A similar assemblage of past abuses can be found in James Madison's original draft of what would become the Fifth Amendment.

In none of these formulations does "process" consist of whatever the government decrees. The process must be what is, in some unspecified sense, "due." The concept of "deprivation" is intimately linked, but logically prior, to the concept of legality. The guarantee with respect to "life, liberty, or property" suggests that those entitlements do not arise solely from positive law that the legislature can alter by statute. If, however, the courts agree with the legislature that there is *no* liberty or property at stake, the government can proceed without legal authority and without fair hearing; the due process clause does not apply. When, however, the government deprives the individual of liberty or property, the deprivation is not illegal per se but subject to review for legality and procedural fairness. For example, a prison sentence for a crime deprives the defendant of liberty; it will survive constitutional challenge only upon a showing that a fair trial determined that the defendant violated a valid preexisting law.

A critical effect of conceiving of due process in this way has been to make the courts the highest authority, not just on the meaning of liberty and property but on what counts as law and what constitutes fair procedure. Intense controversy always has surrounded these questions and probably always will. For now, let us turn our attention to how these controversies erupted in antebellum America, after which time the Fourteenth Amendment will alter the ground of debate.

DUE PROCESS BEFORE THE CIVIL WAR

American jurists of the antebellum era disagreed, bitterly, about unwritten limits on the elective legislature's lawmaking power. As a consequence, they offer support for a variety of historical and constitutional interpretations. The situation is further complicated by the fact that ideas about legality and procedure have changed over time. With these caveats, it is possible to offer some generalizations about due process before the Civil War. Baseline entitlements were understood as established in law as the law stood before the occurrence of the deprivation claimed. Legality was understood at least partially in normative (natural law) terms rather than in wholly positive ones. Fair procedure was understood in historical terms, that is, by reference to custom and common law.

An excellent example of due process so conceived is found in Daniel Webster's famous argument in *Dartmouth College* v. *Woodward*, decided in 1819.[7] Trustees of Dartmouth College appointed under a royal charter granted

---

[7] 17 U.S. 518 (1819).

by George III brought suit, arguing that a New Hampshire statute that removed them from their positions violated the "law of the land" clause of the state constitution. Having been rejected in state court, the due process argument was made again in the US Supreme Court by Webster, now based on the parallel provision in the Fifth Amendment. "By the law of the land," Webster declared,

> is most clearly intended, the general law; a law, which hears before it condemns; which proceeds upon inquiry, and renders judgment only after trial. The meaning is, that every citizen shall hold his life, liberty, property and immunities, under the protection of the general rules which govern society. Everything which may pass under the form of an enactment, is not, therefore, to be considered the law of the land. If this were so, acts of attainder, bills of pains and penalties, acts of confiscation, acts reversing judgments, and acts directly transferring one man's estate to another, legislative judgments, decrees and forfeitures, in all possible forms, would be the law of the land.[8]

Notice how Webster exposes the interdependence of deprivation, legality, and procedure. Without fair hearings, laws that were entirely just could still be the pretext for arbitrary punishments. Fair procedures alone, however, at best implement the substantive law, and that might provide unjustly that A's property is transferred to B or that X is guilty of treason. The "general rules which govern society" – the positive law before the statute challenged as a denial of due process was enacted – define the baseline entitlements. Without constitutional protection for all three components, the other two are "nugatory." The difficulty in this perfectly logical explanation is that Webster does not identify the limits on prior legislation the courts should enforce. Are the instances he offers exclusive or illustrative and, if illustrative, of what general principle? The Constitution establishes a representative democracy that vests "all legislative powers herein granted" to the elected legislature. If the tax or commerce power does not include confiscations and attainders, what *else* does it not include?

In 1836, John Calhoun, Webster's great adversary in the Senate, adopted an understanding of due process similar to Webster's. During this period the Fifth Amendment did not apply to the states, but the Senate was debating a rule to preclude consideration of petitions asking Congress to emancipate slaves in the District of Columbia. Calhoun argued that emancipation in the District would deprive owners of property in violation of the Fifth Amendment Due Process Clause. "[H]ow can Congress take away the property of a master in his slave, in this District, any more than it could his life and liberty? They stand on the same ground."[9] From Calhoun's perspective, a statute emancipating slaves was confiscation, illegal and void, even if the statute provided reasonable compensation and fair procedures.

---

[8] 17 U.S. at 581–82.

[9] Register of Debates, 24th Congress, 1st sess., at 97 (Jan. 7, 1836) (statement of Sen. Calhoun), available online at http://memory.loc.gov/cgi-bin/ampage?collId=llrd&fileName=022/llrd022 .db&recNum=4 (image 97).

Opponents of slavery, including Salmon P. Chase, relied on the same definition of due process but denied that slavery was compatible with any of its three components. For constitutional purposes, a master could not be deprived of his slave, "for man is not, by nature, the subject of ownership."[10] The master could have no legal entitlement to the slave precisely because, according to abolitionists, the slave had a "higher-law" entitlement to "liberty" not subject to any "inferior" law. It also followed that the Fugitive Slave Act offended the legality requirement, being as "unjust" as laws nullifying contracts or making one party judge of his own case.[11] Chase did not, however, feel "obliged to resort to any general principle of the natural law," claiming instead a "firm footing in the Constitution." which forbade "Congress to enact, and this Court to enforce, any law which authorizes unreasonable seizures, or privation of liberty without due process of law."[12] An act that authorized slave catchers, without warrants, to abduct supposed fugitives before, rather than after, a judicial hearing was not fair procedure unless it could be said that "no process" was due process.

In 1856, the Republican platform – adopted at a convention where Lincoln narrowly lost the nomination for vice president – declared that due process both prohibited all local laws implementing slavery and obligated the federal government to suppress pro-slavery forces, "while the present Constitution shall be maintained."[13] One year later, the Supreme Court ruled that due process *protected* slavery in the territories. In *Dred Scott* v. *Sanford*[14] Chief Justice Taney ruled that African Americans were not citizens of the United States and so not entitled to sue in federal court; that the Missouri Compromise barring slavery in the northern territories exceeded congressional power under Article IV, Section 3; and that if an otherwise valid statute had the effect of emancipating slaves lawfully held in a state because they sojourned in federal territory, the act "could hardly be dignified with the name of due process of law."[15]

Significantly, the dissent penned by Justice Curtis proceeds on the same premises, acknowledging, as Taney did not, the roots of the Due Process Clause in Magna Carta.[16] But according to Curtis, slaves were not ordinary property, so no valid deprivation could be claimed. Being contrary to natural right, supported only by the positive law of the slave states, the master's right ended with the slave states' local jurisdiction.

---

[10] Salmon P. Chase, *Reclamation of Fugitives from Service. An Argument for the Defendant, submitted to the Supreme Court of the United States, at the December Term 1846, in the case of Wharton Jones vs. John Vanzandt* (Cincinnati: R.P. Donogh, 1847), 83, available online at http://babel.hathitrust.org/cgi/pt?id=loc.ark:/13960/t1bk1gt5c;view=1up;seq=4.

[11] Ibid. at 93–94.   [12] Ibid. at 96.

[13] Republican Party Platform of 1856, available online at www.ushistory.org/gop/convention_1856republicanplatform.htm.

[14] 60 U.S. 393 (1856).   [15] 60 U.S. at 450.   [16] 60 U.S. at 694–97.

The clash between Taney and Curtis over due process illustrates how judicial review made constitutional questions out of both the baseline deprivation component and the requirement of legality. Was Dred Scott "property" so that a federal law making him free was confiscatory, taking from A and giving to B? Or was Dred Scott a "person" entitled to "life, liberty, and property" anywhere outside the eccentric slave zone recognized by the Constitution of 1789 and thus exempt from Fifth Amendment challenge? The answer turned on whether higher law did, or did not, permit equating property in slaves with other chattels, such as property in, say, horses.

With respect to the third component of due process, fair hearing, which did not arise directly in *Dred Scott*, the leading antebellum case was *Murray's Lessee v. Hoboken Land & Improvement Co.*, decided in 1855.[17] The parties disputed land in New Jersey purchased by Samuel Swartwout. Swartwout was a supporter of Andrew Jackson, who, over the opposition of Vice President Van Buren, named Swartwout to the post of customs collector for New York. After Swartwout's term as collector expired, an investigation instigated by then President Van Buren found Swartwout's accounts were more than a million dollars short.[18] As authorized by an 1820 statute, the Treasury Department filed a "warrant of distress" in the New Jersey district court, placing a lien on Swartwout's property, which the U.S. Marshal then sold to the Hoboken company. Murray's lessee claimed the same property through a sale by Swartwout, which took place before the marshal's sale to Hoboken but after the warrant of distress was filed in the district court. The lessee had not received notice of the warrant and understandably challenged the constitutionality of the statute as violating both Article III and due process.

The distress procedure was not far removed from making a party judge of the case. The Treasury Department's auditor made conclusive findings of fact, without submission to a judge let alone a jury, and indeed without even notice to interested parties. The government had a direct financial interest in finding a deficiency, and there was the more sinister possibility that the investigation had been trumped up at the behest of a vengeful president.

The Supreme Court unanimously upheld the statute. Speaking through Justice Curtis, the same man who would later challenge Taney's due process argument in *Dred Scott*, the Court initially conceded that statutory authorization by Congress did not necessarily amount to "due process of law." The content of the constitutional right to fair procedure, however, posed a difficult challenge. The Constitution contained no description of "due" procedures, allowed or forbidden, or even of principles. Unwilling to

---

[17] 59 U.S. 272 (1855).

[18] Arthur James Weise, *The Swartwout Chronicles* (New York: Trow Printing 1899), a biased but well-documented family history, provides details of the scandal at 402–84, available online at http://memory.loc.gov/master/gdc/scdser01/200401/books_on_film_project/loc06/nov13batchofPDFs/20060523002sw.pdf.

leave the matter to be settled by the mere will of Congress, the Court settled on a historical test. If no provision of the Constitution specified what procedure was "due" in a particular case,

> we must look to those settled usages and modes of proceeding existing in the common and statute law of England, before the emigration of our ancestors, and which are shown not to have been unsuited to their civil and political condition by having been acted on by them after the settlement of this country.[19]

Versions of the distress process to enforce collectors' deficits had been authorized by law for centuries in England and by the American states following independence. It followed that, however unfair or unreliable the procedure might be, it did not conflict with the Fifth Amendment.

THE FOURTEENTH AMENDMENT

When Congress convened in 1866, the Republican majority realized that the Thirteenth Amendment's abolition of slavery had failed to prevent the violent reassertion of white supremacy in the states of the former confederacy. Protecting the civil rights of both freed slaves and southern unionists, however, was largely beyond federal power. Congress had no powers under Article I to legislate on the internal affairs of the states, and the Supreme Court had held in *Barron* v. *Baltimore* (1833) that key Bill of Rights provisions, including the Fifth Amendment Due Process Clause, did not apply to the states.[20]

A Joint Committee on Reconstruction was charged with preparing a new constitutional amendment. After many twists and turns in the drafting process, Congress proposed the Fourteenth Amendment, with, in Section 1, a Due Process Clause applicable to the states.[21] Debates in Congress, the state ratification conventions, the 1866 election campaigns – all paid little if any attention to the details. There was no prominent suggestion that "due process" in the Fourteenth Amendment was to mean anything other than what it meant in the Fifth. The only change made to the language of the Due Process Clause itself was the trivial substitution of the active "deprive" for the passive "nor be deprived." Section 5 gave Congress legislative power to enforce the amendment, but like Section 1, the Due Process Clause was in its terms self-executing and enforceable by the courts. *Dred Scott* was repudiated by making all persons citizens, not by altering the terms of due process.

---

[19] 59 U.S. at 277.   [20] 32 U.S 243 (1833).

[21] Section 1 provides: "All persons born or naturalized in the United States, and subject to the jurisdiction thereof, are citizens of the United States and of the state wherein they reside. No state shall make or enforce any law which shall abridge the privileges or immunities of citizens of the United States; nor shall any state deprive any person of life, liberty, or property, without due process of law; nor deny to any person within its jurisdiction the equal protection of the laws."

In hindsight we can see that the new constitutional guarantees against state governments were bound to raise at least three difficult and, as it turned out, momentous issues. First, the new amendment invited fresh controversies about both the deprivation and legality components. During the nineteenth century, the prevailing view of congressional power under the commerce clause meant that most social-welfare and economic regulation was done by the states. With the Fourteenth Amendment in place, the Court would now hear challenges to state labor laws and rate regulations as unconstitutional deprivations of liberty or property.

Second, the Court now confronted a conflict between the historical test of fair procedure announced in *Murray's Lessee* and the sweeping reform of common law procedure, civil and criminal, going forward in the states.[22] Statute after statute simplified pleading requirements. New statutes swept away the common law system of evidence, based on competency rules that excluded all testimony from interested or disreputable persons. Also, *Murray's Lessee* had involved a federal statute that adopted summary accusation procedures long familiar in Anglo-American law. What about felony informations *ex parte* (only one side represented) on the criminal side or worker's compensation systems on the civil side, both, however fair and efficient, radical departures from established due process?

Third, cutting across all three components of due process, the new amendment reopened the possibility that the Bill of Rights might apply to the states. State statutes restricting free speech, for example, might now be treated as deprivations of liberty. The consistency of these statutes with a "higher-law" understanding of the legality component was now an issue for federal judges, who might see the issues differently than their state counterparts. As for fair hearings, such rights as the Fifth Amendment privilege against self-incrimination or the Seventh Amendment right to a civil jury trial might now apply to the states through *Murray's Lessee*'s historical test of fair procedure.

Generally speaking, supporters of the Fourteenth Amendment disclaimed any intention to significantly curtail the states' existing authority. Justice Miller's majority opinion in the *Slaughterhouse Cases* gave the Privileges or Immunities Clause an interpretation that rendered it all but nugatory but offered a good reason.[23] Since the amendment gave no indication of precisely what "privileges or immunities" meant, it might well, if taken literally, amount to an invitation to the Court to become "perpetual censor" of state legislation. The same dilemma resurfaced in cases raising due process challenges to state laws. But with due process no similar nullifying interpretation was plausible. The Court had consistently denied that Fifth Amendment due process meant whatever the legislature said it meant. How might a new version of the deprivation/legality/fair hearing formula be devised for the Fourteenth Amendment that would also avoid a judicial blank check?

[22] See, e.g., Holden v. Hardy, 169 U.S. 366, 386–87 (1898) (surveying reforms).
[23] 83 U.S. at 78.

With respect for deprivation, for the first thirty years after ratification, the Court adopted a strategy of deference toward state legislatures while maintaining in *dicta* that deference was not abdication. Unlike the federal government, the states were governments of general rather than enumerated powers. That meant states exercised the "police power" to regulate individual conduct to promote the morals, health, and welfare of the community, and by its own lights. If a claimed deprivation could reasonably be said to fall within the police power, the state legislature was entitled to respect concerning the reasonableness and legitimacy of its exercise.

In effect, the legality requirement turned on the deprivation inquiry, just as it had in *Dred Scott*. The Court held that the police power includes the power to tax both persons and property to pay for draining health-threatening swamps,[24] to prohibit liquor as a threat to both morals and health,[25] and to regulate the rates charged by utilities and common carriers, railroads included.[26] Those who invested in any of these businesses did so with knowledge that the police power applied and that its exercise might be changed at the will of the legislature. By this reasoning, due process decisions in these areas continued to maintain that the law was not whatever a legislature might declare it to be.[27] Indeed, with rare exceptions, the early Fourteenth Amendment due process cases maintained that legislation at least theoretically might exceed the police power.[28]

---

[24] Davidson v. New Orleans, 96 U.S. 97 (1878). Davidson's estate challenged taxes assessed to its property for draining swamps. The improvements did not directly benefit the property taxed, and Louisiana law made the owner personally liable, creating the possibility that the city might assess taxes in excess of the value of the property. In upholding the assessments, Justice Miller's majority opinion stated: "[I]t is not possible to hold that a party has, without due process of law, been deprived of his property, when, as regards the issues affecting it, he has, by the laws of the State, a fair trial in a court of justice, according to the modes of proceeding applicable to such a case." 96 U.S. at 105. This passage suggests that while due process might limit statutes changing procedure, no such limits were imposed on legislative substance.

[25] Mugler v. Kansas, 123 U.S. 623 (1887). Mugler had invested $10,000 in a brewery. After Kansas prohibited alcohol, the value sank to $2,500. The Court held that liquor prohibition was within the state's police power and not an unconstitutional deprivation of property.

[26] Munn v. Illinois, 94 U.S. 113 (1877). Munn operated a grain elevator. After the state legislature adopted a "granger law" fixing the prices that could be stored for warehousing grain, Munn charged prices in excess of what the statute allowed. He was convicted of violating the statute and challenged it as a deprivation of property without due process. The Court rejected the challenge, holding that when warehouses acquired a practical monopoly their rates could be regulated.

[27] See, e.g., *Mugler*, 123 U.S. at 661: "It does not at all follow that every statute enacted ostensibly for the promotion of these ends is to be accepted as a legitimate exertion of the police powers of the state ... If, therefore, a statute purporting to have been enacted to protect the public health, the public morals, or the public safety, has no real or substantial relation to those objects, or is a palpable invasion of rights secured by the fundamental law, it is the duty of the courts to so adjudge, and thereby give effect to the constitution."

[28] E.g., *Munn*, 94 U.S. at 125 ("down to the time of the adoption of the Fourteenth Amendment, it was not supposed that statutes regulating the use, or even the price of the use, of private property

The same deference-but-not-abdication approach prevailed with respect to fair procedure. In *Hurtado v. California*,[29] the defendant challenged his state murder conviction because he had been charged by an *ex parte* information filed by the prosecuting attorney rather than an indictment returned by a grand jury. Under the historical test of *Murray's Lessee*, Hurtado should have won, but he lost. The Court qualified the historical analysis in *Murray's Lessee* by characterizing traditional practice as an inclusive rather than exclusive test of fair procedure. States could follow the common law per se or depart from it by statute, so long as the new procedures provided the same protections in practice as the old. In this way, the Court permitted the great procedural reforms of the nineteenth century to move forward.

Procedural cases like *Hurtado* echoed the caveat in the police power cases: legislation was not always valid law. Justice Mathews wrote for the Court that due process in the Fourteenth Amendment "refers to that law of the land in each state which derives its authority from the inherent and reserved powers of the state, exerted within the limits of those fundamental principles of liberty and justice which lie at the base of all our civil and political institutions, and the greatest security for which resides in the right of the people to make their own laws, and alter them at their pleasure."[30] The felony information procedure upheld in *Hurtado* gave the accused the same notice of the charge as a traditional indictment and was therefore constitutional. Only a procedure that offended "fundamental principles" would violate due process.

This approach to entitlements and to fair procedures came to depend on the analysis of legislation's compatibility with higher law; only cases in conflict with "fundamental principles" would exceed the police power just as they would taint procedural innovations with unconstitutional unfairness. Although the Court left the door open to invalidating state legislation on these grounds, the states lost no significant due process cases in the Supreme Court until 1897.

Finally, *Hurtado* had taken the position that, because the Fifth Amendment contained a Due Process Clause and constitutional language should not be treated as surplusage, the Fourteenth Amendment Due Process Clause should be read to *exclude* the application of other Fifth Amendment clauses, like the privilege against self-incrimination and the grand jury.[31] Had the Court maintained this position, nothing in the Fifth Amendment could be imputed to Fourteenth Amendment due process. However, in 1897, it abandoned that inference and heard the appeal of a railroad against the city of Chicago for exercising its eminent domain power to build a street across its land.[32] The

---

necessarily deprived an owner of his property without due process of law. Under some circumstances they may, but not under all.").

[29] Hurtado v. California, 110 U.S. 516 (1884).   [30] *Hurtado*, 110 U.S. at 535.

[31] 110 U.S. at 535 ("if in the adoption of that amendment it had been part of its purpose to perpetuate the institution of the grand jury in all the states, it would have embodied, as did the fifth amendment, express declarations to that effect").

[32] Chicago B. & Q. R. Co. v. Chicago, 166 U.S. 226 (1897).

Court equated uncompensated takings with the classic example of a statute that is not law, that is, a statute purporting to transfer the estate of A to B.[33] Though it proceeded to uphold the jury's award of one dollar's damages as conclusive, the era of deference was about to end.

The *Lochner* Era

During the "*Lochner* era" (roughly speaking, 1897–1937) the Court became less deferential toward the states. *Lochner* itself invalidated New York's working-hours law for bakers.[34] Despite some modern defenders, *Lochner* remains the most notorious example of "substantive due process." In fact, the Court's activism during the period cut across all three components of due process jurisprudence.

The Court embraced an expansive understanding of Fourteenth Amendment "liberty" by equating deprivation and government regulation. In a case before *Lochner*, *Allgeyer* v. *Louisiana*,[35] which struck down a state statute prohibiting in-state owners from insuring property through out-of-state carriers without employing an in-state agent, the Court had adopted language from Justice Bradley's *Slaughterhouse* dissent declaring that "the right to follow any of the common occupations of life is an inalienable right."[36] Unlike the sale of liquor or lottery tickets, which the state could prohibit under its police power, trades like insurance and baking bread were "ordinary" and "lawful," and state statutes could not, under the Constitution, make them illegal.

The outcomes in *Lochner* and *Allgeyer* fit the pro-business, anti-labor stereotype commonly associated with the period. But the Court also invoked due process to protect "liberty" against state deprivations in some different and perhaps surprising contexts. *Meyer* v. *Nebraska* struck down a state statute prohibiting the teaching of foreign languages to schoolchildren until they had passed the eighth grade.[37] *Pierce* v. *Society of Sisters* held a statute requiring attendance at public, as opposed to private, schools unconstitutional.[38] The rubric of legality in both opinions was much like *Lochner*'s: teaching is a lawful occupation, the statute lacked any plausible connection to the police power's legitimate ends, and statutes that worked such deprivations were nullities.

The *Lochner* era Court carried forward the process of incorporating other provisions of the Bill of Rights into Fourteenth Amendment due process. We have seen that the Court's just-compensation decision in 1897 read that clause in the Fourteenth Amendment to protect other rights listed in the Fifth

---

[33] 166 U.S. at 636 ("But if, as this court has adjudged, a legislative enactment, assuming arbitrarily to take the property of one individual and give it to another individual, would not be due process of law, as enjoined by the fourteenth amendment, it must be that the requirement of due process of law in that amendment is applicable to the direct appropriation by the state to public use, and without compensation, of the private property of the citizen.").

[34] Lochner v. New York, 198 U.S. 45 (1905).   [35] 165 U.S. 578 (1897).   [36] 165 U.S. at 590.

[37] 262 U.S. 390 (1923).   [38] 268 U.S. 510 (1925).

Amendment. In *Gitlow* v. *New York*, for example, the Court upheld Gitlow's conviction for fomenting anarchy, but only after declaring that "[we] assume that freedom of speech and of the press – which are protected by the First Amendment from abridgment by Congress – are among the fundamental personal rights and 'liberties' protected by the Due Process Clause of the Fourteenth Amendment from impairment by the States."[39] The Court's procedure was selective. Just-compensation and free-speech and free-press rights were "fundamental" to the "liberty" protected by the Due Process Clause. Grand jury indictment was not "fundamental." The test of "liberty" was higher law, not inclusion in the Bill of Rights.

During these years, the legality of a particular deprivation was a function of the state's legitimate police power. The scope of the police power was indefinite; the line between legitimate paternalism and illegitimate protection of particular interest groups was hard to draw. A few labor regulations survived constitutional scrutiny, as in *Muller* v. *Oregon*,[40] the case won by the famous "Brandeis brief." *Muller* upheld a state statute prohibiting employing women in laundries for more than ten hours a day (and in a majority opinion by Justice Brewer from whose more sexist passages modern readers might well recoil). Unlike *Lochner*, where the public health connection to the police power was judged bogus, here it was at least arguably genuine.[41] As *Muller* shows, however, proponents of labor regulations had to first persuade the legislature and then again persuade the courts about the legislation's connection to public health, welfare or morals. Fifteen years after *Muller*, for example, *Adkins* v. *Children's Hospital*[42] held a federal statute setting minimum wages for women working in the District of Columbia a deprivation of "liberty" contrary to higher-law principles. *Adkins* distinguished minimum wages from maximum hours laws of the sort upheld in *Muller*. Unlike the amount of time worked, the amount paid had only an indirect effect on worker health. The legislature might see such a connection, and its judgment was entitled to respect, but the Court would be the final judge of whether the state's police power had been exceeded.[43]

The Court's willingness to treat statutes as illegal usurpations extended to criminal laws that failed to specify just what conduct was proscribed. In 1914, the Court invalidated a Kentucky statute making it a crime for participants in a

---

[39] 262 U.S. at 666.   [40] 208 U.S. 412 (1908).

[41] 208 U.S. at 421 ("by abundant testimony of the medical fraternity continuance for a long time on her feet at work, repeating this from day to day, tends to injurious effects upon the body, and, as healthy mothers are essential to vigorous offspring, the physical well-being of woman becomes an object of public interest and care in order to preserve the strength and vigor of the race").

[42] 261 U.S. 525 (1923). The challenged statute was adopted in 1918.

[43] 261 U.S. at 564 ("The statute here in question has successfully borne the scrutiny of the legislative branch of the government, which, by enacting it, has affirmed its validity, and that determination must be given great weight ... But, if by clear and indubitable demonstration a statute be opposed to the Constitution, we have no choice but to say so.").

cartel to charge more than the "real value" of their products. Since there was no accessible test of what price the goods would have fetched absent the cartel, the Court found the statute was, functionally, no law at all.[44] Likewise, later rulings struck down state statutes banning raising a red flag as a symbol "of opposition to organized government"[45] and one making it a crime for a person with no lawful business and a criminal record to "be in a gang of two or more persons."[46] In subsequent cases to this day,[47] the justices often disagree about whether a statute is definite enough to count as law. There is all but universal agreement, however, that a penal law so vague that its meaning can only be guessed fails to satisfy the legality criterion.

The Court's new willingness to overrule state policy decisions extended also to the component of fair procedure. *Munn* v. *Illinois*, an 1877 decision upholding a statute providing maximum rates for the storage of grain, went beyond recognizing that the police power encompassed reasonable rate regulation of utilities and common carriers and declared that the state legislature's determination of reasonableness was conclusive.[48] In 1898, the Court reversed itself on this point, deciding in *Smyth* v. *Ames* that because rate regulation was potentially confiscatory, the federal courts had a duty to independently examine the facts in determining reasonableness for purposes of due process analysis.[49] Similarly, the Court for the first time overturned state criminal convictions as contrary to due process on account of unfair trial procedures or brutal police practices. The initial cases involved black defendants convicted in capital cases by southern courts after sham trials characterized by the threats of mob violence,[50] the denial of counsel,[51] or the use of confessions obtained by torture.[52] The Court continued to refuse to incorporate the Fourth, Fifth, and Sixth amendment criminal procedure provisions into the fair hearing component of due process.[53] But it had begun to scrutinize the overall fairness of the criminal process in the states.

1937 and *Carolene Products*

The *Lochner* era ended abruptly when, a month after FDR announced his Court-packing plan, the Court by a bare majority decided *West Coast Hotel* v. *Parrish*, upholding Washington's minimum-wage law, repudiating *Adkins* v.

---

[44] International Harvester v. Kentucky, 234 U.S. 216 (1914); Collins v. Kentucky, 234 U.S. 634 (1914).
[45] Stromberg v. California, 283 U.S. 359 (1931).
[46] Lanzetta v. New Jersey, 306 U.S. 451 (1939).
[47] E.g., Skilling v. United States, 561 U.S. 358 (2010).   [48] 94 U.S. 113 (1877).
[49] 169 U.S. 466, 526 (1898).   [50] Moore v. Dempsey, 261 U.S. 86 (1923).
[51] Powell v. Alabama, 287 U.S. 45 (1932).   [52] Brown v. Mississippi, 297 U.S. 78 (1936).
[53] See, e.g., Palko v. Connecticut, 302 U.S. 319, 328 (1937) (reaffirming "fundamental principles" test).

Children's Hospital openly and *Lochner* by implication.[54] Chief Justice Charles Evans Hughes's *Parrish* opinion said two notable things about due process.

First, the "liberty" protected by the Due Process Clause was "liberty in a social organization which requires the protection of law against the evils which menace the health, safety, morals, and welfare of the people. Liberty under the Constitution is thus necessarily subject to the restraints of due process, and regulation which is reasonable in relation to its subject and is adopted in the interests of the community is due process."[55] At least with respect to social welfare legislation, the Court renounced the project of testing statutes for their consistency with some unwritten higher law.

Second, the Chief Justice denied giving the Due Process Clause any radical new interpretation.[56] This counterintuitive proposition is not implausible. In *Parrish*, there was no ambiguity in the deprivation; the statute clearly cost the employers money. Nor was there any question about fair procedure. The only issue was whether the minimum-wage law was within the legitimate scope of the police power and therefore consistent with the legality component. On that issue "all" the Court did in *Parrish* was return to a broad understanding of the legitimate scope of governmental concerns and a deferential attitude toward legislatures who press against the envelope of their authority.

From this point forward, judicial review generally, and due process jurisprudence in particular, focused increasingly on civil liberties and racial equality, while review of transfer payments, rate-making, wage and hour laws, and health and safety regulations fell into virtual desuetude. The transformation was abrupt, making 1937 as momentous a year in constitutional history as 1791 or 1868, when, respectively, the Bill of Rights and Fourteenth Amendment were ratified.

The New Deal–era transformation was openly announced and deeply theorized. The occasion was *Carolene Products*, a case that raised due process objections to the "Filled Milk Act," a federal statute making it a crime to ship nonfat milk compounded with nondairy coconut oil in interstate commerce. After rejecting the commerce clause challenge, Justice Stone would execute a breathtaking overhaul of the due process jurisprudence. Clearly the statute deprived the company of the "liberty" to contract sales of the product and just as clearly of the "property" to be paid as a fine. The company was entitled to a full-blown criminal trial on the issue of whether it had, in fact, shipped the milk, so the fair hearing component of due process was satisfied. But what about the legality of the deprivation?

The statute itself could not establish its consistency with "the law of the land." Milk production was not a traditionally regulated business like utilities and common carriers. If the act was passed for purely private ends – to enrich dairy farmers at the expense of coconut oil producers – it would be taking from A and giving to B, in violation of due process. But, ostensibly, it had purposes

---

[54] 300 U.S. 379 (1937).   [55] 300 U.S. at 391.   [56] 300 U.S. at 392–97.

other than commercial protectionism. It was intended to promote public health and to prevent fraud. These might be shams, of course, but that depended on the facts. After all, during the *Lochner* era – for example, in *Muller* and in *Smyth* v. *Ames* – the courts had undertaken serious second-guessing of the factual claims necessary to square legislation with unwritten higher law.

Carolene Products did not disavow the higher-law theory of due process in its entirety. Instead, the Court repudiated the judicial duty to independently assess the facts said to support legality. The legislature's factual premises were "presumed" and the presumption would control so long as facts showing a "rational basis" for the statute were "at least debatable."[57] "[R]egulatory legislation affecting ordinary commercial transactions is not to be pronounced unconstitutional unless in the light of the facts made known or generally assumed it is of such a character as to preclude the assumption that it rests upon some rational basis within the knowledge and experience of the legislators."[58]

The key word in that important sentence is "regulatory." To make the point unmistakable, the Court appended the famous footnote 4:

There may be narrower scope for operation of the presumption of constitutionality when legislation appears on its face to be within a specific prohibition of the Constitution, such as those of the first ten Amendments, which are deemed equally specific when held to be embraced within the Fourteenth.

It is unnecessary to consider now whether legislation which restricts those political processes which can ordinarily be expected to bring about repeal of undesirable legislation, is to be subjected to more exacting judicial scrutiny ...

Nor need we enquire whether similar considerations enter into the review of statutes directed at particular religious, or national, or racial minorities ....[59]

Here was the blueprint for due process jurisprudence for the rest of the twentieth century. Henceforth the constitutional law of civil liberties would be the same in state and federal cases. The commerce clause would be equivalent to a federal police power, subject to the same due process constraints as its state counterpart. The now familiar procedural-substantive dichotomy –"procedural due process" a legitimate source of fair-hearing rights and "substantive due process" a sketchy throwback to *Lochner* – is a belated child of *Carolene Products*. The phrase "substantive due process" first appears in the *U.S. Reports* in 1948.[60]

---

[57] 304 U.S. at 152–54.   [58] 304 U.S. at 152 (footnote omitted).
[59] 304 U.S. at 152 (citations omitted).
[60] Republic Natural Gas v. Oklahoma, 334 U.S. 62, 90 (1948) ("The basic question here is really one of substantive due process.") (Rutledge, J., dissenting). Republic Gas appealed an order of the Oklahoma Corporation Commission that reduced Republic's share of gas extracted from a large gas field. The majority declined to rule on Republic's constitutional challenge because the proceedings in the state courts were not yet final. Justice Rutledge thought the Court should have reached Republic's due process claim and rejected it. From inception, then, "substantive due process" has had a pejorative connotation.

What until now had been a collection of rights that were protected coincidentally by the Bill of Rights and by Fourteenth Amendment due process were now understood in terms of specific amendments, among the first eight now being "embraced," or, as the doctrine came to say, "incorporated," by the Fourteenth. "Due process" as there provided, however, was not to be limited to these incorporations. The general requirements of legality and fair procedure remained and were to be policed judicially to make sure no legislation targeted minorities or aimed to insulate political incumbents from the democratic accountability that justified leaving social and economic regulation to the legislative process in the first place.

MODERN DUE PROCESS

After the Great Depression, the New Deal, and World War II, American politics was thoroughly transformed. Even when the Republican Party regained control of Congress in 1946, what followed was more consolidation than reaction. Addressed to the most urgent abuses perceived in New Deal domestic programs, the Taft-Hartley Act balanced in a pro-business direction some of labor's gains under the Wagner Act, and the Administrative Procedure Act reined in the greatly expanded powers of administrative agencies. Additionally, the advent of the Cold War fostered a bipartisan consensus on the need to maintain a powerful peacetime military and to ferret out disloyalty. The Supreme Court was part of this settlement. The justices in 1937 had accepted the turn away from rigorous due process review of social and economic legislation, state or federal. The experience of the war, exposing the horrors of racist persecution and totalitarian repression, did nothing to shake judicial confidence in the new course set by *Carolene Products*. During the second half of the twentieth century, the Court would intervene, sometimes dramatically, on behalf of racial equality and the freedoms enshrined in the Bill of Rights.

If considered in caricature form, as an account of heroic judges successfully foiling a perversely inegalitarian polity, the *Carolene Products* model does not succeed in describing subsequent jurisprudence with complete accuracy. A strong case can be made, for instance, that the model called for much earlier judicial action than the Court eventually took on behalf of, say, suspected communists or women or homosexuals. But with respect to its actual interventions, that decision with its famous footnote correctly anticipated much of what followed. Where the model's explanatory power does arguably flag, however, is in the presence of what were the most furious normative controversies of the period.

The most important change to the deprivation component was the reconceptualization of "liberty" as equality. The Supreme Court's era-defining desegregation case, *Brown* v. *Topeka Board of Education*,[61] had a

---

[61] Brown v. Board of Education, 347 U.S. 483 (1954).

companion case, *Bolling* v. *Sharpe*,[62] in which the plaintiffs raised a
constitutional challenge to racial segregation in the public schools of the
District of Columbia. The principle of *Brown* clearly applied, but the
Fourteenth Amendment on which its ruling rested reads that "no state" shall
deny due process or equal protection, making no provision for acts of the
federal government. This left the Due Process Clause of the Fifth Amendment
as one of the few doctrinal avenues available for imposing *Brown*'s mandate on
the District. So Chief Justice Warren in a brief and seemingly embarrassed
(albeit unanimous) opinion ruled that racial discrimination by the federal
government violates due process. In a throwback to the *Lochner* era, the
Chief Justice wrote: "Segregation in public education is not reasonably related
to any proper governmental objective, and thus it imposes on Negro children of
the District of Columbia a burden that constitutes an arbitrary deprivation of
their liberty in violation of the Due Process Clause."[63]

With respect to the component of legality, *Bolling* unified the constitutional
rights of state and federal citizens and did so without returning to pre–New
Deal–style scrutiny of regulatory laws. For example, in *Heart of Atlanta Motel*
v. *United States*,[64] a business owner challenged the constitutionality of Title II
of the 1964 Civil Rights Act that prohibited, to the full extent of Congress's
interstate commerce power, racial discrimination in places of public
accommodation. Here, the Court followed the *Carolene Products* script,
denying that due process provided a shield for discrimination by private
persons. As the old granger case of *Munn* v. *Illinois* had recognized,
regulation of innkeepers under the common law was a practice several
centuries old; plaintiffs had no baseline entitlement to pick and choose among
the travelers they served. Therefore the Civil Rights act did not "deprive
appellant of liberty or property under the Fifth Amendment."[65] Likewise,
cases on freedom of association turned aside challenges on these grounds
unless they could be shown to abridge the right of "expressive association" by
forcing an organization to alter its membership in ways that contradicted tenets
that were both held and openly espoused.[66]

A more puzzling line of cases has recognized government benefits such as
welfare payments or public employment as "property" for purposes of due
process. In the seminal case, *Goldberg* v. *Kelly*,[67] the Court held that before
public assistance payments could be terminated on a finding of ineligibility, the
welfare agency was constitutionally required to hold a formal adversary
hearing. The benefits cases do not require that public assistance – or pensions

---

[62] 347 U.S. 497 (1954).   [63] 347 U.S. at 500.   [64] 379 U.S. 241 (1964).   [65] 379 U.S. at 258.
[66] Boy Scouts v. Dale, 530 U.S. 640 (2000). In *Dale*, the Boy Scouts of America had expelled a
scoutmaster for being homosexual. The scoutmaster sued for reinstatement under New Jersey's
public accommodations law, which prohibited private discrimination on the basis of sexual
orientation. The Court, in a five-to-four decision, held that the New Jersey law violated the
Scouts' right to free speech.
[67] 397 U.S. 254 (1970).

or university tenure – be provided, nor do they mandate hearings prior to the rejection of initial applications. Still, they refuse to accept the termination procedures in the authorizing statutes as conclusive of the "process" that is "due." In that sense, the government benefit cases seem at best an imperfect fit with the process theory laid out in *Carolene Products*. To be sure, the political system gives little incentive to take account of the interests of the desperately poor. But these decisions also require hearings before terminating public employees for cause[68] or cutting off non-means-tested Social Security disability benefits,[69] even though neither of these beneficiary groups is disabled through prejudice or poverty from participating in the democratic process.

The best explanation seems to be that public benefits have become an ingrained feature of public life, and the "law of the land" therefore includes customary expectations about this so-called "new property." Where statutes and administrative decisions give rise to a "legitimate claim of entitlement," as distinct from purely "unilateral expectation,"[70] deprivations require fair hearings to protect that reliance. The customary law may be a creature of statutes, but it is not their prisoner.

The government benefits puzzle has generated considerable controversy, but one largely confined to the academic literature. The sexual privacy cases, on the other hand, likewise grounded on due process, have provoked controversy that moved out from the law reviews to the ballot box and, as organized protest, into the streets. About the only thing that is uncontroversial seems to be that laws prohibiting sexual conduct, like laws prohibiting any other kind of conduct, deprive citizens of their liberty. Under *Carolene Products*, then, should laws regulating sexual conduct be reviewed as if they were social and economic legislation or, instead, like statutes based on racial discrimination or other obstacles in the democratic process? Gays and lesbians or women might be groups disempowered in the electoral process. Even if one accepts that characterization, however, the timeline of the decisions does not fit the *Carolene Products* template.

The initial case in the sexual-conduct line, *Griswold* v. *Connecticut*,[71] invalidated a state statute prohibiting the sale of contraceptives, making no exception for individuals who were lawfully married. The actual persons prosecuted by the state were leaders of Planned Parenthood, for aiding and abetting the offense. Clearly the criminal conviction deprived the defendants of "liberty," and, just as clearly, the statute itself restricted the "liberty" of individuals to use birth control. The defendants did not raise any claim of unfair trial procedure. The only issue was the legality of their deprivation of liberty. In striking down the Connecticut statute, the justices were

---

[68] E.g., Cleveland Board of Education v. Loudermill, 470 U.S. 532 (1985).
[69] Mathews v. Eldridge, 424 U.S. 319 (1976).
[70] Board of Regents v. Roth, 408 U.S. 564, 577 (1972).   [71] 381 U.S. 479 (1965).

embarrassed, as in *Bolling,* by their evident need to turn back to the *Lochner* era for supporting authority. Justice Douglas for the majority hewed to the Fourteenth Amendment incorporation doctrine but by arguing that particular amendments in the Bill of Rights cast "penumbras" the Court might enforce. In this case, shadows of the Third and Fourth Amendments restricted government interference in what was done in the privacy of the home. Only slightly less eccentric was Justice Goldberg's concurrence, which would have invalidated the statute for violating the Ninth Amendment.

Justice Harlan's concurrence in *Griswold,* based on an earlier dissent in *Poe v. Ullman,* is generally regarded as having provided the soundest justification.[72] Harlan relied on the fundamental fairness approach, finding that the higher law includes not just some protections in the Bill of Rights but "a rational continuum which, broadly speaking, includes a freedom from all substantial arbitrary impositions and purposeless restraints, and which also recognizes, what a reasonable and sensitive judgment must, that certain interests require particularly careful scrutiny of the state needs asserted to justify their abridgment."[73] In fact, *Carolene Products* had accepted this framework but deemed it judicially enforceable, primarily if not exclusively, against statutes that stifled dissent or targeted unpopular minorities. Nothing in the Connecticut law shielded it against repeal through electoral politics. One might characterize the law as burdening women, and women as a disempowered group, but the justices limited the holding to married persons of either gender; only subsequently did they extend the ruling to unmarried persons.[74]

Reliance on *Griswold* as precedent for invalidating state laws against abortion set off a ferocious political controversy, pitting "the right to life" against "the right to choose."[75] Subsequent cases have reaffirmed the leading case, *Roe v. Wade,* over forceful dissent.[76] In this same line, after initially rejecting a due process challenge to criminal sodomy laws in *Bowers v. Hardwick,*[77] the Court eventually reversed course and invalidated them in *Lawrence v. Texas.*[78] Perhaps the most peculiar feature of the sexual privacy cases is not their content but their limits. They do not, for instance, read John Stuart Mill's "harm principle" into the Constitution.[79] The cases disclaim any

---

[72] Poe v. Ullman, 367 U.S. 497 (1961). In *Poe* the majority rejected a challenge to the Connecticut birth-control statute because the plaintiffs lacked standing. Justice Harlan disagreed with the majority's standing analysis, reached the merits, and would have ruled that the statute violated the Due Process Clause.

[73] Ibid. at 543 (Harlan, J., dissenting) (citations omitted).

[74] Eisenstadt v. Baird, 405 U.S. 538 (1972).   [75] Roe v. Wade, 410 U.S. 113 (1973).

[76] E.g., Planned Parenthood v. Casey, 505 U.S. 833 (1992).   [77] 478 U.S. 186 (1986).

[78] 539 U.S. 558 (2003).

[79] Mill famously argued that "the sole end for which mankind are warranted, individually or collectively, in interfering with the liberty of action of any of their number, is self-protection." John Stuart Mill, *On Liberty and Other Writings,* ed. Stefan Collini (Cambridge: Cambridge University Press, 1989), 13.

right to commercial or public sex. Not a term goes by that the Court does not let stand the sentence of some seller of illegal drugs to willing buyers. The privacy decisions seem premised on the special value of autonomy in erotic and reproductive aspects of life, similar to the special value of autonomy over speech and faith. Yet the cases do not articulate and defend that premise in ways that fully satisfy even those who favor their outcomes.

The fair hearing requirement is interesting, for it has dictated quite different standards in criminal, as opposed to civil, cases. The criminal cases were also slower to change. By the time of *Carolene Products*, the Court already had brought the Fifth Amendment takings clause and First Amendment freedoms of speech, press, and free exercise into the domain of Fourteenth Amendment due process. Four years later, in 1942, in a case involving the refusal of a Maryland court to appoint counsel for an indigent defendant accused of a noncapital felony,[80] Justice Black casually reported his view that the Fourteenth Amendment incorporates the Bill of Rights *in toto*. He wrote, however, in dissent. The majority ruled that due process depended on "fundamental fairness" in "the totality of facts in a given case." Six years after that, in *Adamson* v. *California*,[81] a capital case raising a due process challenge to the California practice permitting comment on the failure of the defendant to testify, Justice Black presented a full exposition of his total incorporation theory, relying on the text and legislative history of the Fourteenth Amendment. Three other justices agreed with him, but the majority reaffirmed a prior holding that the privilege against self-incrimination was not "fundamental."

The "fundamental fairness" in the "totality of facts in a given case" approach turned out to be irredeemably vague. It failed to guide police, prosecutors, and state court judges. Its application by federal courts hearing habeas corpus petitions after state supreme courts had affirmed criminal convictions seemed to betray the federalism principles the approach sought to promote. In its wake, in less than a decade, came the "criminal procedure revolution." Beginning in 1961 and *Mapp* v. *Ohio*,[82] which held that due process requires the exclusionary rule to bolster the substantive Fourth Amendment guarantee against unreasonable search and seizure, through 1969 and *Benton* v. *Maryland*,[83] holding that the Fifth Amendment guarantee against double-jeopardy was "fundamental," the Warren Court had incorporated all of the provisions in the Fourth, Fifth, and Sixth Amendments into the Fourteenth,

---

[80] Betts v. Brady, 316 U.S. 455 (1942).
[81] 332 U.S. 46 (1947). Justice Black invoked both "due process" and "privileges or immunities." Substantial contemporary scholarship supports incorporation via "privileges or "immunities," but the Court has not overruled the *Slaughterhouse Cases* and continues to treat incorporation as a matter of due process. See McDonald v. Chicago, 561 U.S. 742 (2010).
[82] 367 U.S. 643 (1961).   [83] 395 U.S. 784 (1969).

leaving out only Fifth Amendment grand jury, with which, in *Hurtado*, the long succession of holdouts had begun almost a century earlier.[84]

Reaction occurred gradually and on several fronts. First, the Warren Court itself, having applied the Bill of Rights to the states, began to interpret its provisions more favorably toward state law enforcement than in the preincorporation federal cases. Second, Richard Nixon, who had campaigned for "law and order," appointed four justices, each of whom was largely sympathetic to law enforcement. The Burger Court did not overrule the incorporation decisions but did take a markedly more pro-government approach to interpreting the Bill of Rights. It diluted the standard of probable cause[85] and both expanded existing exceptions to the exclusionary rule[86] and created new ones. The Court declined to overrule the Warren Court's landmark ruling in *Miranda* v. *Arizona*,[87] which required the famous warnings before evidence gained through custodial interrogations could be admitted at trial, but has read it narrowly.[88] *Gideon* v. *Wainwright*, which declared a constitutional right to counsel for indigent defendants, has also survived, but while the Sixth Amendment continues to require offering all indigent felony defendants appointed counsel, the counsel's deficient performance mandates a new trial only if it can be shown on appeal that the errors were egregious and might have altered the outcome.[89]

Third, the practice of plea bargaining – offering defendants reduced sentences for pleading guilty – came to dominate the criminal process. When the Burger Court heard a due process challenge to a life sentence imposed on a defendant who would have received a five-year sentence if he had pled guilty, it found the penalty following trial consistent with due process.[90] So long as the facts supported the higher charge and the accused had been advised by competent counsel, the plea deal offered by the prosecution was treated as an offer rather than a threat. Today about 95 percent of criminal convictions result from pleas rather than trials. The constitutional rights recognized by the Warren Court still matter overall but primarily as bargaining chips.

In the "new property" or entitlement cases, the scope of the hearing is determined by a balancing or "cost-benefit" test announced in *Mathews* v. *Eldridge*.[91] There, Eldridge had challenged the procedures for terminating his

---

[84] The Court understood its process of incorporation as "selective." It never accepted Justice Black's view that due process required nothing more – or less – in criminal cases than the Bill of Rights provided.

[85] Illinois v. Gates, 462.S. 213 (1983).   [86] E.g., *Havens*, 446 U.S. 620 (1980).

[87] Dickerson v. United States, 530 U.S. 428 (2000) (holding Title II of the 1968 Crime Control Act, which purported to reverse *Miranda* by statute, contrary to *Miranda* and therefore unconstitutional).

[88] E.g., Harris v. New York, 401 U.S. 222 (1971) (holding that defendant's pretrial statement, obtained in violation of *Miranda*, could be admitted to contradict the defendant's testimony at trial).

[89] Strickland v. Washington, 466 U.S. 668 (1984).

[90] Bordenkircher v. Hayes, 434 U.S. 357 (1978).   [91] 424 U.S. 319 (1976).

Social Security disability benefits, which allowed for a recipient to obtain a hearing but only after the benefits were ended. Eldridge had argued that due process required an opportunity to be heard prior to termination, quoting an earlier public assistance case, *Goldberg* v. *Kelly*. The *Mathews* Court, however, announced a new test under which due process generally requires consideration of three distinct factors: "First, the private interest that will be affected by the official action; second, the risk of an erroneous deprivation of such interest through the procedures used, and the probable value, if any, of additional or substitute procedural safeguards; and finally, the Government's interest, including the function involved and the fiscal and administrative burdens that the additional or substitute procedural requirement would entail."[92]

Applying this test, the Court rejected Eldridge's fair hearing argument. Unlike public assistance benefits, disability benefits were not means tested; their termination will not always lead to poverty. Because disability benefits turned on the claimant's medical condition, the pretermination opportunity to present documentary support from medical professionals would be little improved by an adversarial hearing. Therefore, the costs of that hearing would outweigh the benefits.

The benefits and costs of procedural safeguards as calculated by the judiciary have varied across cases less than the weight of the individual interests at stake. The public school student facing suspension for misbehavior has only a right to be told of the supposed misconduct and given a chance to explain.[93] The adult facing indefinite civil commitment for dangerous insanity has a constitutional right to a full adversarial trial under the clear-and-convincing evidence standard.[94] Intermediate cases call for intermediate procedures. In general, however, the Court has refused to apply the *Eldridge* test to criminal cases. Instead, "we have defined the category of infractions that violate fundamental fairness very narrowly based on the recognition that, [b]eyond the specific guarantees enumerated in the Bill of Rights, the Due Process Clause has limited operation."[95] So while procedures for terminating Social Security benefits are reviewed in the interest of accuracy, the procedures for imposing criminal punishment are reviewed for consistency with the historical practices enshrined in the Bill of Rights.

COMMON GROUND IN THE TWENTY-FIRST CENTURY

The bitterness of individual debates can obscure the substantial degree of consensus among the justices about due process. They generally agree that

---

[92] 424 U.S. 319 at 335.   [93] 419 U.S. 565 (1975).
[94] Addington v. Texas, 441 U.S. 418 (1979).
[95] Medina v. California, 505 U.S. 437, 443 (1992) (citations and internal quotation marks omitted). California required criminal defendants claiming incompetence to stand trial to rebut a presumption of competence by a preponderance of the evidence. *Medina* upheld the California procedure.

statute law does not define either the "life, liberty, or property" that is protected against deprivation by government, the legality of deprivations, or the fairness of the hearings that must accompany them. For example, in *Washington* v. *Glucksberg*, rejecting a due process challenge to a state statute prohibiting physician-assisted suicide, Chief Justice Rehnquist accepted Justice Harlan's basic approach in *Griswold*:

> Our established method of substantive-due-process analysis has two primary features: First, we have regularly observed that the Due Process Clause specially protects those fundamental rights and liberties which are, objectively, "deeply rooted in this Nation's history and tradition," and "implicit in the concept of ordered liberty," such that "neither liberty nor justice would exist if they were sacrificed." Second, we have required in substantive-due-process cases a "careful description" of the asserted fundamental liberty interest.[96]

This conservative formulation nonetheless recognizes that due process forbids abridgement of fundamental liberty interests "*at all*, no matter what process is provided, unless the infringement is narrowly tailored to serve a compelling state interest."[97] So too, in the sodomy decisions, no justice has said that the very existence of a formally valid sodomy statute provided a truly lawful basis on which "liberty" might be deprived. Justice White for the *Hardwick* majority, Chief Justice Burger concurring there, and Justice Scalia dissenting in *Lawrence* all thought it necessary to support the challenged statute by invoking legal tradition – that is, not what the legislature had done in the case at hand but how its act compared to what *other* legislatures and judges had done in other cases.

If there is broad consensus that statutes can violate due process without violating a specific constitutional provision, there is at the same time no agreement on any "established" method for assessing the scope of "liberty" protected or of higher-law legality. In *Glucksberg*, five justices – Souter, O'Connor, Ginsburg, Breyer, and Stevens – wrote five separate concurring opinions. In *Lawrence*, the majority did not identify a fundamental right abridged but held that the Texas statute lacked even the rational basis required of social welfare legislation under *Carolene Products*. So it seems fair to say not only that a statute that flunks Chief Justice Rehnquist's *Glucksberg* test will be struck down but also that – as *Lawrence* and *Obergefell*, striking a law against same-sex marriage, suggest – some laws that comport with tradition may also violate due process.

The prevailing law of due process can be summarized, albeit roughly, in a single paragraph. "Life" means life after birth. "Property" means positive law rights to land, chattels, patents, and so on, and also includes reliable

---

[96] 521 U.S. 702, at 720 (1997) (citations omitted).

[97] 521 U.S. at 721 (quoting Reno v. Flores, 507 U.S. 292, 302 [1993]) (emphasis original in both *Flores* and *Glucksberg*).

entitlements to government jobs and benefit payments. "Liberty" means negative liberty, i.e., freedom from restraint by government. "Law" means the (sufficiently specific) positive statute and common law, except insofar as these either violate substantive provisions in the Bill of Rights, such as freedom of speech, or an unenumerated yet "fundamental" right, including most prominently sexual autonomy. In criminal cases, a fair hearing means the fair-trial provisions in the Bill of Rights, supplemented by any other procedures required as a matter of "fundamental fairness." In civil proceedings, a fair hearing means a procedure that satisfies the balancing test of *Mathews* v. *Eldridge*.

The recent cases mentioned at the outset of this discussion show the persistence of this basic framework and the continuing controversy over each of the constituent concepts. *Obergefell* v. *Hodges*[98] presented sharp disagreements about whether laws against same-sex marriage were deprivations of liberty and, if they were deprivations, whether the statutes were consistent with higher law. The majority held that the unenumerated fundamental right to marry recognized in prior cases included the right to marry a partner of the same sex. The fundamental right at stake, according to the majority, was not the right to sexual autonomy vindicated in *Lawrence* but the distinct right to a legal status providing a secure basis for emotional commitment and the nurturing of children.

Justice Thomas, dissenting, challenged this positive understanding of "liberty." In *Lawrence*, the Court barred Texas from doing things *to* same-sex couples, namely, arrest and prosecute them. In *Obergefell*, the Court required the states to do something *for* same-sex couples. Chief Justice Roberts and Justice Scalia, on the other hand, disagreed with the majority on the legality component. Both saw no reason to overrule the democratic process. Chief Justice Roberts cited *Dred Scott* and *Lochner* as cautionary tales. The majority did not resort to *Carolene Products*, instead taking the view that even if there were no deficit of democracy in the instance at hand, delay alone called for decisive and immediate judicial intervention.

In *Johnson* v. *United States*,[99] the Court relied on due process to strike down the residual clause of the federal Armed Career Criminal Act (ACCA). The ACCA increases – "enhances" – the sentence of any defendant convicted of a third violent felony, defining "violent felony" as one in which the use of force against another person is an element of the crime, and includes arson and arson-like crimes, even if they involve no use of force. There is also a residual clause, defining "violent felony" to include a crime that "otherwise involves conduct that presents a serious potential risk of physical injury to another."[100] In *Johnson*, the government sought an enhanced sentence for the defendant. One of his prior convictions was for possessing a sawed-off shotgun, and the issue in

---

[98] 135 S.Ct. 2584 (2015).   [99] 135 S.Ct. 2551 (2015).   [100] 18 U.S.C. 924(b)(2)(b).

the case was whether this conviction was a "violent felony" within the meaning of the residual clause.

The majority, speaking through Justice Scalia, ruled that the ACCA's residual clause was void for vagueness, and therefore the sentencing enhancement, which clearly deprived Johnson of liberty, violated the legality criterion. Justice Thomas concurred in the result because he thought the residual clause was clear enough to be constitutional and that the defense, rather than the government, had the better statutory argument. Nevertheless, he went on to launch a broad attack on the vagueness doctrine generally. Thomas characterized the Court's use of that doctrine as a stealthy version of substantive due process, by means of which majorities could invalidate any statute they disapproved of on grounds of legislative policy, equating the vagueness cases with *Dred Scott* and *Lochner* for good measure.

Finally, *Ohio* v. *Clark*[101] illustrates the fair hearing component of due process. As we have seen, the Court's decisions generally require state compliance with most of the procedures specified in the Bill of Rights and with a more general right to "fundamental fairness." At Clark's trial for child abuse, the trial court allowed preschool teachers to testify to accusations made by a three-year-old, whereas the child did not testify. Clark argued that admitting the teachers' testimony about the child's accusation violated the Sixth Amendment right "to be confronted with the witnesses against him." (Originally applied only to federal prosecutions, the confrontation clause was incorporated into the Fourteenth Amendment's Due Process Clause in 1965[102] as part of the criminal procedure revolution.)

The majority, however, rejected Clark's confrontation clause claim, concluding that a child's accusation to schoolteachers was not equivalent to trial by affidavit, which had been the core abuse prohibited by the confrontation clause. Clark had also argued that even if the confrontation clause did not bar the teachers' testimony, permitting the adults to testify was fundamentally unfair when coupled with the state's exclusion of the child's own testimony. Justice Alito's majority opinion tersely rejected this claim, too, as inconsistent with the legal use of hearsay testimony from an unavailable declarant, as when the court hears a dying declaration reportedly made by the deceased accusing the defendant of the murder. The point remains, however, that due process in criminal cases requires both observance of traditional procedures enshrined in

---

[101] 135 S.Ct. 2173 (2015).

[102] Pointer v. Texas, 380 U.S. 400 (1965). In *Pointer*, a prosecution witness identified Pointer as one of the robbers at a preliminary hearing, where Pointer was present but not represented by counsel. The witness moved out of state before the trial, where the prosecution offered the transcript of the preliminary hearing. The Court held that the Sixth Amendment right of confrontation was fundamental and so incorporated by Fourteenth Amendment due process and that the use at trial of sworn testimony taken at a hearing where the defendant did not have the opportunity to cross-examine the witness through counsel violated the confrontation right.

the Bill of Rights (excepting, in state cases, the grand jury) *and* more generally "fundamental fairness."

Disagreement about due process cases persists. It persists, however, because of general, perhaps even complete, agreement that (1) due process protects certain individual interests against deprivation absent lawful authority and fair procedure and (2) ordinary statutes purporting to define entitlements, authorize deprivations, or provide fair hearings are not conclusive but subject to judicial review. It seems probable that this common ground will continue to frame, but not to settle, debates about due process, just as it has since the birth of the republic.

3

Civil Liberties and the Dual Legacy of the Founding

John W. Compton

In the area of civil liberties, the American framers bequeathed a dual legacy. On the one hand, they authored and ratified constitutions with strikingly open-ended guarantees concerning the freedom of speech, the freedom of religion, the right to trial by jury, and various aspects of criminal procedure. On the other hand, the same Americans who spoke of "inalienable" rights endorsed a range of inherited laws and customary practices that sharply limited the practical consequences of these abstract guarantees. Most of the newly independent states enforced laws against blasphemy, for example, even as their constitutions promised to respect the freedom of speech. Many states also criminalized Sunday labor and barred non-Protestants from holding office, even as their constitutions prohibited religious establishments and promised to respect the freedom of religion. And virtually no one involved in the drafting of the state or federal constitutions believed that civil liberties provisions indicated any change in the legal status of slaves, women, or other subordinate classes of Americans.

There can be little doubt that the authors of Founding-era rights provisions sincerely hoped to protect citizens from the sorts of abuses – from warrantless searches to the forced quartering of soldiers – that had transformed the imperial crisis into a revolution. But most of them were equally determined to guard against the collapse of customary forms of authority that they deemed essential to social stability. Thus, while civil liberties principles certainly played a central role in the American Revolution, it is not at all clear that they occupied a preeminent position in the constitutional order that emerged in its aftermath. Far from elevating civil liberties above inherited forms of authority, the founding generation superimposed the former on the latter, leaving it to future generations to work out the precise nature of the resulting relationships.

This chapter will argue that the framers' dual legacy in the area of civil liberties has cast a long historical shadow. Since the early republic, Americans have invoked constitutional civil liberties provisions to challenge customary forms of authority. Yet establishing the abstract legitimacy of one's claim – that it comports with a particular conception of religious liberty or the freedom of speech, for example – has typically been insufficient to prevail in the courts. In addition, rights claimants have regularly been asked to overcome a competing set of normative commitments – to federalism, to patriarchal family relations, to religiously inspired social mores – that give entrenched authority its own distinct claim to constitutional legitimacy. The most obvious practical effect of this duality, particularly in the early years of the republic, was the frequent subordination of civil liberties to illiberal forms of authority. Yet even as illiberal authority structures have eroded over time, the framers' dual legacy has continued to shape constitutional development in ways both subtle and profound.

Indeed, it is noteworthy that even as Americans have adopted ever more expansive conceptions of particular constitutional liberties, they have continued to disagree, often bitterly, about precisely which forms of inherited authority are so arbitrary or oppressive as to run afoul of these guarantees. They have also disagreed, just as bitterly, over the state's proper role in mitigating the social and political effects of illiberal social authority. Should civil liberties provisions be regarded as purely negative guarantees, offering protection against government action only, and thus not incompatible with social arrangements that, while illiberal, are not clearly underpinned by official authority? Alternatively, do government actors have an affirmative duty to dismantle inherited social structures that render civil liberties all but meaningless for some citizens? And if such an obligation exists, how does one calculate (and justify) the resulting tradeoffs between liberty and equality? If consensus on these questions has proved elusive, it is at least in part because the Constitution, owing to its dual nature, cannot settle the matter.

This chapter divides the history of civil liberties into four periods. The first section covers the period from the founding through the late nineteenth century – a time when a broad moral consensus rooted in Protestant Christianity was said to demarcate a boundary between "liberty" and "license" and when open-ended civil liberties provisions were rarely interpreted in ways that undermined customary patterns of authority. The second section examines the early decades of the twentieth century, a transformative period when the collapse of the Protestant moral consensus, together with the rise of social movements bent on undermining entrenched hierarchies, left the traditional theory of civil liberties in tatters.

The chapter's third section documents the emergence, in the middle decades of the twentieth century, of a new theory centered on promoting individual autonomy and protecting a robust marketplace of ideas. Crucially, the mid-century Supreme Court harnessed its civil liberties jurisprudence to an egalitarian theory of American democracy, aggressively scrutinizing laws that appeared to perpetuate systemic inequality while adopting a deferential approach in cases where state action seemed designed to mitigate flaws in the nation's representative system of government.

The chapter's final section covers the modern period (1970s to the present), an era when the justices have sorted themselves into competing ideological camps, with each camp at times embracing an expansive conception of civil liberties – albeit for very different reasons. In some cases, a "liberal" bloc advocating an uncompromising approach to civil liberties is pitted against a "conservative" bloc advocating deference to traditional mores and local majority sentiment. In others, the ideological valence of civil liberties is reversed, with the conservative bloc adopting an absolutist conception of individual rights and the liberal bloc advocating deference to lawmakers who are purportedly acting to remedy structural inequalities. Because case outcomes have often turned on the vote of a single "swing" justice, modern civil liberties doctrine has grown increasingly incoherent: decisions proclaiming the inviolability of civil liberties principles are followed, often in the same term, by decisions calling for deference to tradition or for subordinating civil liberties to the goal of fostering a more egalitarian society. These doctrinal tensions become comprehensible when viewed in the light of the framers' dual legacy.

CIVIL LIBERTIES IN THE LONG NINETEENTH CENTURY

At first glance, it may seem that the individual rights today referred to as "civil liberties" have always been a core concern – perhaps *the* core concern – of American constitutionalism. Certainly, no subject featured more prominently in the ratification debate of 1787–1788.[1] Most of the delegates tasked with evaluating the Philadelphia Convention's handiwork hailed from states whose constitutions recognized a range of "natural," "inalienable," or "inherent" rights, including the freedom of the press, the freedom of religion, and the right to trial by jury. The bill (or declaration) of rights was typically placed at the head of these documents, thus ensuring, at least in theory, that the new state governments would not lose sight of the higher ends for which they were formed. It is hardly surprising, then, that many delegates cried foul when it was discovered that the proposed federal constitution lacked such protections. In the end, James Madison and other leading Federalists, fearing that the Constitution might go down to defeat, agreed to amend the document. The resulting guarantees, now known collectively as the Bill of Rights, included the freedoms of press and speech; the rights of petition and assembly; the free exercise of religion; a ban on religious establishments; the right to bear arms; and a range of criminal procedure guarantees including, among other things, the right to a fair and speedy trial, a ban on warrantless searches, and a prohibition against "cruel and unusual" punishments.

But for all the ink they spilled in defense of civil liberties, it is far from clear that founding-era Americans understood these guarantees in the same way as twenty-first-century Americans. Indeed, many of the same state convention delegates who demanded a federal bill of rights were alarmed to find that the

---

[1] See, for example, Pauline Maier, *Ratification: The People Debate the Constitution, 1787–1788* (New York: Simon and Schuster, 2010).

proposed Constitution explicitly banned the use of religious test oaths for federal officeholders. This provision raised the specter that "pagans, deists, Mahometans" and even the "pope of Rome" might "obtain offices among us."[2] Although Federalist writers conceded the force of the objection, they rushed to assure skeptical delegates that the Constitution would not interfere with the states' ability to punish "profane swearing, blasphemy ... professed atheism" and other "gross immoralities and impieties."[3]

What should we make of Americans who demanded expansively worded rights guarantees while simultaneously insisting that Catholics be barred from public offices and blasphemy punished as a crime? Two broadly shared convictions allowed Americans to proclaim allegiance to the idea of civil liberties while simultaneously embracing inherited social structures that sharply limited the real-world effects of these written guarantees. First, it was widely agreed that republican government was unlikely to survive in the absence of a morally virtuous citizenry.[4] From this it followed that a Protestant-derived moral consensus marked, or ought to mark, the boundary between liberty and license. Second, even as Americans embraced the Lockean language of natural rights, the enduring force of the common law ensured that they would continue to view their own society in broadly hierarchical terms. Thus James Kent and other early American legal commentators depicted a society composed not of coequal rights-bearing citizens but of legally enforceable relationships featuring dominant and subordinate partners: husbands and wives, masters and servants, guardians and wards.[5] To the limited extent that these writers addressed the tension between inherited legal prerogatives and the Lockean ideal of universal rights, they insisted that the very possibility of republican government presumed a well-ordered society. And a well-ordered society, in turn, presupposed the existence of hierarchically organized subunits, such as families and workplaces.[6]

---

[2] Neil H. Cogan, ed., *The Complete Bill of Rights: The Drafts, Debates, Sources, and Origins* (New York: Oxford University Press, 1997), 63, 67. The quotations are from the North Carolina ratifying convention.

[3] Oliver Ellsworth, "A Landholder, No. 7." In Cogan, ed., *The Complete Bill of Rights*, 78.

[4] Although James Madison arguably believed that a well-designed constitutional system could thrive even in the absence of virtuous officeholders, few of his contemporaries seem to have shared this conviction. Nor is it entirely clear that Madison held the amoral view of political society that is often attributed to him. See, for example, Lance Banning, *The Sacred Fire of Liberty: James Madison and the Founding of the Federal Republic* (Ithaca: Cornell University Press, 1998), 247.

[5] James Kent, *Commentaries on American Law*, Vol. 2 (New York: O. Halstead, 1827).

[6] As William Novak has put the point, the particular bundle of rights to which a nineteenth-century American could lay claim was "highly particularized [and] dependent upon [an] individual's personal pattern of residence, jurisdiction, office, job, service, organization, association, family position, age, gender, race, and capacity." "The Legal Transformation of Citizenship in Nineteenth-Century America," in Meg Jacobs, William J. Novak, and Julian E. Zelizer, eds., *The Democratic Experiment: New Directions in American Political History* (Princeton: Princeton University Press, 2009), 85–119, 95. See also, William J. Novak, *The People's Welfare: Law and Regulation in Nineteenth-Century America* (Chapel Hill: University of North Carolina Press, 1996).

To see this moralized and particularized conception of rights in action, we need only examine a few illustrative cases involving religious liberty and the freedom of the press. Consider the case of John Ruggles, a resident of New York who in 1811 appealed his blasphemy conviction to his state's highest court. At first glance, Ruggles had a strong case. He pointed out that New York's constitution guaranteed the freedom of conscience and barred the establishment of an official religion. Moreover, blasphemy was not explicitly mentioned as a criminal act in any statute enacted by the state legislature. And yet Judge James Kent, in the face of these apparently mitigating facts, affirmed Ruggles's conviction. Although Kent acknowledged that New York had "discarded religious establishments," he insisted that it had not repealed those parts of the common law that served to "inculcate moral discipline" and "bind society together."[7] Blasphemy would continue to be punished as a crime in New York not because it offended "the rights of the church" but because it "tend[ed] to corrupt the morals of the people, and to destroy [the] good order" that was the essential prerequisite of republican government.[8]

If the rights of conscience belonged in the first instance to Protestant Christians, the duties that corresponded to these rights fell disproportionately on nonbelievers and religious minorities. This was nowhere more evident than in early appellate cases involving Sunday labor. In *Commonwealth* v. *Wolf* (1817), the Pennsylvania Supreme Court dismissed a Jewish tradesman's constitutional objections to a state law that criminalized nonessential labor on the Christian Sabbath. Although the state's constitution guaranteed the free exercise of religion, the Court reasoned that Wolf's rights had not been infringed, since nothing in (its reading of) the Jewish sacred texts *commanded* Jews to labor on Sundays. Wolf was free to forego labor on Saturdays, but the state constitution did not guarantee his right to make up for lost time by working on the day when "the great mass" of the state's citizens believed God had commanded them to rest.[9] An 1886 decision of the Georgia Supreme Court employed the same line of reasoning, noting that protections for religious liberty would be but "paper guarantees, unless protected and enforced by legal sanctions," including Sunday closing laws, that ensured a quiet and wholesome environment for "religious worship."[10]

---

[7] People v. Ruggles, 8 Johns. 290, 296, 294 (1811). Most early American commentators accepted John Locke's argument that secular authorities, whose primary responsibility was to safeguard citizens' liberty and property, had no business either prescribing or proscribing particular articles of faith or forms of worship. This conception marked a significant break with English practice in that it generally barred the state from persecuting citizens whose only crime was to belong to an unpopular sect. Yet as Kent's *Ruggles* opinion makes clear, most judges were nonetheless supportive of laws that cultivated respect for religion (read: Protestant Christianity) in the abstract. For Locke's conception of religious liberty, see "A Letter Concerning Toleration," in Ian Shapiro, ed., *Two Treatises of Government and a Letter Concerning Toleration* (New Haven: Yale University Press, 2003), 211–56.

[8] 8 Johns (N.Y.) 290 (1811).   [9] 3 Serg. & Rawle 48; 1817 Pa. LEXIS 10 at 51.

[10] The Trustees of the First Methodist Episcopal Church, South v. The City of Atlanta, 76 Ga. 181, 191, 194–95 (1886).

Similar assumptions governed early interpretations of constitutional free speech provisions. Most commentators agreed that the common law definition of freedom of the press, which barred only the "prior restraint" of speech, was insufficiently protective of individual liberty. And many were also critical of the English doctrine of seditious libel, under which virtually any speaker who criticized a government official in print could be prosecuted, so long as the state acted after the offensive material was published.[11] By the early nineteenth century, most of the states had formally declared – whether by constitutional amendment, judicial decision, or statute – that speakers who, in the judgment of a jury, published factual information with upstanding motives would be guilty of no crime.[12]

Yet even as antebellum Americans enthusiastically exercised the right to criticize officeholders, they steadfastly resisted any suggestion that this newfound freedom implied a broader right to challenge the legitimacy of entrenched authority in the private or "domestic" sphere. This much became clear in the mid-1830s, when President Andrew Jackson authorized US postmasters to destroy the antislavery literature that Northern abolitionists had recently begun mailing to Southern addressees.[13] Jackson's Postmaster General, Amos Kendall, went further, urging Southern states to enact their own laws to prevent the dissemination of abolitionist literature. According to Kendall, neither the First Amendment nor any other provision of the Constitution had disturbed the slave states' right to "fence and protect their interest in slaves by such laws and regulations as, in their sovereign will, they may deem expedient."[14]

Chief Justice Roger Taney's majority opinion in the 1857 *Dred Scott Case* erased any remaining doubt that the scope of constitutional speech rights was determined by an individual's position in a broader matrix of legally enforceable interpersonal relationships. Although the case primarily concerned the legal status of chattel slavery in the territories, Taney went out of his way to declare that even *free* blacks were excluded from the privileges and immunities of

---

[11] Writing in 1789, Thomas Jefferson expressed hope that Americans would "not be deprived or abridged of their right to speak, to write, or otherwise to publish any thing but false facts affecting injuriously the life, property or reputation of others or affecting the peace of the confederacy with foreign nations." Thomas Jefferson to James Madison, August 28, 1789. In Neil H. Cogan, ed., *The Complete Bill of Rights: The Drafts, Debates, Sources, and Origins*, 2nd ed. (New York: Oxford University Press, 2015), 181.

[12] For the most influential statement of this rule, see Judge James Kent's opinion in People v. Croswell, 3 Johns. Cas. 337 (N.Y. 1804).

[13] Jackson used his 1835 Annual Message to Congress to urge passage of "such a law as will prohibit, under severe penalties, the circulation in the Southern States . . . of incendiary publications intended to instigate the slaves to insurrection." Stephen M. Feldman, *Free Expression and Democracy in America: A History* (Chicago: University of Chicago Press, 2009), 130.

[14] Amos quoted in Michael Kent Curtis, *Free Speech, "The People's Darling Privilege": Struggles for Freedom of Expression in American History* (Durham, NC: Duke University Press, 2000), 138.

national citizenship. To recognize free blacks as full citizens, Taney reasoned, would entail the unimaginable consequence that

persons of the negro race, who were recognized as citizens in any one State of the Union, [would enjoy] the right to enter every other State whenever they pleased ... *and it would give them the full liberty of speech in public and in private upon all subjects upon which [a state's] own citizens might speak ... [and] to hold public meetings upon political affairs* ... And all of this would be done in the face of the subject race of the same color ... and inevitably producing discontent and insubordination among them, and endangering the peace and safety of the State.[15]

For Taney, it was simply "impossible to believe" that the Southern framers "could have been so forgetful or regardless of their own safety" as to endorse the existence of rights whose contours were unaffected by their impact upon preexisting authority structures.[16]

One finds the same line of reasoning in countless nineteenth-century cases where an asserted constitutional right of free speech collided with entrenched social hierarchies. Authority relations within the family, for example, remained largely unaffected by developments in the realm of constitutional law. Women in the early republic were regularly prevented from speaking in public, particularly to mixed audiences. State and federal obscenity laws – known as Comstock Laws, after their chief proponent – barred discussion of contraception and family planning. And although women raised constitutional objections to these restrictions (and many others), their pleas typically fell on deaf ears. As Justice Joseph P. Bradley explained in 1873, in a case involving the Illinois state bar's refusal to admit a woman, "the law of the Creator" had decreed that women were to enjoy only those rights that were essential to "fulfill[ing] the noble and benign offices of wife and mother."[17]

Nor did civil liberties provisions significantly interfere with authority relations in the workplace. As nineteenth-century workers who invoked the freedom of speech in defense of the right to organize quickly discovered, the legal prerogatives of the employer trumped – or rather defined the limits of – the constitutional rights of the employee.[18] In some cases, employers and anti-union officials suppressed labor organizing by relying on ordinances that

---

[15] 60 U.S. 393, 416–17 (1857).

[16] Ibid. at 417. Even the most explicit constitutional guarantees, such as the First Amendment right to "petition the Government for a redress of grievances," had little practical effect when the subject in question was slavery. In 1836, the US House adopted a rule – informally known as the "gag rule" – that automatically tabled all slavery-related petitions. See Curtis, *Free Speech: "The People's Darling Privilege,"* 138, 175–81.

[17] Bradwell v. Illinois, 83 U.S. 130, 142 (1873). Bradley, J., concurring.

[18] Karen Orren, *Belated Feudalism: Labor, the Law, and Liberal Development in the United States* (New York: Cambridge University Press, 1991), 92. As Orren puts the point, "The employee lived in a divided political world. One section was governed by public representatives of his own choosing, in rituals festooned and celebrated with the ballyhoo of party politics, peopled by silver-tongued orators and war heroes. The other was sealed off from the public, disciplined and drab, its governance located finally in the somber and mystifying routines of the courtroom."

limited street speaking to certain (typically inconvenient) times and places. In others, they arrested organizers on vague charges that included vagrancy and disturbing the peace. But the most powerful tool in the anti-union arsenal was the labor injunction: a court order that enjoined workers and organizers from picketing, boycotting, or otherwise interfering with the operations of a particular business. Although constitutional free speech provisions were generally understood to bar "prior restraints" of speech, judges reasoned that labor demonstrations, by threatening the employer's property interest in the peaceful operation of his business, crossed the line that divided peaceful advocacy from harmful conduct.[19]

The Union victory in the Civil War is often described as marking a fundamental shift in American thinking about constitutional rights. It is certainly true that Lincoln and his fellow Republicans vehemently contested Justice Taney's assertion that the preservation of slavery trumped all constitutional claims that might be asserted on behalf of free blacks or other residents of free states and territories. Moreover, by the war's end, most northern Americans were convinced that chattel slavery was an affront to the ideals of liberty and equality. And to ensure slavery's demise, all agreed, it would be necessary to nationalize at least some constitutional rights. Thus, the Fourteenth Amendment, adopted in 1868, vested Congress and the courts with the formal authority to ensure that no state denied its residents equal protection of the laws; deprived them of life, liberty, or property without due process; or abridged the "privileges and immunities" of US citizens. But while the Reconstruction amendments granted a measure of liberty to the former slaves, they did not fundamentally alter the definition of liberty itself.

Indeed, many of the same commentators who denounced slavery as a moral evil remained steadfastly supportive of the legally enforced hierarchies that ordered the home and the workplace. Many of them also envisioned a future in which African Americans and other racial minorities would occupy a subordinate position in society. And nearly everyone agreed that traditional standards of personal morality should continue to delimit the boundary between liberty and license. Thus, Thomas M. Cooley reminded readers of his influential *Constitutional Limitations* that the right to publish true statements concerning public affairs did not protect one who published a factually accurate account of a criminal trial where the subject matter was "such as to make it improper that the proceedings should be spread before the public, because of their immoral tendency, or of the blasphemous or indecent character of the evidence exhibited." Nor did religious liberty provisions protect citizens who

---

[19] David M. Rabban, *Free Speech in Its Forgotten Years* (New York: Cambridge University Press, 1997), 171–72; Feldman, *Free Expression and Democracy in America*, 228–30, 235. As the Supreme Court explained in Gompers v. Bucks Stove & Range Co. (1911), printed material backed by the threat of union activity acquired "a force not inhering in the words themselves, and therefore exceeding any possible right of speech which a single individual might have. Under such circumstances they become . . . verbal acts, and as much subject to injunction as the use of any other force whereby property is unlawfully damaged." 221 U.S. 418, 239 (1911).

dared to labor on the Christian Sabbath. Although Sunday labor bans were admittedly less than fair to Jews, nothing in the Constitution barred lawmakers from requiring that a certain amount of "deference ... be paid ... to the ... religious convictions of the majority."[20]

THE BIRTH OF MODERN CIVIL LIBERTIES, 1900–1937

Three developments paved the way for a fundamental shift in Americans' thinking about civil liberties. First, as the nation grew more ethnically and religiously diverse, and as urban elites grew increasingly skeptical of customary moral strictures, it became ever more difficult to maintain that a broad moral consensus defined the boundary between liberty and license. At the same time, activists from traditionally marginalized segments of American society began to challenge the legitimacy of entrenched hierarchies, aggressively asserting novel rights claims both in the courts and in the forum of public opinion. Finally, a major political realignment opened the halls of power – and ultimately the courts – to precisely those Americans who had the most to gain from a more expansive conception of civil liberties.

During the first three decades of the twentieth century, internal divisions within American Protestantism gradually reduced the liberty-license distinction to a shambles. Although the split between modernists (or liberals) and fundamentalists was triggered by theological differences, it was exacerbated by disagreements over the state's role in policing the moral and religious convictions of the citizenry.[21] Liberals, while nominally supportive of efforts to cultivate public morality, tended to adopt a dynamic view of morality and to oppose enforcement of morals laws that appeared out of step with contemporary opinion and intellectual trends.[22] Fundamentalists, in contrast, favored vigorous enforcement of traditional moral and religious prerogatives. Thus, when fundamentalists in Tennessee and elsewhere banned the teaching of evolution in public schools, liberal Protestants condemned the laws as an affront to scientific inquiry and academic freedom.[23] Similarly, in 1930, when the birth control advocate and sex educator Mary Ware Dennett was brought up on federal obscenity charges, mainline

---

[20] Thomas M. Cooley, *A Treatise on the Constitutional Limitations which Rest upon the Legislative Power of the States of the American Union*, 5th ed. (Boston: Little, Brown, 1883), 554, 591.

[21] George M. Marsden, *Fundamentalism and American Culture* (New York: Oxford University Press, 2006); David A. Hollinger, *After Cloven Tongues of Fire: Protestant Liberalism in Modern American History* (Princeton: Princeton University Press, 2013).

[22] On mainline Protestant criticism of traditional morals laws, see John W. Compton, "Evangelical Reform and the Paradoxical Origins of the Right to Privacy," *Maryland Law Review* 75 (2015): 362–82.

[23] P. C. Kemeny, "Power, Ridicule, and the Destruction of Religious Moral Reform Politics in the 1920s," in Christian Smith, ed., *The Secular Revolution: Power, Interests, and Conflict in the Secularization of American Public Life* (Berkeley: University of California Press, 2003): 216–68, 230–32.

Protestant groups including the Federal Council of Churches and the Young Men's Christian Association (YMCA) leaped to her defense.[24] The debacle of national prohibition offered further evidence of a disintegrating moral consensus. Although the Eighteenth Amendment was generally welcomed in rural and small-town America, it met stiff resistance not only from the nation's growing Irish and Italian ethnic communities but also from many well-heeled urban WASPs, who were by now accustomed to living without the moral supervision of their neighbors.

Walter Lippmann provided a trenchant analysis of these developments in *A Preface to Morals*, one of the best-selling books of the late 1920s. Reflecting on events such as the Scopes Monkey Trial, the splintering of American Protestantism, and the evident failure of prohibition, Lippmann concluded that the "acids of modernity" had "dissolve[ed]" the traditional belief systems to which Americans had "habitually conformed." What was worse, it seemed highly unlikely that there would develop "a new orthodoxy into which men can retreat." Whatever boundaries might henceforth be established to constrain individual liberty would not be based on custom or religion but rather on careful deliberation concerning the material needs of society. In the new age of moral relativism and personal freedom, Lippmann concluded, it had become "impossible for the moralist to command. He can only persuade."[25]

At the same time that the illusion of moral consensus was crumbling, various groups of outsiders were beginning to detach the Constitution's civil liberties provisions from their traditional moorings in custom and common law. Reimagined as abstract guarantees, civil liberties could be turned against the very social structures that had long been thought to mark the outer limits of individual liberty in a republican society. Jews and Catholics, for example, began to use constitutional arguments to oppose Protestant proselytizing in the public schools. In several states, elected officials responded by directing public funds to parochial schools, thus implicitly endorsing the right of Catholic children to receive a publicly funded education that did not conflict with the tenets of their faith.[26] Moreover, five state judiciaries – most of them in states with significant Catholic populations – had by 1920 declared that Protestant Bible reading in the public schools amounted to an unconstitutional establishment of religion.[27]

---

[24] By this point, these pillars of the Protestant establishment had concluded that scientifically based sex education, rather than blanket censorship, provided the surest route to a morally upstanding citizenry. Constance M. Chen, *"The Sex Side of Life": Mary Ware Dennett's Pioneering Battle for Birth Control and Sex Education* (New York: The New Press, 1996), 299. Dennett's conviction was eventually overturned in a landmark federal court ruling that substantially narrowed the definition of obscenity under federal law. U.S. v. Dennett, 39 F.2d 564 (1930).

[25] Walter Lippmann, *A Preface to Morals* (New York: Transaction Publishers, 1960), 318, 19–20.

[26] Steven K. Green, *The Bible, the School, and the Constitution: The Clash That Shaped Modern Church-State Doctrine* (New York: Oxford University Press, 2012).

[27] Michael J. Klarman, "Rethinking the Civil Rights and Civil Liberties Revolutions," *Virginia Law Review* (1996): 1–67, 50.

Around the same time, labor activists began to exchange polarizing appeals to class struggle for the more anodyne language of civil liberties.[28] In the early 1920s, the novelist and labor organizer Upton Sinclair declared that there was "one platform upon which it should be possible to get every true American" to stand with labor "for the purpose of bringing about industrial changes." That platform was "free discussion," an "ideal ... carefully embodied by our forefathers in the fundamental law of our nation and of every one of our separate states."[29] In 1920, a group of attorneys and academics with pro-labor sympathies formed the nation's first major civil liberties organization, the American Civil Liberties Union (ACLU), with the primary aim of securing constitutional protection for pickets, boycotts, and other organizing activities. In conjunction with the Industrial Workers of the World (IWW) and other groups from the labor movement's radical wing, the ACLU worked to reframe anti-organizing measures as affronts to the constitutional liberties of average Americans.[30] A particularly successful strategy involved having labor activists who were barred from speaking under local ordinances or injunctions read the Bill of Rights in a public setting, such as a park, with the aim of being arrested. The jailing of citizens whose only apparent crime was to read the Constitution aloud in public led many Americans to conclude that constitutional rights were, in fact, at stake on both sides of the picket line.[31]

The racial order was also undergoing unprecedented changes as large numbers of African Americans began to migrate northward in search of greater economic opportunity in the nation's urban centers. With expanded economic opportunity came the growth of an African American middle class, which in turn facilitated the founding of organizations, such as the NAACP, that were dedicated to publicizing the evils of segregation and funding legal challenges to Jim Crow.[32] In addition, the sudden enfranchisement of large numbers of African Americans, many of them concentrated in a handful of

---

[28] See, for example, Ken I. Kersch, "How Conduct Became Speech and Speech Became Conduct: A Political Development Case Study in Labor Law and the Freedom of Speech," *U. Pa. J. Const. L.* 8 (2006): 255–97, 273–77.

[29] Quoted in Paul L. Murphy, *The Meaning of Freedom of Speech: First Amendment Freedoms from Wilson to FDR* (Westport, CT: Greenwood Press, 1972), 158–59.

[30] See, generally, Murphy, *The Meaning of Freedom of Speech*, 117–30; Michael J. Klarman, "Rethinking the Civil Rights and Civil Liberties Revolutions," *Virginia Law Review* (1996): 1–67, 39–40; Laura M. Weinrib, "Civil Liberties outside the Courts," *Supreme Court Review* 2014 (2014): 297–362, 309–11.

[31] In 1922, for example, the moderate Republican editor William Allen White, after being briefly jailed for defying an industrial court order prohibiting discussion of that year's national railroad strike, penned a Pulitzer prize–winning column on the subject of free speech. Murphy, *The Meaning of Freedom of Speech*, 162–63.

[32] Doug McAdam, *Political Process and the Development of Black Insurgency, 1930–1970*, 2nd ed. (Chicago: University of Chicago Press, 2010); Michael J. Klarman, *From Jim Crow to Civil Rights: The Supreme Court and the Struggle for Racial Equality* (New York: Oxford University Press, 2005).

pivotal swing states, conferred increased political influence and, ultimately, a more favorable reception from the judiciary.[33] Although the Supreme Court would not begin seriously to engage with the problem of racial segregation until the 1940s and 1950s, the NAACP and its allies could by the 1920s point to a handful of Supreme Court decisions that, at the very least, cast doubt on the constitutionality of racial disenfranchisement, residential segregation, and mob-dominated criminal trials.[34]

In the midst of this atmosphere of social upheaval, Justices Oliver Wendell Holmes, Jr., and Louis D. Brandeis penned a series of (mostly dissenting) Supreme Court opinions that are widely seen as marking the birth of modern civil liberties. Word War I and the Red Scare of the early 1920s provided the immediate context for the great Holmes and Brandeis dissents. In 1917, Congress had enacted the Espionage Act, the first federal law since the Sedition Act of 1798 to impose explicit limitations on political speech. As the war drew to a close, and as Russia fell to the Bolsheviks, several states enacted similar anti-syndicalism laws that imposed criminal penalties on speakers who advocated the overthrow of the American political or economic systems. The Supreme Court upheld both types of restrictions, reasoning that the First Amendment did not protect speakers who intended to sow social discord. Holmes and Brandeis, writing in dissent, argued that restrictions on political speech should be upheld only in the event of a "clear and present danger" to an important governmental interest – something that was lacking in cases like *Abrams* v. *U.S.* (1919), where the speaker in question had, according to Holmes, merely thrown a few "silly" anarchist leaflets from a Manhattan rooftop.[35]

Arguably more important than this doctrinal innovation, however, was the secular theory of political society on which it was based. In sharp contrast to nineteenth-century commentators, Holmes doubted that it was possible, on the basis of objective criteria, to distinguish morally worthy ideas from those that were false or dangerous. American society, after all, was currently riven by moral disagreement. And the problem of identifying objective moral principles became even more vexing when one considered the evolution of moral ideas over time. American history was replete with examples of activities and forms of property – from slavery to liquor to lotteries – that were widely accepted or even celebrated in one era only to be condemned as immoral in the next (or vice versa).[36] When one considered that "time ha[d] upset many fighting faiths," it was unclear why notions of morality should play any role at all in the process of

---

[33] Kevin J. McMahon, *Reconsidering Roosevelt on Race: How the Presidency Paved the Road to Brown* (Chicago: University of Chicago Press, 2010).

[34] Buchanan v. Warley, 245 U.S. 60 (1917); Moore v. Dempsey, 261 U.S. 86 (1923); Nixon v. Herndon, 273 U.S. 536 (1927).

[35] 250 U.S. 616, 628 (1919), Holmes, J., dissenting.

[36] Americans' evolving attitudes toward liquor and lottery regulation had a particularly significant impact on Holmes's thinking about the nature of constitutional rights. See John W. Compton,

constitutional interpretation.[37] Better, Holmes reasoned, to interpret the Constitution without regard to the historical "accident of our finding certain opinions natural and familiar or novel and even shocking."[38]

But how would judges delimit the boundaries of free speech, if not by reference to broadly shared mores? Drawing on an argument first advanced by the English philosopher John Stuart Mill, Holmes answered that there was no need for lawmakers or judges to concern themselves with the social effects of particular ideas or creeds. Indeed, censorship was counterproductive, since governments were so often mistaken in their judgments about which ideas were so dangerous or wrongheaded as to justify suppression. And in an open exchange of views, ideas that were socially beneficial would generally triumph over those that were false or dangerous. "[T]he best test of truth," Holmes asserted, was "the power of the thought to get itself accepted in the competition of the market."[39]

Brandeis, in addition to endorsing Holmes's "marketplace" theory of speech, proposed that civil liberties provisions were fundamentally concerned with protecting individual autonomy. The framers of the Bill of Rights, he wrote in an oft-quoted dissent, hoped to "secure conditions favorable to the pursuit of happiness. They recognized the significance of man's spiritual nature, of his feelings, and of his intellect ... They sought to protect Americans in their beliefs, their thoughts, their emotions and their sensations. They conferred ... the right to be let alone – the most comprehensive of rights, and the right most valued by civilized men."[40] Nineteenth-century commentators thus had the relationship between conventional morality and republican government exactly backward: to reach their full potential, what citizens most needed was not the moral tutelage of the law but rather a constitutionally protected private sphere. In addition, an expanded conception of civil liberties would benefit society by allowing citizens to boldly assert their views – whatever they might happen to be – in the public arena, thereby developing their deliberative faculties and stimulating others to do the same. It was not the heterodox thinker who was the "menace to freedom," but rather the "inert" citizen who blindly conformed to inherited mores.[41]

Although the Holmes and Brandeis dissents stimulated a great deal of discussion in academic circles, few of their fellow justices expressed much enthusiasm for the idea that courts should adopt a more assertive stance in civil liberties cases. To be sure, a majority of the Court held for the first time in *Gitlow v. New York* (1925) that the freedom of speech was among the rights protected from state interference by the due process clause of the Fourteenth

---

The Evangelical Origins of the Living Constitution (Cambridge, MA: Harvard University Press, 2014), 136–41.
[37] Abrams v. U.S., 250 U.S. 616 at 630, Holmes, J., dissenting.
[38] Lochner v. New York, 198 U.S. 45, 76 (1905), Holmes, J., dissenting.
[39] Abrams v. U.S., 250 U.S. 616, 630 (1919). Holmes, J., dissenting.
[40] Olmstead v. U.S., 277 U.S. 438, 478 (1928), Brandeis, J., dissenting.
[41] Whitney v. California, 247 U.S. 357, 375–76 (1927), Brandeis, J., concurring.

Amendment.[42] But even as the Court "incorporated" the First Amendment's free speech clause, it declined to expand the substantive definition of "free speech."[43]

Political and intellectual elites were similarly ambivalent. Conservative commentators, while supportive of judicially enforced economic rights, generally opposed enhanced protection for civil liberties, at least where the liberties in question could be claimed by labor organizers.[44] Progressives, while generally supportive of labor organizing, were skeptical of attempts to expand judicial authority at a time when the courts seemed reflexively hostile to economic regulation.[45] The latter group was particularly alarmed by a string of decisions in which the Court had blocked attempts to regulate the wages and hours of workers. In the most notorious of these rulings, *Lochner* v. *New York* (1905), the Court found that a law limiting the working hours of bakery employees was not a legitimate health or safety regulation but rather an unconstitutional interference with the "liberty of contract," a liberty ostensibly enshrined in the Fourteenth Amendment's due process clause.[46] If the justices were simply reading their laissez-faire policy preferences into the Fourteenth Amendment – and progressives were convinced this was case – then it made little sense to provide the Court with yet another doctrinal tool that could be used to thwart the will of democratic majorities.

Skepticism of judicial authority remained de rigueur among left-leaning Americans in 1932, when Franklin D. Roosevelt won the presidency in what would come to be seen as a realigning election. Between 1937 and 1943, Roosevelt would appoint eight justices to the Court. Precisely how this unprecedented personnel turnover would impact constitutional doctrine was unclear, however. On the one hand, as Michael J. Klarman has pointed out, FDR's electoral victories were underwritten by "an extraordinary assemblage of traditional outgroups," including organized labor, religious and ethnic minorities, and, eventually, African Americans.[47] Roosevelt's presidency therefore conferred a degree of political influence on precisely those groups who stood to gain from a more assertive construction of the Constitution's civil liberties provisions. On the other hand, most New Dealers – and even many labor leaders – were initially reluctant to

---

[42] 268 U.S. 652.

[43] 268 U.S. 652 at 658. Thus, the *Gitlow* Court found that the Constitution offered no protection to a speaker who advocated "revolutionary mass action" for the purpose of overthrowing the capitalist economic system.

[44] For an insightful discussion of the conservative libertarian defense of free speech, see Mark A. Graber, *Transforming Free Speech: The Ambiguous Legacy of Civil Libertarianism* (Berkeley: University of California Press, 1990), 17–49.

[45] One major exception to the rule was Zechariah Chaffee, whose writings on the freedom of speech are thought to have influenced Justice Holmes. See, for example, Chaffee's *Freedom of Speech* (New York: Harcourt, Brace and Howe, 1920).

[46] 198 U.S. 45 (1905).

[47] Klarman, "Rethinking the Civil Rights and Civil Liberties Revolutions," 44–45.

augment the Court's authority at a moment when the Democratic Party had a stranglehold on the levers of legislative authority.[48] Moreover, even if the reconstituted Court could be trusted to interpret the Constitution in ways that comported with the programmatic goals of the Democratic regime, it was unclear how, at the level of doctrine, the justices could simultaneously devalue economic rights *and* expand civil liberties protections. To many observers, including future Supreme Court Justice Felix Frankfurter, it seemed that the wiser stance was an across-the-board policy of judicial deference.

Justice Harlan Fiske Stone's majority opinion in *U.S.* v. *Carolene Products* (1938) pointed the way out of this theoretical thicket.[49] In the opinion's famous Footnote Four, Stone offered a pair of theories to explain why an expansive conception of civil liberties was not incompatible with a deferential approach to economic regulation. First, he pointed out that the individual rights enshrined in the "first ten amendments" had a firmer basis in the text than economic due process rights. Where the early-twentieth-century Court had relied on a series of judicially created doctrines – including the "liberty of contract" – to obstruct the rise of the regulatory state, the post–New Deal Court would confine its scrutiny of democratically enacted laws to those that violated textually grounded rights, including the freedoms of speech and religion. Second, Stone noted that in cases where the democratic process had been corrupted or where "discrete and insular minorities" had been singled out for negative treatment, judicial enforcement of individual rights could not fairly be described as undermining democratic principles. True, the exercise of judicial review in such cases would have the effect of overturning laws that reflected (at least superficially) the will of the majority, but in so doing the Court would be preserving the integrity of the underlying democratic system – something that could not be said of the pre–New Deal Court's decisions invalidating broadly popular economic regulations.

When combined with the earlier opinions of Holmes and Brandeis, Stone's *Carolene Products* footnote provided the blueprint for a radically new approach to civil liberties. Instead of relying on inherited mores or religious views to mark the boundary between liberty and license, the Court would now read the Constitution's civil liberties provisions as demanding maximum scope for the free play of ideas and the self-development of individual citizens. And instead of assuming that longstanding inegalitarian features of American society were essential to the survival of republican government and thus deserving of judicial deference, the Court would take a skeptical view of laws that worked to the disadvantage of "discrete and insular minorities." For the next three decades, the First Amendment and other civil liberties provisions would be at their most potent in precisely those cases that Justice Taney and the

---

[48] On organized labor's skeptical attitude towards the judiciary, see Weinrib, "Civil Liberties outside the Courts," 311–15.

[49] 304 U.S. 144 (1938).

Dred Scott majority had rejected as "impossible" to take seriously – that is, cases pitting marginalized citizens against entrenched patterns of state and local authority.

THE RIGHTS REVOLUTION, 1938–1973

Between the late 1930s and the early 1970s, the Supreme Court presided over a "rights revolution" that stood the nineteenth-century theory of the constitutional order on its head. By the end of this period, it was generally accepted that the freedom of speech, the free exercise of religion, and most of the other individual rights enshrined in the Bill of Rights were (1) enjoyed equally by all Americans; (2) binding on all levels of government; and (3) more or less inviolable, save in the event of a compelling threat to public safety or basic governmental functions. The net effect of the new way of thinking was to elevate civil liberties claims above the traditionally superior claims of domestic and local authority. Long relegated to a peripheral position in American constitutional law, civil liberties now became the "fixed star" around which the constitutional system was said to revolve.[50]

If a single decision can be said to epitomize the Court's new approach to civil liberties, it is *West Virginia* v. *Barnette*, a 1943 case involving a group of Jehovah's Witness children who were expelled from public school for refusing to salute the flag.[51] Only three years before, the Court, in an opinion by Justice Frankfurter, had upheld a similar compulsory flag salute law on the grounds that efforts to promote a patriotic citizenry were well within the traditional bounds of state and local authority.[52] But now three justices, perhaps influenced by widespread reports of officially sanctioned mob violence against Jehovah's Witnesses, had come to see the matter differently, and the Court reversed its earlier ruling.[53]

Writing for the *Barnette* majority, Justice Robert Jackson made two key points. First, he denied that the scope of the Constitution's civil liberties guarantees was in any way affected by the admittedly "delicate and highly discretionary functions" of local government. Perhaps he was thinking of the Witnesses' well-publicized travails. Or perhaps he was thinking of several recent cases that had drawn attention to other abuses of local authority, including the routine denial of basic criminal procedure protections to Southern blacks and the use of facially neutral licensing schemes to obstruct labor organizing.[54] In any event, Jackson concluded that "small and local authority," far from serving as the essential guardian of citizens' liberties, was comparatively more likely than national authority to

[50] West Virginia State Bd. of Educ. v. Barnette, 319 U.S. 624, 642 (1943).
[51] 319 U.S. 624, 642 (1943). [52] Minersville School District v. Gobitis, 310 U.S. 586 (1940).
[53] On the possibility that the justices in the *Barnette* majority were influenced by reports of mob violence, see Kevin J. McMahon, *Reconsidering Roosevelt on Race: How the Presidency Paved the Road to Brown* (Chicago: University of Chicago Press, 2010), 140–41.
[54] See, for example, Powell v. Alabama, 287 U.S. 45 (1932); Norris v. Alabama, 294 U.S. 587 (1935); Hague v. Committee for Industrial Organization, 307 U.S. 496 (1939).

threaten them. Instead of deferring to the edicts of "village tyrants," the Court would henceforth be especially diligent in scrutinizing their activities.[55]

Second, Jackson laid to rest the nineteenth-century understanding of the relationship between religious and moral orthodoxy on the one hand and republican government on the other. In sharp contrast to James Kent and the countless nineteenth-century commentators who had defended the constitutionality of blasphemy laws, Jackson's reading of history indicated that attempts to achieve "[c]ompulsory unification of opinion" in matters of religion were destined to fail or else to achieve "only the unanimity of the graveyard." Nor was there any credible evidence to suggest that allowing citizens the "freedom to be intellectually and spiritually diverse" would "disintegrate the social organization."[56] Henceforth, the First Amendment would be understood to require that common convictions be arrived at voluntarily or not at all.

But if *Barnette* indicated that the Court would not hesitate to dismantle entrenched authority in the name of universal rights, it provided little in the way of a broader theory that might delineate a new boundary between individual liberty and official authority. Unable to invoke the idea of a society-wide moral consensus for this purpose, the mid-century Court relied instead on Holmes's marketplace metaphor and Brandeis's autonomy ideal. The marketplace metaphor provided the rationale for a series of decisions that effectively stripped state and local governments of their longstanding authority to regulate public discourse. Laws punishing subversive speech were now unconstitutional in the absence of a "clear and present danger" to an important governmental interest (or, in the later, more stringent formulation, where the speaker seemed likely to unleash "imminent lawless violence").[57] Laws that indirectly restricted speech in the interest of public safety or convenience had to be narrowly tailored and neutral with respect to the viewpoint of the speaker. Requiring licenses of speakers was permissible in certain limited cases (as when a group sought to hold a parade on a busy public street), but license laws were to be purely administrative in nature, leaving officials powerless to discriminate against particular ideas or speakers.[58] The Court's critics – including internal ones like Frankfurter – warned that the new doctrines would leave states and municipalities powerless to combat the social unrest that inevitably accompanied extremist speech making. But a majority of the justices were willing to run the risk of occasional disorder if in so doing they prevented an even greater evil – namely, the "standardization of ideas" by "dominant political or community groups."[59]

---

[55] In addition, Jackson reasoned that constitutional violations at the local level were more likely escape detection, since the "agents of publicity" were typically less diligent in reporting on them. 319 U.S. 624 at 637–38.

[56] West Virginia State Board of Education v. Barnette, 319 U.S. 624, 642 (1943).

[57] Brandenburg v. Ohio, 395 U.S. 444 (1969).

[58] Cantwell v. Connecticut, 310 U.S. 296 (1940); Saia v. New York, 334 U.S. 558 (1948).

[59] Terminiello v. Chicago, 337 U.S. 1, 4 (1949).

In decisions involving constitutional challenges to nineteenth-century morals laws, the Court regularly invoked some version of Brandeis's "right to be let alone," a right that extended beyond spatial privacy to include a guarantee of decisional autonomy with respect to (among other things) matters touching upon sex and reproduction. In *Stanley* v. *Georgia* (1969), for example, the Court invalidated a state law making it a crime to possess obscene material. Writing for the majority, Justice Thurgood Marshall reasoned that "a State has no business telling a man, sitting alone in his own home, what books he may read or what films he may watch."[60]

Century-old laws restricting the sale, distribution, and use of contraceptives met a similar fate in *Griswold* v. *Connecticut* (1965) and *Eisenstadt* v. *Baird* (1972).[61] Although rarely enforced, contraception bans were determined by the Warren-era justices to violate a constitutionally enshrined right to reproductive privacy, a right eventually found to be lodged in the Fourteenth Amendment's due process clause. The underlying problem was that Comstock-era contraception laws inserted "the machinery of the criminal law" into the heart of citizens' most intimate relationships and personally consequential decisions.[62] "If the right of privacy means anything," the Court declared in *Eisenstadt*, it was that citizens were "to be free from unwarranted governmental intrusion into matters so fundamentally affecting a person as the decision whether to bear or beget a child."[63]

Autonomy rationales also figured prominently in a series of contemporaneous decisions that dismantled many longstanding symbols of Protestant cultural hegemony. Writing for the Court in *Everson* v. *Board of Education* (1947), Justice Hugo Black found that the authors of the First Amendment had intended to erect a "high and impregnable" "wall of separation" between church and state.[64] The case turned on the question of whether a local government could use public funds to offset the cost of transporting students to Catholic schools, and a bare majority of the Court answered in the affirmative. But it was Black's reading of the Establishment Clause – as opposed to the rather incongruous holding – that marked the real turning point. Henceforth, the First Amendment would preclude not only the recognition of a national church but virtually any official act that might be construed as encouraging citizens to adopt a particular point of view concerning religion. By the early 1960s, the Court had prohibited teacher-led prayer and Bible reading in the public schools on the

---

[60] Even if legitimate reasons for policing personal morality existed (which Marshall doubted), the "philosophy of the First Amendment" would not permit the state to pursue its goals by policing "private thoughts" or the "private consumption of ideas and information." 394 U.S. 557 at 556–57.

[61] 381 U.S. 479 (1965); 405 U.S. 438, 453 (1972).

[62] Poe v. Ullman, 367 U.S. 497, 553 (1961) Harlan, J., dissenting; Griswold v. Connecticut, 318 U.S. 479 (1965).

[63] Eisenstadt v. Baird, 405 U.S. 438, 453 (1972). Emphasis added.

[64] Everson v. Board of Education, 330 U.S. 1, 18 (1947). The phrase "wall of separation" was borrowed from Thomas Jefferson's 1802 letter to the Danbury Baptist Association.

grounds that these practices exerted "coercive pressure" on children to adopt the religious views of the majority.[65] A similar logic underpinned a subsequent series of religious free exercise decisions that granted religious believers the right to demand exemptions from generally applicable laws. Under the doctrine announced in *Sherbert* v. *Verner* (1965), citizens whose ability to practice their chosen faith was "substantially burdened" by a state or federal law were entitled to relief unless the government could demonstrate that granting an exemption would endanger a compelling governmental interest.[66]

In keeping with the theory of the *Carolene Products* footnote, the mid-century Court was at its most assertive – and creative – in cases where an individual or group could plausibly claim to have been silenced or disenfranchised by structural inequalities or flaws in the nation's representative system of government. Indeed, what gives the period's major civil liberties decisions a sense of coherence, even in the face of bitter disagreement over particulars, is that the Court tended to read both the marketplace and autonomy ideals through the lens of *Carolene Products*. Without necessarily taking a position on the relative importance of liberty and equality as constitutional values, the Court insisted that its *institutional role* demanded a more robust response to alleged civil liberties violations involving traditionally subordinated Americans. Because judicial authority was most legitimate, and thus most potent, in cases where the democratic processes had gone awry, it was incumbent upon the Court to pay careful attention to how authority – whether public, private, or a fusion of the two – was actually experienced by citizens. This would ensure that the marketplace and autonomy ideals were realized in fact, not just in theory.

The guarantee of an unfettered ideological marketplace, for example, demanded more than formal state neutrality with respect to a speaker's identity or message. Even facially neutral speech regulations now posed First Amendment problems when their practical effect was to diminish expressive opportunities for traditionally subordinated groups. Ordinances banning the distribution of handbills were struck down in part because they outlawed a mode of communication favored by labor organizers, Jehovah's Witnesses, and other advocates of "poorly financed causes."[67] State laws banning picketing or

---

[65] Even if children were permitted to opt out of such programs, there remained "an obvious pressure upon the child to attend," and those who refused would likely "have inculcated in them a feeling of separatism." Engel v. Vitale, 370 U.S. 421 at 431; McCollum v. Board of Education, 333 U.S. 203 at 227.

[66] This rule applied even to measures, such as compulsory education laws and unemployment compensation programs, where there was no reason to believe that the state had intended to burden religious practice. As Justice Brennan explained in his opinion for the *Sherbert* majority, the First Amendment did not permit the state to "pressure" a person "to choose between following the precepts of her religion" on the one hand and obeying the law (or receiving benefits) on the other. Sherbert v. Verner, 374 U.S. 398, 404 (1963). Also see Wisconsin v. Yoder, 406 U.S. 205 (1972).

[67] Martin v. Struthers, 319 U.S. 141, 146 (1943). Also see Schneider v. The State, 308 U.S. 147 (1939).

requiring labor organizers to register with the state were similarly problematic, since their practical effect was to silence the traditionally disadvantaged side in an ongoing debate over "the destiny of modern industrial society."[68]

The Court's egalitarian reading of the First Amendment also played a critical role in dismantling the South's racial caste system. As late as the early 1960s, Southern officials had at their disposal a range of legal tools that appeared well suited to turning back challenges to white supremacy. These included statutes regulating the activities of out-of-state corporations, statutes barring outside groups from organizing or funding litigation, and the long-established right of public officials to bring libel suits against groups or individuals who damaged their reputations. Although most of these tools were well within the traditional limits of state and local authority, the Court used the First Amendment to block each of them in turn. In *NAACP* v. *Patterson* (1958), it held that a state could not force a civil rights group to disclose its membership rolls where there was reason to believe that group members would face "economic reprisal, loss of employment, [and the] threat of physical coercion."[69] Similarly, in *NAACP* v. *Button* (1963), the Court refused to "close [its] eyes to the fact" that facially neutral laws targeting champerty and barratry – in essence, the stirring up of frivolous lawsuits – were being used to deprive African Americans of the "sole practicable avenue" by which they might seek redress for injuries suffered at the hands of the "politically dominant [white] community."[70] A final landmark decision, *New York Times* v. *Sullivan* (1964), eviscerated the common law of libel as it applied to public officials.[71] In addition to setting aside an Alabama jury's $500,000 libel award to a police commissioner who had been criticized in print by a civil rights group, *Sullivan* held that public officials hoping to win a libel judgment would henceforth have to meet the high standard of proving "actual malice."[72] Any less stringent standard, the majority reasoned, would have the effect of "chilling First Amendment freedoms in the area of race relations."[73]

At the same time, the mid-century Court adopted a more deferential approach in cases where the state – or, more likely, the federal government – could plausibly claim to be acting with the aim of *mitigating* the effects of structural inequality on American democracy. The justices were particularly skeptical of claims that the First Amendment protected corporate or commercial speakers from the emergent

---

[68] As the Court declared in Thornhill v. Alabama (1940), the first decision to extend constitutional protection to labor picketing, the judiciary's proper role was not to defend the industrial status quo but rather to ensure that "the group in power at any moment [does] not impose penal sanctions" on those who advocate for peaceful political or economic change. 310 U.S. 88, 103, 104 (1940). For the Court's decision on laws requiring labor organizers to register with the state, see Thomas v. Collins, 323 U.S. 516 (1945).

[69] 357 U.S. 449, 462 (1958).   [70] 371 U.S. 415, 430–31 (1963).   [71] 376 U.S. 254 (1965).

[72] That is, that the statement in question was made with knowledge of its falsity or with reckless disregard for the truth.

[73] Ibid. at 301.

regulatory state. In order to discourage such claims, they drew a bright line between expressive activities that were primarily concerned with moneymaking and those that were not. Advertising and soliciting were distinguishable from the core First Amendment activities of "communicating information and disseminating opinion[s]," the Court reasoned, and thus less worthy of judicial protection.[74] A similar line of reasoning produced a decision distinguishing professional lobbying efforts from the expressive activities of ordinary Americans. As Chief Justice Earl Warren wrote for the Court in *U.S. v. Harriss* (1954), new federal regulations requiring lobbyists to register with the Congress and disclose their sources of income were not an affront to First Amendment rights but rather a reasonable means of ensuring that "the voice of the people" was not "drowned out by the voice of special interest groups seeking favored treatment while masquerading as proponents of the public weal."[75]

Laws that made union membership a condition of employment in certain industries also survived First Amendment scrutiny. That some workers should be required to join and contribute to unions followed naturally from the reigning Democratic Party's view that collective bargaining offered the surest route to industrial peace. By the 1950s, however, critics of organized labor had seized on the idea that mandatory union contributions violated the First Amendment by compelling anti-union workers to subsidize expressive activities that they opposed. In *International Association of Machinists* v. *Street* (1961), the Court, speaking through Justice Brennan, agreed that workers could not be compelled to support political activity against their wills. At the same time, Brennan found that workers could be required to contribute to a union, so long as the compelled contributions were used only for core union activities such as organizing elections and representing workers in negotiations with employers. Although the First Amendment offered individual citizens protection against compelled speech, it also guaranteed the right of "the majority" of workers to form and operate a union without "being silenced by the dissenters." Indeed, the Court was constitutionally obligated to balance the rights of individual workers against the rights of workers as a class, protecting "both interests to the maximum extent possible without [permitting] undue impingement of one on the other."[76]

THE REVOLUTION'S TROUBLED LEGACY

Clearly, the middle decades of the twentieth century witnessed a significant restructuring of American society. Still, the question remains: Do these

---

[74] Valentine v. Chrestensen, 316 U.S. 52 at 54.

[75] U.S. v. Harriss, 347 U.S. 612, 625 (1954). The law defined a "lobbyist" as a person "receiving any contributions or expending any money" for the purpose of influencing the passage or defeat of legislation. Chief Justice Warren, speaking for the majority, agreed that the act would have to be read narrowly – as applying only to paid lobbyists who regularly consulted with members of Congress – to survive constitutional scrutiny.

[76] 367 U.S. 740, 773 (1961).

admittedly significant developments amount to a *revolution?* If the term implies a clean break with the governing structures and legitimating principles of the past as well as the successful construction of new arrangements underpinned by alternative principles, then it is at least arguable that the Court's admittedly transformative rulings fell short of this standard. Indeed, two problems – one practical and one theoretical – plagued the mid-century Court's civil liberties jurisprudence, foreshadowing the eventual unraveling of the post–New Deal consensus on civil liberties. The practical problem was that the justices, aware of the Court's limited capacity to enforce its own decisions, often seemed to pull back from principled stands when confronted with credible threats of widespread noncompliance. As a result, the "rights revolution" ended with significant vestiges of the old order still very much in place.

Consider the ill-fated attempt to decouple church and state. The early 1960s decisions on prayer and Bible reading in the schools made clear that the "wall of separation" metaphor was more than empty rhetoric, as did a separate decision invalidating religious tests for state officeholders.[77] And yet the Court's separationist reading of the Establishment Clause was never fully matched by developments on the ground. The school prayer rulings, in particular, proved difficult to enforce; a number of contemporary academic studies found that many public school teachers and administrators simply ignored them.[78]

It is surely no accident that the Court, in the face of widespread opposition to its rulings on religion in the schools, declined to follow Justice Black's metaphor to its logical conclusion.[79] When confronted with a challenge to the tax-exempt status of religious entities in *Walz* v. *Tax Commission* (1970), for example, the justices stopped short of ordering what would surely have been the largest tax increase in American history. Indeed, even Justice Black joined a tortuous majority opinion holding that governments that exempted religious bodies from taxation were not "sponsoring" religion, but merely "abstain[ing] from demanding that the churches support the state."[80] (Never mind that these tax exempt entities received, free of charge, a variety of public services.) Sunday closing laws and legislative prayers likewise survived Establishment Clause challenges.[81] Viewed collectively, these rulings made clear that the rights

---

[77] Torcaso v. Watkins, 367 U.S. 488 (1961).

[78] On local defiance of the Court's school prayer rulings in the 1960s and 1970s, see Lucas A. Powe, Jr., *The Warren Court and American Politics* (Cambridge, MA: Belknap Press, 2000), 362–63; Daniel K. Williams, *God's Own Party: The Making of the Christian Right* (New York: Oxford University Press, 2010), 67.

[79] On the public reaction to *Engel* v. *Vitale*, see Powe, *The Warren Court and American Politics*, 187–90; Williams, *God's Own Party*, 62–67. As Williams points out, between 1962 and 1964 no fewer than 111 members of Congress introduced constitutional amendments overturning the Court's decision barring prayer in the public schools.

[80] Walz v. Tax Commission of City of New York, 397 U.S. 664, 675 (1970).

[81] Although Sunday closing laws were undoubtedly religious in origin, a majority of the Court found that they also served the secular purpose of protecting citizens' "health, safety, recreation, and general well-being." McGowan v. Maryland, 366 U.S. 420, 444 (1961). Legislative prayers,

revolution would not end with the complete secularization of the American state.

A similar gap between principle and doctrine can be seen in the Court's decisions on sexual and reproductive privacy. In striking down a Massachusetts law that prohibited the distribution of contraceptives to unmarried persons, the Court had seemed to suggest that any official intrusion into the "decision whether to bear or beget a child" was a fundamental violation of personal autonomy. The Court's willingness to issue such a sweeping statement of principle may be explained in part by the fact that the nation's contraception laws had all but lapsed into desuetude; in fact, the states that still had such laws on the books defended them by claiming that there was no constitutional injury to redress, since the laws were never enforced.

Regulation of abortion, in contrast, was alive and well in 1973 when the Court decided *Roe* v. *Wade*.[82] This may explain why the Court felt it advisable to adopt a more cautious and pragmatic tone in its landmark abortion decision, even as it broadened the scope of the underlying right. Whatever the reason, Blackmun and the *Roe* majority determined that the primary problem with abortion restrictions was not that they interfered with privacy in the sense of individual autonomy but rather that they impinged upon the patient–physician relationship. Seen in this light, the constitutional right to access abortion services had to be balanced against the state's interest in protecting the health of the mother and, in the latter stages of pregnancy, the health of the fetus.[83] Although *Roe*'s immediate effect was to expand access to abortion services throughout the nation, the medical privacy frame suggested obvious routes by which abortion opponents might narrow, if not negate, the right to terminate a pregnancy.

---

while certainly intended to promote respect for religion, were too "deeply embedded in the [nation's] history and tradition" to be deemed incompatible with the Establishment Clause. Marsh v. Chambers, 463 U.S. 783, 786 (1983).

[82] Daniel K. Williams. "No Happy Medium: The Role of Americans' Ambivalent View of Fetal Rights in Political Conflict over Abortion Legalization," *Journal of Policy History* 25.1 (2013): 42–61. By this point the liberalization movement of the late 1960s, during which numerous states had legalized therapeutic abortions and two had legalized abortion "on demand," had effectively stalled. Williams points out that although numerous states adopted therapeutic laws in the late 1960s, only one (Florida) did so after 1970, and this as a result of a court order. In 1971, twenty-five state legislatures debated such laws, and all the measures were defeated. Moreover, in 1972, voters in two states (Michigan and North Dakota) defeated therapeutic abortion reform in statewide referenda. Also in 1972, the New York legislature repealed that state's liberal abortion law, but the repeal legislation was vetoed by Governor Nelson Rockefeller.

[83] "The Court's decisions recognizing a right of privacy also acknowledge that some state regulation in areas protected by that right is appropriate ... A State may properly assert important interests in safeguarding health, in maintaining medical standards, and in protecting potential life. At some point in pregnancy, these respective interests become sufficiently compelling to sustain regulation of the factors that govern the abortion decision." 410 U.S. 113, 154 (1973).

The theoretical problem that dogged civil liberties jurisprudence in this period concerned the rather murky nature of the relationship between the Court's civil liberties principles and its egalitarian theory of American democracy. We have seen that the Court rejected First Amendment challenges to commercial speech regulations, lobbying regulations, and union shop agreements. But it bears emphasis that each of these decisions provoked spirited dissents arguing that the majority was permitting lawmakers to run roughshod over rights that the Court had earlier declared inviolable. Thus, a 1951 decision finding that the First Amendment did not protect door-to-door commercial solicitation led Justice Black to ask why a salesman hawking subscriptions to the *Saturday Evening Post* should be afforded less constitutional protection than a Jehovah's Witness or labor organizer engaged in the door-to-door distribution of handbills. In each case, Black alleged, the end result of regulation was to "hobble" the free circulation of "religious or political ideas."[84] When the Court in 1955 upheld the Federal Lobbying Act, Justice William O. Douglas wondered why the Court had only ten years before struck down a seemingly similar Texas law that required labor organizers to register with the state. At least to Douglas, it seemed that both laws exerted a chilling effect on speech, forcing speakers to tread cautiously – or else refrain from speaking entirely – for fear of crossing "the prohibited line" that divided constitutionally protected expression from paid organizing or lobbying activities.[85] And when the Court in 1961 upheld the constitutionality of mandatory union contributions, Black attacked his fellow justices for seeming to abandon the core principle of *West Virginia* v. *Barnette* – namely, that citizens could never be forced to endorse or subsidize political speech with which they disagreed.[86]

In theory, the mid-century Court might have produced a body of doctrine that integrated principled commitments to free expression, personal autonomy, and egalitarian democracy into a coherent whole. But this was not to be. All too often, the justices asserted the constitutionality of measures that seemed likely to mitigate the effects of entrenched inequality without offering clear explanations of how particular policies might be reconciled with an expansive conception of personal autonomy or the ideal of an unfettered marketplace of ideas. On other occasions, the justices fractured into competing camps based around irreconcilable theories concerning the relationship between civil liberties

---

[84] Breard v. Alexandria, 341 U.S. 622, 650 (1951). Black, J., dissenting.

[85] U.S. v. Harriss, 347 U.S. 612, 632 (1954). Douglas, J., dissenting.

[86] Black doubted that unions were capable of maintaining strictly separate accounts for political and collective bargaining activities. In all likelihood, he reasoned, the objecting employee would receive only few pennies on the dollar – an amount that might or might not reflect the true extent of the union's political activities. Meanwhile, the employee would remain officially affiliated with an organization whose aims he despised. The union security agreement thus violated "a man's constitutional right to be wholly free from any sort of governmental compulsion in the expression of opinions." International Association of Machinists v. Street, 367 U.S. 740, 797 (1961). Black, J., dissenting.

and the regulatory state. As a result, the rights revolution bequeathed a troubled legacy, leaving behind a body of law that was plagued by internal tensions and, when wielded by justices of a different ideological stripe, easily turned against its original normative commitments.

MODERN CIVIL LIBERTIES: THE AGE OF INCOHERENCE

Richard Nixon's victory in the presidential election of 1968 marked the beginning of the end of the rights revolution. With the nation gripped by urban riots and anti-war protests, Nixon blamed the Court – and its civil liberties rulings in particular – for fostering a general spirit of lawlessness. Nixon's fellow Republican, Ronald Reagan, who was elected president in 1980, directed similar complaints at the Court. By the early 1980s, the rise of the Christian Right had expanded the list of conservative grievances. In addition to attacking the Court's record on "law and order" questions, Reagan and other prominent Republicans now promised to appoint justices who would roll back recent rulings on school prayer, abortion, and pornography.

Republicans would win six of seven presidential contests between 1968 and 1988. Control of the White House provided Republican Presidents with an opportunity to remake the Court in their party's image, much as FDR and the Democrats had done in the late 1930s and early 1940s.[87] The emergence in the 1970s of a conservative legal movement provided the intellectual foundation for this effort.[88] Many of the movement's early leaders, including Robert Bork and Edwin Meese, attacked the Warren Court for ignoring the original intent (or meaning) of the Constitution's text – noting, for example, that the phrase "right to privacy" appears nowhere in the document. Others foresaw that Warren-era civil liberties principles might be applied to conservative ends, such as weakening corporate transparency laws and rolling back campaign finance regulations. As corporate attorney and future Supreme Court justice Lewis Powell explained in an influential 1971 memo, reformers on the left had long ago learned that an "activist Court" was potentially "the most important instrument [in our constitutional system] for social, economic and political change." It was high time that the nation's corporations applied this lesson in defense of "the free enterprise system."[89]

---

[87] Beginning with Nixon's 1969 nomination of Warren Burger to replace Earl Warren as Chief Justice, Republican Presidents would fill ten consecutive vacancies on the Court.

[88] The origins of the conservative legal movement are discussed in Steven M. Teles, *The Rise of the Conservative Legal Movement: The Battle for Control of the Law* (Princeton: Princeton University Press, 2012); Amanda Hollis-Brusky, *Ideas with Consequences: The Federalist Society and the Conservative Counterrevolution* (New York: Oxford University Press, 2015); Ken I. Kersch, "Ecumenicalism through Constitutionalism: The Discursive Development of Constitutional Conservatism in *National Review*, 1955–1980," *Studies in American Political Development* 25 (2011): 86–116.

[89] The Powell Memo can be read online at: http://law2.wlu.edu/deptimages/Powell%20Archives /PowellMemorandumTypescript.pdf.

Identifying and confirming judicial nominees willing to undo the Warren Court's legacy proved more difficult than expected. Yet, beginning with Nixon's 1969 nomination of Warren Burger to replace Earl Warren as Chief Justice, the arrival of a series of Republican appointees began to transform the Court's ideological orientation. By the 1980s, the Court was beginning to steer constitutional doctrine in directions that comported with key Republican policy goals – from weakening the regulatory state to restoring authority to state and local governments to restricting access to abortion. But just as the rights revolution did not sweep away everything that came before it, the Republican ascendancy did not bring about the complete dissolution of Warren-era civil liberties doctrine. Instead, it ushered in a period of bitter ideological division, with the justices clearly divided into "conservative" and "liberal" blocs. If the conservative bloc has prevailed more often than the liberal, internal divisions within the conservative ranks have nonetheless foreclosed the possibility of a return to the constitutional arrangements of the nineteenth century. And, indeed, conservative members of the Burger (1969–1986), Rehnquist (1986–2005), and Roberts (2005–) Courts have at times openly embraced Warren-era civil liberties doctrines, even as they have exploited that framework's internal tensions and applied its core principles to radically new ends.

At the risk of oversimplification, it is possible to trace three distinct lines of development in the Rehnquist and Roberts Courts' major civil liberties decisions. The first consists of the surprisingly small number of areas where the Court has successfully rolled back – or at least limited the influence of – Warren-era civil liberties principles. The second consists of the surprisingly large number of cases where the Court, acting very much in the spirit of the rights revolution, has extended speech and privacy protections to cover novel situations and previously marginalized groups of Americans. The third consists of cases where the Court has advanced conservative policy goals not by rolling back Warren-era protections but by using innovative interpretations of civil liberties provisions to dismantle the previous regime's handiwork.

As an example of the first line of cases, consider the Rehnquist and Roberts Courts' rulings in the area of church–state relations. Beginning in the early 1980s, the Court rejected Establishment Clause challenges to a series of state and local programs that indirectly funded religious activities; examples included state tax write-offs for religious educational expenditures and school voucher programs that offset the cost of attending parochial schools.[90] Although these programs clearly steered public funds to religious entities, a bare majority of the Court reasoned that any aid to religion resulted from the voluntary decisions of private citizens and thus did not constitute an official "establishment" of religion. Viewed collectively, these decisions clearly eroded the Warren-era "wall of separation." At no point, however, did the Court's conservative majority directly repudiate the landmark mid-century church–state precedents. Rather, it

[90] Mueller v. Allen, 463 U.S. 388 (1983); Zelman v. Simmons-Harris, 536 U.S. 639 (2002).

proceeded by building upon or reinforcing doctrinal vestiges of the old order that had survived the "rights revolution" intact.

The Court's 1970 ruling in *Walz* v. *Tax Commission* proved particularly useful in this regard. If tax exemptions for religious institutions did not run afoul of the Establishment Clause, the argument went, then why should similar exemptions for *individuals* pose First Amendment problems? Had not *Walz* definitively rejected the strict separationist position "that any program which in some manner aids an institution with a religious affiliation violates the Establishment Clause"?[91] Moreover, the amount of money that flowed to religious entities as the indirect result of individual tax write-offs and school voucher programs paled in comparison to the financial windfall bestowed by the *Walz* decision. Seen in this light, the newer programs were not "atypical of existing government programs" that had survived even Justice Hugo Black's exacting scrutiny.[92]

In the case of abortion, the Court has mostly stayed above the fray, leaving state and lower federal courts to sort out the question of whether particular forms of regulation are so onerous as to violate a woman's right to terminate a pregnancy.[93] As a result, a patchwork system of regulation has emerged, with access to abortion services varying widely from state to state. In jurisdictions where the lower courts have upheld innovative restrictions – from twenty-four-hour waiting periods to mandatory sonogram procedures to laws requiring that abortion providers have admitting privileges at a nearby hospital – it has become difficult, if not impossible, for women to avail themselves of the constitutional right to terminate a pregnancy in its early stages. But while some pushback was certainly to be expected in light of the Republican party's staunch opposition to abortion, the movement to restrict access could hardly have proceeded so smoothly absent the *Roe* majority's decision to (1) frame the issue in the language of medical privacy and (2) adopt a balancing approach to health and safety regulations. Like the landmark mid-century Establishment Clause decisions, in other words, *Roe* left in place significant vestiges of the traditional regulatory structure, which in turn provided abortion opponents with convenient launching points for attacks on the underlying constitutional right.[94]

---

[91] Mueller v. Allen, 463 U.S. 388, 393 (1983).

[92] Zelman v. Simmons-Harris, 536 U.S. 639, 665, 668 (2002). O'Connor, J., concurring.

[93] The major exception is *Gonzales* v. *Carhart*, in which a bare majority of the Court upheld a state ban on partial-birth abortions. 550 U.S. 124 (2007).

[94] Significantly, the Court in June 2016 invalidated, by a vote of 5–3, a Texas law requiring that doctors performing abortions have admitting privileges at nearby hospitals and also that abortion providers undertake costly upgrades to their existing facilities. Opponents of the measure observed that more than half of the state's abortion clinics had closed within two years of the law's passage, leaving some Texas residents as much as 500 miles from the nearest abortion provider. A majority of the Court, in an opinion by Justice Breyer, found that the medical benefits of the challenged provisions, if any, were not outweighed by the burdens imposed on women seeking abortions. It remains unclear, however, whether the decision signals a broader shift away from the Court's recent practice of deferring to state lawmakers and the lower courts. Whole

In a second line of cases, the Court has carried on the legacy of the Warren Court, embracing both the doctrinal substance and normative spirit of the landmark 1960s civil liberties decisions. Some of the resulting decisions arguably comport with conservative policy preferences. For example, in the early 1990s, at a time when many conservatives were alarmed by the rise of campus speech codes, the Court found that the First Amendment generally precludes the criminalization of hate speech, absent a specific threat to an identifiable individual.[95] Other decisions, however, have cut against the conservative grain. Thus, the Court has recently struck down a number of state and federal laws designed to restrict access to violent or pornographic media content and video games.[96] And, perhaps most surprisingly, the Court in *Lawrence* v. *Texas* (2003) struck down a state-level criminal ban on sodomy, thus extending the right to privacy to cover same-sex intimacy.[97]

At the level of doctrine, these decisions are firmly rooted in the great mid-century free speech and privacy precedents. But doctrine alone cannot explain why the Court, in these particular cases, elected to advance the legacy of the rights revolution. A fuller explanation would begin by noting that many of these cases, in contrast to the abortion and church–state cases, involve forms of regulatory authority that were thoroughly discredited during the heyday of the Warren Court. In the case of free speech, three decades of First Amendment rulings insisting upon the viewpoint neutrality of speech regulations had by the time of the Court's rightward shift effectively stripped states and localities of the ability to discriminate for or against particular speakers, even when the speakers or ideas in question are reviled by mainstream society.[98] To be sure, obscene speech remained theoretically beyond the scope of First Amendment protection, but this category had been narrowed almost to oblivion: works that did not depict explicit sexual acts or that possessed some semblance of "literary, artistic, political or scientific value" were by the late 1970s beyond the reach of the censors.[99] Any attempt to revive the government's traditional role in policing public discourse would have involved far more than overturning a single wayward precedent; it would have meant uprooting a doctrinal framework that had been constructed over several decades and that appeared to enjoy

Woman's Health v. Hellerstedt, 579 U.S. ___ (2016); Mary Tuma, "Only Eight Clinics Expected to Survive Ruling," *The Austin Chronicle*, June 12, 2015.

[95] R.A.V. v. City of St. Paul, 505 U.S. 377 (1992); also see Virginia v. Black, 538 U.S. 343 (2003).

[96] Reno v. American Civil Liberties Union, 521 U.S. 844 (1997); Ashcroft v. Free Speech Coalition, 535 U.S. 234 (2002); Ashcroft v. American Civil Liberties Union, 542 U.S. 656 (2004); Brown v. Entertainment Merchants Association, 564 U.S. ___ (2011); United States v. Stevens, 559 U.S. ___ (2010).

[97] Lawrence v. Texas, 539 U.S. 558 (2003).

[98] This point was driven home by the Seventh Circuit's 1978 decision upholding the right of American Nazi Party members to march through the heavily Jewish enclave of Skokie, Illinois. Collin v. Smith, 578 F.2d 1197 (1978).

[99] Miller v. California, 413 U.S. 15 (1973); Jenkins v. Georgia, 418 U.S. 153 (1974).

broad public support – at least in the abstract. In this area, where doctrinal vestiges were few and far between, even the Court's most conservative members have generally embraced the inherited framework, and even in the most controversial of cases.[100]

To be sure, the Rehnquist Court narrowly affirmed the constitutionality of state-level sodomy bans as late as 1986. But the more important point to note about the Court's decision in *Bowers* v. *Hardwick* is that a generally conservative Court came within a single vote of extending constitutional protection to same-sex intimacy at a time when many in the Republican party viewed homosexuality as a dire threat to the moral and physical health of the nation.[101] The 5–4 decision, with two Republican appointees in the majority and a third only narrowly dissuaded from joining them, testified to the difficulty of reconciling sodomy prosecutions with the major privacy precedents of the 1960s and 1970s.[102] If the Court's earlier rulings had found that private, consensual, noncommercial sexual conduct was generally beyond the reach of the state, it was difficult to see why homosexual conduct should be excluded from the scope of the rule. Moreover, by the 1980s, it was clear that laws prohibiting sodomy, like the earlier bans on contraception, were enforced only rarely and often in an arbitrary and vindictive manner.[103] As in *Griswold*, a strong case could be made that desuetude principles alone provided sufficient grounds for an opinion invalidating the nation's anti-sodomy laws.[104] That *Bowers* was overruled only seventeen years after it was handed down was due in no small part to the efforts of the many activists who, in the intervening years, built a constitutional case for reversal and cultivated public support for decriminalization.[105] But it surely does these activists no disservice to suggest that they were aided by the gradual erosion, over the preceding four decades, of the states' powers of morals police.

---

[100] In *Ashcroft* v. *Free Speech Coalition*, for example, the Court struck down provisions of the Child Pornography Prevention Act of 1996 (CPPA) that prohibited "any visual depiction, including any photograph, film, video, picture, or computer or computer-generated image or picture" that "is, or appears to be, of a minor engaging in sexually explicit conduct." The Court found that the language was overbroad and would potentially apply to works of "serious literary, artistic, political, or scientific value." 535 U.S. 234, 246 (2002). A revised child pornography law was upheld in *U.S.* v. *Williams*. 553 U.S. 285 (2008).

[101] 478 U.S. 186 (1986).

[102] Justice Lewis Powell, a Nixon appointee, originally voted to strike down the sodomy law at issue in *Bowers* but later reversed his vote. Powell later expressed regret for his decision to join the *Bowers* majority. Dale Carpenter, *Flagrant Conduct: The Story of Lawrence v. Texas* (New York: Norton, 2012), 213.

[103] See, for example, Carpenter, *Flagrant Conduct*, 3–25.

[104] For the argument that the *Lawrence* majority's opinion – and the Court's privacy jurisprudence more generally – has been shaped by the principle of desuetude, see Cass R. Sunstein, "What Did Lawrence Hold? Of Autonomy, Desuetude, Sexuality, and Marriage," *University of Chicago Law & Economics, Olin Working Paper* 196 (2003), available online at www.law.uchicago.edu/files/files/196.crs_.lawrence.pdf.

[105] Carpenter, *Flagrant Conduct*, 124–30, 154–79.

But it is the third line of cases that is perhaps the most interesting. In cases involving corporate speakers, the Burger, Rehnquist, and Roberts Courts have enthusiastically embraced the ideals of unfettered public discourse and personal autonomy that undergirded so much of the mid-century Court's civil liberties jurisprudence. But instead of wielding these ideals in the service of a more egalitarian society, it has used them to dismantle key features of the regulatory state. The first signs of a shift came in *Virginia State Board of Pharmacy* v. *Virginia Citizens Consumer Council* (1976), when the Court extended First Amendment protection to commercial speech. If one purpose of the First Amendment was to promote the "societal interest in the fullest possible dissemination of information," then the Court could see no reason why speakers should be stripped of constitutional protection merely because the information they hoped to convey was commercial in nature.[106] On this point, the Court's remaining liberals agreed with the recent Republican appointees: the mid-century Court had erred when it permitted lawmakers to restrict speech solely on the basis of its commercial content.

Sharp disagreements arose, however, when the Court began to consider the precise extent of corporate and commercial First Amendment rights. At bottom, the rift concerned the relationship between civil liberties and economic power. In cases involving corporate speakers, the Court's conservative justices tended to treat the marketplace and autonomy ideals as abstract commands: more speech was always better than less, regardless of who was speaking; and coerced speech was always constitutionally problematic, even when the target of coercion was a corporation and even when the information in question was demonstrably true. In contrast, the Court's liberals tended to adhere to the Warren-era view that civil liberties principles were not to be interpreted in ways that reinforced structural flaws in the nation's representative system of government.

In *First National Bank of Boston* v. *Bellotti* (1978), for example, a bare majority consisting entirely of Republican appointees struck down a Massachusetts law that banned corporations from attempting to influence ballot initiatives "unless the corporation's business interests were directly involved." Relying heavily on the marketplace metaphor, Justice Lewis Powell's majority opinion declared that "the inherent worth of ... speech in terms of its capacity for informing the public" was unaffected by "the identify of its source, whether corporation, association, union, or individual."[107] In contrast, three Democratic appointees and William Rehnquist, a Nixon appointee, would have held that the law was a permissible

---

[106] Central Hudson Gas & Electric v. Public Service Commission, 447 U.S. 557, 561 (1980). Henceforth, factually accurate commercial speech involving lawful activity would be constitutionally protected, unless the state could demonstrate that the challenged regulation "directly advanced" a "substantial government interest" and was "not more extensive than necessary to serve that interest."

[107] First National Bank of Boston v. Bellotti, 435 U.S. 765, 777 (1978).

means of preventing corporations from dominating the airwaves and directing shareholder money to political causes that were only tangentially related to the corporation's bottom line. Far from distorting public discourse, Massachusetts was attempting to preserve the historic "role of the First Amendment as a guarantor of a free marketplace of ideas."[108]

Although the *Bellotti* majority found that the First Amendment protected the right of corporations to influence elections, the precise scope of this right was left undefined. Some language in the opinion suggested that regulations narrowly targeted at the avoidance of corruption (or its appearance) would survive First Amendment scrutiny. And a subsequent 1990 decision upheld a state law that barred corporations from using treasury funds (as opposed to political action committee funds) for political purposes.[109] As a result, an uneasy truce held for the next three decades. Under the Federal Election Campaign Act and the Bipartisan Campaign Reform Act (BCRA), the size of direct contributions to candidates, parties, and political action committees was limited, and corporate and union expenditures were channeled through political action committees. Independent expenditures were also subject to rules designed to prevent corporations and unions from circumventing contribution limits by cutting ads on behalf of specific candidates.

The truce collapsed in 2006, however, following the death of Chief Justice Rehnquist and the retirement of Sandra Day O'Connor. Following the confirmation of John Roberts and Samuel Alito, respectively, to fill the resulting vacancies, it became clear that a bare majority of the Court now favored dismantling most remaining restrictions on corporate electoral activity. The most significant blow to the campaign finance regime came in 2010, when a bare majority held in *Citizens United* v. *Federal Elections Commission* that the First Amendment protects the right of corporations to spend unlimited amounts from their corporate treasuries to influence campaigns, provided they do not coordinate their expenditures with a particular candidate.[110] As in *Bellotti*, the marketplace metaphor undergirded much of the majority opinion. According to Justice Kennedy, laws restricting political spending by corporations distorted the ideological marketplace by depriving average Americans of information they might want or need to hear. To be sure, corporations possessed the capacity to dominate the airwaves in ways that average citizens could never hope to match. But this fact was irrelevant since, under the marketplace theory, the public could be counted on to separate the wheat from the chaff.[111]

---

[108] Ibid. at 810, White, J., dissenting.
[109] Austin v. Michigan Chamber of Commerce, 494 U.S. 652 (1990).
[110] Citizens United v. Federal Election Commission, 558 U.S. 310 (2010).
[111] 558 U.S. 310 at ___ (2010). "By suppressing the speech of ... corporations," Kennedy wrote, "the Government prevent[s] their voices and viewpoints from reaching the public and advising voters on which persons or entities are hostile to their interests ... Factions should be checked by permitting them all to speak, and by entrusting the people to judge what is true and what is false." A subsequent lower court decision, following *Citizens United* to its logical conclusion,

The impact of the Court's corporate speech decisions was not confined to the realm of campaign finance. Following *Virginia Board* and *Bellotti*, the number of First Amendment challenges to corporate transparency and disclosure laws skyrocketed – as did the odds of success. In recent years, roughly half of all First Amendment decisions handed down at the federal appellate level have benefited business corporations and trade groups as opposed to individuals and traditional expressive associations.[112] More to the point, the resulting decisions have cut to the very core of the regulatory state. To list but a few examples, corporations have successfully advanced First Amendment speech challenges to laws prohibiting the buying and selling, without consent, of patient prescription data by data mining and pharmaceutical companies,[113] regulations requiring that health claims used to market food products be supported by at least two randomly controlled trial studies,[114] regulations requiring companies to disclose their use of "conflict minerals,"[115] and regulations requiring tobacco companies to display graphic warning labels on packs of cigarettes.[116]

The autonomy principle and the corollary prohibition against compelled speech have proved particularly useful in this regard. In its opinion upholding the right of tobacco companies to refuse to include graphic warning labels on their products, for example, the D.C. Circuit held that "any attempt by the government to compel individuals to … subsidize speech to which they object" was subject to strict scrutiny. This rule applied even when the speech in question involved "statements of fact the speaker would rather avoid" and regardless of whether the speakers in question were individuals or corporations.[117] A bare majority of the Supreme Court endorsed a similar argument in *Harris* v. *Quinn* (2014), a potentially far-reaching decision invalidating a "fair share" agreement that required publicly subsidized home health care workers to contribute to the costs of union representation.[118] Breaking with a long line of precedent that included *International Association of Machinists* v. *Street*, the *Harris* majority found that, although the collective bargaining system in question furthered legitimate state interests, these interests were not sufficient to overcome the First Amendment rights of employees who objected to paying union dues. To hold otherwise would be to violate the principle

---

held that the First Amendment protects the right of interest groups and political action committees to *raise* unlimited amounts of money, provided, again, that they do not coordinate their expenditures with a particular candidate. SpeechNOW.org v. FEC, 599 F.3d 686 (D.C. Cir. 2010).

[112] John C. Coates IV, "Corporate Speech and the First Amendment: History, Data, and Implications," *Constitutional Commentary* 30 (2015): 223–76.

[113] Sorrell v. IMS Health, 564 U.S. ___ (2011).

[114] POM Wonderful, LLC v. FTC (D.C. Cir. Jan. 30, 2015).

[115] National Association of Manufacturers v. Securities and Exchange Commission, 748 F.3d 359 (D.C. Cir. 2014). The *NAM* decision was, however, overruled by American Meat Institute v. USDA, 760 F.3d 18 (D.C. Cir. 2014) (en banc).

[116] R.J. Reynolds Tobacco Co. v. Food and Drug Administration, 696 F.3d 1205 (D.C. Cir. 2012).

[117] Ibid. at 1211.   [118] Harris v. Quinn, 134 S. Ct. 2618 (2014).

that the government "may not prohibit the dissemination of ideas that it disfavors, nor compel the endorsement of ideas that it approves."[119]

In decisions such as *Virginia Board, Citizens United,* and *Harris v. Quinn,* the reconstituted Court has dealt a series of significant blows to the regulatory state, but not by challenging its authority head-on. Rather, the Court's conservative majority has conceded the legitimacy of the underlying power (e.g., to regulate campaign finance, to mandate corporate transparency, to impose collective bargaining arrangements), only to render regulation impractical through an expansive interpretation of the First Amendment rights of individuals and corporations. Adding to the irony, it has done so using the very doctrines that the mid-century Court used to dismantle the various state and local prerogatives that had long relegated workers and minorities to a subordinate position in American society. To be sure, as Justice Alito acknowledged in his opinion for the *Harris* majority, previous Courts had repeatedly rebuffed First Amendment challenges to the regulatory state. But these earlier precedents were not binding upon the present Court, Alito insisted, as they were the "result of historical accident, not careful application of principles."[120]

CONCLUSION

This last remark from Justice Alito, with its juxtaposition of "principles" and "historical accidents," might well serve as the epitaph for the past century of constitutional development in the area of civil liberties. Since at least the New Deal period, it has been the aspiration of judges and commentators alike to liberate citizens from arbitrary authority structures bequeathed by their forebears. During this period, constitutional interpreters have generally agreed that if official authority is to survive constitutional scrutiny, it should not be because of the judge's irrational prejudice in favor of the familiar but rather because the rights claimant has misunderstood or misstated the nature of the principle at stake – whether the freedom of speech, the freedom of religion, or the right to privacy. The problem – and the explanation for much of the incoherence of recent civil liberties doctrine – is that the distinction between a "historical accident" and a proper "application of principles" often lies in the eye of the beholder.

---

[119] 573 U.S. ___ (2014). Although the specific holding of *Harris* was narrowly targeted at Illinois' regulation of home health care workers, the decision seemed to signal the Court's willingness to reconsider the broader question of compelled union dues. And, indeed, the Court in March 2016 divided 4–4 on the question of whether public sector "agency shop" provisions were in violation of the First Amendment. If not for Justice Scalia's untimely death in February 2016, the Court almost certainly would have handed down a far-reaching decision eviscerating the critical Warren-era precedents concerning union dues and the First Amendment. *Friedrichs v. California Teachers Association,* 578 U.S. ___ (2016).

[120] 573 U.S. ___ (2014)

In the same term that the Court decided *Harris* v. *Quinn*, it also decided *Obergefell* v. *Hodges*, a landmark decision granting same-sex couples the right to marry. In *Obergefell*, Justice Kennedy and the majority found that state laws that limited the right to marry to opposite-sex couples were, in effect, historical accidents. Because the laws in question served no purpose other than to register a longstanding and irrational prejudice against homosexuals, they could only be characterized as an illegitimate denial of "liberty" under the Fourteenth Amendment's Due Process Clause. Although "history and tradition" were certainly relevant to the constitutional inquiry, they did not mark the "outer bounds" of constitutional liberty. The past, Kennedy insisted, would not be "allow[ed] . . . to rule the present."

Now on the opposite side of the "historical accident" formulation, Justice Alito failed to perceive how traditional marriage laws could be characterized as arbitrary relics of a bygone era. In a dissent joined by Justices Scalia and Thomas, Alito suggested that traditional marriage laws served the important purpose of "encourag[ing] potentially procreative conduct to take place within a lasting unit that has long been thought to provide the best atmosphere for raising children." Far from registering an irrational prejudice, existing laws embodied an interest long regarded as legitimate "in a great variety of countries and cultures all around the globe." If anyone was guilty of conflating irrational prejudice and constitutional principle, it was Justice Kennedy and the majority. It was they, not state lawmakers, who had read into "the Constitution a vision of liberty that happen[ed] to coincide with their own."

The core disagreement in *Obergefell* calls to mind Walter Lippmann's warning, issued in the late 1920s, that Americans would increasingly find themselves unable to justify legal authority by reference to shared moral or religious principles. Lippmann was of course referring to the difficulty of enforcing traditional legal prohibitions in a world that was growing more morally heterogeneous by the day. But he might just as easily have formulated the point in the opposite way: with the collapse of traditional belief structures, expansively worded constitutional guarantees – from the "freedom of speech" to the "establishment of religion" to "liberty" itself – would be transformed into highly adaptable tools that could be used to challenge (or buttress) almost any form of authority, whether public or private, national or local, old or new. To be sure, Americans would remain free to invoke tradition as one possible locus of interpretive authority, but the interpretive significance of tradition was itself up for grabs. Whether inherited authority structures furthered legitimate ends or merely reflected parochial prejudices – whether against gays and lesbians or in favor of organized labor – would become increasingly a matter of opinion. Judges and commentators, for their part, would be left to search in vain "for a new orthodoxy into which men can retreat."

4

Political Representation and the US Constitution

Andrew Rehfeld

As the summer of 1787 came to a close, all but three of the original delegates to the Constitutional Convention in Philadelphia gathered to sign the document from which a new representative government would be formed. The Constitution in front of them that Monday morning in September had been written on parchment by the engrosser Jacob Shallus; it was a document that, centuries later, would continue to be an icon of the United States. Displayed to this day in the National Archives, with "We the People" elegantly penned in its upper left corner, the document became a powerful symbol of the rule of law conquering tyranny through the principles of democratic representation.

Given his painstaking work, Shallus must have had a sinking feeling when Nathaniel Gorham rose to propose a last-minute change. Gorham's concern: the House of Representatives appeared to be too small to fully represent the people. George Washington supported Gorham's proposal to expand the House, providing Washington's only recorded contribution to that summer's deliberation. With Washington's assent and the sense that accommodation would be necessary for success, the motion carried. Rather than rewriting the document, Shallus physically changed the otherwise complete parchment: the House of Representatives would now ensure that the number of representatives would "not exceed one for every thirty" – rather than forty – "Thousand" residents and the physical document would forever be imperfect.[1]

The incident itself captures many qualities of political representation that have been reflected in the US Constitution over time. They involve tradeoffs and compromises between conflicting principles on the one hand and practical needs of governance on the other. Like all features of the Constitution, the institutions that established political representation in the United States have changed over time and were never fixed "once and for all." Because of this, it is hard to say

---

[1] Jack Rakove, *Original Meanings: Politics and Ideas in the Making of the Constitution* (New York: Knopf, 1996), 228.

precisely what the founders "intended." But we do know what the founders established and how it was later changed.

It is also hard to establish whether any particular institution was formed for primarily principled reasons or reasons of expediency; in most cases it was a bit of both. And often the very reasons for the provisions have been forgotten, contorted by our own prejudices and presumptions. For example, the infamous clause that counted slaves as "three-fifths" of a person seems to us today obviously demeaning to African Americans. In fact, its inclusion in the constitution was a reflection of a more complicated dynamic. The three-fifths clause established how to enumerate a state's population for purposes of taxation and representation. States with larger populations would receive more representatives in Congress, but they would also be liable to contribute more in taxes to support the federal government. The "three-fifths" calculus was thus a compromise position between slave states that ironically wanted to *count slaves as full persons* for the sake of representation (but not taxation) and opponents of slavery who *did not want to count slaves at all*.[2]

The perceived threat that Gorham's objection posed to the successful conclusion of the deliberations in Philadelphia illustrates the importance of political representation to the establishment of a republican form of government and its dynamism. As we will see, "representation" is not one fixed thing but a dynamic process involving four key parts: (i)*representatives* who (ii) *represent* (iii) constituencies in a manner that may or may not be (iv) descriptively similar (or "representative") of the whole. And this process of political representation is itself different from "representative" or "republican government." Representative government is a form of government in which each of these four parts of political representation is connected to, or constrained by the will of the people and their interests. To be a "representative government" the people (rather than, say, a leader) must be the object of representation. They must choose their own representatives, who in turn must represent them in a manner that is responsive and accountable to them. Additionally, some argue that representatives should bear some descriptive similarity to those whom they represent, whether simply being from the same residential area, or sharing similar traits like race, age, religion or gender. Representative government thus uses the four-part process of political representation to transmit the authority of citizens to the resulting law by establishing a government that acts on behalf of those it rules. And it is for this reason that "representative government" is plausibly a democratic form, a form, that is, that allows us to claim that "We the People" continue to rule despite the people's lack of direct authorship of the laws by which they are ruled. In the case of the United States, the process of representation enacted as representative

---

[2] I thank the editors of the volume for suggesting the emphasis on the role that principle and accident played at any point in time. Population counts of the states were originally used for setting the number of seats in the House of Representatives and for federal taxation. Thus Southern states preferred to count slaves as persons for representation but not at all for taxation, and Northern states wanted the opposite. The three-fifths clause was thus the compromise position.

government by the Constitution would allow the principle of rule by the people to achieve the most stable and arguably just form it has achieved to date.

What was the key to that stability? It may have been because the will of the people was expressed but limited to avoid the most perverse effects of direct democratic rule through what was perceived by the founders to be a Newtonian balance of forces.[3] But the resulting constraints were not limited to countering the rise of demagogues by countering ambition within government through checks and balances (Madison, *Federalist* 51) nor even to forces that balanced conflict externally, which, as Madison would say, was the mechanism to defeat faction (Madison, *Federalist* 10). The limits were, in a sense, limits inherent in the use of political representation: a process that creates a separation between ruled and ruler, creating the space for a deliberative legislature separated from the squabbles of the rabble.[4] Or as Nadia Urbinati has put the point, representation allows the will and judgment of the people to be expressed and weighed in a deliberative manner while minimizing the cacophony and self-interest associated with more directly democratic forms.[5] In this way representation can bring about an arguably purer form of democracy as it allows the people's will to be, in a manner, purified and refined.[6]

In this review essay, we illustrate how democratic political representation is established through the US Constitution. In the first section, we distinguish between the process of political representation and the principles of representative government. The subsequent four sections then illustrate how the US Constitution establishes representative government by limiting each of the four parts of political representation ("constituencies and other objects of representation," "political representatives," "the action of representing," and "representativeness or descriptive representation"). In the process, we demonstrate how, over the course of more than 225 years, political representation and republican government have enhanced the democratic potential of the government even as they have constrained the activities of those in power, for good or ill. (Importantly, while representation can be said to take place throughout all institutions of government, its main expression is through the legislature. In this limited chapter, we therefore focus on the US Congress and treat representation through executive, judicial, and other non-legislative institutions only in passing.)

POLITICAL REPRESENTATION AND REPRESENTATIVE GOVERNMENT

Following the rise of social contract theory in seventeenth-century England – particularly the writing of John Locke – the founding generation justified

---

[3] Douglas Adair, "That Politics May Be Reduced to a Science: David Hume, James Madison and the Tenth Federalist," in Trevor Colbourn, ed., *Fame and the Founding Fathers* (Indianapolis: Liberty Fund, 1974).
[4] Franklin Rudolf Ankersmit, *Political Representation* (Palo Alto: Stanford University Press, 2002).
[5] Nadia Urbinati, *Representative Democracy: Principles and Genealogy* (Chicago: University of Chicago Press, 2006).
[6] David Plotke, "Representation Is Democracy," *Constellations* 4 (1997): 19–34.

government based upon the consent of the governed. The sense that, as Locke would put it, government derived its legitimacy from the consent of the governed reshaped English monarchy during the early eighteenth century and later became the rallying cry for the American colonists who reclaimed government in their own names. Social contract theory and a call to respect the "rights of man" would lead the founding generation to identify popular government as the proper basis of the new republic.

After the US war of independence, the founding generation faced two problems in their efforts to establish popular government over the thirteen colonies. In the first place, democracy had historically seemed to require homogeneity and geographical proximity to foster both "fellow feeling" among citizens and a sense of shared interests and purpose. By contrast, the new American republic would be vast, filled with competing interests and encompassing a geographical expanse greater than any other ruled by democratic forms in history. More troubling was a concern from antiquity that democracies were unstable and liable to the misjudgments, demagogues, and tyranny of the mob. This was the animating impetus that led the founding generation to establish representative government as a mediated form of democracy. Though Alexander Hamilton was perhaps incorrect in his claim that republican government was a new discovery of modern times (*Federalist* 9), he nevertheless had a point that it had never been successfully deployed in so extensive a manner.

We will discuss representative government in much of the remainder of the essay. Before we do, it is critical that we distinguish it from "political representation." Representative or republican government is a set of institutions that creates a form of popular rule in which the people rule in a manner that is mediated by individuals whom they elect and regularly hold to account for their actions. While representative government uses the process of political representation, it is not the same thing.

Political representation by contrast is a system or process involving four related but conceptually different parts: an object of representation, a representative, actions of representing, and descriptive similarity or representativeness. Each component or the entire process can be deployed for democratic or nondemocratic purposes, as we might see a representative at the United Nations representing a totalitarian regime in a manner that is entirely unaccountable to the people.[7] By contrast, representative government denotes a set of institutions that establishes democratic limits on each of the four parts of political representation – for example, requiring that the people will choose their representatives.

More formally, political representation refers to a system in which one thing "stands in for another, in order to do."[8] This formulation emphasizes the fact that representation involves a sense of replacement or substitution ("standing in

---

[7] Andrew Rehfeld, "Towards a General Theory of Political Representation," *Journal of Politics* 68 (2006).

[8] Ibid., 2.

for") *and* that it indicates a specific function or activity for which it is enacted ("in order to do"). Representatives are thus not simply "stand-ins"; they are stand-ins for a reason, for a purpose, and this purpose is related to some form of activity.[9]

The four key components of the process of representation require some elaboration. First, there is an object of representation, the thing that is represented, often called "the constituency." Examples include "the people," "residents of a particular territorial district," or "members of a political party" in systems of proportional representation. Objects of representation have included individuals, communities, states, and even "the common good."[10] Second, political representation involves representatives who individually or as a collective "stand-in-for" the object of representation. In the US House of Representatives, for example, citizens living in territorially contiguous areas (the electoral constituency or district) are separate objects of representation and individual representatives "stand-in-for" them.

Third, political representation in any particular case involves a set of actions that count as "representing."[11] These actions range widely and include "making law," "voting in a legislature," "advocating for a constituency," and so on. From the vantage point of US history, these actions can also include "act as a delegate would and follow the instructions of your constituents" or "act as a trustee would and use your own judgment to determine what is best."[12]

Finally, political representation can sometimes involve a sense of *representativeness*, that is, a descriptive similarity between either the representatives or the action of representing and some feature of the constituency (i.e., the object of representation). These features can range widely from "share our views" to "look like us." "Representativeness" is achieved most often by the use of qualifications for office, rules that restrict who can be a "representative." As we will see, the US Constitution ensures that all representatives in Congress be residents of the states they represent; thus the members of the House of Representatives are in at least one sense descriptively representative of their constituencies.[13]

---

[9] Hanna Pitkin similarly emphasizes the centrality of activity to representation. However, Pitkin does not clearly separate the four parts of the process here identified and collapses the concept itself into the independent limits that representative government places on that process. *The Concept of Representation* (Berkeley: University of California Press, 1967).

[10] Andrew Rehfeld, *The Concept of Constituency: Political Representation, Democratic Legitimacy and Institutional Design* (Cambridge: Cambridge University Press, 2005).

[11] Andrew Rehfeld, "On Representing." *Journal of Political Philosophy*. Forthcoming (Dec 2017).

[12] Pitkin, *The Concept of Representation*. Also see Jane Mansbridge, "Rethinking Representation," *American Political Science Review* 97 (2003): 515–28; Jane Mansbridge, "Clarifying the Concept of Representation," *American Political Science Review* 105 (2011): 621–30.

[13] It is an unfortunate feature of the English language that the same word, "representative," is used for both the noun and the adjective sense. In fact, the noun and adjective of "representative" function quite differently – being descriptively similar in some way (adjective sense of

We can now see why political representation is different from "representative government" and that political representation can "happen," if you will, in a wide variety of nondemocratic situations. When a dictator stands at the United Nations, he is arguably a representative of his nation, representing what he may or may not believe are its interests in a manner that may or may not be descriptively representative of them.[14] In this way it is important to recognize that "political representation" is a broad description of this four-part process and that in any particular case it may or may not be used for democratic purposes.

By contrast, representative government, like that established by the US Constitution, creates limits on the four-stage process of political representation in a manner that arguably transforms it into a democratic form. Representative government – or the "republican principle" as the founders sometimes referred to it – limits each of the four parts of representation in some ways to the will of those governed. In this way it arguably transfers the authority of the people to those who make, execute, and adjudicate the law, thus deploying the process of political representation to establish a plausibly democratic form of government.

Consider how each of the four parts of political representation just described – the object, the representative, representing, and representativeness – can be limited by these democratic controls. For a government to enjoy the label "representative government," the object of representation must be "the people" in some form. To count as a "representative government," the objects of representation may not be "the ruler's interests" or some subgroup like "the wealthy" to the exclusion of the other parts. The famous words of the Preamble of the US Constitution establish this intention, "We the People . . . ." But this is a very broad limit as it leaves entirely to the people how to constitute themselves into constituencies – whether by territorial districts, political parties, or some other way.

Second, a wide range of individuals may conceptually serve as "political representatives" including "whomever the dictator chooses," "whomever controls the army," or "whomever is randomly chosen." By contrast, representative government limits these possibilities by requiring that citizens choose their own representatives. This is typically done through the practice of regular elections. Representatives in representative government are thus said to carry with them the authority of those "in-for-whom they stand" because of this act of election. The authority that is transferred by individual citizens at election

---

"representative") is not the same as being a "stand-in-for" some other person or object (the noun sense of "representative"). The similarity in these two terms has given rise to considerable confusion about whether representatives (noun) have to be representative (adjective) of those they represent (verb!). By focusing on the distinct underlying meanings – one is a noun (*a* representative) and the other is a descriptive feature (representative, without the article "a") – we can ask whether and to what extent representatives ought to be representative of those they represent. Rehfeld, "The Concepts of Representation," *American Political Science Review* 103 (2011): 631–41.

[14] Rehfeld, "Towards a General Theory of Political Representation."

allows the resulting legislature to claim a collective authority or legitimacy to pass laws that can arguably obligate citizens to obey.[15] This is why a key feature of the legitimacy of a representative government is whether it maintains the proper conditions of free and fair elections, by which citizen authority can be transferred to representatives without coercion and with appropriate information. In the US Constitution, these limits involve the specification of the nature and manner of elections, voting rights, and the terms of office by which an individual may need to renew the authority by which he or she holds office.

Third, just as "political representatives" need not be democratic, so too political representing as an activity may be more or less democratic, connected, that is, to the public will. Representing becomes "democratic" and thus consistent with the principles of representative government when the actions of representing are done in a manner that pursues the *interests* of those represented and/or in a manner that is *responsive to them*.[16] As we will see, the US Constitution specifies what counts as representing ("making law," for example) but leaves to individual representatives enormous discretion in deciding how best to pursue their constituents' interests. The Constitution creates an incentive for representatives to pursue the people's interest based on their individual desire to be reelected but does not restrict the actual conduct of representing relative to constituents' interests while in office.

Finally, the idea of representativeness or descriptive similarity between representatives and those in-for-whom they stand becomes democratic – or, more appropriately, just – as a part of republican government when specific qualities of a government correspond to the underlying features of the people it represents. This can happen for reasons of expediency, stability, or justice. Thus, as many democracies around the world have now established, we might say that a legislature *should be* representative of women – in the sense of its members bearing a descriptive similarity of gender to the body politic – in order to be democratic, legitimate, or just. Similarly, individual actions may serve to secure a kind of representativeness when, for example, a member of a minority group is appointed to serve on a committee or judiciary in order to make that body more "representative" of the nation as a whole (in the sense of descriptive similarity). Finally, although this descriptive similarity is most often described in terms based on objective attributes of people (age, gender, race, geography,

---

[15] The position here presumes that authority can and is transferred by the people to their representatives through free and fair elections as this was the governing presumption of the founding generation and perhaps most American citizens today. However, we recognize the considerable disagreement among moral and political philosophers on the substantive question: Do elections in fact confer upon a legislature the real authority of the people, and even if they do, are people bound to obey a legislature's laws without regard to the content of the law itself?

[16] This view of democratic representation has been clearly articulated by Hanna Pitkin, though she attributes these two conditions to the very action of representing rather than seeing them as democratic conditions to a broader range of actions denoted by the term "representing." Rehfeld, "On Representing."

profession, class, wealth, and religion), it can also apply to ideas. As Anne Phillips has pointed out, elections may help ensure that representatives are descriptively representative of their constituents' opinions but may not be good at ensuring a descriptive similarity of their persons (what Phillips has contrasted as a "politics of ideas" versus a "politics of presence").[17] As we will see, the US Constitution secures representativeness through various qualifications for office to ensure that a certain kind of descriptive similarity between the government and some feature of the underlying body is captured in the legislature or in government generally. These tools include age, residency, citizenship, and other qualifications for office that we will explore.

Representative government of any kind thus aspires to be a democratic form by deploying the four-part process of political representation in a manner that is limited by principles of self-rule. It creates a legislature that buffers the people from the making of the law that governs them. It is arguably democratic insofar as the people's authority is given to the representatives in the legislature to make law standing-in-for the people themselves. And it retains certain "aristocratic" elements because it does not presume, as direct democracy does, that all individuals have an equal right to rule and make law nor that "whatever the people want" is worthy of enacting. Indeed, one virtue of representative government over direct democracy may be its claim to elevate citizens of distinction into the legislature, thus raising the virtue of those who make the law. And in the end, for the founders, the creation of the space between the people and the making of their laws made "filtration" possible, allowing elections to elevate people of distinction, limiting the threats to the public of instability and exposure to mob rule.[18]

Thus, for representative government to remain democratic, the people must be able to elect those who will rule them *and* they must retain the right to be the ultimate arbiters of the law – either through their control of their representatives in office or ultimately through the amendment provisions of the Constitution. Representative government can be said to be superior to democratic forms insofar as it prevents a deleterious exercise of the people's will without creating a rule of the elite, for it creates a space in which representatives can exercise their judgment or have their choice set constrained toward objects of justice.

With this distinction between political representation and representative government established, we can now examine how the US Constitution establishes the four parts of political representation and the democratic limits it imposes on each of them in order to establish representative government. We trace the features of representation in the US Constitution by illustrating the historical transfer of authority from the people to the government through various openings and expansions of access to power. However, such an

---

[17] Anne Phillips, *The Politics of Presence* (Oxford: Clarendon Press, 1995).
[18] Bernard Manin, *The Principles of Representative Government* (New York: Cambridge University Press, 1997).

analysis sheds apocryphal light on institutional design and development, for it must be remembered that the US Constitution was not a wholly new form, and many of its institutions came directly from the colonies' experiments with republican forms in the eighteenth century. Thus the analysis here provides a normative frame to understand the mechanisms of representation even as we recognize the decidedly historical and contingent path traced by its development.

OBJECTS OF REPRESENTATION: THE PEOPLE, THE STATES, AND THE NATION AS A WHOLE

The first part of the process of political representation is the existence of an object that is to be "stood in for," that is, an object to be represented. This object – often called a "constituency"[19] – is that which a representative will later "represent." Constituencies can be either formal or informal. Within democratic political institutions, representatives have a relationship to their formal constituencies through the mechanism of elections. Informal constituencies are ones that a representative may hope to represent in the future and arise from various practices, like the advocacy of a group's interests by a friend who does not have a formal relationship to this group through the process of "virtual" representation or because the formal constituency is a mere proxy for an intangible object of representation. A good example of "virtual" representation is the case of Edward Kennedy, a wealthy US senator from Massachusetts, who often represented the interests of the poor despite the fact that they were not a formal constituency of his. A good example of an intangible object of representation is "the national interest," which was meant to be the object of representation for the President of the United States but was achieved only indirectly through the institutional creation of an electoral college.

As a result of important debates during the summer of 1787, the two primary objects of representation as established in the US Constitution are the "people" and the "states," thus exhibiting the joint federal and national structure of the US government. As a national entity, the US government would represent the people directly and exclusively. As a federation of states and localities, the US government would represent local political units as political units. Both are then combined in three ways: through territorial constituencies that introduce a measure of localism into the House of Representatives; through state representation in the US Senate; and through a combination of both as objects of representation for the President, as reflected in the make up of the electoral college.

---

[19] Rehfeld, *The Concept of Constituency.*

The key passages establishing the states and the people as the two different objects of representation can be identified on the basis of who was given electoral rights and how representatives were apportioned. In the House, individual citizens would be granted the right to select their representatives on the basis of rough population equality. In the Senate, individual state legislatures would select representatives for their state as US senators, each state being given an equal number of representatives (two) regardless of its underlying population. And for the President, both individual citizens and state legislatures would select electors that would be apportioned on the basis of a combination of population and equality of the states.

Two key provisions establish that the people are to be the object of representation – the "thing" to be represented – in the House of Representatives. Article I, Section 2, establishes that "the House of Representatives shall be composed of Members chosen every second Year by the People of the several States." This section further establishes the principle that representatives should be apportioned to each state "according to their respective Numbers," establishing a principle of rough population equality (what the founding generation termed "proportional representation") among those who were represented. Importantly, as originally ratified, both sections excluded African Americans by denying them voting rights in many states and then counting them as only three-fifths of a person for the sake of apportionment. Thus while it is rhetorically offensive that they were counted as "three-fifths" a person, those who advocated for their full "humanness" were paradoxically trying to prevent them from being counted at all. The apportionment criteria was ultimately changed in 1868 through the ratification of the Fourteenth Amendment (Section 2) and a century later through the Voting Rights Acts of 1965.

The apportionment of representatives to the states based on rough population equality established that the object of representation in the House was the people themselves. However, it may today seem as if representation in the House is still "place-based" due to the practice of territorial districting – the practice, that is, of defining single member electoral districts by geographical lines. While electing representatives to the House based on where their electors live does create the effect that "all politics is local," it was neither the intention nor the expectation of the founders that this would occur. And that is because both supporters and opponents believed the size of each individual congressional district would be too large to allow for the specific interests of any particular "place" to be transmitted to the legislature. Supporters of the Constitution, like James Madison, took the large size of the district as an important reason to support the plan; opponents found the size of the congressional district to be a singular failure.[20]

---

[20] Rehfeld, *The Concept of Constituency.*

The dynamics of these arguments help to illustrate how institutions can help support general normative aims. While representatives from the House were expected to communicate knowledge of local laws and customs to the benefit of national legislation, they were not expected to represent local interests per se because of the scale of representation. At the time of the founding, state legislative districts were on average comprised of 3,000 individuals. Districts then almost always followed the existing political boundaries of the local unit that in state legislatures served as the object of representation: the town, county, or borough. But as described in the opening of this chapter, with the establishment of a representative for every 30,000 people, any grouping – territorial or otherwise – would have been far too large to capture the distinct interests of a particularly town.

Both supporters and opponents of the constitution recognized this fundamental shift in the object of representation moving from local political units like towns to a direct representation of the people themselves. Supporters of the Constitution – particularly James Madison in *Federalist* 10 – believed that the largeness of the district would make it difficult for any candidate to win election by coordinating on any particular local interest; voters would be forced to choose the candidate with the best character and virtue since no single issue would dominate. Opponents of the Constitution agreed that this dynamic would occur, and for them it was a problem: because the scale of representation would eliminate any kind of local interests in the US House, the plan should be opposed. Both sides agreed that the principle of representation in the House would be "the people" as districts would be too large to capture or represent any other object.[21]

Consistent with this view that the people, not even local towns or counties, were to be represented in the House, it must be noted that nowhere in the US Constitution are territorial districts themselves required. Rather, the Constitution grants full authority to the states to determine how their citizens would be represented. Taking advantage of this opportunity, some states

---

[21] The view presented here is different from the conventional view that Madison believed the extended republic would combat interests throughout the nation rather than in the individual constituency. The evidence for the present view is based on an analysis of Madison's preceding writings on an "extended republic" that featured prominently in *Federalist* 10. It is additionally based on argument itself. As Madison puts it, the inability to communicate and coordinate will impede partial interests from taking over the national good. This would have had to refer to dynamics outside of the national body, as a group of what was then going to be about sixty-five people would have had no problem communicating and coordinating with each other. For a complete presentation of the evidence supporting the constituency view, see Rehfeld, *The Concept of Constituency*, 98–107. See also Wilson's speech of Dec. 4, 1787, as quoted in Manin, *The Principles of Representative Government*, 122; and David Epstein, *The Political Theory of the Federalist* (Chicago: University of Chicago Press). For a good example of the more conventional view, see Adair, "That Politics May Be Reduced to a Science." For an overview of the politics of state size in the early founding era, see Rosemarie Zagarri, *Politics of Size: Representation in the United States, 1776–1850* (Ithaca: Cornell University Press, 1987).

experimented with statewide "winner-take-all" elections in the decade after the ratification of the Constitution. This allowed newly forming political parties to capitalize on population density.[22] Thus in the first election of the House of Representatives in Pennsylvania, a statewide delegation of all Federalists was elected to the exclusion of any Democrat-Republicans. While the practice has seldom been replicated, it is widely accepted that states could experiment with different electoral choices beyond the territorial district and be fully compliant with the provisions of the US Constitution.[23]

While the object of representation in the House was based on rough population equality, the Senate treated the states themselves as its object of representation. This is indicated by the assignment of electoral rights for choosing senators to state legislatures and also by the equal apportionment of senators to states without regard to their underlying populations. Both of these principles were established in Article I, Section 3. However, with the passage of the Seventeenth Amendment in 1913, electoral rights were taken from the state legislatures and handed to the people of each state without compromising the state basis of apportionment. Thus, while the state legislatures are no longer the source of a senator's selection, the object of representation in the Senate must still be seen as the state itself, though in a more compromised manner than when originally established.

The establishment of the states themselves as an object of representation for the Senate was a core feature of the original US Constitution, and it remains one of the more important institutional features of federalism still in the document. As the upper chamber of a bicameral legislature, the Senate provided an internal check on legislation, limiting the process of political representation to outcomes that, it was hoped, would be more consistent with justice. This bicameral structure had its origins in two separate but related concerns: that the

---

[22] As a historical footnote, the unexpected rise of political parties after the founding undermined the arguments of both supporters and opponents about the dynamics of the district. Political parties allowed close coordination and communication between individual voters and communities and thus undermined the canceling effects of the large district on interests. Added to that, political leadership quickly used territorial district lines to self-select the groups that would count as an electoral constituency. The term "gerrymandering" was based on a political cartoon that appeared in 1804 lambasting Governor Gerry's creation of a salamander-shaped electoral district in order to maximize party gain in an election. Over the next 150 years, the distortion of population equality between districts became extreme and would be ultimately resolved when the Supreme Court in the 1960s mandated equality of population between electoral districts. However, paradoxically, the practice of districting and redistricting would become more pronounced and politicized by the further requirements of racial equity and the development of more precise and sophisticated computer programs that allow for greater precision in the drawing of districts. Today, redistricting is widely seen as a powerful tool that allows majority parties in state legislatures to retain their majority status by spreading their voters strategically to ensure that a maximum number of their party retain seats and concentrating the opposing party in districts in order to minimize the number of representatives it can elect.

[23] Robert Richie and Steven Hill, *Reflecting All of Us: The Case for Proportional Representation* (Boston: Beacon Press, 1999).

interests of both large and small states be adequately represented and that the federal structure be preserved by formally representing the underlying sovereignty of the states.

The idea that large and small states had different sets of interests was partly but not entirely due to distinct interests in slavery. Most of the population expansion at the time of the founding was expected to occur in the Southern states of Virginia, the Carolinas, and Georgia. And because smaller states were more abundant in the North, it was believed that having a Senate whose objects of representation were the states would protect the North's interests against the future growth of the South. A second related but distinct motivation was that the states, under Articles of Confederation, had enjoyed a considerable degree of autonomy. Eager to maintain that autonomy and not wishing to be swallowed up by the larger states – whether Virginia or Massachusetts – delegates from smaller states – whether Delaware or Connecticut – argued that the federal nature of the republic depended on the preservation of their distinct voice in the legislature.

Indeed, the debate about whether to use people or states as the object of representation provided one of the key fault lines during the summer of 1787. It ultimately produced the "great compromise," which established a bicameral legislature in which both the states (as states) and roughly equal groups of people would be represented. The compromise helped the delegates resolve a thorny political problem while leaving future generations to grapple with the ongoing legacy of the division. In the early twenty-first century, legislation can now pass the US Senate with the support of senators representing an increasingly small minority of the nation's population. The control of the Senate by a small minority of the nation's voters explains why, in part, broadly popular initiatives in areas concerning climate change, health care access, and gun control are more difficult to pass.

Finally, we must recognize that no matter what object of representation was established by the intent of the founding generation, the effective object of representation would be determined as a practical matter by who was allowed to vote for the candidate. In practice, the selection of US senators by state legislatures created multiple problems. These included turning statewide elections for senators into proxy competitions for the US Senate, deadlocked legislatures unable to agree on a candidate, and a general sense that the selection of US senators was taking up too much of the state legislatures' time and energy. Further, a string of sensational bribery scandals in the late nineteenth and early twentieth centuries that involved would-be senators essentially purchasing their seats from state legislatures coalesced public support for an institutional change – a good example of a messy mix of principle and accident creating a motive for reform.[24] The resulting ratification of the Seventeenth Amendment in 1913 ensured that the people of each state would vote directly for their US senators.

---

[24] I thank John Compton for suggesting this additional factor.

If voting dynamics effectively established the object of representation in the Senate, it had a similar effect for the House. While the US Constitution provides for representatives selected "by the People," it does not provide any definition of "the People." Instead, it links voting rights for members of the House of Representatives to the procedures used to select state legislators in each state (Article I, Section 2). This meant that until the Fourteenth Amendment was ratified in 1868, states enjoyed considerable leeway to restrict voting rights – leeway that they used to limit the franchise to white males (and in some cases to property owners or taxpayers).[25]

The ratification of the Fourteenth and Fifteenth Amendments began a process of legally guaranteeing universal suffrage to all US citizens. In 1868, the Fourteenth Amendment imposed penalties on states for denying voting rights to any male who had attained the age of twenty-one, but it was not until the Fifteenth Amendment was ratified two years later that states were explicitly prohibited from denying or abridging voting rights "on account of race, color, or previous condition of servitude." Significantly, the Fourteenth Amendment introduced a gender limit on rights for the first time in the US Constitution by protecting only men from voting rights infringements.[26] It was not until the Nineteenth Amendment was ratified in 1920 that voting rights were guaranteed to women as a group.

Other restrictions were removed over the remainder of the twentieth century. The Twenty-Fourth Amendment, ratified in 1964, eliminated poll taxes, and in 1971 the ratification of the Twenty-Sixth Amendment established the voting age of eighteen. By the end of the twentieth century, formal voting rights for all citizens over the age of eighteen were firmly and clearly established by the US Constitution. And of course there would continue to be legal and political disputes over the execution of these

[25] For an excellent overview of the history of voting rights in the United States, see Alexander Keyssar, *The Right to Vote: The Contested History of Democracy in the United States* (New York: Basic Books, 2000). As documented there, gender and racial restrictions were not universal. Also, most property requirements for voting were dropped by the early nineteenth century, but some remained through the mid-1800s: Connecticut (removed in 1850), New Jersey (1844), North Carolina (1854), and Virginia (1850). As late as 1855, Rhode Island, New York, and South Carolina still had property requirements, though they were restricted to non-native-born citizens (in Rhode Island) and African Americans (in New York) and provided a residency alternative in South Carolina. Ibid., Table A.3 "Chronology of Property Requirements for Suffrage: 1790–1855."

[26] Section 2 of the Fourteenth Amendment reads, "Representatives shall be apportioned among the several States according to their respective numbers, counting the whole number of persons in each State, excluding Indians not taxed. But when the right to vote at any election for the choice of electors for President and Vice President of the United States, Representatives in Congress, the Executive and Judicial officers of a State, or the members of the Legislature thereof, is denied to any of the male inhabitants of such State, being twenty-one years of age, and citizens of the United States, or in any way abridged, except for participation in rebellion, or other crime, the basis of representation therein shall be reduced in the proportion which the number of such male citizens shall bear to the whole number of male citizens twenty-one years of age in such State."

guarantees in practice.[27] Once again, these changes in institutional design were due to a combination of political will and simple accident or opportunity. For example, the lowering of the voting age was long discussed whenever the United States mobilized soldiers under the age of twenty-one to fight in its wars. As Keyssar notes, there were efforts made to amend the Constitution during both world wars and the Korean conflict. The measure to decrease the voting age to eighteen was finally adopted in 1971 when the impetus of another war, combined with significant cultural shifts, created a political environment favorable to reform.

REPRESENTATIVES: WHO STANDS IN FOR OTHERS?

After an object of representation is identified or created, "political representatives" can then stand-in-for that object in order to execute a surprisingly wide range of actions including voting, deliberating, and advocacy, among other possibilities.[28] These representatives may be individuals (as they are in the United States), or they may be groups of individuals like political parties (as they are in most of Europe and other global democracies). In this section we consider the process by which individuals become representatives in the House and the Senate through the formalization of "rules of recognition" that guide audiences to judge that one person stands-in-for either the people or the state (as the case may be).

In all cases of political representation, individuals or groups (like political parties) become representatives only when they are taken as stand-ins for other individuals or groups by a relevant audience. People can claim to be representatives,[29] but unless and until a relevant audience accepts them as such, they do not have the social authority to function in that role and thus are not properly characterized as representatives. Audiences are "relevant" insofar as they have the specific authority to invest a person or group with the power to perform a set of actions for which the particular case of representation is invoked. This recognition by an audience explains why one individual – say, the winner of an election – is the representative of a group but someone else is not. It also explains why, in the case of a contested election, it is the audience's acceptance of the fitness of the rules, and not the actual facts per se, that resolves a matter. The general point is that the decision of the relevant parties is all that matters to denote political representatives. The fact that the audience may use the results of an election to determine their decision should not be mistaken as evidence that the results speak for themselves.[30]

---

[27] Keyssar, *The Right to Vote.*
[28] Rehfeld, "Towards a General Theory of Political Representation"; Rehfeld, "The Concepts of Representation."
[29] Michael Saward, *The Representative Claim* (Oxford: Oxford University Press, 2010).
[30] Rehfeld, "Towards a General Theory of Political Representation."

The US Constitution deploys representatives in order to make laws (Article I, Section 1). "Making law" is thus the function of political representation in the US legislature. The US Constitution further invests in Congress the authority to determine for itself who stands-in-for each state (in the US Senate) or each state's delegation (in the US House) (Article I, Section 4). That makes Congress the relevant audience to determine who each representative will be, for it means that Congress and Congress alone has the political authority to invest its members with the social authority of making law that their role as representative requires them to have. Put differently, the only way that an individual can come to have the standing of "member of Congress" with the accompanying rights of casting a vote that counts on legislation is for the other members of Congress to determine that that individual has that standing.

Of course, members of Congress make their judgments not arbitrarily but based on a set of public and reliable rules. This is how most cases of formal, institutional representation operate: audiences use rules of recognition to guide their judgment about whom to recognize as stand-ins for other individuals or groups. The US Constitution establishes three key rules of recognition that the US Congress (as the relevant audience) should use in its determination of who should be recognized as the representative of a district or state. These rules establish that (i) the will of the people should be followed (ii) according to elections regulated by the state and (iii) with candidates limited to those who meet a set of qualifications for office. We will take each in turn.

The first rule of recognition, established in Article I, Section 2 – as modified by the Seventeenth Amendment – establishes that *the people's will* should be followed on a regular basis (either every two or six years). In the case of the House, it "shall be composed of Members chosen every second year by the People of the several States ...." Post Seventeenth Amendment, US Senators are to be "elected by the people [of each state] for six years." It is important to see that, consistent with the structure of any case of political representation, the people's will itself (via election results) does *not* make a person a representative. Rather it is, as the Constitution establishes, Congress's judgment about what constitutes the people's will. (Of course, as with most provisions, the Supreme Court remains the ultimate arbiter of the interpretation of these passages, so that more precisely it is Congress's judgment unless or until the Supreme Court modifies its practice.) The second rule of recognition specifies who is eligible to establish valid election rules. Article I, Section 4, provides that the state legislatures shall set "the times, places and manner of holding elections" and thus gives more clarity in contested cases. However, it also reserves the right of Congress to "alter such regulations" with the exception of the "places of choosing Senators."

Historically, the combination of these first two rules of recognition meant that voting rights would be limited to favored groups of people. In particular, voting eligibility for US House elections was originally limited by qualifications that each state set for voters in its own state elections (Article I, Section 2.) This would soon change, but the process of expanding the suffrage involved a good deal of "backsliding and sideshifting"; sometimes restrictions were imposed on a class of voters only after those voters began exercising rights that had not been explicitly taken away.[31] This was the case with women, who in some places like New Jersey were originally permitted to vote and only later – 1807 in New Jersey – had the right taken away. The constitutional legality of prohibitions established by the Fifteenth Amendment ensured voting rights only for men but again did not prohibit women from voting.

If the first rule of recognition (post Seventeenth Amendment) established that Congress should follow the people's choice and the second rule helped Congress to identify how the people's choice was to be determined, the third rule of recognition established limits on the kinds of individuals whom voters could choose to serve in the role of representative. Qualifications for office formally limit voter choice and can also ensure that the legislature is representative (in the descriptive sense) of the nation, a point we will take up later.[32] Current qualifications for either branch of Congress cover three key dimensions: age, duration of US citizenship, and residency. Age qualifications were meant to secure increasing political maturity[33] in each of the branches of office (and ultimately in the executive as well). US citizenship requirements are meant to ensure that legislators have a sufficient stake in the country over which they legislate and are fully subject to its laws. These citizenship requirements increase with relative legislative power: seven years for members of the House and nine years for the US Senate. In order to prevent undue foreign influence, additional requirements were added for the executive, who was required to be "natural born." Finally, residency qualifications required that members of Congress – whether in the House or Senate – be "inhabitants" of their particular state.

The three rules that Congress uses to determine who becomes a representative can thus be summarized this way: the people must choose; their choice must be based on free and fair elections; and they must choose from among a candidate pool that is limited by age, citizenship, and residency requirements. Reflecting on these three key rules of recognition, it is clear that representatives are not simply "whomever the people want" nor "whoever won an election." Further, it is also the case that Congress's judgment about the election results and not the election results themselves establish who the representative will be. The reliance upon and determination by the relevant audience follow the general structure of all cases of representation,[34] and the US Constitution explicitly establishes it for both the House of Representatives and the US Senate.

---

[31] Keyssar, *The Right to Vote*, 53–80.
[32] Andrew Rehfeld, "On Quotas and Qualifications for Office," *Political Representation* (2010): 236–68.
[33] Andrew Rehfeld, "The Child as Democratic Citizen," *The ANNALS of the American Academy of Political and Social Science* 633 (2011): 141–66.
[34] Rehfeld, "Towards a General Theory of Political Representation."

Because the Constitution stipulates that Congress as a body must determine its own membership, there is in fact a circularity problem at the heart the matter: in order to be a member of Congress, an individual has to be recognized by the other members of Congress as having met the three rules of recognition described previously. Yet those other members of Congress are not formally members of Congress until they themselves are recognized by members of Congress as having met the rules of recognition for the body. In the US House, the circularity problem is faced every two years as the entire body is dissolved and has to be reconstituted. (It is not faced in the US Senate because only a third of that house stands for reelection in any given election year.) Though this circularity problem is a real theoretical issue, in practice it is of little consequence as the vast majority of election returns are clear and uncontested. Thus, the potential audience "self-constitutes," as it were, mutually recognizing each other and then handling the very few cases of close calls that might arise after the body has been constituted by mutual recognition.

WHAT COUNTS AS "REPRESENTING"?

We have now specified the first two stages of the process of representation – the objects of representation (the people and the states) and the establishment of representatives through three rules of recognition who the representatives of these objects are. We move now to the third stage of political representation and ask what the US Constitution takes to be the *activity* of representing.

The activity of representing – what it means "to represent" another – gets us to the heart of the most controversial issues surrounding political representation. How closely should the actions of our representatives correspond to the interests of those whom they represent? Should there be formal legal limits on what representatives can do in the form of legal instructions from their constituents? Should representatives act as mere delegates, their actions limited by binding instructions from those in-for-whom they stand (the people or the states)? Or should representatives be allowed to act with a degree of independence, holding the interests of their constituents and that of the nation as a whole in trusteeship? And how do we understand the actions of a representative when he or she seems to be acting to advance the interests of a constituency to whom the representative is not formally linked?

Before we address these questions, however, we need to recognize the difficulty of pinning down the general category of actions that we might call "representing" in the first place. Sometimes we say that lawmakers are engaged in the activity of representing when they are writing law, voting on legislation, or deliberating in Congress. At other times, lawmakers are said to be representing when they speak with their constituents or visit a foreign nation on an official delegation. Depending on the context, the activity of representing seems to cover almost anything.

The breadth of scope of the activity of representing is in marked contrast with other activities. We generally know what it means "to run" or "to write" or "to cook dinner." To use an obvious example, we know that the action of "drinking a soda" would not be confused for the activity of "writing." But if "drinking" might generally refer to actions that involve swallowing liquid and "writing" to actions that involve arranging words (on paper or a screen) in a coherent manner, what precisely counts as the actions of "representing"? One prominent definition of the activity of "representing" comes from Hanna Pitkin's seminal work, *The Concept of Representation*, a work that relies on many examples from the founding period in America, England, and Europe. Pitkin finds two key features of the activity: "pursuing the interests of those represented in a manner responsive to them." Call these two features "interest-pursuing" and "responsiveness." For Pitkin, an activity counts as "representing," then, to the extent it pursues the interests of those represented in a manner responsive to them.[35]

Upon just a bit of reflection we can see that these two features of "interest-pursuing" and "responsiveness" do not actually describe the activity of "representing," for we can imagine many examples in which both parts are achieved and yet no "representing" actually occurs. If a person were to make his friend coffee he might be acting in a manner that pursued his friend's interests in a manner that was responsive to his friend. But "making coffee" in this case would not be a case of "representing." And we can also imagine cases where neither of the two features was achieved yet we would want to say that "representing" happened all the same. When Representative Margorie Margolies Mezvinsky cast the last vote in favor of US President Bill Clinton's 1993 budget, she acted in a manner that was presumed to be counter to her wealthy constituents' interests and preferences. Further, we could imagine the vote was taken in a way that was not responsive to her constituents' concerns. In such a case we might say that the person represented their constituents *poorly* or *undemocratically* or *without reference to the common good*. But that judgment depends on our being able to treat the voting itself as an action of representing, such that we can say it was bad representing (if it was). By contrast, in this particular context many other activities would clearly have been "not representing at all": swimming in Barbados, drinking tea, going for a walk in the woods. By voting for the legislation Mezvinsky *was* representing her constituents. She may have done the activity poorly or unjustly or *represented* them against their own will in order to pursue a greater good. No matter how you describe her voting, the activity itself should count as an instance of representing.

Pitkin's two conditions of interest and responsiveness should thus be understood as a theory of how the activity of representing can become more democratic or just. "Representing" is more just, perhaps, when it is done in a

---

[35] Pitkin, *The Concept of Representation*.

manner that pursues the interests of those represented (the object of representation). "Representing" is more democratic, perhaps, when it is done in a manner that is responsive to those who are represented. And to the extent representatives limit their activity of representing to meet these two ethical standards, they act in a manner that comports with the normative ideals of republican government. Pitkin's two conditions thus help us evaluate whether the activity of representing was done in a good way, a way consistent with values of democracy or justice. But they do not explain what counts as representing itself.

What then should count as the activity of "representing" if not the features of "interest-pursuing" and "responsiveness"? At a formal level, "representing" denotes the exercise of the social power that audiences give stand-ins upon recognizing them as "representatives" – the activity for which they "stand-in-for" others to achieve. This reflects the fact that political representation is always deployed in order to execute a function or to perform some activity.[36]

In the case of the US Congress, as stipulated by the US Constitution, the action of representing is "lawmaking," and representatives "represent" their constituents primarily when they engage in all the varied activities involved in making law. This is why they "represent" their constituents when they deliberate, vote, negotiate, and also "stand up" to express the views of those in-for-whom they stand. And this is why they do not "represent" them when they are swimming in Barbados, drinking tea, or walking in the woods (except to the extent these activities are related to lawmaking). Sometimes the activity they engage in is more symbolic or merely constituted by an individual "showing up," much as a monarch might "represent" her subjects when she attends a state funeral because she is "doing" what it is she as a representative has the social power to "stand in" to do in that case – convey the symbolic presence of the nation at a time of mourning.

In all these cases, "representing" denotes both the active exercise of the social power the representative has on account of being a representative in that context and also the passive capacity to exercise that power. This passive capacity explains why we can say of an individual representative that "she represents us" simply when she is serving her term in office and thus possessing the power that a representative has. In this case, the representative "represents us" not by virtue of walking in the woods but by virtue of having the social power to make law that others who are not representatives do not have. The activity of political representing thus refers to an incredibly broad set of actions. To determine what counts as "representing" we have always to look explicitly at the power that individual representatives have invested in them on account of being stand-ins-for their constituents. Whether they execute that power well or poorly – consistent with a theory of representative government – will be a question to be asked later.

---

[36] Rehfeld, "Towards a General Theory of Political Representation."

As we have seen, the US Constitution specifies the activities for which representatives "stand in for others in order to do" and thus helps define what counts as "representing" for a member of Congress. But each house of Congress has slightly different powers. For example, representatives in the House have the authority to impeach the executive, but representatives in the Senate (i.e., senators) may not. This is why members of the House can represent their constituents by *impeaching* the president but members of the US Senate cannot (the inverse applies for trying impeachments). Similarly the Constitution establishes that senators have the power to advise the President on appointments to the Supreme Court, something that representatives in the House cannot formally do even if they wanted to; thus members of the House cannot represent their constituents in this particular way. This advisory role of senators is an act of "representing" precisely because they are exercising the power that is granted to them as senators as representatives of their states.

Beyond these broad categories, the Constitution specifies very little for representatives to do, leaving a wide swath of legislative activity as detailed in Section 8 of Article I to count as "representing." Indeed, the US Constitution says nothing explicitly about what it means "to represent" per se, even as it sets up all kinds of institutions to ensure some correspondence between the actions of representing and the will of the people. The verb "represent" appears nowhere in the US Constitution, including its amendments. The abstract noun that is sometimes used to indicate activity ("representation") appears only twice in the main text (both in Article II, Section 2) and in three subsequent amendments (Twelfth, Fourteenth, and Seventeenth). In each of these cases, the word denotes individual representatives rather than the activity itself – for example, "the representation of each state having one vote" (Twelfth) or "When vacancies happen in the representation of any State ..." (Seventeenth Amendment). Both of these use "representation" to refer to qualities of the representatives, not the activities that they might perform.

The lack of limitations on what will count as "representing" is likely due to both conceptual and normative considerations. Conceptually, and as just noted, "making law" entails a wide range of activities. Normatively, however, the lack of limits on how that activity should be carried out reflects the self-conscious effort of the founding generation to create in our representative government a deliberative filter that can mediate between the people's will, passions, and interests and the laws that govern them. In this way, the Constitution embodies the ideals articulated by Plotke, Ankersmit, and Urbinati in which representative government presents a space to elevate the people's will before it becomes law.[37]

Practical considerations were also important. For example, many of the framers were concerned by the practice of issuing "instructions," which some states had experimented with during the colonial period. Instructions allowed

---

[37] Plotke, "Representation Is Democracy"; Ankersmit, *Political Representation*; Urbinati, *Representative Democracy*.

constituencies to legally bind their representatives in how they could vote or otherwise act as representatives. Indeed, the most important theoretical questions and debates surrounding political representation have historically come from the questions that were intimated by Pitkin: how closely the activity of representing (passing laws, etc.) should correspond to the will of the people and the states (the objects of representation). This question, along with the expansion of the suffrage, helps determine whether the government itself is plausibly a democratic form of republican government. On the one hand, biding instructions ensure that representatives within a legislature perfectly communicate and act as their constituents wanted them to, thus ensuring a perfect correspondence between constituent will and a representative's vote. On the other hand, the presumed benefits of republican or representative government included its ability to create a deliberative space in which individual representatives could decide the public good only after debate.[38] This process of deliberation and decision could only occur if individual representatives were free from binding precommitments.

There was, in any case, a great deal of ambivalence about whether the people could influence legislative activity when the legislature was not close by. During the colonial era, for example, Massachusetts towns had a constitutional right to bind their representatives to the state legislature with instructions. Yet many towns did not send a representative, deciding it would be better to be fined for nonrepresentation than to pay for a representative whose single voice and vote were unlikely to have a major impact on the actions of the larger legislative body.[39] The scale of the proposed national government magnified these pragmatic concerns about "instructions." But perhaps more important was the normative aim to create a deliberative space in which representatives would be free to change their minds based on a stronger argument. For while instructions allow the will of the people to be conveyed into the legislature, they do so at the cost of representatives exercising their own will and judgment about an issue by learning from others in the legislature or responding to contingencies. Though Edmund Burke's support of independent legislators was aimed at the British Parliament, in 1774 his reasons for opposing instructed representatives were generally supported by the founding generation:

To deliver an opinion, is the right of all men; that of constituents is a weighty and respectable opinion, which a representative ought always to rejoice to hear; and which he ought always most seriously to consider. But authoritative instructions; mandates issued, which the member is bound blindly and implicitly to obey, to vote, and to argue for,

---

[38] Manin, *The Principles of Representative Government.*

[39] "The town records show again and again that when the cost of being assessed for the support of a member throughout the legislative sessions was considered by a community, the gains to be had from representation frequently did not seem worth the price." J. R. Pole, *Political Representation in England and the Origins of the American Republic* (New York: MacMillan, 1966), 234.

though contrary to the clearest conviction of his judgment and conscience, – these are things utterly unknown to the laws of this land, and which arise from a fundamental mistake of the whole order and tenor of our constitution. Parliament is not a congress of ambassadors from different and hostile interests; which interests each must maintain, as an agent and advocate, against other agents and advocates; but parliament is a deliberative assembly of one nation, with one interest, that of the whole; where, not local purposes, not local prejudices, ought to guide, but the general good, resulting from the general reason of the whole.[40]

Allowing individuals to have the freedom to exercise their judgment provided a moderating influence on the perceived extremism and instability of direct democracy. Indeed, as we saw, while Massachusetts in the 1780s provided a constitutional right of constituencies to instruct their representatives to the lower house, its state senators were under no such restrictions. This was because they were "required to be men of substance."[41] This identifies the important "filtration" idea inherent in many defenses of representative government.[42] So long as representatives were bound prior to deliberation in the legislature, there would be no way to achieve a deliberative body in which the better arguments could prevail. Thus, by not requiring the use of instructions, the Constitution allowed individual representatives to act on their own best judgment about how to vote in any particular case.

The distinction is thus made between whether representatives should act like "trustees" or "delegates."[43] At a conceptual level, this binary distinction oversimplifies three key variables we should track when describing the activity of representing within most democratic situations, in particular the decision about whether to vote for a law.[44] First, we can ask "what standards should be used" to evaluate a law, for example, whether the law should advance the interests of a representatives' constituents or the nation as a whole. Second, we can ask "who should judge" whether the proposed law meets the whatever standards we establish: Should that be the representative herself or her constituents or the nation as a whole? Finally we can ask "what level of responsiveness" should the representative have to her constituents. Should she be in regular communication providing feedback and soliciting their views? Or should she follow the guidance of her own internal "gyroscope"[45] and proceed based on a set of preexisting values?

---

[40] Edmund Burke, Speech to the Electors of Bristol, Nov. 3, 1774. Available online at http://press-pubs.uchicago.edu/founders/documents/v1ch13s7.html.

[41] Pole, *Political Representation in England*, 231.

[42] Manin, *The Principles of Representative Government*.

[43] Pitkin refers to this as the "Mandate-Independence Controversy" and provides a very good historical and theoretical review. *The Concept of Representation*, 145–67. This and the next two paragraphs summarize an argument presented in full in Andrew Rehfeld, "Representation Rethought: On Trustees, Delegates, and Gyroscopes in the Study of Political Representation and Democracy," *American Political Science Review* 103 (2009): 214–30.

[44] Rehfeld, "Representation Rethought," 214–30.

[45] Mansbridge, "Rethinking Representation."

These three variables of (i) standards, (ii) judgment, and (iii) level of responsiveness range on two ends of a spectrum. Standards are based on a range between "good for the constituency" to "good for all." Judgment ranges between "based on the constituency's judgment" to "based on the representative's judgment." And level of responsiveness ranges from "complete" to "not at all." With three variables each expressed on a scale with two extremes, there are eight possibilities, six more than the mere "trustee" and "delegate" labels cover. The traditional "delegate" model is a conflation of a representative who seeks (i) the interests of her constituents; (ii) based on their constituents' own judgment (iii) in a manner completely responsive to them. The traditional "trustee" model is a conflation of (i) a representative who seeks the interests of the nation as a whole (ii) based on the representative's own judgment of what is best (iii) in a manner that is less responsive to his constituents. There are six more conceptual possibilities that go well beyond these two labels.[46]

Rather than specifying any of the eight possible combinations that might follow from these three variables, the US Constitution leaves the manner of representing completely up to the individual representatives. In fact there was very little discussion of instructing representatives during the constitutional convention. The right to recall a representative that had existed in the Articles of Confederation was not included in the Constitution, and proposed constitutional amendments in the first and second congresses to include instructions failed. Ultimately the practice was left to individual states to deploy, which they tried to do for a period after the founding until efforts died out.[47]

Rather than using instructions, the US Constitution relies on the practice of reelection and variable term limits to constrain representatives toward the popular will. The prospect of reelection leverages the natural ambition of politicians back to the will of their constituents on a regular basis. Individual representatives thus retain considerable degrees of freedom to judge as they believe is right, to seek the aims of either their constituents or the general public good, and to do so in a manner that is more or less responsive to their constituents. But they do so with the knowledge that after a set period of time they will be held accountable, which thus constrains their actions in the direction of securing some measure of the people's will.

Because the US Constitution provides a democratic limit on representing through the prospect of reelection, the conditions under which elections occur must be seen as affecting the democratic quality of the system as a whole. To this extent, conditions that allow some citizens to have more effective power over others systematically as a group stand to undermine the claims of the system to be democratic.

---

[46] Rehfeld, "Representation Rethought," 214–30; Rehfeld, "The Concepts of Representation." Also see Mansbridge "Clarifying the Concept of Representation."

[47] Christopher Terranova, "The Constitutional Life of Legislative Instructions in America," *New York University Law Review* 84 (2009): 1337–49.

To begin with, so long as the voting rights of some groups are limited by law or custom, the government is said to be only imperfectly a democratic form. Here, even in the early twenty-first century, voting rights are restricted to the politically mature (those eighteen and older) and thus the consideration of the interests of children may not be as fully realized in the actions of representing by members of Congress.[48] Similarly, to the extent that there is a strong majority of one kind of voter in a particular district or state, the activity of representing will be more constrained to support that majority view because of the representative's interest in being reelected. This is why any redistricting plan that creates districts of overwhelming majorities can limit the outcomes of a legislature. When districts have a supermajority of voters of one party or ethnicity (majority-minority African American districts, for example), fewer members of that party or ethnicity remain in other districts. That means that representatives from both districts are less able to compromise on measures that may be required for the good of all.[49] With advanced computer modeling and robust data, in the first two decades of the twenty-first century, partisan gerrymandering has exacerbated these problems.

Far more important at the end of the twenty-first century is the influence of money on politics. The Supreme Court's decision in 2011 in *Citizens United* established that the government could not limit the amount of money spent on political speech. This ruling allowed individuals and corporations to invest significantly, if indirectly, in political campaigns. Since money is critical to reelection efforts, the ability of individual candidates to win an election depends on attracting funders, much like attracting voters. While this may seem to be a move away from democracy, some have argued that unlimited spending enhances the democratic process by allowing the expression of a wide range of viewpoints, or by allowing individuals to express the intensity of their preferences based on the amounts that they can contribute. In any event, these changes stand to have a dramatic influence on the manner in which representatives represent. If Pitkin's description of the activity of (democratic) representing centered on the pursuit of the interests of the people in a manner responsive to them, the decision in *Citizens United* creates a different incentive, one that redirects their efforts to satisfying their investors rather than the people themselves. This could change the fundamental nature of the US government, threatening to turn it into a democracy on paper that because of the practices of representing becomes effectively an oligarchy.

REPRESENTATIVENESS: DESCRIPTIVE REPRESENTATION AND THE UNITED STATES

The last stage of the four-part process of political representation is captured by the quality of "representativeness," the extent to which there is a descriptive

---

[48] Rehfeld, "The Concepts of Representation,".
[49] David Lublin, "The Election of African Americans and Latinos to the U.S. House of Representatives, 1972–1994," *American Politics Quarterly* 25 (1997): 269–86.

similarity or formal correspondence between an object of representation, the representative, or the activity of representing, and some other stipulated feature, usually of the whole. Thus we might say that a constituency is "representative" of the nation to the extent that certain features of the constituency – the distribution of ethnicities, ages, professions, etc. – reflect the nation as a whole.[50] Similarly a representative (noun) may be representative (adjective) of the nation to the extent that his or her views are descriptively similar to the median views of the nation on some particular issue.

In purely descriptive terms, an individual (or group) is representative (adjective) of the whole insofar as some aspect of that individual or group corresponds to some specified feature of the whole. Note that a person may be *a* representative (noun) of the whole whether or not the person is representative (adjective) of the whole. This distinction helps explain why a member of a minority group who is *a* representative (noun) of a group may or may not be representative (adjective) of the group. (The similarity of language explains why debates on these matters can sometimes be confused and confusing.)[51]

Representativeness is also referred to as "descriptive representation" and can occur when a subgroup's proportion of the population is reflected in the proportion of representatives in a nation's legislature. At its broadest level, descriptive representation may be desired to ensure a close correspondence between the attitudes, ideas, and general "fellow feeling" between representatives and those who live far away. Creating that tie was important in debates on representation during the colonial period. For example, in the "Essex Result," critics of the proposed 1780 Massachusetts state constitution argued that "[t]he rights of representation should be so equally and impartially distributed, that the representatives should have the same views, and interests with the people at large. They should think, feel, and act like them, and in fine, should be an exact miniature of their constituents. They should be (if we may use the expression) the whole body politic, with all its property, rights, and priviledges, [sic] reduced to a smaller scale, every part being diminished in just proportion." To remedy the deficiency, the authors looked to institutional changes, namely, that "the legislative body should be so constructed, that every law affecting property, should have the consent of those who hold a majority of the property."[52] However, while this concern with creating a "fellow feeling" between a group of representatives and their constituents was important, it was never formally institutionalized except, as we will see in a moment, in the manner of broad qualifications for office.

---

[50] Rehfeld, *The Concept of Constituency.*   [51] Rehfeld, "The Concepts of Representation."
[52] Oscar Handlin, and Mary Handlin, eds. *The Popular Sources of Political Authority: Documents on the Massachusetts Constitution of 1780* (Cambridge, MA: Belknap Press of Harvard University Press, 1966), 341.

As an example of the descriptive correspondence between representatives and those they represent, the US Congress in 2016 is not representative of women in its composition because it contains about 19 percent women when the population is just over 50 percent female. But representativeness is always a question of "with respect to what?" Thus Congress may be more representative of women with respect to the policies it enacts if they are descriptively similar to the policies that women support or descriptively similar to policies that would help women. The US Congress is more closely representative of underlying support for the major political parties in the United States, where the number of members of each political party is similar to the number of citizens identified as Republicans and Democrats. However this correspondence is inexact by a large margin as only 43 percent of the representatives in 2016 were Democrats compared to 47 percent of the population that was registered Democrat and 56 percent Republican compared to only 40 percent of the population that is registered Republican. The US House is not representative of any other party – in this sense of "descriptively similar." Finally, in terms of wealth and income, the US Congress is not representative at all, as the people it represents are in the median descriptively less wealthy than those who represent them.

To ensure representative features of their legislatures, representative governments use general qualifications for office that apply to all individuals running for a particular branch of government or house of a legislature as well as the establishment of specific qualifications for each individual seat. In European governments, this is usually achieved by using some form of proportional representation that reflects the underlying support for each party in the proportion of seats that are awarded in the legislature.[53] Similarly, European governments in the late twentieth century secured women's descriptive representation by setting gender qualifications for office that require parties to establish a minimum number of women on their party lists or establishing that certain seats were eligible to be won only by women.

There are provisions in the US Constitution that ensure descriptive representation of the politically mature via age requirements,[54] citizenship, and residency. More recently, the idea of representativeness has focused on ensuring the descriptive correspondence between underrepresented ethnic and racial populations and the ethnicity and race of those who serve in the legislature. While other representative governments around the world have developed quota systems that effectively established qualifications for office to limit a seat or office to members of a particular group (women, linguistic minorities, etc.), in the United States advocates have used the concentration of minorities into districts in order to ensure that they may elect one of their own. This strategy has successfully increased the numbers of African American legislators elected into the US House. But the strategy is limited to securing

---

[53] Rehfeld, *The Concept of Constituency.*
[54] Rehfeld, "On Quotas and Qualifications for Office," 236–68.

descriptive representation to groups who can be geographically concentrated. Guaranteeing the descriptive representation of women, for example, would require changing the qualifications for office for various seats in Congress based on gender.

CONCLUSION

This essay has outlined the way that concepts of political representation play out in the US constitutional system. It has defined political representation as entailing a four-stage process: (i) the establishment of states and people as the two objects of representation, (ii) representatives who stand-in-for states in the Senate and the people in the House (iii) in order to "pass law" (the specific activity that counts as "representing"), and (iv) doing all three in a way that is more or less representative of (in the sense of descriptively similar to) the people and states that are represented. But more than that, the Constitution specifically limits each of these four parts by tying them to either the people's will or principles of justice. In doing so, the US Constitution can be said to create a republican form of government – a government that deploys political representation limited by principles of democracy and justice.

5

Equality

Ken I. Kersch[*]

Conventional accounts of the path of constitutional equality in the United States conceptualize its development as a trajectory – secular, long-term, and linear. Some find a creedal commitment to equality present, if not realized, from the nation's inception, articulated, for instance, in the Declaration of Independence's pronouncement "We hold these truths to be self-evident, that all men are created equal."[1] Others hold the accommodations and protections the Constitution afforded to chattel slavery or to economic elites, among other failings, to have rendered this pronouncement a nullity, if not a mockery.[2] Still

---

[*] Work on this essay was supported in part by Bowdoin College, where I was Tallman Scholar in Government (in residence) in the fall of 2015. I considered some of my themes here in my Tallman Lecture at Bowdoin. I am especially grateful to John Compton and Karen Orren for their insightful comments and suggestions.
[1] See, e.g., Gunnar Myrdal, *An American Dilemma: The Negro Problem and Modern Democracy* (Harper and Bros., 1944); Danielle Allen, *Our Declaration: A Reading of the Declaration of Independence in Defense of Equality* (Liveright, 2015); Alexander Tsesis, *For Liberty and Equality: The Life and Times of the Declaration of Independence* (Oxford University Press, 2012); Harry V. Jaffa, *Crisis of the House Divided: An Interpretation of the Issues in the Lincoln-Douglas Debates* (University of Chicago Press, 1959); John Courtney Murray, S.J., *We Hold These Truths: Catholic Reflections on the American Proposition* (Sheed and Ward, 1960). See also Frederick Douglass, "What the Fourth of July Means to the American Negro," in Herbert Storing, ed., *What Country Have I? Political Writings by Black Americans* (St. Martins, 1970); Abraham Lincoln, Gettysburg Address (1863); and the more general observations of Alexis de Tocqueville in the 1830s emphasizing the degree to which the USA's democratic political culture was suffused with an egalitarian ethos. Alexis de Tocqueville, *Democracy in America* (Harvey Mansfield and Delba Winthrop, trans. and eds.) (University of Chicago Press, 2000).
[2] See, e.g., Paul Finkelman, "Making a Covenant with Death: Slavery and the Constitutional Convention," in Finkelman, ed., *Slavery and the Founders: Race and Liberty in the Age of Jefferson* (M.E. Sharpe, 1996). Within the abolitionist movement, the former position is associated with Frederick Douglass and his followers and the latter with William Lloyd Garrison and the "Garrisonians." See also Gordon Wood, *The Creation of the American Republic, 1776–1787* (University of North Carolina Press, 1969); Woody Holton, *Unruly Americans and the Origins of the Constitution* (Hill and Wang, 2007).

others acknowledge the initial statement's significance as an articulated abstraction and dimly apprehended aspiration while shifting the primary focus to the unruly, outsider political and social movements that fought to realize its promise: Jacksonian democracy, abolitionism, first-wave feminism, the labor and Granger movements, populism, progressivism, socialism, New Deal liberalism, second-wave Feminism, civil rights, black power, and the gay rights movement, among others. The Civil War Amendments, particularly the Fourteenth Amendment's guarantee that no state shall deprive any person of the "equal protection of the laws," belatedly inscribed the commitment to equality in the Constitution's text.

Some interpreters have read that clause narrowly and formalistically, by the lights of an "anti-classification" or "anti-differentiation" principle that guarantees only formal equality under law. Others have read it broadly and aspirationally, as promising substantive fairness, by the lights of an "anti-subordination" or anti-caste principle rooted in robust understandings of civic equality in fact. In either case, the Civil War Amendments marked a significant stride forward.[3] Progress was an "unsteady march," but the road was at least discernable.[4]

These same accounts map this forward movement along a set of well-known political and legal/doctrinal dimensions. New claims were made for the equality principle's applicability to previously unseen or unacknowledged classifications, once assumed to be natural or self-evidently relevant and rationally related to legitimate public objectives but, in time, newly held to be disturbingly, and perhaps illegitimately, "suspect." Across time, new claims challenged the

---

[3] For the formalist, anti-classification/anti-differentiation approach, see Andrew Kull, *The Color-Blind Constitution* (Harvard University Press, 1992); Herman Belz, *Equality Transformed: A Quarter Century of Affirmative Action* (Transaction, 1991). For the anti-subordination approach, see Catherine MacKinnon, *Toward a Feminist Theory of the State* (Harvard University Press, 1989); Kenneth Karst, "The Supreme Court, 1976 Term – Foreword: Equal Citizenship under the Fourteenth Amendment," *Harvard Law Review* 91 (1977): 1–68; Ruth Colker, "Anti-Subordination above All: Sex, Race, and Equal Protection," *New York University Law Review* 61 (1986): 1003–66; Cass Sunstein, "The Anticaste Principle," *Michigan Law Review* 92 (1994): 2410–55; Reva Siegel, "Equality Talk: Anti-Subordination and Anti-Classification Values in Constitutional Struggles over *Brown*," *Harvard Law Review* 117 (2004): 1470–1547. For a historian's aspirational understanding of the Civil War Amendments, see Michael Vorenberg, "Bringing the Constitution Back In: Amendment, Innovation, and Popular Democracy during the Civil War Era," in Meg Jacobs, William Novak, and Julien Zelizer, eds., *The Democratic Experiment: New Directions in American Political History* (Princeton University Press, 2003); Hendrick Hartog, "The Constitution of Aspiration and 'The Rights That Belong to Us All,'" *Journal of American History* 74 (December 1987): 1013–34. See also John W. Compton, *The Evangelical Origins of the Living Constitution* (Harvard University Press, 2014). On the contemporary Supreme Court, the anti-classification approach has been articulated by Chief Justice John Roberts, Parents Involved in Community Schools v. Seattle School District No. 1, 551 U.S. 701 (2007), and an approach more akin to anti-subordination by Ruth Bader Ginsburg, United States v. Virginia, 518 U.S. 515 (1996).

[4] Philip Klinkner and Rogers M. Smith, *The Unsteady March: The Rise and Decline of Racial Equality in America* (University of Chicago Press, 2002).

disparate treatment of men without property; the poor; women; and racial, ethnic, sexual, gender, and linguistic minorities. Assessments of the legitimacy of these claims involved an acknowledgment, first, of the fundamental and cognizable likeness of all within the class and, second, of the problematic nature of government's disparate treatment between those within and those outside it. This also entailed the problematizing and, ultimately, the delegitimating of the ostensible public purposes adduced to justify the disparate treatment. Subsequent movement along the path involved the gradual enlargement of the circle of protection – the enforcement of the antidiscrimination principle against an expanding array of governmental and nongovernmental institutions: from the federal government to the states to private entities, including private employers, labor unions, private businesses, clubs, and associations.[5]

While true in many important respects, the smooth, ineluctable logic of this familiar template for understanding rights and liberties involving equality in the American constitutional tradition obscures significant dynamics of US constitutional development. As against these conventional understandings, this chapter proposes a pluralist configurative model concerning constitutional equality involving a dynamically unfolding process operating on three distinct but interacting planes: (1) principled, (2) spatial, and (3) temporal.

The principled dimension frankly recognizes *both* the anti-classification *and* the anti-subordination principles as foundational to the nation's (genuinely) creedal commitment to liberty, equality, and justice under law. It signs onto this dual recognition on both normative and positive grounds: that is, on the grounds that it is both *good* and *it is us* – always has been and likely always will be (put otherwise, this plurally principled [or agonistic] creed is constitutive of the US political and constitutional culture).[6]

---

[5] This radiating process commonly involved: (1) the renegotiation and redefinition of the boundaries of the public and private spheres in the interest of augmenting the pervasiveness of the new norms and (2) the deconstruction of the boundaries between (or compartmentalization of) allegedly distinctive "types" of rights (political, economic, social), typically as a prelude to disassembling wonted social frames separating matters of public (political/legal) concern from others spheres once held to be most appropriately governed by the norms, traditions, and ministrations of civil society. See Mark Tushnet, "An Essay on Rights," *Texas Law Review* 62 (1984): 1363–1403. As Pamela Brandwein has demonstrated, it also potentially involved a willingness to enforce the principle of the equal protection of the laws in a way that required that states take an active role in meeting those guarantees. That is, it could be used to challenge not just "state action" but state inaction as well. Pamela Brandwein, "The Lost Language of State Neglect," in Ronald Kahn and Ken I. Kersch, eds., *The Supreme Court and American Political Development* (University Press of Kansas, 2006); Pamela Brandwein, *Rethinking the Judicial Settlement of Reconstruction* (Cambridge University Press, 2011). See also William Stuntz, *The Collapse of American Criminal Justice* (Belknap, 2011). This, however, was a path untaken. See United States v. Reese, 92 U.S. 214 (1876); United States v. Cruikshank, 92 U.S. 542 (1875).

[6] On "agonistic liberalism," see John Gray, *Isaiah Berlin: An Interpretation of His Thought* (Princeton University Press, 2013).

The spatial dimension accounts for the USA's distinctive constitutional architecture and geography, structured by diverse jurisdictional spaces situated in an "overgrown" landscape rich in shared, overlapping, and oppositional powers and institutions.[7] This jurisdictional and institutional hyper-pluralism provides an almost infinite array of beachheads for diverse claims and claimants, and opportunities for enforcement, and resistance, all with some plausible claim to legitimacy.[8]

Finally, contention over principle and jurisdiction (or space) takes place, in the nature of things, across time – time in which concepts, ideologies, and ideas develop, are adopted, and are discarded; institutions evolve, flourish, and decay; processes are fashioned, are instituted, operate, and are played out; events occur in disparate registers at different rates, altering and in some cases transforming the institutional, ideational, political, and social landscapes; and enterprising agents, in ordinary or contentious politics, pursue their objectives.[9]

In sum, so far as equality is concerned, both claim-making and official recognition and enforcement of claims against purportedly discriminatory public and private actors take place in a variegated landscape of jurisdictional and institutional space, characterized by multiple orders that both operate independently and intercur.[10] Both claim-makers and governing institutions and officials have recourse to diverse, even contradictory conceptual logics involving anti-classification and anti-subordination principles, both considered legitimate in the broader legal and political culture. Both claim-making and official recognition and enforcement of those claims are, more-over, subject to time's vicissitudes and dynamics, which occasion complex patterns of settlement and change.[11]

Over the course of US constitutional development, any relatively settled time period will be structured by a multiplicity of *equality configurations*. These micro- and macro-regimes instantiate institutional settlements following a

---

[7] See Karen Orren and Stephen Skowronek's description of the American polity as resembling "downtown Tokyo." *The Search for American Political Development* (Cambridge University Press, 2004), 22–23.

[8] See Ronald Kahn, *The Supreme Court and Constitutional Theory, 1953–1993* (University of Kansas Press, 1994), on the application of "polity" (structural/jurisdictional) versus "rights" principles by the US Supreme Court.

[9] See Ken I. Kersch, *Constructing Civil Liberties: Discontinuities in the Development of American Constitutional Law* (Cambridge University Press, 2004); Ken I. Kersch, "The Talking Cure: How Constitutional Argument Drives Constitutional Development," *Boston University Law Review* 94 (May 2014): 1083–1108. See also Samuel Huntington, *American Politics: The Promise of Disharmony* (Belknap, 1981).

[10] See Orren and Skowronek, *Search for American Political Development*; Karen Orren and Stephen Skowronek, "Beyond the Iconography of Order: Notes for a New Institutionalism," in Lawrence Dodd and Calvin Jillson, eds., *The Dynamics of American Politics* (Westview, 1994).

[11] See Paul Pierson, *Politics in Time: History, Institutions, and Social Analysis* (Princeton University Press, 2004).

robust moment of claim-making during which the equality claims of some square off against potentially countervailing equality, democracy, and liberty claims of others in ways that implicate the countervailing conceptual logics of the polity's diverse jurisdictional spaces. As such, the development of constitutional equality in the United States is consistently characterized by a dynamic that involves the repudiation of formerly countervailing, historically sanctioned, and (in the abstract, at least) normatively desirable, if not sacrosanct, rights claims. These have included claims involving "states rights" (rights of sovereign self-determination of subsidiary political units), property rights, free association and free expression, and religious liberty. Because the principles underlying these countervailing claims are typically held – over the long term and in the broader polity – as not only valued and valuable but, indeed, still in force, such reconfigurative dynamics are systematically erased from the "whiggish" stories of progress that are inherent in conventional readings of history and historical change.[12]

The equality configurations structuring these settlements are durable in that they lock in particular adjudications of this contestation, rendering them stable and path dependent. But they are not unalterably or irreversibly so. As such, the pluralist configurative understanding of constitutional equality I advance here is consistent with "regime politics" models of constitutional development subject to "punctuated equilibria."[13] It does not, however, assume that the regime enforces a hegemonic, cross-cutting ethos or governing order concerning equality. The regime settlement is itself pluralistic, inhabiting the fragmented institutional spaces of the US constitutional order. So, for instance, the anti-classification principle may be held to govern certain regulatory spaces in the public or private spheres, while the anti-subordination principle may be enforced in others, while in still other spaces, other normatively desirable principles (such as majoritarian democracy, private property rights, religious liberty) may be afforded precedence to either of these equality principles.

In particular time-delimited cases, claimants and/or adjudicators will insist that either one or the other is the "true" or proper understanding of constitutional equality or that other normatively desirable principles take precedence over equality considerations. But in the distinctively variegated and pluralistic American constitutional order, multiple settlements inevitably exist simultaneously, applying different equality configurations as the foundational ordering frameworks for the polity's diverse social, political, and

---

[12] Kersch, *Constructing Civil Liberties*.

[13] Institutions can be knocked off paths and new possibilities opened by "exogenous shocks" such as crises (such as wars and violence, economic collapses, high-profile scandals), political challenges (whether from an opposition party or social movements), "slow-moving" abrasions of intercurrent orders, or other dynamics of incremental change, such as those common to common law legal systems. See Pierson, *Politics in Time*; Orren and Skowronek, *Search for American Political Development*; Benjamin Cardozo, *The Nature of the Judicial Process* (Yale University Press, 1921).

constitutional spaces. Within these spaces, particular equality configurations, operating as micro-regimes, temporarily and provisionally govern particular spaces – whether it be the fifty states, the workplace, the public school, the street, the family, the household, religious institutions, land ownership, public employment, or some other domain. These may be either consonant with or antagonistic to the configurations (regimes) that govern other spaces: there is no reason to believe that one form of configuration will structure all of the polity's significant social spaces in a pervasive manner, across the board.[14]

A PLURALIST CONFIGURATIVE HISTORY: OUTLINE AND DEVELOPMENTAL OVERVIEW

Rights configurations concerning constitutional equality structure both the routine adjudication of normative claims involving equality within a governing regime and the governing frameworks in which this contestation takes place. These configurations are innumerable. While some micro-configurations structure more delimited jurisdictional spaces, others are prominent, overarching, and well known. The most robust big-picture equality claims (national-level party politics) from the early republic through the Jacksonian era involved economic concentrations and the exclusions wrought by economic power. These inequalities were implicated in contention over a range of national constitutional and public policy issues including federal taxation, universal (white) male suffrage, the National Bank, internal improvements, bankruptcy law, the embargo, the tariff, the autonomy of business corporations, monopolies, and the terms of admission of new states. Appealing to the core principles of the contemporary anti-classification principle (as vouchsafing not equality of result but the equality of opportunity promised by an abstracted equal treatment under law), Andrew Jackson's bank veto message (1832) characteristically recognized that "[d]istinctions in society will always exist under every just government," that "[e]quality of talents, of education, or of wealth can not be produced by human institutions," and that "[i]n the full enjoyment of the gifts of Heaven and the fruits of superior industry, economy, and virtue, every man is entitled to protection by law ...." In his very next breath, however, Jackson insisted that the shibboleth of equal treatment under law should not blind anyone to the ways in which appeals to equality can serve to mask class interest, privilege, and subordination – that is, the dynamics of power. "[W]hen the laws undertake to add to these natural and just advantages artificial distinctions ... the humble members of society ... who have neither the time nor the means of securing like favors to themselves, have a right to

---

[14] See generally Elmer E. Schattschneider, *The Semi-Sovereign People: A Realist's View of Democracy in America* (Holt, Rinehart and Winston, 1960). Dynamics of norm or policy diffusion will be common features of such an order.

complain of the injustice of their Government," Jackson propounded, invok-ing the purportedly contrary anti-subordination principle. For President Jack-son, the pursuit of class equality – which, for him, focused on "the [humble] farmer, mechanics, and laborers" – meant instituting robust majoritarian democracy with an expanded (universal, white male) suffrage, operated on a "winner-take-all" model: when the people rule, the equality of the common man will govern, with equal privileges for all, as opposed to special privileges for the few.[15]

In its time and place, the Jeffersonian egalitarianism advanced by Jacksonian democracy at the national level counseled a respect for government generally, and the national government certainly ("Its evils exist only in its abuses"), but also a heavy emphasis on the constitutional limitations placed on the federal government and a corresponding securing, as against the federal government, of the powers of the states – that is, a relatively strict adherence to the jurisdictional boundaries set by the USA's constitutionally specified federal structure. The general government's "true strength," Jackson maintained, "consists in leaving individuals and states as much as possible to themselves."[16]

Later, this understanding of the relationship between the anti-subordination principle and the arrangement of authority within the US constitutional system was reversed. The late-nineteenth-century Populist Movement, arising from the country's rural Midwestern and southern periphery in response to the social and economic upheaval wrought by industrial and finance capitalism, expressly invoked Jefferson in its push to "restore the government of the Republic to the hands of the 'plain people' with which class it originated," a restoration Populists held to be "identical with the purposes of the National Constitution." This meant stronger government where power was authorized but a government largely limited by the Constitution's terms, thus entailing a large dose of constitutional formalism.[17] Once the Populists and (later) the Progressives captured legislatures, however, the forces pursuing the advancement of the anti-subordination principle in the economic sphere began to deemphasize the constitutional limitations of government, arguing that equality was best furthered by majoritarian presumptions at both the state and federal levels. "Progressive" constitutional theory critical of the aggressive exercise of the judicial review power by courts, as articulated, for instance, by James Bradley Thayer and Oliver Wendell Holmes, Jr., in turn placed a heavy emphasis on the claims of democracy, anchored in the idea of the civic equality entailed by popular rule, as against the countervailing claims of a ruling elite. A powerful state, as Herbert

[15] See generally John Gerring, *Party Ideologies in America, 1828–1996* (Cambridge University Press, 1998) See also Joseph Fishkin and William E. Forbath, "The Anti-Oligarchy Constitution," *Boston University Law Review* 94 (2014): 669–696.

[16] Andrew Jackson, Bank Veto Message (1832).

[17] People's Party Platform (1892); M. Elizabeth Sanders, *Roots of Reform: Farmers, Workers, and the American State, 1877–1917* (University of Chicago Press, 1999); Charles Postel, *The Populist Vision* (Oxford University Press, 2007). See Gerard Magliocca, *Andrew Jackson and the Constitution: The Rise and Fall of Generational Regimes* (University of Kansas Press, 2007).

Croly would have it, was under modern conditions indispensible to the project of remedying pervasive structural economic inequality.[18]

Even as this general macro-configuration took shape, however, new reform imperatives[19] were brewing that would ultimately prompt the construction of a new constitutional architecture concerning equality. The Progressive movement sided with the governing claims of legislatures and administrative agencies on grounds of both democratic legitimacy and institutional competence and expertise. New theories of democracy – most prominently, the Deweyian pragmatism that had motivated and structured key strains of progressivism – helped construct and privilege new theories concerning the freedom of speech, especially of outsiders to, or vocal opponents of, the decisions made by government officials and popular majorities. These ultimately informed and underwrote a constitutional jurisprudence enforced by counter-majoritarian courts emphasizing the value of equal voice, regardless of content or viewpoint.[20] Invoking the Fourteenth Amendment's equal protection clause and the First Amendment's free exercise clause, racial and religious minorities began to demand equal legal and civic status. Both types of claims were recognized and then implemented by courts, legislatures, and executives at both the state and federal levels.[21]

---

[18] James Bradley Thayer, "The Origin and Scope of the American Doctrine of Constitutional Law," *Harvard Law Review* 7 (1893): 129. Lochner v. New York, 198 U.S. 45 (1905) (J. Holmes, dissenting); Herbert Croly, *The Promise of American Life* (Macmillan, 1909).

[19] Kersch, *Constructing Civil Liberties*. New refusals – doubling down on particular commitments and understandings in a more conservative spirit – might also arise, in particular contexts, and will: political actors will react negatively to bad experiences, which motivate them to staunchly resist particular policies and reform imperatives to vindicate core, traditional principles and traditions or emphasize one core value (e.g., liberty, property) over drives toward innovation. See Kim Lane Scheppele, "Aspirational and Aversive Constitutionalism: The Case for Studying Constitutional Influence through Negative Models," *I-CON* 1 (2003): 296–324. See also Richard Primus, *The American Language of Rights* (Cambridge University Press, 1999).

[20] Abrams v. United States, 250 U.S. 616 (1919) (J. Holmes, dissenting); West Virginia v. Barnette, 319 U.S. 624 (1943); Police Department of Chicago v. Mosley, 408 U.S. 92 (1972) (using equal protection analysis to resolve free speech issue); Carey v. Brown, 447 U.S. 455 (1980) (using equal protection analysis to resolve free speech issue); Texas v. Johnson, 491 U.S. 397 (1989); Ward v. Rock Against Racism, 491 U.S. 781 (1989); R.A.V. v. St. Paul, 505 U.S. 377 (1992). See Erwin Chemerinsky, "Content Neutrality as a Central Problem of Freedom of Speech: Problems of the Supreme Court's Application," *Southern California Law Review* 74 (2000): 49–64.

[21] On Fourteenth Amendment equal protection as applied to race, see, e.g., Yick Wo v. Hopkins, 118 U.S. 356 (1886); Shelley v. Kraemer, 334 U.S. 1 (1948); Brown v. Board of Education, 347 U.S. 483 (1954); City of Richmond v. Croson, 448 U.S. 469 (1989); Adarand v. Pena, 515 U.S. 200 (1995). See Hugh Davis Graham, *The Civil Rights Era: Origin and Development of National Policy, 1960–1972* (Oxford University Press, 1990); John Skrentny, *The Minority Rights Revolution* (Belknap, 2002). On First Amendment free exercise considered through the prism of equality, see Lamb's Chapel v. Center Moriches, 508 U.S. 384 (1993); Rosenberger v. University of Virginia, 515 U.S. 819 (1995); Good News Club v. Milford, 533 U.S. 98 (2001); Locke v. Davey, 540 U.S. 712 (2004); Christian Legal Society v. Martinez, 561 U.S. 661 (2010). See generally U.S. v. Carolene Products, 304 U.S. 144, fn. 4 (1938).

Considered in this way, it is clear that concerns for constitutional and civic equality overspill the legalistic category of the Supreme Court's Fourteenth Amendment equal protection jurisprudence. Clearly, claims involving constitutional equality played a major role in popular disputes over public policy well before the words "equal protection" were added to the Constitution's text. And even after the adoption of the equal protection clause, Americans often linked equality claims to other sorts of principled claims, including those involving economic and civil liberties. Within the Supreme Court, the Fourteenth Amendment's equal protection clause, read by the lights of an anti-classification principle proscribing "class legislation," was a pillar of nineteenth-century economic liberties jurisprudence, with race, sex, and other modern classifications rarely figuring in the period's major decisions.[22] Similarly, in the contemporary (post–New Deal) era, equality considerations are plainly implicated in the Court's jurisprudence concerning other liberties, including those involving Congress's power to regulate interstate commerce (which was pioneered by New Deal policy initiatives to enforce anti-subordination principles in the economic sphere) and the individual rights provisions of the First Amendment (to say nothing of the criminal process provisions of the Bill of Rights, which were revised pursuant to a reform imperative concerning race).[23]

PRINCIPLE IN TIME: POWER, JUSTICE, AND EQUALITY THROUGH A DEVELOPMENTAL LENS

From a developmental perspective, the problem of constitutional equality involves a consideration of normative requirements in and across time. A core social-political problem facing morally aspirational societies like the United States is the problem of justice, requiring that each person be afforded his *due*.[24] The reality of power, however, rooted in human appetites and wants – the greed, envy, partiality, bigotry, and pride inherent in human nature – poses a problem for justice.[25] As a society moves forward in time, the many who act upon these desires get and leverage what they get to get more, seeking, winning, and accumulating power. In this way, political and economic development in free, liberal capitalist societies conduces to the uneven distribution – the concentration – of political, economic,

---

[22] Howard Gillman, *The Constitution Besieged: The Rise and Demise of Lochner Era Police Powers Jurisprudence* (Duke University Press, 1995).

[23] See Kersch, *Constructing Civil Liberties*; Lucas A. Powe, Jr., *The Warren Court and American Politics* (Harvard University Press, 2000); Mary Dudziak, *Cold War Civil Rights: Race and the Image of American Democracy* (Princeton University Press, 2001).

[24] See Aristotle, *The Nichomachean Ethics*, Book V (Lesley Brown, ed.; David Ross, trans.) (Oxford University Press, 2009). This, importantly, is different from a requirement that each is entitled to *the same*. See US Constitution, Preamble; Sotirios Barber, *Welfare and the Constitution* (Princeton University Press, 2003).

[25] See, e.g., Thomas Hobbes, *Leviathan* (Richard Tuck, ed.) (Cambridge University Press, 1996).

and social power. As such, development in these societies generates "structural" inequalities: it is a hothouse for the germination of new obstacles to justice not present at earlier stages of development. Because, on balance, people in free societies will privilege their own needs and those of the groups to which they belong to those of other individuals and groups, development perpetually gives rise to new theoretical problems concerning the relationship of power to justice.[26]

These problems are dealt with in the unique guises in which they present themselves across time in a changing institutional and political context. This means that every moment in time inherently raises questions about the ways in which existing institutions meet the problems that concentrations of power pose for justice. The result is a collective determination, arrived at deliberately or ipso facto, that currently existing institutions are successful or at least adequate in meeting the requirements of justice or that these institutions are sufficiently settled, and perhaps sacrosanct, and that justice is best, albeit imperfectly, served by the institutional status quo. Or, alternatively, it is determined that reform, if not revolution, is imperative to advance equality in the service of justice. This second determination is possible because human beings are also capable of sympathy, empathy, critical reflection, and moral aspiration. They can see and recognize injustice and are capable of benevolence, selflessness, and sacrifice in organizing around a "reform imperative" in challenging it.[27] Political theory tells us that the situation is further complicated by the fact that problems of political (and constitutional) equality are commonly problems of groups. Partiality and selfishness are to be expected in pluralist polities because selflessness and magnanimity are rare between groups, perhaps even more so than between individuals: human collectivities are inherently morally obtuse. As Hobbes recognized long ago, social and political aggregations pose a challenge to the realization of more inclusive loyalties and higher collective aspirations.[28]

Over time, the "moral attitudes" of powerful or privileged groups will diverge from those of disempowered groups. The former, often self-deceptively, will

---

[26] Reinhold Niebuhr, *Moral Man and Immoral Society: A Study in Ethics and Politics* (Louisville, KY: Westminster John Knox Press, 2013)[1932], 1–3, 16, 11 ["MMIS"]. See also James Madison, *Federalist* 51. I draw extensively in the discussion that follows on the political thought of Reinhold Niebuhr and, to a lesser extent, John Dewey.

[27] See J. David Greenstone, *The Lincoln Persuasion: Remaking American Liberalism* (Princeton, 1993).

[28] Reinhold Niebuhr, *The Children of Light and The Children of Darkness: A Vindication of Democracy and a Critique of Its Traditional Defense* (Charles Scribner's Sons, 1944)["CLCD"], 122; MMIS, 47, 272, 267–68. See also Hobbes, *Leviathan*. The group nature of modern US politics, of course, has been recognized by modern political science, dispassionately, approvingly, and critically. See, e.g., Arthur Bentley, *The Process of Government: A Study of Social Pressures* (University of Chicago Press, 1908); Robert Dahl, *A Preface to Democratic Theory* (University of Chicago Press, 1956); Grant McConnell, *Private Power and American Democracy* (Knopf, 1966); Theodore J. Lowi, *The End of Liberalism: The Second Republic of the United States* (W.W. Norton, 1969).

identify their special, personal interests with universal values and the general public interest. They will go to great lengths to do so, seeking to prove these consonances through elaborate intellectual demonstrations that what is best for them personally – the privileges they have claimed – are products of the natural order and the just reward for the application in the economic, political, and social spheres of their uniquely serviceable character, merit, and effort.[29]

Thus equality, where it exists in pluralistic and morally aspirational liberal capitalist polities, tends to be an in-group commitment, afforded only rarely as a matter of course to out-groups, even in relatively enlightened (large) communities. Rivals of roughly equivalent privilege and power are treated as members of the club – respected as worthy opponents in the game – and those of lesser status as the subject of (appropriate) philanthropy.[30]

Given the nature of contemporary constitutional debates in the United States, in which historically informed constitutional theories are sometimes attacked as fatally positivist and without foundations,[31] it is worth underlining that while the framework set out earlier is "historicist" and "relativist," it does not entail a denial of "timeless" moral principles (including justice and the natural equality of man) and foundational eternal truths (like "human nature"). Nor does it downgrade their status as fundamental or even "God given." It simply recognizes and accounts for the fact that those principles live and are applied in the real world, to real human beings, alive in a certain place, time, and context – in the world, if you will, as God created it. So too with the problem of justice.[32]

THE HISTORICAL TRAJECTORY: THE EVOLUTION OF EQUALITY IN THE ANGLO-AMERICAN POLITICAL TRADITION

Although space does not permit a full survey, this section will attempt to situate the American debate over equality within the much longer stream of Anglo-American – and European – thinking about power and justice. One of the most perceptive modern commentators on this subject was the twentieth-century

---

[29] MMIS, 117. Niebuhr – a vocal anti-communist – observes that this is the mirror image of the equally erroneous communist view that unequal rewards are always unjust.

[30] MMIS, 13. On the clubby membership dynamic, see also C. Wright Mills, *The Power Elite* (Oxford University Press, 1956).

[31] Ken I. Kersch, "Constitutional Conservatives Remember The Progressive Era," in Stephen Skowronek, Stephen Engel, and Bruce Ackerman, eds., *The Progressives' Century: Democratic Reform and Constitutional Government in the United States* (Yale, 2016); Ken I. Kersch, "Beyond Originalism: Conservative Declarationism and Constitutional Redemption," *Maryland Law Review* 71 (2011): 229–82.

[32] In this sense, contra the Kantian idealism of much of the constitutional theory in this era (John Rawls, Ronald Dworkin), which shares much with natural law/natural rights approaches (Harry Jaffa, Robert P. George, Randy Barnett), this approach is Humean – and, given Hume's extensive influence on the Founders, thus has a robust "originalist" pedigree. See James Harris, *David Hume: An Intellectual Biography* (Cambridge University Press, 2015).

Protestant theologian Reinhold Niebuhr. Niebuhr was particularly attentive to the ways in which ideas concerning equality have been shaped by tectonic shifts in social organization. In what follows, I draw on Niebuhr (and, to a lesser extent, the works of John Dewey) in tracing four distinct historical stages: from bourgeois liberalism to "free market" industrial capitalism to the era of the modern state and, finally, the era of civil rights. As we shall see, American constitutional doctrine in the area of equality was not forged in a vacuum; rather, it emerged from a prolonged encounter with the practical problems entailed in justifying, or else challenging, entrenched forms of social, political, and economic authority.

Bourgeois Liberalism

Individual liberty (freedom) in its modern sense was forged under particular historical conditions involving opposition by rising claimants to the cultural, social, economic, and political dominance and subordination instituted and sustained by feudal institutions. In the emergent "bourgeois" society, the demand for middle-class (economic, then political) liberty was made by a vital advancing class understanding the conditions of its own liberation as universal: the freedom achieved in opposition to the feudal order's oppressions was understood as an end in itself. The era's established authority, rooted in claims of divine right and will, reinforced the status quo. Those challenging this monolith appealed to inalienable claims inherent in the rebelling individuals – to pre-political, natural, individual rights. In this way, the revolt against society's limiting hierarchies and associations was theorized as a set of claims confirming the inherent rights of the individual to be free from any and all associations, except those he entered into through his own free (individual) will. Government existed both as a product of this consent (the state of nature and the subsequent social contract) and to preserve the individual's rights, which were his by nature. In moving from claims on behalf of the natural rights of individuals to the establishment of new forms of government, bourgeois liberalism promised to reconcile what Niebuhr described as the "two dimensions of human existence . . . man's spiritual stature [inherent in his status as an individual] and his social character [his status as a member of the community]"; that is, "the uniqueness and variety of life, [and] . . . the common necessities of all men." Henceforth, the core political questions would be held to involve the relationship between liberty and order, that is, bringing the claims of the individual and those of the community into proper relation.[33]

---

[33] John Dewey, *The Public and Its Problems* (Henry Holt, 1927) ["PP"], 86–87; CLCD, 2–4, 6–7, 42–43, 52–53. See also John Locke, *Second Treatise of Civil Government* (1689); Isaac Kramnick, *Republicanism and Bourgeois Radicalism: Political Ideology in Late Eighteenth Century England and America* (Cornell University Press, 1990); Louis Hartz, *The Liberal Tradition in America* (Harcourt, Brace, 1955). Recent work in analytic constitutional theory has brought us right back to this very same point. See, e.g., James Fleming and Linda McClain, *Ordered Liberty: Rights, Responsibilities, and Virtues* (Harvard University Press, 2013). See Ken I. Kersch, "Bringing It All Back Home?" *Constitutional Commentary* 28 (Fall 2013): 407–19.

At this early stage, the potential menace of individual rapacity and anarchy – alien concepts, other than theoretically – was hardly considered. The reform imperative that stimulated the invention of bourgeois liberalism called for the removal of political fetters from economic activity: as such, this moment's anti-subordination imperative was realized through the new protections that would be afforded by governments to "natural" economic liberties. The emergent theory justifying this reform did not regard new concentrations of economic power as significant threats under the new order, which had, after all, reversed the then-extant dynamics by undermining feudal and then mercantilist controls. The rivalrous interaction of free, self-seeking individuals in the market, the theory assumed, would keep potentially overweening economic power roughly in check, with a broader view informed by "enlightened self-interest" serving as a stopgap in cases of periodic maladjustment between the interests of the individual and those of the community. As Niebuhr put the point, bourgeois liberalism's "serene confidence in the possibilities of social harmony" was derived both from the genuine achievements of a commercial culture (wealth creation, economic growth, and scientific and technological advance) and from the illusions natural to that culture.[34]

This new liberalism, however, assumed a natural equilibrium of economic power in the community that in the long run simply did not hold. Economic power accumulated, and those who got leveraged what they got to get more. The strong took advantage of the weak. Under the sway of this stage's reigning creed and their understanding of their place within it, the powerful made what they understood to be sensible demands upon the community that the broader community increasingly apprehended as inordinate.[35]

"Free Market" Industrial Capitalism in the Nineteenth-Century United States

Like feudalism before it, bourgeois liberalism lent itself to unique aggrandizements of power. In nineteenth-century England and the United States, the commercial classes converted the precepts of a liberating, anti-hierarchical liberalism into a set of dogmas holding the emancipated to be imbued with special virtues uniquely qualifying them to rule in ways neatly coinciding with their interests.[36] They called for the removal of political restraints upon economic activity and sharp constitutional limits on state power (often justified with

---

[34] PP, 86–87; CLCD, 2–4, 6–7, 42–43, 52–53. See also Adam Smith, *The Wealth of Nations* (1776).
[35] CLCD, 23, n. 4., 26, 76, 114; Reinhold Niebuhr, *The Irony of American History* (University of Chicago, 1952) ["IAH"], 92–95.
[36] See, e.g., William Graham Sumner, *What the Social Classes Owe to Each Other* (Harper and Bros., 1883); Andrew Carnegie, "Wealth," *North American Review* 148 (June 1889): 653–65; Herbert Spencer, *Social Statics, of the Conditions Essential to Happiness Specified, and the First of Them Developed* (John Chapman, 1851); PP, 204. See also Carol Nackenoff, *The Fictional Republic: Horatio Alger and American Political Discourse* (Oxford University Press, 1994); Hartz, *Liberal Tradition in America*.

reference to the anti-classification conception of equality). While liberal political and economic theorists like William Graham Sumner and constitutional theorists like Christopher Tiedemann stridently condemned the active use of governmental power to advance private interests – Sumner called it "jobbery," underwriting "plutocracy," and Tiedemann held it to be (unconstitutional) "class legislation" – the actual liberal regime ended up proscribing the use of governmental power where it might have been leveraged to equilibrate increasingly cavernous economic power disparities (such as between employers and employees in the emergent wage labor system) and standing down when it was enlisted to advance the interests of the already powerful and well connected.[37] The effect of this under industrial capitalism was to render unprecedentedly coercive concentrations of economic power with significant implications for social well-being largely outside of social control.[38] Classical liberal theory – pioneered in its more ideological laissez-faire version not by Adam Smith and John Locke, empiricists who might have been more sensitive to actual historical developments, but by the more doctrinaire, scientistic French physiocrats like Turgot, Condorcet, and Quesnay (whom Smith criticized as dogmatic) – did not account for the inordinate and disproportionate development of economic power.[39] At its most naïve and self-serving, the ideology posited, as an afterthought, a superintending dogma that the general welfare is advanced by imposing the fewest possible limits on economic activity. As such, the interests of the profit-seeking individual or corporation and the public interest were, by definition, one and the same.[40] These understandings were, in turn, reflected in the jurisprudence of the late-nineteenth- and early-twentieth-century US Supreme Court.[41]

Over time, the accumulation of social power by those who initially won and succeeded was leveraged through relentless enterprise to secure new conquests,

---

[37] See, e.g., Richard White, *Railroaded: The Transcontinentals and the Making of Modern America* (W.W. Norton, 2011).

[38] MMIS, 14–15.

[39] See CLCD, 108–9. Emma Rothschild, *Economic Sentiments: Adam Smith, Condorcet, and the Enlightenment* (Harvard University Press, 2013); Martin Albaum, "The Moral Defenses of the Physiocrats Laissez-Faire," *Journal of the History of Ideas*, 16 (1955): 179–97.

[40] MMIS, 8–9, 33; CLCD, 29. Some have held this to be a later development, not attributable to the original physiocrats, but nevertheless ensconced by the nineteenth century. See Thomas P. Neill, "The Physiocrats' Concept of Economics," *The Quarterly Journal of Economics*, 63 (1949): 532–53.

[41] IAH, 99. See, e.g., *Slaughterhouse Cases*, 83 U.S. 36 (1873) (J. Field, dissenting); Munn v. Illinois, 94 U.S. 113 (1877) (J. Field, dissenting); Lochner v. New York, 198 U.S. 45 (1905) (J. Holmes, dissenting). See also Thomas Cooley, *A Treatise on the Constitutional Limitations Which Rest Upon the Legislative Power of the States of the American Union* (Little, Brown, 1868); David J. Brewer, "The Nation's Safeguard," in *Proceedings of the New York State Bar Association, Sixteenth Annual Meeting* (New York State Bar Association, 1893).

greater gains, and the acquisition of even more property – unimpeded save by would-be state coercion in the interest of justice.[42]

Contentious Politics and the Countervailing Power of the Modern American State

The sense of many late-nineteenth and early-twentieth-century Americans that they were living by the dictates of inordinate economic (and, in turn, social and political) power paralleled the dynamics that had first occasioned the birth of liberal individualism. The new claimants, as Niebuhr put it, had lost confidence in their power to navigate the world as self-determining individual agents; they felt themselves to be "not ... individual[s], as more privileged persons are ...."[43] Their grievance was accentuated by the cognitive dissonance inherent in their sense of growing powerlessness as individuals at the very moment which celebrated to the point of myth the agency, power, and value of the self-directed individual.[44] It was precisely this predicament that was registered first by the Granger movement, then by Populists, and, in turn, by the labor movement and the Progressives, the last of whom began calling for a more active government focused on creating the conditions for giving all Americans a "Square Deal."[45] Its understandings were ultimately incorporated into the constitutional reasoning of Supreme Court justices like John Marshall Harlan and Charles Evans Hughes, who were willing to rethink the entrenched dogmas of their wonted analytical frameworks by accepting, for instance, the plausibility of a legislature's determination that employer and employee did not stand on the equal footing assumed by the prevailing doctrine of "liberty of contract."[46]

In their initial incarnations, these rising claimant movements commonly appealed to the countervailing sensibilities of fraternity and solidarity – that

---

[42] While this diagnosis and prescription are largely synonymous with the "Madisonian" diagnosis of the political problem posed by faction and the institutional solution of simultaneously empowering and limiting government (see, e.g., George Thomas, *The Madisonian Constitution* [Johns Hopkins, 2008]), Niebuhr argued that Madison's *Federalist* 10 attached "too great a significance ... to inequality of faculty as the basis of inequality of privilege." What Madison did not recognize was that "unequal [economic] power ... is a social and historical accretion." CLCD, 65–66. "Differences in faculty and function do indeed help to originate inequality of privilege." But "they never justify the degree of inequality created, and they are frequently not even relevant to the type of inequality perpetuated in a social system." MMIS, 114. The situation in the late-nineteenth- and early-twentieth-century United States was particularly egregious in this regard. CLCD, 98–100.

[43] MMIS, 176–77; CLCD, 57.

[44] PP, 95–97. See also Woodrow Wilson, *The New Freedom: A Call for the Emancipation of the Generous Energies of a People* (Doubleday, 1913).

[45] Croly, *Promise of American Life*; Theodore Roosevelt, *The New Nationalism* (The Outlook Company, 1910).

[46] Lochner v. New York, 198 U.S. 45, 69 (1905) (J. Harlan, dissenting); West Coast Hotel v. Parrish, 300 U.S. 370, 493–394 (1937) (C. J. Hughes, for the Court). See also PP, 62–63.

is, to the claims of community. When legislatures targeted by Populist, Progressive, and labor movement reformists moved to mitigate power imbalances through group-oriented regulatory and social reform legislation (e.g., antitrust laws, rate regulation, legal support for unionization, the removal of sanctions for strikes and boycotts, workplace health and safety laws, minimum wage and maximum hours laws, mothers' and old-age pensions), their animating paradigm clashed with the then regnant liberal individualist jurisprudence predominating on the courts. Opponents of reform – from Supreme Court Justice Stephen J. Field to legal commentators like Tiedemann – apprehended and anathematized the novel forms of regulation as not only aberrant but heretical in their purported hostility to individual liberty.[47]

This clash was thought to be – or at least described as – existential, and it fueled considerable violence and resistance.[48] Confronting strikes, boycotts, sabotage, and even, at the extremes, targeted assassinations (by anarchists), liberal individualists identified the status quo with social peace, order, and the rule of law. They identified their antagonists with violence, strife, disorder, lawlessness, class warfare, and anarchism.[49] Because liberal individualists saw themselves as defending common sense morality and basic decency, they rarely hesitated to call upon the state's police powers to defend society from the forces of nihilism and immorality. The police power, in turn, was described as neutral and impartial, though it is clear, at least in hindsight, that it was closely aligned with the forces of the status quo.[50]

[47] MMIS, 176–77. See Munn v. Illinois, 94 U.S. 113 (1877) (J. Field, dissenting); U.S. v. E.C. Knight, 156 U.S. 1 (1895); Pollack v. Farmers' Loan and Trust Co., 157 U.S. 429 (1894) (Argument of Joseph H. Choate, for appellant). See generally Joseph Postell and Johnathan O'Neill, eds., *Toward an American Conservatism: Constitutional Conservatism during the Progressive Era* (Palgrave Macmillan, 2013).

[48] See Robert Justin Goldstein, *Political Repression in Modern America, 1870 to the Present* (Schenckman Publishing Co., 1978); Nick Salvatore, *Eugene V. Debs: Citizen and Socialist* (University of Illinois Press, 1982); David Rabban, *Free Speech in Its Forgotten Years, 1870–1920* (Cambridge University Press, 1999); William G. Ross, *A Muted Fury: Populists, Progressives, and Labor Unions Confront the Courts, 1890–1937* (Princeton University Press, 1994).

[49] See, e.g., Rabban, *Free Speech in Its Forgotten Years;* Victoria Hattam, *Labor Visions and State Power: The Origins of Business Unionism in the United States* (Princeton University Press, 1993); Daniel Ernst, *Lawyers Against Labor: From Individual Rights to Corporate Liberalism* (University of Illinois Press, 1995); MMIS, 129–31. See also Emma Goldman, "Anarchism: What It Really Stands For," in Goldman, ed., *Anarchism and Other Essays* (Mother Earth, 1910).

[50] MMIS, 129–31. See *In re Debs*, 158 U.S. 564 (1895). Liberal individualists, of course, understood their own violence as provoked, defensive, and in the service of law and order – and, hence, justified. See also Risa Goluboff, *Vagrant Nation: Police Power, Constitutional Change, and the Making of the 1960s* (Oxford University Press, 2016).

From Economics to Civil Rights: The Case of Subsequent Subject Classes in US Constitutional Development

The long New Deal restructured the animating logic of the state to account for imbalances of economic power in the interest of justice. The new liberal constitutionalism that authorized and justified this new status quo assimilated its ethos and logic. While initially formulated in the economic realm, it was in turn applied to other areas raising long-standing and significant problems of equality, including, most importantly, race and gender. The main lines of advocacy and debate in both areas had long tracked the (classical) liberal individualism that came to predominate in the economic sphere: appeals were made to timeless natural rights, understood by the lights of the laws of nature, as vouchsafed, for instance, by the Declaration of Independence. The new liberalism and its concerns for the real-world actualities of hierarchical power relations (as sanctioned by natural law theories) set the stage for the possibility of alternative theories concerning constitutional equality. The doctrinal adjustments made to incorporate into constitutional law the historical realities of the relationship between power, justice, and the state in the economic realm came to foundationally structure the New Deal liberal state. Stated otherwise, they became part of its governing logic and ethos and were thus, in turn, subsequently applied by state actors and institutions to other forms of unequal group power.[51]

The ideational landscape, however, was complicated by the developmental trajectory. Many Progressives and their progenitors, starting from strong republican or Christian premises, placed significant if not surpassing emphasis on the claims of community, with some like Lester Ward and Henry Wallace boldly proclaiming the age of the individual to have passed.[52] Others, however, appealed to liberal individualist frameworks, recognizing the realities of power according to the "race of life" metaphor: the race run by free individuals to claim the prize was not fair if some were hobbled or handicapped at the starting line.[53] Herbert Croly and Theodore Roosevelt insisted on a more active, power-cognizant state in

---

[51] The typically cited harbinger in the Supreme Court's jurisprudence is U.S. v. Carolene Products, 303 U.S. 144, fn. 4. See generally David Plotke, *Building a Democratic Political Order – Re-shaping American Liberalism in the 1930s and 1940s* (Cambridge University Press, 1996); Anne Kornhauser, *Debating the American State: Liberal Anxieties and the New Leviathan, 1930–1970* (University of Pennsylvania Press, 2015); Kevin J. McMahon, *Reconsidering Roosevelt on Race: How the Presidency Paved the Road to Brown* (University of Chicago Press, 2004).

[52] Lester F. Ward, *The Psychic Factors of Civilization* (Ginn & Co., 1893) ("How can society escape this last conquest of power by the egoistic intellect? ... There is one power and only one that is greater than that which now chiefly rules society. That power is society itself ... The individual has reigned long enough. The day has come for society to take its affairs into its own hands and shape its own destinies."); Henry A. Wallace, *New Frontiers: A Study of the Mind of America and the Way That Lies Ahead* (Reynal & Hitchcock, 1934) ("The keynote of the new frontier is cooperation just as that of old frontier was individualistic competition.").

[53] Abraham Lincoln, Message to Congress (July 4, 1861); Abraham Lincoln, Speech to the 166th Ohio Regiment (Washington, D.C., August 22, 1864). See Isaac Kramnick, "Equal Opportunity and 'The Race of Life': Reflections on Liberal Ideology," *Dissent* (Spring, 1981): 178–87; Isaac

formulating their theory of the "Square Deal," as Woodrow Wilson did in setting out his "New Freedom" and then Franklin Roosevelt in explaining and implementing his "New Deal." Thus, while twentieth-century "New" or "New Deal" liberals routinely advocated for the expansion of state capacities, they also insisted that the claims of the community were important precisely because they were essential to the (re)liberation of the individual.[54]

About the same time, liberals committed to civil rights began to challenge conventional understandings of women's "nature" that had long confined women to the roles of wife and mother and largely excluded them from work outside the home and from political participation in the public sphere.[55] Once more, privilege and power were justified as resulting not from political choices but rather from the dictate of nature's eternal laws. Here, both bourgeois liberal individualism and a cognizance of the dynamics of consolidated group power (as analogized to the former position of labor under industrial capitalism) served potentially liberating functions when husbands, and men more generally, were held to occupy a position in which they could potentially wield tyrannical power (patriarchy as feudal or oligarchic). In this context, full political voice for women as civic equals required both equal voting rights and, in turn, the option (if not reality) of economic independence. Historical developments set the stage for the recognition of the status quo in these regards as fundamentally unjust.[56]

Religious hierarchies, too, began to appear suspect. In the late nineteenth and early twentieth centuries, the mass immigration of Roman Catholics, Jews, and other non-Protestants, together with the leaps-and-bounds advance of scientific rationalism and understandings of human evolution (undermining widespread literal and traditional understandings of the Bible), posed challenges to the authority and privileged status of Protestant Christianity. Niebuhr contemplated the possibilities for a comprehensive solution to this decline in the authority of the country's traditionally constitutive religion(s) that might be consonant with the governing ethos of the New Deal liberal order. He concluded that three approaches to religious and cultural diversity were available to the twentieth-century liberal West. The first, followed by (pre–Vatican II) Roman Catholicism, insists that diversity be overcome and the

---

Kramnick, "The Ideals of the Enlightenment," in Kramnick, ed., *The Portable Enlightenment Reader* (Viking Penguin, 1995).

[54] See Steve Fraser, *The Age of Acquiescence: The Life and Death of American Resistance to Organized Wealth and Power* (Little, Brown and Co., 2015). This Square Deal understanding is the (unacknowledged) basis and predecessor of the "justice as fairness" understandings of Kantian liberal political theory of the late twentieth century as framed, most prominently, by John Rawls. John Rawls, *A Theory of Justice* (Harvard University Press, 1971).

[55] The boundaries of these roles were reworked for nonwhites: African American women, for instance, often worked outside the home.

[56] CLCD, 76–77; MMIS, 46–47. See Bradwell v. Illinois, 83 U.S. 130 (1873); Jane Addams, "If Men Were Seeking the Franchise," *Ladies Home Journal* 30 (June 1913), 21.

original unity of the one "True Faith" and culture be restored. The second, secularism (akin to the French model of *laicite*), disavows society's traditional religions. The third recognizes religious vitality while supporting and celebrating religious diversity. Where religion is concerned, single-mindedness, if not fanaticism, is common, and humility and tolerance rare (toleration, after all, "requires that religious convictions be sincerely and devoutly held while yet the sinful and finite corruptions of these convictions be humbly acknowledged; and the actual fruits of other faiths be generously estimated"). Niebuhr advocated the third option, which was the option most consonant with the liberal, New Deal order and was, in fact, instituted by the US Supreme Court in its First Amendment doctrine, in decisions initiated, instituted, and implemented under the broader rubric of civil liberties.[57]

When confronted with challenges to white supremacy, many Progressive social scientists found support for racial hierarchy, subordination, and privilege in modern science. But others, drawing from new departures in anthropology, insisted upon racism's irrationality and looked hopefully to education to solve "the problem of the color line."[58] For those fighting for genuine civil equality, the actual historical situation posed innumerable challenges. The dominant, as is usually the case, strived to maintain their place in the social and civil hierarchy.[59] And within that hierarchy, American blacks were both the subject class and race, denied equality "on any terms," whether current incapacity (assuming an inability to act as self-directing liberal individuals) or ascriptive (congenital/genetic) incapacity – whatever it took.[60]

---

[57] CLCD, 120, 126, 130, 137. Niebuhr was an outspoken critic of "the inflexible authoritarianism of the [pre–Vatican II] Catholic religion." CLCD, 128. Cantwell v. Connecticut, 310 U.S. 296 (1940); Everson v. Ewing, 330 U.S. 1 (1947); Zorach v. Clauson, 343 U.S. 306 (1952); Engel v. Vitale, 370 U.S. 421 (1962); Sherbert v. Verner, 374 U.S. 398 (1963); Lemon v. Kurtzman, 403 U.S. 602 (1971); Wisconsin v. Yoder, 406 U.S. 205 (1972); Employment Division v. Smith, 494 U.S. 872 (1990); Lee v. Weisman, 505 U.S. 577 (1992); Rosenberger v. University v. Virginia, 515 U.S. 819 (1995); Good News Club v. Milford, 553 U.S. 98 (2001); McCreary v. ACLU of Kentucky, 545 U.S. 844 (2005). See Kersch, *Constructing Civil Liberties*; Howard Gillman, "Party Politics and Constitutional Change: The Political Origins of Liberal Judicial Activism," in Kahn and Kersch, *Supreme Court and American Political Development*; Kahn, *Supreme Court and Political Theory*; Powe, *Warren Court and American Politics*. See also Murray, *We Hold These Truths*, setting out the Vatican II Roman Catholic constitutional theory that sought to reconcile traditional Catholic theology with this modern, New Deal liberal understanding; John F. Kennedy, Speech to the Greater Houston Ministerial Association (September 12, 1960).

[58] See, e.g., Franz Boas, "The Instability of Human Types," in Gustav Spiller, ed., *Papers on Interracial Problems Communicated to the First Universal Races Congress Held at the University of London, July 26–29 (1911)* (Ginn and Co., 1912), 99–103; Franz Boas, "New Evidence in Regard to the Instability of Human Types," *Proceedings of the National Academy of Sciences of the United States of America*, 2 (December 15, 1916): 713–18. W. E. B. DuBois, *The Souls of Black Folk: Essays and Sketches* (A.C. McClung and Co., 1903).

[59] CLCD, 138–39; MMIS, 253.

[60] MMIS, 119–20. See Rogers M. Smith, "Beyond Tocqueville, Myrdal, and Hartz: The Multiple Traditions in America," *American Political Science Review* 87 (September 1993): 549–66.

Southern blacks were denied the vote on the grounds of their ignorance and illiteracy but at the same time denied the education that would have remedied this debility. Where blacks, southern and otherwise, were in fact literate and educated, other reasons – or no reasons – were adduced to justify the denial of those same rights; ultimately, subjection itself was the only point. "The real crime of any minority group," Niebuhr insisted, "is that it diverges from the dominant type; most of the accusations leveled at these groups are rationalizations of the prejudice aroused by this divergence. The particular crime of the Negroes is that they diverge too obviously from type," thus presenting the problem of power and the group in its purest form.[61] The same dynamics met immigrants to the United States from unfamiliar regions of the world, like southern and eastern Europe or Asia: the possibility of assimilation was perpetually bedeviled by belief, *tout court*, in northern European superiority.[62] It was this that the Civil Rights Movement fought, ultimately achieving notable victories in all three branches of the federal government and in states as well – victories that implemented new regimes and micro-regimes newly enforcing, in disparate spaces, both the anti-classification and anti-subordination principles.[63]

BEYOND THE "WHIGGISH" NARRATIVE OF CONSTITUTIONAL EQUALITY

In the middle decades of the twentieth century, the familiar characterization of the developmental path of constitutional equality – as unidimensional, linear, and culminating in the establishment and consolidation of the New Deal liberal constitutional order – began to acquire the status of orthodoxy. A good deal of history was buried in the process. Before the 1930s, as we have seen, courts did not have robust equality jurisprudences conceptually and doctrinally distinct from their (usually economic) liberty jurisprudences.[64] And yet claims involving charges of the illegitimate operation of unequal power nonetheless figured prominently in political party and social movement contestation. Given that nineteenth- and early-twentieth-century courts, in their constitutional, common law, and statutory rulings alike, were indifferent if not hostile to these claims,[65]

---

[61] CLCD, 141.   [62] CLCD, 140, 143–44. See PP, 115.
[63] Mark Tushnet, *The NAACP's Legal Strategy against Segregated Education, 1925–1950* (University of North Carolina Press, 1987); Michael J. Klarman, *From Jim Crow to Civil Rights* (Oxford University Press, 2004); Graham, *Civil Rights Era*; Skrentny, *Minority Rights Revolution*; Doug McAdam, *Political Process and the Development of Black Insurgency, 1930–1970* (University of Chicago Press, 1999); Bruce Ackerman, *We the People, Volume 3: The Civil Rights Revolution* (Harvard University Press, 2014).
[64] See, e.g., Bradwell v. Illinois, 83 U.S. 130 (1873); U.S. v. Susan B. Anthony, 24 Fed. Cas. 899 (1873); Yick Wo v. Hopkins, 188 U.S. 356 (1886); Plessy v. Ferguson, 163 U.S. 537 (1896); Buchanan v. Warley, 245 U.S. 60 (1917).
[65] See, e.g., Karen Orren, *Belated Feudalism: Labor, the Law, and Liberal Development in the United States* (Cambridge University Press, 1991); Hattam, *Labor Visions and State Power*;

Populist and Progressive reformers typically advocated for judicial deference to legislatures. Lawmakers, not judges, would be empowered to confront the problem of unequal economic power directly through the enactment of new forms of tax, regulatory, administrative, and social welfare legislation.[66] Once these movements had achieved political victory and launched the New Deal and post–New Deal liberal state, however, the true nature of constitutional equality in the United States – and, in particular, the long history of contestation between conflicting rights claims – went underground. Politicians and theorists with systematizing ambitions alike claimed that their ruling program had all but resolved the purported conflicts between liberty and equality.[67] The regulatory, redistributive, and jurisprudential policies of the liberal Democrats, the constitutional understandings of their judges, and the governing regime they established promised, at long last, a permanently free and equal United States.

This, of course, was not and could never have been true given the nature constitutional principle in the nation's complex, heterogeneous, pluralistic, liberal democratic constitutional order. My own work has documented the ways in which earlier movements concerned with unequal power relations frankly pitted their own claims against the plausible, contending constitutional rights claims of others, both extant and future.[68] The consolidation and construction of the New Deal rendered the resolution of these oppositions automatic, mechanical – a matter of routine administration, the technical business of governance. This new regime was not simply Progressivism carried forward. Rather, it involved the implementation of a complex system of rights administration in which different social spaces – the school; the workplace; the streets; the economic marketplace; the public and private spheres generally; national, state, and local jurisdictions; and so forth – were each configured by bespoke micro-governance regimes, each entailing a distinctive, rank-ordered preferencing of the competing claims democracy (collective self-determination through public deliberation), community (forging a common social identity), or management (instrumental rationalities employed to create the conditions to accomplish specific policy goals) deemed most appropriate for

Rabban, *Free Speech in Its Forgotten Years*; George Lovell, *Legislative Deferrals: Statutory Ambiguity, Judicial Power, and American Democracy* (Cambridge University Press, 2010). See also Ross, *Muted Fury*.

[66] Ken I. Kersch, "The Gilded Age through the Progressive Era," in Mark Tushnet, Mark Graber, and Sanford Levinson, eds., *Oxford Handbook on the United States Constitution* (Oxford University Press, 2015); Stephen Skowronek, *Building a New American State: The Expansion of National Administrative Capacities, 1877–1920* (Cambridge University Press, 1982); Sanders, *Roots of Reform*; Eldon Eisenach, *The Lost Promise of Progressivism* (University of Kansas Press, 1994); Fraser, *Age of Acquiescence*.

[67] See Rawls, *Theory of Justice*; Ronald Dworkin, *Taking Rights Seriously* (Harvard University Press, 1977). See Lawrence Lessig, "Post Constitutionalism," *Michigan Law Review* 94 (1986): 1422–70; Bernard Williams, "Why Philosophy Needs History," in Williams, ed., *Essays and Reviews, 1959–2002* (Princeton University Press, 2014).

[68] Kersch, *Constructing Civil Liberties*.

that space.[69] To complicate things further, these regimes did not (necessarily) remain stable: they and the broader New Deal liberal regime, after all, were perpetually moving forward in time, with all the developmental dynamics that process entails: changing institutions and political coalitions, exogenous shocks (wars, economic crises, scandals), and social movement pressures altering the ideational landscape and perceptions of reform imperatives.[70]

As an illustration of these dynamics, consider the case of the labor movement and its relation to the New Deal/Great Society liberal state. Earlier work has mapped the ways in which, under the National Labor Relations Act (Wagner Act), organized labor won broad rights to organize and, in turn, bargain collectively in the workplace under National Labor Relations Board (NLRB) supervision. This triumph, and the new governing order for the workplace it instituted, proudly flew under the banners of both (majoritarian) democracy and equality (the equalization of economic power). But once the next equality reform imperative arrived – racial equality/civil rights – union claims of (democratic) autonomy and power were newly understood as *barriers* to equality. Recognizing this, the courts, in turn, renegotiated – that is, placed new limits upon – labor union democracy and autonomy (power) to allow for the achievement of new goals concerning race discrimination in the workplace.[71]

As part of the project of empowering labor union democracy in the immediate aftermath of the establishment of this new managerial order for the workplace, moreover, the NLRB worked actively and aggressively to manage political speech associated with labor union elections by inventing and applying a "laboratory conditions" model for speech that authorized the active regulatory policing of electoral speech in the interest of ensuring nonemotional, reasoned, and rational discussion and political debate and cleansing the electoral process of manifestations and assertions of unequal discursive power.[72] This managerial

---

[69] Robert C. Post, *Constitutional Domains: Democracy, Community, Management* (Harvard University Press, 1995).

[70] See David Karol, *Party Position Change in American Politics: Coalition Management* (Cambridge University Press, 2009); Edward Carmines and James Stimson, *Issue Evolution: Race and the Transformation of American Politics* (Princeton University Press, 1990); Frank Baumgartner and Bryan Jones, *Agendas and Instability in American Politics*, 2nd ed. (University of Chicago Press, 2009); Gerald Berk, Dennis Galvan, and Victoria Hattam, eds., *Political Creativity: Reconfiguring Institutional Order and Change* (University of Pennsylvania Press, 2013).

[71] Ken I. Kersch, "The New Deal Triumph as the End of History? The Judicial Negotiation of Labor Rights and Civil Rights," in Kahn and Kersch, *Supreme Court and American Political Development* (2006); Reuel Schiller, *Forging Rivals: Race, Class, Law, and the Collapse of Postwar Liberalism* (Cambridge University Press, 2015); Sophia Z. Lee, *The Workplace Constitution: From the New Deal to the New Right* (Cambridge University Press, 2014). These initiatives were ultimately capped by the enactment of the Civil Rights Act of 1964.

[72] Ken I. Kersch, "How Conduct Became Speech and Speech Became Conduct: A Political Development Case Study in Labor Law and the Freedom of Speech," *University of Pennsylvania Journal of Constitutional Law* 8 (March 2006): 255–97.

understanding of free speech flatly contradicted the ostensible First Amendment requirements of free speech in other domains that emphasized the foundational value in a democracy of speech that was "uninhibited, robust, and wide-open," with "political" speech of the sort associated with elections the foundational and quintessential category of "high value" speech secured by these norms.[73] Moving forward, both of these models of speech – the managerial (concerned with power inequalities) and the libertarian (concerned with individual autonomy) – remained available for adoption as the governing norm in the polity's diverse social spaces. When the managerial model, as applied to a particular space in the modern liberal pluralist polity, was confronted with First Amendment challenges, courts often held that the matter did not implicate free speech questions at all.

In the aftermath of the New Deal and the "rights revolution," the managerial model concerned with power relations pioneered by organized labor and its state sponsors was adopted and promoted by (many) feminists and civil rights activists, underwriting sharp limits on workplace (and college and university) speech under "hostile environment" understandings of sexual harassment and so-called "hate speech" and calls for the regulation of campaign finance. This is not to say that courts did not reject this managerial model as applied to other spheres, domains, and contexts: they did, to growing effect as Republicans/conservatives drew attention to the managerial nature of particular domains and the ways their governing regimes ran counter to the libertarian model commonly applied in other spheres – a model that was more consistent with the rhetorical ballast underwriting modern free speech doctrine.[74] Such conflicts between equality claims and other legitimate and important rights claims involving, for instance, religious liberty, the freedom of association, property rights, or rights to democratic self-government are endemic to – indeed, constitutive of – the complex, decentralized, rights-suffused, pluralistic, multi-jurisdictional modern liberal US constitutional order.

---

[73] New York Times v. Sullivan, 376 U.S. 254 (1964). See also Whitney v. California, 274 U.S. 357 (1927) (J. Brandeis, concurring); Palko v. Connecticut, 302 U.S. 319 (1937); West Virginia v. Barnette, 319 U.S. 624 (1943); Brandenberg v. Ohio, 395 U.S. 444 (1969).

[74] See, e.g., Citizens United v. FEC, 558 U.S. 310 (2010); Rosenberger v. University of Virginia, 515 U.S. 819 (1995); Hurley v. Irish-American Gay, Lesbian, and Bi-Sexual Group of Boston, 515 U.S. 557 (1995). See Catherine MacKinnon, *Sexual Harassment of Working Women: A Case of Sex Discrimination* (Yale University Press, 1979); Mari Matsuda, Charles Lawrence III, Richard Delgado, and Kimberlé Williams Crenshaw, *Words That Wound: Critical Race Theory, Assaultive Speech, and the First Amendment* (Westview, 1993); David E. Bernstein, *You Can't Say That! The Growing Threat to Civil Liberties from Anti-Discrimination Laws* (Cato Institute, 2003); Alan Kors and Harvey Silverglate, *The Shadow University: The Betrayal of Liberty on America's Campus's* (Harper Perennial, 1999); Robert P. George, *Conscience and Its Enemies: Confronting the Dogmas of Liberal Secularism* (Intercollegiate Studies Institute, 2016); Ryan T. Anderson, *Truth Overruled: The Future of Marriage and Religious Freedom* (Regnery, 2015).

CONCLUSION: NATURAL LAW, LIVING CONSTITUTIONALISM,
AND THE PURSUIT OF JUSTICE

While a natural law/natural rights framework advanced in the right spirit is of immense value to those committed to liberty, equality, and justice, those who wield it as dogma tend to vitiate both that framework's value and its promise. This is necessarily the case in complex, pluralistic, morally aspirational modern societies like the United States. While individuals and communities may aspire to virtue and justice, most will nevertheless in the end incline toward advancing their own individual interest or that of their associated group (faction), entailing conflict if not violence.[75] The fact that the appeal has been made to the laws of nature and nature's God determines little, since in politics pure reason and morality are applied by actual human beings – creatures of bias, interest, or "Original Sin."[76] When employed in politics, natural rights/natural law principles cannot be offered purely: they are by nature relative and contingent – mediated by virtue of being interpreted and applied by actual human beings in complex contemporaneous contexts. When the question involves the reach and powers of government in free liberal states – limited to preserve the liberty of the individual and strengthened and extended to advance the collective interest of the whole – the precise balance cannot be resolved apodictically.[77]

Put otherwise, moral principles in the abstract and moral principles in politics are not the same thing. Equality is a transcendent principle of timeless natural law. But if the principle of equality is welded too securely to a particular historical understanding of its requirements, it can function as a defense of unwarranted privilege. Political principles, moreover, are not the same thing as particular *applications* of political principles. Specific applications mean different things in different contexts or periods, which are inevitably characterized by different constellations of power and ambition.

In the United States, at least, appeals to pure principle are a coin of the realm, the currency used both to attack and rationalize unjust systems of power. There is no simple formula for deciding when, under particular historical circumstances and conditions, the invocation of the principle is performing one function rather than the other. For this reason, the sanctification of pure principle and the dogmatic claim that a faith in that principle is one's "special possession" – exempting one, one's group, and one's application of the principle from attack for the way that they have (ostensibly) applied it to a particular set of contingent arrangements – ultimately betray the prospects for the future realization the principle itself, and the truths it entails, to public life.[78]

Moral realism thus foists upon the polity the perpetual responsibility of reassessing the balance in public policy between the claims of the individual

---

[75] MMIS, 257–59. See Madison, *Federalist* 51 ("If men were angels, no government would be necessary.").

[76] CLCD, 72.   [77] CLCD, 54, 73.   [78] CLCD, 74–75.

and the community. Instead of apodictically applying natural rights theories to politics – or else attempting to reconcile the principles of liberty and equality via a formulation of justice that stands outside of history – commentators would do better to attend to "the indeterminate possibilities of historic vitalities, as they express themselves in both individual and collective terms."[79] Political responsibility, political morality, and political ethics require endless elaboration and accommodation by law.[80] Living constitutionalism provides the space for this elaboration. This process does not, as is sometimes alleged, banish morality and ethics from politics but rather provides space for these ideals and commitments to be realized across the unfolding of political time. Good and effective – indeed, truly principled – governance requires attentiveness to the conditions and problems a society actually faces in a changing interconnected, complex modern social and economic order.[81] As the nation's constitutional institutions (the Presidency, the states and their governments, Congress, the Supreme Court) and its political institutions (political parties, administrative agencies, etc.) move forward through time, while social and economic institutions (the family, the business corporation) change and are changed around them, institutions no longer fill, or fill in the same way, the functions those who created them intended or imagined. Constitutional scholars, to say nothing of constitutional and political actors, *must* confront these changes, since they constitute the setting for actual, lived constitutional and political life.[82]

The point is not simply to observe that conflicts over the meaning of equality are endemic to modern liberal democracies and require resolution as part of the ordinary business of constitutional politics and law. It is that these conflicts are inherently and, from a philosophical and political science point of view, irremediably historical and developmental: they cannot be resolved as a "matter of principle" without undertaking the more grounded task of considering them in their historical, developmental context. Questions of constitutional equality cannot be either understood or resolved in isolation from questions of constitutional history and development.

---

[79] CLCD, 59.   [80] See CLCD, 61.

[81] PP, 46–47. See Graham Wallas, *The Great Society: A Psychological Analysis* (Macmillan Co., 1914).

[82] CLCD, 101. This was no heresy to an earlier generation of seminal Straussian constitutional theorists either. See, e.g., Martin Diamond, "What the Framers Meant by Federalism," in Robert Goldwin, ed., *A Nation of States* (Rand McNally, 1963).

PART II

STRUCTURE

Placing a group of essays on the Constitution under the heading "structure" will, to a modern reader, seem entirely natural. As it turns out, structure as we understand it today is a relatively recent idea, not often encountered before the eighteenth century. To be sure, political theorists as ancient as Aristotle and Polybius classified constitutional "forms" according to how their differing arrangements of rulers and peoples expressed diverse principles of government. By the time of the American framers, "structure" meant something more abstract, more scientific, that is, a stable positioning of parts within any larger whole, no longer a matter of classification but a product of active endeavor. When the author of *The Federalist* writes that the greatest error made by the architects of the Articles of Confederation was in "the structure of the Union," he doesn't attribute the mistake to flawed principles but to a failure to design "the building" correctly. In this regard, the Constitution was a new undertaking in human history: "It seems to have been reserved to the people of this country, by their conduct and example, to decide the important question, whether societies of men are really capable or not of establishing good government from reflection and choice, or whether they are forever destined to depend for their political constitutions on accident and force."[1]

In Supreme Court opinions before the Civil War, the word "structure" appears only sparingly; it is far less frequently used than the word "principles." This gap in usage narrows over time, while "structure" itself broadens its meaning. Originally connoting at the start a permanent framework, in the nineteenth century it takes on a more flexible meaning of *arrangement*; today's understanding includes the idea of coherence and functionality, even integrity.[2] Unvarying, however, in this legal-historical setting is a preoccupation with problems *of* structure, under the name of sovereignty, to refer to the structure's

---

[1] James Madison, *Federalist* 1 and 14. http://avalon.law.yale.edu/18th_century/fed01.asp.
[2] John Compton and Karen Orren, "Categories of Constitutional Analysis: An Historical Inquiry," paper presented at the meeting of the Law and Society Association meetings, Seattle, 2015.

final and appropriate distribution of authority. The structure of the US Constitution is intended throughout to embody "popular sovereignty."

The optimal structure to meet this standard has been a subject of contention among statesmen, jurists, and diverse commentators. Situating the question against the background of contemporaneous ideas and practices concerning sovereignty goes a long way to explaining pivotal constitutional change. The framer's own outlook took shape a century after the Glorious Revolution of 1688, when remnants of the royal prerogative remained intact but the center of lawmaking in English government had shifted decisively to Parliament. As a consequence, their project lived halfway between the parliamentary sovereignty propounded by William Blackstone, constrained by natural law, and the more positivist, totalizing parliamentary sovereignty associated with thinkers such as Jeremy Bentham. Application of the one had fueled the American Revolution; a version of the second idea influenced state governments in the Confederation. The framers, for their part, eschewed the debate, summarily discarding the premise of parliamentary sovereignty altogether, adopting in its place the three-branch government structure. Untoward ambitions of officers of one branch would be counteracted by ambitions of officers in the others, thus ensuring the sovereignty of the people; in a short time, the carefully delineated legislative authority of Congress would reappear in state constitutions based on the federal model.

What had not been anticipated was the profound strain on these safeguards produced by the reception of English statutes and common law, which were also in a process of transition. At the end of the eighteenth century, the business of Parliament insofar as it involved passing new statutes was still limited. But Parliament already enjoyed the last word in lawmaking as it concerned religion, commerce (pertaining to all buying and selling and their appurtenances), and the organization and conduct of public offices; other subjects, including the relations of persons at common law – master and servant, husband and wife, parent and child, guardian and ward – were still the jurisdiction of judges. This arrangement transferred wholesale into the United States, with the added complication that parallel systems, exhibiting the same divisions, are established in national and state governments. The Constitution says nothing expressly about the details of this scheme, although the Ninth Amendment may be understood to include the common law rights enumerated earlier, administration of which under the Tenth Amendment is "reserved" to the states.

Evidence of the transfer is further demonstrated by the appearance in American law of one of the few royal prerogatives that survived the Bill of Rights of 1689 and the Act of Settlement of 1701. This was the sovereign's right not to be sued in his own courts without his permission. In a sense ground zero for constitutional development historically, just where such "sovereign immunity" fit, if anywhere, in the American structure of government very quickly posed a conundrum. It arose early, in 1793, in the Supreme Court case of *Chisholm* v. *Georgia*. Could the justices hear a creditor's claim against the state of Georgia for its Revolutionary War debt over Georgia's objection that a "sovereign" state was immune to suit? Nothing in the Constitution or on the statute books suggested otherwise, and the majority held that the suit could proceed, opining eloquently on its oddity in a republic.[3] Soon afterward, in a somewhat perverse expression of popular sovereignty, this judgment was reversed by the passage of Eleventh Amendment.[4]

Sovereign immunity provides the conceptual grounding of "Overcoming Sovereign Immunity: Causes of Action for Enforcing the Constitution," written by Ann Woolhandler and Michael G. Collins. They uncover the twisting succession of legal contrivances by which lawmakers have, over two centuries, maneuvered around this legacy to hold government and its officers accountable for acts injurious to complaining parties. Anticipating further discussion in our "Actions" section later, the authors depict a highly formal structure of intersecting doctrines and rules – concerning modes of pleading, redressable injuries, available remedies, sources of law – resting on a scaffolding of purportedly predefined jurisdictions. This proceeds over time in a pattern of rearrangement among pieces, moving from common law to constitutional causes, with attendant shifts toward federal courts and a greater role for Congress. All the familiar social and political landmarks appear, impetus here as elsewhere. Yet the overall tenor of development is one of discrete legal steps, allotted and withdrawn, from "above." This is in keeping with the institutionally protective idea of sovereign immunity that remains the default position throughout.

Traces of eighteenth-century England are far from limited to anomalies like sovereign immunity. In "Federalism," Barry Cushman sets the stage for his analysis by observing that Americans, as former citizens of the British Empire, were acquainted with parallel governments in arrangements that were "varied, contested, fluctuating, and in many respects underspecified." The structure of their new Constitution had rendered this condition permanent. Cushman recounts how the Supreme Court adjusted the division of nation and state to the scaffolding described to both accommodate and resist state and federal legislation. From the slavery controversy forward, a stimulus to both these imperatives has been a deep reserve of rights – property rights, due process rights, states' rights, common law rights, rights against harm to public safety and morals, vested rights, rights of sovereign immunity, constitutional rights, statutory rights. Each a rule of its own, in Cushman's telling these variously combine and turn back on one another to become the successive versions of the federal idea. Over time, these reflect the increasing instrumentalism and loosening of boundaries that today characterize constitutional law more broadly.

---

[3] 2 U.S. 419 (1793).
[4] Passed in 1795, the Eleventh Amendment reads: "The judicial power of the United States shall not be construed to extend to any suit in law or equity, commenced or prosecuted against one of the United States by citizens of another state, or by citizens or subjects of any foreign state."

The loosening-of-boundaries theme continues in Mark Graber's essay, "Separation of Powers." Along with federalism, the separation of powers among the three branches comprises the core structures of American government. Graber argues that a stable meaning of this separation, that is to say, acceptance of the purpose of each branch's sovereignty sufficient to legitimize its regular operations, waited until the advent of political parties in the 1830s. The resulting settlement rejected rigid compartments in favor of flexible interbranch coordination managed by partisans, thereby generating and accomplishing mandates of the public. Graber locates the emergence of the judiciary's pervasive role at the end of the nineteenth century when Congress, attentive primarily to the details of reelection, sloughed off policymaking to the President and the bureaucracy, necessitating an umpire to arbitrate the turf wars that ensued. The papering over of the interbranch conflict in the name of popular sovereignty was successful as long as members of both political parties shared overlapping and compatible ideologies. When this condition gave way in the 1970s, one divide over policy became stacked upon another in various configurations, with the party-ridden umpire not exempt.

In "Executive Power and National Security Power" by Andrew Kent and Julian Davis Mortenson, we see that perhaps no structural feature of the Constitution has been invoked more insistently or more often debated than the divide between the executive and legislative branches concerning military affairs. This trail, too, leads back to the circumstances of its authorship. In a bid for international power, Congress was given essentially the same powers in this area enjoyed by Parliament. Having experienced the disarray of war with no effective political head, the framers designated the President as "Commander-in-Chief," providing little further elaboration. Kent and Mortenson identify the strain created by this scant provision and show how it has been relieved during different historical crises. The solution arrived at today rests on broadly worded legislation that seeks to support whatever presidential moves might be anticipated in advance. Under these statutes, the President is able to act decisively while the authority of Congress is honored mainly in the breach. Not connected directly to social reordering, this original structure has seen only minor modification at the edges.

The framers' allocation of military authority appears in Ed Rubin's essay, "The Administrative State," as demonstration of an administrative impulse recently acquired by governments of the period. That impulse was to articulate, in design and in words, for particular specified purposes, discrete and permanent structures of rule that before this had been fungible, overlapping, and changeable at the discretion of monarchs. Rubin construes the Constitution itself to represent the first episode in a continuous stream of administrative governance. His formulation answers the criticism that today's bureaucratic establishments within the executive branch and the independent-regulatory sector signal a severe derangement of American constitutionalism. Taking the Supreme Court as the ultimate arbiter of this claim and reviewing decisions from the early republic, Rubin finds corrective interventions rather than resistance to essential administrative features. The exception is the "Lochner era" in the early twentieth century, which he characterizes as the judiciary's principled resistance to unprecedented change via legislation.

6

Overcoming Sovereign Immunity: Causes of Action for Enforcing the Constitution

Ann Woolhandler and Michael G. Collins

When a person is deprived of rights guaranteed by the Constitution, it might be supposed that federal statutes or the Constitution itself would provide a right to sue – a federally created cause of action – to redress the deprivation. Today, for example, if a state official arrests someone without probable cause, the individual has a federal cause of action against the official for violation of Fourth Amendment rights. A congressional statute, 42 U.S.C. § 1983, provides such an action against state and local officers who deprive others of their federal constitutional rights. Victims of constitutional deprivations may therefore recover damages for past injuries and injunctive relief when the unconstitutional action is ongoing as well as against them.

Such federal causes of action alleging constitutional violations as a central element of the plaintiff's complaint, however, were not a feature of traditional practice. Rather, the Constitution was enforced through ordinary proceedings in which the Constitution would supply relevant law but not a cause of action. For example, when a state prosecutor brought charges against a criminal defendant, the defendant could raise, by way of defense, that the law under which he was prosecuted was unconstitutional. In addition, plaintiffs whose person or property was injured by government officials' enforcing unconstitutional laws might bring common law actions, particularly actions in the nature of trespass, against government officers sued as individual tortfeasors for invading plaintiffs' interests in person and property. Over time, however, the causes of action brought by plaintiffs became more constitutionally based and less grounded in the common law. This chapter will address the movement in constitutional litigation from common law–based to more constitutionally based causes of action.

Nearly all constitutional restrictions are limitations on governmental action. But because of sovereign immunity, individuals cannot sue the federal or state governments directly – absent consent of the sovereign being sued. Naming the sovereign as a defendant is sometimes said to be inconsistent with its dignity; in all events, the inability to name the government as a defendant protects the treasury from ruinous monetary liability. Because of sovereign immunity, if a government officer committed a trespass in enforcing a state law, the injured party could not bring a suit naming the state as the defendant. So too, if the state borrowed money, the creditor could not sue the state to enforce the debt. (Historically, however, local governments and municipalities enjoyed no similar immunity, although other doctrines make recovery against them difficult.) As a result of sovereign immunity and other doctrines limiting the liability of government itself, the availability of actions against individual officers is of critical importance in redressing constitutional violations

Over time, the Court added to the wrongs for which the officer could be sued. This chapter – in addition to tracing the move from common law–based to constitutionally based actions – will therefore also trace expansions of what constituted good claims against individual officers, such that the actions were not barred by sovereign immunity. Primary focus will be on constitutional violations by state officers.

A final issue involves whether actions for the deprivation of constitutional rights can be brought in state or federal courts. Litigants have generally viewed the federal courts as a preferable forum for enforcing constitutional limitations on government – particularly limitations on state and local officers. And the gradual move from common law forms of action to actions in which the Constitution was treated as a source of the plaintiff's claim increased the availability of a federal forum for plaintiffs raising constitutional claims.

BACKGROUND ON THE STATE AND FEDERAL COURTS AND CAUSES OF ACTIONS[1]

Federal Courts, State Courts, and Their Subject Matter Jurisdiction

The US court system has both state and federal courts. State courts are creatures of state law; state constitutions and state statutes create state courts and define their jurisdiction. State courts typically have general subject matter jurisdiction, which means that the state law that created these courts does not ordinarily limit the type of cases that they can hear. State courts thus can take jurisdiction of almost any type of civil claim, including cases under the law of other states and under federal law.

Federal courts are creatures of the federal Constitution and federal statutes. Unlike state courts, federal court subject matter jurisdiction is limited by Article III of the federal Constitution and by federal statutes enacted thereunder. To proceed in the federal courts, a case generally needs to fall within Article III's provision for federal judicial power over controversies between citizens of different states (diversity jurisdiction) or be a case arising under federal law or

---

[1] Those familiar with the American legal system may wish to skip this section.

the Constitution (federal question jurisdiction). While the Constitution called for a Supreme Court, it did not similarly provide for lower federal courts, and Congress was largely free to decide whether to create such lower courts and to decide how much of the jurisdiction provided for in Article III they could exercise. Consequently, for a lower federal court to have subject matter jurisdiction, the case must be within the Article III grant and also within a congressional statutory grant of jurisdiction.

Despite their general civil jurisdiction, state courts only have jurisdiction to hear criminal cases brought under their own laws and by their own prosecutors. Similarly, federal prosecutions only proceed in federal courts. The US Supreme Court, as well as having jurisdiction to hear appeals from most cases heard in the federal courts, can review federal issues decided in state court cases, both civil and criminal.

Federal, State, and General Law Causes of Action

To bring a case, a private litigant must file a "complaint" with the court, which is the document that alleges the elements of the plaintiff's cause of action. (For federal courts, given their limited jurisdiction, the plaintiff must also allege a basis for subject matter jurisdiction – e.g., diversity or federal question.) "Cause of action" refers to a civil claim for relief that the courts recognize. It is not enough for a plaintiff to show that a defendant's acts violated the law and caused plaintiff some harm thereby. Rather, the law also needs to give the plaintiff a right to seek a remedy against the defendant in a court of law.

Modern lawyers tend to identify causes of action by the source of law that provides the plaintiff's right to bring a claim against a defendant. A "federal cause of action" is one that derives from federal law sources – particularly congressional statutes but also federal common law (federal judge-made law) or the federal Constitution. Typically, a federal cause of action is one where federal law provides the law that the defendant is alleged to have violated as well as the right of the plaintiff to seek relief in a court of law. Today, a plaintiff with a federal cause of action may almost always file her complaint in a federal court, under the "federal question" jurisdiction for cases that "arise under" federal law, but state courts generally can also hear federal causes of action.

The sources of state causes of action are state statutes passed by state legislatures, state judge-made law, and state constitutions. A state cause of action may be brought in state court or in federal court provided there is a basis for federal court jurisdiction. The most common basis for a federal court to hear state causes of action is "diversity" jurisdiction, which generally requires adverse parties to be from different states. For diversity jurisdiction, it does not matter which sovereign's law supplies the cause of action so long as the parties are from different states.

Historically, however, not all causes of action were treated as having such definite sources in federal or state law. Lawyers and judges did not necessarily see common law claims – for example, in trespass (tort) or contract – as deriving from a particular sovereign source. When federal courts entertained such actions under diversity jurisdiction, they might perceive the causes of action as being state law or "general law" causes of action. The federal courts continued until 1938 to treat many common law actions in diversity as general law claims.

As noted, a trespass (tort) claim was a common law claim and thus might be seen as a state law or general law cause of action. The typical elements of a trespass claim that a plaintiff would need to allege in her complaint were that the defendant had invaded the person or property of the plaintiff and thereby caused damage or injury to plaintiff. Here, too, the plaintiff could file such an action in state court or in a federal court if there were a basis for jurisdiction, such as diversity of citizenship. Another type of common law claim was a breach of contract claim. Typically a plaintiff would have to allege that the plaintiff and defendant had a contract and that the defendant breached the bargain and thereby caused a loss to the plaintiff. Again, such claims might proceed in state courts or in federal courts if there were a basis for jurisdiction such as diversity of citizenship.

THE ANTEBELLUM PERIOD

The Constitution did not of itself create causes of action. Rather, it was assumed that the courts, including the federal courts, would hear ordinary common law and equitable causes of action. State courts, which did not owe their existence to the Constitution, already heard such claims. Moreover, the Constitution's grant in Article III of "judicial power" as to specified "cases" and "controversies" in law and equity to the Supreme Court – as well as to such lower federal courts as Congress might create – similarly indicated that the federal courts would handle such familiar judicial business. Roughly speaking, actions at law were civil actions for damages as well as criminal prosecutions. Actions in equity were claims for injunctive relief. As the supreme law of the land, the Constitution could provide relevant law in cases that arose in both state and federal courts.

As noted previously, for a case – whether for damages or injunctive relief – to be within the limited subject matter jurisdiction of the federal courts, it would generally need to fall within Article III's provision for federal judicial power over controversies between citizens of different states (diversity jurisdiction) or be a case arising under federal law or the Constitution (federal question jurisdiction). And a congressional grant of jurisdiction was also necessary for cases to be litigated in the lower federal courts. In the first Judiciary Act, enacted in 1789, Congress established lower federal courts and provided for diversity jurisdiction if the amount in controversy were over $500. The 1789 Judiciary Act, however, did not have a general provision for federal question jurisdiction in the lower federal courts. Section 25 of the 1789 Act, however, provided for obligatory Supreme Court appellate review of final state court decisions when a party claimed that federal rights or federal power had gone underenforced.

During the antebellum period, there was no cause of action for the violation of the Constitution as such, and the violation of the Constitution was not an element of a cause of action under federal, state, or general law. Rather, constitutional issues would surface in the federal courts in the course of the litigation of state or general law claims, such as trespass and contract claims, that litigants brought under the diversity statute. In addition, constitutional issues might arise in other actions for which Congress had provided lower federal court jurisdiction, such as federal criminal prosecutions. The Supreme Court could exercise review over many cases arising in the lower federal courts. And finally, constitutional issues would come to the Supreme Court under § 25 as they arose in state court actions, whether civil or criminal.

The following discussion is organized around certain constitutional issues that were salient in the antebellum period: issues of power allocation between the state and federal governments and issues involving the Contracts Clause. As to such issues, the section discusses the types of civil and criminal cases that occasioned constitutional rulings. Particular attention is given to the impact of sovereign immunity on the type of claim, the availability of causes of action against individual officers, and the availability of federal court jurisdiction.

Cases Raising Constitutional Issues of Power Allocation

A number of early cases involved the delineation of the respective spheres of power in the state and federal governments. The Constitution granted Congress various powers, including the power to "regulate Commerce with foreign Nations, and among the several States, and with the Indian Tribes," and such grants often effectively restricted state power to legislate in the same area. The Constitution's enumeration of congressional power, moreover, also meant that federal statutes could not exceed the enumeration. Inevitably state legislatures and Congress passed laws that arguably fell outside of their respective spheres of power, causing consternation to officials of the government whose powers were arguably being trenched upon as well as to the parties subject to the questionable regulation.

Defenses to Enforcement Actions in State Courts; Suits between Private Parties

Issues of the lines between federal power and state power to regulate did not, however, arise in lawsuits directly between the state and federal governments. Such competing claims between sovereigns to exercise governmental power would not have stated a recognized cause of action in law or equity. Rather, if one government believed it had power to regulate in a particular area in which another government may have regulated, it would simply legislate rather than sue the other government. It might then seek to enforce the regulation against a private party who violated it by bringing a prosecution in its own courts. The defendant seeking to avoid conviction would allege in defense that the law under which he was being prosecuted was unconstitutional in that it exceeded the power of the particular sovereign bringing the prosecution. A court then would review the constitutionality of the statute as it arose in the defendant's defense to the state (or federal) prosecution.

For example, in *Worcester* v. *Georgia*, the State of Georgia brought a criminal prosecution against Worcester for failing to comply with a state statute that required a state license for non-Cherokees to live in Cherokee territory.[2] Worcester raised as a defense that he was a missionary authorized by the federal government to live in Cherokee territory and that the state lacked power to regulate commerce with the Indians. Although he was convicted in the Georgia courts, the US Supreme Court on appellate review under § 25 held that the state law could not be the basis for a valid prosecution because Congress had exclusive power to regulate relations with Native Americans under the Indian Commerce Clause. Similarly, in *Brown* v. *Maryland*, the Supreme Court reversed a Maryland conviction for the defendant's failure to pay for a state license on imported goods.[3] The Court held that the state law could not be a valid ground for prosecution because it was contrary to the Constitution's provision that "[n]o State shall, without the Consent of Congress, lay any Imposts or Duties on Imports or Exports: except what may be absolutely necessary for executing its inspection Laws." And in *Prigg* v. *Pennsylvania*, the Court reversed a criminal conviction of a slave catcher under Pennsylvania's kidnapping statute, reasoning, inter alia, that the statute was inconsistent with what it held to be Congress's exclusive power to enforce the Constitution's Fugitive Slave Clause.[4]

As noted previously, sovereign immunity prevents suits from being brought directly against the state in its own name. And if no claim can be stated in law or equity against the state officer as an individual, sovereign immunity will often effectively bar any relief. Criminal prosecutions such as those in *Worcester*, *Brown*, and *Prigg*, however, were brought in the name of the state. Because the state was the original complainant rather than the defendant, sovereign immunity was not a bar to the Court's review; the Court had previously held this in *Cohens* v. *Virginia*.[5] Similarly, to the extent issues of state versus federal power arose in litigation between private parties, no issue of sovereign immunity arose. For example, in *Gibbons* v. *Ogden*, a party with a state-granted monopoly brought suit in state court to enjoin the defendant's operation of steamships under a federal license that interfered with the state-granted monopoly.[6] On appellate review of the state court judgment granting the injunction, the Supreme Court reversed and held that the plaintiff's state-granted monopoly could not affect the defendant's federally granted power to engage in the coastal trade.

---

[2] 31 U.S. (6 Pet.) 515 (1832). Our case selection was aided by David P. Currie, *The Constitution in the Supreme Court: The First Hundred Years 1789–1888* (Chicago: University of Chicago Press, 1985).

[3] 25 U.S. (12 Wheat.) 419 (1827).   [4] 41 U.S. (16 Pet.) 539 (1842).

[5] 19 U.S. (6 Wheat.) 264 (1821).   [6] 22 U.S. (9 Wheat.) 1 (1824).

Tort and Injunctive Actions against Officers Sued as Individuals

Sometimes a plaintiff would have a good claim against a government officer, thus avoiding the problem of sovereign immunity entailed in suing the state itself. Such actions existed, for example, when the officer had committed a tortious act against an individual – such as the seizure of goods – even if the tortious action was undertaken because a state statute purported to authorize the seizure. Under general agency law, one who commits a tort, even on the instruction of another, is still personally liable for the tort. Analogously, if the officer's action was taken pursuant to an unconstitutional state law, the officer would be liable as an ordinary tortfeasor.

Osborn v. *Bank of the United States* provides an example of such an individual-officer liability suit in the context of a dispute about state and federal power.[7] Congress had chartered the Second Bank of the United States in 1816. Many believed that doing so went beyond the federal government's constitutionally enumerated powers despite the Court's having upheld the constitutionality of the Bank in *McCulloch* v. *Maryland*.[8] In a challenge to that power, the legislature of Ohio imposed a $50,000 tax on each office of the Bank. When the Bank did not pay the tax, State Auditor Osborn forcibly collected the tax by seizing Bank assets.

The Bank then sued Osborn in federal court for an injunction to return the seized assets. Federal court jurisdiction was based on a statute that gave federal courts power to hear cases in which the Bank was a party. Osborn's defense was that the Ohio tax law justified his otherwise trespassory seizure of the Bank's assets. But because the Court concluded that Ohio's tax was inconsistent with federal laws that had constitutionally established the Bank, that defense of justification under Ohio law failed. Osborn in addition claimed that the suit against him was effectively against the State of Ohio and therefore barred by sovereign immunity. But because the Bank was suing Osborn as an individual for the trespassory wrong that he committed without legal justification, his sovereign immunity defense failed as well.

A party's tort action that followed on a seizure of property such as in *Osborn* was essentially a defensive action in the sense that the government had disturbed status quo allocations of property by the seizure. The issue of state versus federal power could also have arisen if Ohio had sued the Bank in the Ohio courts to collect the tax. Had that happened, the Bank could have raised the invalidity of the tax as a defense to collection, and the Supreme Court could have reviewed a state court rejection of that defense under § 25. But when the state acted through a state officer's seizure of the taxpayer's property, the taxpayer would generally have a common law trespass action against the individual wrongdoing officer.

---

[7] 22 U.S. (9 Wheat.) 738 (1824).   [8] 17 U.S. (4 Wheat.) 316 (1819).

Cases Raising Contracts Clause Issues

Another source of constitutional disputes during the antebellum period (and thereafter) was the Contracts Clause, which provides that no state shall pass any "Law impairing the Obligation of Contracts." Contracts Clause questions typically arose in ordinary civil suits, based on state law or general law, between private individuals, and in civil suits by private parties against state officers sued as individuals. Some such suits were litigated in state courts, and some were litigated in lower federal courts pursuant to the grant of diversity of citizenship jurisdiction, with Supreme Court review a possibility for cases originating in either the state or federal courts.

The apparent aim of the clause was to protect creditors from retrospective state debtor-protective legislation – legislation that delayed, reduced, or obliterated debtors' preexisting obligations to pay. A creditor who was diverse from a debtor and who met the amount in controversy might choose a federal forum in which to litigate such issues – an attractive option given federal courts' tendency to be more protective of interstate commerce and contracts than many state courts. For example, in *Sturges* v. *Crowninshield*, the plaintiff sued in diversity to collect on two promissory notes, and the defendant raised a defense of discharge under a New York statute.[9] The Supreme Court held the discharge defense unavailing because the New York law violated the Contracts Clause. Indeed, the framers of Article III and the 1789 Judiciary Act may well have anticipated that the diversity jurisdiction would provide a vehicle for out-of-state creditors to sue to collect on debts and to escape hostile state courts and state laws.

In the antebellum period, however, the Contracts Clause would become important not merely as a restriction on state discharges of insolvent debtors but also as a restriction on the states' ability to abrogate their own promises by subsequent legislation. The use of the Contracts Clause to enforce governmental promises, however, could in some circumstances run up against the defense of sovereign immunity in a way that suits between private parties raising Contract Clause issues would not. So, for example, if a creditor of a state complained that the state failed to pay its sovereign debts, the creditor could not sue the state as a defendant, at least absent state consent. Nor would it work to sue a state officer, such as the state treasurer, to compel payment. Under general agency law, a party who acts as the disclosed agent of another as to borrowing and dispersing funds is not personally liable on the debt. Thus, there were generally no common law actions against individual officers to compel them to pay on state government bonds.[10] Indeed, because creditors had to rely on the "full

---

[9] 17 U.S. (4 Wheat.) 122 (1819).
[10] See David E. Engdahl, "Immunity and Accountability for Positive Government Wrongs," 44 *U. Colo. L. Rev.* 1, 15–16 (1972).

faith and credit" of the sovereign to repay its debts, it was not clearly a Contracts Clause violation for a legislature to repudiate or otherwise refuse to pay, at least absent additional promises by the state – as discussed later. And because the state's nonpayment of its debts typically did not result in a seizure of private party assets, there was no trespass action against the individual officer as there had been in *Osborn*. As a result, there might be no common law action that the creditors could bring against the government officers. And sovereign immunity would bar suit against the state itself.

Nevertheless, some potential Contracts Clause cases could fit within the tort model. For example, in an 1845 statute, the State of Ohio promised state-chartered banks that their taxes would be limited to a fixed percentage of their profits. At the time, the Supreme Court treated a state's promise of favorable treatment contained in a corporate charter as a contract by the state subject to the Contracts Clause. Ohio, however, later amended its constitution and legislatively raised taxes on the banks incorporated under the 1845 statute. A state officer's forcible collection of taxes against a nonpaying corporation could therefore subject the state officer to a trespass-type suit. The officer's defense of reliance on state law would be unavailing because the law ran afoul of the Contracts Clause.

For example, in *Deshler* v. *Dodge*, the state collector had seized bank notes to collect the newly imposed tax from an Ohio-chartered bank.[11] Similar to the situation of the federally chartered bank in *Osborn*, the bank was effectively able to sue the collector as an individual on a trespass-type theory (replevin) for return of the notes. And in *Dodge* v. *Woolsey*, shareholders of a bank were able to sue a state official in equity to enjoin collection of the tax at a rate higher than promised in the state charter.[12] The officer could be sued as an individual because he was threatening a trespass against the bank.

In both *Deshler* and *Woolsey*, the banks were able to avail themselves of the federal courts' diversity jurisdiction – jurisdiction for suits between citizens of different states. Use of diversity required some maneuvering by the banks because the tax collectors were citizens of Ohio and the banks were also citizens of Ohio by virtue of their incorporation in that state. In *Deshler*, however, the bank had assigned its claim to the bank notes to an out-of-state party. And in *Woolsey*, an out-of-state shareholder sued on behalf of the bank in a shareholders' derivative action. The Supreme Court in both cases allowed for the jurisdictional manipulation, perhaps manifesting its desire to make the lower federal courts available for cases that raised Contracts Clause issues and that affected interstate investment and commerce. Until well into the twentieth century, using an out-of-state shareholder to bring a suit on behalf of a corporation remained a good avenue to diversity jurisdiction for corporations challenging the actions of state officials.

---

[11] 57 U.S. (16 How.) 622 (1854).   [12] 59 U.S. (18 How.) 331 (1856).

AFTERMATH OF CIVIL WAR AND THE RISE OF THE LOCHNER ERA

The traditional ways of raising constitutional issues described previously continued after the Civil War. Constitutional issues could arise in the course of state prosecutions, in suits between private parties, and in tort suits and suits to enjoin trespasses brought by private parties against government officials. Diversity jurisdiction would remain an avenue for civil cases raising constitutional issues to be brought in the federal courts.

The Reconstruction Amendments and statutes, however, wrought important changes. The Fourteenth Amendment to the Constitution added new restrictions on state and local governments by providing that no state shall "deprive any person of life, liberty or property, without due process of law; nor deny to any person within its jurisdiction the equal protection of the laws." In addition, in 1867, the Reconstruction Congress extended the power of federal courts to entertain writs of habeas corpus to those held in state or local custody "in violation of the Constitution." Prior to that time, under an older grant of habeas jurisdiction to the federal courts, the writ had generally been available only to those held in federal custody and then primarily for those held without judicial process or where jurisdiction was lacking. What is more, in 1875, Congress finally provided so-called general federal question jurisdiction by giving lower federal courts jurisdiction over all civil cases arising under the Constitution, laws, and treaties of the United States when more than $500 was in controversy. The ratification of the Fourteenth Amendment and Congress's statutory extensions of federal court jurisdiction, together with the Court's interpretation of both the amendment and the statutes, would open new possibilities for raising constitutional issues in the federal courts.

As before, the discussion that follows is organized around constitutional issues that loomed large at the time. In the early post-bellum era, the Contracts Clause remained an important issue. As the *Lochner* era took off in the 1890s, Fourteenth Amendment due process issues eventually eclipsed the Contracts Clause as a source of constitutional litigation. The discussion addresses the type of cases in which Contracts Clause and due process issues arose with emphasis on the move from common law to more constitutionally based causes of action. Attention is also accorded to the impact of sovereign immunity, the ability to sue individual officers, and access to lower federal court jurisdiction.

Cases Raising Contract Clause Issues in the Post-Bellum Era

Before the *Lochner* era, Contracts Clause issues remained an important area of constitutional dispute. Cases raising such questions not only would exhibit continuity with earlier cases but also pointed the way toward expansions of causes of action and the use of the 1875 general federal question statute as a basis for jurisdiction – expansions that would later be consolidated with the rise of due process litigation. A primary example of post-Reconstruction Contracts Clause cases involved southern states' repudiation of their sovereign debt.

The antebellum assumptions that sovereign immunity generally disallowed suits against the state or its officers for payment continued to hold sway. Indeed, when an in-state creditor in *Hans* v. *Louisiana* attempted to sue Louisiana in its own name in federal court under the 1875 federal question statute, the Court held that sovereign immunity barred the suit to recover on state bonds.[13] The result in *Hans* was consistent with other attempted suits against states (and sometimes state officials) to compel direct payment of their sovereign debt.

Creditors, however, were more successful in cases involving Virginia's repudiation of its debts because they were able to slot their claims against collection officers into trespass actions. When Virginia sought to reduce its indebtedness by encouraging creditors to turn in their old bonds for new ones, the state promised that the interest coupons on the new bonds could be used in payment of state taxes. The ability to use the coupons to pay state taxes seemed to provide a way to enforce the state's obligations outside the fruitless attempt to sue the state or state officials directly for payment. Virginia, however, later repudiated the new bond issue and prohibited its tax collectors from accepting the coupons in payment of taxes. Resourceful coupon holders nevertheless tendered the coupons to the tax collector and sued the tax collector for trespass after he seized taxpayer property to satisfy the tax. The collector's defense to the trespass action was that state law forbade his taking the coupons in satisfaction of taxes, but the defense failed because the Supreme Court held that the law forbidding receipt of the coupons for taxes violated the Contracts Clause.

While adhering to the old individual officer model of liability for trespasses, the *Virginia Coupon Cases*[14] foreshadowed the shape of things to come. A plaintiff in one of those cases, *White* v. *Greenhow*, brought his action in federal court under the 1875 general federal question statute, and the Supreme Court upheld such jurisdiction. To file an action originally in the lower federal courts under the 1875 statute, however, a plaintiff presumptively needed to allege an issue of federal law in his or her complaint. But to state a good claim of trespass, a plaintiff needed to state little more than that the individual defendant had seized his property; the plaintiff had no need to allege a violation of the Constitution. The officer would allege justification under state law as a defense, and the plaintiff would reply that the Contracts Clause invalidated the defense. Nevertheless, in *White*, the Court allowed the plaintiff to obtain lower federal court jurisdiction under the 1875 general federal question provision by alleging – as part of his complaint – that the statute the officer was acting under violated the Contracts Clause.[15] Thus the traditional trespass complaint was now apparently treated as having a federal ingredient that

[13] 134 U.S. 1 (1890).   [14] 114 U.S. 269 (1885).   [15] 114 U.S. 307 (1885).

allowed the suit to be brought as one arising under federal law under the 1875 statute.

Habeas corpus, traditionally limited to executive detention and jurisdictional defects of the convicting court, contemporaneously expanded to allow challenges to convictions under unconstitutional statutes. In *Ex parte Royall*, for example, the state of Virginia prosecuted Royall for having failed to comply with expensive licensing requirements the state had imposed on the sale of bond coupons and on bringing any suits on the coupons.[16] The Court indicated that challenges to convictions under unconstitutional laws could now be considered jurisdictional defects that would allow habeas[17] and also that being held pursuant to such a conviction would be considered to be "custody in violation of the Constitution" under the 1867 habeas provision. The Court would gradually expand the availability of habeas, such that by the mid-twentieth century the Court allowed collateral attack for most reversible constitutional error. Reforms in the 1990s somewhat limited the availability of such collateral attacks, but habeas remains a much used cause of action to remedy constitutional violations that would affect the fact of or duration of one's custody – whether pursuant to judicial process or otherwise.

Cases Raising Fourteenth Amendment Issues

The trend toward viewing the constitutional violation as part of the plaintiff's complaint would be reinforced as parties increasingly turned to the Due Process Clause to challenge state regulation. The Court read the clause as invalidating state laws that did not, according to the Court, fit within a state's police powers, i.e., powers to protect health, safety, and morals. Absent such a justification, the state was effectively engaged in illicitly advancing the interests of one group of citizens over another and taking the property of one person and giving it to another in violation of due process.

To be sure, many of the famous examples of the Court's striking down economic regulation arose in cases in which the state was enforcing its regulatory statutes in its own courts. Indeed, *Lochner v. New York*, the case that gave the era its name, was a criminal prosecution by the State of New York against a bakery owner who had not complied with state statutes setting maximum hours for bakery workers.[18] The bakery owner raised the defense that the statute was outside of the state's legitimate police power and violated his due process right to contract with employees – an argument that the Court upheld when it reversed his state court conviction on appellate review from the New York state courts.

[16] 117 U.S. 241 (1886).
[17] Ibid. at 248; Ex parte Siebold, 100 U.S. 373, 376 (1880); Ex parte Yarborough, 110 U.S. 651, 654 (1884).
[18] 198 U.S. 45 (1905).

But the *Lochner* era was also one in which the Court expanded the boundaries of causes of action against individual officers. Such actions, moreover, would not violate state sovereign immunity, and they met the conditions for federal question jurisdiction. These innovations emerged from railroads' challenges to state regulations that required railroads to charge no more than prescribed maximum rates. The railroads in these cases alleged that the rate ceilings were so low as to confiscate their property devoted to the public service.

Ex parte Young provides the exemplar of such innovations,[19] although it had predecessors in earlier decisions. Railroad shareholders sued Young, the Minnesota Attorney General, to enjoin his enforcement of new maximum rates against the railroad. The Court allowed an equity action in which the constitutional violation was alleged as part of the plaintiffs' complaint. Predecessor decisions as in the Virginia Coupon litigation had similarly allowed plaintiffs to include reference to a constitutional violation as an element of their trespass claims – trespasses arising from tax collectors' seizures of property for taxes. In the railroad rate cases, however, the threat of a traditional trespass was lacking. Rather, the threat was that the state would bring enforcement actions in state courts against the railroad or its agents if they failed to comply with state law. The Court in *Ex parte Young* nevertheless treated the threatened prosecution as equivalent to a trespass. The threat of the enforcement of the allegedly unconstitutional law, even without an immediately threatened physical trespass, now stated a cause of action.

To be sure, liberty and property would be at stake if the state were to bring actions to enforce the large penalties for each violation of the maximum rates. The Court, however, had previously held that threats of a government official to bring prosecutions or other enforcement lawsuits in the name of the state were not equivalent to threats of an immediate seizure of property. Rather, in *In re Ayers*, the Court had held that a federal court suit to enjoin enforcement actions by state officers in state courts did not state a good claim against the individual officer but rather was effectively a suit against the state and therefore barred by sovereign immunity.[20] After all, the state itself would be the proper party complainant in any state-court prosecutions. In *Ex parte Young*, however, the Court held that a suit against the state's Attorney General to enjoin his threatened enforcement of the allegedly unconstitutional law was a good claim as against the individual officer and was not barred by sovereign immunity.

In addition to expanding actions available against the individual officer that would not be barred by sovereign immunity, *Ex parte Young* furthered the use of the general federal question jurisdiction by allowing the allegation that the challenged statute violated the Constitution as part of the complaint. As noted earlier, shareholder suits had been a way for corporations seeking to challenge state laws to obtain diversity jurisdiction

---

[19] 209 U.S. 123 (1908).   [20] 123 U.S. 443 (1887).

in the federal courts. In the particular action that had led to the proceedings in *Young*, however, one of the named plaintiffs was from Minnesota – which was also the state of citizenship of the Attorney General – thus destroying diversity jurisdiction. The Court nevertheless allowed the case to proceed as a federal question case based on the constitutional violations alleged in the complaint. The *Virginia Coupon Cases* had foreshadowed this development, albeit in the context of a more traditional trespass action. As a result, the use of shareholder suits under the rubric of diversity jurisdiction as a vehicle for raising constitutional challenges to state laws would decline because corporations could now sue to enjoin allegedly unconstitutional state regulation under the federal question statute.

At this point, then, it is possible to say that the type of wrong that would allow a plaintiff to bring an action against an officer as an individual had expanded. The threat of enforcement of an unconstitutional law, even if that enforcement would have proceeded through a state court enforcement action rather than a direct seizure, could count as an individual wrong by the officer, and a federal court suit to enjoin such enforcement was not blocked by sovereign immunity. What is more, rather than being closely tied to a traditional trespass as in the *Virginia Coupon Cases*, some form of injury resulting from an alleged constitutional violation was itself becoming the basis for the complaint. And the constitutional violation's being central to the complaint meant that federal question jurisdiction was available.

LOCHNER'S DEMISE AND THE PROGRESSIVE ASCENT

By the late 1930s, the Court began to back away from its *Lochner*-era willingness to overturn social and economic legislation. Many viewed *Ex parte Young* actions seeking to enjoin enforcement of state regulation in federal courts as the jurisdictional counterpart of the Court's expansive substantive interpretations of the Fourteenth Amendment, and both fell out of favor. By legislation in 1934 and 1937, Congress forbade the federal courts from entering injunctions in most cases challenging state rate regulation and state taxes – both important sources of *Lochner*-era constitutional litigation. The Court itself directed other constitutional challenges to state courts in the first instance through the judicial development of abstention doctrines. Under such doctrines, the Supreme Court instructed lower federal courts to decline to hear some cases that were otherwise within their jurisdiction in favor of allowing the state courts to hear them initially. For example, the Court held that the lower federal courts should have withheld any decision on whether a city's requirement that milk be sold only in "standard milk bottles" violated the Constitution to await a state court determination of whether the state court might interpret the statute to allow sale in paper cartons.[21]

---

[21] Chicago v. Fieldcrest Dairies, 316 U.S. 168 (1942).

The era, however, was not totally one of retrenchment. Business challenges to state economic regulation under the Commerce Clause continued to enjoy some success, sometimes after initial diversion from the federal to the state courts under abstention doctrines.[22] And plaintiffs were advancing First Amendment and race discrimination claims by a variety of means in state and federal courts. In addition to alleging their federal court actions for injunctive relief pursuant to *Ex parte Young* and the general federal question statute, plaintiffs in First Amendment and desegregation cases also sometimes styled their claims as actions under the 1871 Civil Rights Act – current 42 U.S.C. § 1983. At least in hindsight, the use of § 1983 would prove important for future developments.

This Reconstruction-era statute provided a cause of action for damages and injunctive relief against any person who, "under color of any statute, ordinance, regulation, custom or usage" of any State, subjected any person "to the deprivation of any rights, privileges or immunities secured by the Constitution." Its jurisdictional provisions allowed federal court access without requiring an amount in controversy, unlike the general federal question statute, which had such a requirement until 1980. Section 1983, moreover, made allegations of violation of the Constitution central to the complaint. Nevertheless, § 1983 remained largely in disuse for decades after its enactment. Many litigants and courts assumed that the statute was particularly directed to claims for racial equality – claims that did not get much traction until the mid-twentieth century. And the Court narrowly read § 1983's reference to "rights secured by" the Constitution as not including all constitutional rights but rather some subset that was uniquely secured by the Constitution. For example, claims alleging confiscation of property, as in the railroad rate cases, were presumptively excluded because property rights preexisted the Constitution. Contract Clause claims and dormant Commerce Clause claims were also outside the "rights secured by" language.[23] Similarly limiting the statute's effectiveness was the provision requiring that the challenged action be "under color of" state law – language that, until the modern era, was generally read as requiring that the actions of defendant officers be taken pursuant to state statutory authorization or its near equivalent.

The school desegregation cases of the in the 1940s and 1950s, however, fit within even these narrow interpretations of § 1983. Plaintiffs thus often pleaded their actions at least in part under that statute,[24] in addition to using *Ex parte Young*–style equity actions. What is more, the Court in *Hague* v. *CIO* allowed an action under the 1871 Act to enjoin enforcement of ordinances that local

---

[22] See, e.g., Spector Motor Services v. O'Connor, 340 U.S. 602 (1951).

[23] Carter v. Greenhow, 114 U.S. 317 (1885); Bowman v. Chicago & Northwestern Ry., 115 U.S. 611 (1885).

[24] Jack Greenberg, *Race Relations and American Law* (New York: Columbia University Press, 1959), 270.

officials had used to interfere with labor organization.[25] By allowing such a First Amendment claim under the Act, the Court indicated that the scope of rights "secured by" the Constitution would not be as limited as may have once been true. Thereafter, First Amendment injunction actions could rely on § 1983 and its jurisdictional counterpart, in addition to *Ex parte Young* actions and general federal question jurisdiction. Many First Amendment challenges, however, came to the Supreme Court on review of state criminal convictions or other state court suits. For example, the Court in several cases reversed criminal convictions of Jehovah's Witnesses who had failed to comply with local anti-solicitation ordinances.[26]

The desegregation cases as well as others indicated that constitutional claims had expanded to injuries that might not have constituted traditional trespasses nor even their equivalent in the threat of enforcement actions, as in *Ex parte Young*. Students seeking a desegregated education in cases such as *Brown* v. *Board of Education* neither were deprived of traditional property nor were threatened with enforcement suits.[27]

While constitutionally based injunctive actions were becoming ever more firmly entrenched during this time, the same could not be said of damages actions. To a large extent, damages actions retained their tie to trespass suits and were not widely pleaded as constitutionally based actions. For example, a random unreasonable search and seizure by the police typically would be addressed by a state law trespass action against the officer. And absent diversity of citizenship between the parties, such actions would proceed in the state courts. Nor were such suits thought to be covered by § 1983 for many of the reasons noted above, and particularly given that the random and unauthorized violation of the Fourth Amendment would not have been viewed as being "under color of" law within the meaning of § 1983.

THE WARREN COURT AND BEYOND

In 1961 the Court decided *Monroe* v. *Pape*,[28] which opened up the constitutional damages action under § 1983. In *Monroe*, the plaintiff brought an action for damages, after police officers broke into his home without a warrant, made him stand naked in the living room, and ransacked his house. The Court held that the plaintiff had stated a good cause of action for damages under § 1983 for a violation of his Fourth Amendment rights to be free from unreasonable searches and seizures. The case was not one for race discrimination, thus reflecting that the Court no longer adhered to a limited view of rights secured by the Constitution – a development earlier signaled in the Court's First Amendment cases. And significantly, the Court interpreted § 1983's language of "under color of" state law to include not only statutory and

---

[25] 307 U.S. 496 (1939).   [26] See, e.g., Murdock v. Pennsylvania, 319 U.S. 105 (1943).
[27] 347 U.S. 483 (1954).   [28] 365 U.S. 167 (1961).

systemic violations but even ad hoc violations of the Constitution like the search at issue in *Monroe*. The Court thus read under color of state law to mean something more like "under color of office." After *Monroe*, any violation of the Constitution by a state or local officer, even if totally unauthorized by state law, could potentially evoke a federal cause of action with federal jurisdiction. With a damages action now available for such constitutional violations, the move from the trespass action to across-the-board constitutionally based actions against state officers was largely complete.

In addition to opening up constitutionally based damages actions, *Monroe* would lead constitutional litigants who might have once brought their claims for injunctive relief under *Ex parte Young* and the federal question statute to plead their claims under § 1983. And when, in the 1976 Civil Rights Attorney's Fee Awards Act, Congress made attorneys' fees available for prevailing plaintiffs in § 1983 actions, pleading under § 1983 became even more desirable. That is because no similar fee shifting was possible for *Ex parte Young* actions that did not go forward as § 1983 suits (and that could not be slotted into one of the other statutory civil rights actions for which fees could be awarded). *Monroe* also provided the model for constitutionally based damages actions against federal officers, although no federal statute analogous to § 1983 has ever existed. Instead, in *Bivens* v. *Six Unknown Agents of the Federal Bureau of Narcotics*, the Court implied a private right of action for damages directly under the Constitution, actionable in federal court as a case arising under federal law.[29]

Just as *Ex parte Young* had been the cause-of-action and federal-court-jurisdictional counterpart to the *Lochner* Court's protection of economic rights, *Monroe*'s opening up of § 1983 may be seen as the cause-of-action and federal-court-jurisdictional counterpart to the Warren Court's vast expansion of federal constitutional rights. The Court stepped up the pace of school desegregation, engaged in redistricting of voting districts for malapportionment and race discrimination, expanded First Amendment rights, and extended certain other Bill of Rights guarantees – originally applicable against only the federal government – to the states. There were more constitutional rights to enforce, and the Supreme Court made it easier to enforce them in federal court with the § 1983 action. Nevertheless, Supreme Court review of state criminal convictions and federal court post-conviction habeas corpus would be the primary avenues for applying constitutional criminal procedural guarantees to the states.

As the causes of action that ran against individual officers expanded, the practical reach of sovereign immunity diminished. To the extent individuals increasingly could bring § 1983 damages suits against individual officers, sovereign immunity was not a problem because judgments ran against the individuals' assets rather than the government's, even if governments frequently indemnified their officers. A significant inroad into sovereign immunity occurred,

---

[29] 403 U.S. 388 (1971).

however, when the Court approved affirmative injunctions that restructured school systems, that redrew voting districts, and that required improved prison conditions. Such decrees typically required state expenditures to bring state institutions into compliance with the Constitution on a forward-looking basis. The Court allowed such treasury-reaching effects, although the decrees were (and still are) styled as running against the officer. Injunctive suits against state officers generally name the officer as defendant in his individual and official capacities, even though the Supreme Court has stated that a suit against an officer in his or her official capacity is a suit against the entity that employs the officer.

Despite the allowance of prospective injunctive relief that effectively required state expenditures, sovereign immunity retains substantial vigor. One still cannot sue the state or its treasurer to pay its sovereign debt. And even in cases in which plaintiffs can sue state officials for ongoing injunctive relief to bring the state into compliance with federal law and the Constitution, the Court has disallowed damages or other retrospective monetary relief that would more directly run against the state treasury. In *Edelman* v. *Jordan*, the Court implicitly approved a decree that ordered a state to bring its welfare system into compliance with federal law by providing certain payments to beneficiaries in the future consistent with federal law, thus affirming prior cases that had allowed for prospective injunctions that would cost the state money.[30] But the Court explicitly disapproved an order that would have required the state to provide monetary relief to redress its past failures to make certain welfare payments called for by federal law. The Court held that sovereign immunity barred such retroactive monetary relief against the state treasury.

Thus one could say that sovereign immunity law has remained somewhat consistent over time with some adjustments. The causes of action available against individual officers have expanded from the initial trespass suits and injunctions against trespasses to injunctions against enforcement of unconstitutional laws to even affirmative injunctions that would cost the state money going forward if necessary to bring the state into prospective compliance with the Constitution. But the core of treasury protection – disallowing suits on sovereign debt and for retrospective damages relief – has remained. The states thus continue to be largely protected from potentially ruinous damages judgments, although they are not protected from injunctive decrees with their attendant costs.

Perhaps more discordant with prior law was the Court's 1976 decision allowing Congress to abrogate state sovereign immunity if Congress was sufficiently clear and acted under § 5 of the Fourteenth Amendment, which provides that "Congress shall have power to enforce, by appropriate legislation, the provisions" of the amendment. In *Fitzpatrick* v. *Bitzer*, the Court indicated that a federal court could enter a judgment against the state itself for retroactive damages relief under Title VII, the principal federal employment discrimination

[30] 415 U.S. 651 (1974).

law that applies to both private and public employers.[31] The Court held that Congress was properly acting within its § 5 powers to enforce the Fourteenth Amendment's Equal Protection Clause in making states themselves liable under Title VII. Although the Court for a time seemed willing to permit Congress to abrogate state sovereign immunity when acting under powers in the original Constitution (such as its commerce powers), the Court largely put a stop to that possibility in *Seminole Tribe* v. *Florida*.[32] In addition, the Court has since indicated that it will police whether a congressional abrogation of state sovereign immunity is congruent and proportional to addressing Fourteenth Amendment violations that the Court itself has recognized.

It is interesting to note, however, that Congress did not abrogate state sovereign immunity in § 1983, even though it would now be possible for Congress to do so to the extent that § 1983 provides remedies for Fourteenth Amendment violations, including incorporated Bill of Rights guarantees. That the Reconstruction Congress in § 1983 only made "persons" and not states liable suggests that the framers of the Fourteenth Amendment did not think abrogation of immunity was necessary for its enforcement. And because § 1983 liability remains limited to "persons," sovereign immunity continues to apply in § 1983 actions. (By contrast, local governments enjoy no similar immunity, and they may be sued under § 1983 if their "custom or policy" caused the constitutional violation of which the plaintiff complains.)

CONTINUITY AND CHANGE IN CONSTITUTIONAL ACTIONS

Some areas have remained constant in litigation implicating constitutional issues. Raising a constitutional defense to an enforcement suit remains a common mode of constitutional challenge, and constitutional issues may arise in ordinary litigation between private parties if a determination of the constitutional validity of a state statute or other form of state action is necessary to decide the case. Supreme Court review of state criminal and civil actions remains an important avenue for federal court decisions of constitutional issues.

As to civil actions against government officials for damages and injunctive relief in the federal courts, the story involves significant continuity but also change. The cause of action against the officer as an individual remains the paradigm, but those causes of action have greatly expanded over time. This chapter has traced the move from constitutional issues arising primarily within preexisting common law causes of action such as trespass suits, where the Constitution was not part of the complaint but typically came in by way of reply to a defense of justification under state law. Over time, however, the constitutional issue became an element of the complaint, particularly in injunctive actions against enforcement of unconstitutional laws. And eventually the Court did not require the plaintiff to show she would be subject to a state

---

[31] 427 U.S. 445 (1976).   [32] 517 U.S. 44 (1996).

enforcement suit to bring such injunctive actions. The modern Court's breathing life into § 1983 confirmed these developments and made them applicable to damages actions in addition to injunctive claims.

Sovereign immunity has also remained a constant, although its scope has undergone change. From the outset, to the extent that a private party stated a good action against an individual officer, sovereign immunity would not bar the action. And as causes of action against individual officers expanded, sovereign immunity contracted. Nevertheless, sovereign immunity doctrine has retained its core treasury-protective function, with its continuing prohibitions on suits for collection of sovereign debt and for retrospective monetary relief that runs against the state treasury.

Finally, there have also been jurisdictional shifts over time. Before the 1875 general federal question statute, civil actions against state officers primarily came into lower federal courts based on diversity of citizenship. Absent diversity, they could only be heard in the state courts with a possibility of Supreme Court review. After 1875, parties increasingly pleaded the Constitution as part of their complaints with a view to securing a federal forum, at the same time reshaping causes of action into their more constitutionally based form. So, too, the modern development of § 1983 actions provided access to lower federal court jurisdiction for constitutional damages as well as injunctive actions.

7

Federalism

Barry Cushman

American constitutional federalism emerged from a complex matrix comprised by multiple intellectual, institutional, and experiential sources: from political theorists ranging from Machiavelli to Montesquieu and from Harrington to Hume; from colonial analogies to other dominions connected to the English realm through a common monarch, such as Ireland and seventeenth-century Scotland; and from an assortment of colonial customs, practices, and formal and informal institutional arrangements that were varied, fluctuating, contested, and in many respects underspecified.[1] The multiplicity and diversity of these conceptual and historical inputs ensured that the nature and implementation of the federal idea would be matters of continuing political and theoretical debate.

Though the Supreme Court of the United States has played a preeminent role in the liquidation of the federal idea, its contours have been shaped by contributions from multiple centers: by state and federal legislators in decisions

[1] See, e.g., Alison L. LaCroix, *The Ideological Origins of American Federalism* (Cambridge, MA: Harvard University Press, 2010); Edward A. Purcell, Jr., *Originalism, Federalism, and the American Constitutional Enterprise: A Historical Inquiry* (New Haven: Yale University Press, 2007); Daniel J. Hulsebosch, *Constituting Empire: New York and the Transformation of Constitutionalism in the Atlantic World, 1664–1830* (Chapel Hill, NC: University of North Carolina Press, 2005); Mary Sarah Bilder, *The Transatlantic Constitution: Colonial Legal Culture and the Empire* (Cambridge, MA: Harvard University Press, 2004); John Phillip Reid, *Constitutional History of the American Revolution* (Madison, WI: University of Wisconsin Press, 1995); Jack P. Greene, *Negotiated Authorities: Essays in Colonial Political and Constitutional History* (Charlottesville, VA: University of Virginia Press, 1994); Samuel H. Beer, *To Make a Nation: The Rediscovery of American Federalism* (Cambridge, MA: Belknap Press, 1993); Jack P. Greene, *Peripheries and Center: Constitutional Development in the Extended Polities of the British Empire* (Athens, GA: University of Georgia Press, 1985); John Phillip Reid, *In a Defiant Stance: The Conditions of Law in Massachusetts Bay, the Irish Comparison, and the Coming of the American Revolution* (University Park: Pennsylvania State University Press, 1977); J. G. A. Pocock, *The Machiavellian Moment: Florentine Political Thought and the Atlantic Republican Tradition* (Princeton, NJ: Princeton University Press, 1975); Douglass Adair, *Fame and the Founding Fathers* (New York: Norton, 1974); Gordon S. Wood, *The Creation of the American Republic, 1776–1787* (Chapel Hill, NC: University of North Carolina Press, 1969).

whether to initiate or enact legislation; by state and federal executives determining whether to approve or veto legislation with which they were presented; by state and federal judges reviewing legislation for constitutionality or determining which rules of decision to apply in cases coming before them; by statesmen and commentators motivated by combinations of high principle and immediate interest; and by the people by whom such officials were elected to or retired from office. Much of the work of constructing a working federal system has been performed incrementally, as actors in each of the branches of government, and judges most particularly, have sought in the context of particular cases or issues to find solutions to the practical problems arising from the coexistence of two semiautonomous levels of government within a single territory. Though the subjects addressed by this accumulative process have varied from generation to generation, many of the themes and tensions have proven remarkably durable. Still, the fallout from two exogenous shocks to the federal system has fundamentally reoriented the trajectory of American constitutional federalism. The first was the Civil War and the Reconstruction that followed; the second was the Great Depression and the resulting New Deal, which in the domain of political economy transformed American federalism from a regime constituted by a set of judicially enforced rules into a system constituted by a collection of political values entrusted to the democratic process. In the domain of civil rights, meanwhile, the "rights revolution" saw the federal judiciary claim authority to decide questions previously left to state and local governments.

This chapter proceeds in four parts. The first part discusses salient developments in American constitutional federalism between the ratification of the Constitution and the Civil War. The second part examines the impact of the Civil War and Reconstruction on the federal equilibrium, particularly with respect to the domain of civil rights. The third part explores the intricate body of constitutional doctrine that the post–Civil War Court constructed to address the complex governance issues presented by a rapidly integrating and industrializing economy in a federal system, and the disintegration of that body of doctrine during the crisis of the Great Depression. The fourth part analyzes the evolution of American constitutional federalism in the post–New Deal era.

THE ANTEBELLUM PERIOD

The Constitution that emerged from the Philadelphia Convention created a federal government of limited and enumerated powers. The powers of Congress were listed in Article I, Section 8, and included authority to regulate commerce among the several states and with foreign nations, to tax and spend for the general welfare, and to establish lower federal courts. In addition, the section's final provision granted Congress power "To make all Laws which shall be necessary and proper for carrying into Execution the foregoing Powers." The Bill of Rights, ratified in 1791, imposed a series of affirmative limitations on federal power dealing principally with freedoms of speech, of the press, and of religion; the right to keep and bear arms; takings or deprivations of private property; and matters concerning the investigation, prosecution, and adjudication of alleged criminal offenses. The Tenth Amendment provided that "[t]he powers not delegated to the United States by the Constitution, nor prohibited by it to the States, are reserved to the States respectively, or to the people." Article I, Section 10, imposed limitations on the power of state governments to engage in foreign policy, tax foreign trade, regulate currency, and enact retrospective laws, and the Supremacy Clause of Article VI bound state judges to enforce the federal Constitution, valid federal statutes, and national treaties, even where they conflicted with a state constitution or state law. In other respects the Constitution left the states with broad legislative, executive, and judicial powers.

The Supreme Court's assertion and establishment in the early years of the Republic of the power to review state and federal legislation for compliance with the Constitution brought to the Court a series of litigants claiming that either a state or the federal government had transgressed limitations imposed by the national charter. During the antebellum period, the justices settled a handful of important questions concerning the nature of the federal republic that ratification of the Constitution had created. Several of these had to do with the jurisdiction of the federal courts. In *Martin* v. *Hunter's Lessee*,[2] the justices upheld the constitutionality of Section 25 of the Judiciary Act of 1789, which conferred upon the Supreme Court appellate jurisdiction over certain state court decisions involving the Constitution, treaties, or federal statutes. In *Cohens* v. *Virginia*,[3] the Court extended this holding to cases in which one of the states was a party. These two decisions consolidated the vision of a national judicial system in which the state courts would serve in some respects as lower federal courts.

Three significant restraints on federal judicial power emerged from different sources. The ratification of the Eleventh Amendment in 1795 overruled the Court's decision in *Chisholm* v. *Georgia*,[4] which had provoked fierce objections from the states, and established that the federal courts did not have jurisdiction in cases in which a citizen of one state sued another state. In *United States* v. *Hudson & Goodwin*,[5] a narrowly divided Court declined to follow the path blazed by several lower court decisions in the 1790s and declared that the lower federal courts had no jurisdiction to try cases charging criminal offenses at common law. Such courts could exercise jurisdiction only where the infraction alleged had been made criminal by congressional statute. And in connection with efforts by Georgia officials to force the Cherokee from the state to the western Indian Territory, the Court held in *Cherokee Nation* v. *Georgia*[6] that Native American nations were not foreign nations within the

---

[2] 14 U.S. 304 (1816).   [3] 19 U.S. 264 (1821).   [4] 2 U.S. 419 (1793).   [5] 11 U.S. 32 (1812).
[6] 30 U.S. 1 (1831).

meaning of Article III of the Constitution but instead "domestic dependent nations" without standing to invoke the Court's original jurisdiction.

These curtailments of jurisdiction were, however, accompanied by three modes of expansion. First, in *The Genessee Chief* v. *Fitzhugh*,[7] the Court overruled the precedent of the *Steamboat Thomas Jefferson*,[8] which had held that the federal admiralty jurisdiction extended only to the ebb and flow of the tide. Henceforth, that jurisdiction would extend to all navigable inland waterways as well. Second, in *Louisville Railroad Co.* v. *Letson*[9] and *Marshall* v. *B&O Railroad Co.*,[10] the Court departed from earlier precedents and, through the use of a legal fiction, effectively held that corporations were citizens for purposes of suing and being sued in federal court under Article III's grant of jurisdiction over cases involving citizens of different states ("diversity" jurisdiction). And third, decisions such as *Swift* v. *Tyson*[11] held that federal courts in diversity cases were not obliged by Section 34 of the Judiciary Act to apply the decisional law of the states in which they sat but could instead apply what they determined to be the "general" common law governing the controversies before them. Over time, the domain of the general common law came to include the law of contracts, commercial transactions, torts, insurance, common carriers, and eventually even real property.

Though there were few questions concerning the scope of Congress's enumerated powers that generated significant litigation before the Civil War, those that did produced some of the period's most celebrated and vilified decisions. Secretary of the Treasury Alexander Hamilton's financial system was among the most divisive issues of the early republic, and his proposal for a congressionally chartered Bank of the United States elicited considerable constitutional controversy. James Madison, arguing for a narrow construction of Congress's enumerated powers, observed that the Constitution conferred no such power to charter a bank. Indeed, Madison's own motion that the federal government be empowered to grant corporate charters had been rejected at the Philadelphia Convention. As for Article I's Necessary and Proper Clause, Madison maintained, it should be read so as to authorize only such powers as arose by "unavoidable implication" from those specifically enumerated. Secretary of State Thomas Jefferson, asked by President Washington for his views on the constitutionality of the Bank Bill, replied that it was beyond congressional power. Construing the text strictly, Jefferson observed that the Constitution conferred no express power to charter a bank, and maintained that the term "necessary" should be read not to mean merely "convenient" but instead should be rendered as "indispensable." Hamilton, by contrast, insisted that the Constitution conferred both express and implied powers on Congress, and he gave the Necessary and Proper Clause its classic broad construction: "If the end be clearly contemplated within any of the specified powers, and if the

---

[7] 53 U.S. 443 (1851).   [8] 23 U.S. 428 (1825).   [9] 43 U.S. 497 (1844).
[10] 57 U.S. 314 (1853).   [11] 41 U.S. 1 (1842).

measure have an obvious relation to that end, and is not forbidden by any particular provision of the Constitution, it may be safely be deemed to come within the compass of the national authority."

Washington signed the bill, but the charter lapsed of its own terms in 1811. When then-President Madison was faced with a bill to charter a Second Bank in 1816, his opinion on the constitutional issue had not changed. But because he believed that the actions of the political branches and the American people had settled the question in favor of the Bank's constitutionality, he declined to veto the bill. When a unanimous Supreme Court placed its constitutional imprimatur on the Bank in *McCulloch* v. *Maryland*,[12] Chief Justice John Marshall's exposition of the Necessary and Proper Clause simply paraphrased the construction rendered by Hamilton nearly three decades earlier: "Let the end be legitimate, let it be within the scope of the Constitution, and all means which are appropriate, which are plainly adapted to that end, which are not prohibited, but consist with the letter and spirit of the Constitution, are Constitutional."[13] In 1832, however, Congress preemptively sent a bill renewing the Bank's charter to a hostile President Andrew Jackson. Invoking departmental principles of constitutional interpretation, Jackson vetoed the bill on the ground that Congress lacked the constitutional power to enact it. Continued domination of the presidency by Democratic successors ensured that Jackson's views of the Bank's constitutionality would prevail throughout the antebellum period.

In *Gibbons* v. *Ogden*,[14] the Court offered its principal antebellum exposition of the congressional power to regulate interstate commerce. The case involved the validity of New York's grant of a monopoly in steamboat navigation on the Hudson River between New York and New Jersey. Here Chief Justice Marshall established that "commerce among the several states" included not merely "traffic," i.e., the buying and selling of goods, but all commercial "intercourse," including interstate navigation. Associate Justice William Johnson maintained that congressional power to regulate interstate commerce was exclusive and that the grant of this power to Congress implicitly deprived the states of legislative jurisdiction over the subject. Marshall found it unnecessary to reach this question, finding that the New York legislation conflicted with a 1793 federal coastal licensing statute and was therefore void under the provision of Article VI declaring statutes enacted pursuant to Congress's constitutional authority "the Supreme Law of the Land."

Despite the Court's seemingly broad formulation of the Commerce Clause in *Gibbons*, the antebellum Congress hesitated to call upon that power as a source of regulatory authority. Perhaps most notable in this regard was the failure of Congress seriously to consider regulation or prohibition of the interstate trade in slaves.[15] Instead, the three decades following *Gibbons* witnessed the justices

---

[12] 17 U.S. 316 (1819).   [13] Id. at 421.   [14] 22 U.S. 1 (1824).
[15] See Arthur Bestor, "The American Civil War as a Constitutional Crisis," 69 *Am. Hist. Rev.* 327 (1964).

engaging in a divisive debate over whether and to what extent the "negative implications" of the Constitution's grant of power over interstate commerce to Congress imposed restraints on the taxing and regulatory powers of the states. Though they disagreed over whether the commerce power was exclusive or concurrent and the extent to which it qualified the states' police powers to regulate for the health, safety, and welfare of their inhabitants, the members of the Court on the whole upheld state measures challenged under what came to be known as the "dormant" Commerce Clause. Ultimately, in *Cooley* v. *Pennsylvania Board of Wardens*,[16] six of the nine justices joined an opinion that split their differences. They agreed that some aspects of interstate commerce were national in character and therefore could be regulated only by Congress. With respect to the regulation of such activities, congressional power was exclusive. Other aspects, by contrast, were local in character. The states were permitted to regulate these aspects of interstate commerce unless and until Congress had legislated with respect to them. With respect to these activities, state power was concurrent, though federal power was paramount. The majority justices agreed that Pennsylvania's challenged regulation of pilotage fell into the latter category, but the determination of which activities fell into which category was for the most part left open to the case-by-case determination of future Courts. As one scholar has put it, the *Cooley* decision's most "significant feature" was "not the formulation of a definitive doctrine but the court's tacit agreement to stop looking for one."[17]

Federalism also played a central role in the law of freedom and slavery. In 1776, slavery was legal in all of the North American colonies. But the Constitution left the decision over whether to countenance slavery to the several states, and over the next three decades eight northern states took steps to emancipate their slave populations, either gradually or at a stroke. For the remainder of the antebellum period, new free and new slave states were admitted to the Union in nearly equal proportions, so that in 1858 Abraham Lincoln could with reason describe the nation as "half slave and half free." The heterogeneity of state policy positions on the issue gave rise to a series of controversies over states' rights and federal power.

Article IV, Section 2, of the Constitution provided that "[t]he citizens of each state shall be entitled to all the privileges and immunities of citizens of the several states." This provision was understood to require that, with regard to the enjoyment of certain privileges and immunities, a citizen of one state traveling in a second state must be treated by that state as if he were one of its own citizens. The question of whether free blacks from northern states were citizens entitled to the equal enjoyment of such privileges and immunities when traveling to unfree states arose in two contexts.

The first concerned the so-called Negro Seamen's Laws, enacted by the legislatures of South Carolina and six other coastal slave states. Those statutes

---

[16] 53 U.S. 299 (1851).

[17] R. Kent Newmyer, *The Supreme Court under Marshall and Taney*, 2nd ed. (Wheeling, IL: Harlan Davidson, 2006), 107.

prescribed that black sailors be incarcerated in local jails for the periods during which their ships were in port. In 1823 Justice Johnson, sitting in his capacity as a federal circuit judge, heard a constitutional challenge to South Carolina's statute. Anticipating his concurring opinion in *Gibbons*, Johnson held that the statute offended the dormant Commerce Clause.[18] South Carolina and its sister states nevertheless persisted in enforcing their laws, and in 1832, President Andrew Jackson's Attorney General, Roger Taney, wrote an opinion concluding that the southern statutes did not violate Article IV's Privileges and Immunities Clause. Anticipating his own decision a quarter century later in *Dred Scott* v. *Sandford*,[19] Taney wrote that "[t]he African race in the United States, even when free, are everywhere a degraded class, and exercise no political influence. The privileges they are allowed to enjoy, are accorded to them as a matter of kindness and benevolence rather than of right ... They were not looked upon as citizens by the contracting parties who formed the Constitution ... and were not intended to be embraced in any of the provisions of that Constitution but those which point to them in terms not to be mistaken."[20]

The second context in which the Privileges and Immunities issue arose concerned the so-called exclusion laws. Most southern states enacted legislation prohibiting free blacks from entering their states, and by 1857, four northern states had joined their ranks. No successful constitutional challenge to these measures ever was mounted, and an 1856 decision of the Indiana Supreme Court enforcing that state's statute appeared to assume its constitutionality.[21]

Article IV, Section 2, also provided that "No Person held to Service or Labor in one State, under the Laws thereof, escaping into another, shall, in Consequence of any Law or Regulation therein, be discharged from such Service or Labor, but shall be delivered up on Claim of the Party to whom such Service or Labor may be due." This Fugitive Slave Clause did not specify the means by which its directives were to be enforced, but in 1793 Congress assumed powers of enforcement by enacting the first Fugitive Slave Act. The act permitted the owner of a fugitive slave or the owner's agent to seize the alleged slave and to bring him before either a federal or state judge in the free state in which the alleged slave was located. If the owner or agent could prove title to the fugitive by affidavit or oral testimony, the judge was to issue the captor a certificate of removal permitting the captor to leave the jurisdiction with the

---

[18] Elkison v. Deliesseline, 8 Fed. Cas. 493 (C.C.D. S.C., 1823).   [19] 60 U.S. 393 (1857).

[20] Opinion and supplement accompanying letters of Taney to Secretary of State Edward Livingston, dated May 28 and June 9, 1832, Miscellaneous Letters, Department of State Papers, National Archives, quoted in Don E. Fehrenbacher, *The Dred Scott Case: Its Significance in American Law and Politics* (New York: Oxford University Press, 1978), 70. In Bank of Augusta v. Earle, 38 U.S. 519 (1839), then-Chief Justice Taney would similarly hold that corporations were not citizens for purposes of the Privileges and Immunities Clause.

[21] Barkshire v. State, 7 Ind. 389 (1856).

fugitive. In addition, the act imposed criminal penalties for obstructing the capture and for rescuing, harboring, aiding, or hiding an alleged fugitive slave.

Northern antislavery lawyers and legislators, construing the Constitution strictly, maintained that, because the Constitution was silent on the mechanism for rendition of fugitives, the matter had been left to the several states. Anxious to protect their free black citizens from wrongful abduction, they persuaded legislators in most northern states to enact anti-kidnapping statutes providing procedural protections for alleged fugitive slaves in proceedings before state judges. In the 1842 case of *Prigg* v. *Pennsylvania*,[22] the Supreme Court struck down Pennsylvania's anti-kidnapping statute on the ground that it conflicted with the 1793 Fugitive Slave Act and was therefore invalid under the Supremacy Clause. At the same time, however, the Court maintained that the federal government could not compel state governments to enforce the federal act. Such a requirement would be an infringement on states' rights. Justice Story's majority opinion further acknowledged that the states could refuse to allow their officers and officials to enforce the federal law. In response, northern states withdrew the assistance of their law enforcement officials in helping slave owners recapture fugitive slaves. Several state legislatures enacted personal liberty laws, prohibiting state officials from enforcing the federal act, or repealed statutes that had directed state officials to enforce it. And numerous state court judges cited *Prigg* in holding that they were without power to issue a certificate of removal or otherwise entertain proceedings concerning fugitive slaves. Slave owners could proceed to the federal courts, but they were few and far between and might be more than a hundred miles away and not even in session. The protections that the personal liberty laws provided for free blacks and fugitive slaves prompted John C. Calhoun to denounce them as "one of the most fatal blows ever received by the South and the Union." They had, he lamented, rendered the constitutional obligation to return runaways "of non-effect, and with so much success that it may be regarded now as practically expunged from the Constitution."[23]

In 1850, in response to southern demands for a more stringent federal law prompted by the passage of the new northern personal liberty laws, Congress enacted a statute beefing up the enforcement provisions of the 1793 act with the creation of federal fugitive slave commissioners, who were granted authority to issue certificates authorizing the removal of a captured fugitive from a free state. Several northern states responded by enacting new personal liberty laws designed to frustrate the federal rendition process by denying slave catchers the assistance of state officials or the use of state jails, appointing commissioners to defend anyone claimed as a fugitive, strictly punishing anyone guilty of

---

[22] 41 U.S. 539 (1842).
[23] Richard Cralle, ed., *The Works of John C. Calhoun* (New York: D. Appleton, 1870), 6:292. Quoted in Thomas D. Morris, *Free Men All: The Personal Liberty Laws of the North, 1780–1861* (Baltimore: Johns Hopkins University Press, 1974), 130.

seizing a free man, and supplying alleged fugitives with substantial procedural guarantees. In some states, such as Massachusetts, slave catchers were so intimidated by the obstacles to rendition that they simply stopped pursuing those who managed to reach free soil. Southern politicians complained that these personal liberty laws had rendered the federal statute a dead letter, and South Carolina's Declaration of the Causes of Secession of 1860 listed the personal liberty laws as the first of its grievances against the northern states. The declaration charged that "fourteen of the States have deliberately refused, for years past, to fulfill their constitutional obligations" by enacting "laws which either nullify" the Fugitive Slave Laws of Congress "or render useless any attempt to execute" those laws.[24]

Occasionally a slave owner traveling to or through a free state would voluntarily bring with him one or more of his slaves. Before the mid-1830s, free states generally extended comity to the law of southern states by allowing masters to sojourn in the North accompanied by their slaves. If, however, the master established a domicile in the northern state, then the slaves accompanying him became free. The question of domicile usually turned on the intentions of the master, but states such as Pennsylvania and New York enacted statutes providing that the master became a domiciliary of their states if he remained there for longer than six or nine months, respectively. Similarly, if the master returned to his southern home after having established a domicile in a free state, southern state courts extended comity to northern state laws by holding that slaves that had accompanied the master were as a result now free.[25]

Beginning in the 1836, however, under the spur of rising abolitionist sentiment and Joseph Story's 1834 treatise on *The Conflict of Laws*, northern state courts began to grant freedom to slaves that had been brought into their jurisdictions for much shorter periods of time.[26] The Supreme Judicial Court of Massachusetts led the way with its 1836 decision in *Commonwealth v. Aves*,[27] but over the next two decades every northern state other than Indiana and New Jersey followed suit. Pennsylvania and New York repealed their comity statutes, with the effect that slaves traveling through those states could now be freed as soon as they crossed the border.[28] In 1860, the New York Court of Appeals would hold that Virginia slaves who had spent a mere three days in a New York hotel awaiting passage on a ship were free.[29] Slaves who escaped to free states remained enslaved under federal law, but slaves who were brought to a free state by their masters became free by virtue of state law.

[24] *Declaration of the Immediate Causes Which Induce and Justify the Secession of South Carolina from the Federal Union* (Charleston, SC: Evans and Cogswell, 1860).
[25] Paul Finkelman, *An Imperfect Union: Slavery, Federalism, and Comity* (Chapel Hill, NC: University of North Carolina Press, 1981).
[26] Joseph M. Story, *Commentaries on the Conflict of Laws, Foreign and Domestic* (Boston: Hilliard, Gray, 1834).
[27] 35 Mass. 193 (1836).   [28] Finkelman, *An Imperfect Union.*
[29] Lemmon v. People, 20 N.Y. 562 (1860).

Southern state courts responded by ceasing to extend comity to the northern law of freedom. Even if a northern court would have ruled that a slave had become free under the terms of the law of the jurisdiction into which his master had taken him, if the slave did not secure his freedom in the North but instead returned with his master to the South, southern courts began to rule that his status as a slave had "reattached" upon his return.[30] The most famous such instance involved the slave Dred Scott, whose master, an army physician, had taken Scott with him for two-year postings in both the free state of Illinois and the free Minnesota Territory. Scott sued for his freedom when he returned, and the Missouri Supreme Court, refusing to extend comity to the laws of Illinois and the federal territory, held that Scott remained a slave.[31] After Dr. Emerson died, Scott sought his freedom in federal court by suing the estate's executor, Sanford. The defendant was a citizen of New York and thus might have been amenable to suit under the federal court's jurisdiction involving citizens of different states.[32] But Chief Justice Taney reprised his interpretation of Article IV while Attorney General, holding that the federal courts lacked jurisdiction to hear the case because, as an African American, Scott could not be a citizen for purposes of Article III even if he were free. Taney and his colleagues went on to hold that Scott was not free in any event because the provision of the Missouri Compromise (1820) making the federal territory free was beyond congressional power to enact, and the slave state of Missouri was not required to extend comity to the law of the free state of Illinois.[33]

The period's central unresolved question in constitutional federalism, which became ever more pressing as time wore on, concerned the character of the Union. Was it a single, compound republic, partly national and partly federal, or was it instead merely a compact among sovereign states? Was the Union perpetual, or were states at liberty to withdraw from it? Though in connection with these inquiries intelligent contemporaries and subsequent commentators have lavished a great deal of attention on the question of whether the nation preceded the states in time or vice versa, it does not appear that anything of consequence turns on the resolution of this issue. If in fact the states preceded the nation in time, it does not follow that the states were at liberty to secede from the Union formed by the Constitution. Similarly, if the nation preceded the states, it does not follow that the states were precluded by the Constitution from departing the Union. The relevant question was what sort of union did the ratification of the Constitution call into being? The Constitution's silence on that question ensured that it would remain a disputed one.

The issue was first prominently joined when the Federalist Congress enacted the Alien & Sedition Acts in 1798. In anonymous pamphlets authored respectively by James Madison and Thomas Jefferson, the Virginia and Kentucky Resolutions maintained that Congress was without power to enact the legislation in question.

---

[30] Finkelman, *An Imperfect Union.*   [31] Scott v. Emerson, 15 Mo. 576 (1852).
[32] Fehrenbacher, *The Dred Scott Case.*   [33] 60 U.S. 393 (1857).

Madison's Virginia Resolutions maintained that the sovereign states were empowered to judge independently the constitutionality of congressional legislation and had the right and duty to "interpose" in order to preserve their rightful authority and to protect the rights and liberties of their people "in case of a deliberate, palpable, and dangerous exercise" of powers not granted by the federal "compact." Jefferson's Kentucky Resolutions went further, claiming in addition that the proper remedy for federal overreaching was state "nullification" of such unconstitutional federal enactments. Though each of the documents called upon other states to cooperate in efforts to resist usurpation by the federal government, no sister states rallied to the cause. The issue soon was mooted by the expiration of the objectionable legislation, which lapsed before Jefferson's inauguration as president in March 1801.

The issue again came to a head in 1832, however, when a South Carolina convention disgruntled by the allegedly unconstitutional 1828 federal "Tariff of Abominations" drew upon the compact theory of the Union articulated in Vice President John C. Calhoun's anonymously authored 1828 *South Carolina Exposition* and his 1831 *Fort Hill Address* in adopting an ordinance purporting to "nullify" the tariff within South Carolina. The ordinance declared unlawful any efforts by state or federal authorities to enforce the tariff and directed the legislature to enact measures to prevent such enforcement. Moreover, the authors of the ordinance took a position that Madison and Jefferson had not advocated, and that Madison later disavowed, by threatening secession from the Union should the federal government attempt to coerce South Carolina in the matter. Like the authors of the South Carolina ordinance, most of the statesmen who had spoken on the issue to this point in the nation's history appeared not to regard the Union as necessarily perpetual. President Andrew Jackson, however, responded with a message denouncing both nullification and secession as unconstitutional, and Congress supported his position with the Force Act of 1833. The conflict ultimately was settled peacefully through negotiated compromise, but even in its measure repealing the ordinance, the South Carolina convention pointedly preserved its constitutional claims by expressly purporting to nullify the Force Act. As John Quincy Adams wrote of the issue of whether the Union was perpetual, "It is the odious nature of the question that it can be settled only at the cannon's mouth."[34]

CIVIL WAR AND RECONSTRUCTION

And so it was. When South Carolina and ten other states enacted ordinances seceding from the Union in 1860 and 1861, President Abraham Lincoln denounced the actions as unconstitutional and mobilized the remaining states for

[34] William Freehling, *Prelude to Civil War: The Nullification Crisis in South Carolina, 1816–1836* (New York: Harper and Roe, 1965); Kenneth Stampp, "The Concept of a Perpetual Union," 65 *J.A. H.* 5 (1978).

a war to preserve the Union. Secessionists maintained that the federal government was the creature and agent of the people of the states, who remained the ultimate locus of sovereignty and had retained the power to withdraw from the Union. Lincoln and others insisted that sovereign authority rested with the people of the United States rather than those of the states severally, and that the perpetuity of the Union they had together created was implicit in its fundamental law. After the Union Army emerged victorious at Appomattox, Chief Justice Salmon P. Chase of the Supreme Court of the United States articulated in memorable prose what many believed had been won on the battlefield. In pronouncing the Texas ordinance of secession a legal nullity, Chase declared in *Texas* v. *White*[35] that "[t]he Constitution, in all its provisions, looks to an indestructible Union composed of indestructible States." Notwithstanding some contrary theories seeking to explain and justify the fact that the delegations of several southern states had yet to be seated in Congress and that large swaths of the South remained under extensive federal supervision, Chase insisted that the Confederate States never had been outside the Union. "When, therefore, Texas became one of the United States, she entered into an indissoluble relation . . . The act which consummated her admission into the Union was something more than a compact; it was the incorporation of a new member into the political body. And it was final. The union between Texas and the other States was as complete, as perpetual, and as indissoluble as the union between the original States." At the same time, Chase cautioned, "the perpetuity and indissolubility of the Union by no means implies the loss of distinct and individual existence, or of the right of self-government, by the States." Under the Constitution, "all powers not delegated to the United States nor prohibited to the States, are reserved to the States respectively, or to the people."[36] With the question of the Union's essential character definitively resolved, the Court would now devote its efforts to defining and policing the boundaries between state and federal legislative jurisdiction in a federal system transformed by three constitutional amendments and a series of landmark statutes.

A particularly pressing question concerned the extent to which the constitutional amendments ratified in the wake of the Civil War had transformed the federal equilibrium. The Reconstruction Amendments were the first to withdraw power from the states and to grant additional power to Congress. The Thirteenth Amendment (1865) abolished slavery and involuntary servitude throughout the nation. The Fourteenth Amendment (1868), overruling *Dred Scott*, declared that all persons born or naturalized in the United States, and subject to their jurisdiction, were citizens of the United States and of the states wherein they resided. That amendment also prohibited the states from abridging the privileges or immunities of citizens; from depriving any person of life, liberty, or property without due process of law; and from denying to any person equal protection of the laws. The

---

[35] 74 U.S. 700 (1869).

[36] *Id.* at 725–26. Of course, not everyone was persuaded. See Cynthia Nicoletti, *Secession on Trial: The Treason Prosecution of Jefferson Davis* (New York: Cambridge University Press, 2017).

Fifteenth Amendment (1870) further prohibited both the state and federal governments from denying the right to vote based on race, color, or previous condition of servitude. Moreover, each of the three Reconstruction Amendments granted Congress authority to enforce their provisions by appropriate legislation. In the ensuing two decades, the Court would repeatedly confront the question of whether legislation enacted pursuant to these new grants of authority lay within the power of Congress.

In a number of cases, the justices held that Reconstruction legislation exceeded congressional authority. In *United States* v. *Reese*,[37] for example, the Court held that two provisions of the Enforcement Act of 1870 that sought to protect voting rights exceeded the power conferred by the Fifteenth Amendment because they did not confine their protections to racially discriminatory conduct. Similarly, in *United States* v. *Cruikshank*,[38] the Court invalidated indictments of defendants charged with the massacre of dozens of African American voters on the ground that those indictments did not allege that the conduct was motivated by racial animus. In *United States* v. *Harris*,[39] the Court unanimously invalidated a section of the Ku Klux Klan Act of 1871 that made conspiracies to deprive any person of the equal protection of the laws a federal crime. Twenty members of a lynch mob had been convicted under that section for abducting four prisoners from the custody of a Tennessee deputy sheriff and savagely beating them, one to death. The statute could not be sustained as an enforcement of the guarantees of the Thirteenth or Fifteenth Amendments, the Court held, because those amendments secured protection only against actions taken because of the victim's race, color, or previous condition of servitude. (In fact, though in all likelihood unbeknownst to the justices, each of the victims in the case was white.) Nor could the Fourteenth Amendment supply a foundation for the challenged provision, as Section 1 of that Amendment secured a guarantee of equal protection against state action, and no such action had been alleged in this case. That same year, in the *Civil Rights Cases*,[40] the justices likewise invalidated the public accommodations provisions of the Civil Rights Act of 1875 on the grounds that the Fourteenth Amendment empowered Congress to reach racial discrimination perpetrated only by state officials and not by private individuals.

Many scholars have viewed these decisions as comprising a judicially led "retreat" from Reconstruction. On this account, the justices construed the power conferred upon Congress by the Reconstruction Amendments with an unduly narrow vision, thereby aiding the war-fatigued political branches in their program of forging sectional reconciliation on the backs and with the blood of the freedmen. Others have argued that this perspective credits the members of the Reconstruction Congresses with greater racial egalitarianism and a more robust desire to transform the federal system than they deserve. On this account, the Court's decisions were instead coherent and principled applications of the more

[37] 92 U.S. 214 (1876). [38] 92 U.S. 542 (1876). [39] 106 U.S. 629 (1883).
[40] 109 U.S. 3 (1883).

moderate aspirations of those who framed and ratified the Reconstruction Amendments. Indeed, some scholars maintain that several of the Court's decisions clearly left open constitutional pathways for Congress and federal prosecutors to reach racial discrimination, intimidation, and violence, in many cases even where perpetrated by private individuals. On this view, the federal officials to blame for the outrages of the Jim Crow South were not the justices of the Supreme Court but instead those in the political branches who lost the will to deliver on the promise of the Reconstruction Amendments.[41]

This latter interpretation finds some support when these Reconstruction decisions are read against the broader backdrop of the Court's congruent contemporary federalism jurisprudence. First, the justices recognized that the possession by the states of "all of the powers essential to separate and independent existence" placed inherent limitations of the powers of the federal government. In *Lane County* v. *Oregon*,[42] for example, the Court held the state of Oregon was not required to take federal greenbacks from its counties in payment of their state tax obligations. Notwithstanding federal legislation making the paper currency legal tender for all debts public and private, Congress could not prescribe to the state the currency in which its power to tax might be satisfied. Similarly, in *Collector* v. *Day*,[43] which along with *McCulloch* v. *Maryland* launched what would become a vast and complex body of case law identifying limits on the power of the state and federal governments to tax one another's officials and instrumentalities, the Court held that the salary of a state judge could not be subjected to federal income tax. As Chief Justice Marshall had put it in *McCulloch* v. *Maryland* when striking down the state's taxation of the Bank of the United States, the power to tax involved "the power to destroy."[44] Were one government permitted to tax the officials or instrumentalities of the other, it might make the tax so burdensome as to be insupportable and thus destructive of the powers necessary to its separate and independent existence. From this it followed, as *McCulloch* had made clear, that the existence of the federal government placed inherent limitations on state power as well. So, for example, in *Tarble's Case*,[45] the justices ruled as they had in *Abelman* v. *Booth*[46] that federal officials having custody of federal prisoners were not amenable to writs of habeas corpus issued by state courts.[47]

---

[41] Pamela Brandwein, *Rethinking the Judicial Settlement of Reconstruction* (New York: Cambridge University Press, 2011); Michael Collins, "Justice Bradley's Civil Rights Odyssey Revisited," 70 *Tul. L. Rev.* 1979 (1996); Michael Collins, "'Economic Rights,' Implied Constitutional Actions, and the Scope of Section 1983," 77 *Geo. L. J.* 1493 (1989); Michael Les Benedict, "Preserving Federalism: Reconstruction and the Waite Court," 1978 Sup. *Ct. Rev.* 39 (1979); Michael Les Benedict, "Preserving the Constitution: The Conservative Basis of Radical Reconstruction," 61 *J.A.H.* 65 (1974).
[42] 74 U.S. 71 (1869).   [43] 78 U.S. 113 (1871).   [44] 17 U.S. at 431.   [45] 80 U.S. 391 (1871).
[46] 62 U.S. 506 (1859).
[47] Charles W. McCurdy, "Federalism and the Judicial Mind in a Conservative Age: Stephen Field," in Harry N. Scheiber and Malcom Feeley, eds., *Power Divided: Essays on the Theory and Practice of Federalism* (Berkeley, CA: Institute of Governmental Studies, 1989).

Such manifestations of what came to be called "dual federalism" were thus apparent both in cases that involved racial issues and in those that did not. The Court's post-bellum preoccupation with policing the respective boundaries of state and federal authority was animated by the conviction that the federal and state governments occupied separate spheres of authority within which they were entitled to exercise all of the powers that they had been granted or retained, and that neither was permitted to trespass upon nor impede the exercise of the sovereign prerogatives of the other. Thus, the very existence of the state and federal governments implicitly limited the powers of each.[48]

At the same time, however, the Court also recognized that the very existence of the federal government entailed the possession by Congress of certain inherent powers beyond those specifically enumerated in the Constitution. In *Kohl* v. *United States*,[49] for instance, notwithstanding language in the constitutional text suggesting that Congress could acquire land within a state only by purchasing it with the consent of the state's legislature, the Court held that the federal government had an inherent eminent domain power that could not be obstructed by intransigent persons or states. It was upon such notions of inherent federal power that the Court relied in upholding a conviction under the Enforcement Act in *Ex parte Yarbrough*.[50] The case concerned the same section of the act that had been unsuccessfully deployed in *Cruikshank* eight years earlier. But whereas *Cruikshank* had involved horrific violence in connection with a state election, the black voter beaten by Yarbrough had been intercepted on his way to vote in a federal election.[51]

Critics of the judicial "retreat from Reconstruction" hypothesis point to *Yarbrough* and other lesser-known decisions as evidence indicating that, even if the justices could be justifiably faulted for a callous focus on structural concerns in the face of pressing needs to safeguard southern blacks' rights to personal security, liberty, and equal protection, they were by no means implacably opposed to federal intervention to secure these rights. First, *Reese, Cruikshank*, and *Harris* indicated that statutes and indictments that were more narrowly tailored to target only racial discrimination with respect to rights secured by the Thirteenth and Fifteenth Amendments would pass constitutional muster. Moreover, such critics contend, both *Cruikshank* and *Harris* appeared rather casually to read the state action requirement out of the Fifteenth Amendment, leaving open the possibility of federal enforcement legislation criminalizing private efforts to deny the right to vote on the basis of race. In addition, some opinions have been read to suggest that the failure of state officials to protect their African American citizens from private violence – a sort of state *inaction* – might constitute state *action* denying those citizens the equal protection of the laws, and that this in turn could authorize Congress to enact legislation punishing

---

[48] Edward S. Corwin, "The Passing of Dual Federalism," 36 *Va. L. Rev.* 1 (1950).
[49] 91 U.S. 367 (1876).   [50] 110 U.S. 651 (1884).
[51] McCurdy, "Federalism and the Judicial Mind."

perpetrators pursuant to the enforcement power of the Fourteenth Amendment. On this account, those potentialities lay unrealized because a Congress in which representatives of all of the former states of the Confederacy had now been seated refused to take up the Court's invitations.[52]

Prior to its withdrawal from the field, however, Congress did enact a series of statutes enlarging the jurisdiction of the federal courts, thereby offering mistreated people who previously could seek redress only from state courts new opportunities to vindicate their rights before a more sympathetic federal tribunal. First, the Civil Rights Act of 1866, enacted in response to the infamously discriminatory southern "black codes," guaranteed to the freedmen equal legal treatment with respect to rights of contract, property, and access to courts, as well as "the full and equal benefit of all laws and proceedings for the security of persons and property." The act further provided that anyone sued or arrested under a discriminatory law impinging upon the rights enumerated in that statute could remove his case to federal court. Second, before the Civil War, persons seeking habeas corpus from state custody could resort only to state courts. The Habeas Corpus Act of 1867, by contrast, authorized federal courts to issue writs of habeas corpus "in all cases where any person may be restrained of his or her liberty in violation of the constitution, or any treaty or law of the United States." Third, the Judiciary Act of 1875 granted the lower federal courts jurisdiction over all cases involving questions of federal law and made all such cases initiated in state courts removable to a federal forum. Though the Supreme Court had enjoyed appellate jurisdiction over such cases since 1789, state courts had held monopolies over the trial and initial levels of appeal in all such "federal question" cases except those arising in specific areas, such as intellectual property, over which Congress had expressly conferred jurisdiction on the lower federal courts.

Throughout the period between the "end" of Reconstruction in 1877 and the late New Deal, the Court generally upheld efforts to employ the Reconstruction Amendments to protect what were at the time considered the "civil" rights – those of contract, property, and vocational liberty – of the freedmen. In the 1867 federal circuit court case of *In re Turner*,[53] for example, Chief Justice Chase struck down a racially discriminatory Maryland apprenticeship law. In *Yick Wo v. Hopkins*,[54] the Court unanimously invalidated a conviction for violating a building code regulation that was discriminatorily administered against Chinese laundry owners with "an evil eye and an unequal hand" by local authorities. In *Bailey v. Alabama*[55] and *United States v. Reynolds*,[56] the Court invalidated southern labor regulations that ensnared impecunious African Americans in webs of debt peonage and forced servitude. And in *Buchanan v. Warley*,[57] the

---

[52] Brandwein, *Rethinking the Judicial Settlement*; Collins, "Justice Bradley's Civil Rights Odyssey"; Benedict, "Preserving Federalism."

[53] 24 F. Cas. 337 (C.C.D. Md. 1867).   [54] 118 U.S. 356 (1886).   [55] 219 U.S. 219 (1911).
[56] 235 U.S. 133 (1914).   [57] 245 U.S. 60 (1917).

Court unanimously struck down a residential housing ordinance that prohibited whites and blacks from buying homes from one another.

These interventions did little to change realities on the ground, however. Southern authorities either openly defied or found ways to circumvent the Court's rulings, and African Americans faced the prospect of economic coercion or private violence were they to pursue legal redress. Moreover, unlike the California Chinese, whose financial backing from Cantonese merchants enabled them to mount successful challenges to numerous discriminatory business and employment regulations in the federal courts, southern blacks generally lacked access to the legal services necessary to enforce their rights. Notwithstanding these important judicial vindications of federal authority, the domain of "civil" rights remained governed almost exclusively by state law and local custom.[58]

The justices also often vindicated the "political" rights of the freedmen. In a pair of cases decided in 1880, the Court held that the Fourteenth Amendment protected the rights of African Americans to sit on juries and the rights of black defendants to juries from which African Americans were not categorically excluded, and conferred upon Congress the power to protect those rights through positive legislation.[59] In *Guinn* v. *United States*,[60] the Court unanimously struck down an Oklahoma statute that required passage of a literacy test for all prospective voters whose ancestors had not been eligible to vote before 1866. And in *Nixon* v. *Herndon*[61] and *Nixon* v. *Condon*,[62] the justices invalidated Texas statutes commanding or authorizing exclusion of African American voters from Democratic primary elections.

Here again, however, state resistance and black subordination were obstacles to realizing the promise of such decisions. The practice of striking African Americans from jury venires through peremptory and for-cause challenges continued unimpeded. Oklahoma authorities cynically circumvented the *Guinn* decision in a manner that persisted for nearly a quarter century until a case successfully challenging the scheme finally reached the Court in 1939.[63] The Texas legislature maintained its white primary by withdrawing from its regulation and simply leaving the "private" Democratic Party to do as it liked. With state action no longer involved, the Court unanimously rejected a constitutional challenge to the party's rules excluding black primary voters in *Grovey* v. *Townsend*.[64] Meanwhile, poll taxes, private intimidation, and

[58] Charles J. McClain, *In Search of Equality: The Chinese Struggle Against Discrimination in Nineteenth-Century America* (Berkeley, CA: University of California Press, 1994); Alexander M. Bickel and Benno C. Schmidt, *The Judiciary and Responsible Government, 1910–1921* (New York: Macmillan, 1984); Daniel A. Novak, *The Wheel of Servitude: Black Forced Labor after Slavery* (Lexington: University Press of Kentucky, 1978); Pete Daniel, *The Shadow of Slavery: Peonage in the South, 1901–1969* (Urbana: University of Illinois Press, 1972).
[59] Strauder v. West Virginia, 100 U.S. 303 (1880); Ex parte Virginia, 100 U.S. 339 (1880).
[60] 238 U.S. 347 (1915). [61] 273 U.S. 536 (1927). [62] 286 U.S. 73 (1932).
[63] Lane v. Wilson, 307 U.S. 268 (1939). [64] 295 U.S. 45 (1935).

discriminatorily administered literacy tests functioned to exclude vast numbers of southern blacks from the franchise and, as a consequence, from eligibility to serve as jurors. The general spirit of judicial resignation was captured by Justice Oliver Wendell Holmes's opinion in *Giles* v. *Harris*,[65] where he confessed that, without the aid of the political branches, the Court had little power to correct systemic voting discrimination in the South. Here again, the Reconstruction Amendments and enforcing legislation notwithstanding, the applicable "law in action" was state and local.

In the domain of "social equality," by contrast, southern authorities and Supreme Court justices were in agreement on the law. Just as the Court had held in the *Civil Rights Cases* that Congress was without power to prohibit private discrimination in hotels, restaurants, theaters, and the like, so the justices of this period upheld state and local regulations prescribing racial segregation in public schools (*Cumming* v. *Richmond Board of Education*,[66] *Gong Lum* v. *Rice*[67]) and public transportation (*Plessy* v. *Ferguson*[68]) as well statutes prohibiting interracial marriage or cohabitation (*Pace* v. *Alabama*[69]). Regulation of such matters was left both legally and functionally to state and local authorities.

FROM THE GILDED AGE THROUGH THE NEW DEAL

Along with such questions of minority rights, a central concern of the Court's post-bellum federalism jurisprudence was the scope of state and federal power to regulate business. If scholars sometimes have described the resulting body of case law as incoherent, it may be because they have not fully appreciated two key features of "dual federalism." The first feature concerns the interconnected nature of the Court's "dormant" and "affirmative" Commerce Clause decisions. Although the Court's dormant Commerce Clause cases were facially concerned with defining the scope of *state* regulatory authority over commercial subjects left unregulated by Congress, we shall see that the categories developed in these decisions also played an important role in defining the extent of Congress's affirmative commerce power. Similarly, New Deal transformations in affirmative Commerce Clause doctrine would entail a reorientation of dormant Commerce Clause jurisprudence. The second neglected feature of post-bellum federalism jurisprudence concerns the relationship between the Commerce Clause and due process. As we shall see, the law of vested rights and due process played a critical role in defining the boundary between state and federal regulatory authority. The New Deal–era collapse of dual federalism can thus be seen as resulting, at least in part, from the Court's prior abandonment of traditional due process limitations. After a review of the New Deal Court's transformative Commerce Clause decisions and of coordinate developments concerning the congressional powers to tax and spend, this section concludes with a brief examination of some significant

[65] 189 U.S. 475 (1903).   [66] 175 U.S. 528 (1899).   [67] 275 U.S. 78 (1927).
[68] 163 U.S. 537 (1896).   [69] 106 U.S. 583 (1883).

constitutional amendments and a discussion of contemporaneous developments concerning the treaty power, state sovereign immunity, rules governing diversity jurisdiction, and the law of intergovernmental tax immunities.

The Court's dormant Commerce Clause docket expanded considerably in the period following the Civil War, as an increasing number of enterprises carrying on an interstate business sought to dismantle time-honored schemes of state and local economic protectionism. In case after case, the justices found that long-standing programs of licensure, taxation, and inspection of out-of-state goods and salesmen failed to pass muster.[70] Though the field of concurrent power recognized by *Cooley* persisted, it came to represent an increasingly small slice of dormant Commerce Clause doctrine. Instead, justices and commentators characteristically referred to Congress's power to regulate interstate commerce as "exclusive," thereby placing the subject matter beyond the legislative jurisdiction of the states. The doctrine was animated by a frankly instrumental impulse to break down state and local barriers to interstate commercial traffic in an increasingly vibrant and integrated economy, and it functioned to open up a zone of free trade among the states.[71]

At the same time, however, it was recognized that the theory of exclusive congressional jurisdiction, unless properly qualified, might be destructive of necessary state and local powers to tax and regulate. If every activity, tax, or regulation that had an effect on interstate commerce lay beyond the powers of state and local government, then the states and localities would be deprived of significant portions of their tax bases, and Congress alone would have the power to regulate such matters. Were Congress not to act, such activities would necessarily remain entirely free of regulation. The justices rightly doubted that Congress was prepared to take on such a herculean task, and in light of the great variation in local conditions and circumstances, they doubted as well that Congress could perform the task effectively even were it to try.[72]

The Court therefore formulated the doctrine so as to leave room for a broad range of state and local taxation and regulation. To be sure, where a state or local regulation touched on a "national" matter or burdened interstate commerce "directly," it would be held invalid. But as to "local" matters, any otherwise valid exercise of the police or taxing powers that affected interstate commerce only "incidentally," "indirectly," or "remotely" would be sustained. With such analytic distinctions at the ready, the justices upheld a broad range of nondiscriminatory programs of licensure, taxation, and regulation at the state and local level. Moreover, goods that had not yet begun their interstate transit or had concluded their interstate journey and had come to rest in the destination

---

[70] Charles W. McCurdy, "American Law and the Marketing Structure of the Large Corporation, 1875–1890," 38 *J. Econ. Hist.* 331 (1978).

[71] Barry Cushman, "Formalism and Realism in Commerce Clause Jurisprudence," 67 *U. Chi. L. Rev.* 1089 (2000).

[72] Id.

state remained subject to state and local legislative jurisdiction. The overall effect of the doctrine was to remove impediments to free trade without simultaneously opening an enormous regulatory vacuum.[73]

The paradigmatically "local" activities the regulation of which the doctrine left to state and local authorities were those of "production" – agriculture, mining, and manufacturing. Thus, for example, state taxation or regulation of coal mining, iron mining, petroleum production, and the production of electricity each survived dormant Commerce Clause challenges. Regulations restricting the conditions under which cotton-seed oil companies could own or operate cotton gins and prohibiting the manufacture of such controversial products as liquor and oleomargarine colored to resemble butter were likewise upheld. Production, even if intended for interstate sale, preceded interstate commerce, the Court held, and its regulation affected such commerce only "indirectly." Were it otherwise, Congress would be saddled with the impossible task of enacting a vast array of "only locally applicable and utterly inconsistent" statutes regulating every act of human industry that contemplated an interstate market, while at the same time leaving to local regulators those acts that did not. This would "paralyze" state governments and create interminable tensions and confusions between federal and local authorities.[74]

These dormant Commerce Clause decisions created the categories and set the terms within which the Court developed its jurisprudence concerning the scope of congressional power to regulate commerce among the several states. The justices regularly relied upon dormant Commerce Clause precedents in holding that the Sherman Antitrust Act could not reach acts of corporate consolidation in the manufacturing sector (e.g., *U.S.* v. *E.C. Knight*[75]) or labor strikes or boycotts of manufacturing enterprises (e.g., *United Leather Workers* v. *Herkert & Meisel Trunk Co.*[76]). The effect of such actions on interstate commerce was only "indirect." During the New Deal the Court similarly reasoned to the conclusions that Congress could not regulate employment terms and relations between coal companies and their employees (*Carter* v. *Carter Coal Co.*[77]) nor those of a Brooklyn Kosher butchery that sold all of its meat locally (*Schechter Poultry Corp.* v. *U.S.*[78]). The Justice Department enjoyed considerable success in prosecuting anticompetitive behavior both in the interstate railroad industry and among independent enterprises that entered into agreements not to compete with one another in interstate markets. The Court also recognized federal jurisdiction over mergers, acquisitions, and labor disturbances that were demonstrably undertaken with the intent to restrain interstate trade. There the effects on interstate commerce were "direct." But in the absence of such evidence, the justices insisted that the regulation of activities of production was a matter reserved to the states.[79]

---

[73] Id.   [74] Id.   [75] 156 U.S. 1 (1895).   [76] 265 U.S. 457 (1924).   [77] 298 U.S. 238 (1936).
[78] 295 U.S. 495 (1935).   [79] Cushman, "Formalism and Realism."

During this period, then, much of affirmative Commerce Clause jurisprudence was the mirror image of its dormant counterpart. Matters subject to the legislative jurisdiction of one sovereign lay beyond that of the other. But just as the *Cooley* doctrine permitted states and localities to regulate provisionally some matters that were subject to the jurisdiction of Congress, two affirmative Commerce Clause doctrines recognized the power of Congress to regulate activities that would otherwise have been considered "local." They were the "stream of commerce doctrine," first announced in *Swift* v. *U.S.*,[80] and the "*Shreveport* doctrine," inaugurated in the so-called *Shreveport Rate Case*.[81] Where these doctrines applied, the local activity regulated by Congress was deemed to have a "direct" effect on interstate commerce.[82]

The stream of commerce doctrine recognized the power of Congress to regulate local activities, even those falling into the category of production, where those activities were both preceded and followed by interstate shipment of the item in question. Thus, for example, the Court held in *Stafford* v. *Wallace*[83] that Congress could regulate the charges imposed by owners of stockyards for housing, feeding, watering, and caring for livestock that had arrived from out of state and would continue its interstate journey after sale or slaughter. The *Shreveport* doctrine recognized congressional power to regulate rates for intrastate rail travel where necessary to prevent destructive competition with federally regulated interstate carriers. Under each doctrine the activity in question was subject to state regulation, but Congress was free to step in and preempt local authority with a scheme of its own.

In order to appreciate how narrowly circumscribed the domains of these two doctrines were, it is necessary to understand the important role that concepts of vested rights and substantive due process played in configuring the federal equilibrium. During this period, the Due Process Clause of the Fourteenth Amendment performed a role analogous to that played in the antebellum period by Article I, Section 10's prohibition on state laws impairing the obligation of contract. In each case, the constitutional provision placed constraints on the policy options available to states and localities in the realm of political economy. Though substantive due process is conventionally most closely associated with decisions invalidating certain regulations of the employment relationship, its broadest application came in cases involving the regulation of prices and rates charged by businesses and utilities.[84]

Following its 1877 decision upholding the regulation of rates charged by grain elevators in *Munn* v. *Illinois*,[85] the Court repeatedly held that the prices of

---

[80] 196 U.S. 375 (1905).   [81] 234 U.S. 342 (1914).

[82] Barry Cushman, *Rethinking the New Deal Court: The Structure of a Constitutional Revolution* (New York: Oxford University Press, 1998).

[83] 258 U.S. 495 (1922).

[84] Barry Cushman, "Some Varieties and Vicissitudes of Lochnerism," 85 *B.U. L. Rev.* 881 (2005).

[85] 94 U.S. 113 (1877).

goods and services provided by ordinary private enterprises were not amenable
to government regulation. An enterprise was subject to price and certain other
forms of regulation only if it were a "business affected with a public interest."
Though there was some disagreement among the justices concerning where the
outer boundaries of this category lay, at its core were those businesses that
provided a necessary or indispensable good or service for which the market
provided no substitute. Because the public was forced to deal with such "virtual
monopolies," they could extract from their customers "exorbitant charges."
No one had a vested right to a monopoly rent, however, so regulation of their
prices that still allowed them a "reasonable return" on their investment did not
deprive them of property without due process of law. The rather brief list of
enterprises that fell into this narrow category included railroads, power and
water utilities, public stockyards, public grain exchanges, and grain elevators,[86]
which, as Chief Justice Morrison Waite put it in *Munn*, stood "in the very
gateway of commerce," taking "toll from all who pass."[87]

It was just such enterprises that occupied a monopolistic position in streams of
interstate commerce, and it was only such activities that were held to be subject to
federal regulation under the stream of commerce doctrine. Of the four stream of
commerce cases the Court decided during this period, three involved public
stockyards[88] and the other involved a major public grain exchange.[89] In order
to be a local business subject to federal regulation under the stream of commerce
doctrine, it was necessary that such a business be affected with a public interest.
The stream of commerce doctrine thus cut a very narrow channel, leaving the
overwhelming majority of local enterprises free from federal regulation.

The *Shreveport* doctrine was similarly constrained by due process limitations.
There, congressional power to regulate intrastate rates for rail carriage was
derived from its power to regulate interstate rates. Of course, Congress had
power to regulate such interstate rates – and therefore intrastate rates – only
because railroads were businesses affected with a public interest. Indeed, between
the time that the doctrine was announced in 1914 and 1937, all of the cases in
which the Court applied the *Shreveport* case involved railroads. No other area of
local economic activity fell within the doctrine's purview.[90]

The Court abandoned this category of due process jurisprudence in the 1934
case of *Nebbia* v. *New York*,[91] declaring that there was "no closed class or
category of businesses affected with a public interest." Henceforth, that term
would mean only that "an industry, for adequate reason, [was] subject to
control for the public good." Due process required "only that the law shall
not be unreasonable, arbitrary or capricious, and that the means selected shall

[86] Cushman, "Some Varieties and Vicissitudes."   [87] 94 U.S. at 132.
[88] Tagg Bros. & Moorhead v. U.S., 280 U.S. 420 (1930); Stafford v. Wallace, 258 U.S. 495 (1922);
     Swift & Co. v. U.S., 196 U.S. 375 (1905).
[89] Chicago Board of Trade v. Olsen, 262 U.S. 1 (1923).
[90] Cushman, "Formalism and Realism."   [91] 291 U.S. 502 (1934).

have a real and substantial relation to the object sought to be attained."[92] The remarkable relaxation of this due process limitation opened vast new frontiers for regulation underwritten by the Commerce Clause doctrines that it had previously constrained. The stream of commerce, now free to overflow its former banks, could justify a flood of federal regulation. Attorneys defending the constitutionality of the National Labor Relations Act deliberately selected as test cases disputes at manufacturing plants that acquired most of their raw materials from other states and then shipped their finished products across state lines. Such formerly "private" enterprises, they now claimed, stood astride a stream of interstate commerce and were accordingly subject to federal regulation.[93] Their efforts were rewarded with success in the *Labor Board Cases*,[94] and such broadened stream of commerce arguments continued to play a prominent role in legal arguments, scholarly commentary, and judicial decisions throughout the late 1930s.[95]

This revolution in due process jurisprudence likewise dramatically expanded the range of application of the *Shreveport* doctrine. Now that the due process clause no longer limited price regulation to a narrow class of businesses affected with a public interest, Congress was free to prescribe reasonable prices at which items such as coal, milk, and a variety of agricultural commodities could be sold in interstate commerce. And because the successful regulation of interstate prices required that Congress also regulate prices and marketing in intrastate transactions, the Court repeatedly held that the *Shreveport* doctrine authorized such regulation. Thus, by reorienting its regulatory efforts toward marketing rather than production, Congress could wield substantial control over national and local markets.[96]

These transformations alone, however, did not extend congressional jurisdiction to most of the "local" activities previously regulated only by states and localities. The stream of commerce did not extend to local production, such as mining or agriculture, which preceded interstate commerce. Nor did it reach local activities conducted after the stream of interstate commerce had come to its terminus in a destination state. Similarly, the *Shreveport* doctrine did not authorize federal regulation of intrastate activity unless it were necessary and proper to maintain the efficacy of a program that the commerce power authorized Congress to enact. Indeed, the Court cautioned that the liberalized Commerce Clause doctrines must be applied "in the light of our dual system of government and may not be extended so as to embrace effects upon interstate commerce so indirect and remote that to embrace them, in view of our complex

---

[92] Id. at 510–11, 515–16.

[93] Cushman, *Rethinking the New Deal Court*; Peter Irons, *The New Deal Lawyers* (New York: Oxford University Press, 1982); Richard C. Cortner, *The Jones & Laughlin Case* (New York: Knopf, 1970).

[94] NLRB v. Jones & Laughlin Steel Corp., 301 U.S. 1 (1937); NLRB v. Fruehauf Trailer Co., 301 U.S. 49 (1937); NLRB v. Friedman-Harry Marks Clothing Co., 301 U.S. 58 (1937).

[95] Cushman, *Rethinking the New Deal Court*.   [96] Id.

society, would effectually obliterate the distinction between what is national and
what is local and create a completely centralized government."[97] The justices
continued throughout the late 1930s to employ the same categories and
vocabulary that had governed both affirmative and dormant Commerce Clause
jurisprudence for decades.[98]

That long-standing, coordinated jurisprudential enterprise came to an end with
Wickard v. *Filburn*.[99] There the Court upheld federal regulations limiting the
acreage that a farmer could plant during any given season. The farmer who had
planted more wheat than was authorized claimed that his excess wheat would be
marketed neither in interstate nor in intrastate commerce, but would instead be
consumed on his own farm. The Court nevertheless reasoned that such a means of
satisfying one's own demand for wheat, if pursued by many others similarly situated,
could have a significant effect on the aggregate demand for wheat. This in turn could
have a significant effect on the price at which wheat traded in interstate commerce.
And because Congress had the power to regulate the price at which wheat was
marketed in interstate commerce, it therefore had the power to regulate local
activities where it was necessary and proper to make effective its program of
interstate marketing regulation. In arriving at this conclusion, Justice Robert
Jackson's unanimous opinion for the Court rejected the analytic categories that
had bound affirmative and dormant Commerce Clause jurisprudence together for
half a century. Now it was of no significance that the activity Congress purported to
regulate was one of production; nor would questions of congressional power any
longer turn on whether the effect of an activity on interstate commerce was "direct"
or "indirect." The only question was whether the aggregate effect of such activities
on interstate commerce was "substantial."

This recognition of virtually plenary congressional power under the Commerce
Clause had immediate and dramatic implications for dormant Commerce Clause
jurisprudence. If congressional power to regulate interstate commerce was both
plenary and exclusive, then long-standing state powers to regulate and tax what
previously had been regarded as "local" activities would be implicitly preempted,
and the regulatory vacuum feared by late-nineteenth-century jurists and
commentators would have become a reality. The Court avoided this consequence
by quickly abandoning the premise of congressional exclusivity, replacing it with the
premise that, in the absence of statutory preemption, state and federal governments
enjoyed concurrent power to regulate matters over which the Commerce and
Necessary and Proper Clauses together conferred power on Congress. Dormant
Commerce Clause jurisprudence was thereby reoriented from a focus on the scope of
legislative jurisdiction to inquiries into whether state or local regulations
discriminated against or unduly burdened interstate commerce.[100]

[97] NLRB v. Jones & Laughlin Steel Corp., 301 U.S. at 37.
[98] Cushman, *Rethinking the New Deal Court*.   [99] 317 U.S. 111 (1942).
[100] Cushman, "Formalism and Realism."

This doctrinal decoupling of affirmative and dormant Commerce Clause jurisprudence, however, obscured a common underlying theoretical foundation. Jackson had come to regard questions of congressional power under the Commerce Clause as political questions not only because economic integration had made judicial line-drawing impracticable but also because he believed that state and local interests were adequately protected in the national political process through their representation in Congress.[101] By contrast, as Justice Harlan Fiske Stone observed in the dormant Commerce Clause case of *South Carolina Highway Department* v. *Barnwell Brothers*,[102] the interests of sister states were not adequately represented in state and local legislative bodies, and for this reason it was appropriate for those interests to be safeguarded by judicial review. This "representation-reinforcement" conception of federalism, famously articulated by Marshall in *McCulloch*, thus became a central organizing principle of Commerce Clause jurisprudence.

The line of affirmative Commerce Clause doctrine just described concerned the power of Congress to regulate local activities because of their relationship to interstate commerce. Another line of affirmative Commerce Clause doctrine concerned the power of Congress to prohibit the interstate shipment or transport of disfavored items. This line of doctrine similarly followed a course of development influenced by both dormant Commerce Clause and substantive due process jurisprudence. Beginning in the late nineteenth century, the Court began to infer from the grant of the commerce power to Congress a disability on the part of states to exclude from their borders such controversial items as liquor, oleomargarine, and cigarettes. Even though the Due Process Clause would permit extensive regulation of such items under state and local police powers once they had become intermingled with the general property of the state, so long as they remained in their "original packages" they fell within the exclusive regulatory jurisdiction of Congress.[103]

Congress responded to the opening of such regulatory lacunae in three ways. The first was with legislation "divesting" the article of its interstate character upon its arrival in the destination state, even while it remained in its original package, thereby permitting state regulation of the article's disposition under the police power. Congress enacted such measures with respect to alcoholic beverages, oleomargarine colored to resemble butter, and eventually convict-made goods, and the Court upheld these statutes when they were challenged. The second generation of such "cooperative" statutes prohibited interstate transport of an article, such as liquor or convict-made goods, into a state where it was to be used, sold, or possessed in violation of the destination state's law. The Court likewise sustained these measures. The third legislative response was to prohibit interstate transportation of an article altogether,

---

[101] Cushman, *Rethinking the New Deal Court.* [102] 303 U.S. 177 (1938).

[103] Barry Cushman, "*Carolene Products* and Constitutional Structure," 2012 *Sup. Ct. Rev.* 321 (2013).

irrespective of whether its use, possession, or disposition would violate the law of a destination state. The Court upheld such statutes prohibiting interstate transport of lottery tickets and of impure or mislabeled food and drugs. But in *Hammer* v. *Dagenhart*,[104] a narrowly divided Court struck down a statute prohibiting the interstate shipment of goods produced by firms employing children under specified ages and for certain hours.[105]

The apparent inconsistency in this line of cases presents a puzzle. The majority maintained that the Child Labor Act was a regulation of production, but this claim suffered from two deficiencies pointed out by the dissent. First, the act regulated only the interstate transportation of the firm's products, not the conditions of their production. Second, to the extent that the prohibition on shipment indirectly affected conditions of production in the firm, it was not distinguishable from the Lottery Act, which by eliminating the interstate market in lottery tickets reduced the volume of their production, nor from the Pure Food and Drugs Act, which by prohibiting interstate shipment of articles not meeting the standards prescribed by the act naturally affected the conditions of their production. The majority sought to distinguish those statutes on the ground that they prohibited interstate shipment of goods that were "harmful," whereas child-made goods were "of themselves harmless" and would, unlike lottery tickets or impure food, inflict no harm in the state of destination. This distinction was undermined seven years later when, to the howls of *Hammer*'s many critics, the Court unanimously upheld a federal prohibition on the interstate transportation of stolen automobiles without explaining how such articles were "of themselves" harmful.[106]

Reconciliation of this line of cases requires a recognition that their differing results are explicable in terms of vested rights and substantive due process. The structure of the doctrine rested on the proposition that once a property right in an item had vested under the applicable state law, the Due Process Clauses prohibited either Congress or sister state legislatures from disadvantageously regulating the disposition of that item unless such a disposition threatened the infliction of a cognizable harm within the legislative jurisdiction of the regulating sovereign. In the absence of a threat that such a cognizable harm might be inflicted within Congress's legislative jurisdiction, therefore, a federal prohibition on the interstate shipment of an item deprived its owner of property without due process of law. Were the threat of such a harm present, however, a prohibition on interstate shipment would not deprive the owner of property without due process, for no one could have a vested right to inflict harm on public health, safety, or morals.[107]

Thus, Congress was competent to prohibit interstate transportation of intoxicating liquors due to the threat that they posed to public health, safety, and morals in states of destination. Just as the states could prohibit their manufacture and sale without violating the Fourteenth Amendment's Due

---

[104] 247 U.S. 251 (1918).   [105] Cushman, "*Carolene Products.*"   [106] Id.   [107] Id.

Process Clause, so Congress could exclude them from interstate commerce without violating the corresponding provision of the Fifth Amendment. As it was equally well established that states were empowered to outlaw the sale of lottery tickets due to their tendencies to corrupt morals and contribute to penury, so it followed that Congress impaired no vested right by excluding lottery tickets from interstate channels. And because no one enjoyed a vested right to harm public health and safety through the distribution of impure foods or medicines, nor to defraud the public by deceptively labeling such goods, congressional prohibition of interstate shipment of such products deprived no one of property without due process. Because in each of these instances the original package doctrine made possible the infliction of the threatened harm while the article in question remained within the federal legislative jurisdiction, Congress had power under the Commerce Clause to guard against such an eventuality.[108]

For similar reasons, federal statutes prohibiting interstate transportation of wild game or petroleum acquired in violation of the law of the state of origin weathered judicial review. Because neither the poacher nor the wildcat driller obtained a vested right in the article illegally taken, laws forbidding such interstate transport did not deprive their possessors of property without due process. Nor was a prohibition on the interstate transport of stolen cars constitutionally problematic. For though a stolen car might in itself be no more dangerous than a shoe made by a child, neither the thief nor anyone knowingly taking from him had any vested right in the pilfered motor vehicle. In each of these cases, the legislation was valid not because it prevented infliction of a harm within the federal legislative jurisdiction, but instead because it impaired no vested right.[109]

The Child Labor Act was the one such federal initiative that fell within neither of these safe harbors. To be sure, it was established that there was no constitutional right to employ children, and any state was free to prohibit such employment. But if, for example, the state of North Carolina chose to permit the employment of children in its factories, then the employer of that labor acquired a vested right in its product under the law of that state. The power of Congress to exclude that product from interstate commerce thus turned on whether the good threatened to inflict a cognizable harm outside the legislative jurisdiction of the state of its production.[110]

This made a great deal turn on which types of extraterritorial harms the Court regarded as legally privileged and which it recognized as falling outside the protection of the Due Process Clause. In *Hammer*, the government contended that the extraterritorial harm inflicted was competitive in nature. A firm employing children could pay them less than adults, which reduced its overhead as compared with that of competing firms in states with more restrictive child labor laws. This "unfair competition" would cause economic

[108] Id.   [109] Id.   [110] Id.

harm to firms in more child-protective states, which would induce them to pressure their legislatures to relax their own child labor standards and thereby jeopardize the health and safety of that state's children. But the *Hammer* majority refused to recognize the threat of such competitive harms as a justification for federal intervention, pronounced child-made goods of themselves harmless, and invalidated the statute. It was this narrow conception of what constituted a cognizable harm under the Due Process Clause that restrained congressional power to prohibit interstate shipment.[111]

In *United States* v. *Carolene Products Co.*,[112] however, the Court upheld a federal prohibition on interstate transport of filled milk. In his opinion for the Court, Justice Stone expressly disaggregated from the Commerce Clause analysis the due process analysis with which it had been conflated by the *Hammer* majority. Prohibitions on interstate shipment were exercises of the commerce power, Stone declared, constrained only by other provisions of the Constitution such as the Fifth Amendment's Due Process Clause. Moreover, Stone announced that henceforth in cases involving challenges to economic regulation under the Due Process Clauses, the Court would accord a broad measure of deference to legislative judgments concerning harm. This relaxation of the due process constraint on the commerce power paved the way for the recognition in *United States* v. *Darby Lumber Co.*[113] that the sort of unfair competition generated by firms employing child laborers or underpaid workers was a harm that Congress was empowered to remedy through prohibitions on the interstate shipment of goods produced by such firms. *Darby* thus overruled *Hammer*, rendering congressional power to prohibit interstate shipments as unimpeded by judicial review as *Wickard* would make the power to regulate local activities affecting interstate commerce the following year. The interjurisdictional regulatory competition and policy heterogeneity among the states that had been underwritten by the restrictions that the Court's protection of vested rights had placed on federal regulatory authority thus gave way to national policies implemented through exercises of a commerce power no longer constrained by due process limitations.[114]

Thus, during this period the economic rights protected by the Due Process Clause functioned as structural mechanisms, not only marking the boundaries between individual liberty and sovereign authority but also allocating regulatory power among the state and federal governments.[115] This was true not only with respect to the commerce power but also with respect to exercises of the congressional fiscal powers. In the late nineteenth century, Congress began to take an interest in regulating substances and activities that lay beyond the reach of its commerce power by imposing prohibitive excise taxes on them. Critics of such measures claimed that they did not impose true taxes but instead regulated matters reserved to the states. When this claim was

---

[111] Id.   [112] 304 U.S. 144 (1938).   [113] 312 U.S. 100 (1941).
[114] Cushman, "*Carolene Products.*"   [115] Id.

presented to the Court in *McCray* v. *United States*,[116] however, the justices maintained that the question was not justiciable. In upholding a ten cent per pound excise on oleomargarine colored to resemble butter, Chief Justice Edward White insisted that only the political branches were competent to determine whether a purported tax constituted a true exercise of the taxing power or was instead "the exercise of an authority not conferred" by the Constitution. Under only one condition would the Court intervene: "[W]here it was plain to the judicial mind that the power had been called into play not for revenue but solely for the purpose of destroying rights which could not be rightfully destroyed consistently with the principles of freedom and justice upon which the Constitution rests." Only if an interest of the sort protected by the Due Process Clause were implicated would the justices address the question of whether Congress had encroached on the domain of the states by seeking the accomplishment of objectives not entrusted to the government. That principle was inapplicable in *McCray*, White observed, because the Court's Fourteenth Amendment due process decisions had established that "the manufacture of artificially colored oleomargarine may be prohibited by a free government without a violation of fundamental rights."[117]

The doctrinal structure that emerged from *McCray* thus entwined Fifth Amendment, Tenth Amendment, and separation of powers concerns in a unique configuration. As a general rule, principles of separation of powers would preclude the Court from inquiring into whether a regulatory tax was intended to invade the regulatory space reserved to the states by the Tenth Amendment and thus was merely the pretextual exercise of an enumerated power. Only where a fundamental individual right was imperiled would the Court vindicate the Tenth Amendment interest in confining Congress to exercising only those powers conferred by the Constitution. So long as federal regulatory taxation did not transgress the limitations that the Fourteenth Amendment imposed upon the states' police powers, there would be no occasion for the Court to subject such pretextual enactments to searching judicial scrutiny. And by remaining within this safe harbor, over the next several decades Congress managed to secure judicial validation of excises not only on oleomargarine but also on narcotics, certain firearms, marijuana, gambling, and ticket scalping. Thus, it was the Fifth Amendment, rather than the Tenth, that imposed the constitutional restraint on congressional power to regulate through taxation. Only by asserting a Fifth Amendment interest could one secure judicial vindication of the Tenth Amendment limitation.[118]

It would not be long, however, before two unusually aggressive exercises of the taxing power prompted the Court to qualify this position. In 1922 the

---

[116] 195 U.S. 27 (1904).   [117] Id. at 64.

[118] Barry Cushman, "*NFIB* v. *Sebelius* and the Transformation of the Taxing Power," 89 *Notre Dame L. Rev.* 133 (2013); Barry Cushman, "The Structure of Classical Public Law," 75 *U. Chi. L. Rev.* 1917 (2008).

justices invalidated a heavy tax on the net profits of firms employing child labor and a prohibitive excise on options contracts in grain futures. No one could seriously contend that regulation of such activities transgressed the limitations of the Due Process Clause, as the Court had sustained earlier state prohibitions of the taxed conduct. But the Court found that, unlike the other taxes that it had upheld and would later uphold, these taxes imposed heavy exactions for deviations from a prescribed, detailed, and specified course of conduct. Were the Court to sustain such a measure, then Congress could regulate any and all matters simply by prescribing rules of conduct and imposing excises on violators. The result would be a federal government of plenary rather than enumerated powers. The justices therefore declared the exactions "penalties" rather than true taxes and thus beyond the power of Congress to impose.[119]

With the taxing power now foreclosed as a means of realizing comprehensive programs of federal regulation, Congress turned to the spending power. The scope of this power had been the subject of debate from the earliest years of the republic. James Madison had construed the power narrowly, maintaining that Congress could appropriate funds only as an incident to the exercise of its other enumerated powers. Alexander Hamilton, by contrast, insisted that the power to spend was a great and independent power limited only by the requirement that it be exercised to provide for the general welfare of the United States. Throughout the nineteenth and early twentieth centuries, Congress regularly appropriated funds for a range of purposes, including relief of those suffering from various disasters, and several antebellum presidents vetoed bills underwriting internal improvement projects believed to lie beyond the power of the federal legislature. Yet no case directly presenting the question of the spending power's scope reached the Court until nearly 150 years after the ratification of the Constitution. In *United States* v. *Butler*,[120] however, the Court relied upon its review of "the writings of public men and commentators" and "the legislative practice" in resolving the dispute in favor of Hamilton. It was on the basis of this resolution that the Court upheld the old-age pension and unemployment compensation provisions of the Social Security Act in *Helvering* v. *Davis*[121] and *Steward Machine Co.* v. *Davis*.[122]

The lengthy delay preceding *Butler*'s pronouncement on the scope of the spending power was attributable in no small part to a feature of the Court's justiciability doctrine. In 1921, Congress enacted the Sheppard-Towner Maternity Act, which established a grant-in-aid program for the reduction of maternal and infant mortality. Under the statute, Congress appropriated funds to be disbursed to states that established qualifying programs for the promotion of infant and maternal health. A taxpayer in Massachusetts asserted that Congress

---

[119] Bailey v. Drexel Furniture Co., 259 U.S. 20 (1922); Hill v. Wallace, 259 U.S. 44 (1922); Cushman, "Transformation of the Taxing Power"; Cushman, "The Structure of Classical Public Law."

[120] 297 U.S. 1 (1936).   [121] 301 U.S. 619 (1937).   [122] 301 U.S. 548 (1937).

was without authority to spend for such a purpose, and that the taxation necessary to fund the program would deprive her of her property without due process of law in violation of the Fifth Amendment. In *Frothingham* v. *Mellon*,[123] the justices unanimously rejected her challenge, maintaining that she had no standing to bring it. The Court ruled that Frothingham's interest in the moneys of the federal treasury, which was shared with millions of others, was simply too "minute and indeterminable" to support a justiciable claim of injury entitling her to appeal to "the preventive powers of a court of equity" "to enjoin the execution of a federal appropriation act."[124]

This "taxpayer standing doctrine" had profound implications for federal spending policy during the New Deal. So long as Congress appropriated funds for federal spending programs from general revenue rather than from the proceeds of a specially dedicated tax, no one would have standing to challenge any such expenditures. Numerous public works, relief, and recovery spending programs designed with this counsel in mind managed for that very reason to elude judicial review. Under such a regime of justiciability, it mattered little whether the Court espoused a Madisonian or a Hamiltonian reading of the General Welfare Clause. The system was functionally Hamiltonian.[125]

United States v. *Butler* came to the Court precisely because the Agricultural Adjustment Act of 1933 was not designed to fit within the taxpayer standing doctrine's safe harbor. In an effort to bolster depressed prices brought on by chronic agricultural surpluses, the act authorized the Secretary of Agriculture to enter into contracts with farmers, paying them to reduce their production of specified commodities. These benefit payments were funded by a special, designated tax on the processors of these commodities. The receiver of an insolvent textile mill thus had standing to challenge the earmarked exaction, and argued that taxing the processor in order to provide a benefit payment to a farmer took the processor's property for a private rather than a public purpose and thereby denied it rights protected by the Fifth Amendment. The Court agreed that an "expropriation of money from one group for the benefit of another" (as distinguished from an "exaction for the support of the Government") was "not a true tax," and struck down the exaction as a step in a scheme to usurp the states' regulatory authority over agricultural production. Here again, the Tenth Amendment interest could be vindicated only because a Fifth Amendment interest was also implicated.[126]

Congress responded by eliminating the Fifth Amendment interest. Under the Soil Conservation and Domestic Allotment Act, which was enacted within two months of the decision in *Butler*, farmers were paid to shift their acreage from soil-depleting, surplus crops to soil-building crops such as grasses and legumes.

---

[123] 262 U.S. 447 (1923).   [124] Id. at 486–87.
[125] Barry Cushman, "The Hughes Court and Constitutional Consultation," 23–1 *J. Sup. Ct. Hist.* 79 (1998).
[126] 297 U.S. at 61.

The payments under the act were made from general revenue rather than from the proceeds of an earmarked tax, with the result that no taxpayer had any Fifth Amendment interest that would give him standing to challenge the program. With the Fifth Amendment no longer implicated, restraints on the spending power would be supplied, if at all, only by the political branches.[127]

Before leaving this period, a few other developments should be noted briefly. First, the eight years between 1913 and 1920 witnessed the ratification of the first four amendments to the Constitution since Reconstruction. The Sixteenth Amendment (1913) empowered Congress to enact a federal income tax – a power that a narrowly divided Supreme Court had determined that Congress did not possess in *Pollock* v. *Farmers' Loan & Trust Co.*[128] It would not be long before the resulting increase in federal revenue would underwrite vast new federal programs both of direct subsidy and of regulation through conditional expenditure. What was long regarded as one of the structural safeguards of federalism fell when the Seventeenth Amendment (1913) prescribed that US senators would henceforth be selected not by state legislatures but instead by popular, statewide election. The Nineteenth Amendment (1920) prohibited the federal and state governments from denying or abridging the right to vote on the basis of sex. And the Eighteenth Amendment (1919) launched the federal government on a decade-long experiment in federal enforcement throughout the country of prohibitions on the manufacture, sale, and transportation of intoxicating liquors. Those efforts received mixed reviews at best, and regulation of such matters was returned to the states with the ratification of the Twenty-First Amendment in 1933.

In the domain of case law, the Court held in *Missouri* v. *Holland*[129] that federal legislation implementing treaties with foreign nations need not fall within the scope of Congress's other enumerated powers. Though this decision held the potential to transform the federal equilibrium at the time, Congress did not rely upon this principle in order to achieve its desired ends, and the dramatic expansion of the commerce power by 1942 rendered doing so unnecessary. *Hans* v. *Louisiana*[130] held that principles of sovereign immunity protected states from suits in federal court brought by their own citizens, thus supplying states with an immunity analogous to that which they had long enjoyed under the Eleventh Amendment. The Court soon made it clear in *Ex parte Young*,[131] however, that these principles did not preclude suits against state *officers* who had acted unconstitutionally.

The Constitutional Revolution of the New Deal Era also witnessed a "Copernican Revolution" concerning the rules of decision applied by federal courts sitting in diversity. In *Erie Railroad.* v. *Tompkins*,[132] the Court overruled *Swift* v. *Tyson* and the line of cases it represented. Declaring that there was no

---

[127] Cushman, "Constitutional Consultation"; Cushman, "The Structure of Classical Public Law."
[128] 158 U.S. 601 (1895).   [129] 252 U.S. 416 (1920).   [130] 134 U.S. 1 (1890).
[131] 209 U.S. 123 (1908).   [132] 304 U.S. 64 (1938).

federal general common law, the Court announced that henceforth in diversity cases federal judges would be obliged to apply the relevant state decisional law. Finally, in a series of cases decided in the late 1930s, the justices substantially curtailed long-standing principles of intergovernmental tax immunity.

The dramatic expansion of federal power during this period by no means heralded the total displacement of state authority. Indeed, the demise of economic substantive due process during the 1930s "unshackled" state governments, thereby permitting them to engage in forms of regulation that previous decisions had forbidden.[133] State and local government would continue to exert primary control over the content of such expansive realms of positive law as contracts and commercial transactions, property and land use, torts and insurance, marriage and divorce, wills, trusts, inheritance, corporate law, and criminal law. In the wake of the New Deal constitutional settlement, however, the contours of the federal equilibrium with respect to such matters were largely left to the discretion of federal legislators.

CONSTITUTIONAL FEDERALISM SINCE THE NEW DEAL

In May 1939, Harold Laski published an article in *The New Republic* titled "The Obsolescence of Federalism." Laski opined that "the federal form of state is unsuitable to the stage of economic and social development that America has reached" and declared that "the epoch of federalism is over."[134] Rather than a blessing to be celebrated, federalism was a problem to be solved. Later scholars would go so far as to declare federalism "a national neurosis."[135] In the decades following the New Deal Constitutional Revolution, it became the reigning orthodoxy that the political process alone was sufficient to impose whatever limits on federal power might remain desirable and that judicial review no longer had a meaningful role to play.[136] Congress enacted and the Court approved uses of the commerce power to regulate not only ever-widening swaths of the economy, but a variety of other matters ranging from civil rights to street crime as well. Through the extensive use of conditional grants of federal funds and conditional preemption of fields of regulation, Congress induced state legislatures

---

[133] Stephen Gardbaum, "New Deal Constitutionalism and the Unshackling of the States," 64 *U. Chi. L. Rev.* 483 (1997).

[134] Harold J. Laski, "The Obsolescence of Federalism," 98 *The New Republic* 367 (1939).

[135] Edward L. Rubin and Malcolm Feeley, "Federalism: Some Notes on a National Neurosis," 41 *UCLA L. Rev.* 903 (1994).

[136] John Hart Ely, *Democracy and Distrust: A Theory of Judicial Review* (Cambridge, MA: Harvard University Press, 1980); Jesse H. Choper, *Judicial Review and the National Political Process: A Functional Reconsideration of the Role of the Supreme Court* (Chicago: University of Chicago Press, 1980); Herbert Wechsler, "The Political Safeguards of Federalism: The Role of the States in the Composition and Selection of the National Government," 54 *Colum. L. Rev.* 543 (1954).

to enact programs to facilitate the achievement of a broad array of federal goals concerning areas as diverse as health care, education and training, job counseling, child care, housing, conservation, transportation, and urban redevelopment.[137] All of this was achieved without meaningful judicial resistance. By mid-century Professor Edward S. Corwin would proclaim "the passing of dual federalism," and joined others in hailing the rise of a new "cooperative federalism."[138] Social scientists valorizing the displacement of dual federalism by "intergovernmental relations" declared that the federal and state governments were now so intermingled and interdependent in matters of public administration that the federal system was no longer a "layer cake" but instead a "marble cake."[139] By 1968, Professor Phillip Kurland would announce that "federalism as a viable constitutional principle" was "moribund if it is not dead."[140]

One can readily understand why observers such as Kurland had come to such a conclusion. The decades following the Great Depression were characterized not only by significant expansion of the federal regulatory apparatus but also by the judicial imposition of new constitutional constraints in areas of governance traditionally left to state and local authorities. These inhibitions emerged from two related jurisprudential developments: the Court's application to the states of limitations contained in the Bill of Rights, and an ever-broadening construction of the restraints imposed by the Due Process and Equal Protection Clauses of the Fourteenth Amendment. After discussing these developments, this section will turn to the federalism "revival" of the late twentieth and early twenty-first centuries. This period witnessed the resuscitation of modest limits on congressional power under the Commerce Clause and Section 5 of the Fourteenth Amendment as well as the emergence of a more robust doctrine of state sovereign immunity. At the same time, however, broad readings of the taxing power, the Necessary and Proper Clause, and, most importantly, the spending power continued to supply Congress with virtually plenary regulatory authority that was constrained only by the Bill of Rights and the political process.

In *Barron* v. *Baltimore*,[141] the Marshall Court had established that the Bill of Rights imposed limitations only on Congress and did not apply to the states. This view was controversial in some contemporary quarters, and after the ratification of the Fourteenth Amendment, the Court was confronted with claims that among the privileges or immunities protected against state abridgment by the amendment were the rights enumerated in most if not all of the Constitution's first eight amendments. Though recent scholarship has unearthed significant evidence in

---

[137] Harry N. Scheiber, "American Federalism and the Diffusion of Power: Historical and Contemporary Perspectives," 9 *Toledo L. Rev.* 619 (1978).

[138] Edward S. Corwin, "The Passing of Dual Federalism," 36 *Va. L. Rev.* 1 (1950).

[139] See, e.g., Morton Grodzins, *The American System: A New View of Government in the United States* (Chicago: Rand McNally, 1966).

[140] Philip B. Kurland, "The Impotence of Reticence," 4 *Duke L. J.* 619, 620 (1968).

[141] 32 U.S. 243 (1833).

support of such a claim,[142] for many years it was the conventional wisdom that the contention was mistaken.[143] This was the view taken by a Court majority anxious to limit the scope of Section One's guarantees lest Section Five's enforcement power be understood to authorize congressional regulation of virtually every aspect of local conduct. In 1873 the justices gave the Privileges or Immunities Clause a remarkably narrow reading in *The Slaughterhouse Cases*,[144] and held in a series of subsequent decisions that various provisions of the Bill of Rights did not protect citizens from their own state governments.[145]

Over the next several decades, the Court would moderate this position, holding that the Fourteenth Amendment applied against the states only those provisions of the Bill of Rights embodying a "principle of justice so rooted in the traditions and conscience of our people as to be ranked as fundamental."[146] By 1940 the justices had determined that rights of free speech,[147] freedom of the press,[148] peaceable assembly,[149] and free exercise of religion[150] met that standard, whereas the right to indictment by grand jury,[151] the right to trial by jury in civil and criminal cases,[152] the privilege against self-incrimination,[153] and the prohibition on double jeopardy did not.[154]

During the 1940s this "selective incorporation" approach came under attack from Justice Hugo Black, who argued that the Fourteenth Amendment imposed on the states all of the restraints of the Bill of Rights.[155] Though the Court never embraced Black's theory of "total incorporation," the process of selective incorporation proceeded at such a dizzying pace under the Chief Justiceship of Earl Warren that it would not be long before Black's vision would be very nearly realized. At the same time, expansive new readings of the incorporated First Amendment placed new limits on the role that religion could play in public schools,[156] the power of state and local officials to curb speech to which they

---

[142] See, e.g., Akhil Amar, *The Bill of Rights: Creation and Reconstruction* (New Haven, CT: Yale University Press, 1998); Richard L. Aynes, "On Misreading John Bingham and the Fourteenth Amendment," 103 *Yale L. J.* 57 (1993); Michael Kent Curtis, *No State Shall Abridge: The Fourteenth Amendment and the Bill of Rights* (Durham, NC: Duke University Press, 1986).

[143] The leading defense of this view was Charles Fairman, "Does the Fourteenth Amendment Incorporate the Bill of Rights? The Original Understanding," 2 *Stan. L. Rev.* 5 (1949).

[144] 83 U.S. 36 (1873).   [145] See infra notes 151–54.

[146] Snyder v. Massachusetts, 291 U.S. 97, 105 (1934).

[147] Gitlow v. New York, 268 U.S. 652 (1925).   [148] Near v. Minnesota, 283 U.S. 697 (1931).

[149] DeJonge v. Oregon, 299 U.S. 353 (1937).

[150] Cantwell v. Connecticut, 310 U.S. 296 (1940).

[151] Hurtado v. California, 110 U.S. 516 (1884).

[152] Pearson v. Yewdall, 95 U.S. 294 (1877); Minneapolis & St. Louis. R. Co. v. Bombolis, 241 U.S. 211 (1916); Maxwell v. Dow, 176 U.S. 581 (1900); Snyder v. Massachusetts, 291 U.S. 97 (1934).

[153] Twining v. New Jersey, 211 U.S. 78 (1908).

[154] Palko v. Connecticut, 302 U.S. 319 (1937).

[155] See, e.g., Adamson v. California, 332 U.S. 46, 68 (1947) (Black, J., dissenting).

[156] See, e.g., Abingdon School District v. Schempp, 374 U.S. 203 (1963); Engel v. Vitale, 370 U.S. 421 (1962).

objected,[157] and the authority of courts to sanction defamatory publications.[158] Similarly momentous were novel and sometimes elaborate constructions of the Fourth, Fifth, Sixth, and Eighth Amendments, which curtailed the power and discretion of state and local officials with a judicially crafted, uniform, national code of criminal procedure.[159]

A revolution in the Court's interpretation of the Equal Protection Clause similarly curtailed long-standing state and local powers to formulate and implement social policy. In case after case, the Court announced that racial segregation in public universities, public primary and secondary schools, public transportation, and such public facilities as parks, swimming pools, and golf courses was inconsistent with the guaranties of the Fourteenth Amendment. The Court's landmark decision in *Brown* v. *Board of Education*[160] did not produce significant racial integration in southern public schools, however. Instead, orders to desegregate were met with "massive resistance" in the South, and tangible integration began to materialize in the mid-1960s only as a result of conditioning eligibility for federal educational grants-in-aid on local compliance with federally established desegregation standards. Soon lingering prohibitions on interracial marriage were invalidated in the aptly titled case of *Loving* v. *Virginia*.[161] In addition, *Baker* v. *Carr*[162] and *Reynolds* v. *Sims*[163] saw the Court entering the "political thicket" and requiring that state legislative districts be apportioned so as to conform to the standard of "one person, one vote."

Soon this luxuriation of equal protection jurisprudence spread to new domains, as the Court invalidated a variety of state and local measures disadvantaging women, aliens, nonmarital children, hippies, those with mental disabilities, and, eventually, sexual minorities. In tandem with the near-total incorporation of the Bill of Rights, this expanded domain of equal protection produced a wave of structural reform litigation that placed a large number of state or local schools, prisons, jails, mental health facilities, housing authorities, and public employers under the ongoing supervision and control of federal courts. Innovative and often controversial interpretations of the Fourteenth Amendment's Due Process Clause similarly expanded the domain of federal rights at the expense of local regulatory power. Decisions from the 1920s had recognized the rights of parents to direct the educations of their children,[164] but in the decades following 1965 the justices further extended rights to be free from traditional state and local regulations in

---

[157] See, e.g., Cohen v. California, 403 U.S. 15 (1971); Brandenberg v. Ohio, 395 U.S. 444 (1969); Tinker v. Des Moines Independent Community School District, 393 U.S. 503 (1969).

[158] New York Times v. Sullivan, 376 U.S. 254 (1964).

[159] See, e.g., Furman v. Georgia, 408 U.S. 238 (1972); Miranda v. Arizona, 348 U.S. 436 (1966); Escobedo v. Illinois, 378 U.S. 478 (1964); Henry J. Friendly, "The Bill of Rights as a Code of Criminal Procedure," 53 *Cal. L. Rev.* 929 (1965).

[160] 347 U.S. 483 (1954).   [161] 388 U.S. 1 (1967).   [162] 369 U.S. 186 (1962).

[163] 377 U.S. 533 (1964).

[164] Pierce v. Society of Sisters, 268 U.S. 510 (1925); Meyer v. Nebraska, 262 U.S. 390 (1923).

such matters as the distribution of contraceptives, the provision of abortion, sexual conduct, and marriage.[165]

By the mid-1970s, the judicial "consensus" surrounding the claim that the national political process was adequate to safeguard the values of federalism had begun to unravel. In *National League of Cities* v. *Usery*,[166] a Court transformed by four Nixon appointments held that the Commerce Clause did not empower Congress to prescribe minimum wages and maximum hours for state and local government employees engaged in "traditional governmental functions" such as fire prevention, police protection, sanitation, public health, and parks and recreation. A change of mind on the part of one justice resulted in the overruling of that decision nine years later in *Garcia* v. *San Antonio Metropolitan Transit Authority*,[167] and it seemed that the political process approach had been restored to its former primacy. But soon the Court began to qualify its position by holding that federal statutes did not reach traditional governmental functions of states and localities unless they contained a "clear statement" of intent to do so.[168] At the same time, the justices became less inclined to find that Congress had preempted state or local regulation by "occupying the field," instead requiring a showing that the challenged state or local law was expressly preempted by the language of the federal statute or "conflicted" with provisions of the federal program. And though the Supremacy Clause required state judges to apply and enforce relevant federal law, the Court held in *New York* v. *United States*[169] and *Printz* v. *United States*,[170] respectively, that Congress could not command state legislatures to enact nor state and local executive officials to enforce federal regulatory programs.

Meanwhile, in *Seminole Tribe of Florida* v. *Florida*,[171] the Court overruled the recent decision of *Pennsylvania* v. *Union Gas Co.*[172] and held that Congress could not exercise the commerce power so as to abrogate state sovereign immunity in suits brought in federal court. Three years later *Alden* v. *Maine*[173] extended this principle both to all of Congress's Article I powers and to suits brought in state courts. Suits against state officers remained available, however, and Congress continued to be free to abrogate state sovereign immunity when it was exercising its powers to enforce the guaranties of the Fourteenth or Fifteenth Amendments. Yet in a series of decisions beginning with *City of Boerne* v. *Flores*,[174] the justices began to construe those powers more narrowly than had such earlier decisions as *Katzenbach* v. *Morgan*.[175] In holding that the Religious

---

[165] Griswold v. Connecticut, 381 U.S. 479 (1965); Roe v. Wade, 410 U.S. 113 (1973); Lawrence v. Texas, 539 U.S. 558 (2003); Obergefell v. Hodges, 135 S. Ct. 2584 (2015).
[166] 426 U.S. 833 (1976).   [167] 469 U.S. 529 (1985).
[168] Gregory v. Ashcroft, 501 U.S. 452 (1991).   [169] 505 U.S. 144 (1992).
[170] 521 U.S. 898 (1997).   [171] 517 U.S. 44 (1996).   [172] 491 U.S. 1 (1989).
[173] 527 U.S. 706 (1999).   [174] 521 U.S. 507 (1997).   [175] 384 U.S. 641 (1966).

Freedom Restoration Act of 1993 could not be enforced against state and local governments, the Court declared that Congress did not possess "the power to decree the substance of the Fourteenth Amendment's restrictions on the states." That was a matter for judicial determination, and congressional exercises of the enforcement powers were required to bear a "congruence and proportionality" between the constitutional "injury to be prevented or remedied and the means adopted to that end."[176] The interaction of reduced congressional latitude to enforce the Fourteenth Amendment with the Court's sovereign immunity jurisprudence produced a patchwork of cases holding that states were not amenable to suit under the Age Discrimination in Employment Act,[177] that they were so amenable under the Family and Medical Leave Act,[178] and that they could be sued under some provisions of the Americans with Disabilities Act[179] but not under others.[180]

The high-water mark in the revival of judicially imposed limits on congressional power came in *United States* v. *Lopez*[181] and *United States* v. *Morrison*.[182] *Lopez* struck down a federal statute that proscribed possession of a firearm within 1,000 feet of a school on the ground that the activity regulated was not "economic" but instead pertained to crime and education, two traditional areas of state and local concern. *Morrison* followed *Lopez* in striking down a provision of the Violence against Women Act of 1994 that created a federal civil remedy for gender-based violence. In each case the Court held that the effect of the regulated activity on interstate commerce was too attenuated to be "substantial," and that because the activities in question were not economic in nature, *Wickard*'s principle of aggregation did not apply. The *Morrison* Court further relied upon the state action doctrine in holding that the provision lay beyond Congress's power to enforce the guaranties of the Equal Protection Clause.

It soon became clear, however, how limited the effects of the Court's new federalism jurisprudence would be. In the immediate wake of *Lopez*, Congress enacted a revised statute prohibiting possession within 1,000 feet of a school of any firearm "that has moved in or that otherwise affects interstate or foreign commerce." Armed with this new jurisdictional hook, the statute was uniformly upheld in the lower federal courts. The decision in *Morrison*, though certainly more consequential, left standing the legions of other provisions comprising the act's massive federal initiative to protect women across the country from violent abuse. In *Gonzales* v. *Raich*,[183] the Court upheld congressional prohibition of the production and use of homegrown marijuana for medicinal purposes even where such conduct had been authorized by the state legislature. And in

---

[176] 521 U.S. at 520.   [177] Kimel v. Florida Board of Regents, 528 U.S. 62 (2000).
[178] Nevada Dept. of Human Resources v. Hibbs, 538 U.S. 721 (2003).
[179] United States v. Georgia, 546 U.S. 151 (2006); Tennessee v. Lane, 541 U.S. 509 (2004).
[180] Board of Trustees v. Garrett, 531 U.S. 356 (2001).   [181] 514 U.S. 549 (1995).
[182] 529 U.S. 598 (2000).   [183] 545 U.S. 1 (2005).

National Federation of Independent Businesses v. *Sebelius*,[184] the justices held that though the commerce power could not underwrite a federal exaction imposed on persons who failed to acquire health insurance, the taxing power was adequate to the task.

Behind all of these developments lurked the capacious power of Congress to subsidize and regulate local activity through its spending power, even where such regulation lay beyond the reach of its other enumerated powers. Just as the federal government had desegregated southern public schools through the use of the power of the purse, so it continued to induce the states to enact other desired regulations by conditioning receipt of federal funds on compliance with federal directives. The scope of the conditional spending power was resoundingly affirmed in *South Dakota* v. *Dole*,[185] where the Court upheld a regulation conditioning state eligibility for certain federal highway funds on the states raising the drinking age to twenty-one. And even where Congress transgressed limitations on the use of the conditional spending power, it remained free to provide direct subsidies. Thus, even though *Sebelius* struck down as unconstitutionally coercive the Affordable Care Act's provision requiring the states to expand eligibility for Medicaid or forfeit all of their federal Medicaid funding, federal authorities nevertheless provided funding necessary to subsidize the expansion in the many states that elected to do so, and no constitutional obstacle prevented a direct federal appropriation subsidizing health insurance for persons living in states that elected against expansion. Meanwhile, many other vast programs of congressional regulation through conditional spending continued, unimpeded by judicial let or hindrance, even as the justices repeatedly approved uses of the necessary and proper power in conjunction with both the spending power and other enumerated powers. In nearly all cases, it seemed, one or more of Congress's enumerated powers would suffice to achieve the desired objective. Notwithstanding some comparatively modest judicial tinkering at the margins, it remained the case that effective restraints on the exercise of congressional power "must," as Justice Jackson wrote in *Wickard*, "proceed from political rather than from judicial processes."[186]

---

[184] 132 S. Ct. 2566 (2012).   [185] 483 U.S. 203 (1987).   [186] 317 U.S. at 120.

8

Separation of Powers

Mark A. Graber

American constitutional politics – the processes by which constitutional norms, texts, and processes constrain, construct, and constitute politics[1] – is increasingly dysfunctional. Some commentators insist that an eighteenth-century constitution neither entrenches acceptable principles nor delineates adequate processes for governing a twenty-first century polity.[2] Those who take that position, however, fail to explain why an eighteenth-century constitution managed to govern a mid-twentieth-century polity.[3] Constitutional senility apparently sets in only at 200 years. The better view is that a centuries-old struggle that began during the English Civil War has mutated in ways that prevent Americans from operating the constitutional separation of powers within contemporary two-party politics.

King Charles I is a great-grandfather of the Constitution of the United States. Responding to the Nineteen Propositions, Charles I in 1642 provided what became the foundations for the Federalist conception of the separation of powers. His defense of regal authority insisted that each branch of government play a distinct and independent role. "In this Kingdom," Charles stated,

> the Laws are jointly made by a King, by a House of Peers, and by a House of Commons chosen by the People, all having free Votes and particular Privileges. The Government according to these Laws, is trusted to the King ..., the House of Commons ... is solely entrusted with the first Propositions concerning the Levies of Monies ..., [a]nd the Lords (are) trusted with a Judicatory Power.[4]

---

[1] See Mark A. Graber, *A New Introduction to American Constitutionalism* (New York: Oxford University Press, 2013).

[2] See, e.g., Sanford Levinson, *Our Undemocratic Constitution: Where the Constitution Goes Wrong (And How We the People Can Correct It)* (New York: Oxford University Press, 2006); Robert A. Dahl, *How Democratic Is the American Constitution* (2nd ed.) (New Haven: Yale University Press, 2003).

[3] See Mark A. Graber, "Belling the Partisan Cats: Preliminary Thoughts on Identifying and Mending a Dysfunctional Constitutional Order," 94 *Boston University Law Review* 611, 628–39 (2014).

[4] "His Majesty's Answer to the Nineteen Propositions of both Houses of Parliament, tending towards a Peace, June 18, 1642," *The Complete American Constitutionalism*

Chief Justice Warren Burger in 1983 echoed Charles I's sentiments when he stated, "Explicit and unambiguous provisions of the Constitution prescribe and define the respective functions of the Congress and of the Executive in the legislative process."[5]

John Pym and the parliamentarians who challenged royal authority are also great-grandfathers of the Constitution of the United States. Pym insisted that governing institutions work in unison. The king (and the courts), in his judgment, was responsible for implementing the policies made by Parliament and did not act independently in any matter affecting the realm. The Nineteen Propositions insisted that parliamentary consent is necessary for all royal policies, all royal appointments, and even all royal weddings. "That no Marriage shall be concluded, or treated for any of the King's Children," one proposition stated, "without the Consent of Parliament." The next proposition denies independent royal authority to determine how parliamentary edicts will be implemented. "That the laws in force against Jesuits, Priests and Popish Recusants," Pym wrote, "be strictly put in Execution, without any Toleration or Dispensation to the contrary."[6] Nearly 300 years later, Franklin Roosevelt articulated a similar demand that government institutions function harmoniously when he criticized the Supreme Court for not working with the president and Congress to secure shared goals.

Last Thursday I described the American form of government as a three-horse team provided by the Constitution to the American people so that their field might be plowed ... Two of the horses, the Congress and the executive, are pulling in unison today ... It is the American people themselves who expect the third horse (the courts) to fall in unison with the other two.[7]

Warren Burger, Franklin Roosevelt, and other Americans have replayed the conflict between Charles I and John Pym for more than 200 years. The venerated and venerable Constitution of the United States divides government into legislative, executive, and judicial branches, but the text does not explain the purpose of that division or of the framing decision to divide the national legislature into the House of Representatives and the Senate. Charles I's constitutional descendants maintain that the constitutionally mandated separation of powers makes the Constitution work though a system of checks and balances that prevents constitutional violations and promotes more deliberate policy. The legislative, executive, and judicial branches of government are analogous to independent buyers and sellers in an unregulated marketplace. Contests for power or goods between these rivals

(Vol. I) (edited by Mark A. Graber and Howard Gillman) (New York: Oxford University Press, 2014), p. 278.
5 Immigration and Naturalization Service v. Chadha, 462 U.S. 919, 945 (1983).
6 "The Humble Petition and Advice of both Houses of Parliament, with Nineteenth Propositions sent unto his Majesty, June 2, 1642," *The Complete American Constitutionalism*, p. 277.
7 Franklin D. Roosevelt, "Fireside Chat on Court-Packing Plan," *American Constitutionalism* (Vol. I) (edited by Howard Gillman, Mark A. Graber and Keith E. Whittington) (New York: Oxford University Press, 2013), p. 502.

are expected to produce constitutional policy or efficient prices, respectively; *Federalist* 47 proclaims, "The accumulation of all powers, legislative, executive, and judiciary, in the same hands, whether of one, a few, or many, and whether hereditary, self-appointed, or elective, may justly be pronounced the very definition of tyranny."[8] John Pym's constitutional descendants maintain that the constitutionally mandated separation of powers makes the Constitution work by promoting a functional division of labor that enables the party of the people who are loyal to the Constitution to make their constitutional vision the official law of the land. The legislative, executive, and judicial branches of government are analogous to the brass, woodwind, and string sections of an orchestra (or different positions on a sports team). Each branch or section has a different part to play in achieving a shared constitutional vision or performing a common musical score. Justice Robert Jackson observed that the Constitution "contemplates that practice will integrate the dispersed powers into a workable government. It enjoins upon its branches separateness but interdependence, autonomy but reciprocity."[9]

American constitutional politics is nevertheless something other than an ongoing struggle between the heirs of Charles I and Parliament or even a cycle in which Charles I and John Pym's visions alternate as the dominant constitutional ethos. Official constitutional practice evolves in light of changes in the political system that influence how more formal and more functional understandings of the separation of powers develop as well as how they exist and operate in any particular political era. Constitutional practice in the late eighteenth and early nineteenth century was structured by the classical conception of the separation of powers, in which a sharp division of powers between the elected branches of government and departmentalism[10] was thought the best means for preserving the Constitution and constitutional democracy. Americans from the Jacksonian Era to the end of the nineteenth century experienced a partisan conception of the separation of powers in which separate branches of government were conceptualized as a division of labor among members of the dominant party of the people loyal to the Constitution whose maintenance in power was necessary for preserving the Constitution and constitutional democracy. Americans from the end of the nineteenth century until the last quarter of the twentieth century lived when courts (and later administrative agencies) were largely responsible for making the basic rules, leaving presidents free to conduct foreign policy and the legislative and executive branches to negotiate over domestic policy and patronage. Conventional wisdom maintained that the Constitution and constitutional democracy were best preserved by an independent judiciary empowered to resolve all disputes over the scope of national power and over the interpretation of constitutional rights. Americans presently live in a

---

[8] Alexander Hamilton, James Madison, and John Jay, *The Federalist Papers* (New York: New American Library, 1961), p. 301.

[9] Youngstown Sheet & Tube Co. v. Sawyer, 343 U.S. 579, 635 (1952) (Jackson, J. concurring).

[10] For a brief introduction to departmentalism, see Graber, *A New Introduction*, pp. 113–18.

polarized regime in which each party claims to be the party of the people loyal to the Constitution, aggrandizes the power of the national institutions they control, weakens the powers of those institutions controlled by the rival coalition, and engages in near-death struggles over control of the national judiciary. The Constitution and constitutional democracy are best preserved, conservatives and liberals have concluded, when the branch of government controlled by one's partisans makes crucial governing decisions and the true party of the people loyal to the Constitution gains secure control over the federal judiciary.

Americans have not experienced a political regime in which the separation of powers was conceptualized primarily in terms of representation for the different interests in society or what Aristotle called the one, the few, and the many.[11] John Adams aside,[12] this political arrangement plays surprisingly little role in American constitutional development. Neither Charles I nor Parliament when debating the Nineteen Propositions conceptualized the different governmental institutions of England as representing distinctive interests, even though that was their classical justification. Their debate was over the extent to which the different government institutions should be coordinated or independent. Although some Americans at the founding thought that the upper house of the state legislature should represent property and that the Senate of the United States should represent states, over time the distinctive representational functions of the different houses of state legislatures diminished to the point of vanishing and on matters of state sovereignty the Senate has not been essentially different than the House.[13]

The far more common notion throughout American history is that all branches of government represent different aspects of all Americans rather than represent different groups of Americans. James Wilson declared, "The executive and judicial powers are now drawn from the same source, are now animated by the same principles, and are now directed to the same ends, with the legislative authority: they who execute, and they who administer the laws, are so much the servants, and therefore as much the friends of the people, as those who make them."[14] The most salient and ongoing controversies over the separation of powers in the United States are about whether different government institutions playing different functions ought to be coordinated, a functional conception to the separation of powers, or should be independent, a formal approach to the separation of powers, rather than over which branch of government represents what people or which interests.

[11] Aristotle, *The Politics* (revised ed.) (translated by T. A. Sinclair) (revised by Trevor Saunders) (New York: Penguin Books, 1981), pp. 262–73.
[12] See Gordon Wood, *The Creation of the American Republic, 1776–1787* (Chapel Hill: University of North Carolina Press, 1969), pp. 574–80.
[13] See Elaine K. Swift, *The Making of an American Senate: Reconstitutive Change in Congress* (Ann Arbor: University of Michigan Press, 1996).
[14] James Wilson, *The Works of the Honourable James Wilson, L.L.D.* (Vol. I) (edited by Bird Wilson) (Philadelphia, PA: Lorenzo Press, 1804), p. 399.

The American constitutional experience with the separation of powers is a story about courts and political parties as well as the relationships between the legislative and the executive branches of government. Conceptions of the proper role of the legislative and executive branches of the national government throughout American history are intertwined with conceptions of the proper role of the federal judiciary. Jeffersonian departmentalists relied on the same separation of powers logic when justifying presidents challenging constitutional interpretations by the judiciary and members of congress challenging constitutional interpretations by the president. The *Carolene Products* footnote[15] assigned economic policy to the elected branches of the national government and civil rights to federal courts. The structure of partisan competition at a given time is similarly intertwined with the dominant conceptions of the relationships between national institutions. The framers designed the constitutional separation of powers to prevent the rise of political parties they thought inimical to constitutional democracy. Democrats and Republicans formed strong political parties during the mid-nineteenth century to concentrate power and largely obliterate the ways in which the classical separation of powers, in their judgment, enabled aristocratic elites to distort the Constitution. Presidential and judicial power increased during the late nineteenth century as parties weakened. Contemporary conflict over the separation of powers is largely a conflict between two parties, each of which controls some branches of the national government and not others.

The separation of powers throughout American history has functioned in four different ways to structure the American constitutional experience, even though Americans have developed only three coherent conceptions of how the Constitution should work to preserve constitutional boundaries and realize constitutional commitments. From 1787 to 1970, a rough congruence existed between how the constitutional separation of powers actually worked and the dominant theory of how the separation of powers should work. The Constitution might construct a constitutional politics that accepted constitutional limits on national power and protected constitutional rights if, as the framing generation thought, different governing branches checked each other; if, as mid-nineteenth-century partisans preferred, the party of the people loyal to the Constitution controlled all governing institutions; or if, as the governing consensus during most of the twentieth century maintained, an independent judiciary aggressively policed the constitutional borders.

No rough fit exists between constitutional practice and constitutional theory in the twenty-first century. Instead, liberal Democrats and conservative Republicans articulate incoherent amalgamations of previous constitutional norms. Political activists on both the left and right seem committed to the proposition that "[t]he Constitution will work if the true party of the people loyal to the Constitution controls all three branches of the national government, but in the meantime as much power as possible must be syphoned to whatever

---

[15] United States v. Carolene Products Co., 304 U.S. 144, 152–53 n.4 (1938).

governing institutions that coalition presently controls" and the proposition that "[t]he Constitution works when an independent judiciary aggressively polices constitutional borders, provided the true party of the Constitution controls the judiciary." The result is too often incoherence, when different institutions controlled by different parties make inconsistent policy decisions; gridlock, when different institutions controlled by different parties are successfully only when they block rival institutions from acting; and bitter struggles over control of the judiciary. Whether Americans trapped in this regime can escape to some version of the first three constitutional orders or find a conception of the separation of powers that enables a polarized polity to make the Constitution work is the challenge for the future.

IN THE BEGINNING

In the beginning, there was the English Civil War and the Glorious Revolution. The central debates that framed the American Revolution, state constitution making, and the Constitution of the United States concerned the proper interpretation and lessons to be learned from the English constitutional experience during the seventeenth century. The most famous debate was over the meaning of taxation without representation.[16] English authorities interpreted that battle cry of the English Civil War as a demand that executives not raise revenues without legislative permission. Americans interpreted that battle cry as a demand that people be taxed only by legislatures in which they were actually represented. American revolutionaries nevertheless disagreed among themselves about the more general principle underlying the constitutional commitment to having the power of the purse vested in the national legislature. Thomas Paine and more democratic revolutionaries believed that the seventeenth-century English revolutionaries had stood for the supremacy of the legislature, a principle being corrupted in eighteenth-century Great Britain. James Madison and more conservative revolutionaries believed that the English revolutionaries had merely wanted to rebalance the powers of the executive and legislature, a constitutional commitment being corrupted in eighteenth-century England. These two different interpretations of the causes of the American Revolution help explain the controversies over American constitutionalism that broke out as Americans were declaring independence from Great Britain. More democratic American revolutionaries favored constitutional arrangements in which all other branches of government were servants of a single legislative body. More conservative revolutionaries favored arrangements in which the executive and judicial branch of the government exercised independent authority. The latter

---

[16] See Mark A. Graber and Howard Gillman, eds., *The Complete American Constitutionalism* (Vol. I) (New York: Oxford University Press, 2014), pp. 179–81.

forces emerged victorious, both in state constitutional debate and during the framing and ratification of the Constitution of the United States.

American revolutionaries also offered two distinctive explanations for the English government's repeated violations of colonial rights during the crisis of the 1760s and early 1770s.[17] Those who took the perspective of John Pym claimed that the monarch had corrupted Parliament through the use of patronage. They complained of royal ministers whose "power and interest is so great that they can, and do procure whatever laws they please, having (by power, Interest, and the application of the people's money, to placement, and pensioners) the whole legislative authority at their command."[18] The proper remedy for this ill was the near elimination of independent executive authority. Those who took the perspective of Charles I claimed that an enfeebled monarch was unable to veto unconstitutional parliamentary legislation. James Wilson insisted, "The people of America did not oppose the British King but the parliament – the opposition was not against an Unity but a corrupt multitude."[19] The proper remedy for this ill was to reconstruct the monarchical prerogative along republican lines.

Thomas Paine was the leading champion of the parliamentary conception of the separation of powers. Although *Common Sense* is mostly remembered for the attack on monarchy, the essay was deeply suspicious of executive power no matter how popular the credentials of the executive wielding authority.[20] In *Common Sense* and other works written in 1776, Paine championed government by a single legislature that had the authority to appoint and recall all other governing officials. "The forms of government are numerous, and perhaps the simplest is the best," Paine wrote in *Four Letters on Interesting Subjects*. "The notion of checking by having different houses, has but little weight in it, when inquired into, and in all cases it tends to embarrass and prolong business."[21] Paine's vision was embodied in the Constitution of Pennsylvania and the Constitution of Vermont, which largely imitated Pennsylvania.[22] Both constitutions vested all power in the General Assembly. Members of the General Assembly selected a governor who could not corrupt the general assembly by patronage, because the governor had no appointment

---

[17] This paragraph relies heavily on Eric Nelson, *The Royalist Revolution: Monarchy and the American Founding* (Cambridge, MA: Harvard University Press, 2014), especially, pp. 148–49, 189–91.

[18] Nelson, *The Royalist Revolution*, p. 22.

[19] Nelson, *The Royalist Revolution*, p. 1 (quoting James Wilson).

[20] Thomas Paine, *The Political Works of Thomas Paine* (London: Holyoake and Co., 1857), p. 24.

[21] Thomas Paine, "Four Letters on Interesting Subjects," *Classic of American Political and Constitutional Thought* (Vol. I) (edited by Scott J. Hammond, Kevin R. Hardwick, and Howard L. Lubert) (Indianapolis: Hackett Publishing Company, Inc., 2007), p. 297.

[22] See Robert F. Williams, "The State Constitutions of the Founding Decade: Pennsylvania's Radical 1776 Constitution and Its Influences on American Constitutionalism," 62 *Temple Law Review* 541, 551–55, 570 (1989).

power, or by threats of a veto, because the governor had no power to veto legislation.[23]

More conservative Americans abhorred the Pennsylvania constitution. Benjamin Rush claimed that Pennsylvanians had established a "mobocracy."[24] Their gripe with George III was not that he was the true author of British policy toward the colonies but that he had passively allowed parliament to dictate an unconstitutional policy.[25] Conservatives wanted the traditional balanced constitution restored in the more modern sense of all power being checked rather than the classic conception of different social orders being represented in different institutions. Thomas Jefferson famously declared, "[A]n elective despotism was not the government we fought for."[26] The Massachusetts Constitution of 1780 was the first clear triumph for this conservative understanding of the separation of powers. That constitution required that the governor be elected separately from the legislature, gave the governor substantial appointment powers, and vested the governor with the authority to veto legislation.[27] A decade later, Massachusetts had become the model for all state constitutions including Pennsylvania, which in 1790 adopted a new constitution with a strong executive.[28]

These differences over executive authority were rooted as much in substantial policy commitments as in abstract notions of good government or theories about the failure of policymaking in Great Britain. Proponents of simple government in the states were proponents of confiscating loyalist property, printing paper money, and debtor relief legislation. Proponents of a sharper separation of powers opposed such measures.[29] While some conservative opponents of confiscation, paper money, and debtor relief legislation turned to courts, most maintained that the most effective barrier to unconstitutional interferences with property rights was an independent executive with veto powers. The citizens of

---

[23] See "Constitution of Pennsylvania," *The Federal and State Constitutions, Colonial Charters, and Other Organic Laws* (Vol. V) (edited by Francis Newton Thorpe (Washington, DC: Government Printing Office, 1909), pp. 3081–92; "Constitution of Vermont – 1777," *The Federal and State Constitutions, Colonial Charters, and Other Organic Laws* (Vol. VI) (edited by Francis Newton Thorpe (Washington, DC: Government Printing Office, 1909), pp. 3737–49.

[24] Williams, "Pennsylvania's Radical Constitution," p. 559 (quoting Benjamin Rush to John Adams, January 22, 1789).

[25] See Nelson, *The Royalist Revolution*, p. 4.

[26] Thomas Jefferson, *The Writings of Thomas Jefferson* (Vol. II) (edited by Andrew A. Lipscomb) (Washington, DC: The Thomas Jefferson Memorial Society, 1904), p. 163.

[27] See "Constitution or Form of Government for the Commonwealth of Massachusetts – 1780," *The Federal and State Constitutions, Colonial Charters, and Other Organic Laws* (Vol. V) (edited by Francis Newton Thorpe) (Washington, DC: Government Printing Office, 1909), pp. 1888–1911.

[28] See "Constitution of Pennsylvania," *The Federal and State Constitutions, Colonial Charters, and Other Organic Laws* (Vol. V) (edited by Francis Newton Thorpe) (Washington, DC: Government Printing Office, 1909), pp. 3092–3103.

[29] See generally Merrill Jensen, *The New Nation: A History of the United States during the Confederation, 1781–1789* (New York: Random House Inc., 1966).

Essex rejected the first proposed constitution of Massachusetts because they were unable to "discover ... in any part of the constitution that the executive power is entrusted with a check upon the legislative power."[30] "The danger," if any, they feared, was that a governor "would be too cautious of using his negative for the interest of the state."[31] The state judiciary played little role in their conception of constitutional authority.

Constitutional politics during the late 1770s centered on the government institutions most likely to protect fundamental rights. While no parties existed on a national level in this period, proto-parties organized in many states as political actors with similar purposes began to act in concert. Politics in Pennsylvania was structured by conflicts between the Constitutionalists, who favored the legislative supremacy mandated by the 1777 state constitution, and Republicans, who opposed that constitution as insufficiently attentive to the need for a strong separation of powers.[32] Similar patterns, if less stark, appear in other new states, if not necessarily in the Continental Congress.[33] Americans linked attitudes toward popular parties and attitudes toward the separation of powers. Constitutionalists in Pennsylvania celebrated state constitutional arrangements for enabling ordinary people to prevent the constitution from being corrupted by undemocratic elites. Conservatives demanded a more complex government with a strong separation of powers that would prevent well-organized popular majorities from violating constitutional rights.

The Constitution of the United States was a clear victory for proponents of a sharp separation of powers. Federalists at the drafting convention successfully pointed to the legislative supremacy mandated by the Constitution of Pennsylvania as the paradigm of a constitutional design that fostered usurpations of power.[34] The Constitution they drafted resembled the Constitution of Massachusetts in that the president is elected separately from the legislature, the president has considerable appointment powers, and the president has the power to veto legislation. Conservatives did not fully triumph. The Senate must confirm presidential appointees, and a two-thirds majority of both houses of Congress may overturn a presidential veto. Still, the president of the United States was far more powerful than any existing state governor and, while in office, wielded more power than George III did in 1789. Mercy Warren was one of many

---

[30] Theophilus Parsons, *Memoir of Theophilus Parsons* (Boston: Ticknor and Fields, 1859), p. 387.

[31] Parsons, *Memoir*, p. 398.

[32] See Robert L. Brunhouse, *The Counter-Revolution in Pennsylvania 1776–1790* (Harrisburg, PA: Pennsylvania Historical Commission, 1942).

[33] See Edward Countryman, *A People in Revolution: The American Revolution and Political Society in New York, 1760–1790* (Baltimore: Johns Hopkins University Press, 1981); Jensen, *The New Nation*. Jensen's thesis has been contested with respect to national politics but not with respect to state politics.

[34] See Williams, "Pennsylvania's Radical Constitution," pp. 575–78.

Anti-Federalists who complained about a "Republican form of government, founded on the principles of monarchy."[35]

The Constitution was also a victory for conservatives who feared the proto-party politics that had developed in Pennsylvania and in other localities. They self-consciously crafted what Richard Hofstadter later described as "a Constitution against parties."[36] Madison in *Federalist* 10 celebrated the Constitution for constructing a politics that obstructed what he perceived were overly partisan struggles for power taking place in the states. "Extend the sphere," he asserted,

[a]nd you take in a greater variety of parties and interests; you make it less probable that a majority of the whole will have a common motive to invade the rights of other citizens; or if such a common motive exists, it will be more difficult for all who feel it to discover their own strength and act in unison with each other.[37]

The separation of powers contributed to the anti-partisan politics envisioned by the framers. By dividing government power, Madison declared, "the society itself will be broken up into so many parts ... that the rights of individuals, or of the minority, will be in little danger from interested combinations of the majority," such as he and other Federalists believed had formed in Pennsylvania.[38]

Other essays in *The Federalist Papers* highlight how the Stuart conception of the separation of powers influenced the American constitutional order. *Federalist* 51 emphasizes how the different branches of government will check one another and are not merely divided by function. "Ambition must be made to counteract ambition," Madison declared.[39] Hamilton's papers on the executive branch are even more royalist. The New York Federalist insisted upon an energetic executive[40] with strong veto powers necessary to prevent the more popular branches of the national government from violating fundamental rights. *Federalist* 73 states,

The propensity of the legislative department to intrude upon the rights, and to absorb the powers, of the other departments has been already more than once suggested. The insufficiency of a mere parchment delineation of the boundaries of each has also been remarked upon; and the necessity of furnishing each with constitutional arms for its own defense has been inferred and proved. From these clear and indubitable principles results the propriety of a negative, either absolute or qualified, in the executive upon the acts of the legislative branches.[41]

[35] Mercy Warren ("A Columbia Patriot"), "Observations on the New Constitution, and on the Federal and State Conventions," *The Complete Anti-Federalist* (edited by Herbert Storing) (Chicago: University of Chicago Press, 1981), p. 275.
[36] Richard Hofstadter, *The Idea of a Party System: The Rise of Legitimate Opposition in the United States, 1780 to 1849* (Berkeley: University of California Press: Berkeley, 1969), p. 40.
[37] The Federalist Papers, p. 83.   [38] *The Federalist Papers*, p. 324.
[39] The Federalist Papers, p. 322.
[40] See *The Federalist Papers*, p. 424 ("energy" is "the most necessary qualification" of the executive).
[41] *The Federalist Papers*, p. 442.

The presidency in *The Federalist Papers* is the main check on unconstitutional legislation, not the Supreme Court. Hamilton maintained that the Supreme Court will be an effective check on the national government only when supported by the president. The judiciary, he wrote, "must ultimately depend upon the aid of the executive arm even for the efficacy of its judgments."[42]

Thomas Jefferson and James Madison's departmentalism was grounded in their underlying commitment to the separation of powers as a vital means for preserving constitutional arrangements. Jefferson claimed a presidential power to interpret the Constitution independently from the federal judiciary. When explaining to Abigail Adams why he pardoned as unconstitutionally convicted persons the federal judiciary ruled had been constitutionally convicted, the third president asserted,

> You seem to think it devolved on the judges to decide on the validity of the sedition law. But nothing in the Constitution has given them a right to decide for the Executive, more than to the Executive to decide to them. The judges, believing the law constitutional, had a right to pass a sentence of fine and imprisonment; because the power was placed in their hands by the Constitution. But the Executive, believing the law to be unconstitutional, was bound to remit the execution of it, because that power has been confided to him by the Constitution. That instrument meant that its co-ordinate branches should be checks on each other.[43]

Madison when discussing the allocation of constitutional authority between the president and Congress during the debates over the Jay Treaty of 1795 championed the same departmentalist commitment to the power of all national institutions to interpret the Constitution independently. The constitutional issue being considered when Madison spoke was whether Congress could constitutionally request the president to turn over executive papers relevant to the negotiations between members of the Washington administration and Great Britain. President George Washington vigorously denied that legislative authority. He wrote, "To admit . . . a right in the House of Representatives to demand, and to have . . . all the papers respecting a negotiation with a foreign Power, would be to establish a dangerous precedent."[44] Madison in response recognized both a legislative right to ask for papers and an executive right to refuse compliance. He asserted, "The House must have a right . . . to ask for information which might assist their deliberations on the subjects submitted to them by the Constitution," but that "the Executive had a right, under due responsibility, also, to withhold information, when of a nature that did not permit a disclosure of it at the time."[45] Anticipating Jefferson's response to Abigail Adams, Madison concluded,

---

[42] *The Federalist Papers*, p. 465.
[43] Thomas Jefferson, *The Writings of Thomas Jefferson* (Vol. 10) (edited by Paul Leicester Ford) (New York: G.P. Putnam's Sons, 1899), p. 88.
[44] *Annals of Congress*, 4th Cong., 1st Sess., p. 760.
[45] *Annals of Congress*, 4th Cong., 1st Sess., p. 772.

[When] different branches of the Government should disagree in the construction of their powers ... each branch must judge for itself; and the judgment of the Executive in this case can be no more an authority for overruling the judgment of the House than the judgment of the House could be an authority for overruling that of the Executive.[46]

This shared commitment to a sharp separation of powers helps explain why politicians in the early republic regarded judicial supremacy on almost all constitutional disputes and executive supremacy on the remaining constitutional questions as the practical alternative to departmentalism. Such Federalists as John Marshall and Alexander Hamilton believed that the federal judiciary should have the final say on the proper interpretation of the Constitution.[47] Washington believed the president was the only official who could make constitutional judgments on whether executive documents were constitutionally privileged.[48] These Federalists and mainstream Jeffersonian Republicans agreed that the separation of powers was the vital means for independent branches of government to check each other. Federalists believed that the executive and judiciary branches could best prevent legislative usurpations when each was given absolute authority over certain constitutional questions (and the president given a qualified veto on other matters). Mainstream Jeffersonian Republicans believed the branches best checked each other when each had independent constitutional authority. Only a few radical Jeffersonians favored arrangements similar to those mandated by the 1777 Constitution of Pennsylvania in which the legislature had the final say on all questions of constitutional law (subject to the Council of Censors, elected every seven years). William Giles, possibly the most radical legislative supremacist at the turn of the nineteenth century, when claiming, "The theory of three distinct department in government is, perhaps, not critically correct," nevertheless confessed that "it is obvious that the framers of our Constitution proceeded upon this theory in its formation."[49]

PARTY TIME

During the nineteenth century, party replaced the separation of powers as the main vehicle for preserving constitutional commitments. Such party stalwarts as Martin Van Buren and Abraham Lincoln agreed that ordinary citizens could best prevent undemocratic elites from perverting the American constitutional order by joining a political party and accepting party discipline. Van Buren and his fellow Democrats organized to oppose what they perceived was an aristocratic money power. Lincoln and his fellow Republicans organized to oppose what they perceived was an aristocratic slave power. What united Jacksonian Democrats and antislavery Republicans was their shared belief that rights were best protected when the party of the people loyal to the

---

[46] *Annals of Congress*, 4th Cong., 1st Sess., p. 780.
[47] McCulloch v. Maryland, 17 U.S. 316, 401 (1819).   [48] See note 44 and the relevant text.
[49] *Annals of Congress*, 10th Cong., 1st Sess., p. 114.

Constitution controlled all branches of the national government. Although Andrew Jackson and others occasionally gave lip service to an inherited departmentalism, Jackson, Lincoln, and their supporters developed a theory of partisan supremacy in which constitutional authority was vested in whatever party gained control of the national government by winning national elections. The Republicans most responsible for the Fourteenth Amendment designed that text to enable the party of the majority of the people who remained loyal to the Union to retain the control over the national government necessary to ensure that Americans realized the broad constitutional commitments made by the Thirteenth Amendment.

The self-conscious partisan politicians of the Jacksonian era, the Civil War, and Reconstruction were the direct descendants of the parliamentarians who drafted the Nineteen Propositions and the democratic revolutionaries who framed the Pennsylvania Constitution. Pym, Paine, Van Buren, and Lincoln believed that concentrated, as opposed to divided, political power was the best means for preserving fundamental regime commitments. Van Buren and Lincoln, who could not write on a clean slate, claimed to venerate the Constitution of the United States, scorning those who called for novel constitutional reforms more consistent with generational priorities. Lincoln insisted, "Don't interfere with anything in the Constitution. That must be maintained, for it is the only safeguard of our liberties."[50] Nevertheless, Jacksonian Democrats and antislavery Republicans altered inherited regime understandings of the separation of powers and constitutional authority, even as they invoked the framers as authority for their actions. Rather than concentrate power in government, as Pym and Paine had done, they sought to concentrate power outside of government through the institution of a political party that would first gain election and then coordinate the actions of officeholders in different institutions. Contrary to the framers, Americans during the Jacksonian era, the Civil War, and Reconstruction believed, "Party is indispensable to every Administration – it is essential to the existence of our institutions."[51] Martin Van Buren maintained that an organized political party was the best, if not only, means for preserving the constitutional commitment to democracy. Gerald Leonard notes the Van Burenite commitment to the proposition that "[a]s long as elections were free and organized by constitutional parties, the democracy would forever be equipped to spy and defeat all attempts to re-create a society of anti-democratic dependency. And every election ... would yield an overwhelming Democratic majority."[52] Abraham Lincoln believed that an organized party was the best means for preserving the constitutional commitment to limiting and eventually abolishing slavery. Lincoln wrote,

---

[50] Abraham Lincoln, *The Collected Works of Abraham Lincoln* (Vol. II) (edited by Roy P. Basler).

[51] *Debates in Congress*, 19th Cong., 1st Sess., p. 1545 (speech of Representative Churchill Cambreleng of New York).

[52] Gerald Leonard, "Party as a 'Political Safeguard of Federalism': Martin Van Buren and the Constitutional Theory of Party Politics," 54 *Rutgers Law Review* 221, 249 (2001).

Upon those men who are, in sentiment, opposed to the spread, and nationalization of slavery, rests the task of preventing it. The Republican organization is the embodiment of that sentiment ... In spite of old differences, prejudices, and animosities, it's members were drawn together by a paramount common danger. They formed and maneuvered in the face of the disciplined enemy, and in the teeth of all his persistent misrepresentations. Of course, they fell far short of gathering in all of their own. And yet, a year ago, they stood up, an army over thirteen hundred thousand strong. That army is, to-day, the best hope of the nation, and of the world.[53]

Elections became the central means by which constitutional commitments were maintained. Political parties during the second third of the nineteenth century strove to make their constitutional vision the law of the land by gaining control over all branches of the national government, a control that reduced the tendency of any one branch to check the others. Democrats and Republicans recognized that different offices in government performed different functions. At times, they spoke the inherited language of departmentalism and separation of powers.[54] Nevertheless, the separation of powers was at most a temporary expedient for resolving matters until the true party of the people gained sufficient control of the national government. Persistent disagreements, partisan activists believed, should be settled by the victors in the next round of elections rather than by those officeholders whose ambitions Madison thought would counteract each other in ways that produced constitutional policies in the public interest. "If different interpretations are put upon the Constitution by the different departments, the people is the tribunal to settle the dispute," Van Buren declared. "Each of the departments is the agent of the people, doing their business according to the powers conferred; and where there is a disagreement as to the extent of these powers, the people themselves, through the ballot-boxes, must settle it."[55]

Andrew Jackson justified his unprecedented use of the veto power by pointing to the electoral process rather than to the original understanding that the executive veto was a check on majoritarian power in the legislature. Jackson insisted that he was "the direct representative of the American people,"[56] a participant in the partisan politics of the time, rather than a figure whose office required occupants to rise above the political fray. When vetoing the

---

[53] Abraham Lincoln, "Fragment on the Formation of the Republican Party," *The Collected Works of Abraham Lincoln* (Vol. 2) (edited by Roy P. Basler) (New Brunswick, NJ: Rutgers University Press, 1953), p. 391.

[54] See Andrew Jackson, "Veto Message," *A Compilation of the Messages and Papers of the Presidents, 1789–1897* (edited by James D. Richardson) (Vol. II) (Washington, DC: Government Printing Office, 1997), p. 582; Martin Van Buren, *Inquiry into the Origins and Course of Political Parties of the United States* (New York: Augustus M. Kelley, 1967), pp. 315–16.

[55] Van Buren, *Inquiry*, p. 330.

[56] Andrew Jackson, "Protest," *A Compilation of the Messages and Papers of the Presidents, 1789–1897* (edited by James D. Richardson) (Vol. III) (Washington, DC: Government Printing Office, 1997), p. 90.

rechartering of the national bank, Jackson pointed to the upcoming election as the event ultimately responsible for determining the constitutionality of that measure:

A general discussion will now take place, eliciting new light and settling important principles; and a new Congress, elected in the middle of such discussion, and furnishing an equal representation of the people according to the last census, will bear to the Capitol the verdict of public opinion, and, I doubt not, bring this important question to a satisfactory result.[57]

Jackson subsequently interpreted his reelection in 1832 as settling questions concerning the constitutionality of the national bank. "Whatever may be the opinions of others," Jackson declared when insisting that federal deposits be removed from that institution, "the President considers his reelection as a decision of the people against the bank"[58]

The controversy over the Censure Resolution witnessed another contest between the Jacksonian descendants of John Pym and the Whig descendants of Charles I. That resolution raised separation of powers questions concerning the president's power to remove deposits from the Bank of the United States without congressional permission and the Senate's power to censure the president. After a Whig-controlled Senate censured Jackson in 1834 for withholding documents relating to his decision to defund the Bank, the Democrats regained the Senate in 1836 and immediately moved to expunge the censure from the record. Madison might have expected members of Congress to defend the prerogatives of their branch, particularly with respect to the Senate's power to censure the president. Instead, Jackson's allies in the Senate placed party first, consistently supporting their partisan allies in a rival institution rather than their partisan rivals in their home institution. Gerard Magliocca observes, "For Jacksonian Democrats, the popular sovereignty expressed by several recent elections was every bit as authoritative as the popular sovereignty embodied by our constitutional structure."[59]

Abraham Lincoln's first inaugural address elaborated this commitment to a partisan supremacy justified by electoral success. Lincoln is commonly considered a departmentalist because he claimed that the Supreme Court did not have the final authority to determine what the Constitution means. His first inaugural address, however, discusses the power of the people to challenge judicial decisions, not the power of any particular officeholders to engage in independent constitutional interpretation. Lincoln said,

---

[57] Andrew Jackson, "Veto Message," p. 589.

[58] Andrew Jackson, "Removal of the Public Deposits," *A Compilation of the Messages and Papers of the Presidents, 1789–1897* (edited by James D. Richardson) (Vol. III) (Washington, DC: Government Printing Office, 1997), p. 7.

[59] Gerard N. Magliocca, "Veto! The Jacksonian Revolution in Constitutional Law," 78 *Nebraska Law Review* 206, 244 (1999).

[T]he candid citizen must confess that if the policy of the government, upon vital questions, affecting the whole people, is to be irrevocably fixed by decisions of the Supreme Court, the instant they are made, in ordinary litigation between parties, in personal actions, the people will have ceased, to be their own rulers, having, to that extent, practically resigned their government, into the hands of that eminent tribunal. Nor is there, in this view, any assault upon the court, or the judges.[60]

In sharp contrast to Jefferson, Lincoln in his first inaugural address or in other speeches never claimed that he had authority to challenge decisions of the Supreme Court because he was president of the United States or held some other office. He spoke of the right of the people through elections to challenge judicial decisions. *Dred Scott* v. *Sandford*, Lincoln stated, expressed the constitutional philosophy of the Democratic Party. "The *Dred Scott* decision," he asserted, "never would have been made in its present form if the party that made it had not been sustained previously by the elections."[61] Reversing *Dred Scott* was the constitutional philosophy of the Republican Party. Republicans were entitled to reverse *Dred Scott*, Lincoln maintained, because that party had through elections demonstrated that a majority of the people shared its antislavery constitutional vision. Immediately before this famous attack on the Supreme Court, the sixteenth president asserted, "A majority, held in restraint by constitutional checks, and limitations, and always changing easily, with deliberate changes of popular opinions and sentiments, is the only true sovereign of a free people."[62] John Pym and Andrew Jackson would have agreed.

The two major separation of powers questions decided by the Supreme Court during the Civil War and early Reconstruction highlight the absence of intractable separation of powers controversies among party regulars and do not articulate any distinctive Republican commitment to a particular conception of the distinctive roles of different governing institutions. The *Prize Cases* held that President Lincoln was constitutionally authorized to blockade southern ports.[63] *Ex parte Milligan* held that neither President Lincoln nor Congress could impose martial law in loyal states where the courts were still open.[64] Neither resolved a live separation of powers dispute between the legislative and executive branches of the national government. Congress immediately ratified Lincoln's blockade upon meeting in the summer of 1861. The only issue in the *Prize Cases* was whether retroactive justification was necessary or sufficient to ratify Lincoln's actions, a matter on which Republicans in the White House and Congress agreed. President Lincoln and Republicans in Congress had more substantial disagreements over

---

[60] Abraham Lincoln, "First Inaugural Address – Final Text," *The Collected Works of Abraham Lincoln* (Vol. 4) (edited by Roy P. Basler) (New Brunswick, NJ: Rutgers University Press, 1953), p. 268.

[61] Abraham Lincoln, "Mr. Lincoln's Speech, Fifth Debate with Stephen A. Douglas, at Galesburg, Illinois," *The Collected Works of Abraham Lincoln* (Vol. 4) (edited by Roy P. Basler) (New Brunswick, NJ: Rutgers University Press, 1953), p. 232.

[62] Lincoln, "First Inaugural," p. 268.   [63] 67 U.S. 635 (1862).   [64] 71 U.S. 2 (1866).

presidential power to suspend habeas corpus and suspend martial law. While the Civil War raged, these conflicts were fought out by the negotiations that led to such measures as the Habeas Corpus Act of 1863. *Milligan* was decided only after the Civil War ended and Lincoln administration's policies were being abandoned.[65]

Republicans sought to entrench partisan supremacy when framing and ratifying the Fourteenth Amendment.[66] Thaddeus Stevens and other party leaders during the summer of 1865 feared that Democrats would soon regain control of the national government. The Thirteenth Amendment, they realized, gave the white South a thirty-vote bonus in the House of Representatives and Electoral College by requiring that historically disenfranchised persons of color be counted as whole persons, rather than three-fifths of a person, when apportioning House members and members of the Electoral College. John Bingham aside, Republicans thought existing constitutional rights and powers more than adequate for protecting former slaves. They assumed the Thirteenth Amendment combined with the Guaranty Clause of Article IV empowered Congress to do whatever Republicans thought necessary to promote racial equality throughout the nation. Bingham was the only prominent Republican who expressed doubts about the constitutionality of the Civil Rights Act of 1866, which exercised congressional power under the Thirteenth Amendment to prohibit black codes and provide persons of color with substantial rights. Confident that they had the necessary constitutional power to secure Republican constitutional visions but concerned they might soon lack the necessary political power, Stevens and his partisan allies sought to fashion a constitutional politics that privileged the party of the people who remained loyal during the Civil War.

When the Thirty-Ninth Congress met, Stevens emphasized the need for a constitutional amendment "to secure perpetual ascendancy to the party of the Union; and so as to render our republican Government firm and stable forever."[67] No Republican championed the founding rule that constitutional commitments would be preserved as long as national institutions remained independent. The Republican Party was the vehicle for maintaining the post–Civil War Constitution, not the separation of powers. Senator of Henry Wilson spoke for his fellow antislavery constitutionalists when he declared,

No political party in any country or in any age has fought on a plain so lofty, or achieved so much for country, republican institutions, the cause of freedom, of justice, and of Christian civilization. If it should perish now in the pride of strength and of power, by the

---

[65] Mark E. Neely, *The Fate of Liberty: Abraham Lincoln and Civil Liberties* (New York: Oxford University Press, 1991).

[66] The following three paragraphs summarize the central thesis of Mark A. Graber, *Constructing Constitutional Politics: Thaddeus Stevens, John Bingham and the Forgotten Fourteenth Amendment* (Lawrence, KS: University Press of Kansas, under contract).

[67] *Congressional Globe*, 39th Congress, 1st Sess., p. 74.

hands of suicide, or by the follies or treacheries of men it has generously trusted, it will leave to after times a brilliant record of honor and of glory. The enduring interests of the regenerated nation, the rights of man, and the elevation of an emancipated race alike demand that the great Union Republican party, the outgrowth and development of advancing civilization in America, shall continue to administer the Government it preserved, and frame the laws for the nation it saved.[68]

These concerns explain why Congress debated with great care and at great length what became Sections 2 and 3 of the Fourteenth Amendment but, John Bingham aside, paid almost no attention to what became Section 1. Section 2 of the Fourteenth Amendment reduced a state's representation in Congress to the extent that states disenfranchised adult male voters. Section 3 prohibited some former Confederates from holding office and, as originally proposed, prohibited most former Confederates from voting. Combined, Republicans hoped, Sections 2 and 3 would ensure that Republicans controlled the meaning of the post–Civil War Constitution.[69] The Constitution of 1865 would be maintained because Republicans in all branches of government would defeat southern efforts to repeal in practice the Thirteenth Amendment. The Thirteenth and Fourteenth Amendments would be interpreted in a manner consistent with the Republican antislavery constitutional vision, Republicans thought, because for the foreseeable future only Republicans would be doing the interpreting.

Convinced that constitutional arrangements that preserved the power of the only party committed to realizing the fruits of the Northern victory in the Civil War were necessary to preserve in practice the rights protected by the Thirteenth Amendment,[70] Republicans, when framing the Fourteenth Amendment, were unconcerned with potential future conflicts between Republicans in different branches of the national government over what constituted appropriate legislation for ensuring that former slaves and persons of color enjoyed the blessings of liberty. Republican exhibited this disinterest even though in 1865 and 1866 separation of powers conflicts had broken out between Republicans in Congress and a president, who was a former Democrat, and between Republicans in Congress and a Supreme Court composed of many former Democrats.[71] Stevens and other prominent Republicans flirted with resurrecting John Pym when suggesting a legislative supremacy that might propel Andrew Johnson and the judicial majority in *Milligan* toward greater harmony with the Republican majority in Congress. Nevertheless, Republicans in the immediate aftermath of

---

[68] *Congressional Globe*, 39th Cong., 1st Sess. App., p. 142. See *Congressional Globe*, 39th Cong., 1st Sess., p. 3038 (Yates) ("I always feel perfectly safe when I am in the hands of a good Republican Union party").

[69] Although more radicals feared that the final version of Sections 2 and 3 were too weak to prevent white supremacists from returning to national power. See *Congressional Globe*, 39th Cong., 1st Sess., p. 3148 (speech of Thaddeus Stevens).

[70] See Graber, Constructing Constitutional Politics.

[71] See Mark A. Graber, "The Jacksonian Origins of Chase Court Activism," 25 *Journal of Supreme Court History* 17 (2000).

the Civil War never reached a consensus or made a sustained effort to develop a consensus on the place of the separation of powers in the post–Civil War constitutional regime. They regarded institutional conflicts with Johnson and the federal courts as temporary aberrations requiring only short-term solutions until Republicans recaptured control of the White House and Supreme Court.[72] Republicans when debating the Fourteenth Amendment barely alluded to the possibility of foreseeable future disputes between Republicans in Congress and Republicans in the White House. Demonstrating their Jacksonian antipathy to a sharp separation of powers, they never considered the possibility, after Andrew Johnson left office, of sustained conflict between Republicans in Congress and Republicans in the White House.

THE STATE OF COURTS, PARTIES, AND AGENCIES

The partisan constitutional order envisioned by the Republicans responsible for the Fourteenth Amendment was transformed during the late nineteenth century. Initially in this new political regime, nonideological parties distributed the benefits of government while courts made the substantive rules.[73] During and immediately after the New Deal, what Stephen Skowronek describes as the "state of courts and parties" evolved into what might be described as the "state of courts, parties, bureaucrats, and presidents" or, more briefly, "the state of courts, parties, and agencies." In this political universe, nonideological parties continued to distribute the benefits of government while bureaucrats made domestic policy, presidents managed the bureaucracies and made foreign policy, and the Supreme Court determined what civil rights the states (and the national government) were constitutionally obligated to respect.[74]

Institutional functions changed in response to these developments. The separation of powers became the vehicle by which Congress delegated or sloughed off, depending on one's perspective, responsibilities to other governing institutions on the theory that those institutions were better suited to make the policy in question than the national legislature. The Supreme Court became the institution responsible for determining what Congress had delegated and when Congress could delegate. The justices initially fought a rearguard action against the administrative state. When liberals gained control over courts, bureaucracies and executive agencies, judges became more tolerant of legislative delegations. A federal judiciary charged by political activists in

---

[72] See Stanley I. Kutler, *Judicial Power and Reconstruction Politics* (Chicago: University of Chicago Press, 1969); William Lasser, *The Limits of Judicial Power: The Supreme Court in American Politics* (Chapel Hill: University of North Carolina Press, 1989).

[73] Stephen Skowronek, *Building a New American State: The Expansion of National Administrative Capacities, 1877–1920* (New York: Cambridge University Press, 1982), pp. 39–42.

[74] See Graber, "Belling the Partisan Cats," pp. 611, 628–39; Lucas A. Powe, Jr., *The Warren Court and American Politics* (Cambridge, MA: Harvard University Press, 2000).

both parties with the responsibility for policing constitutional limits and protecting constitutional rights handed down an increasing number of important decisions on the constitutional relationships between the elected branches of government, even though clashes between the elected branches of government did not increase during this period.

By the turn of the twentieth century, Jacksonian parties committed to preserving the Constitution had been replaced by Downsian parties committed to adopting centrist positions likely to win elections.[75] The Republican Party in 1900 and 1940 was no longer united by a shared commitment to preserving the fruits of the Northern victory in the Civil War. Democrats continued to celebrate Jackson Day dinners while disputing and eventually abandoning Jacksonian commitments to limited national power and federalism. During the first two-thirds of the twentieth century, both parties had strong liberal and strong conservative wings. From 1930 until 1970, the presidency and courts were controlled by the liberal wings of each party, while conservatives in both parties exercised more influence in Congress. The lack of strong parties that the framers feared did not foster the strong identification with particular branches of the national government that Madison in *Federalist* 51 promised. Progressive and liberal Democrats in the White House often cooperated with progressive and liberal Republicans in Congress in struggles again a powerful coalition of conservative southern Democrats and Midwestern Republicans. Section counted more than party on many issues. Bipartisan sectional coalitions formed to pass such measures as the Taft-Hartley Act and the Civil Rights Act of 1964.

A functional separation of powers thrived in the absence of strong ideologically coherent parties. As ideological diversity and internal congressional reforms weakened the capacity or will of the majority party in Congress to present the united front necessary to take the lead on policymaking and advancing a distinctive constitutional vision, those functions were foisted off, drifted, or were seized by other governing institutions. Presidents assumed the role of party leader and policy driver. Theodore Roosevelt claimed that "it was not only his right but his duty to do anything the needs of the Nation demanded unless such action was forbidden by the Constitution or by the laws."[76] The more powerful presidency was spurred by such developments as mass communications, which enabled presidents to speak directly to the American people;[77] a more complex society, which often demanded immediate responses to social problems; and the increased role of foreign policy in American political life. Complaints about an "imperial presidency" that began when Theodore Roosevelt was in office became conventional political

---

[75] See Anthony Downs, *An Economic Theory of Democracy* (New York: Harper and Row, 1957).

[76] Theodore Roosevelt, "The Presidency: Making an Old Party Progressive," 105 *The Outlook* 631, 638 (1913).

[77] See Jeffrey K. Tulis, *The Rhetorical Presidency* (Princeton: Princeton University Press, 1987).

science wisdom by the 1960s.[78] Executive agencies and independent regulatory commissions gained increased authority. Nonideological parties unable to agree on much substantive policy helped fashion an administrative state as a substitute. Much legislation in the early twentieth century merely identified a problem and charged a regulatory agency with the responsibility for solving the problem. The Sherman Anti-Trust Act forbade "contracts in restraint of trade," leaving bureaucrats, executive branch officials, and judges responsible for determining what contracts sufficiently restrained trade to merit prohibition.[79] The vague phrases in most statutes passed during the Progressive Era were models of clarity when compared to the language of New Deal legislation.

Judges were the other governing officials who gained power during this period. The late nineteenth century witnessed the emergence of judicial supremacy as the dominant theory of constitutional authority in the United States. Federal judges always insisted that they were the ultimate arbiters of constitutional meaning,[80] and prominent members of the national legislature and executive consistently supported these judicial pretensions.[81] Nevertheless, for the first century of American constitutional life, most important constitutional decisions were made outside of the courts. Federalist and Jeffersonian elected officials resolved constitutional debates over presidential power to remove executive branch officials, the Louisiana Purchase, and Sedition Act of 1798 with no or very limited judicial participation.[82] The constitutionality of Henry Clay's American System was settled by Jacksonian vetoes rather than by judicial edict.[83] The revival of *Marbury* v. *Madison*[84] in the 1880s and 1890s[85] symbolized the new status of federal courts as practically supreme in their interpretation of the Constitution and the institution responsible for resolving the most important constitutional questions facing the nation, such as the status of the Constitution in American territories, the rights of unions and their members, antitrust policy, the income tax, and race relations in the South.[86] New Dealers retained this commitment to judicial supremacy. The difference between New Deal Court and the more

---

[78] Arthur M. Schlesinger, Jr., *The Imperial Presidency* (Boston: Houghton Mifflin, 1973).

[79] See Mark A. Graber, "The Nonmajoritarian Difficulty: Legislative Deference to the Judiciary," 7 *Studies in American Political Development* 35, 50–53 (1993).

[80] See McCulloch v. Maryland, 17 U.S. 316, 401 (1819).

[81] See Mark A. Graber, "James Buchanan as Savior," 88 *Oregon Law Review* 95 (2009).

[82] See Gillman, Graber, and Whittington, *American Constitutionalism* (Vol. I), pp. 139–41, 170–73; Gillman, Graber, and Whittington, *American Constitutionalism* (Vol. II), pp. 175–78.

[83] See Mark A. Graber, "Resolving Political Questions into Judicial Questions: Tocqueville's Aphorism Revisited," 21 *Constitutional Commentary* 485 (2004).

[84] 5 U.S. 137 (1803).

[85] See Robert Lowry Clinton, *Marbury v. Madison and Judicial Review* (Lawrence, KS: University Press of Kansas, 1989).

[86] See Downes v. Bidwell, 182 U.S. 244 (1901); In re Debs, 158 U.S. 564 (1895); United States v. E. C. Knight, 156 U.S. 1 (1895); Pollock v. Farmers' Loan & Trust Co., 157 U.S. 429 (1895); Plessy v. Ferguson, 163 U.S. 437 (1896).

conservative Fuller, White, and Taft Courts was that New Dealers championed very different constitutional limits on the national and state governments than had previously been the case.[87]

Congressional action and inaction spurred the dispersion of power in this new constitutional regime. Federal statutes frequently empowered other institutions. The Judiciary Acts of 1875 and 1891 reflected and spurred increased commitments to judicial supremacy.[88] The Executive Reorganization Act of 1939 enabled the president to better manage the bureaucracy. During the Progressive Era, Congress created numerous independent regulatory commissions and charged them with regulating wide swaths of public life. Independent commissions, presidents, and courts often took relatively autonomous actions, confident that their allies in Congress could at least prevent the national legislature from reversing their decisions. Isolationists carped when President Franklin Roosevelt, acting unilaterally, gave substantial support to England and France after hostilities broke out in Europe, but Roosevelt's critics lacked the numbers in Congress to challenge those executive decisions. Conservatives prevented progressives from amending the federal code when federal courts interpreted narrowly statutes progressives hoped would increase legal protections for employees.[89]

Much of the constitutional law concerning the separation of powers that emerged from this period was forged during struggles between courts and bureaucracies over their proper boundaries. From the 1880s until the 1940s, the Supreme Court considered a series of cases raising questions about what powers Congress had delegated to a regulatory agency and what powers Congress could constitutionally delegate to a regulatory agency. The justices when considering the legality of various delegations more often policed accords between the national legislature and national executive than refereed disputes between Congress and the president over the scope of their respective constitutional powers. These cases did not pit Congress against the president because members of both branches agreed on the actual powers that had been delegated and on the constitutional power of Congress to delegate those powers. The delegation doctrine concerned the extent to which courts or bureaucracies were responsible for rule-making. The first judicial decisions on delegation indicated clear limits on what legislatures could delegate to executive branch officials and bureaucrats. The Supreme Court until 1935 did not declare delegations unconstitutional (although some lower federal courts did) but defined narrowly the scope of agency power under federal statutory law, often in ways inconsistent with what members of the elected branches of the national

---

[87] See especially, United States v. Carolene Products Co., 304 U.S. 144, 152–53 n.4 (1938).

[88] See Howard Gillman, "How Political Parties Can Use the Courts to Advance Their Agendas: Federal Courts in the United States, 1875–1891," 96 *American Political Science Review* 511 (2002).

[89] See George I. Lovell, *Legislative Deferrals: Statutory Ambiguity, Judicial Power, and American Democracy* (New York: Cambridge University Press, 2003).

government had intended.[90] During the early New Deal, the requirement that delegations be rooted in an "intelligible principle" gained additional bite when the justices declared unconstitutional several legislative efforts to foist policymaking responsibility off to administrative agencies.[91] Justice Benjamin Cardozo condemned the National Recovery Act as "delegation running riot."[92] That judicial effort to police delegation soon became a casualty of the New Deal Constitutional Revolution. Within a decade, the justices gave up trying to limit legislative delegations.[93] Justice Robert Jackson expressed the conventional wisdom of the state of courts, parties, and agencies when he declared that executive officials could act with congressional sanction unless no institution in the federal government could perform the action in question. His concurring opinion in *Youngstown Sheet & Tube Co.* v. *Sawyer* maintained that a congressional delegation was unconstitutional only if "the Federal Government as an undivided whole lacks power."[94]

The Supreme Court more proactively constrained presidential power when presidents challenged federal statutes limiting executive control over the administrative state. In *Myers* v. *United States* (1926) the justices for the first time entered the long-standing constitutional controversy over whether presidents were authorized to fire executive branch officials. Chief Justice William Howard Taft when declaring unconstitutional statutory job protections for postmasters supported presidential power to defy Congress. He declared, "The vesting of the executive power in the President was essentially a grant of the power to execute the laws and as his selection of administrative officers is essential to the execution of the laws by him, so much be his power of removing those for whom he can not continue to be responsible."[95] A decade later, the justices in *Humphrey's Executor* v. *United States* (1935) supported congressional power to prohibit presidential action when unanimously sustaining legislation prohibited the president from removing without good cause a commissioner of the Federal Trade Commission. In an opinion that legitimated independent regulatory commissions, Justice George Sutherland stated, "The Federal Trade Commission is an administrative body created by Congress to carry into effect legislative policies embodied in the statute accordance with the legislative standard therein prescribed."[96]

Whether *Myers* or *Humphrey's Executor* resolved a live controversy between the executive and legislative branches of the national government is doubtful. *Humphrey's Executor* almost certainly and *Myers* to a fair degree are better conceptualized as instances when federal justices exercised their constitutional

[90] See Skowronek, *Building the New American State*, pp. 150–60.
[91] See Panama Refining Co. v. Ryan, 293 U.S.388 (1935); A.L.A. Schechter Poultry Corporation v. United States, 295 U.S. 495 (1935).
[92] *Schechter*, at 553 (Cardozo, J., concurring).
[93] See Yakus v. United States, 321 U.S. 414 (1944).
[94] 343 U.S. 579, 636–37 (Jackson, J., concurring).
[95] Myers v. United States, 272 U.S. 52, 117 (1926).
[96] Humphrey's Executor v. United States, 295 U.S. 602, 628 (1935).

authority to inform Congress and the president how they should perform their constitutional duties, even when Congress and the president had agreed on a different conception of their job responsibilities. New Dealers in Congress urged Roosevelt to fire Humphrey. Frank Myers sued under a statute passed during the late nineteenth century. Presidents and members of Congress during the early twentieth century took no consistent stand on presidential control of the executive branch. President Woodrow Wilson successfully vetoed a bill that imposed further limits on presidential capacity to remove executive branch officials. President Warren Harding routinely signed such measures without constitutional objection.[97] The "ambition counteracted ambition" in *Myers* and *Humphrey's Executor* was the ambition of bureaucrats to keep their jobs confronting presidential ambitions to control the bureaucracy.

United States v. *Curtiss-Wright Export Corporation*[98] is typical of the separation of powers cases decided by the Supreme Court during the first two-thirds of the twentieth century. The issue in that case was whether Congress could delegate to President Franklin Roosevelt the power to determine whether to prohibit arms sales to warring Paraguay and Bolivia. The Supreme Court by a 7–1 vote ruled that the delegation was constitutional. Justice George Sutherland's majority opinion is best known for the ringing endorsement of presidential power in foreign affairs. He asserted, "In this vast external realm, with its important, complicated, delicate and manifold problems, the President alone has the power to speak or listen as a representative of the nation."[99] Proponents of executive power in a different era cited that passage and others in *Curtiss-Wright* for the proposition that presidents when making foreign policy may act without congressional authorization and in the face of congressional prohibition. No such contest for foreign policy authority took place during *Curtiss-Wright*. President Roosevelt issued the order in controversy a mere four days after both Houses of Congress explicitly authorized the order.[100] Charles I could only have dreamed for such legislative support for executive power.

Youngstown Sheet & Tube Co. v. *Sawyer* is the great exception to the ordinary constitutional politics of the state of courts, parties, and agencies. The *Steel Seizure Case* is an instance of a clear conflict between Congress and the president fought out in the courts. President Harry Truman seized steel factories in defiance of clear legislative commands to the contrary. The justices by a 6–3 vote declared the seizure unconstitutional. Justice Hugo Black's opinion for the Court was grounded in constitutional formalism. "The President's power," he wrote, "must stem either from an act of Congress or

---

[97] For the political background of *Humphrey's Executor* and *Myers*, see J. David Alvis, Jeremy D. Bailey, and F. Flagg Taylor IV, *The Contested Removal Power* (Lawrence, KS: University Press of Kansas, 2012), pp. 126, 160–61.

[98] 299 U.S. 304 (1936). [99] *Curtiss-Wright*, at 319.

[100] See Charles A. Lofgren, "United States v. Curtiss-Wright Export Corporation: An Historical Reassessment," 83 *Yale Law Journal* 1 (1971).

from the Constitution itself."[101] Finding no authorizing text, Black rejected Truman's authority. Justice Robert Jackson's concurring opinion was grounded in constitutional functionalism. Jackson discussed three circumstances in which separation of powers controversies might arise: when the president's actions were authorized by Congress, when the president was acting "in absence of either a congressional grant or denial of authority," and when presidential action was "incompatible with the expressed or implied will of Congress."[102] Truman's seizure was unconstitutional, Jackson concluded, because that action fell into the third category, when presidential "power is at its lowest ebb."[103] Jackson's categories structured constitutional analysis in a later era marked by pervasive and partisan conflict between the president and Congress.[104] Most exercises of presidential power during the remaining years of this period belonged in or near the first category, as Congress with different degrees of enthusiasm continued delegating most policies to bureaucracies, executive agencies, and courts, the latter being the institution charged in the twentieth century with the responsibility for maintained the rules of the constitutional order, including the rules governing the separation of powers.[105]

TWO JOHN PYMS: THE POLARIZED POLITY

The United States experienced a new form of constitutional politics during the late twentieth century. A system in which two ideologically polarized parties struggled for dominance replaced the long state of courts and nonideological parties.[106] The Democratic Party became the coalition of choice for liberals. The Republican Party became the coalition of choice for conservatives. Constitutional controversies over the separation of powers more resembled a debate between two clones of John Pym, each trying to maximize the power of the institutions they control, than the debate between the Pym and Charles I over the merits of a system in which different government institutions exercised different powers and functioned independently.

Contemporary political polarization differs from the semi-polarized politics of the mid-nineteenth century. Partisan divisions in Jacksonian America were limited to debates over national power to promote commercial enterprise. Partisan divisions during the Civil War and Reconstruction were over the constitutional status of slavery and racial equality. Twenty-first century Republicans and Democrats fight over the entire national agenda. Democratic political activists are liberals on all issues, from foreign policy to capital

---

[101] *Youngstown* at 585.   [102] *Youngstown*, at 637 (Jackson, J., concurring).
[103] *Youngstown*, at 637 (Jackson, J., concurring).
[104] Seventeen of the eighteen Supreme Court cases that discuss Jackson's opinion were decided after Richard Nixon took office.
[105] Seventeen of the eighteen cases that subsequently cited Jackson's categories were decided after 1970.
[106] See Graber, "Belling the Partisan Cats," p. 611.

punishment. Republican political activists are conservatives on all issues, from same-sex marriage to the merits of torturing suspected terrorists.[107] In sharp contrast to the mid-nineteenth century, no dominant party emerged in contemporary politics. Democrats won most American national elections from 1832 until 1860. Republicans were the dominant party afterward. Contemporary Republicans and Democrats fight each other to a draw. From 1968 until the present, one party has controlled all elected branch of the national government for only twelve years. In only four of the forty-eight years before 2017 did one party control the presidency, both houses of Congress, and the Supreme Court of the United States.

How the separation of powers functions in the contemporary United States is structured by the polarization of contemporary politics. Struggles between Congress and the president are pervasive and intense. More so than at any point in American history, contests over the separation of powers are fought by a Congress controlled by one party and an executive branch controlled by the other party. Political actors and academics champion constitutional understandings that magnify the power of the governing institutions they control at the expense of the institution their rivals control. Bitter conflicts routinely break out between Democrats and Republicans over the staffing of the federal court system in part because the federal judges have retained their inherited capacity to declare the official constitutional law of the land on the scope of constitutional powers and rights and in part because the Supreme Court has assumed the role of referee when contests break out between the national legislature and the national executive.

Constitutional politics in the United States presently lacks a justification. Prominent political actors do not claim that the constitutional separation of powers can be successfully operated by two equally powerful polarized parties. No contemporary analogue to *Federalist 51*, Van Buren's *Inquiry into the Origins and Course of Political Parties in the United States*, or the *Carolene Products* footnote exists that claims that specific or any constitutional ends can best be achieved when two polarized parties control different national institutions. Instead, the separation of powers in polarized America is best described as a distorted amalgam of the different guiding principles that structured the three previous constitutional regimes. Both Democrats and Republicans characterize their coalition as the party of the people who are loyal to the Constitution and, following Pym and Van Buren, believe the Constitution can best be maintained if their party gains control of all national governing institutions. Neither party has achieved this control for any sustained period of time. Their power concentrated in particular national institutions, partisans often imitate Charles I when celebrating a strict separation of powers, but only when they claim a national institution they do not control should not

---

[107] See Geoffrey C. Layman and Thomas M. Carsey, "Party Polarization and 'Conflict Extension' in the American Electorate," 46 *American Journal of Political Science* 786 (2002).

interfere with policies made by the national institution they do control. Republicans and Democrats engage in prolonged struggles for control over the federal judicial institutions that the dominant theory of the previous century held responsible for maintaining constitutional order. The governing theory of constitutional authority remains judicial supremacy, but only when the true party of the Constitution controls the Supreme Court or when the particular judicial decision advances the values and interests of that true party of the Constitution.

The constitutional politics of polarization is responsible for the increased discordance between empirical theories about the way the Constitution works and normative theories about the way the Constitution should work. For much of American history, a rough congruence existed between how the constitutional separation of powers functioned and theories about how the constitutional separation of powers best functioned. Presidents, bureaucrats, and judges gained power during the twentieth century because prominent leaders in both parties believed these government officials were better able to perform some tasks than Congress. The *Carolene Products* footnote, which declared that elected officials were best able to make economic policy and federal judges best able to protect democratic processes and unpopular minorities, provides a fair description of how the New Deal/Great Society order actually operated. No self-conscious political choice explains why presidents, bureaucrats, and judges continue to gain power in the contemporary political regime. Rather, a gridlocked Congress enfeebled by polarization often cannot prevent unilateral presidential action, and gridlock between Congress and the president prevents elected officials from constraining administrative and judicial policymaking. Justice Anthony Kennedy waxes poetic when claiming that "[l]iberty is always at stake when one or more of the branches seek to transgress the separation of powers" and that "[s]eparation of powers helps to ensure the ability of each branch to be vigorous in asserting its proper authority."[108] He does not seem to notice that while the separation of powers in the anti-partisan regime of 1787 may have preserved liberty by enabling each branch of government "to be vigorous in asserting its proper authority," the present separation of powers functions as the vehicle by which the two parties try to steer as much power to the branch of government they control while minimizing the power of the branch of government they do not control, a governing philosophy more rooted in the expedience of the moment than any enduring commitment to a set of practices that enable a regime of polarized parties to make the Constitution work effectively.

The Richard Nixon presidency witnessed the first sustained fights between Congress and the president since the Lincoln/Johnson administration. Nixon insisted that the president was authorized to expand hostilities in Southeast Asia, he sought to impound funds appropriated by Congress, and he aggressively resisted

---

[108] Clinton v. City of New York, at 451, 452 (Kennedy, J., concurring).

congressional probes into the Watergate affairs. The Democratic majority in Congress fought back, most notably with the Watergate investigation and the War Powers Act of 1973. Still, from the perspective of the early 1970s, the events of Nixon administration seemed aberrational, more a consequence of Nixon's idiosyncrasies than the result of structural change in American politics. While Democrats led the fight for Congressional power, many liberal Republicans joined Democrats when they sought to combat presidential efforts to act independently in domestic affairs, send troops abroad, and withhold information from Congress. Many conservative Democrats supported Nixon when he expanded military conflict in Southeast Asia and sought to curb the growth of the welfare state.

The contemporary constitutional politics of the separation of powers became entrenched during the Reagan and Bush I administrations. While Republicans controlled the White House from 1980 until 1992, Democrats controlled the House of Representatives during that time period and controlled the Senate from 1986 until 1994. Much conventional wisdom during the 1970s and 1980s maintained that American politics had become structured in ways that privileged Republican candidates for the presidency and Democratic candidates for Congress.[109] Liberals in the national legislature battled conservatives in the national executive as Reagan and Bush I struggled to gain control of administrative agencies, maintain a stronger anti-communist policy in Latin America than Congress thought appropriate, and establish a conservative majority in the federal courts.

The institutional base of each party temporarily flipped during the late 1990s. Republicans controlled both Houses of Congress from 1994 to 2000 while Democrats controlled the White House. Continuing a trend that began during the Nixon and Reagan administrations, members of the majority party in the national legislature aggressively investigated their rivals in the national executive. At a time when the public seemed evenly divided between the two parties, many political activists concluded the best strategy to gain control of the government was to accuse partisan rivals of corruption rather than persuade swing voters that their coalition was the true party of the Constitution.[110] From 1994 to 2000, President Bill Clinton, Hillary Clinton, and their political associates were almost always being investigated for some misdeed. When a special prosecutor concluded that President Clinton had lied under oath about a sexual affair, the House of Representatives promptly started impeachment procedures. Pretty much every Republican reached the conclusion that lying under oath was an impeachable high crime or misdemeanor. Pretty much every Democrat reached the conclusion that Clinton had not committed an

---

[109] See Martin P. Wattenburg, "The Republican Presidential Advantage in the Age of Party Disunity," *The Politics of Divided Government* (Boulder, CO: Westview Press, 1991).

[110] See Benjamin Ginsburg, *Politics by Other Means: Politicians, Prosecutors, and the Press from Watergate to Whitewater* (3rd ed.) (New York: W.W. Norton & Company, 2002).

impeachable offense because his conduct had nothing to do with his official duties. One consequence of the Clinton impeachment was the end of special prosecutors, a tool Democrats had originally devised to investigate Republicans.

Separation of powers controversies did not diminish even when George W. Bush was elected president and Republicans controlled all three branches of the national government from 2002 to 2006. To the consternation of Democrats and some Republicans in Congress, the Bush II administration insisted on exercising almost complete control over the war against terrorism. When Congress attempted to rein in the administration, the administration often issued signing statements declaring certain parts of the law the president had signed unconstitutional. The precise import of these statements was unclear, but they did little to restore harmony between the governing branches, particularly after Democrats regained control of the House and Senate in the 2006 national elections.

After a two-year period of united Democratic Party rule from 2008 to 2010, renewed separation of powers controversies erupted after Republicans gained control of the House of Representatives in the 2010 national election and the Senate in the 2014 national election. President Barack Obama consistently did end runs around Congress when operating an executive-centered foreign policy similar to that of the Bush II administration. Despite the sometimes vigorous objections of congressional Republicans, Obama administration officials more often than not found reason to act unilaterally when engaging in domestic surveillance, conducting drone strikes on suspected terrorists, or determining the American response to regional civil wars. In addition, Obama frequently acted unilaterally when making ordinary domestic policy. The administration resorted to recess appointments when Congress delayed confirming nominees and relied on executive orders in the absence of any updated legislation on illegal immigrants and immigration.

No dominant theory about the place of the separation of powers in the American constitutional scheme emerged at the turn of the twenty-first century. Many Republicans and conservatives defend what became known as the "unitary president." On this view, the Constitution forbids any congressional interference with an executive power unless explicit constitutional text clearly mandates the contrary, although what constitutes an executive power that may be exercised solely by an executive branch official often seems to depend on whether a Democrat or a Republican sat in the Oval Office. Democrats are more comfortable with a functionalist rhetoric that justifies a substantial role for Congress in theory when Congress is willing to play that role. Democratic presidents when engaged in unilateral executive actions eschew the unitary executive rationales trumpeted by members of the Reagan, Bush I, and Bush II administrations, preferring to claim only specific constitutional or legislative authority to perform that executive action under consideration, leaving Democrats in Congress free to challenge a Republican president who takes a somewhat different action.

Proponents of the unitary executive emphasize the clause in Article II declaring, "The Executive Power shall be vested in the President of the United States." They claim this provision vests the entire executive power of the United States in the president of the United States or in an executive official who is entirely under the control of the president of the United States. Congress may delegate legislative powers to other governing institutions, but Article II prohibits parceling out executive power to any person not directly responsible to the president. Leading proponents of the unitary executive maintain,

The Constitution gives and ought to give all the executive power to one, and only one, person: the president of the United States. According to this view, the Constitution creates a unitary executive to ensure energetic enforcement of the law and to promote accountability by making it crystal clear who is to blame for maladministration. The Constitution's creation of a unitary executive eliminates conflicts in law enforcement and regulatory policy by ensuring that all of the cabinet departments and agencies that make up the federal government will execute the law in a consistent manner and in accordance with the president's wishes.[111]

If the decision whether to prosecute an individual is an executive decision, then proponents of the unitary president maintain that the decision to prosecute must be made either by the president or by an official responsible to the president and the president must have the power to fire for any reason all federal prosecutors.

Many conservative Republicans also inferred from the constitutional text that the president had unenumerated executive powers. Article I explicitly enumerates the powers of Congress. That text begins, "All legislative powers herein granted shall be vested in the Congress of the United States." This contrasts to Article II, which omits the words "herein granted." John Yoo and other Bush II administration officials insisted this language provided the textual hook for their conclusion that the president may exercise any power that is executive in nature unless the Constitution plainly forbids presidential exercise of that power. They maintain that "the constitutional structure requires that any ambiguities in the allocation of a power that is executive in nature, such as the power to conduct military hostilities, must be resolved in favor of the executive branch," enabling the president to exercise "inherent executive powers that are unenumerated in the Constitution."[112] If sending troops into hostile combat in a foreign nation is an executive power, then the president has

---

[111] Steven G. Calabresi and Christopher Yoo, *The Unitary Executive: Presidential Power from Washington to Bush* (New Haven: Yale University Press, 2008), p. 3.

[112] Robert J. Delahunty and John C. Yoo, "The President's Constitutional Authority to Conduct Military Operations against Terrorist Organizations and the Nations That Harbor or Support Them," 25 *Harvard Journal of Law & Public Policy* 487, 494 (2002).

that power, even if no constitutional provision expressly assigns that power to the president.

Democrats in the White House adopt more piecemeal defenses of their frequent attempts to take unilateral executive action. The Obama administration was typical in this regard. Obama often made foreign and domestic policy without seeking legislative approval, but he eschewed broad defenses of presidential powers when doing so. Republican administrations routinely claimed that the War Powers Act of 1973 unconstitutionally constrains presidential power. The Obama administration, when bombing Libya, claimed that its actions did not fall under the War Powers Act.[113] Obama when issuing an order suspending the deportation proceedings for thousands of alleged illegal aliens claimed to be doing nothing more than implementing a congressional policy.[114] Obama administrative officials during the summer of 2015 insisted that an agreement reached with Iran on nuclear proliferation was not a treaty that required Senate approval.[115]

The contemporary judicial role in delineating the separation of powers is unique in scope and function. The Supreme Court over the past forty-five years has adjudicated more important disputes over the separation of powers than that tribunal had considered during the previous 190 years, and for the first time in American history the Supreme Court consistently officiates constitutional contests between the national executive and national legislature. These changes reflect both inherited understandings of the judicial role and the newer political dynamics of the polarized polity. During the first half of the twentieth century, the Supreme Court became the institution that settled all controversies over the scope of national power and the meaning of constitutional rights. This previous restructuring of constitutional authority helps explain why contemporary institutions controlled by different ideological parties cannot reach agreements on the constitutional balance of power between the national legislature and national executive. Governing officials and distressed litigants alike assume the national judiciary will settle these constitutional differences. Federal judges almost always prove eager referees. The political questions doctrine, born in an era when the national legislature and national executive could be trusted to work out most disputes over their respective powers, became largely moribund by the early twenty-first century.[116]

[113] See Caoline D. Krass, "Memorandum Opinion on the Authority to Use Military Force in Libya," *American Constitutionalism* (Vol. I), pp. 696–99.
[114] See Office of Legal Counsel, "The Department of Homeland Security's Authority to Prioritize Removal of Certain Aliens Unlawfully Present in the United States and to Defer Removal of Others," November 19, 2014.
[115] See Jack Goldsmith, "More Weak Arguments for the Illegality of the Iran Deal," *Lawfare*, July 27, 2015.
[116] See Rachel E. Barkow, "More Supreme Than Court? The Fall of the Political Question Doctrine and the Rise of Judicial Supremacy," 102 *Columbia Law Review* 237 (2002).

Most constitutional law on the separation of powers dates from no earlier than the late Nixon administration. From 1789 to 1973, the Supreme Court played a peripheral role when most disputes arose over the respective powers of the elected branches of the national government. During the late eighteenth and nineteenth centuries, members of the elected branches of government resolved their differences over presidential power to remove executive branch officials.[117] During the state of courts, parties, and agencies, presidents and congressional leaders resolved fights over legislative vetoes without asking for a judicial referee.[118] While federal courts never refrained from resolving all separation of powers questions, Justice William Brennan's opinion in *Baker* v. *Carr* could point to many controversies over the separation of powers as the paradigm examples of non-justiciable political questions.[119] The justices with considerable support from Nixon's opponents in Congress abandoned this hands-off approach during the 1970s and have aggressively policed the boundaries between the national legislature and national executive ever since. Major judicial decisions on the separation of powers from 1974 to the present include *United States* v. *Nixon* (no generalized presidential power to withhold information),[120] *Train* v. *City of New York* (no inherent presidential power to impound funds),[121] *INS* v. *Chadha* (legislative veto unconstitutional),[122] *Bowsher* v. *Synar* (member of legislative branch cannot be entrusted with executive powers),[123] *Morrison* v. *Olson* (special prosecutors may constitutionally be appointed by non-executive officials),[124] *Clinton* v. *City of New York* (Congress may not vest the president with a line-item veto),[125] *Hamdi* v. *Rumsfeld* (president may not detain an American citizen without some kind of hearing),[126] *Hamdan* v. *Rumsfeld* (president may not try terrorists for conspiracy in the absence of a federal statute),[127] *Clinton* v. *Jones* (presidents are not constitutionally immune to civil lawsuits while in office),[128] *Chaney* v. *United States District Court* (executive branch official may withhold certain documents from the general public),[129] *Zivotofsky* v. *Kerry* (presidents have the sole power to recognize foreign nations),[130] and *National Labor Relations Board* v. *Noel Canning* (presidents may not make recess appointments when Congress has not formally recessed).[131] With the important exception of unilateral presidential power to order American troops into foreign combat, the Burger, Rehnquist, and

---

[117] J. David Alvis, Jeremy D. Bailey, and F. Flagg Taylor, IV, *The Contested Removal Power, 1789–2010* (Lawrence, KS: University Press of Kansas, 2013).

[118] See Barbara Craig, *Chadha: The Story of An Epic Constitutional Struggle* (New York: Oxford University Press, 1987).

[119] Baker v. Carr, 369 U.S. 186, 211–14 (1962). One prominent academic proposed that all separation of powers questions be non-justiciable. See Jesse H. Choper, *Judicial Review and the National Political Process: A Functional Reconsideration of the Role of the Supreme Court* (Chicago: University of Chicago Press, 1980).

[120] 418 U.S. 683 (1974).   [121] 420 U.S. 35 (1975).   [122] 462 U.S. 919 (1983).

[123] 478 U.S. 714 (1986).   [124] 487 U.S. 654 (1988).   [125] 524 U.S. 417 (1998).

[126] 542 U.S. 507 (2004).   [127] 548 U.S. 557 (2006).   [128] 520 U.S. 681 (1997).

[129] 542 U.S. 267 (2004).   [130] ___ U.S. ___ (2015).   [131] 573 U.S. ___ (2014).

Roberts Courts have had their say on the most important separation of powers disputes dividing the nation. Their decisions range from presidential power to withhold information from Congress to the management of the war against terror, from the precise allocation of power to manage the contemporary welfare state to investigations and convictions of the president and other executive branch members.

The contemporary Supreme Court when making separation of powers decisions frequently serves as a referee between Congress and the president rather than, as was previously the case, as the institution that polices how Congress and the president have mutually decided to do business. *Youngstown* aside, cases adjudicated before 1974 concerning the balance of power between the national legislature and the national executive were typically brought by litigants who opposed existing arrangements between the Congress and president. Contemporary litigants are more often allied with, if not proxies for, different branches of the national government in their partisan struggles over the allocation of power. *Train* v. *City of New York* was part of the effort by Democrats in Congress to prevent Richard Nixon from impounded funds. *Morrison* v. *Olson* was an episode in the struggle between Democrats in Congress and Republicans in the White House over the investigative authority of special prosecutors. *Noel Canning* moved fights between President Obama and Republicans in Congress over presidential appointments from legislative committees to judicial chambers.

Federal courts when adjudicating separation of powers controversies initially resisted the partisan tides engulfing other governing institutions, but recent decisions increasingly evince similar ideological divisions to those structuring contemporary decision making outside the courts on most civil liberties issues. The Supreme Court on major separation of powers cases decided during the last quarter of the twentieth century was often unanimous. The divisions that occured were idiosyncratic. The unanimous decisions in *United States* v. *Nixon* and *Clinton* v. *Jones* demonstrate that both Democrats and Republicans on the Supreme Court are willing to damage a president of their party, particularly when doing so is perceived as contributing to the integrity of the judicial process. Justices Scalia, Breyer, and O'Connor, an uncommon judicial trio, were the dissenters in *Clinton* v. *City of New York*. The judicial divisions in more recent separation of powers cases better reflect both the ideological/partisan divisions on the Court and the ideological/partisan polarization in contemporary American politics. The judicial divisions in *Hamdan, Noel Canning*, and *Zivotofsky* are more similar to the judicial divisions in such recent civil rights cases as *Citizens United* v. *Federal Elections Commission*,[132] *Shelby County* v. *Holder*,[133] and *Obergefell* v. *Hodges*[134] than any previous judicial division in a separation of powers case. Justices Stephen Breyer, Ruth Bader Ginsburg, Sonia Sotomayor, and Elana

[132] 558 U.S. 310 (2010).   [133] 570 U.S. ___ (2013).   [134] ___ U.S. ___ (2015).

Kagan have voted as a bloc in favor of the more liberal position in recent separation of powers cases. The more conservative justices also tend to vote as a bloc, although, as is the case in many contemporary civil liberties cases, the liberal block often picks off one or two conservative justices.

Unelected contemporary justices are no more able than contemporary elected officials to agree on a common constitutional approach to the separation of powers. Chief Justice Burger's constitutional formalism in *Chadha*[135] coexists with the more functional approach that Chief Justice Rehnquist took in *Morrison*.[136] Justices Byron White and Stephen Breyer claim that the justices should ratify whatever arrangements Congress and the president find workable.[137] Justice Antonin Scalia defended the unitary executive.[138] Justice Clarence Thomas insists that presidents have inherent constitutional powers.[139] None of these claims consistently garners even three of the five votes necessary to become the official constitutional law of the land.

THE DESCENDANTS OF CHARLES I AND JOHN PYM

Daryl Levinson and Richard Pildes in a celebrated article recognize and seek to mitigate how partisan competition in the United States has weakened if not obliterated the constitutional commitment to the separation of powers. Their paper describes the interplay between partisan and institutional competition for power. Levinson and Pildes note,

[T]he degree and kind of competition between the legislative and executive branches vary significantly, and may all but disappear, depending on whether the House, Senate, and presidency are divided or unified by political party. The practical distinction between party-divided and party-unified government rivals in significance, and often dominates, the constitutional distinction between the branches in predicting and explaining inter-branch political dynamics.[140]

They propose Americans confront the challenges strong parties present to the separation of powers by augmenting existing constitutional arrangements that

---

[135] See note 5 and the relevant text.

[136] See *Morrison*, at 691 ("the real question is whether the removal restrictions are of such a nature that they impede the President's ability to perform his constitutional duty").

[137] See Clinton v. City of New York, at 497 (Breyer J., dissenting) (claiming that the Court should have regarded the line-item veto as "an experiment that may, or may not, help representative government work better").

[138] See *Morrison*, at 709 ("It is not for us to determine ... how much of the purely executive powers of government must be within the full control of the President. The Constitution prescribes that they all are.").

[139] See *Zivotofsky*, at ___ (Thomas J., concurring and dissenting) (the Constitution "vests the residual foreign affairs powers of the Federal Government – i.e., those not specifically enumerated in the Constitution – in the President by way of Article II's Vesting Clause").

[140] Daryl J. Levinson and Richard H. Pildes, "Separation of Parties, Not Powers," 119 *Harvard Law Review* 2311, 2315 (2006).

divide powers between different national institutions with new constitutional mechanisms that divide powers between the major parties.[141] Rather than conceptualize the constitutional universe as divided between a monarchy controlled by Charles I and a Parliament under the leadership of John Pym and adjust the powers of each institution in light of their inherited functions, Levinson and Pildes conceive of the constitutional universe as divided between the party of Charles I and the party of John Pym and balance their powers in light of their popular support.

The problem with proposals to separate both parties and governing institutions is that the very purpose of ideological political parties, as John Pym, Martin Van Buren, Abraham Lincoln, and Newt Gingrich understood, is to obliterate the separation of powers. Strong partisan leaders dispute the Federalist claim that constitutional limits are best respected and constitutional rights are best protected when authority is dispersed throughout the national government. They regard the separation of powers as a functional convenience at best and at worse the vehicle that enables elites, from the money power to contemporary special interest groups, to warp American constitutional commitments by using control over various veto points to hold government hostage to their illegitimate demands. The strongly pro-same-sex marriage twenty-first-century Democrat is as convinced as the strongly antislavery nineteenth-century Republican that American constitutional commitments will be preserved and American constitutional promises redeemed only when the true party of the Constitution controls all three branches of the national government. Dividing power between different branches of national government or the major political parties may facilitate compromises that prevent an enfeebling gridlock. Still, whatever the virtue of making abortion legal but heavily regulated or mending rather than ending affirmative action, contemporary Republican and Democrat party activists believe that the national government is likely to respect constitutional limits and honor constitutional rights only to the extent that their coalition commands of the entire national government. The Levinson/Pildes call to divide power between parties from the perspective of ideological parties more resembles an effort to update Charles I than a compromise between the separation of powers championed by Stuart monarchs and the party government championed by their parliamentary rivals.

This essay focuses on the interaction between parties and the separation of powers during particular periods of American history rather than on the mechanisms that have driven transitions from one era to another. That essay on regime change might investigate usual suspects; constitutional transitions are structured by governing practices, the structure of partisan competition, and external events. Consider the transition from the party-driven politics of the nineteenth century to the state of courts, parties, and agencies. The

---

[141] Levinson and Pildes, pp. 2347–85.

constitutional separation of powers provided presidents from Theodore Roosevelt to Lyndon Johnson with the capacity to act independently from Congress and to seize a leadership role in policymaking. The Australian ballot, which diminished straight-ticket voting, was part of a series of progressive reforms that, by weakening the power of parties in the national legislature, increased the power of bureaucrats, executives, and judges.[142] The events responsible for the end of Reconstruction reduced the salience of racial issues, which weakened the capacity of Republican leaders to maintain a strong ideological party and halted any tendency toward legislative supremacy in the United States.[143]

Political pundits complain that Congress is broken,[144] the executive has run amok,[145] the judiciary has seized constitutional authority from the people,[146] and, even, the Constitution of the United States desperately needs to be replaced by a text that restores either the balances preferred by Charles I or the strong majoritarian government championed by John Pym.[147] Whatever constitutional transition occurs, however, is likely to be structured by the political leaders, political practices, and political institutions of our present constitutional regime.[148] The dynamics of non-revolutionary constitutional transition suggest that the next constitutional order in the United States will feature a separation of powers structured to achieve the constitutional vision of either the newly dominant Democratic Party or newly dominant Republican Party or, less likely, a separation of powers designed to keep power in the hands of the newly strengthened moderate wings of both parties.[149] That constitutional politics may resemble the party-driven constitutional politics of the nineteenth century, revive the constitutional politics of the first two-thirds of the twentieth century, or introduce a new

---

[142] See Walter Dean Burnham, *The Current Crisis in American Politics* (New York: Oxford University Press, 1983).

[143] See "Symposium: America's Political Dysfunction: Constitutional Connections, Causes, and Cures," 94 *Boston University Law Review* 575 (2014).

[144] Thomas E. Mann and Norman J. Ornstein, *The Broken Branch: How Congress is Failing America and How to Get It Back on Track* (New York: Oxford University Press, 2008).

[145] See Peter M. Shane, *Madison's Nightmare: How Executive Power Threatens American Democracy* (New York: University of Chicago Press, 2009); Stephen M. Griffin, *Long Wars and the Constitution* (Cambridge, MA: Harvard University Press, 2013).

[146] See Larry D. Kramer, *The People Themselves: Popular Constitutionalism and Judicial Review* (New York: Oxford University Press, 2004).

[147] See Sanford Levinson, *Our Undemocratic Constitution: Where the Constitution Goes Wrong (and How We the People Can Correct It)* (New York: Oxford University Press, 2006); Larry J. Sabato, *A More Perfect Constitution: Ideas to Inspire a New Generation* (New York: Walker Publishing Company, Inc., 2007).

[148] Skowronek, *Building a New American State*, p. 285; Graber, "Belling the Partisan Cats," p. 615.

[149] Whether President Trump creates an entirely different constitutional regime, fashions a partisan regime dominated by Republicans, or has little influence on an ongoing process in which partisan control of the White House shifts on an eight-year basis is for the future to determine.

scheme for making constitutional institutions work to achieve constitutional ends. The most unlikely outcome is a return to the Stuart/Federalist commitments of the framing. Charles I is now beheaded in both the United States and England, and as Keith Whittington observes, "James Madison has left the building."[150]

[150] Keith E. Whittington, "James Madison Has Left the Building," 72 *University of Chicago Review* 1137 (2005).

9

Executive Power and National Security Power

Andrew Kent and Julian Davis Mortenson

The constitutional text governing national security law is notoriously underspecified. The first thing the Constitution does after vesting "the executive power" in the President is to name the chief executive "commander in chief of the Army and Navy of the United States" and of the state militias "when called into the actual service of the United States." After that, clauses granting specific powers to the President are few and far between. If two thirds of the Senate concurs, the President can "make treaties." "On extraordinary occasions," the President can convene both houses of Congress. The President has an overarching obligation to "take care that the laws be faithfully executed" and must take an oath to "preserve, protect and defend the Constitution of the United States," perhaps implying a grant of power to do so. When it comes to Article II powers that plausibly bear on national security, that's more or less it.[1]

This lack of particularized authority creates two related problems. First, the federal government has no general police power to promote the public welfare; rather, it possesses only specific and limited powers. Just as Congress can only enact statutes pursuant to a specifically enumerated or implied constitutional power,[2] presidential action must likewise be grounded in some constitutional authority. Second, the defining role of the executive in US constitutional governance is *to execute* – to perform tasks assigned by statute or the Constitution and thereby to serve as the active arm of the popular will as it has been expressed through positive law. Both of these traditions complicate national security action by a chief executive who is armed with such sparse constitutional text – a difficulty with which American Presidents have wrestled since the first generation of US constitutional practice.

---

[1] The text of the Constitution also grants the President power of foreign intercourse, specifically the power to "receive ambassadors and other public ministers" and, with the consent of the Senate, to "nominate" and "appoint" US diplomats.

[2] This fundamental rule is not vitiated by the controversial case law suggesting that Congress may derive some legislative power directly from the law of nations or by virtue of the country's status as a sovereign nation. *See, e.g.*, United States v. Curtiss-Wright Exp. Corp., 299 U.S. 304, 318 (1936); Chae Chan Ping v. United States, 130 U.S. 581, 609 (1889).

This chapter will assess the national security powers of the President through the lens of what we call the authorization principle, which requires not just Presidents but all federal actors to identify particularized authority for their actions. In perhaps the most important opinion in all of separation of powers law, Justice Robert Jackson focused on authorization in its legislative guise as the central organizing principle for constitutional inquiry. In an analysis that was later formally adopted by a majority of the Supreme Court,[3] he described a constitutional spectrum divided loosely into three zones, each defined by the relationship between a presidential action and the existing statutory framework.[4] Zone 1 cases are those where "the President acts pursuant to an express or implied authorization of Congress"; Zone 2 cases involve executive "acts in absence of either a congressional grant or denial of authority"; and Zone 3 cases involve executive "measures incompatible with the express or implied will of Congress." The harder it is to ground a presidential act in specific legislative authorization, the harder it is to justify that act under the Constitution.

This instinct remains remarkably consistent throughout the course of American constitutional history. But the authorization principle has played out very differently over time. In the early republic, Congress often had to authorize national security action on an ad hoc basis. Today, blanket ex ante statutory authorizations are so broad that Presidents can often take action without needing to seek contemporaneous legislative approval at all. This of course tracks a larger trend in American constitutionalism, where broad delegations of power to the executive branch have become the dominant mode of regulation across a wide range of policy areas. In that sense, the national security realm is not unique – but its particularly high-stakes combination of urgency and uncertainty has resulted in a scheme of extraordinarily open-ended legislative delegation that probably exceeds any other area of American governance. This chapter sketches the contours of that evolution by focusing, in accordance with the structure of each contribution to this volume, on three moments in American history.

The first period is the early republic. Using three exemplary episodes – the Whiskey Rebellion, the Neutrality Proclamation, and the Quasi-War with France – the chapter traces the consistent instinct of Presidents in this period to seek highly particularized authorization from the two other constitutional branches of government. It emphasizes in particular how *modest* were the Presidents' claims of direct constitutional authorization and how *precise* were their requests for (and compliance with the terms of) specific statutory or judicial instructions. While very much alive to the risks of statehood in a complex and violent international order, this was a political culture that remained anxious about an excessively powerful – and ambiguously and

---

[3] Zivotofsky v. Kerry, 135 S. Ct. 2076, 2083–84 (2015); Hamdan v. Rumsfeld, 548 U.S. 557, 638 (2006); Dames & Moore v. Regan, 453 U.S. 654, 668–69 (1981).

[4] Youngstown Sheet & Tube Co. v. Sawyer, 343 U.S. 579, 635–38 (1952) (Jackson, J., concurring).

permanently authorized – executive branch. And so the instinct of Presidents was to seek approval from other constitutional actors, often in quite precise detail.

The second period is the Civil War. Given the existential upheaval of this period, it is perhaps unsurprising that it came to be defined by far more aggressive presidential claims that the Constitution itself grants a range of inherent ex ante authorities. While the authorization principle still dominated as an organizing concept, the *sources* of authority actually invoked were very different. During the early republic, national security authorization had been sought primarily in the contemporaneous acts of a then-sitting Congress. The Civil War period saw a dramatically increased tendency to seek authorization in the century-old terms of the Constitution. The chapter focuses on four presidential decisions to act without specific legislative authorization: the decisions to treat the Confederacy as subject to war powers, to blockade its ports, to suspend habeas corpus, and to emancipate slaves. Predictably, the more assertive posture of the Civil War presidency triggered severe constitutional controversy at each point.

Shifting frames to the post–Cold War period, the chapter concludes by showing how this constitutional pressure was eventually alleviated. Essentially, the solution has been for Congress – drawing on the legacy of the New Deal, World War II, and the Cold War alike – to enact a broad set of permanent and interlocking ex ante statutory authorizations, the collective effect of which is to allow the President to take virtually any national security action that seems needful. Combined with aggressive statutory interpretation and a large standing military, these statutes have enabled Presidents to take an extraordinarily wide range of significant national security measures without seeking particularized, contemporaneous authorization from any other constitutional actor. To make this point, the chapter will focus on three illustrative episodes: the detention of suspected terrorists throughout the world pursuant to Congress's 2001 Authorization for Use of Military Force, the use of power under the International Emergency Economic Powers Act (IEEPA) to both impose and lift sanctions on foreign powers, and the interpretive inversion of the War Powers Resolution to claim authorization for low-level presidential military interventions overseas.

The upshot is a constitutional arrangement that relies on remarkably open-ended statutory authorization to mitigate anxieties about both power and constraint – about the risks of a disempowered presidency in a dangerous world but also about the risks of letting Presidents rely on abstract constitutional text as the sole basis for coercive action. While these authorizations don't purport to constrain the executive branch with anything approaching the specificity of statutory regimes in earlier eras, their nature as legislative enactments entails a more meaningful possibility of authoritative supervision and even revision via subsequent democratic enactment than the Constitution ever could.

Our argument is not that no one in the founding era made aggressive constitutional claims or that no one in the modern era has challenged presidential claims of statutory authorization. But the patterns in this chapter mark out the lived experience of presidential power in the national security realm: underspecified at the founding, filled in on an ad hoc basis by congressional action in the early republic, expanded by aggressive reading of Constitutional text during the Civil War, and authorized ex ante by open-ended modern statutes that seek to resolve most plausibly necessary scenarios in advance. Constitutional law is never simply a matter of looking at founding text and subsequent precedent; here especially presidential practice must be understood with reference to the statutory background from which it emerges.

THE EARLY REPUBLIC

The defining constitutional commitment of the earliest American Presidents was a belief that executive action requires particularized rule-of-law authorization, even in the realm of national security. For a modern audience, early Presidents' scrupulous efforts to ground their national security actions in precise authorization can be surprising.[5] But it is demonstrably the case that Congress expected Presidents to seek authorization even for emergency action and that the earliest Presidents – far from challenging that expectation – complied with it painstakingly.

Start with President George Washington's response to the Whiskey Rebellion, a domestic disturbance that was viewed in many quarters as implicating adventurism by European powers.[6] The trouble began in March 1791, when Congress enacted a tax "upon Spirits distilled within the United States."[7] The tax was a central element of the national government's fiscal

---

[5] It actually makes perfect sense in a world where commanders-in-chief had long been viewed as answerable to the legislative power – not only on strategy but even on tactics. David J. Barron and Martin S. Lederman, The Commander in Chief at the Lowest Ebb – Framing the Problem, Doctrine, and Original Understanding, 121 *Harv. L. Rev.* 689, 772–80 (2008). This is at odds with the frequent modern assertion that at least low-level tactical determinations are within the preclusive discretion of the President. *See, e.g.*, John Hart Ely, *War and Responsibility: Constitutional Lessons of Vietnam and Its Aftermath* 5 (Princeton University Press 1993) ("The president, as 'commander in chief,' would assume tactical control (without constant congressional interference) of the way they were conducted."); *Ex parte Milligan*, 71 U.S. (4 Wall.) 2, 139 (1866) (arguing that Congress may not "interfere[] with the [President's] command of the forces and the conduct of [military] campaigns") (Chase, C.J. concurring).

[6] *See, e.g.*, Thomas P. Slaughter, *The Whiskey Rebellion: Frontier Epilogue to the American Revolution* 155–57, 190–92, 198–200 (Oxford University Press 1986). Slaughter's book is probably the most thorough modern treatment of the subject. *See also* Leland D. Baldwin, *Whiskey Rebels: The Story of a Frontier Uprising* 69, 104–9 (Pittsburgh University Press 1939) (focusing on events in Pennsylvania).

[7] Act of Mar. 3, 1791, ch. 15, 1 Stat. 199.

strategy – indeed, the second largest source of federal income[8] – and it prompted angry opposition, particularly in the western territories.[9] Despite legislative moderation of the tax regime,[10] trouble continued to brew and armed resistance broke out across Pennsylvania in 1794.[11]

Washington's ability to respond was governed by the Calling Forth Act of 1792,[12] which imposed strict limits on his ability to mobilize state militias.[13] First, the state where the insurrection was occurring had to petition for federal assistance.[14] Second, a federal judge had to certify that "the laws of the United States [had been] opposed, or the execution thereof obstructed, ... by combinations too powerful to be suppressed by the ordinary course of judicial proceedings, or by the powers vested in the marshals by this act[.]"[15] Third, before calling forth the militia, the act required the President to, "by proclamation, command such insurgents to disperse, and retire peaceably to their respective abodes, within a limited time."[16] Even then, the statute permitted mobilization only of the local militia in the state facing insurrection,

---

[8] Ron Chernow, *Alexander Hamilton* 468 (Penguin Books 2004).

[9] *Id.* (noting that federal tax collectors "were shunned, tarred, feathered, blindfolded, and whipped"). *See also* Townsend Ward, *The Insurrection of the Year 1794, in the Western Counties of Pennsylvania, in* 6 Memoirs of the Historical Society of Pennsylvania 119–27 (1858) (noting that distilling alcohol "was considered to be as clear a national right as to convert grain into flour").

[10] Congress reduced the tax on distillers in cities, towns or villages from nine to twenty-five cents per gallon to seven to eighteen cents per gallon. Act of May 8, 1792, ch. 32, 1 Stat. 267.

[11] Slaughter, *supra* note 6, at 3 ("[S]ome 7000 western Pennsylvanians advanced against the town of Pittsburgh, threatened its residents, feigned an attack on Fort Pitt and the federal arsenal there, banished seven members of the community, and destroyed the property of several others. Violence spread to western Maryland, where a Hagerstown crowd joined in, raised liberty poles, and began a march on the arsenal at Frederick. At about the same time, sympathetic 'friends of liberty' arose in Carlisle, Pennsylvania, and back-country regions of Virginia and Kentucky. Reports reached the federal government in Philadelphia that the western country was ablaze and that rebels were negotiating with representatives of Great Britain and Spain, two of the nation's most formidable European competitors, for aid in a frontier-wide separatist movement.").

[12] Act of May 2, 1792, ch. 23, 1 Stat. 264 ("Calling Forth Act"), codified as amended at 10 U.S.C. § 334.

[13] The intricacy of these checks was no accident. The proposal to allow the President to call out the militia to execute federal law was controversial and much debated. It passed only after the initial bill was amended to add precisely the procedural checks that Washington later followed so carefully. *See* David E. Engdahl, Soldiers, Riots, and Revolution: The Law and History of Military Troops in Civil Disorders, 57 *Iowa L. Rev.* 1, 44–48 (1971). Even then it was limited by a three-year sunset provision. Calling Forth Act § 10. Washington's compliance with the laws was thus no empty formality; it was both politically salient and of deeply substantive significance.

[14] Calling Forth Act § 1 ("[I]t shall be lawful for the President of the United States, on application of the legislature of such state, or of the executive (when the legislature cannot be convened) to call forth such number of the militia of any other state or states, as may be applied for, or as he may judge sufficient to suppress such insurrection.").

[15] *Id.* § 2.   [16] *Id.* § 3.

unless that militia refused to comply or was ineffective, in which case the President could call up militia from other states if Congress was not then in session.[17]

Far from defying these comprehensive restrictions in a moment of crisis, Washington satisfied their every requirement in scrupulous detail. He submitted a statement to Justice James Wilson of the Supreme Court describing the situation in Pennsylvania and requesting statutory certification.[18] He waited to muster the troops until Wilson had issued a letter reciting the requisite statutory language (after first requiring the President to present authentication of the underlying reports and verification of their handwriting).[19] And Washington issued the requisite proclamation ordering the Whiskey Rebels to disperse.[20] Nor did his compliance with statutory restrictions cease once his forces were in the field. Since Congress had not been not in session when he issued the call-up order, Washington was authorized by statute to mobilize militias from other states besides Pennsylvania – but only "until the expiration of thirty days after the commencement of the ensuing [congressional] session."[21] When it became clear that the Pennsylvania campaign would take longer than that, Washington went back to Congress to petition for extension of the statutory time limit that would otherwise have required him to disband his troops.[22] The story of the Whiskey Rebellion, in short, is one of a famously vigorous leader adhering to statutory limits in exacting detail, regardless of the inconvenience involved.

A similar instinct for seeking external legal approval characterized Washington's approach to the diplomatic imbroglio that eventually resulted

---

[17] See id. § 2.
[18] See Letter from James Wilson to George Washington (Aug. 4, 1794), reprinted in Walter Lowrie and Walter S. Franklin, eds., 1 *American State Papers: Miscellaneous* 85 (Gales & Seaton 1834).
[19] See Stanley Elkins and Eric McKitrick, *The Age of Federalism* 478 (Oxford University Press 1993); Letter from James Wilson to George Washington (Aug. 4, 1794), reprinted in Walter Lowrie and Walter S. Franklin, eds., 1 *American State Papers: Miscellaneous* 85 (Gales & Seaton 1834). *See also* Slaughter, *supra* note 6, at 3 ("President Washington nationalized 12,950 militiamen from New Jersey, Pennsylvania, Maryland, and Virginia – an army approximating in size the Continental force that followed him during the Revolution – and personally led the 'Watermelon Army' west to shatter the insurgency.").
[20] Calling Forth Act § 3 (requiring the President to issue a proclamation ordering insurgents to "disperse, and retire peaceably to their respective abodes"); George Washington, *A Proclamation* (Aug. 7, 1794), reprinted in James D. Richardson, ed., 1 *A Compilation of the Messages and Papers of the Presidents, 1789–1897* at 158, 158–60 (Government Printing Office 1896) (making the required proclamation). *See also* Baldwin, *supra* note 6, at 183–85 (describing course of mobilization); Glenn A. Phelps, *George Washington and American Constitutionalism* 134 (University Press of Kansas 1993) (noting that Washington resisted calls to summon the militia without congressional support).
[21] Calling Forth Act § 2.
[22] See William C. Banks, Providing "Supplemental Security": The Insurrection Act and the Military Role in Responding to Domestic Crises, 3 *J. Nat'l Sec. L. & Pol.* 39, 59 (2009); Stephen I. Vladeck, Emergency Power and the Militia Acts, 114 *Yale L. J.* 149, 161 (2004).

in the Neutrality Proclamation of 1793.[23] The proclamation was prompted by the ongoing fallout of the French Revolution, and in particular by revolutionary France's declaration of war on both Great Britain and the Netherlands. The difficulty for the United States was not just diplomatic but legal. In addition to treaties pledging perpetual peace with both France and Great Britain,[24] the United States had also entered a 1778 agreement with the old French regime under which the United States undertook to protect "from the present time and forever against all other powers ... the present possessions of the Crown of France in America, as well as those which it may acquire by the future treaty of peace."[25] As a policy matter, Washington was committed to keeping the United States out of the war in Europe;[26] the legal question was whether the 1778 agreement with France permitted him to do so.

The controversy spurred sharp disagreement among members of Washington's cabinet and other statesmen about a number of key decisions, including which side of the conflict to prefer, what the various treaties required, and whether and how to engage the other branches of government.[27] Despite these disputes, the entire cabinet supported Washington when he issued his Neutrality Proclamation in April 1793. Asserting that "the duty and interest of the United States require that they should with sincerity and good faith adopt and pursue a conduct friendly and impartial toward the belligerent powers," the proclamation warned American citizens that "prosecutions [would] be instituted against all persons who shall, within the cognizance of the courts of the United States, violate the law of nations with respect to the powers at war, or any of them."[28]

The key legal point was the administration's conclusion – implicit in the proclamation and quite explicit in the internal deliberations – that the 1778 agreements did not require the United States to offer affirmative assistance to France in this case and that the more recent treaties of perpetual peace applied in

---

[23] For an excellent short treatment of how the Neutrality Proclamation was drafted, see Elkins and McKitrick, *supra* note 19, at 336–41. For an analysis of the legal issues involved, see Martin S. Flaherty, The Story of the Neutrality Controversy: Struggling over Presidential Power Outside the Courts, in Christopher H. Schroeder and Curtis A. Bradley, eds., *Presidential Power Stories* 21 (Foundation Press 2009).

[24] Treaty of Amity and Commerce Between the United States of American and His Most Christian Majesty (Feb. 6, 1778), reprinted in Government Printing Office, *Treaties and Conventions Concluded between the United States of America and Other Powers since July 4, 1776*, at 244–53 (1873); Definitive Treaty of Peace between the United States of America and His Britannic Majesty (Sept. 3, 1783), reprinted in *id.* at 314–18.

[25] Treaty of Alliance Between the United States of America and His Most Christian Majesty (Feb. 6, 1778), reprinted in *id.* at 241–44.

[26] William R. Casto, *Foreign Affairs and the Constitution in the Age of Fighting Sail* 26 (University of South Carolina Press 2006); Flaherty, *supra* note 23, at 23–25.

[27] *See* Chernow, *supra* note 8, at 435–44; Casto, *supra* note 26, at 29–31; Flaherty, *supra* note 23, at 28–42.

[28] Richardson, *supra* note 20, at 156–57.

full. The Neutrality Proclamation, in this sense, represented a President taking seriously the nation's obligations under international law.[29] Even Alexander Hamilton, the most aggressive proponent of executive power in the cabinet, grounded his defense of the proclamation principally in the assertion that Washington had not just a right but a duty to assess his legal obligations as executor of public law: "He, who is to execute the laws, must first judge for himself of their meaning."[30]

Notably, Washington went out of his way to seek approval of his legal assessment by both the Supreme Court and Congress. The administration began by asking the Supreme Court to resolve the treaty and neutrality questions more definitively:

The war which has taken place among the powers of Europe produces frequent transactions within our ports and limits, on which questions arise of considerable difficulty, and of greater importance to the peace of the US ... Yet their decision is so little analogous to the ordinary functions of the Executive, as to occasion much embarrassment and difficulty to them. The President would therefore be much relieved if he found himself free to refer questions of this description to the opinions of the Judges of the supreme court of the US. whose knolege of the subject would secure us against errors dangerous to the peace of the US. and their authority ensure the respect of all parties.[31]

---

[29] *See* Flaherty, *supra* note 23, at 49; Robert J. Reinstein, *Executive Power and the Law of Nations in the Washington Administration*, 46 Univ. Richmond L. Rev. 373, 409–33 (2012). The proposition "[i]nternational law is part of our law" was much less controversial for much of United States history than it is now. *See, e.g.*, The Paquette Habana, 175 U.S. 677, 700 (1900).

[30] Alexander Hamilton, Pacificus No 1 (June 29, 1793), in J. Gideon and G. S. Gideon, *Letters of Pacificus and Helvidius (1845) with the Letters of Americanus* 5, 14–15 (Scholars' Facsimiles & Reprints 1976) ("In order to the observance of that conduct which the laws of nations, combined with our treaties, prescribed to this country, in reference to the present war in Europe, it was necessary for the president to judge for himself, whether there was any thing in our treaties, incompatible with an adherence to neutrality."). A contrary view frames the Neutrality Proclamation as asserting a wide-ranging residual foreign affairs power. *See* Saikrishna B. Prakash and Michael D. Ramsey, *The Executive Power over Foreign Affairs*, 111 Yale L.J. 231, 324–39 (2001). The evidence for this assertion is not convincing. *Compare* Curtis A. Bradley and Martin S. Flaherty, *Executive Power Essentialism and Foreign Affairs*, 102 Mich. L. Rev. 545, 669 n. 603 (2004) (citing the lack of cabinet discussion about the existence of an exclusive constitutional authority to issue the Neutrality Proclamation), *with* Prakash and Ramsey, supra, at 324–27 (arguing that this belief was implicit in the discussions). Washington's failure to consult Congress seems of little more legal significance, standing alone, than any executive officer's failure to consult Congress or the courts about the proper interpretation of an important statute. We would hardly conclude from the latter scenario that the President was asserting the "sole" power to interpret statutes.

[31] Letter from Thomas Jefferson, Sec'y of State, to the Justices of the Supreme Court (July 8, 1793), http://founders.archives.gov/documents/Jefferson/01-26-02-0462. Accompanying the letter was a list of twenty-nine specific questions regarding the neutrality crisis. Enclosure to Letter from Thomas Jefferson, Sec'y of State, to the Justices of the Supreme Court (July 8, 1793), http:// founders.archives.gov/documents/Washington/05-13-02-0164-0002.

When the Court refused to issue an advisory opinion,[32] Washington turned to Congress. He appeared before a joint session to describe his actions and to invite the legislature to overrule him if it disagreed with his course of action. Since Congress had not been in session, he said, "[i]t seemed ... to be my duty to admonish our citizens of the consequences of a contraband trade, and of hostile acts to any of the parties"; "[u]nder these impressions, the [Neutrality] Proclamation ... was issued." There was no equivocation in Washington's recognition of legislative supremacy on the underlying question: "It rests with the wisdom of Congress to correct, improve, *or* enforce this plan of procedure" regarding neutrality.[33]

Washington's successor John Adams continued the previous administration's practice of seeking and then following contemporaneous congressional authorization – sometimes in flyspecking detail – even during an open military conflict with a foreign nation.[34] During the European wars following the French Revolution, the French (and other belligerents) had been seizing American merchant ships and cargos under various pretexts. After the United States' partial reconciliation with Great Britain through the Jay Treaty, France in 1796 and 1797 increased the quantity and outrageousness of its seizures,[35] taking hundreds of vessels.[36]

In the face of these provocations, the Adams administration cautiously tried to preserve peace – both for policy reasons and because, like during the

---

[32] "The Lines of Separation drawn by the Constitution between the three Departments of Government – their being in certain Respects checks on each other – and our being Judges of a court in the last Resort – are Considerations which afford strong arguments against the Propriety of our extrajudicially deciding the questions alluded to; especially as the Power given by the Constitution to the President of calling on the Heads of Departments for opinions, seems to have been *purposely* as well as expressly limited to *executive* Departments." Letter from the Justices of the United States Supreme Court, to George Washington (Aug. 8, 1793), http://founders .archives.gov/documents/Washington/05-13-02-0263. *See also* Phelps, *supra* note 20, at 164–67; Neal Kumar Katyal, Judges as Advicegivers, 50 *Stan. L. Rev.* 1709, 1742–46 (1998).

[33] *Address of George Washington*, 4 Annals of Cong. 11 (Dec. 3, 1793) (emphasis added). Note the disjunctive nature of his last sentence: this was not merely a request that Congress provide for the enforcement of Washington's announced policy; it was a recognition that Congress might instead choose to change it. *See generally* Robert J. Reinstein, Is the President's Recognition Power Exclusive?, 86 *Temp. L. Rev.* 1, 13–14 (2013) ("Washington understood that he was exercising power that was concurrent with, and ultimately subordinate to, the will of Congress.").

[34] Nor does the tradition end with Adams. If anything, Presidents Jefferson and Madison were even more scrupulous about framing their national security activities within an affirmative structure of statutory authorization. *See, e.g.,* the discussion in Julian Davis Mortenson, Executive Power and the Discipline of History, 78 *U. Chi. L. Rev.* 377, 404–5, 433–36 (2011).

[35] *See* Alexander DeConde, *The Quasi-War: The Politics and Diplomacy of the Undeclared War with France, 1797–1801,* at 8–9 (Charles Scribner's Sons 1966); Elkins and McKitrick, *supra* note 19, at 537–38.

[36] Deconde, *supra* note 35, at 9; Bradford Perkins, 1 *The Cambridge History of American Foreign Relations: The Creation of a Republican Empire, 1776–1865,* at 105 (Cambridge University Press 1993).

Washington administration, the President and his advisors understood that only Congress had constitutional authority to decide to take the country to war.

In his inaugural address in March 1797, President Adams announced his "determination to maintain peace" and US neutrality in the European war, a policy that had been "solemnly sanctioned by both Houses of Congress," until such as time as another policy "shall be otherwise ordained by Congress."[37] If he could not maintain peace, the President said he would "lay the facts before the Legislature, that they may consider what further measures the honor and interest of the Government and its constituents demand."[38] As French attacks on US shipping continued, Adams called the legislature into special session so Congress could "determine on such measures as in their wisdom shall be deemed meet for the safety and welfare" of the country.[39] Adams recommended, among other measures, that Congress increase the number of armed public vessels, raise a provisional army, allow US naval vessels to convoy unarmed merchant ships, and allow merchantmen to arm and defend themselves, stressing however that this decision "remain[ed] for Congress" to make.[40]

Adams repeatedly deferred to Congress on decisions about how to respond to France,[41] and Congress indeed set its own course. It began a gradual program of rearmament and defensive preparations and over time authorized increasingly vigorous military responses by the executive. The congressional statutes governing military action directed that only naval forces could be used to defend or attack the French and specified that particular classes of vessels could be used "for particular sorts of actions against French vessels, in particular locations, for particular purposes."[42] A "provisional army" was authorized to be raised and deployed

---

[37] Inaugural Address of President John Adams (Mar. 4, 1797), in 1 James D. Richardson, ed., *A Compilation of the Messages and Papers of the Presidents* 218, 221 (Bureau of National Literature, Inc., New York, 1897).

[38] *Id.* at 221–22.

[39] Proclamation of the President of the United States, Mar. 25, 1797, *in id.* at 222, 223.

[40] *Id.* at 227–28. Both Adams and the Congress agreed, in the words of the House, that "management of our foreign negotiations" was given by the Constitution to "the control of the Executive power," Address of the House of Representatives to John Adams, President of the United States, Nov. 26, 1800, *in id.* at 300, 301, and so Adams on his own initiative nominated and instructed three special envoys to go to France to seek a peaceful resolution, see Special Message of President Adams to the Senate, May 31, 1797, *in id.* at 236, 236.

[41] *See generally* Perkins, *supra* note 36, at 105–6 (noting that Adams sought to preserve peace during the entire period).

[42] David J. Barron & Martin S. Lederman, The Commander in Chief at the Lowest Ebb—A Constitutional History, 121 Harv. L. Rev. 941, 967 (2008). For congressional authorizations (and limitations) on the President's use of the military, see, for example, Act of July 1, 1797, § 12, ch. 7, 1 Stat. 523, 525 (authorizing the President to use revenue cutters—not larger ships of war—to "defend the seacoast, and … repel any hostility to their vessels and commerce"); Act of May 28, 1798, ch. 48, 1 Stat. 561, 561 (authorizing the President to use armed public vessels to seize armed French vessels that had committed "depredations on the vessels belonging to citizens" of the United States or were "hovering on the coasts of the United States" for that purpose); Act of July 9, 1798, ch. 68, 1 Stat. 578, 578, § 1 (authorizing the President to instruct

only until the next session of Congress and "in the event of a declaration of war against the United States, or of actual invasion of their territory, by a foreign power, or of imminent danger of such invasion."[43] Even amid the increased pace of French attacks, with French cruisers hovering along the seacoast at Long Island, the entrance of Delaware Bay, and elsewhere,[44] Adams considered himself limited by the metes and bounds of congressional authorizations and acted accordingly.

The Adams administration did occasionally cut some corners during a covert part of the Quasi War. To weaken France without risking escalation to total war, Adams secretly and cautiously aided Toussaint Louverture's rebels who were fighting a civil war against France on the island of St. Domingue (today's Haiti). In the course of rendering this assistance, Adams sent one shipment of supplies to the rebels prior to complying with necessary statutory formalities that would have legalized the transaction.[45] On another occasion, and without either congressional authorization or specific orders from the administration itself, an American naval vessel at St. Domingue blockaded a harbor and bombarded the fort of a pro-French local force.[46]

For its part, the Supreme Court did not equivocate in upholding the supremacy of Congress when confronted with a specific case where an executive officer had gone beyond statutory authorization at St. Domingue. Notably, the issue did not involve armed confrontation with the enemy but rather seizure of a vessel for allegedly violating a narrowly drawn nonintercourse statute. The Secretary of Navy adopted a plausible though broad view of the means needed to implement the statutory policy, but the Supreme Court held that since "the legislature seem to have prescribed ... the manner in which this law shall be carried into execution," the executive was bound to follow statutory directions strictly.[47]

Consistent with Adam's deferential posture elsewhere, the administration did not challenge the courts' authority to decide the case and did not argue that Article II overrode Congress's choice of means for carrying out policy embodied in a wartime statute. Viewed as a whole, the actions of the Adams administration thus continued Washington's policy of seeking and then following contemporaneous congressional authorization to respond to national security crises.

U.S. naval vessels to "seize and take any armed French vessel, which shall be found within the jurisdictional limits of the United States, or elsewhere, on the high seas").

[43] Act of May 28, 1798, ch. 47, 1 Stat. 558, 558, § 1.

[44] Elkins and McKitrick, *supra* note 19, at 645, 652.

[45] *See* Robert J. Reinstein, Slavery, Executive Power, and International Law: The Haitian Revolution and American Constitutionalism, 53 *Am. J. Leg. Hist.* 141, 164, 173–74 (2013).

[46] *Id.* at 175–76.   [47] Little v. Barreme, 6 U.S. (2 Cranch) 170, 177–78 (1804).

THE CIVIL WAR ERA

The existential crisis of the Civil War and expansive constitutional vision of the presidency held by Abraham Lincoln inaugurated a new era in executive-congressional relations and a new approach for the executive toward the problem of authorization. There were some standing statutory authorities that could be taken off the shelf and used to respond to the rebellion, and the President did so aggressively. But when the scale and pace of the crisis rendered these few preexisting authorities insufficient almost immediately, Lincoln did not refrain from vital military measures simply because the statutory framework had important gaps. Instead, the President asserted a broad, inherent ex ante authority to defend the Union and preserve constitutional government, granted to the executive by the Constitution itself. Former Supreme Court justice Benjamin Curtis described Lincoln's position as amounting to a claim of "transcendent executive power,"[48] and Lincoln himself explained to a group of Chicago ministers that "as commander-in-chief of the army and navy, in time of war, I suppose I have a right to take *any* measure which may best subdue the enemy."[49]

Lincoln's reliance on constitutional authorization and an expansive reading of the power to execute the laws, rather than on the detailed, bespoke authorization statutes favored by earlier Presidents, caused significant legal and political controversy. Four examples are addressed in what follows: the legal characterization of both the Confederacy and the war, the decision to order a naval blockade, the suspension of habeas corpus, and the emancipation of slaves.

That said, while Lincoln had a broad view of executive power under the Constitution, he did not slight the other branches of government. Rather he saw himself as protecting and preserving a constitutional order in which Congress by design played a dominant role. Each of the legal-policy decisions examined here were supported by key members of Congress and ultimately endorsed, wholly or largely, by formal acts of the full Congress. Three of the decisions by Lincoln occurred at the outset of the war, before Congress was in session, and therefore the legislature was not able to offer its formal views beforehand. But on the one issue where it could – the emancipation of slaves, which unfolded over the course of 1861 and 1862 – Lincoln's policies were spurred and shaped in significant part by congressional priorities embodied in statute. Lincoln also conceded that his actions could be overruled by Congress.

Moreover, Lincoln chose policies knowing that the federal judiciary would assert the authority to approve or reject his decisions about blockade, emancipation, and the legal nature of the war. It was not a forgone conclusion that the President's decisions would be endorsed by the federal courts. Hence Lincoln worked within a framework of shared authority over

---

[48] B[enjamin] R. Curtis, *Executive Power* 9 (Little, Brown & Co. 1862).
[49] Reply to Emancipation Memorial Presented by Chicago Christians of All Denominations, Sept. 13, 1862, *in* Roy P. Basler, ed., 5 *The Collected Works of Abraham Lincoln* 419, 421 (Rutgers 1953) (emphasis added).

war and national security even as he exerted much more power, with much less statutory authorization, than any of his predecessors.[50]

* * *

By the time Lincoln was inaugurated in early March 1861, the lower South had purported to secede from the Union, almost all federal property and installations there had been abandoned or confiscated, and the government of the new Confederate States of America (CSA) had formed.[51] In mid-April, the rebels' attack on Fort Sumter in the harbor of Charleston, South Carolina, inaugurated the shooting war.[52]

Congress was not in session, so the President and his advisers needed to decide how to respond to armed rebellion based on existing legal authorities. Decades-old statutes authorized the President to deploy the militia or army "whenever the laws of the United States shall be opposed, or the execution thereof obstructed, by combinations too powerful to be suppressed by the ordinary course of judicial proceedings."[53] But the available troops were few. And the Buchanan administration had recently taken the position that it would be "wholly illegal" to use federal armed forces against seceding states if the closure of federal courts and resignations of federal officials had left no effective criminal justice machinery in place to enforce the civil law.[54]

While the attack on Sumter raised a host of military problems for the Lincoln administration, there was also a constitutional and strategic issue of immense import: how to characterize the legal status of the CSA and its residents. Lincoln's inaugural address had rejected the constitutionality of secession and promised to continue to enforce federal law nationwide.[55] Congress was not consulted before Lincoln made this declaration, but attempting to maintain the status quo and to faithfully execute the laws until Congress gave contrary direction was the President's acknowledged duty under the Constitution.[56] Especially after Sumter, Lincoln had broad public support in declaring that, "in view of the Constitution and the laws[,] the Union [wa]s unbroken."[57] So

---

[50] For a description of actions by Lincoln in spring 1861 that contravened statutory and constitutional limits, see Barron and Lederman, *supra* note 42, at 1001–3.

[51] *See* David M. Potter, *The Impending Crisis, 1848–1861*, at 485–554 (Harper Colophon 1976); E. B. Long and Barbara Long, *The Civil War Day by Day* 11–33 (Doubleday & Co. 1971).

[52] *See* David Herbert Donald, *Lincoln* 285–92 (Simon & Schuster 1995); Craig L. Symonds, *Lincoln and His Admirals* 3–36 (Oxford University Press 2008); Long and Long, *supra* note 51, at 56–57.

[53] Act of Feb. 28, 1795, ch. 36, 1 Stat. 424, § 2; Act of Mar. 3, 1807, ch. 39, 2 Stat. 443, § 1.

[54] Power of the President in Executing the Laws, 9 Op. Att'y Gen. 516, 518, 522–23 (1860).

[55] Abraham Lincoln, First Inaugural Address, Mar. 4, 1861, in 4 Basler, *supra* note 49, at 262–71.

[56] *Id.* at 265; *see also* U.S. Const. art. II, § 3 ("[The President] shall take care that the laws be faithfully executed.").

[57] First Inaugural Address, *in* 4 Basler, *supra* note 49, at 265. On popular opinion in the north, see James McPherson, *Battle Cry of Freedom* 274–75 (Oxford University Press 1988); Donald, *supra* note 52, at 295–96, 305.

secession would be treated as null and void, the CSA would not be recognized as an independent nation, CSA residents' citizenship and duty of allegiance to the United States would be deemed unimpaired, and federal criminal laws would be enforced where possible.[58]

The problem for Lincoln was that important strands of legal thought at the time held that domestic rebels could only be checked by individually singling out the guilty for criminal punishment using methods based on preexisting statutory authority, overseen by courts and respecting individual constitutional rights. The militia or army could be called out to assist the civil authorities and meet fire with fire if resisted. But unlike in a foreign war, whole regions or states or classes of citizens could not be deemed outside the protection of domestic law and indiscriminately targeted with the methods of warfare, whether armed attack or property seizure.[59] This criminal law-based approach, however, faced a practical problem: a large region of the country, home to several million people, claimed to have seceded and become independent and was raising armies and naval forces to attack the United States. Domestic law enforcement was plainly not up to the task; merely executing the statutory laws on the books would not save the Union.

There was also a separation of powers angle to consider before the methods and rules of warfare could be employed. Some thought that only Congress had the constitutional authority to take the United States from a state of peace – where ordinary, domestic processes prevailed and the President had a duty to faithfully execute preexisting law against guilty individuals – into a state of war where opponents of the United States could be treated *en bloc* as enemies and belligerents under the international laws of war and where the President would enjoy discretion as Commander in Chief to take actions that would otherwise be unconstitutional. But Congress, as noted, was not in session.

Lincoln acted decisively. On April 19, he ordered the US Navy to blockade the seven states of the CSA and added Virginia and North Carolina when they also took steps to secede.[60] Blockade was only lawful when a state of war existed between belligerent parties, and it acted against all of the people of the blockaded area and anyone trying to trade with them, not just individually guilty malefactors.[61] Hence the blockade proclamation amounted to a presidential decision that the rebellion would be treated as a war, not a law enforcement operation. The 1795 and 1807 insurrection statutes authorized the President to call out the militia, army, and navy to enforce the laws of the United States in the event of "insurrection," but they did not purport to authorize the employment of

---

[58] *See* Donald, *supra* note 52, at 302–3; Andrew Kent, The Constitution and the Laws of War during the Civil War, 85 *Notre Dame L. Rev.* 1839, 1850–53, 1863–85 (2010).

[59] *See id.*

[60] Proclamation of a Blockade, Apr. 19, 1861, in 4 Basler, *supra* note 49, at 338–39; Proclamation of a Blockade, Apr. 27, 1861, *in id.* at 346–47.

[61] *See* Thomas H. Lee and Michael D. Ramsey, *The Story of the Prize Cases: Executive Action and Judicial Review in Wartime*, in Schroeder and Bradley, *supra* note 23, at 53, 60.

military force against persons innocent of involvement in insurrection, whether residents of insurrectionary districts or neutral foreigners.[62] Hence Article II of the Constitution, invoking authority under the laws of war rather than under congressional statutes, was the source of the power asserted.[63]

Many supporters of the administration had argued that to avoid implying a recognition of the Confederacy and to make clear to European powers that the rebellion was a purely domestic issue, Lincoln should have ordered the closure of the ports in the CSA rather than their blockade.[64] This would have barred all traffic in and out and subjected violators to arrest and prosecution under US criminal laws. At the suggestion of Secretary of State Seward, Lincoln chose instead to blockade because it would reduce the chance of conflict with Great Britain. The international rules of blockade were well known and accepted, and getting caught running a blockade resulted in, at most, the forfeiture of vessel and cargo in a court applying the law of nations, not criminal punishment imposed under domestic law.[65]

Opponents of the administration in the North and many Southerners argued that the blockade proclamation was unconstitutional. Critics claimed that only Congress had authority to regulate commerce; the blockade was a discriminatory preference for some ports of the United States over others; blockades were only appropriate in nation-to-nation wars, not insurrections; and the United States could not make war against its states and, even if it could, only Congress could move the nation into a state of war.[66]

Neither the President nor any member of his cabinet publicly outlined the legal reasons why they believed that the President had constitutional authority to order the blockade and seizure of vessels violating it. But in an 1863 letter written to James Conkling, intended to be read at a pro-Union political rally, Lincoln explained, in the context of defending the Emancipation Proclamation, the President's constitutional right to order the seizure of property from enemies, whether combatants or not: "I think the constitution invests its

---

[62] Act of Mar. 3, 1807, ch. 39, 2 Stat. 443 and Act of Feb. 28, 1795, ch. 36, 1 Stat. 424. *See also* Kent, *supra* note 58, at 1897 n. 209; Thomas H. Lee, The Civil War in U.S. Foreign Relations Law: A Dress Rehearsal for Modern Transformations, 53 *St. Louis U. L.J.* 53, 63–64 (2008).

[63] *See* Kent, *supra* note 58, at 1864–65; Lee and Ramsey, *supra* note 61, at 77–78, 88.

[64] *See, e.g.,* John Fabian Witt, *Lincoln's Code: The Laws of War in American History* 145 (Free Press 2012) (reporting the views of Secretary of the Navy Gideon Welles, Attorney General Edward Bates and Postmaster General Montgomery Blair); Charles M. Segal ed., *Conversations with Lincoln* 113–14 (G.P. Putnam's Sons 1961) (recounting conversation between Lincoln and Rep. Thaddeus Stevens on Apr. 19, 1861).

[65] Witt, *supra* note 64, at 143–47.

[66] *See, e.g.,* Cong. Globe, 37th Cong., 1st Sess. 48–49, 67 (statements of Sen. Polk); Cong. Globe, 37th Cong., 1st Sess. 69 (statements of Sen. Powell); Cong. Globe, 37th Cong., 1st Sess. 57 (statement of Rep. Vallandigham). *See also* U.S. Const. art. I, § 8, cl. 3 ("The Congress shall have power … [t]o regulate commerce with foreign nations, and among the several states" and "declare war"); *id.* § 9, cl. 6 ("No preference shall be given by any regulation of commerce or revenue to the ports of one state over those of another.").

commander-in-chief, with the law of war, in time of war ... Is there – has there ever been – any question that by the law of war, property... of enemies ... may be taken when needed?"[67]

The legal issues were more fully developed in litigation before the US Supreme Court. Counsel for vessels seized during the blockade argued that the President had usurped Congress' constitutional role: "Congress had not declared war to begin, or to exist already, at the date in question. Therefore, war did not exist; blockade did not exist; and there could be no capture for breach of blockade, or intent to break it."[68]

Richard A. Dana, one of the administration's lawyers, responded that if war is to be initiated by the United States, it is true that only Congress may decide do to so. "But there are two parties to a war. War is *a state of things*, and not an act of legislative will. If a foreign power springs a war upon us by sea and land, during a recess of Congress, exercising all belligerent rights of capture, the question is, whether the President can repel war with war ...?"[69] The answer was obvious, he thought: "It is enough to state the proposition. If it be not so, there is no protection to the State."[70] Dana then argued that the same rule must necessarily apply to rebellions of the scale that occurred in 1861.

The President's assertion of Article II power to blockade was bold but did not seek to shut out other constitutional actors. In his July 4 address to Congress, he indicated that he hoped that Congress would agree that his policy choices made during the recess had been appropriate but that he would be guided now, "as ever," by the laws of the United States.[71] When Congress convened for its special emergency session, it authorized the President to close the ports of states in insurrection and barred commercial intercourse between states in insurrection and the rest of the United States.[72] Congress retroactively approved the blockade in both that statute and in a general ratification act.[73]

The President also knew from the outset that federal courts applying the law of nations would rule on the legality of the blockade when captured vessels and cargo were brought to court to adjudicate whether they were proper prizes of war. It was not until spring 1863 that the Supreme Court agreed that the President had possessed authority under Article II to implement the blockade

[67] Letter from Abraham Lincoln to James Conkling, Aug. 26, 1863, in 6 Basler, *supra* note 49, at 406, 408.

[68] The Prize Cases, 67 U.S. 635, 649 (1863) (argument of James Carlisle).

[69] *Id.* at 659 (argument of Richard Dana).   [70] *Id.* at 660 (argument of Richard Dana).

[71] Abraham Lincoln, Message to Congress in Special Session, July 4, 1861, in 4 Basler, *supra* note 49, at 421, 439.

[72] Non-Intercourse Act, ch. 3, 12 Stat. 255, §§ 4–6 (July 13, 1861).

[73] Act of August 6, 1861, ch. 63, § 3, 12 Stat. 326 ("[A]ll the acts, proclamations and orders of the President ... after the fourth of March, [1861], respecting the army and navy of the United States, and calling out or relating to the militia or volunteers from the states, are hereby approved and in all respects legalized and made valid, to the same intent and with the same effect as if they had been issued and done under the previous express authority and direction of the Congress of the United States.").

in April 1861.[74] Even then, four dissenting justices, including Chief Justice Roger Taney, contended that the blockade had been unlawful until authorized by Congress in the Non-Intercourse Act.[75]

More controversial than the blockade were the President's orders authorizing military commanders to suspend the privilege of the writ of habeas corpus. Lincoln first authorized suspension of the writ along the military lines between Philadelphia and Washington, DC, on April 27, 1861.[76] With the secession of Virginia and pro-secession rioting and sabotage occurring in Maryland, there was a real possibility that the capital might be cut off from the North and overrun. Some Marylanders were burning railroad bridges, destroying telegraph lines, and attempting to bar the passage of Union troops through to Washington.[77] The US Army arrested numerous rebels in Maryland, many of whom were imprisoned at Fort McHenry in Baltimore harbor.[78]

The Constitution provided that "[t]he privilege of the writ of habeas corpus shall not be suspended, unless when in cases of rebellion or invasion the public safety may require it."[79] It was widely assumed at the time, though rarely had it been actively debated, that only Congress could suspend habeas corpus and that suspension authorization would need to be given expressly.[80]

Lincoln's July 4 address made a special point to defend his invocation of an Article II power to suspend habeas corpus. His first claim was a more modest one, built on his duty to faithfully execute the laws of the United States – in the so-called Take Care Clause of Article II – rather than an assertion of executive prerogative. In the states in insurrection, all of the federal "forts, arsenals, dockyards, custom-houses, and the like, including the movable and stationary property in and about them, had been seized" by rebels, and federal officials had either defected to the rebels or been expelled.[81] "The whole of the laws which were required to be faithfully executed were being resisted and failing of execution in nearly one-third of the States."[82] Even assuming, Lincoln argued, that only Congress could authorize suspension of habeas corpus, he was faced with an impossible position where constitutional duties clashed. His Take Care Clause duty required him to faithfully execute federal statutes making criminal the

---

[74] The Prize Cases, 67 U.S. (2 Black) 635, 665–82 (1863).

[75] *Id.* at 688–89, 98–99 (Nelson, J., dissenting).

[76] Letter from Abraham Lincoln to Gen. Winfield Scott, Apr. 27, 1861, in 4 Basler, *supra* note 49, at 347.

[77] Donald, *supra* note 52, at 297–99; Long and Long, *supra* note 51, at 62–63.

[78] Donald, *supra* note 52, at 299; McPherson, *supra* note 57, at 284–89.

[79] U.S. Const. art. I, § 9, cl. 2.

[80] *See* Cong. Globe, 37th Cong., 3d Sess. 31 (Dec. 9, 1862) (statement of Sen. Trumbull); Sidney George Fisher, The Suspension of Habeas Corpus during the War of the Rebellion, 3 *Pol. Sci. Q.* 454, 458–59 (1888).

[81] Abraham Lincoln, Message to Congress in Special Session, July 4, 1861, in 4 Basler, *supra* note 49, at 421, 422.

[82] *Id.* at 430.

levying of war against the United States, the robbing or embezzling of federal property from forts and places of exclusive federal control, and the obstruction of federal officials in the performance of their duties.[83] And his Article II oath and position as President compelled him to protect and defend the Constitution and the nation and national government it constituted.[84] But if US law allowed only Congress to suspend habeas corpus, the President's Take Care Clause duty also required him to preserve habeas corpus, even for rebels who might use the courts to gain their freedom and tie up military resources in the process. The chief executive needed to choose, Lincoln argued, and his choice was to let one law "go unexecuted" – the law protecting habeas corpus – so that he could attempt to save the nation in its moment of gravest crisis, preserve the government and the legal order, and execute all the other laws.[85]

But, Lincoln continued, he did not in fact "believe[] that any law was violated" by his suspension orders. The Constitution contemplated that habeas could be suspended in extreme emergencies, but did not specify who could do the suspending. When the safety of the national government and nation was at stake, Congress was not in session, and organized rebels were attempting to cut off access to the capital city and hence prevent Congress from reconvening, did it really make sense, Lincoln asked, to think that the Constitution required the President to allow this to happen? Did not his duty to protect and defend the Constitution and nation instead suggest that he should temporarily suspend habeas corpus? Lincoln again defended his Article II power to suspend in June 1863 in a public letter to Erastus Corning and other New York Democrats. He contended that the Suspension Clause of the Constitution "plainly attests the understanding of those who made the constitution that ordinary courts of justice are inadequate to 'cases of Rebellion' – attests their purpose that in such cases, men may be held in custody whom the courts acting on ordinary rules, would discharge."[86] Lincoln did not address the separation of powers question about who could suspend the writ except to note that he had acted "without ruinous waste of time,"[87] referencing the dire circumstances in April and May 1861 when Congress was not in session.

To say that Lincoln's suspensions were controversial is an understatement. Of course supporters of the CSA and anti-war Democrats in the North declared them

---

[83] Crimes Act of 1790, ch. 9, §§ 1, 16-17, 22, 1 Stat. 112, 112, 116–17 (Apr. 30, 1790).

[84] See U.S. Const. art. II, § 1, cl. 8 ("Before he enter on the Execution of his Office, [the President] shall take the following Oath or Affirmation:–'I do solemnly swear (or affirm) that I will faithfully execute the Office of President of the United States, and will to the best of my Ability, preserve, protect and defend the Constitution of the United States.'").

[85] Abraham Lincoln, Message to Congress in Special Session, July 4, 1861, in 4 Basler, *supra* note 49, at 421, 430.

[86] Letter from Abraham Lincoln to Erastus Corning and Others, June 12, 1863, in 6 Basler, *supra* note 49, at 260, 264 (quoting U.S. Const. art. I, § 9, cl. 2).

[87] *Id.* at 263.

to be unconstitutional and outrageous.[88] But even some staunch Republicans were inclined to the view that only Congress could suspend habeas corpus.[89] And Chief Justice Roger Taney of *Dred Scott* fame, sitting as a circuit judge in spring 1861, held in a habeas corpus case arising out of the military arrest of a pro-rebel militiaman in Maryland that only Congress could suspend.[90] The Lincoln administration and the military declined to concede that Taney had the authority to overrule the President, going so far as to block service of the writ at Fort McHenry – but released the detained militiaman on bail the month after Taney's order was published.[91]

In 1861 and 1862, Congress debated but could not decide whether to expressly endorse or repudiate presidential habeas suspension; nor could it decide whether, if it legislated about the issue, it should assert that only Congress could suspend or admit that the President might also. The vaguely worded ratification statute passed in August 1861 was taken by some to have retrospectively approved the President's habeas suspension, among other emergency measures of spring 1861.[92] The legislative history, however, suggests that it was not meant to address suspension.[93] There were many in Congress who wanted to enact a habeas suspension authorization statute that would imply that only Congress could suspend, but sufficient numbers of important Republicans in Congress believed that the President had acted lawfully to block any efforts to do so.[94] Hence no legislation concerning habeas corpus was enacted until spring 1863. And then Congress' enactment was deliberately ambiguous as to whether the President had constitutional authority to suspend.[95] In the meantime, the President had continued and even expanded the suspensions of habeas corpus, thereby keeping alive the issue of his constitutional power to do so for the first two years of the war.[96]

---

[88] *See, e.g.*, Mark E. Neely, Jr., *The Fate of Liberty: Abraham Lincoln and Civil Liberties* 187–99 (Oxford University Press 1991); Carl B. Swisher, *History of the Supreme Court of the United States: The Taney Period 1836–64*, at 916–17 (Macmillan Publishing Co. 1974).

[89] *See, e.g.*, George Clarke Sellery, Lincoln's Suspension of Habeas Corpus as Viewed by Congress, 1 *Bulletin of the Univ. of Wisconsin, Hist. Series* 213, 228, 236–37 n. 55 (1907) (reprinting views of Senator John Sherman).

[90] *Ex parte* Merryman, 17 F. Cas. 144 (C.C.D. Md. 1861) (No. 9487). *See also* Brian McGinty, *Lincoln and the Court* 65–91 (Harvard University Press 2008).

[91] Donald, *supra* note 52, at 299; McGinty, *supra* note 90, at 87–88.

[92] For the text, see *supra* note 73.   [93] Sellery, *supra* note 85, at 223–38.   [94] *Id.* at 223–63.

[95] *Id.* at 264.

[96] *See* Proclamation Suspending the Writ of Habeas Corpus in Florida, May 10, 1861, in 4 Basler, *supra* note 49, at 364–65; Order from the President to Gen. Winfield Scott, June 20, 1861, *in id.* at 414 (authorizing suspension of habeas corpus as to "Major Chase, lately of the Engineer Corps of the Army of the United States"); Order from the President to Gen. Winfield Scott, July 2, 1861, *in id.* at 419 (authorizing suspension of habeas corpus along military lines between New York City and Washington); Order from the President to Gen. Henry W. Halleck, Dec. 2, 1861, *in* 5 Basler, *supra* note 49, at 35 (authorizing suspension of habeas corpus in Missouri); Proclamation Suspending the Writ of Habeas Corpus, Sept. 24, 1862, *in id.* at 436–37 (ordering nationwide suspension of habeas corpus for all persons arrested and detained by the military).

The emancipation of slaves was another area where Lincoln asserted expansive Article II authority. But emancipation was in no sense solely a presidential initiative; Congress was deeply involved in the process that freed the slaves, and the Emancipation Proclamation was just a step – a very important step, but still just a step – toward universal freedom. Unlike in earlier eras where Presidents sought specific legislative authorization for their actions and generally disclaimed reliance on constitutional authorities, President Lincoln neither requested nor received congressional authorization for everything that the Emancipation Proclamation accomplished. And so emancipation involved assertion of Article II powers, even as Congress provided the main legal impetus and support.

A steady stream of legislation, resolutions, speeches, and private pressure came from Republicans in Congress in 1861 and 1862 pushing forward the project of emancipation. Many Radicals in and out of Congress believed from the outset that the President could emancipate with his Commander in Chief war powers.[97] Senator Charles Sumner went to the White House as soon as he heard the news about Sumter on April 14, 1861, and announced to the President that he should emancipate the slaves of rebels with wartime authority newly gained from the international laws of war.[98] Two resolutions introduced in the House in late 1861 asserted the power of the President under the laws of war to emancipate slaves of the enemy.[99] Members of Congress also endorsed military emancipation by the President in public speeches and private communications to Lincoln.[100]

Immediate military emancipation was not popular in the country at large, however, and many Republicans – including the President and many Radicals – believed that Congress lacked authority to directly eliminate slavery within the states.[101] As late as fall 1861, Lincoln was privately expressing the view that he lacked authority to emancipate as a war measure.[102]

But congressional legislation nevertheless pushed forward the cause of emancipation through 1861 and 1862. The First Confiscation Act, passed in

[97] *See* James Oakes, *The Scorpion's Sting: Antislavery and the Coming of the Civil War* 139–60 (W.W. Norton & Co. 2014); James Oakes, *Freedom National: The Destruction of Slavery in the United States, 1861–1865*, at 34–42 (W.W. Norton & Co. 2013).

[98] *See* David Herbert Donald, *Charles Sumner and the Coming of the Civil War* 323 (Sourcebooks 2009 ed.).

[99] *See* Cong. Globe, 37th Cong., 2d Sess. 5 (Dec. 2, 1861) (Rep. Eliot of Massachusetts); Cong. Globe, 37th Cong., 2d Sess. 6 (Dec. 2, 1861) (Rep. Stevens of Pennsylvania).

[100] *See, e.g., Union and Peace! How They Shall be Restored: Speech of Charles Sumner before the Republican State Convention, at Worcester, October 1, 1861*, at 7 (Wright & Potter 1861); Letter from Orville H. Browning to Abraham Lincoln, Sept. 30, 1861, reprinted in Burrus M. Carnahan, *Act of Justice: Lincoln's Emancipation Proclamation and the Law of War* 148, 150–55 (University Press of Kentucky 2007).

[101] Allen G. Guelzo, *Lincoln's Emancipation Proclamation and the End of Slavery in America* 18–40 (Simon & Schuster 2004).

[102] Letter from Abraham Lincoln to Orville H. Browning, Sept. 22, 1861, in 4 Basler, *supra* note 49, at 531, 531–32.

August 1861, provided that any slave used to fight or otherwise work for the Confederate military cause was free.[103] In March 1862, Congress prohibited the US military from being employed "for the purpose of returning fugitives from service or labor, who may have escaped" from their claimed owners.[104] In April, Congress freed all slaves in Washington, DC, with compensation to loyal owners, and also passed a Joint Resolution, requested by the President, declaring that the United States ought to cooperate with states and provide funds to assist the "gradual abolishment of slavery."[105] In June, Congress banned slavery in all current and future federal territories, without compensation – repudiating the loathed *Dred Scott* decision.[106]

By spring 1862, Lincoln seems to have shifted his thinking about his power to order military emancipation. While revoking orders of US generals decreeing emancipation in districts they commanded, Lincoln implied that the President might have the authority to make such an order, if "it shall have become a necessity indispensable to the maintenance of the government."[107]

July 1862, the month that Lincoln announced to his cabinet that he would issue the Emancipation Proclamation,[108] was the most important month yet in Congress. Congress carried into effect the treaty the United States had recently signed with Great Britain to use the navy and international courts to suppress the international slave trade.[109] It authorized the President to enlist "persons of African descent" in the military[110] and declared that any slave of an enemy who rendered service to the US military was free, along with his mother, wife, and children.[111] Finally, the Second Confiscation Act contained important emancipation provisions. As punishment for crime, it freed the slaves of anyone convicted of treason or inciting, supporting, or engaging in rebellion or insurrection. It declared that escaped slaves of those persons engaging in or aiding rebellion were, if they came within the control of the US Army, free. And it provided that slaves escaping into free states, the District of Columbia, or any federal territory would not be returned unless the owner proved to be loyal.

These statutes provided crucial political and legal support for the President's later proclamation, but they did not fully authorize it. The Preliminary Emancipation Proclamation of September 22, 1862, suggested that it was

---

[103] First Confiscation Act, 12 Stat. 319, ch. 60, § 4 (Aug. 6, 1861).

[104] Act of Mar. 13, 1862, 12 Stat. 354, ch. 40, § 1.

[105] District of Columbia Emancipation Act, 12 Stat. 376, ch. 54, §§ 1–3 (Apr. 16, 1862); J. Res. No. 26, 12 Stat. 617 (Apr. 10, 1862).

[106] Act of June 19, 1862, 12 Stat. 432, ch. 111, § 1.

[107] Abraham Lincoln, Proclamation Revoking General Hunter's Order of Military Emancipation, May 19, 1863, in 5 Basler, *supra* note 49, at 222.

[108] Abraham Lincoln, Emancipation Proclamation – First Draft, in 5 Basler, *supra* note 49, at 336–37.

[109] Act of July 11, 1862, 12 Stat. 531, ch. 140.

[110] Act of July 17, 1862, ch. 201, 12 Stat. 597, 599, § 12; Second Confiscation Act, 12 Stat. 589, 592, ch. 195, § 11 (July 17, 1862).

[111] Act of July 17, 1862, 12 Stat. 597, 599, ch. 201, § 13.

enforcing the act of Congress prohibiting the army from returning fugitive slaves and section nine of the Second Confiscation Act, which had declared freedom for slaves of rebels who came within the control of the army.[112] But certainly as a formal matter, the Preliminary Proclamation went further than the statutes, announcing that as of January 1, "all persons held as slaves within any State, or designated part of a State, the people whereof shall then be in rebellion against the United States shall be then, thenceforward, and forever free."[113] During the gap between the September announcement of the policy and its implementation in the new year, a midterm election occurred and the outgoing Congress reconvened. Lincoln therefore knowingly held his emancipation policy up to the scrutiny of the voters and their representatives. And after Lincoln announced his policy in the Preliminary Proclamation but before the policy went into effect, the House of Representatives expressly approved it.[114]

Because the proclamation went beyond what Congress had done by statute, it necessarily relied on claims of executive power. The proclamation issued on January 1 did not cite any acts of Congress but rather stated that it was issued "by virtue of the power in me vested as Commander-in-Chief of the Army and Navy of the United States ... and as a fit and necessary war measure for suppressing said rebellion."[115] Further congressional approval for this measure of executive power can be found in legislative action in 1863 and 1864.[116] And Congress of course ultimately endorsed universal freedom when it enacted the proposed addition to the Constitution that became the Thirteenth Amendment.

* * *

The Civil War era differed from the early republic because there was a standing statutory framework for authorizing presidential responses to national security crises. But that framework was quite skimpy, even when supplemented during the war years. The unprecedented scope of the crisis facing the Lincoln administration at the outset of the war in spring 1861 meant as a practical matter that this thin statutory framework had to be filled out extensively by aggressive assertions of Article II power. Throughout the war, the President

---

[112] Preliminary Emancipation Proclamation, Sept. 22, 1862, in 5 Basler, *supra* note 49, at 433–36.

[113] *Id.* at 434–35.

[114] *See* Cong. Globe, 37th Cong., 3d Sess. 92 (Dec. 15, 1862) (declaring that the proclamation was "warranted by the Constitution" and "well chosen as a war measure"). *See also* Guelzo, *supra* note 101, at 177–79 (describing positive reaction to the preliminary Proclamation among Radical Republicans and abolitionists, in and out of Congress).

[115] Emancipation Proclamation, Jan. 1, 1863, in 6 Basler, *supra* note 49, at 28, 29. *See also id.* at 30 (stating that the Proclamation was "sincerely believed to be an act of justice, warranted by the Constitution upon military necessity").

[116] Congress provided that no civil or military officer of the federal government could be held liable for carrying out presidential directives concerning any "search, seizure, arrest, or imprisonment." Act of Mar. 3, 1863, ch. 81, § 4, 12 Stat. 755, 756. And Congress in the Wade-Davis bill provided for the emancipation of slaves in rebel states. Cong. Globe, 38th, 1st Sess. 3449 (July 1, 1864). The bill passed both houses, *see id.* 2107–8, 3491, 3535, but Lincoln pocket vetoed it.

only rarely sought specific statutory authorization for actions he was contemplating and continued to rely on expansive Article II claims. Even though Lincoln neither sought to challenge Congress directly nor asserted an authority to disregard enacted legislation, this era nevertheless represents a decisive turn toward the modern empowered executive aggressively asserting broad ex ante authority to confront threats to the national security.

POST–COLD WAR ERA

In the modern era, the constitutional landscape has shifted further still in the direction of presidential unilateralism. The key legal difference from the Civil War era is that legislative authorization has now become so comprehensive and open-ended that, while presidential aggrandizement has certainly continued, it has more typically done so through assertion of statutory authority. The space allotted to this chapter does not suffice to explore in detail how the pressures of World War II and the Cold War catalyzed this legal transition.[117] Partly it came in response to massively increasing stakes and complexity of modern foreign policy.[118] Partly it can be characterized as a passing of the buck.[119] But the result is clear: in our post–Cold War era, even the most "forward-leaning"[120] examples of presidential assertion generally come in the form of aggressive interpretation of statutes rather than of the Constitution itself.

Perhaps the best-known example of this kind of amorphous ex ante authorization is the International Economic Emergency Powers Act (IEEPA).[121] Since 1977, it has given Presidents the authority to alter or even terminate an extraordinary range of property interests[122] for reasons expressed in statutory terms that are simple, vague, and far-reaching:

[117] For discussions of accelerating legal flexibility for national security action during both World War II and the Cold War, *see, e.g.,* Louis Fisher, *Presidential War Power* 61–113 (1995); Stephen M. Griffin, *Long Wars and the Constitution* 52–119 (2013); Matthew C. Waxman, The Power to Threaten War, 123 *Yale L. J.,* 1626, 1658–59 (2014). For a caution about overreading the legal implications of increased presidential political unilateralism during this period, see Mortenson, *supra* note 34, at 401–3, 415–16.

[118] Julian Davis Mortenson, A Theory of Republican Prerogative, 88 *S. Cal. L. Rev.* 45, 52–61, 90–91 (2015) (discussing broad statutory delegations as one solution to the rule of law's "Anticipation Problem").

[119] *See, e.g.,* Jules Lobel, Emergency Power and the Decline of Liberalism, 98 *Yale L. J.* 1385 (1989).

[120] Dawn Johnsen, What's a President to Do?, 88 *B.U. L. Rev.* 395, 419 (2008) (quoting former associate White House counsel Bradford Berenson); *see also* Michael V. Hayden, Director, U.S. Central Intelligence Agency, Address at Duquesne University Commencement (May 4, 2007) ("I had a duty to play aggressively – 'right up to' the line. Playing back from the line protected me but didn't protect America. I made it clear I would always play in fair territory, but that there would be no chalk dust on my cleats.").

[121] Pub. L. 95-223, 91 Stat. 1625 (1977) (codified as amended at 50 U.S.C. §§ 1701–1706 [2012]).

[122] "At the times and to the extent specified in section 202, the President may, under such regulations as he may prescribe, by means of instructions, licenses, or otherwise –,

Any authority granted to the President by [the IEEPA] may be exercised to deal with any unusual and extraordinary threat, which has its source in whole or substantial part outside the United States, to the national security, foreign policy, or economy of the United States, if the President declares a national emergency with respect to such threat ....[123]

This authority has been used by Presidents to respond to an extraordinary range of problems.[124]

In 1979, for example, the Shah of Iran was toppled by his people. Anti-American sentiment featured prominently, and revolutionary leaders seized the US embassy and took its staff hostage.[125] In response, President Carter invoked the IEEPA, declaring a national emergency,[126] freezing approximately $12 billion[127] in "all property and interests in property" of Iran and the Central Bank of Iran, and prohibiting all non-humanitarian trade with Iran.[128]

The hostage crisis was ultimately settled by the Algiers Accords.[129] In exchange for the release of the hostages, the United States agreed to restore the financial position of Iran to that which existed prior to Executive Order 12170 and to refer all claims by US citizens against Iran to binding arbitration through the Iran–United States Claims Tribunal.[130] Shortly after reaching that agreement, President Carter invoked the IEEPA to revoke all prohibitions on transactions involving Iran[131] and to order US banks holding Iranian government assets to transfer them to specified holding banks.[132] All

(A) investigate, regulate, or prohibit –
   (i)   any transactions in foreign exchange,
   (ii) transfers of credit or payments between, by, through, or to any banking institution, to the extent that such transfers or payments involve any interest of any foreign country or a national thereof,
   (iii) the importing or exporting of currency or securities; and
(B) investigate, regulate, direct and compel, nullify, void, prevent or prohibit, any acquisition, holding, withholding, use, transfer, withdrawal, transportation, importation or exportation of, or dealing in, or exercising any right, power, or privilege with respect to, or transactions involving, any property in which any foreign country or a national thereof has any interest; by any person, or with respect to any property, subject to the jurisdiction of the United States." 50 U.S.C. § 1702.

[123] *Id.*§ 1701.
[124] Patrick A. Thronson, Note, Toward Comprehensive Reform of America's Emergency Law Regime, 46 *U. Mich. J. L. Reform* 737, 756–59 (2013) (documenting thirty states of emergency then in effect); Gregory Korte, Special Report: America's Perpetual State of Emergency, *USA Today* (Oct. 23, 2014), www.usatoday.com/story/news/politics/2014/10/22/president-obama-states-of-emergency/16851775/ (documenting 53 states of emergency declared since 1976).
[125] See generally James F. Larson, *Taken Hostage: The Iran Hostage Crisis and America's First Encounter with Radical Islam* (Princeton University Press 2005).
[126] Exec. Order No. 12,170, 44 Fed. Reg. 65729 (Nov. 14, 1979).
[127] Gary Sick, *The Carter Administration*, in *United States Institute of Peace: The Iran Primer*, http://iranprimer.usip.org/resource/carter-administration-0.
[128] Exec. Order No. 12,205, 45 Fed. Reg. 24,099 (Apr. 7, 1980).
[129] Algiers Accords, U.S.-Iran, Jan. 19, 1981.   [130] *Id.*
[131] Exec. Order No. 12,282, 46 Fed. Reg. 7925 (Jan. 19, 1981).
[132] Exec. Order No. 12,279, 46 Fed. Reg. 7919 (Jan. 19, 1981).

American hostages were released the next day. A little more than one month later, newly elected President Ronald Reagan invoked the IEEPA in issuing an executive order that suspended all claims against Iran that could be presented to the Iran–United States Claims Tribunal.[133]

The IEEPA played a similar role in the long-standing face-off between Cuba and the United States. In May 1960, Fidel Castro's revolutionary government nationalized all American-owned oil refineries in Cuba.[134] In response, first President Eisenhower[135] and then President Kennedy[136] instituted the Cuba sanctions regime under statutes that conferred sweeping, largely unspecified grants of executive authority.[137] For years thereafter, Congress tinkered with the scope of presidential power and the scope of the embargo, repeatedly amending the authorizing statutes.[138] Notably, even when Congress declined to renew a key authorization for sanctions in 1983, President Reagan simply declared a national emergency under the IEEPA that essentially reinstated the provisions of the expiring embargo authorization.[139] Subsequent administrations have followed Reagan's lead when faced with similar lapses in embargo authority,[140] and President Obama relied on broad statutory authority in deciding to relieve important elements of the embargo as part of the two states' broader rapprochement.[141]

---

[133] Dames & Moore v. Regan, 453 U.S. 654, 666 (1981).

[134] Diane E. Rennack and Mark P. Sullivan, Cong. Res. Serv., Cuba Sanctions: Legislative Restrictions Limiting the Normalization of Relations 1 n. 2 (2015). *See also A Guide to the United States' History Of Recognition, Diplomatic, and Consular Relations, by Country, since 1776: Cuba*, U.S. Department of State, Office of the Historian, at http://history.state.gov /countries/cuba (last visited June 19, 2015); Rupinder Hans, The United States' Economic Embargo of Cuba: International Implications of the Cuban Liberty and Democratic Solidarity Act of 1995, 5 *J. Int'l L. & Prac.* 327, 330 (1996).

[135] Export Regs., 25 Fed. Reg. 10006–13 (Oct. 20, 1960).

[136] Proclamation 3447, Embargo on All Trade with Cuba, 27 Fed. Reg. 1085, 3 C.F.R. 26 (1963); *see also* Cuban Import Regulations, 27 Fed. Reg. 1116 (Feb. 7, 1962); Cuban Import Regulations, 27 Fed. Reg. 2765 (Mar. 24, 1962).

[137] Export Control Act of 1949, Pub. L. No. 11-548 § 3(a), 63 Stat. 7, 7; Foreign Assistance Act of 1961, Pub. L. No. 87-195, 75 Stat. 424; Trading with the Enemy Act of 1917, Pub. L. No. 65-91, 40 Stat. 411.

[138] *E.g.*, Amendments to the Trading with the Enemy Act, Pub. L. No. 95–223, § 101(a), 91 Stat. 1625 (1977); Export Administration Act of 1979, Pub. L. No. 96-72, 93 Stat. 503.

[139] Exec. Order No. 12444, 48 Fed. Reg. 48,215 (Oct. 18, 1983). *See* Ian F. Fergusson, Congressional Research Service, *The Export Administration Act: Evolution, Provisions, and Debate* 13–14 (2009) (describing slight modifications of the embargo under IEEPA authority).

[140] *E.g., Notice – Continuation of the National Emergency with Respect to Export Control Regulations*, The White House, Office of the Press Secretary (Aug. 7, 2015), www.whitehouse .gov/the-press-office/2015/08/07/notice-continuation-national-emergency-respect-export-control.

[141] *Statement by the President on Cuba Policy Changes*, The White House (Dec. 17, 2014), at https:// www.whitehouse.gov/the-press-office/2014/12/17/statement-president-cuba-policy-changes. *See also Fact Sheet: Treasury and Commerce Announce Regulatory Amendments to the Cuba Sanctions*, U.S. Department of the Treasury (Jan. 15, 2015), www.treasury.gov/press-center /press-releases/Pages/jl9740.aspx; *Rescission of Cuba as a State Sponsor of Terror*, The U.S. Department of State (May 29, 2015), www.state.gov/r/pa/prs/ps/2015/05/242986.htm; *Press*

Presidents have also used the IEEPA to impose sanctions on individuals rather than states. While such sanctions have most often been imposed on foreign officials acting in a public capacity,[142] authority has also been asserted to impose them even on individuals who have acted only in a private capacity. In April 2015, President Obama announced that sanctions would be imposed on individuals and entities found to have perpetrated malicious cyberactivities "that are reasonably likely to result in, or have materially contributed to, a significant threat to the national security, foreign policy, or economic health or financial stability of the United States."[143] Under such sanctions, no property located in the United States or under the control of any US person may be "transferred, paid, exported, withdrawn, or otherwise dealt in."[144] Notably, the order targets not just cyberattacks that destroy technology infrastructure but also cyberexploits perpetrated in the service of economic espionage.

While statutory authority to use military force has not expanded quite as broadly as the powers granted by the IEEPA, it has often been broad gauged indeed. A central example is the 2001 Authorization for the Use of Military Force ("AUMF"). Enacted seven days after the September 11 terrorist attacks in New York City and Washington, the AUMF authorized the President to use all necessary and appropriate force against those nations, organizations, or persons he determines planned, authorized, committed, or aided the terrorist attacks that occurred on September 11, 2001, or harbored such organizations or persons, in

---

Briefing by Press Secretary Josh Earnest, The White House (Dec. 18, 2014), www.whitehouse .gov/the-press-office/2014/12/18/press-briefing-press-secretary-josh-earnest-121814 (having made revisions that "are well within his executive authority as President," Obama "has done all that he can do using his executive authority, and the remaining restrictions can only be removed through congressional action"). For more detail on the interlocking statutory regime within which Obama was operating, see Rennack and Sullivan, *supra* note 134.

[142] *See, e.g.*, Exec. Order No. 13,660, 79 Fed. Reg. 13,493 (Mar. 6, 2014) (authorizing individual sanctions against those undermining the democratic process in Ukraine, namely Russian officials); Exec. Order No. 13,553, 75 Fed. Reg. 60,567 (Sept. 28, 2010) (authorizing individual sanctions on Iranian officials responsible for human rights violations on or after June 2009); Exec. Order No. 13,219, 66 Fed. Reg. 34,777 (June 26, 2001) (authorizing sanctions against individuals supporting extremist violence in former Yugoslavia or undermining NATO efforts in the region).

[143] Exec. Order 13,694, 80 Fed. Reg. 18,077, 18,077 (Apr. 2, 2015) (stating that "the increasing prevalence and severity of malicious cyber-enabled activities" by actors located outside the United States constituted an "unusual and extraordinary threat" to the United States); *Statement by the President on Executive Order "Blocking the Property of Certain Persons Engaging in Significant Malicious Cyber-Enabled Activities,"* The White House (Apr. 1, 2015), www.whitehouse.gov/the-press-office/2015/04/01/statement-president-executive -order-blocking-property-certain-persons-en.

[144] Exec. Order No. 13,694, 80 Fed. Reg. at 18,077; *see also* 109 Amer. J. Int'l L. 643, 674. (Special Assistant to the President and Cybersecurity Coordinator Michael Daniel acknowledging that the order is "the first of its kind in this space where we don't have to rely on a sanctions regime that is, in fact, targeted at a particular country or group of actors within a country, but is more broad-brushed than that.").

order to prevent any future acts of international terrorism against the United States by such nations, organizations, or persons.[145]

While Congress had rejected an even more open-ended version,[146] two successive administrations have understood the enacted text to authorize an extraordinarily wide variety of counterterrorism operations against an extraordinarily diverse range of targets – including groups that did not even exist at the time the statute was enacted.

Consider as one example the case of Anouar Al Aulaki – an American citizen who was accused of being a propagandist and operational organizer for Al Qaeda in the Arabian Peninsula ("AQAP"). His 2011 killing by drone strike in Yemen was legally justified by the US government as an exercise of "necessary and appropriate force" under the 2001 AUMF. But the argument undergirding this conclusion was convoluted. The AUMF was originally intended to authorize force as a military response to the particular attacks that were perpetrated by a particular group on September 11. So the groups that it targeted were defined in two categories: those who perpetrated the terrorist attacks (al Qaeda) and those who harbored the perpetrators (the Afghan Taliban).[147] The problem was that while AQAP was sympathetic to al Qaeda, shared many of al Qaeda's goals, and even worked with al Qaeda, it was widely understood to be organizationally distinct.

How then did the government justify its theory of the AUMF? In the most extensive publicly available discussion, the Justice Department asserted that

the AUMF applies with respect to forces "associated with" al-Qaida that are engaged in hostilities against the U.S. or its coalition partners, and a decision-maker could reasonably conclude that the AQAP forces of which al-Aulaqi is a leader are "associated with" al Qaida forces for purposes of the AUMF. On [this] view, DoD would carry out its contemplated operation against a leader of an organization that is within the scope of the AUMF, and therefore DoD would in that respect be operating in accord with a grant of statutory authority.[148]

---

[145] Authorization for Use of Military Force, Pub. L. No. 107-40, 115 Stat. 224 (2001).

[146] Cong. Research Serv., *Authorization for Use of Military Force in Response to the 9/11 Attacks (Pub. L. 107-40): Legislative History* 2-2 (2007) (noting original presidential proposal authorizing military action "to deter and pre-empt *any* future acts of terrorism or aggression against the United States") (emphasis added).

[147] For what remains the best single treatment of this question, see Robert M. Chesney, Beyond the Battlefield, Beyond Al Qaeda: The Destabilizing Legal Architecture of Counterterrorism, 112 *Mich. L. Rev.* 163 (2013).

[148] The government also argued in the alternative that al Aulaki was himself a member of al Qaeda. David J. Barron, Acting Assistant Attorney General, Memorandum for the Attorney General Re: Applicability of Federal Criminal Laws and the Constitution to Contemplated Lethal Operations Against Shaykh Anwar al-Aulaqi (July 16, 2010), www.washingtonpost.com/r/2010-2019/WashingtonPost/2014/06/23/National-Security/Graphics/memodrones.pdf. In 2013, the Justice Department had released a much shorter white paper addressing some of the same issues. Department of Justice White Paper, *Lawfulness of a Lethal Operation Directed Against a U.S.*

This was not a new theory. Apparently aware of this gap in the scheme from early on, the White House had as early as 2004 publicly adopted a detention standard covering "an[y] individual who was part of or supporting Taliban or al Qaeda forces, *or associated forces* that are engaged in hostilities against the United States or its coalition partners,"[149] notwithstanding the lack of specific textual basis for that extension in the AUMF itself.[150]

As another example of how the AUMF has been applied, consider the armed response to the Islamic State of Iraq and the Levant ("ISIL"). The latest incarnation of an armed group that rose to prominence in Iraq after the 2003 fall of Saddam Hussein,[151] ISIL managed to establish a de facto state in a sprawling area covering large swaths of Iraq and Syria. In September 2014, President Obama announced that the United States would lead a coalition of nations to "degrade and ultimately destroy ISIL through a comprehensive and sustained counterterrorism strategy"[152] in both Syria and Iraq. The President disclaimed any need for additional congressional authorization, stating that he "[had] the authority to address the threat from ISIL"[153] under the 2001 AUMF.[154] The White House later explained that that the President "can rely

Citizen Who Is a Senior Operational Leader of Al-Qai'da or an Associated Force (Feb. 4, 2013), http://msnbcmedia.msn.com/i/msnbc/sections/news/020413_DOJ_White_Paper.pdf.

[149] Memorandum from Paul Wolfowitz, Deputy Sec'y. of Def., to Sec'y. of the Navy (July 7, 2004); see also Hamdi v. Rumsfeld, 542 U.S. 507, 515 (2004) (describing detention authority claimed by executive in legal briefing); Hedges v. Obama, Brief for the Appellants at *6–7, 724 F.3d 170 (2d Cir. 2013) (reflecting the Obama administration's retention of "associated forces" extension with minor revisions).

[150] The "associated forces" extension is apparently grounded in the international law concept of co-belligerency. For an illuminating exchange on the question of cobelligerency as a theory under the AUMF, compare Rebecca Ingber, Untangling Belligerency from Neutrality in the Conflict with Al-Qaeda, 47 *Tex. Int'l. L. J.* 75 (2011) and Karl S. Chang, Enemy Status and Military Detention in the War against Al-Qaeda, 47 *Tex. Int'l. L. J.* 1 (2011). In 2012, Congress adopted this standard for detention (but not for lethal force) in the National Defense Authorization Act for FY2012, Pub. L. No. 112-81.

[151] Graeme Baker, *ISIL: Rising Power in Iraq and* Syria, Al Jazeera, June 11, 2014, www.aljazeera .com/news/middleeast/2014/06/isil-eminent-threat-iraq-syria-20146101543970327.html.

[152] White House Press Release, Statement by the President on ISIL (Sept. 10, 2014), www.whitehouse .gov/the-press-office/2014/09/10/statement-president-isil-1.

[153] White House Press Release, Statement by the President on ISIL (Sept. 10, 2014), www.whitehouse .gov/the-press-office/2014/09/10/statement-president-isil-1.

[154] A few days after the President's speech, the White House claimed that a second statute – the 2002 Authorization for the Use of Military Force in Iraq (2002 AUMF) – could also serve as legal authority for airstrikes. Charlie Savage, Obama Sees Iraq Resolution as a Legal Basis for Airstrikes, Official Says, *N.Y. Times*, Sept. 13, 2014, at A8. The 2002 AUMF provides that "[t]he President is authorized to use the Armed Forces of the United States as he determines to be necessary and appropriate in order to – (1) defend the national security of the United States against the continuing threat posed by Iraq; and (2) enforce all relevant United Nations Security Council resolutions regarding Iraq" Pub. L. No. 107-243, 116 Stat. 1498 (2002) (codified at 50 U.S. § 1541 note (2012)). For additional background on the 2002 AUMF, see Sean D. Murphy, Contemporary Practice of the United States, 97 *Am. J. Int'l L.* 419 (2003); 96 *Am. J. Int'l L.* 956 (2002).

on the 2001 AUMF as statutory authority for the military airstrike operations he is directing against ISIL."[155]

This too was a tricky sell: ISIL didn't even *exist* in September 2001, and by 2014 its relationship with al Qaeda had deteriorated to the point of outright hostility. And yet the administration claimed that the 2001 AUMF provided a legal basis for strikes in Syria because under the long-standing executive branch interpretation, the AUMF "applies to al Qaeda, the Taliban, and associated forces."[156] Since ISIL's former leader in 2004 had "publicly pledged his group's allegiance to bin Laden"[157] and since ISIL was "known as al Qaeda in Iraq for a number of years,"[158] the administration therefore concluded that ISIL was covered by the 2001 AUMF. It was "only recently that they split with al Qaeda," and the administration "[didn't] believe that Congress would have intended to remove the President's authority to use force against this group simply because the group had a disagreement with al Qaeda leadership."[159] Despite eventually proposing a new ISIL-specific AUMF,[160] as of this writing the White House has maintained its position that operations against ISIL in Syria are fully authorized under the 2001 AUMF.[161]

---

[155] White House Press Release, Background Conference Call on the President's Address to the Nation (Sept. 10, 2014), www.whitehouse.gov/the-press-office/2014/09/10/background-conference-call -presidents-address-nation. *See also* White House Press Release, Letter from the President – War Powers Resolution Regarding Syria (Sept. 23, 2014), www.whitehouse.gov/the-press-office/2014 /09/23/letter-president-war-powers-resolution-regarding-syria.

[156] White House Press Release, Background Conference Call on Airstrikes in Syria (Sept. 23, 2014), www.whitehouse.gov/the-press-office/2014/09/23/background-conference-call-airstrikes -syria (emphasis added); *see also* Robert Chesney, The 2001 AUMF: From Associated Forces to (Disassociated) Successor Forces, *Lawfare* (Sept. 10, 2014), www.lawfareblog.com/2014/09 /the-2001-aumf-from-associated-forces-to-disassociated-successor-forces (describing the asso- ciated forces theory).

[157] Stephen W. Preston, General Counsel, Department of Defense, Address at the Annual Meeting of the American Society of International Law: The Legal Framework for the United States' Use of Military Force since 9/11 (Apr. 10, 2015).

[158] White House Press Release, Background Conference Call on Airstrikes in Syria (Sept. 23, 2014), www.whitehouse.gov/the-press-office/2014/09/23/background-conference-call-airstrikes-syria.

[159] *Id.*

[160] Joint Resolution to Authorize the Limited Use of the United States Armed Forces against the Islamic State of Iraq and the Levant, at www.whitehouse.gov/sites/default/files/docs /aumf_02112015.pdf ("Draft Force Authorization") ("The President is authorized, subject to the limitations in subsection (c), to use the Armed Forces of the United States as the President determines to be necessary and appropriate against ISIL or associated persons or forces as defined in section 5"). It defines "associated persons or forces" to mean "individuals and organizations fighting for, on behalf of, or alongside ISIL or any closely related successor entity in hostilities against the United States or its coalition partners."

[161] White House Press Briefing (Nov. 6, 2014), www.whitehouse.gov/the-press-office/2014/11/06 /press-briefing-press-secretary-josh-earnest-1162014.

Even where statutes have been intended to restrain the President, Presidents have found ways to interpret them as actually extending authorization.[162] For example, the War Powers Resolution of 1973 (WPR), enacted in response to the war in Vietnam and neighboring countries, was intended to restrain unilateral presidential initiations of armed conflict.[163] Congress had to pass it over President Nixon's veto, which was prompted by his view that the WPR unconstitutionally restricted the president's Article II powers to use force abroad.[164] In recent years, however, the executive branch has asserted that the WPR "recognizes and presupposes the existence of unilateral presidential authority" under the Constitution to deploy armed forces into hostilities.[165] On this view, Congress is thus said to have provided some statutory support for independent presidential action,[166] notwithstanding an express proviso in the WPR stating that it shall not be "construed as granting any authority to the President with respect to the introduction of United States Armed Forces into hostilities."[167]

* * *

Compared to the founding and Civil War periods, modern Presidents in the post-Cold War era have vastly greater statutory authority to act without consulting a then-sitting Congress – and without generating constitutional controversy – because of comprehensive authorization statutes. This is not to say that the modern era has left constitutional controversy behind. To the contrary, we have seen fierce debates over claims of exclusive Article II power at the margins of the wide-ranging statutory authorizations. But most of the time, sitting administrations flex their arguments about statutory authorization much more seriously than their claims to constitutional authority. The controversial memorandum justifying torture thus focused principally on a statutory argument about the criminal torture prohibition;[168] the executive's arguments for why the WPR did not require termination of the use of military force in Kosovo relied on

---

[162] The IEEPA itself is in some respects an example of this phenomenon. *See* Thronson, *supra* note 124, at 757–59.

[163] 50 U.S.C. § 1541.

[164] *See* Richard M. Nixon, Oct. 24, 1973, www.presidency.ucsb.edu/ws/?pid=4021.

[165] *See, e.g.,* Deployment of United States Armed Forces into Haiti, 18 Op. Off. Legal Counsel 173, 175 (Sept. 27, 1994); Authority to Use Military Force in Libya, 35 Op. Off. Legal Counsel 8 (Apr. 1, 2011).

[166] Proposed Deployment of United States Armed Forces into Bosnia, 19 Op. Off. Legal Counsel 327, 334-35 (Nov. 30, 1995).

[167] 50 U.S.C. § 1547(d)(2).

[168] Memorandum from Jay Bybee, Assistant Att'y Gen., Off. Legal Counsel, to Alberto R. Gonzales, Counsel to the President, Re: Standards of Conduct for Interrogation under 18 U.S.C. 2340-2340A (Aug. 1, 2002), http://www.justice.gov/sites/default/files/olc/legacy/2010/08/05/memo-gonzales-aug2002.pdf (withdrawn and replaced by Daniel Levin, Acting Assistant Att'y General, Office of Legal Counsel, Memorandum for James B. Comey, Deputy Attorney General [Dec. 30, 2004]).

claims of implicit legislative authorization;[169] and even the controversial memorandum justifying wiretaps in violation of FISA spent most of its analytic energy on a statutory argument grounded in the 2001 AUMF.[170]

Such frequent presidential resort to statutory rather than constitutional authorization might seem to augur a greater role for the legislature in responding to national security crises. But the willingness of modern Congresses to pre-delegate significant authority in broad framework statutes that sit on the books for decades – and can only be modified or withdrawn over a presidential veto – has in practice meant that Presidents typically operate with great freedom.

The upshot is a constitutional arrangement that relies on remarkably open-ended statutory authorization to mitigate anxieties about both power and constraint – about the risks of a disempowered presidency in a dangerous world but also about the risks of letting Presidents rely on abstract constitutional text as the sole basis for violent action. While these authorizations don't purport to constrain the executive branch with anything like the specificity of statutory regimes in earlier eras, their nature as legislative enactments entails a more meaningful possibility of authoritative supervision and even revision via subsequent democratic enactment than the Constitution ever could. Whether this resolution is satisfactory is another question entirely.

---

[169] Authorization for Continuing Hostilities in Kosovo, 24 Op. Off. Legal Counsel 327 (Dec. 19, 2000).

[170] Department of Justice White Paper, Legal Authorities Supporting the Activities of the National Security Agency Described by the President 10–27 (Jan. 19, 2006) (unsigned white paper).

10

The Constitution and the Administrative State

Edward L. Rubin

In some sense, all of American constitutional law involves the administrative state. Constitutional decisions address government actors and our government is an administrative one. To take just three of the most momentous decisions of the current era, *Brown* v. *Board of Education* (1954) concerns the admission practices of public schools, which are state-funded and operated institutions providing services to citizens – a typical and distinctive element of administrative government. *Roe* v. *Wade* (1973) tells public prosecutors, who are members of an administrative agency, that they can no longer treat abortion as a crime. *Miranda* v. *Arizona* (1966) issues instructions to police officers – Michael Lipsky's "street-level bureaucrats" – that countermand the instructions from their administrative superiors.[1]

This observation, however, does not appear to provide a particularly useful way to understand the relationship between the US Constitution and the modern administrative state. It is a bit like including an analysis of Shakespeare's plays and Tolstoy's novels in a book describing the Earth's atmosphere on the basis of the irrefutable observation that these works would not have been produced if the Earth lacked an atmosphere. The contours of academic inquiry are generally established according to their explanatory value, not their extended causal connections. In exploring the relationship between the US Constitution and the administrative state, the question is not whether the two are connected to each other at some point – they almost always are – but rather how constitutional doctrine has affected, and been affected by, those features of the modern state that are distinctively and inherently administrative.

From this perspective, the connection between constitutional doctrine and the administrative state appears episodic and, while important, secondary. There were two relatively delimited periods when the Supreme Court actively engaged in defining the contours and content of administrative action. One is

---

[1] Michael Lipsky, *Street-Level Bureaucracy: Dilemmas of the Individual in Public Service* (New York: Russell Sage Foundation, 1983).

the first third of the twentieth century, called the Lochner era after its most characteristic decision (*Lochner* v. *New York*, 1905), when the Court attempted to distinguish between valid and invalid forms of economic regulation on the basis of rights-related limits on government power, both federal and state. The second is the group of due process decisions of the 1970s and 1980s that were part of the Court's human rights initiative and extended procedural protections developed for civil trials to a wide variety of administrative adjudications, again both federal and state. The delimited nature of these two constitutional interventions into administrative governance is underscored by the fact that the Supreme Court entirely abandoned the first one after 1937 and no longer asserts any constitutionally based supervision over economic regulation. Procedural due process restrictions on administrative adjudications remain fully in force, but the doctrine is now regarded as largely albeit rather awkwardly settled and no longer generates a significant component of the Supreme Court's docket.

A notable feature of the Supreme Court's permissive attitude toward the administrative state has been its rejection of several proposed and sometimes ardently advocated doctrines that would have provided the basis for a much more extensive constitutionally based intervention, and possibly created severe impediments to the development of administrative governance – impediments that could not possibly be left in place but would have required constitutional amendments to remove. These doctrines fall into two historically distinct categories. The first set consists of compact federalism, dual federalism, and the strict construction of Congress's enumerated powers and the President's implied powers. These positions, which will be explained as the discussion proceeds, received strong support, often from state governments and sometimes from the President, during the so-called "Federal era," that is, the first seventy years of the Republic. The second set of potentially restrictive doctrines, more fully voiced in the modern era and at least partially inspired by current anti-regulatory sentiment, includes strict separation of powers, dual federalism (again), and regulatory takings.

This chapter will discuss four episodes in the relationship of constitutional law to the administrative state. Before proceeding, however, it is necessary to reconsider the initial contention, which is that it is useful to approach the relationship between the US Constitution and the administrative state in this manner. The jagged trajectory of the Court's concerns and the overall permissiveness of its approach suggest that some deeper pattern may be operating, some more general principle that first section remains to be identified. first section of this chapter, therefore, will address precisely the issue that originally seemed advisable to avoid, that is, the administrative character of American government in its entirety, and the consequences of such a broad perspective. It will do so, however, not as a matter of causal or casual or casuistic connection but rather at the level of foundational concepts. That inquiry will then allow the four episodes of Supreme Court forbearance or intervention to be understood in context.

THE CONSTITUTION'S ESSENTIALLY ADMINISTRATIVE CHARACTER

In order to appreciate the fundamental relationship between the Constitution and the administrative state, it is necessary to identify the distinctive features of modern administrative governance. Weber's well-known definition of bureaucracy focuses on the operational features of the administrative agency.[2] This can be placed in the context of government in general, as I have previously suggested in other writings, by invoking the idea of articulation.[3] There are at least two ordinary language usages of the term "articulation" that provide a more substantive and neutral definition of modern government than calling it a bureaucracy. One usage is the connection of discrete components of a unified structure or system by visible ligatures or joints in an arrangement that preserves the individual identities of the components. Modern government displays an articulated structure in this sense; it is divided into functional units, typically called agencies, each of which is defined by the specific substantive task it is assigned to perform. A second usage of the term "articulation" refers to the process of expressing something in explicit verbal terms. Modern government is articulated in this sense as well. Each principal action taken by the government is explicitly identified and justified by its potential benefit to the citizens. This dual usage distinguishes modern governments from their monarchical predecessors, whose various components evolved from the divisions of the king's household, thereby possessing vaguely defined, often overlapping jurisdictions, and where the government itself was regarded as either divinely authorized or inherently empowered to act and thereby exempt from justifying or even explaining its specific actions.

The transition from these monarchical systems to modern administrative government occurred during the last quarter of the eighteenth century, and it occurred with a rapidity and ubiquity that suggest genuine conceptual transformation.[4] In France, the Revolution abolished the tradition-bound, casually organized structure of monarchical government along with the monarchy itself and almost immediately installed subject-specific ministries of Foreign Affairs, War, Navy, Interior, Justice, and Finance. At the same time, Joseph II of Austria, France's archenemy (Marie Antoinette was his sister), reorganized his government along similar lines, replacing the genially run departments led by members of the nobility with ministries that recruited on the basis of credentials, required all major officers to be full-time salaried employees, and demanded that they report their activities through extensive, biannual questionnaires. In Britain, Lord North resigned from the Prime Minister's position in 1782, at which point, and for the first time, all the other

---

[2] Max Weber, *Economy and Society*, Guenther Roth and Claus Wittach, eds. (Berkeley: University of California Press, 1978), 217–26, 956–68.

[3] Edward L. Rubin, *Beyond Camelot: Rethinking Politics and Law for the Modern State* (Princeton, NJ: Princeton University Press, 2005), 22–29; *Soul, Self, and Society: The New Morality and the Modern State* (New York: Oxford University Press, 2015), 117–22.

[4] Rubin, *Soul, Self, and Society*, 113–58.

ministers resigned with him, establishing the principle that they were all heads of government departments, not servants of the king. Over the course of the next two decades, Lord North's successor, William Pitt the Younger (served 1783–1801, 1804–1806) established rationalized ministries staffed by salaried employees, which required buying out – often at enormous cost – the incumbents who held those offices as private property.

Along with this change in structure was a change in the understanding of the government's purposes. During the last quarter of the eighteenth century, governmental action was reconceived as consciously designed policy intended to serve particular purposes. Traditional monarchies in Austria and Prussia redefined their role as benefiting their citizens and maintaining political stability.[5] It was Joseph II who said that the goal of government is to provide the greatest good for the greatest number.[6] At this same time, democratic regimes were first established in Western Europe, in Britain as the result of gradual evolution, in France as the result of a cataclysmic uprising. These regimes advanced and secured the articulation of government purposes by making the demands of the citizens a major factor in determining government policy and requiring the government, even though still dominated by elites, to articulate the rationale for its policies in publicly acceptable terms.

The US Constitution was conceived, drafted, ratified, and put into operation at the same time that these momentous events occurred in Europe. But the connection between the Constitution and administrative government is not immediately apparent from its text. As is well known, the Constitution makes no effort to define the administrative structure of the government that it creates. While Article I contains a substantial amount of detail about the way the legislature is structured and the nature of the powers that it exercises, Article II is virtually silent about the structure and powers of the executive. Most of its relatively brief text (it is less than half as long as Article I) is devoted to the election of the President and his qualifications for office. The remainder provides a cursory and seemingly amorphous list of his powers; there is not a word about the authority of other executive officers and just a brief provision regarding their appointment.[7]

The only reference to an administrative apparatus in Article II is the enigmatic Opinion Clause, which states that the President "may require the Opinion, in writing, of the principal Officer in each of the executive Departments upon any Subject relating to the Duties of their respective Offices" (Art. II, sec. 2, cl. 1). What makes this enigmatic is that the authority it establishes would seem to be inherent in the President's hierarchical command over the executive branch, an authority

---

[5] Andre Wakefield, *The Disordered Police State: German Cameralism as Science and Practice* (Chicago: University of Chicago Press, 2009).

[6] Saul K. Padover, *The Revolutionary Emperor: Joseph II* (New York: Robert O. Ballou, 1934).

[7] That provision declares that those public officials who qualify as "Officers" must be nominated by the President and approved by the Senate (Art. II, sec. 2, cl. 2).

that is not described or even mentioned but, as everyone recognizes, is necessarily implied. Why does the text explicitly provide for this one relatively minor aspect of the overall relationship while leaving the relationship itself unspecified? While there have been several efforts to read significance into this textual oddity,[8] the most plausible explanation is that the drafters of the Constitution, having flirted with the idea of specifying the executive departments and thought better of it,[9] inadvertently left this fragment of their efforts as they turned their attention to more contentious issues.

The relationship between the US Constitution and the advent of the administrative state, however, goes far beyond the presence or absence of any particular clause. As the timing of the two developments reveals, the drafting and ratification of the Constitution are themselves expressions of the modern administrative concept of government. The point can be demonstrated by considering not only what the Constitution means but what it means to have a constitution. To begin with, any constitution, and the US Constitution in particular, articulates the structure of government in the process of creating it. Western Europe's monarchies were conceived as being established by some higher power, whether divine or customary. As already suggested, they were unitary structures, with all power centered in the king, who could reorganize and reshuffle the components at will. The theory of sovereignty projected this plenary power.[10] A constitution, in contrast, creates the government through the specific action of identifiable human beings. In doing so, it articulates a structure, defining the authority of each component of the government, the mechanism by which its leaders are selected, and the procedure by which it reaches its decisions (if only to say that it can determine that procedure for itself). In other words, a constitution must do exactly the same things as a regulatory statute does when it creates an administrative agency.

The basic structural articulation in the Constitution is the division of government into executive, legislative, and judicial units, or branches. This division is functional; that is, each component is defined in terms of the type of governmental task it carries out. It has its origins in the English Civil War, about a century prior to the advent of the administrative state, and in theoretical writings by Locke and Montesquieu that point toward modern concepts of government but are not specifically administrative in character. There is little if

---

[8] Akhil Reed Amar, "Some Opinions on the Opinions Clause," *Virginia Law Review* 82 (1996): 647; Steven G. Calabresi and Kevin H. Rhodes "The Structural Constitution: Unitary Executive and Plural Judiciary," *Harvard Law Review* 105 (1992): 1153, 1206–7; Lawrence Lessig and Cass R. Sunstein, "The President and the Administration," *Columbia Law Review* 94 (1994): 1, 32–38.

[9] Max Farrand, *The Records of the Federal Convention of 1787*, vol. II (New Haven, CT: Yale University Press, 1966), 135–36, 158, 334–37.

[10] Robert Jackson, *Sovereignty: The Evolution of an Idea* (Cambridge: Polity Press, 2007); Dieter Grim, *Sovereignty: The Origin and Future of a Political and Legal Concept* (New York: Columbia University Press, 2015).

any articulation of structure in the Constitution on the basis of subject matter as opposed to function. The President is instructed to "take Care that the Laws be faithfully executed" (Art. II, sec. 3), which presumably means all the laws that Congress passes. He is designated as "Commander in Chief of the Army and Navy of the United States, and of the Militia of the several States, when called into the actual service of the United States" (Art II., sec. 2, cl. 1), but the document fails to specify the way in which this authority is distinct from the seven separate enumerated powers granted to Congress regarding the armed forces, the militia, and the use of force in foreign affairs.

The articulation of structure characteristic of administrative governance at the operational level has a different character. It tends to define the components of government by subject matter rather than function; that is, each agency is assigned to an operational area of responsibility but then combines executive, legislative, and judicial functions in carrying out its tasks.[11] The movement of administrative governance toward substantive as opposed to functional divisions results from the complexity of modern knowledge and technology. In order to understand and manage virtually any subject area of contemporary society, a government agency must possess substantive knowledge, or expertise. This simultaneously requires that the agency limit itself to a particular area and that it deal with that area in ways that combine executive, legislative, and judicial functions.

Thus, both the US Constitution and the administrative approach to governance feature an articulated structure, but the divisions they make are based on different and indeed crosscutting principles. Conceivably, the difference in the approach to structural articulation between the Constitution and the administrative state could have led to a strongly interventionist stance by constitutional courts. The courts could have invoked separation of powers doctrine to prohibit or place major limitations on the typical administrative agency that combines these functions. A few cases in the modern era have been decided on these grounds, but they have often increased rather than constrained agency authority.

In terms of constitutional doctrine, the Supreme Court's relatively rare use of the separation of powers doctrine is typically explained by an absence of textual support and by the countervailing principle of checks and balances. Although the first three Articles of the Constitution provide for the legislative, executive, and judicial branch in turn, there is no explicit statement that they should be understood to create strict and inviolable boundaries. At the time the Constitution was adopted, several of the state constitutions had explicit separation of powers provisions; Madison proposed such a provision together with the Bill of Rights, but Congress rejected it. The constitutional principle of checks and balances, moreover, requires that the functions overlap; for example, the President can veto legislation and the Senate approves treaties and executive

---

[11] Peter L. Strauss, "The Place of Agencies in Government: Separation of Powers and the Fourth Branch," *Columbia Law Review* 84 (1984): 573.

appointments. A more theoretical reason why federal courts have rarely enforced a strict separation of power lies in the doctrine of popular sovereignty, the variation of traditional sovereignty doctrine that the American revolutionaries developed.[12] If the basic moral authority for government rests with the people, then the people's representatives should be able to divide that power in any manner which the people approve, and the considerations that militate against the division of a unitary sovereign would not apply.

There is a still more important reason for judicial nonintervention. Given the state of modern knowledge and technology, administrative government could not function if agencies were unable to deploy all the functions of governance in their defined area of expertise. While this sounds like the most pragmatic basis for the non-interventionist approach, it is in fact the most conceptual, as it is inherently consistent with constitutional values. Congress's basic obligation is to articulate the agencies it creates, to specify their area of jurisdiction, whether functional or substantive, because a government created by a constitution is necessarily an articulated one. In other words, the basic meaning of the US Constitution is that it creates a structure that can achieve the pragmatic functions of government in the real-world context in which that government must function.

The articulated purposes of modern government, as embodied in the US Constitution, authorized by the Constitution, and reiterated by the statutes that it authorizes, can be explicated by contrasting the Constitution and its statutes with the other leading feature of revolutionary America's legal system, which was English common law. Common law can be defined as a set of legal rules established by incremental judicial decision-making. It was the prevailing law in Britain and Britain's American colonies at the time of the Revolution. Contrary to the myth – adamantly believed by the revolutionary generation and for a century thereafter – British common law does not date back into England's misty Anglo-Saxon past.[13] Rather, the first of the Angevin kings, Henry II, initiated the common law by statutory enactment, in part because he wanted to establish a uniform (hence "common") law to eliminate overlapping feudal jurisdictions and in part because he wanted to resolve the conflicting land grants issued by previous monarchs.[14] In both cases, Henry simply did not care about the content of the legal rules involved; he merely wanted the rules to be uniform and to resolve the dangerous disputes between conflicting factions of the English nobility. Consequently, he allowed the royal judges whom his statutes authorized to develop whatever rules they chose. Thus, the essential feature of English and then British common law is that its rules

---

[12] Bernard Bailyn, *The Ideological Origins of the American Revolution*, rev. ed. (Cambridge, MA: Belknap Press, 1992), 198–229; Gordon S. Wood, *The Creation of the American Republic, 1776–1787* (New York: W.W. Norton, 1969), 445–46, 524–36.

[13] J. G. A. Pocock, *The Ancient Constitution and the Feudal Law: A Study of English Historical Thought in the Seventeenth Century* (Cambridge: Cambridge University Press, 1987).

[14] W. L. Warren, *Henry II* (Berkeley: University of California Press, 1977), 317–61.

are developed by the courts and not by the monarch, or, in the modern context, by the legislature.

Although the American revolutionaries rejected the authority of the British monarch – they were, after all, revolutionaries – they happily preserved a legal system established by Britain's royal judges. They had no articulated goals regarding the resolution of private disputes that differed from the rules that English and British common law judges had developed over time. But the Constitution does not codify or endorse this important continuity. Rather, the Constitution's main concern, consistent with its essentially administrative character, is to establish a procedure for enacting statutes, that is, positive enactments that have the power to displace common law. In other words, its concern is to achieve its general, articulated purpose of promoting the citizens' welfare by authorizing the federal legislature to enact statutes that achieve specific articulated purposes. This is exactly what has happened over time, of course. As industrialization, urbanization, and commercialization rendered economic relationships between private parties a matter of intense public concern, the federal legislature began to displace common law by using its constitutional authority to enact regulatory statutes designed to alter those relationships. In other words, it rejected the premodern common law that lay outside the conscious, legislating authority of the federal government with statutes that display the essentially administrative character of the Constitution that authorized them.

There is a substantial amount of modern scholarship that appears to contest the intrinsically administrative nature of constitutions in general, and the US Constitution in particular, by arguing that basic features of the administrative state are in fact unconstitutional, that is, that they conflict with various provisions in the text.[15] But virtually all of these works are in full agreement with the principal argument that this chapter advances. They concede that the prevailing interpretation of the Constitution by the courts has been highly deferential to the realities of modern administrative government. Their argument is that this permissive attitude represents a betrayal of the framers' intentions. Even if one concedes this point, it remains necessary to explain why judges, along with the majority of scholars, have consistently engaged in this alleged betrayal. Any answer that relies on disloyalty, corruption, or incompetence misses the point. Rather, the explanation must be that the federal judiciary, with the exception of the Lochner era (discussed later), has always taken the position that the Constitution is fully consistent with an administrative government.

[15] Randy E. Barnett, *Restoring the Lost Constitution* (Princeton, NJ: Princeton University Press, 2013); Richard A. Epstein, *How Progressives Rewrote the Constitution* (Washington, DC: Cato Institute, 2007); *Takings: Private Property and the Power of Eminent Domain* (Cambridge, MA: Harvard University Press, 1985); Philip Hamburger, *Is Administrative Law Unlawful?* (Chicago: University of Chicago Press, 2014); David Schoenbrod, *Power Without Responsibility: How Congress Abuses the People through Delegation* (New Haven, CT: Yale University Press, 1993).

Nor should the substance of the critics' claim be conceded. It depends upon an interpretation of the Constitution that is, at the very least, contestable. For example, most of these writers insist that the framers were intent on protecting private property against government intrusion. The original document, however, never refers to private property; it uses the term "property" only once, when referring to the "Property belonging to the United States" (Art. IV, sec. 3, cl. 2). More basically, they imagine, perhaps on the basis of their own political predilections, that the Constitution's basic purpose is to protect people, and specifically to protect their liberty, against governmental depredations of one sort or another. This confuses the Constitution with the various premodern documents that asserted the rights of private persons, whether nobles or commoners, against royal authority. In English history, the Magna Carta and the Glorious Revolution's Bill of Rights are famous examples. But modern constitutions are entirely different. Rather than beginning with an existing government, whose basic structure and legitimacy are assumed, and then attempting to place limits on that government's actions, modern constitutions – consistent with modern social contract theory – create a government ab initio. The basic purpose or meaning of such constitutions is the administrative one – to establish a political regime with the articulated structure necessary for concerted, goal-oriented action and with the articulated goal of serving the citizenry's needs. Protections for liberty then function as side constraints on the way in which that basic purpose is achieved.[16]

THE REJECTION OF INTERVENTIONIST APPROACHES DURING THE FEDERAL ERA (1789–1860)

During the Federal era (1789–1860), the federal courts established the basic relationship between American constitutional law and the administrative state: that the development of administrative government by the political branches was entirely consistent with the Constitution and should be endorsed, rather than impeded, by the process of judicial review. There is little question that this statement accurately describes Supreme Court doctrine, as there are no decisions from this era striking down administrative programs. In order for the statement to be meaningful, however, it is necessary to determine whether there existed any administrative programs for the Court to strike down. preceding section does not provide an answer. It only asserts that the drafters of the Constitution shared the same view of government that led to the creation of administrative states in Western Europe and that the government they created was not something other than an administrative state, such as a traditional or divine right monarchy. The general view of historians is that even if such claims are true, the national government was not an

---

[16] Robert Nozick, *Anarchy, State and Utopia* (New York: Basic Books, 1974), 28–33.

administrative state during the Federal period but a minimalist one, performing few functions other than those necessary to maintain its basic territorial integrity. According to this view, the essentially administrative approach embodied in the Constitution was not instantiated in actual or pragmatic governmental action until after the Civil War. This might well explain the paucity of constitutional decisions regarding the national government during this period.[17]

Recent investigations have qualified this notion of a minimalist national government, suggesting that the national government not only carried out a wide variety of functions but that it directly affected the lives of American citizens in doing so.[18] The Post Office has always been recognized as an exception to any minimalist view. Dwarfing any private enterprise in the nation and employing three-quarters of the federal government's civilian work force, it reached into every town of even modest size, often serving as its social center. It was the primary means by which people communicated with each across the nation's vast distances and also the primary source of public information because it transported newspapers at subsidized rates to facilitate their circulation. It also played a crucial role in passenger travel by providing an essential source of revenue for private stagecoach lines, which proudly announced their role as mail carriers.[19]

The Post Office was hardly the only federal administrative agency nor the only one that produced direct effects on the lives of its citizens. The federal government administered the vast tracts of land that had not yet been divided into states, a function that only ended, ironically enough, during the Progressive Era when other federal functions expanded so dramatically. The extent of federally administered territory was already large when the United States achieved independence but was greatly expanded during the Federal era through direct and decisive action by the national government. First came the Louisiana Purchase, a treaty that President Jefferson entered into by swallowing his own objections to national government authority. This was followed by the annexation of Texas, a war with Mexico, and another treaty, this time with Britain, the world's leading military power. Not only did the federal government

---

[17] The only two federal laws declared unconstitutional were a provision of the Judiciary Act of 1789, struck down by Chief Justice Marshall in *Marbury* v. *Madison* as a way of resolving a difficult political quandary and to establish the principle of judicial review; and the Missouri Compromise, struck down in the disastrous decision of *Dred Scott* v. *Sanford* (1856). Moreover, these two decisions involve justices of the peace and slavery, both of which predate the administrative state and have no necessary connection to it.

[18] Brian Balogh, *A Government Out of Sight: The Mystery of National Authority in Nineteenth Century America* (Cambridge: Cambridge University Press, 2009), 220–26.

[19] This was, incidentally, the very same role that the Post Office played in developing passenger airline travel in the early part of the twentieth century, when the importance of the federal government was no longer in doubt. T. A. Heppenheimer, *Turbulent Skies: The History of Commercial Aviation* (New York: John Wiley, 1995); Nick A. Komons, *Bonfires to Beacons: Federal Civil Aviation Policy under the Air Commerce Act, 1926–1938* (Washington, DC: Smithsonian Institution Press, 1989).

provide all public services in the new regions, it also sold land to private citizens through administrative agencies, first the Treasury Department and then the specially constituted General Land Office. Many historians would argue that these federal responsibilities produced direct effects on virtually every citizen, not just those residing in the territories, since the availability, price, safety, and accessibility of frontier land were factors in so many people's personal decision-making about where they would live and how they would earn their living.[20]

Another administrative agency of the Federal era was the Bank of the United States. To be sure, it was a private institution, but it was authorized and partially owned by the federal government and performed a number of public functions in accordance with that authority.[21] The First Bank of the United States was the work of Alexander Hamilton and was partially responsible for the defection of Jefferson and Madison from Washington's cabinet. The Second Bank was initiated by Madison, as President, who managed to overcome ongoing objections to government authority inherited from Jefferson. In both its incarnations, the Bank, like the Post Office, directly affected nearly every citizen in the nation as it imposed fiscal discipline on state banks and stabilized the paper currency on which the economy depended.[22] After the Second Bank was effectively destroyed by President Jackson, the nation went through a period of financial instability, then instituted the sub-Treasury system under James Polk that had some but fewer regulatory features, and stumbled along until the creation of the Federal Reserve.[23]

A fourth but certainly not final example of Federal era administration was the safety regulation of steamboats by the Board of Supervising Inspectors (the Steamboat Board), authorized by statute in 1852 after more limited regulatory efforts had failed. This board, described in Jerry Mashaw's *Creating the Administrative Constitution*, was in many ways equivalent to a modern independent agency, headed by a collegium of people with recognized expertise, controlling private parties within its jurisdiction by licensing, possessing both rulemaking and adjudicatory authority, enforcing its decisions through administrative sanctions, and relying on a staff of salaried employees.[24] The

---

[20] Frederick Jackson Turner, *The Significance of the Frontier in American History* (New York: Henry Holt & Co., 1921); Everett S. Lee, "The Turner Thesis Reexamined," *American Quarterly* 13 (1961): 77–83; George Rogers Taylor, *The Turner Thesis: Concerning the Role of the Frontier in American History* (Lexington, MA: D.C. Heath, 1972).

[21] We fully recognize such hybrid institutions as administrative agencies at present; the Federal Reserve Banks have some of the same characteristics, and the Public Company Accounting Oversight Board is a private corporation authorized by the Sarbanes-Oxley Act to perform a variety of public functions.

[22] Bray Hammond, *Banks and Politics in America: From the Revolution to the Civil War* (Princeton, NJ: Princeton University Press, 1957).

[23] Ibid. at 718–39; Jerry L. Mashaw, *Creating the Administrative Constitution: The Lost One Hundred Years of American Administrative Law* (New Haven, CT: Yale University Press, 2012), 167–74.

[24] Mashaw, *Creating the Administrative Constitution*, 187–208.

dramatic improvement in steamboat design and operation that this system of regulation achieved saved a considerable number of lives and provided an increased sense of security for the many people who traveled, or contemplated traveling, on steamboats.

With these examples of Federal era regulation in view, the federal judiciary's nonintervention can be seen as at least an implicit endorsement of the administrative state rather than the result of any lack of opportunity to intervene. The Post Office was legally impregnable, being specifically authorized as one of Congress's enumerated powers, but agencies such as the Bank of the United States and the Steamboat Board lacked textual support and were innovative in both structure and purpose. Yet the courts never struck down any federal program on constitutional grounds and never voiced any serious concerns about their legality.[25] They regarded articulated organizations that existed outside the three traditional branches – combining the functions of all three, designed to achieve articulated purposes, and exercising wide-ranging effects on the populace – as fully constituent with the federal government's constitutional authority.

This implicit endorsement was translated into explicit constitutional doctrine by the Supreme Court when individual states challenged the federal government's authority to establish administrative programs. *McCulloch* v. *Maryland* (1819) involved a tax that the state of Maryland imposed on the Second Bank of the United States and on its circulating notes.[26] In assessing the constitutionality of this tax, Chief Justice Marshall famously observed that "the power to tax involves the power to destroy."[27] Whether this is true in general, it is true with respect to circulating notes, and that was in fact the goal of the Maryland legislation. The question was whether a state can take action of this sort against a federal instrumentality. Counsel for Maryland advanced a highly restrictive view of federal power, sometimes known as compact federalism. "The powers of the General Government ... are delegated by the States, who alone are truly sovereign, and must be exercised in subordination to the States, who alone possess supreme dominion."[28] In other words, the federal government resulted from a compact or agreement among sovereign states and is subject to their superior authority.

Chief Justice James Marshall, a devout Federalist appointed by John Adams to perpetuate that party's position after Adams's electoral defeat, rejected this assertion in ringing terms. "The government proceeds directly from the people; is 'ordained and established' in the name of the people, and is declared to be ordained, 'in order to form a more perfect union, establish justice, insure domestic tranquility, and secure the blessings of liberty to themselves and to

---

[25] Balogh, *A Government Out of Sight*, 250–64; Mashaw, *Creating the Administrative Constitution*, 188.

[26] Mark Killenbeck, *M'Culloch v. Maryland: Securing a Nation* (Lawrence, KS: University Press of Kansas, 2006).

[27] 17 U.S. 316 at 431.   [28] Ibid. at 402.

their posterity.'"[29] Marshall insisted that it is the people, not the states, who are truly sovereign so that, in creating a national government, they were subordinating the states to that government, as they had power to do. In other words, he carried forward the view of the Revolutionary generation that located sovereignty in the people, who could empower any delegate or number of delegates that they wished, much as the sovereign king could empower any type and number of subordinates.[30]

Marshall's grand pronouncements were not sufficient to decide the case, however. The national government established by the Constitution, even if accepted as the people's creation and the states' superior, is nonetheless a government of enumerated powers. It can displace state law only if it acts legally, that is, within its allotted jurisdiction. Maryland asserted that it did not have the authority to establish a national bank because that authority, unlike the authority to create a post office, is not one of those enumerated powers. Marshall responded to this challenge with another of the decision's famous aphorisms: "In considering this question, then, we must never forget that it is *a Constitution* we are expounding."[31] Not simply argument by typeface, this states the basic interpretive principle that constitutional language is to be read in accordance with the Preamble's aspiration to create a strong, effective central government, "a more perfect Union." Marshall then applied this general principle to the Necessary and Proper Clause, which on its own terms can be seen as an instruction to interpret Congress's enumerated powers in an expansive way but becomes an even greater source of national authority if the instruction itself understood broadly. In another famous quote from this most quotable Supreme Court opinion, Marshall declared: "Let the end be legitimate, let it be within the scope of the Constitution, and all means which are appropriate, which are plainly adapted to that end, which are not prohibited, but consist with the letter and spirit of the Constitution, are Constitutional."[32] The end, of course, is the articulated purpose of the action in question, and "all the means appropriate" can be taken as a synonym for articulated administrative mechanisms.

Gibbons v. *Ogden* (1824) provided another doctrinal endorsement of the administrative state. Gibbons possessed a license to operate a vessel in coastal trade under a 1793 federal statute. This was not itself an administrative statute, licenses to carry out various kinds of business having been a common feature of premodern European monarchies. But the scope of federal power to control commerce in this manner would become one of the basic grounds for many

[29] Ibid. at 403–4.
[30] Marshall's decision did not put the theory of compact federalism to rest. Having been invoked by his own party in opposition to the War of 1812 (and thereby ensuring its demise), it served as South Carolina's rationale in the Nullification Crisis of Jackson's administration and then as the basis of the Southern states' secession. It was the Union armies in the Civil War that finally interred this doctrine.
[31] 17 U.S. 316 at 407.   [32] Ibid. at 421.

regulatory statutes, including the 1852 Steamboat Safety Act and, in the twentieth century, the Federal Communications Act, the Securities Exchange Act, the Federal Aviation Act, the Clean Air Act, and the Endangered Species Act. The case arose when New York State granted the exclusive right of operating steamboats in New York waters to two people – Robert Livingston, one of the wealthiest and most prominent men in the nation, and Robert Fulton, who himself invented the steamboat – and they, in turn, assigned their rights to Aaron Ogden. Ogden obtained an injunction from the New York courts to stop Gibbons from operating a ferry service between New Jersey and New York on the ground that its ferries entered New York waters.[33]

In argument before the Supreme Court, Ogden based his case on dual federalism, a more delimited claim than compact federalism. Conceding that New York State was bound by the US Constitution, he argued that control over ship traffic in state waters was a right retained by the states under the Tenth Amendment. To reject this claim, Chief Justice Marshall first established that the federal license fit within the enumerated power to regulate "Commerce with foreign Nations, and among the several States," reflecting the expansive interpretive approach he had declared in *McCulloch*. He then held that the Tenth Amendment did not limit this authority because the authority is "complete in itself, may be exercised to its utmost extent, and acknowledges no limitations except those prescribed in the constitution. If, as has always been understood, the sovereignty of Congress, though limited to specified objects, is plenary as to those objects, the power over commerce . . . is vested in Congress as absolutely as it would be in a single government."[34]

Here again Marshall opposed the idea, carried over from the pre-administrative era, that a nation must be ruled by a unitary sovereign. He did so in this case by asserting, contrary to that theory, the joint or parallel operation of two sovereigns with their respective jurisdictions carefully defined. Unlike compact federalism, which eventually would die with the Civil War, dual federalism remains a viable doctrine today. Bolstered by the Tenth Amendment, it would be revived in subsequent constitutional history, first during the Lochner era and then in recent times.

Although the federal judiciary evinced few concerns about federal administrative authority during the Federal era, that was decidedly untrue for the political branches of government. The Democratic-Republican Party in the early decades of the era and the Jacksonian Democracy that succeeded it made discomfort with federal administration one of its defining issues. Its leaders succeeded in defeating a number of bills in Congress for federal infrastructure development (called "internal improvements"). Even more strikingly, concern

---

[33] Herbert A. Johnson, *Gibbons v. Ogden: John Marshall Steamboats, and Interstate Commerce* (Lawrence, KS: University Press of Kansas, 2010).
[34] 22 U.S. 1 at 196–97.

about the scope of federal authority was strongly voiced by a number of Presidents, including Jefferson, Madison, Jackson, and Van Buren.[35] Jackson vetoed the Second Bank bill on explicitly constitutional grounds, arguing that Congress did not have the authority to charter a national bank.

The national government was unable to sustain this position however. Jefferson and Madison, adopted the pro-national policies of the opposing Federalists, managing to deprive that party of its issues.[36] Jackson, who was willing to maintain his anti-national views about the Second Bank and destroy the economy instead, nonetheless presided over a significant expansion of the central government.[37] That such sophisticated political thinkers as Jefferson and Madison and such a forceful leader as Jackson were unable to abide by their own principles indicates not only the potent current of political developments but also the organic link between constitutionalism and administrative government.[38]

THE INTERVENTIONS OF THE LOCHNER ERA (1897–1937)

The federal judiciary's endorsement of the administrative state continued after the Civil War. But in the first third of the twentieth century, a dramatic reversal occurred. During this period – the "Lochner era" – federal courts, for the first and only time, struck down a number of major regulatory statutes on constitutional grounds. Precisely why they did so was a much-debated question and has continued to be a matter of concern and reflection for both judges and commentators, even after the authority of the decisions themselves has been definitively rejected. Significant for present purposes is to identify the source and scope of the judiciary's hostility toward administrative governance and to highlight the contrast between that attitude and the remainder of American constitutional history.

Following the Civil War, life in the United States was transformed by what is generally described as the Second Industrial Revolution. The explosive growth of cities, the rigors and oppressions of factory work, the promise and threat of new technologies, the extreme concentrations of wealth and its accompanying

---

[35] Daniel Walker Howe, *What Hath God Wrought: The Transformation of America, 1815–1848* (New York: Oxford University Press. 2007); Sean Wilentz, *The Rise of American Democracy: Jefferson to Lincoln* (New York: W.W. Norton, 2005).

[36] George Dangerfield, *The Era of Good Feelings* (New York: Harcourt, Brace & Co., 1953).

[37] Mashaw, *Creating the Administrative Constitution*, 147–55, 209–24.

[38] Jackson's constitutional assertions have never been recognized as doctrine. This does not mean that he is viewed as having acted illegally. Accepted constitutional doctrine permits the President to exercise the veto on any grounds he chooses and certainly does not discourage either the President or members of Congress from acting on their own view of constitutional authority. But Jackson's argument that his views defined the power of the federal government in general and limited the reach of the national administrative state were never accepted by the judiciary, and modern doctrine provides that the judiciary has the final say.

corruptions generated demands for increased government intervention at both the state and federal levels.[39] For a variety of reasons that historians of the "gilded age" have fully documented, the reaction to these demands was slow.[40] Stephen Skowronek describes the federal response between 1865 and 1900 as a "patchwork" focused heavily on the civil service and the military.[41] The one exception that directly affected people's lives was the regulation of railroads through the creation of the first modern independent agency, the Interstate Commerce Commission.[42] Railroads, by their nature, projected themselves into every city and most moderate-sized towns in America, overwhelming local elites with economic power derived from the nationwide scale of their operations. State and local laws were uneven and were eventually turned aside by the courts, creating demand for coordinated national regulation, both from captains of industry and from people of more modest means – farmers, sharecroppers, workers, tenement dwellers, and consumers.

The preemptive name of the "Interstate Commerce" Commission, which was, after all, a railroad regulator, anticipated constitutional challenges based on the scope of Congress's powers under Article I. To be sure, the Marshall Court decisions created a formidable impediment to their success. But the passage of the Civil War Amendments provided a new argument against regulatory law. The Fourteenth Amendment applied the language of the Fifth Amendment's Due Process Clause to the states: "[N]or shall any state deprive any person of life, liberty or property, without due process of law." In the *Slaughter House Cases* (1873), a Louisiana law granting a twenty-five-year monopoly in the slaughtering business to a private company was challenged on the ground that it prevented others from pursuing their trade and thus violated their economic liberty granted by the Due Process Clause. Similar challenges were raised against state laws setting maximum rates for grain storage (*Munn* v. *Illinois*, 1877), setting railroad rates (*Railroad Commission Cases*, 1886), and prohibiting the sale of alcoholic beverages (*Mugler* v. *Kansas*, 1887). Continuing its noninterventionist stance, the Supreme Court rejected all these challenges, holding that legislation of this sort was within the constitutional authority of a state.

---

[39] Sean Dennis Cashman, *America in the Gilded Age: From the Death of Lincoln to the Rise of Theodore Roosevelt*, 3rd ed. (New York: New York University Press, 1984); Glenn Porter, "Industrialization and the Rise of Big Business," in Charles W. Calhoun, ed. *The Gilded Age: Perspectives on the Origins of Modern America*, 2nd ed. (Lanham, MD: Rowman & Littlefield, 2007).

[40] Charles W. Calhoun, "The Political Culture: Public Life and the Conduct of Politics," in Charles W. Calhoun, ed. *The Gilded Age*; Stephen Skowronek, *Building a New American State: The Expansion of National Administrative Capacities, 1877–1920* (Cambridge: Cambridge University Press, 1982).

[41] Skowronek, *Building a New American State*, 37–120.

[42] Thomas K. McCraw, *Prophets of Regulation: Charles Francis Adams, Louis D. Brandeis, James M. Landis, Alfred E. Kahn* (Cambridge, MA: Belknap Press, 1986); Skowronek, *Building a New American State*, 121–62.

By the turn of the century, however, the pace of regulatory legislation had accelerated, reflecting what historians describe as the transition from the Gilded Age to the Progressive Era.[43] This process was viewed with increasing alarm by the Supreme Court, now filled with Justices appointed by several decades of conservative, pro-business Presidents. The first decisions that adopted the due process rationale to strike down regulatory legislation were *Missouri Pacific R. Co. v. Nebraska* (1896) and *Allgeyer v. Louisiana* (1897), but the one that became famous, and gave its name to four decades of Supreme Court decisions, was *Lochner v. New York* (1905). That decision invalidated a New York law setting a maximum of sixty hours per week and ten hours per day that an employee in the baking industry could work. Such a law, the Court declared, violated the Due Process Clause by denying persons the right to form whatever contracts they chose. Because decisions such as this used the Due Process Clause to impose limits on the subject matter of enacted law, rather than on the procedures by which laws were passed and enforced, the doctrine became known as substantive due process; because the laws struck down generally involved the rights of businesses, it is also known as economic due process.

During the following decades, the Court invalidated a succession of federal and state regulatory laws on substantive due process grounds. These included state minimum wage laws for women (*Adkins v. Children's Hospital*, 1923; *Morehead v. New York ex rel. Tipaldo*, 1936), federal and state laws prohibiting employers from hiring only non-union workers (*Adair v. United States*, 1908; *Coppage v. Kansas*, 1915), state laws limiting sale prices of particular products (*Tyson & Brother v. Banton*, 1927), state laws requiring licenses for certain types of businesses (*New State Ice Co. v. Liebmann*, 1932), and state laws that restricted the kinds of products that businesses could sell to the public (*Jay Burns Baking Co. v. Bryan*, 1924; *Weaver v. Palmer Bros.*, 1926). Overall, approximately 200 laws were struck down on these grounds.

A standard view of these decisions has been that they were essentially political in nature – efforts by conservative justices to hold back the tide of legislation that was transforming the nation's legal landscape. Certainly, the Supreme Court's action exercised a significant effect on ordinary people's lives, denying them protections that political majorities perceived as necessary. Recently, however, scholars have suggested that these decisions need to be read more carefully.[44] After all, the amount of regulatory legislation in the Progressive Era was extensive, and the Court affirmatively upheld a good deal

---

[43] John Whiteclay Chambers II, *The Tyranny of Change: America in the Progressive Era, 1890–1920* (New Brunswick, NJ: Rutgers University Press, 2000); Robert H. Wiebe, *The Search for Order, 1877–1920* (New York: Hill and Wang, 1967), 164–95.

[44] David E. Bernstein, *Rehabilitating Lochner: Defending Individual Rights against Progressive Reform* (Chicago: University of Chicago Press, 2011); Howard Gillman, *The Constitution Besieged: The Rise and Demise of Lochner Era Police Powers Jurisprudence* (Durham, NC: Duke University Press, 1993); Paul Kens, *Lochner v. New York: Economic Regulation on Trial* (Lawrence, KS: University Press of Kansas, 1998); Noga Morag-Levine, *Chasing the Wind:*

of it, including maximum hours laws for women (*Muller* v. *Oregon*, 1908); maximum hours laws in manufacturing (*Bunting* v. *Oregon*, 1917), zoning laws (*Euclid* v. *Ambler Realty Co.*, 1926); workmen's compensation laws (*New York Central R. Co.* v. *White*, 1917); laws fixing prices for certain products, such as milk (*Nebbia* v. *New York*, 1932); and laws ordering the destruction of diseased trees (*Miller* v. *Schoene*, 1928). The Court, moreover, justified this differential treatment with a fully developed doctrine, one that was admittedly less than precise but no worse in that respect than many others that the federal judiciary has advanced. Its basic premise was that people's intrinsic right to make contracts and enter whatever line of business they desired could only be constrained by legislation if the legislature could demonstrate that the limits it was imposing served an important public purpose, such as the health of workers or the citizenry.

Howard Gillman has suggested that the Lochner Court was motivated by its concern about what it perceived to be "arbitrary class legislation."[45] This was the use of political power to favor one group of people over another, thus violating the neutrality – the basic sense of fairness – typically regarded as a characteristic of American government.[46] Regulatory laws that lacked a demonstrable connection to the protection of public health or welfare would, by default, fall into this forbidden category. It was one thing to require someone to obtain a license to practice medicine but quite another to require someone to obtain a license to manufacture ice; one thing to limit the hours that "weak and vulnerable" women could work but another to apply such limits to men. This interpretation of the substantive due process cases treats them as more principled by connecting them to the motivating concern of the Fourteenth Amendment, which was the equal treatment of all citizens. In fact, many of the cases finding that regulatory legislation violated the Due Process Clause simultaneously found that it violated the Equal Protection Clause.

At the same time, however, the Court struck down a number of regulatory laws by reviving the dual federalism doctrine. Employing a restrictive definition of interstate commerce, the Supreme Court struck down federal laws that prohibited interstate shipment of goods produced by child labor (*Hammer* v. *Dagenhart*, 1918), that established a pension system for railroad employees (*Railroad Retirement Board* v. *Alton R.R. Co.*, 1935), that attempted to raise the price of agricultural products by inducing farmers to decrease production (*United States* v. *Butler*, 1936), and that set maximum hours for coal miners (*Carter* v. *Carter Coal Co.*, 1936). The Court also eviscerated the Sherman Act, the nation's first antitrust statute, by holding that manufacturing, since it

---

Regulating Air Pollution in the Common Law State (Princeton, NJ: Princeton University Press, 2003).
45 Gillman, *The Constitution Besieged.*
46 Cass Sunstein, "Naked Preferences and the Constitution," *Columbia Law Review* 84 (1984): 1689–1732.

occurred in a single place, was not interstate commerce, even if the manufactured goods were then shipped across the country (*United States* v. *E.C. Knight*, 1895). Applying this same type of restrictive interpretation to a different enumerated power, the Court held that a tax on goods produced with child labor exceeded Congress's taxation authority (*Bailey* v. *Drexel Furniture Co.*, 1922). Moreover, in two unique decisions, the Court invalidated the National Industrial Recovery Act (NIRA), the centerpiece of Franklin Roosevelt's New Deal, on the ground that it represented an excessive delegation of legislative authority by Congress (*Panama Refining Co.* v. *Ryan*, 1935; *A.L.A. Schechter Poultry Corp.*, v. *United States*, 1935).

It is a creditable academic strategy to avoid conclusory and ultimately unhelpful characterizations of the Court's Lochner era jurisprudence as simply conservative. But if one seeks a single theme that would unify the controversial decisions that characterize this era, it would appear to be a position that is closely aligned with conservative politics, namely, an abiding concern about the expansion of the administrative state. Legislation often works to the advantage of some particular group in society and to the disadvantage of others, and those in the disadvantaged group will often perceive the particular statute as an arbitrary preference. The truly distinguishing feature of the statutes that the Court struck down, reversing its prior noninterventionist stance, was the unprecedented scope of these statutes and their novel use of government authority.

There is a more conceptual reading of the substantive due process decisions that emphasizes their essentially anti-regulatory character. Where did the Court get the idea that there was a right to contract or to enter whatever line of business one chose? The original Constitution certainly has no language to this effect, as critics of the Court pointed out, and the Due Process Clause had always been understood to provide only procedural protection, as will be discussed later. One source of the Court's doctrine was common law, which in fact included the principle that parties could enter into any contractual agreement they chose unless it contravened public policy.[47] As noted earlier in the chapter, the essential feature of common law is that its rules are developed by judges, not by the legislature, and thus do not embody the conscious or "positive" policies of the ruler. As long as Americans were content with the rules developed by English royal judges and their American successors, common law remained in force. The Progressives, however, were intensely dissatisfied with these rules, which they saw as favoring the established elite, if not originally then certainly as a result of the massive changes that industrialization, urbanization, and commercialization had produced. They thus proceeded to displace common law rules with statutes designed to achieve the articulated purposes of protecting workers, city dwellers, and consumers. Substantive due process was an effort to grant the common law rules constitutional stature, thus overturning specific regulatory efforts that contravened those rules and, more

---

[47] Morag-Levine, *Chasing the Wind*; Orren, *Belated Feudalism*, 145–54.

generally, assigning the development of legal rules to the judiciary and placing them beyond the reach of the Progressive legislatures.

A second and related rationale for substantive due process was natural law. This abiding theme in Western legal thought, extending back at least to Cicero, holds that certain principles are either built into the structure of the universe or, in the Christian version, ordained by God.[48] It became a building block of seventeenth-century social contract theory as the source of the natural freedom that individuals relinquished, in whole or part, in order to form an orderly society. As Weber points out, if natural law provides that people are only bound by a legal system to which they have freely agreed, then one can discern the boundaries of that system by asking what people would reasonably agree to.[49] The answer given by the Supreme Court is that people would not agree to relinquish their natural liberty to form agreements, the very basis of the social contract in the first place, unless there was a convincing public purpose for the limitation.

What is notable about these two related rationales for economic due process is not only that they are hostile to regulation but that they are extra-constitutional. That is, they do not purport to be either strict or loose interpretations of the constitutional text but rather principles that stand outside that text and control its reach. Common law, according to the myth, emerges from the mists of Anglo-Saxon England and thus long predates the Constitution's drafting and ratification. Natural law claims a still more ancient and distinguished pedigree. The extra-constitutional character of these two rationales emphasizes the essentially administrative character of constitutions in general and the US Constitution in particular. It is difficult to derive a doctrine that is hostile to the regulatory process from the Constitution because the Constitution is itself regulatory in character. It establishes a government of articulated components that take action designed to achieve articulated purposes. A regulatory regime is based on the same conception. The Constitution might include provisions that preclude particular regulatory practices, such as racial segregation, but it will not yield the general distrust of regulatory efforts that the Lochner Court was seeking. For that approach, the Court needed to draw on extra-constitutional principles such as common law and natural law.

The Lochner Era was the only time in US Constitutional history that the federal judiciary developed doctrines that opposed the administrative state. This turned out to be both a conceptually and politically unsustainable position. The politics are well-known and undoubtedly the dominant factor in the demise of economic due process, the restrictive reading of the Commerce Clause, and the other elements of the Supreme Court's anti-regulatory stance. President Roosevelt first tried to "pack" the Court by obtaining legislative

---

[48] Cicero, *The Republic and The Laws*, Niall Rudd, trans. (Oxford: Oxford University Press, 1998), 102–9, 123–28.
[49] Weber, *Economy and Society*, 868–69.

authority to appoint additional justices, then managed to intimidate it, and ultimately replaced most of its members with committed New Dealers. But the unconvincing nature of the Lochner Court's doctrines contributed to the rapidity and totality of these doctrines' rejection. In the single year of 1937, the Supreme Court declared the end of both doctrines (*West Coast Hotel* v. *Parrish; NLRB* v. *Jones & Laughlin Steel Corp.*). Even more definitive rejections followed (*United States* v. *Carolene Products Co.*, 1938; *United States* v. *Darby*, 1941; *Williamson* v. *Lee Optical*, 1955). Many other Supreme Court decisions have been definitively rejected, such as *Dred Scott* v. *Sanford* (1957) and *Plessy* v. *Ferguson* (1896). But the Lochner era anti-regulatory cases are the only ones that have been rejected wholesale.

THE HUMAN RIGHTS ERA (1965–1986)

With the appointment of Earl Warren as Chief Justice in 1954, the Supreme Court shifted focus and undertook a dramatic expansion of the constitutional protections for human rights, a focus that continued, although with decreased intensity, after Warren was replaced by Warren Burger and can be regarded as ending roughly when Ronald Reagan elevated William Rehnquist to Chief Justice and added Antonin Scalia to the Court in 1986. As mentioned in the Introduction, the Warren and Burger Court cases can be generally described as involving the administrative state because constitutional rights generally mean rights against the government and American government was fully administrative by the 1950s. The leading cases do not involve the administrative character of America government as such and are better discussed in other chapters in this volume. There were, however, several groups of cases, beginning roughly in the mid-1960s, dealing with government in its administrative capacity, the two most notable concerning procedural due process and institutional reform. Although invalidating governmental action as unconstitutional, they cannot be described as anti-administrative in either effect or tone. In fact, administration, far from being seen as the problem by the Court's decisions, was typically seen as the solution. That is, the fault that the Court found with the government's action was typically a lack of regularity in administrative practice, and the solution that was often imposed was more regularity or, more bluntly, more bureaucracy.[50]

The procedural due process decisions began with a finding – an insight – that was even more pro-administrative – and more path-breaking – than the administrative remedies the Supreme Court ultimately imposed. While substantive due process continued to be controversial during this era, the procedural content of the Due Process Clause was unquestioned and was regarded – quite correctly in this case – as tracing its origin back more than 700 years to Magna Carta.[51] There was no

---

[50] Malcolm M. Feeley and Edward L. Rubin, *Judicial Policy Making and the Modern State* (New York: Cambridge University Press, 1998), 271–96.
[51] J. C. Holt, *Magna Carta* (Cambridge: Cambridge University Press, 1992), 9–14, 378–405.

question in anyone's mind that the clause, originally applicable to the federal government through the Fifth Amendment and extended to the states in the Fourteenth, imposed a variety of requirements on the way that the government conducted civil and criminal trials. With regard to civil trial, which is the form relevant to administrative law, the content of those requirements, although of course contestable at their margins, was about as clear as any aspect of the American legal system. But it was also clear by the 1960s that those requirements only applied to trials where rights granted by common law or statutes that codified common law were at stake.[52]

The idea that due process protections applied only to common law rights was in fact a holdover from the traditionalist thinking in Lochner era decisions. Those decisions, as discussed in the preceding section, rested on the belief that the contours of the common law possessed constitutional significance and that a legislature could not alter common law rights without providing a more definitive justification than it would need when it took a different type of action, such as creating a new benefit. The obverse of this position was that only common law rights were of constitutional significance and thus could not be taken or impaired without due process of law. Licenses or benefits that were established by regulatory legislation and were unknown to common law did not merit constitutional protection, according to this view, and the government could therefore deal with them in any way it chose. This became known as the right-privilege distinction, with any grant to individuals outside the contours of the common law being relegated to the category of unprotected privileges, like a promise given without consideration.

According to this doctrine, government employment was a privilege. But arbitrary dismissals of government employees under the loyalty-security programs of the 1950s caused distress among the Justices of the Supreme Court, which they expressed in a variety of uncertain and half-hearted decisions when challenges to the dismissals came before them (*Cafeteria & Restaurant Workers Union v. McElroy*, 1961; *Slochower v. Board of Higher Education*, 1957). The source of their discomfort was crystalized by Charles Reich's famous law review article arguing that government benefits were a new form of property, as important to many people as traditional property recognized by common law.[53] A further conceptual building block was an earlier decision, *Mullane v. Central Hanover Trust* (1950), in which a New York statute provided that the rights of beneficiaries in common fund trusts could be settled after notice to the parties provided by publication of the

---

[52] This linkage between due process and common law was entrenched in Anglo-American legal doctrine and in fact went back to Magna Carta as well. What the leading barons who signed the document were demanding, in its famous Chapter 39 was that they be subject to the same common law rules (the *legem terre*, or "law of the land") that governed their subordinates rather than to the feudal obligations that King John had been using to extract money from them for his military campaigns. Ibid. at 277–79, 327–31.

[53] Charles Reich, "The New Property," *Yale Law Journal* 73 (1964): 733–87.

intended action in the newspaper. Justice Jackson, writing for the Court, held that when the address of the beneficiaries was known to the trustee, newspaper publication constituted inadequate notice and the trustee was required to provide notification by ordinary mail. Jackson thus detached the concept of notice from its traditional moorings and established that it was a general obligation of the government to be pragmatic and provide due process in a manner that was effective and practical. He identified another crucial element of due process as a hearing, with the implication that this requirement might be treated in the same pragmatic fashion.

These two conceptual advances combined in the seminal case of *Goldberg* v. *Kelly* (1970), which involved the termination of benefits to welfare recipients. Indicative of social changes occurring at the time, New York City, the defendant, had no desire to argue that welfare benefits were a privilege that could be terminated by the government at will and had already changed its rules to provide a post-termination hearing. The Supreme Court held that a post-termination hearing was not sufficient, given the crucial importance of these benefits for the recipients, and that the Due Process Clause required a pre-termination hearing. In doing so, the Court established the principle that common law, in the procedural as well as the substantive due process context, has no constitutional significance; a benefit granted by statute merits equal treatment to a property right created by common law. In addition, the decision identified the essential elements of due process as notice, a hearing, and an impartial decision maker and possibly an oral hearing, representation by counsel, and a statement of reasons as additional elements, depending on the circumstances.

Goldberg is one of the most significant decisions in modern constitutional law. Both the federal government and the states routinely cancel benefits and discipline or fire their employees across the full range of administrative programs. *Goldberg* had the potential to transform the majority of the interactions between ordinary citizens and government. In fact, the impact was especially severe on state government because nearly all the federal administrative actions involved are subject to the Administrative Procedure Act (APA), which requires procedures that are generally as extensive as those a constitutional court would impose under *Goldberg* and its successors; thus federal adjudications rarely conflict with the requirements of due process, and those that do can be decided on statutory grounds, a preferable approach.

But this was not the case with state administrative actions, which are much more varied and subject to a much greater variety of statutory provisions or, in some cases, to none at all. Thus, the Court had to fashion doctrinal rules to determine both when the Due Process Clause applied and which of its elements would be constitutionally required. The principle arrived at is that due process is required when the government takes action on an individual basis, against specific persons, but not when it acts generally. In other words, the purpose of due process is to decide whether a specific person fits within a legislatively established category, not to evaluate the validity of the category itself. This distinction finds convincing confirmation in democratic theory; individuals rarely have access to the political process, and thus need due process protection against arbitrary or oppressive government action, but groups can compete with one another in that process, and this competition, being the essence of self-government, should not be subject to judicially imposed constraints.

This distinction between generalized legislation and determinations regarding specific individuals, while implicitly adopted by the Supreme Court, turned out to be insufficient to quiet the Justices' concerns that they had wrought havoc on state administrative practice. Thus, only two terms after *Goldberg*, in *Roth* v. *Board of Regents* (1972), the Court imposed a further limitation on the decision's scope by interpreting the phrase "life, liberty, or property," words that had previously been regarded as a formulaic expression for some sort of personal interest. Now the Court declared that due process only applied when the personal interest fell within one of the three specified categories. With respect to the interest at stake in the case under consideration, a teaching position at a public university, it would only qualify as "property" if the individual had more than an "abstract need ... desire ... [or] unilateral expectation ... He must, instead, have a legitimate claim of entitlement to it. It is a purpose of the ancient institution of property to protect those claims upon which people rely in their daily lives."[54] Property interests of this sort, in a case involving state administrative practices, were created by state law, and it was to this law that the Court must turn to determine whether such interests were present. Thus, the plaintiff in *Roth*, who had only a one-year position renewable at will, did not have a property interest in that position, while the plaintiff in the companion case, *Perry* v. *Sindermann* (1972), who had de facto tenure by established state practice, had such an interest and was entitled to due process before being terminated.

Roth initiated several decades of widespread litigation, and multiple Supreme Court decisions, to determine whether various forms of public employment (*Arnett* v. *Kennedy*, 1974; *Bishop* v. *Wood*, 1976; *Cleveland Board of Education* v. *Loudermill*, 1985), government licenses (*Bell* v. *Burson*, 1971; *O'Bannon* v. *Town Court Nursing Center*, 1980), and government benefits (*Goss* v. *Lopez*, 1975; *Memphis Light, Gas, & Water Div.* v. *Craft*, 1978) constituted property. While the Court ultimately managed to delineate a moderately stable doctrine, the whole enterprise suffered from at least three conceptual problems that caused the Court to revisit the issue on a regular basis. First, the doctrine meant that federal courts deciding claims under the Constitution had to interpret state law, often on grounds that had never been addressed by the state courts. Second, many of the government benefits to which the doctrine potentially applied, such as a nursing home's certification to receive Medicare reimbursement or a child's continued attendance at public school, had

---

[54] 408 U.S. 564 at 577.

very little connection with the "ancient institution of property," compelling the Court to fashion a series of convoluted rules to determine when a person had a "legitimate expectation." Third, as Justice Rehnquist declared in his plurality opinion in *Arnett* v. *Kennedy*, if the government could determine by statute whether a property interest was present, it could also attempt to determine the procedures that would accompany that grant of property as well, thus undermining any constitutional protection. This compelled the Court to fashion the conceptually awkward doctrine that state law determines when property is present but federal law determines what procedures attach to that interest.

Having thus struggled with its effort to define property, the Court found that it faced equal if not greater challenges in defining liberty. It quickly concluded that liberty, unlike property but like the scope of procedural protection in general, was a matter of federal law. This demanded resolutions to a series of intricate questions involving prison practices (*Meachum* v. *Fano*, 1976; *Olim* v. *Wakinekona*, 1983; *Hewitt* v. *Helms*, 1983), parole and probation (*Morrissey* v. *Brewer*, 1972; *Gagnon* v. *Scarpelli*, 1973; *Greenholtz* v. *Inmates*, 1979), termination of parental rights (*Stanley* v. *Illinois*, 1972; *Santosky* v. *Kramer*, 1982; *Quillion* v. *Walcott*, 1978), and damage to reputation (*Wisconsin* v. *Constantineau*, 1971; *Goss* v. *Lopez*, 1975; *Owen* v. *City of Independence*, 1980). In addition to the liberty interests based directly on federal law, the Court held that such interests, like property interests, could be created by state law. The basic test was whether the state law in question limited a decision maker's discretion, thus creating a reasonable expectation that procedural protections would be provided. In the contemporary era to be discussed in the next section, the Court has scaled back this second source of liberty interests however (Sandin v. Connor, 1995).

Another question that the Court needed to address after *Goldberg* was the amount of process that was due in a variety of particular circumstances. Here, the Court developed a much more consistent doctrine than it had been able to achieve for the preliminary question of whether due process protection applied. This doctrine, announced in *Mathews* v. *Eldridge* (1976), was that courts should balance three relevant factors: first, the nature of the private interest involved; second, the government's interest, specifically the costs that would be imposed by additional procedures; and third, the risk of error that would result if a particular procedural protection was not provided and the possibility that procedural protection would reduce this error rate. The *Mathews* balancing test has been used by the Court ever since, in part because it comprises most of the factors that the Court considers relevant, in part because it reflects the same cost-benefit approach that was being used in other administrative settings and in part because it was indeterminate enough to allow for a variety of results.

The due process cases clearly represent a major intervention by the federal courts into administrative practice. Unlike the economic due process decisions of the Lochner era, however, this latter group of decisions evinces no hostility toward the administrative state. Both the limits that the Court placed on the scope of due process protection and the criteria that the Court used to determine how much process is due are motivated by an explicitly stated solicitude for the difficulties that government agencies face and the ways in which expanded due process protection can impose costs or inflexibility on administrative adjudications. At a deeper level, the due process decisions are pro-administration in the sense that the requirements imposed are administrative in character. Thus, while these decisions clearly intervene in the administrative process, the remedy imposed is that the government must become more administrative, not less. Providing due process is the opposite of acting arbitrarily; it means that the government is following regular, standardized procedures in making determinations regarding individuals.

This same attitude toward administrative government is further expressed in the leading decision regarding administrative searches, a closely related issue. In *Marshall* v. *Barlow's, Inc.* (1978), the Supreme Court demanded that a regulatory agency, in this case the Occupational Safety and Health Administration (OSHA), must obtain a warrant showing probable cause in order to search a private party's premises. But the Court went on to hold that the warrant could be obtained "on the basis of a general administrative plan for the enforcement of the Act derived from neutral sources."[55] Here again the Court was demanding that the agency act fairly toward individuals but showing concern for the practical demands of regulatory governance. "We doubt that the consumption of enforcement energies in the obtaining of such warrants will exceed manageable proportions," it explained.[56] Again, the remedy that the Court imposed was greater regularity in the administrative process. To have a "general administrative plan" governing the use of searches is not only a means of protecting the rights of private parties but also effective administrative practice.

Other cases decided during this period involved institutional reform. Some concerned institutions with only partial control of their clientele, such as public schools, or that provided a service to people who were otherwise left in private circumstances, such as police and welfare. These cases did not produce any transformative effects on the institution itself. Others involved what Erving Goffman described as "total institutions," primarily prisons and mental hospitals. In these, the federal courts, relying on the Eighth Amendment – which the Supreme Court declared applicable to the states in *Robinson* v. *California* (1962) – went so far as to hold entire systems of institutions unconstitutional, issued structural injunctions affecting nearly every operational aspect of the institution, and appointed special masters to take control and implement the terms of the injunction.[57]

---

[55] 436 U.S. 307 at 321. [56] Ibid. at 321.

[57] Ben M. Crouch and James R. Marquart, *An Appeal to Justice: Litigated Reform of Texas Prisons* (Austin, TX: University of Texas Press, 1989); Feeley and Rubin, *Judicial Policy Making and the Modern State*; Steve J. Martin and Sheldon Ekland-Olson, *Texas Prisons: The Walls Came Tumbling Down* (Austin, TX: Texas Monthly Press, 1987); Larry Yackle, *Reform and Regret:*

Some of the most famous decisions of the human rights era involved intimate relations, establishing a constitutional right to marry (*Loving* v. *Virginia*, 1967; *Boddie* v. *Connecticut*, 1971; *Zablocki* v. *Redhail*, 1978), use contraception (*Griswold* v. *Connecticut*, 1965; *Eisenstadt* v. *Baird*, 1972), or obtain an abortion (*Roe* v. *Wade*, 1972; *Planned Parenthood* v. *Casey*, 1992). These decisions could sometimes be based on the Equal Protection Clause, but prohibitions that applied to everyone required a different rationale. Substantive due process was the most natural choice, but as previous section argued, this rationale is extra-constitutional. While it seemed an acceptable basis for decision by the anti-administrative Lochner era Court, the Court in the human rights era displayed a notable reluctance to rely on it, precisely because it wanted to avoid its extra-constitutional implications. Instead, the Court struggled to identify a rationale based on the constitutional text, most notably the idea that a right of privacy emerged from the implications, or penumbra, of the Bill of Rights. The Court did not explicitly connect this to the administrative state, but its aversion to substantive due process and natural law can be seen as a link between its acceptance of the administrative state in the human rights era and the administrative character of the US Constitution.

THE CONTEMPORARY ERA (SINCE 1980)

The Supreme Court decisions of the past quarter century are difficult to describe with precision. They rest on shifting political alliances rather than consistent doctrinal approaches. One theme that emerges, however, is the Court's willingness to consider, and sometimes endorse, challenges to government action based on structural arguments that hearken back to earlier eras. In particular, it has revisited separation of powers, federalism, and the strict interpretation of Congress's enumerated powers as well as anti-regulatory arguments based on the Takings Clause of the Fifth and Fourteenth Amendments. These issues could readily lead to a revival of the Court's prior anti-administrative efforts, in part because they had previously been used in this manner, in part because they seem allied with a conservative political views that also display hostility to regulatory law. It is notable, therefore, that the Court's renewed concern about structural issues has produced few significant anti-administrative decisions. In fact, the actions that the Court has taken in addressing these issues have generally had the effect of expanding the authority and discretion of administrative agencies.

An emphasis on separation of powers, as opposed to checks and balances, tends to produce anti-administrative results because administrative agencies are articulated, in terms of both structure and purpose, to focus on subject matter issues such as public health, agriculture, or nuclear power while combining the

The Story of Federal Judicial Involvement in the Alabama Prison System (New York: Oxford University Press, 1989).

functional distinctions between executive, legislative, and judicial power. Moreover, the traditional branches defined by the Constitution – the President, Congress, and the federal courts – must work together in new ways to define and control the articulated agencies. The separation of powers doctrine that would produce the most restrictive effects on the administrative state is probably nondelegation, that is, the assertion that Congress may not enact broadly worded statutes that delegate "legislative" authority to an administrative agency but must draft the precise rules that it wants the agency to enforce. Modern political conservatives have been enamored of this idea because it would invalidate many regulatory statutes and make new ones difficult to enact.[58] *Schechter Poultry*, the Lochner era decision that invalidated the NIRA based on the non-delegation doctrine, has never been overruled. Chief Justice Rehnquist and Justice Scalia have attempted to invoke nondelegation several times (*Industrial Union Dept. v. American Petroleum Inst.*, 1980: 687; *American Textile Manufacturers v. Donovan*, 1981: 543; *Mistretta v. United States*, 1989: 414), but the Court as a whole has rejected it decisively. When a D.C. Court of Appeals judge held that a broadly written statute violated the nondelegation doctrine unless the agency drafted precise rules for its enforcement, the Court overturned the decision by unanimous vote (*Whitman v. American Trucking Associations, Inc.*, 2001).

A different separation of powers issue that has attracted a number of modern commentators is the unitary executive theory, the idea that Congress may not insulate an agency from direct presidential control, a result Congress regularly achieves by providing that the President may remove an agency's politically appointed leadership only "for cause," that is, outright corruption or malfeasance.[59] While this theory would not, by itself, reduce the regulatory authority of the federal government as a whole, it would eliminate the independent agency, a basic instrumentality of the American regulatory system since the creation of the Interstate Commerce Commission in the 1880s. The Court seemed to be headed in that direction when it decided *Myers v. United States* (1926), a massive opinion by Chief Justice Taft holding that Congress could not grant itself the authority to remove an executive officer and strongly implying that no constraint on the President's removal authority would be constitutional. In less than a decade, however, the Court rejected a challenge to the independence of the Federal Trade Commissioners by unanimous vote, holding that the commission was "quasi-

[58] F. A. Hayek, *The Road to Serfdom* (Chicago: University of Chicago Press, 1944), 80–96; Theodore J. Lowi, *The End of Liberalism: The Second Republic of the United States*, 2nd ed. (New York: W.W. Norton, 1979), 92–126; Schoenbrod, *Power without Responsibility*.

[59] Steven G. Calabresi and Christopher S. Yoo, *The Unitary Executive: Presidential Power from Washington to Bush* (New Haven, CT: Yale University Press, 2008); Calabresi and Rhodes, "The Structural Constitution"; Geoffrey P. Miller, "Independent Agencies," *Supreme Court Review* 41 (1986); Saikrishna Prakash, "Removal and Tenure in Office," *Virginia Law Review* 92 (2006): 1779.

legislative" and "quasi-judicial" and thus validly insulated from presidential control.[60]

The Supreme Court revisited this issue in *Morrison* v. *Olson* (1988), which involved the independent counsel's office created in the wake of the Watergate scandal, and concluded that the separation of powers principle was violated only if one of the branches was disabled from carrying out its basic, constitutionally assigned responsibilities. In *Free Enterprise Fund* v. *Public Company Accounting Oversight Board* (2009), the Court invalidated a provision of the Sarbanes-Oxley Act providing that the politically appointed members of the Oversight Board could only be removed for cause by the Securities Exchange Commission, whose members, in turn, could only be removed for cause by the President.[61] That was one too many levels of protection according to the Court. If an agency is itself insulated from direct presidential policy control, like the SEC, any agency it supervises cannot have leaders who are similarly insulated; the second-level leaders must be subject to the policy control of the supervising agency. This decision has the capacity to invalidate much more typical features of agency independence, but the Supreme Court has yet to give any indication that it intends to extend this decision or pursue its possible consequences.

This era's general approach to administrative government, which can be characterized as ranging somewhere between calm acceptance and enthusiastic embrace, is underscored by two of the three truly momentous administrative law decisions of the contemporary era – *Chevron USA* v. *NRDC* (1984) and *Vermont Yankee Nuclear Power Corp.* v. *NRDC* (1978). These are not constitutional cases, but unlike the third important decision, *Motor Vehicle Manufacturers Assn* v. *State Farm Ins.* (1983), they are not interpretations of the Administrative Procedure Act (APA) either. They can be called federal common law, but their level of generality renders them major declarations of the judiciary's relationship to the administrative state, almost at the level of a constitutional decision. *Chevron* held that the agency assigned to enforce a regulatory statute is the primary interpreter of that statute. Reversing the long-standing doctrine that appellate courts defer to courts or agencies whose decisions they are reviewing only on questions of fact, and not on questions of law, the Supreme Court, in a unanimous decision, held that statutory ambiguity represented Congress's intention that the agency, and not the reviewing court, should interpret the law. *Vermont Yankee* held that a reviewing court may not require an agency to adopt additional procedures, not required by the APA, in

---

[60] Humphrey's Executor v. U.S., 295 U.S. 602 (1935).

[61] In fact, the organic statute does not provide the members of the Securities Exchange Commission with this protection. Everyone assumes that it intended to do so, however, an indication of the extent to which agency independence has become an intrinsic element in modern administrative law. In fact, the United States has been a world leader in this arena. Most advanced industrial nations, even those without a tradition of agency independence, have separated their central banks from political control, and most economists applaud this development.

order to reach a decision that is acceptable under the APA's standards for review. The broad discretion that these cases grant administrative agencies serves as background for the Court's unwillingness to interfere with the agency's decision when presented with constitutional challenges to agency action.

In addition to reviving separation of powers doctrine, the contemporary Supreme Court has also revived federalism, combining a stricter reading of Congress's enumerated powers with a more expansive reading of the Tenth Amendment. The constitutional decisions invalidated the Gun-Free School Zones Act of 1990 (*United States* v. *Lopez,* 1995) on the ground that the statutory prohibition lacked a sufficient connection to commerce and the private lawsuit provision of the Violence Against Women Act on the same basis (*United States* v. *Morrison,* 2000). They came as a surprise, since, with one minor exception that was soon overruled (*National League of Cities* v. *Usery,* 1976; *Garcia* v. *San Antonio Met. Trans. Auth.,* 1985), the Court had not invalidated any federal statute as exceeding Congress's Commerce Clause authority since the end of the Lochner era. They were followed by *NFIB* v. *Sebelius* (2012), a challenge to what is perhaps the most extensive expansion of federal regulatory authority since the 1970s, the Patient Protection and Affordable Care Act of 2010. The Court, in an opinion by Chief Justice Roberts, held that the statute's individual mandate, a provision requiring that those who fail to obtain insurance coverage must pay a financial penalty, was beyond Congress's Commerce Clause authority because it regulated inactivity rather than an affirmative act. The Court upheld the individual mandate nonetheless, on the ground that it was a valid use of Congress's taxing power.

In *New York* v. *United States* (1997) the Court fashioned a new federalism doctrine. The case challenged a federal statute that required states to take title to any radioactive waste produced within their borders and not properly stored and then be subject to liability for all damages that the waste produced. Although the statute had originally been developed by the National Governors' Association, the Court held that it violated the rights of states under the Tenth Amendment. In the majority opinion, Justice O'Connor declared that "Congress may not simply 'commandee[r] the legislative processes of the States by directly compelling them to enact and enforce a federal regulatory program.'"[62] This commandeering rationale was then applied in *Printz* v. *United States* (1997), which struck down a provision of the Brady Handgun Violence Prevention Act because it "commandeered" state and local officials to conduct background checks on people who want to buy a gun.

Unlike the Court's separation of powers decisions, these dual federalism decisions can hardly be characterized as endorsements of administrative agency discretion. But it is difficult to regard them as revealing anti-

---

[62] 505 U.S. 144 at 161 (quoting *Hodel v. Virginia Surface Mining* [1981], which unanimously upheld the federal statute at issue).

administrative attitudes. *Lopez* and *Morrison*, involved criminal statutes of a sort that were common in pre-administrative times. Both statutes have been reenacted in a revised form that has survived judicial scrutiny, and the Court has subsequently upheld other adventuresome uses of the federal Commerce Clause authority (*Pierce County* v. *Guillen*, 2003; *Gonzales* v. *Raich*, 2005). Whether the Commerce Clause holding in *NFIB* turns out to have any doctrinal significance remains to be seen. Assuming that the distinction between activity and inactivity is coherent, there are not many federal regulatory statutes that can be reasonably categorized as penalizing inactivity, and those that do can probably be interpreted as taxes. The Tenth Amendment or commandeering decisions, *New York* and *Printz*, did invalidate programs of a clearly regulatory nature. In contrast to the federalism decisions of the Lochner era, however, the opinions in these cases left little doubt that the federal government had the authority to enact both programs; what the Court held was only that state officials could not be recruited, by force of law, for this purpose.

The contemporary era has also seen challenges to one more means of expanding federal administrative power under the Commerce Clause, namely the conditional grant. No one questions that Congress, when making monetary grants available to states, can impose conditions on the way the funds are used. In many cases, however, the conditions imposed have only an indirect relationship to the use of the funds and instead provide a means by which Congress can influence or alter state activity that might not be reachable under its enumerated powers. A challenge to this practice was definitively rejected (*South Dakota* v. *Dole*, 1987), and the issue seemed to have been resolved in the typically pro-administrative manner until *NFIB* v. *Sebelius*. Although upholding the individual mandate, the Court struck down a different provision that gave states an option to expand their Medicaid coverage but provided that they would lose the entirety of their federal Medicaid funding if they failed to do so. That was simply too coercive in the majority's view. But in striking down this provision, essentially a retrofitted conditional grant, the Court added a series of qualifications that for the time being have seriously narrowed its holding.

Finally worth considering is the idea that regulation, which often lowers the value of property by placing restrictions on its use, constitutes a taking that requires compensation for the difference in value. Because the implementation of this idea would hobble the administrative state, it has attracted the interest of various conservative commentators.[63] In the seminal Supreme Court decision, rooted in the Lochner era but still viewed as good law, the Court, in an opinion written by Justice Holmes, held that a total deprivation of value rose to the level of a taking and required compensation (*Pennsylvania Coal* v. *Mahon*, 1932). In the contemporary era, the pattern has been mixed. A few cases have declared

---

[63] Epstein, *Takings*; Timothy Sandefur, *Cornerstone of Liberty: Property Rights in 21st Century America* (Washington, DC: Cato Institute, 2006), 75–90.

regulatory programs to be takings, for instance, and perhaps oddly, New York's law authorizing cable companies to install transmission wires in multiple dwellings without the landlord's consent (*Loretto* v. *Teleprompter Manhattan CATV Corp.*, 1982; see also *Lucas* v. *South Carolina Coastal Council*, 1992). The majority of decisions in this era rejected such claims, however, finding that the laws in question were regulatory in nature and either allowed the affected property to retain sufficient value (*Penn Central Transp. Co.* v. *New York City*, 1978; *Palazzolo* v. *Rhode Island*, 2001; *Tahoe-Sierra Preservation Council* v. *Tahoe Regional Planning Agency*, 2002) or were valid regardless of their effect on property values (*Agins* v. *City of Tiburon*, 1980; *Lingle* v. *Chevron USA, Inc.*, 2005).

Most recently, the Court held that a regulatory program amounted to a taking that required compensation (*Horne* v. *Department of Agriculture*, 2015). It came to this conclusion because the regulatory program at issue controlled the price of raisins by having the government take possession of actual raisins produced in excess of the specified quantities rather than limiting the amount of raisins that the farmers could produce. The majority decision reached its conclusion by noting the similarity of this approach to the permanent and total taking of physical land by the government. At the same time, it conceded that the alternative approach of limiting raisin production at the outset would not have triggered the compensation requirement. Like many decisions in the contemporary era, the Court has given credence in this case to a constitutional doctrine that could potentially impose significant limits on regulatory government. Like many such decisions, however, the opinion provides a variety of limitations and qualifications on the doctrine it announces, thereby limiting its scope.

CONCLUSION

The Constitution of the United States is a product of a particular era. It was drafted during the crucial quarter century when governments throughout the Western world were shedding their monarchical origins and transforming themselves – by revolution, fiat, or reform – into modern administrative states. Its design reflects the mode of thought that produced, and was produced by, this transformation. The Constitution creates an articulated structure, empowering that structure to enact statutes with articulated purposes and to create articulated agencies to implement those statutes. As a result, the Constitution's pragmatic function, which is to facilitate and not impair modern administrative government, is also its most deeply conceptual role.

While American government always exercised administrative functions, the accelerated industrialization and urbanization of the late nineteenth century produced demands for the kind of extensive and intensified regulation that had previously been associated with the more crowded and class-oriented nations of

Western Europe. For the only time in its history, the federal judiciary reacted by adopting an oppositional stance toward the administrative state. It did not, and knew well that it could not, reverse this powerful historical trend, but it attempted to slow down and constrain the growth of regulatory governance. With a change in the Supreme Court's personnel, the decisions that embodied this effort were overruled with unparalleled finality, and they remain the only body of Supreme Court opinions that have been repudiated en masse. The Court then turned to other issues, first involving human rights and now involving an unstable mixture of rights and structural design, continuing its policy of allowing the American administrative state to develop and expand in accordance with its own dynamics.

PART III

ACTIONS

Actions, in their legal meaning as judicial proceedings initiated by one party against another to remedy an injury to a right, are perhaps the most constant reminder that the framing generation's adoption of the constitutional text also entailed the adoption of English law. Article III, extending the judicial power to cases in "law and equity" – the two great divisions in English and American legal procedure – shows this was all but taken for granted. From the first case decided by the Supreme Court in 1791, *West* v. *Barnes*, on a writ of error, this and other common law actions, as well as those added later by US statutes and by the judiciary's own devise, have been the sole vehicles by which constitutional provisions are authoritatively interpreted and constitutional rights affirmed. Indeed, in the case-by-case method of proceeding followed by federal and state judges, these are one and the same thing. It is not putting matters too strongly to say that without the existence of an action by which a constitutional right may be claimed in court, no constitutional right exists in any enforceable sense.

The embedding of constitutional claims within the ordinary processes and institutions of private litigation is a distinctive feature of Anglo-American constitutionalism. As a contrasting example, consider the present-day Republic of Germany, where a wider variety of parties, including state entities and officers as well as private individuals, may, without particularized injury, bring constitutional questions for decision to a Federal Constitutional Court with original and final authority. In the United States, apart from the Constitution's jurisdictional grants to the Supreme Court, judicial organization and court rules are, likewise, subject to ordinary legislation. This has meant that legal actions, while still heavily dependent on English common law, have from the first been subject to political controversy. This tendency has become more pronounced over the past half century, when judges have increasingly considered themselves less bound by existing precedent. Actions are not unique in this regard; other procedural rules like standing, diversity jurisdiction, and availability of jury trial are subject to similar influence.

Actions are also interesting because of their nonlegal but constitutionally relevant counterparts in colloquial understanding, that is, actions as they are undertaken by individuals and groups in everyday settings. This is not a linguistic accident. The interplay of formal actions as they work "inside" constitutional operations and actions "out of doors," sometimes known as popular constitutionalism, is an integral dimension of constitutional development. The "inside" or formal actions today are the direct descendants of the standardized, if still highly specified, writs introduced by King Henry II in the twelfth century. These, issued by his royal chancery for a fee, singled out the rights of the realm he most sought to enforce. Their aim in part was to replace the prevailing system of "self-help," by which the strongest party in any dispute seized lands and other valued objects (like absconding wives) on their own volition. To the extent that "self-help" had contributed to a disorderly society, this was "lawlessness"; that said, it continued to be relied upon in circumstances of legal uncertainty and weak government and has remained an acknowledged category in common law until today.

Here, too, the specific timing of the framing at Philadelphia against the background of English history helps explain the divided posture of the Constitution toward self-help. The previous century in England had been rife with all manner of anti-royalist protests, including the colonial rebellion in North America; the constitutional liberties in the Bill of Rights bear their lasting impression. More immediately in rear view was a revolt centered in Massachusetts in 1786–1787. Known as Shay's rebellion, farmers – burdened by debt, threatened by summary actions of dispossession and imprisonment, their entreaties to government for relief turned aside – ransacked and forcibly shut down local courthouses. What this might portend for the future encouraged George Washington to come out of retirement and join the plan under way to strengthen the Union. Other equally distinguished onlookers regarded this self-help, though violent, as justifiable. Thomas Jefferson, at the time Minister in Paris, wrote Madison: "Even this evil is productive of good ... Unsuccessful rebellions, indeed, generally establish the encroachments on the rights of the people which have produced them."[1]

The new Constitution was a retreat from the more populist-leaning Articles of Confederation. It provided for the establishment of a standing army, authority to suppress local rebellions, and suspension of the writ of habeas corpus in emergencies. Still, self-help in its multifarious forms has continued as an enduring feature of American constitutional life. These, in turn, have had a direct effect on the content and availability of formal legal actions. The first important change in the habeas writ occurs in 1833, in the face of resistance by the people and officers of South Carolina to the tariff of the previous year. The civil rights action today known as the Section 1983 suit against state officers

[1] Julian P. Boyd, *The Papers of Thomas Jefferson*, vol. XI (Princeton, NJ: Princeton University Press, 1950), 61.

was aimed squarely at the Ku Klux Klan. In the 1930s, under pressure of the labor movement, the Supreme Court made Section 1983 available for vindicating a broad sweep of constitutional rights besides those of minority citizens.[2] The modern class action and other group-based suits were vehicles used by civil rights groups of the 1950s and championed by consumer, environmental, and gender-equality movements in the decades that followed.

Over the longer perspective, this sequence has brought the connection of formal legal actions and informal actions of collective self-help full circle. Beginning as historic antidotes to one another, the targeting of court procedures has become an important tactic for achieving group goals. This merger can be associated with the interpretive division described earlier. Consider the class action, by which plaintiffs today are certified to represent a large number of persons who claim their rights have been similarly injured. Extra-foundationists regard this as a welcome complement to protections afforded by the Constitution to individualized interests like property, whereas Foundationists insist that Article III authorizes judges to remedy only injuries proven in "cases and controversies" before them.

In "Constitutional Judgment," Howard Schweber argues that federal judges have seldom agreed among themselves about their constitutional role. During the nineteenth century, when they adopted a legalistic jurisprudence and abandoned the broad philosophical principles that guided members of an earlier generation, they divided over whether to stress historical tradition or contemporary commercial practices in their readings of common law. Schweber further describes the gradual emergence in the New Deal period of a distinctive "constitutional" judgment, which he sees to be in some respects a return to the more philosophical style of the early Republic. This new approach served to legitimate the proliferation of constitutional rights and the broadened scope of federal authority, but it did not vanquish its rivals. In fact, Schweber shows that the present-day Court remains sharply divided over questions of interpretative methodology and judicial competence, as evidenced by its recent 5–4 decision on the subject of same-sex marriage.

James Pfander's essay, "Suits against Officeholders," revisits the structure of government accountability with a fine-grained analysis of several such suits "in action" over the course of American history. In the nature of the case, these suits occur against the background of the steadily growing administrative state. They begin in the antebellum period with an ordinary tort claim of wrongful arrest and detention against a US postmaster, heard by a local jury, and end with a twenty-first-century constitutional claim of a Fourth Amendment violation by a child-protection agency in the state of Oregon, heard in federal court. In between occurs a dense, crisscrossing web of statutes and judge-made rules. Following the Civil War, most constitutional violations were seen to arise from the protections of the Fourteenth Amendment in what came to be Section 1983

---

[2] Hague v. Committee for Industrial Organization, 307 U.S. 496 (1939).

suits. During the mid-twentieth century, as provisions in the Bill of Rights were steadily "incorporated" into that amendment and old common law rights holders were one by one displaced, eligible injuries and their occasion for remediation multiplied apace. In response, more recent decades have featured such pro-defendant doctrines as qualified immunity, objective reasonableness, and plausibility pleading. The viability of suits against officeholders has withstood this turmoil, but Pfander questions the net gain for meritorious plaintiffs.

The suits against officers just mentioned offer civil remedies – damages and injunctions – usually after the fact. Yet as the Fourth, Fifth, Sixth, and Eighth Amendments attest, the Constitution also aimed at more directly mitigating the harshness of the criminal law. This brings us to the writ of habeas corpus, a variation available only for use against wardens and other executive officers by persons held or facing confinement under their charge. An ancient common law writ in England, it had by the late eighteenth century evolved to the point of ensuring that imprisonment and criminal trial conformed to the King's laws, even if the crime was one against the state and, as Ann Tyler stresses in "Habeas Corpus," even in wartime, unless the writ was suspended by Parliament. Habeas in the new American Constitution followed on the English model, with the still greater reservation that Congress could suspend the writ only "when in cases of rebellion or invasion the public safety may require it." Tyler attributes the view held by some framers that a Bill of Rights was unnecessary to the vigor of the suspension clause. Indeed, historically, the habeas writ has been the vehicle by which many a landmark constitutional decision was brought before the Court, with far-reaching effects not only on rights to criminal protection but also on religious, civil, and personal liberty. Tyler's essay recounts the transformation of the English writ in the United States, focusing on national security, through a series of vignettes of imprisoned Americans from the colonial to the present era.

All suits against the government, including those discussed in the two previously described essays, provide enforcement of a kind, penalizing official wrongdoing and expected to apply in future cases. Through a logic of deterrence, they act prospectively also to the extent that the constitutional rights affirmed will be respected by other state and federal officeholders. The role of judges in enforcing public policy more generally is the subject addressed by John Hanley and Gordon Silverstein in their essay, "The Supreme Court, the Constitution, and American Public Policy." Epitomized by court supervision of school integration through the 1960s and 1970s, the judicial branch has increasingly taken on this duty where constitutional rights are at issue, not without controversy. Viewed in the light of earlier themes, their discussion offers a kind of finale: the crossing of government-branch divisions, incursions on lines of federalism, the pervasive role of bureaucracy, procedures for group suits, permitting new and large groups to bring lawsuits, inconstant adherence to court rules, judges' ongoing discretion. Hanley and Silverstein show how such constitutional enforcement proceeds in the face of limited resources and room for maneuver, running the gamut from judges' issuing standards like "no undue burden" in abortion cases to following through on orders given other institutions, like schools and prisons, to overseeing the realization of procedures and goals mandated by legislatures and administrative agencies.

Tomiko Brown-Nagin's essay "Constitutional Law and Social Change: Mapping Pathways of Influence" views the Constitution from the angle of social activism. The ambiguity of the framers' heritage, their accent on liberty, and the importation of common law form a template upon which social movement leaders plan strategy and tactics. The dependence on law that Brown-Nagin describes has its roots in the original structural inheritance of partial legislative sovereignty, with legislation closed to questions of slavery and women. That barrier removed, minority and socially subordinate status still recommended court-sponsored change, however, with the caveat that the disadvantages of relying on the judiciary chronicled by Hanley and Silverstein promise compromised results. One feature of Brown-Nagin's analysis dovetails with an important element in the dispute over constitutional interpretation. Brown quotes W. E. B. Dubois as having called the period immediately following the Civil War African Americans' "brief moment in the sun." Some prominent Foundationists have seen these same years as a "second founding of the republic," with the Thirteenth, Fourteenth, and Fifteenth Amendments, now as original text, serving to absolve these commentators of the taint of an undemocratic antiquarianism.[3]

Orin Kerr's "Balancing Privacy and National Security: A Rule of Lenity for National Security Surveillance Law" addresses an issue that has vexed lawmakers across the constitutional spectrum, namely how the mounting demands for information and for the means to obtain it, made by semi-closeted agencies in charge of foreign and domestic intelligence, can be reconciled with civil liberties. Kerr considers the authority of the present "FISA" Court, with jurisdiction to issue secret wiretap orders upon petition of the US Justice Department, proposing that Congress enact a rule borrowed from criminal law providing that all enabling laws be strictly construed. Rather than make FISA proceedings more like those of other courts through "amicus" participation and certification of disputed questions to higher venues, this proposed "rule of lenity" would reinforce the authority of the directly popular branch.

While not intended by its author, Kerr's essay brings our consideration of "actions" full circle. Forthrightly normative, it highlights the purposeful efforts of legal scholars to influence what Schweber calls "constitutional judgment,"

---

[3] See, for example, Michael W. McConnell, "Originalism and the Desegregation Decisions," *Virginia Law Review* 81 (1995): 947–1140; Randy E. Barnett, "Whence Comes Section One: The Abolitionist Origins of the Fourteenth Amendment," *Journal of Legal Analysis* 3 (2011): 165–263; Akhil Amar, *The Bill of Rights: Creation and Reconstruction* (New Haven, CT: Yale University Press, 1998).

whether through writings that turn up as footnotes in judicial opinions or, as here, expert advice on statutory reform. Note that on its face such influence would seem to comport more readily with Extra-foundationist than with Foundationist understandings of the Constitution, the former being in principle more open-ended, participatory, even experimental. Kerr's article demonstrates the opposite, advocating pushing lawmaking "back to Congress where it belongs." It is also worth remarking that, although the issue of privacy arises here in the context of national security, the importance of privacy as a constitutional value has been considerably strengthened by the purely domestic rulings of the "rights revolution" of recent decades.

11

Constitutional Judgment

Howard Schweber

When current Chief Justice John Roberts was undergoing confirmation hearings in 2005, he used a sports analogy to describe his conception of the role of a judge in strictly formal, legalistic, and restrained terms. "Judges are like umpires. Umpires don't make the rules; they apply them. The role of an umpire and a judge is critical. They make sure everybody plays by the rules. But it is a limited role. Nobody ever went to a ball game to see the umpire. Judges have to have the humility to recognize that they operate within a system of precedent, shaped by other judges equally striving to live up to the judicial oath."[1]

The merits of the umpire analogy are debatable.[2] Nonetheless, Roberts' comment points to the fact that a consideration of the proper role of a judge in a court is central to any discussion of American constitutionalism. The question of what is the proper role and function of a constitutional judge is inseparable from the question of judicial review, but focusing on the actions of judges moves the inquiry away from an abstract institutional question ("What is the proper relationship among the branches of government?") to the concrete experience of real people ("What will/should this judge do when my case comes up?"). Those expectations change across historical periods. Across all eras, however, the question "What does the Constitution mean?" has more often than not meant "What will (or should) a judge interpreting the Constitution in a court do?" A statute may be enforced by a police officer, a regulation may be implemented by a bureaucrat, and all of these activities have constitutional dimensions. Ultimately, however, constitutional principles are determined and applied by judges presiding over courts.[3]

---

[1] Available at www.cnn.com/2005/POLITICS/09/12/roberts.statement (last visited September 12, 2015).

[2] *See, e.g.,* Mark A. Graber, "Law and Sports Officiating: A Misunderstood and Justly Neglected Relationship," *Constitutional Commentary* 16 (1999), 293.

[3] Inevitably, the discussion in this article will overlap to some extent with a more general discussion of American constitutional doctrine and its development. For excellent treatments of this larger topic, including extensive bibliographical references, *see*: Mark Graber, *A New Introduction to*

There are historical reasons for the central importance of judging in American constitutional thought and practice. American constitutionalism is grounded in an American sense of law, and historically that has meant an understanding that begins with an inherited idea of common law. The system of English common law had ancient roots in customary practice. In 1470 an English magistrate, confronted by a claim that royal prerogative predated the creation of a common law court's jurisdiction, declared that "common law has existed since the creation of the world." As historian John H. Baker puts is, "it is not improbable that he meant it."[4] What the magistrate was getting at was the idea that the law was an expression of ancient customs that antedated all political institutions, the society precedent to the state.

One expression of that understanding appears in the fact that at every stage, common law judgments reflected the irreducible exercise of human judgment. In its earliest forms, English law was a pure jury system in which groups of community members would judge a case. Later the institution of judges in courts and later still the institution of written opinions and a system of recorded precedents added institutional formality, but in the common law tradition, "law" did not operate outside of the exercise of judgment in a specific case.[5] Up to modern times, this approach to thinking about the sources of legal authority has distinguished Anglo-American law from the civil tradition of deductive "legal science" championed by many European writers.[6] James Wilson expressed the idea with his usual eloquence in 1790. "Judicial decisions are the principal and most authentic evidence, which can be given, of the existence of such a custom as is entitled to form a part of the common law."[7]

One reason to look for connections between common law judging and constitutional judging is the fact that in the Unites States, nearly uniquely, the same judges who decide constitutional questions decide private disputes, criminal cases, and the meaning of state and federal laws and regulations. Moreover, American constitutional decisions take the form of case adjudications. Again almost uniquely in the world, American constitutional judges do not issue

---

American Constitutionalism (New York: Oxford University Press, 2013); Neil Duxbury, *Patterns of American Jurisprudence* (Oxford: Clarendon Press, 1995); *see also* bibliographies compiled in Howard Gillman, Mark Graber, and Keith Whittington, *American Constitutionalism* 2 vols. (New York: Oxford University Press, 2012).

4 John H. Baker, *Introduction to English Legal History* 3rd ed. (London: Butterworths, 1990), 1.
5 *See* Richard Ross, "The Memorial Culture of Early Modern English Lawyers: Memory as Keyword, Shelter, and Identity, 1560–1640," *Yale Journal of Law and the Humanities* 10 (1998): 229–326.
6 Michael H. Hoeflich ed., *The Gladsome Light of Jurisprudence: Learning the Law in England and the United States in the Eighteenth and Nineteenth Centuries* (Westport, CT: Greenwood Press, 1987).
7 James Wilson, "Lectures on the Law" Part 2, Chapt. V: "Of the Constituent Parts of Courts: Of the Judges," in Mark David Hall and Kermit Hall eds., *The Collected Works of James Wilson* 2 vols. (Indianapolis: Liberty Fund, 2009) vol. 2: 828–1084, 953.

abstract statements about the validity of proposed statutes or the propriety of government actions. Instead, the act of constitutional judging in the American context involves the resolution of concrete disputes among specific parties, and the interpretation of the Constitution in a given case is authoritative only insofar as it is an element of a judgment in a case. The scope of "judgment," in other words, defines the scope of constitutional interpretation; it is only through a series of constitutional judgments that American constitutional law is expressed.

There are a number of results of this unusual arrangement. For one thing, American constitutional law is announced in the manner of a mosaic, with a sparkling tile here and a brightly colored tile there and empty spaces in between waiting to be filled in. It is never clear what the final picture will look like or whether there will ever be a completed picture at all. It is not even clear that a completed picture is the goal.[8] In addition, constitutional arguments are specifically legal: there is no sharp distinction between constitutional lawyering and the art (or craft or science) practiced by lawyers in general. Yet constitutional and legal judgments have at times been thought of as different in kind. Indeed, it is not an exaggeration to say that the different versions of American constitutional interpretation – originalism, living constitutionalism, interpretivism, textualism – are different descriptions of the relationship between constitutional and ordinary legal judgment.

The exploration that follows is divided by historical period. Any attempt to define sharp breaks among historical periods is to some extent a distortion. An idea that is claimed to originate at a given time will turn out to have earlier antecedents, and supposedly obsolete modes of reasoning persist across imagined barriers between epochs. In the American case, moreover, we are confronted by Faulkner's dictum: the past not only isn't dead, it isn't even past. To a truly remarkable extent, debates about the nature of constitutional judgment in 2015 reiterate debates that were taking place in 1790, 1870, and 1937. And it goes without saying that any historical period is marked by a plurality of modes of reasoning, theories, and historical understandings too complex to be reduced to a formulaic recitation of a single "dominant" mode of thought. Nonetheless, and keeping all these cautionary notes in mind, it is useful to consider the ways in which the prevailing understandings of constitutional judgment have changed across different historical periods in response to shifts in prevailing judicial practices, elite constitutional ideology, and academic legal discourse.

COMMON LAW JUDGING: 1765–1803

To an American legal historian, the significance of the year 1765 is immediately obvious: it was the year of the publication of the first volume of William Blackstone's *Commentaries on the Common Law*. Blackstone followed in a

---

[8] Cass Sunstein, *The Partial Constitution* (Cambridge, MA: Harvard University Press, 1993).

tradition established by Coke, Selden, and Hale, among others,[9] but his treatment was exceptional for its systematic approach. Indeed, a good deal of Blackstone's purported descriptions of English legal practice comprised idealized fictions that masked enormous local variation in actual legal practice. Possibly as a result, the work was never very influential in Great Britain. The colonies, however, were a different story. The American Revolution has been justifiably called politically radical but legally conservative; the radical political proposition was that traditional legal rights could not be violated by acts of Crown or Parliament, but the content of those rights was English common law. For most American colonists "English common law" meant Blackstone.[10] Blackstone's idealized version of common law doctrine was not only the basis for legal practice, it was one of the most widely read and cited sources for political ideas.[11] One study has found that between 1760 and 1805 it was one of the three most cited sources in American political writing, after Montesquieu and ahead of Locke.[12]

The importance of these common law roots is that Blackstone was the most plausible basis for the common understanding of the role of a constitutional judge, fundamentally similar to that of judges in common law courts. Furthermore, the American version of Blackstone established the basis for state and local law with which the new Constitution would interact. The idea of a "higher law" form of constitutionalism – that is, the idea that a constitution articulates legal principles such that ordinary legislative enactments that violate those principles are invalid – was not new. Limitations on the exercise of legislative and executive power contained in written documents enforceable by courts were elements of the American intellectual landscape at least as early as the Massachusetts Body of Liberties of 1641 (and, less clearly, the Fundamental Orders of Connecticut 1639). Later documents such as the Massachusetts Constitution of 1780 and the Virginia Constitution and Declaration of Rights of 1776 were direct influences on the drafting of the Constitution. Nor was the influence of this intellectual tradition limited to America. The Baron de Lafayette drew heavily on his observations of American state constitutions during the Revolution when he proposed the first Declaration of the Rights of Man in the Paris Assembly on July 11,

---

[9] Harold J. Berman, "The Origins of Historical Jurisprudence: Coke, Selden, Hale," *Yale Law Journal* 103 (1994): 1651–1738.

[10] Hendrik Hartog, *Law in the American Revolution and the Revolution in the Law* (New York: New York University Press, 1981); Beverley Zweiben, *How Blackstone Lost the Colonies: English Law, Colonial Lawyers, and the American Revolution* (New York: Garland, 1990).

[11] Craig Evan Klafter, *Reason over Precedents: Origins of American Legal Thought* (Westport, CT: Greenwood Press, 1993).

[12] Donald S. Lutz. "The Relative Influence of European Writers on Late Eighteenth-Century American Political Thought," *American Political Science Review* 78 (1986): 189–97.

1789.[13] This was the beginning of a phenomenon: the American model of constitutionally guaranteed and legally enforceable rights would be influential in constitution making around the world. Other examples include the Constitution of Poland of 1791[14] and the Constitution of Norway of 1814.[15] These constitutional efforts did not follow the American model in all respects, but they incorporated the idea of substantive, higher law judicial review that required an articulation of a specifically constitutional form of judgment.

None of this was lost on the architects of the American constitutional text. Federalists and Antifederalists alike recognized that the new Constitution would require federal courts to exercise novel and far-reaching supervisory authority over other branches and levels of government. The difference was in the different writers' reactions to that proposition. The Federalist Hamilton welcomed the new arrangement.

The complete independence of the courts of justice is peculiarly essential in a limited Constitution … Limitations of this kind can be preserved in practice no other way than through the medium of courts of justice, whose duty it must be to declare all acts contrary to the manifest tenor of the Constitution void. Without this, all the reservations of particular rights or privileges would amount to nothing.[16]

Antifederalist Robert Yates strongly disapproved of the idea of empowering federal courts in this way, but he did not doubt that Hamilton was accurately describing the new role of the judiciary. For Yates, this was an innovation to be decried as a departure from the less republican, more directly democratic English traditions of legislative supremacy. "[Judges] will give the sense of every article of the constitution, that may from time to time come before them. And in their decisions they will not confine themselves to any fixed or established rules, but will determine, according to what appears to them, the reason and spirit of the constitution. The opinions of the supreme court, whatever they may be, will have the force of law; because there is no power provided in the constitution, that can correct their errors, or control their adjudications. From this court there is no appeal."[17]

---

[13] Georg Jellinek, *The Declaration of the Rights of Man and of Citizens: A Contribution to Modern Constitutional History*, Max Farrand trans. (New York: Holt, 1901); see also Lynn A. Hunt, *Inventing Human Rights: A History*, (New York: W. W. Norton, 2007), 121–26.

[14] Brzezinski, Mark F. (1991). "Constitutional Heritage and Renewal: The Case of Poland," *Virginia Law Review* 77 (1): 49–112.

[15] Louis Henkin and Albert J. Rosenthal eds., *Constitutionalism and Rights: The Influence of the United States Constitution Abroad* (New York, 1990); George Athan Billias, *American Constitutionalism Heard Round the World, 1776–1989: A Global Perspective* (New York: Columbia University Press, 2009).

[16] Alexander Hamilton, "Federalist 78: Duration in Office, Good Behavior. Why Needed," in George W. Carey and James McClellan eds., *The Federalist* (Indianapolis: Liberty Fund, 2001), 495–503.

[17] Robert Yates, "Brutus, Letter #11," in Bernard Bailyn ed., *The Debate on the Constitution: Federalists and Antifederalist Speeches, Part Two: January to August 1788* (New York: Library of America, 1993), 129–36, 134.

While the idea of substantive judicial review was recognized, it would require practice and time to work out the meaning of constitutional judgment in that context. What were judges enforcing the Constitution supposed to do, exactly? The Constitution was a political and philosophical document as well as a set of legal principles: new institutions had been created and given new powers, old political understandings had been explicitly or implicitly jettisoned. What would be the role of political as opposed to legal judgment in the judicial role?

In the early years of the Constitution, Supreme Court Justices Chase and Wilson followed Blackstone's common law model, drawing freely on custom and natural law. One implication of this approach was that judges clearly viewed their role as involving the exercise of political as well as legal judgment. Three iconic moments stand out. First, there was a declaration of the superiority of federal law to state law in *Ware* v. *Hylton* (1796, stating that under the Supremacy Clause of Article IV the provisions of a treaty automatically supersede a contrary state law).[18] The simple act of bootstrapping contained in the statement that the Constitution could declare one law superior to another because the Constitution said it could do so hid an enormous shift in political consciousness. The adoption of the Constitution meant a new legal order, in which the role of judges presiding over constitutional cases might be different from the familiar roles of common law judges.

In *Calder* v. *Bull*, a simple dispute over a will gave Samuel Chase an opportunity to embrace a broad Blackstonian conception of his role as the enforcer of a pre-constitutional social contract.

The purposes for which men enter into society will determine the *nature* and *terms* of the *social* compact; and as *they* will decide what are the *proper* objects of it: The *nature*, and *ends of legislative* power will limit the *exercise* of it … An act of the Legislature (for I cannot call it a *law*) contrary to the *great first principles* of the *social compact*, cannot be considered a *rightful exercise of legislative* authority. The obligation of a law in governments established on *express compact, and on republican principles*, must be determined by the *nature* of the *power*, on which it is founded.[19]

Chase did not appeal to the authority of the constitutional text to strike down the actions of the Connecticut legislature; according to his argument, the Constitution was merely the written record of underlying principles, not their source. The appeal to social contract theory, "republican principles," and "the nature and ends of legislative power" emphasizes the philosophical rather than legal character of the judgment. The Constitution, by this analysis, secured a political philosophical tradition, and it was the role of constitutional judges to preserve that tradition.

While he agreed with the outcome in the case, Justice Iredell of North Carolina found Chase's reliance on Lockean political philosophy disturbing. Iredell argued that the role of a constitutional judge should be understood in more strictly legal

---

[18] Ware v. Hylton, 3 U.S. 199 (1796).   [19] Calder v. Bull, 3 U.S. 386, 388 (1798).

terms. Others agreed, and the Blackstonian approach to constitutional judgment became a focus of public criticism. Most controversial of all was the decision in *Chisholm v. Georgia*, holding that a state government was not immune from being sued in federal court. Chief Justice John Jay based his conclusion on a review of theories of sovereignty. James Wilson went even further. Wilson used the occasion to deliver what was essentially a summary of his *Lectures on the United States Constitution* delivered in Philadelphia between 1788 and 1791,[20] the first published work of American constitutional theory. Wilson explored theories of sovereignty, the relationship between a state and its people, Scottish Common Sense philosophy, the relationship between the US Constitution and other forms of law, federalism, and the nature of rule by the people. In the end, Wilson concluded that a state's assertion of sovereign prerogatives contradicted the fundamental principle of national self-rule. "[T]he people of the United states intended to form themselves into a nation for national purposes. They instituted for such purposes a national government, complete in all its parts, with powers legislative, executive and judicial, and in all those powers extending over the whole nation. Is it congruous that, with regard to such purposes, any man or body of men, any person natural or artificial, should be permitted to claim successfully an entire exemption from the jurisdiction of the national government? Would not such claims, crowned with success, be repugnant to our very existence as a nation?"[21]

The political and doctrinal reaction against the ruling in *Chisholm* was predictable and extreme. The Eleventh Amendment, the very first constitutional amendment after 1791, was adopted to establish state sovereign immunity. What was at least as provocative as the outcome, however, was the implicit description of the role of the constitutional judge as guardians of virtue and the national political experiment. This view of constitutional judges was strongly associated with the Federalist and later the Whig conception of the role of the courts. Simon Greenleaf, upon his inauguration as the first Royall Professor of Law at Harvard in 1834, articulated the principle: "[I]n later days, when the integrity of that charter has been invaded, its spirit violated, and its language perverted, whether to gratify the mad ambition of one partisan, or the cupidity of many; to whom have all eyes been imploringly directed for its preservation, but to the living and honored champions and expounders of constitutional law?"[22]

These images of judges as the guardians of political virtue grated on the sensibilities of Jeffersonians and later of Jacksonian Democrats. If constitutional judges were empowered to use the national government to enforce such broadly

---

[20] James Wilson, "Lectures on Law Delivered at the College of Pennsylvania, 1790–1791," in Mark David Hall, Kermit Hall, and eds., *supra.* n. 5.

[21] *Chisholm*, 2 U.S. 419, 465 (1793).

[22] Simon Greenleaf, *A Discourse Pronounced at the Inauguration of the Author as Royall Professor of Law in Harvard University* (Cambridge, MA: James Munroe and Company, 1834), 137.

conceived philosophical concepts, what other traditional prerogatives might be swept away? With the election of Thomas Jefferson in 1800, the Democratic-Republican Party – heirs to much of the philosophy of the Antifederalists – challenged the prevailing Federalist view of constitutional judging. Most directly, Jefferson directed an effort to eliminate Federalist judges from the federal bench, an effort that eventually resulted in the impeachment of Samuel Chase in 1804.

Jefferson's attempt to purge the judiciary of Federalist judges led to the deepest judicial exploration of the relationship between constitutional and common law judgment in 1803 in *Marbury* v. *Madison*.[23] *Marbury* is perhaps the most famous case in all of American constitutional history, and it is usually regarded in terms of its implications for the exercise of substantive judicial review over the federal government and the elevation of the principle of jurisdiction over remedies (and for the complicated gamesmanship involved in Marshall's construction of his arguments). But it is equally the case that Marshall's *Marbury* opinion represented a critical shift toward a legal as opposed to a political conception of constitutional judgment, away from the broad mandate of Blackstonian common law that had been embraced by Chase and Wilson and toward something closer to Iredell's legalistic understanding. In modern terms, Marshall announced an approach known as "interpretivism,"[24] in which the legal exegesis of the constitutional text is the mark of legitimate constitutional judgment.

Marshall's approach had complicated consequences. In one sense, the range of constitutional judgment had been narrowed by the exclusion of "political" issues and the implicit rejection of appeals to extratextual sources, and the proper role of constitutional judges and lawyers was therefore limited to making legal rather than political arguments. On the other hand, if the exercise of constitutional judgment was to be a technical and legal endeavor, there could be no explicitly political constraints on the range of legal arguments. The full range of creativity of lawyers – drawing on centuries of practice – could be brought to bear. In particular, in the decades that followed, common law property rights were read directly into the Constitution as constraints on the actions of legislatures. Constitutional and common law ideas were not separate and opposing ways of thinking; they were potentially conflicting, potentially reinforcing vocabularies available to constitutional judges.

CLASSICAL CONSTITUTIONAL JUDGMENT: 1803–1868

Following *Marbury* and the decline of the philosophical style of constitutional judging, the question of constitutional judgment divided into two distinct roles.

---

[23] There is an enormous literature on *Marbury*. For a recent treatment of the legal background to the case, including a review of the general literature, *see* Karen Orren and Christopher Walker, "Cold Case File: *Marbury v. Madison* and Officer Accountability," *American Political Science Review* 107 (2013): 241–58.

[24] John Hart Ely, *Democracy and Distrust* (Cambridge, MA: Harvard University Press, 1980).

First, judges were expected to interpret and apply the Constitution in ways consistent with the common law tradition of "police powers," the principle that local (or state) governments had broad authority to regulate social and economic activities for the promotion of the common good. Chief Justice Lemuel Shaw of the Massachusetts Supreme Court provided one of the most authoritative and widely quoted formulations of this concept:

All property in this commonwealth, as well that in the interior as that bordering on tide waters, is derived directly or indirectly from the government, and held subject to those general regulations, which are necessary to the common good and general welfare. Rights of property, like all other social and conventional rights, are subject to such reasonable limitations in their enjoyment, as shall prevent them from being injurious, and to such reasonable restraints and regulations established by law, as the legislature, under the governing and controlling power vested in them by the constitution, may think necessary and expedient.[25]

Shaw spoke of the (state) constitution only in terms of a grant of power to the legislature. Federal judges, however, read the US Constitution to protect traditional common law property rights *against* legislative action, taking on a role quite different from that of the common law judge described by Shaw. For example, in *Fletcher* v. *Peck* (1810) the Supreme Court held that the fact that a legislature had accepted bribes to convey land on fraudulent terms could not justify revocation of those titles because a "vested contract right" trumped the political authority of legislatures to undo the effects of past fraud.[26] This constitutionalization of common law property rights created a rift in the traditional idea of the judicial role. Rather than speaking for the community as it existed at the time, constitutional judges were taking it upon themselves to speak for the community's historical heritage and traditional legal mores. Common law, legislation, and constitutional law could now be seen as three separate and distinct forms of "law," with constitutional judges playing the role of determining when one source of authority took precedence over the others.

The position of judges in applying a constitutionalized conception of common law was not always traditionalist. Constitutional judges sometimes took it upon themselves to push a general project of reform and modernization in legal doctrines based on legislatures' police powers in ways that would further the goal of creating a commercial republic. In 1837, Roger Taney rejected an appeal to a customary understanding about the meaning of property rights protected by the Constitution's Contracts Clause. Instead, Taney ruled that in the case of public as opposed to private contracts, the written terms of the text should be interpreted in a way to maximize the benefit for public policy.[27] Later cases similarly applied the principle that the law governing public projects should be

---

[25] Commonwealth v. Alger, 61 Mass. 53, 84–85(1851).   [26] Fletcher v. Peck, 10 U.S. 87 (1810).
[27] Charles River Bridge v. Warren Bridge, 36 U.S. 420 (1837).

flexible enough to accommodate current needs.[28] Creative application of common law doctrines provided the opportunity to bring concepts of "public good" into the discussion of constitutional protections in strictly legal rather than philosophical terms, thus conforming to expectations that constitutional questions were matters to be decided according to a special body of legal principles that modified the operations of more familiar, traditional bodies of law.[29]

The willingness of constitutional judges to think creatively about common law doctrines paralleled the development of common law doctrines in the industrial states of the North, which saw the emergence of the familiar categories – tort, contract, bailments, securities – that define private legal relations in the United States to this day.[30] State and federal statutes similarly displayed new ideas such as the "general business corporation," and courts invented new common law principles to accommodate them within the constitutional framework of property rights. Thus constitutional judgments about rights claims continued to be couched in the language of ordinary law, but both had become vehicles of transformative change rather than declarations of ancient custom. And where the Constitution's role as creator of institutions and power relations among governments was concerned, Marshall and his colleagues continued to apply political principles such as federalism that had no direct source in the language of purely legal argumentation.

The pattern of common law modernization in state courts in the 1850s was specific to the North. In the South the path of legal development was entirely different. Courts and legislatures alike stubbornly resisted modernization of legal doctrines at the same time and for the same reason they resisted the intrusion of railroads and national corporations. The reason was slavery. Southern writers, judges, and citizens alike were convinced that traditional common law protections of property, sovereignty, and police powers were the shields against political attempts to end their peculiar institution. Legal reforms that favored industrial capitalism and constitutional reforms that favored national authority alike threatened the continued dominance of local elites on this most critical question.

Both politically and legally, the combination of common law property rights and constitutional interpretivism fell apart with the case of *Dred Scott*

---

[28] State of Pennsylvania v. Wheeling and Belmont Bridge, 59 U.S. 421 (1852). *See* Elizabeth Brand Munroe. *The Wheeling Bridge Case: Its Significance in American Law and Technology* (Boston: Northeastern University Press, 1992).

[29] William M. Wiecek, *The Lost World of Classical Legal Thought: Law and Ideology in America, 1886–1937* (New York: Oxford University Press, 1998); Morton J. Horwitz, *The Transformation of American Law, 1870–1960: The Crisis of Legal Orthodoxy* (New York: Oxford University Press, 1992); James Willard Hurst, *Law and the Conditions of Freedom in the Nineteenth Century United States* 2nd ed. (Madison, WI: University of Wisconsin Press, 1964).

[30] Howard Schweber, *The Creation of American Common Law, 1850–1880: Technology, Politics, and the Construction of Citizenship* (New York: Cambridge University Press, 2004).

v. *Sanford*. The case is far too complex to review, but one of its outcomes was a public focus on the proper roles of constitutional judges. In his First Inaugural Address, Abraham Lincoln declared, "The candid citizen must confess that if the policy of the Government upon vital questions affecting the whole people is to be irrevocably fixed by decisions of the Supreme Court, the people will have ceased to be their own rulers, having to that extent practically resigned their Government into the hands of that eminent tribunal. Nor is there in this view any assault upon the court or the judges. It is a duty from which they may not shrink, to decide cases properly brought before them; and it is no fault of theirs if others seek to turn their decisions to political purposes."[31] It is important to recognize that Lincoln did not propose resistance or defiance as a response. In an 1857 speech, he declared, "We think [the Court's] decisions on Constitutional questions, when fully settled, should control, not only the particular cases decided, but the general policy of the country, subject to be disturbed only by amendments of the Constitution as provided in that instrument itself. More than this would be revolution. But we think the Dred Scott decision is erroneous. We know the court that made it, has often over-ruled its own decisions, and we shall do what we can to have it to over-rule this. We offer no resistance to it."[32]

As a reflection on the prevailing understandings of constitutional judging, it is clear that there was a widespread perception that something had gone terribly wrong. Trying to capture exactly what that "something" was, however, is difficult. Later writers have insisted that the problem with *Dred Scott* was that the judges reached beyond the law and interposed their political views, but legal historians have noted a good argument can be made that Chief Justice Taney's analysis was legally sound.[33] Perhaps from a strategic perspective a more judicious course might have been to avoid the case altogether. Regardless, the willingness of the Supreme Court to set aside major national legislation (the Missouri Compromise) raised the question of the limits of constitutional judgment in starker terms than ever before. After the most devastating military conflict in American history was completed, that question was addressed by the adoption of the Twelfth, Fourteenth, and Fifteenth Amendments.

"GUARDIANS OF THE CONSTITUTION BESIEGED": 1868–1937

The Fourteenth Amendment, in particular, dramatically altered the terms of the debate. Its adoption constituted that rarest of events, a genuine change in

---

[31] Abraham Lincoln, "First Inaugural Address," March 4, 1861, available at www.abrahamlin-colnonline.org/lincoln/speeches/1inaug.htm (last viewed September 16, 2015).

[32] Abraham Lincoln, "Speech on the Dred Scott Decision," June 26, 1857, available at http://teachingamericanhistory.org/library/document/speech-on-the-dred-scott-decision/ (last viewed October 29, 2015).

[33] Mark Graber, *Dred Scott and the Problem of Constitutional Evil* (New York: Cambridge University Press, 2006).

historical epoch. The amendment's guarantees of state and federal birthright citizenship, equal protection, due process of law, and the privileges and immunities of citizenship, plus a grant of authority to Congress as well as federal courts to enforce those rights against states, represented a dramatic reconceptualization of basic categories of American constitutionalism. Some of these principles referred to old ideas in new terms; others were entirely new elements of the national Constitution. What would and what should be the role of judges in interpreting and applying these new principles? The new principles invited an interpretation that made constitutional protections of rights absolute limits on *all* forms of government including states' traditional exercise of police powers. The question, as always, was one of judging: a narrow, legalistic interpretation that drew on common law traditions could limit the scope of newly guaranteed rights. Conversely, a broad political reading might result in a radical reconception of the relationship between constitutional and ordinary law.

Initially, judges schooled in an earlier tradition wrestled to keep the constitutional text within legal bounds, thus minimizing the radicalism of its implications. The new Privileges and Immunities Clause of the Fourteenth Amendment was held not to convey any broad new set of substantive rights, while Congress's authority was limited to correcting formal acts of discrimination by state governments.[34] Over time, however, judges in both state and federal courts began to interpret the Fourteenth Amendment in ways that introduced a new role. The adoption of the Reconstruction Amendments came to be understood as empowering judges to strike down long-established common law principles and traditional exercises of police powers, especially with respect to economic activities.

These arguments were often couched in common law terms, suggesting that as had been the case in earlier periods the courts had a newly created constitutional mandate to protect traditional legal "liberties" against political innovation. Like the American Revolution itself, this approach to interpreting the Fourteenth Amendment might be described as "politically radical but legally conservative."[35] It was politically radical in the aggressive willingness of courts to strike down laws duly enacted by elected legislatures, but it was legally conservative in that the judges involved claimed, at least, to be preserving property rights and liberties against the threat of mass politics. It was in that sense of protecting the rule of law against the threat of politics that Justice Field could describe judges as "guardians of a constitution besieged."[36]

---

[34] *Slaughterhouse Cases* 83 U.S. 36 (1873); *Civil Rights Cases* 109 U.S. 3 (1883).

[35] Shannon C. Stimson, *The American Revolution in the Law: Anglo-American Jurisprudence before John Marshall* (Princeton, NJ: Princeton University Press, 1990).

[36] Howard Gillman, *The Constitution Besieged: The Rise and Demise of Lochner Era Police Powers Jurisprudence* (Durham, NC: Duke University Press, 1995). Gillman describes judges in this period as "giving voice to the founders' conception of appropriate and inappropriate legislation in a commercial republic ... elaborated, clarified and transformed into a workable set

Two key concepts were "class legislation" and "arbitrary" lawmaking. While neither idea is specifically mentioned in the constitutional text, they were loosely associated with the Equal Protection Clause and the Due Process Clause, respectively. But each concept also drew on earlier ideas rooted in common law as well as philosophical notions. The basic idea was a variant of the one articulated by Chase in *Calder* v. *Bull*: that a law that does not serve the public good is not properly a "law" at all but rather an arbitrary exercise of power and that favoring one private party over another can never properly be understood as serving the public good.

The most famous case of the period was *Lochner* v. *New York* (1905); among legal historians, in fact, this entire period is frequently referred to as "the *Lochner* era."[37] In that case the Supreme Court struck down a New York law regulating the working hours of bakers on the grounds that it served no public purpose (hence "arbitrary") and favored some private actors over others (hence "unequal" or "class legislation"). As an expression of traditional police powers jurisprudence, Justice Peckham's majority opinion relied on the questionable proposition that regulation of economic relations could never serve a public good. "There is no reasonable ground for interfering with the liberty of person or the right of free contract by determining the hours of labor in the occupation of a baker." The only justifiable basis for regulating the hours of bakers, according to Peckham, would be a finding that there were exceptional risks to health involved in the work. Here, Peckham writing for the majority refused to give credence to the legislature's findings, instead substituting his own view that "[w]e think that there can be no fair doubt that the trade of a baker, in and of itself, is not an unhealthy one to that degree which would authorize the legislature to interfere with the right to labor, and with the right of free contract on the part of the individual, either as employer or employee."[38]

---

of doctrines by state court judges." Ibid., 20. The reference to a commercial republic emphasizes the ways in which American common law in the nineteenth century had departed from older English traditions.

[37] There is an extensive literature about *Lochner* v. *New York* and its significance for American constitutional development. Some writers view the case as exemplifying a judicial tendency to favor capitol over labor. Others, however, see the case and others like it as early expressions of the idea that the Fourteenth Amendment secures strong substantive rights against government action. Still other writers understand the case as a legal expression of larger intellectual currents, arguing that what was new was the incorporation of extra-legal principles into legal reasoning. *See, e.g.*, David Bernstein, *Rehabilitating Lochner: Defending Individual Rights against Progressive Reform* (Chicago: University of Chicago Press, 2010); Victoria Nourse, "A Tale of Two Lochners: The Untold History of Substantive Due Process and the Idea of Fundamental Rights," *California Law Review* 97 (2009): 751–99; Paul Kens, *Lochner v. New York: Economic Regulation on Trial* (Lawrence, KS: University Press of Kansas, 1998); Howard Gillman, *The Constitution Besieged, supra.*, n. 31. For a review of historiographical treatments of the case, *see* Schweber, "Lochner v New York and the Challenge of Legal Historiography," *Law and Social Inquiry* 39 (2014), 242.

[38] Lochner v. New York, 198 U.S. at 57, 59.

Dissenting, Justice John Marshall Harlan protested that regulation of economic relations fell squarely within the traditional bounds of police powers. The more famous dissenting opinion, however, was by Justice Oliver Wendell Holmes Jr.:

[A] constitution is not intended to embody a particular economic theory, whether of paternalism and the organic relation of the citizen to the State or of *laissez faire*. It is made for people of fundamentally differing views, and the accident of our finding certain opinions natural and familiar or novel and even shocking ought not to conclude our judgment ... I think that the word liberty in the Fourteenth Amendment is perverted when it is held to prevent the natural outcome of a dominant opinion, unless it can be said that a rational and fair man necessarily would admit that the statute proposed would infringe fundamental principles as they have been understood by the traditions of our people and our law.[39]

The reference to "traditions of our people" saves the argument from being one of complete deference to democratic decision-making. Instead, Holmes' opinion sounds a great deal like Lemuel Shaw's description of traditional police powers, "such reasonable restraints and regulations established by law, as the legislature ... may think necessary and expedient." Thus Holmes emerges as the defender of traditional deference to the judgment of local authorities, while the justices of the majority – despite their claims of preserving common law property rights – take on the role of innovators in the field of constitutional judgment.

Holmes's critique of the *Lochner* majority was an appeal to Iredellian idea of constitutional judging as legalistic interpretivism. The majority opinion, authored by Chief Justice Rufus Peckham, arguably reflected a more natural law–driven idea of the Constitution as a guarantor of a political conception of "liberty" that gave courts authority to review the substantive merits of legislation. "In every case that comes before this court, therefore, where legislation of this character is concerned and where the protection of the Federal Constitution is sought, the question necessarily arises: Is this a fair, reasonable and appropriate exercise of the police power of the State?"[40] In addition, the majority took it upon itself to review the empirical conclusions of the New York legislature on the question of whether baking was a particularly hazardous occupation.

It was difficult for observers to miss the point that in the *Lochner* era far more often than not it was the interests of capital – particularly corporate capital – that ended up the winners. The degree to which constitutional judges would defer to legislatures' claims, too, varied with the topic: nine years earlier, four of the five justices in the *Lochner* majority (Brown, Peckham, Fuller, and Brewer) had been in the majority in *Plessy* v. *Ferguson*, in which they accepted Louisiana's assertion that racial segregation was a proper exercise of police

---

[39] *Lochner*, 198 U.S.at 75–76.   [40] *Lochner* 1905, 53, 56

powers to prevent social conflict.[41] The constitutional treatment of efforts to organize labor in response to the corporate consolidation of capital was particularly telling; consistently, courts used constitutional principles to prevent workers from acting collectively at the same time that they shielded the collective activities of corporate employers.[42] As a result, critics increasingly came to suspect that the actions of judges were merely those of "politicians in robes."[43] Among some legal thinkers, this observation was taken as an affirmative invitation to engage in treating constitutional judgment as an articulation of policy preferences; among tradition-minded legalists it was a cause for dismay at the decline in the legitimacy of the enterprise.[44]

The term "legalist" requires some explanation. In the context of constitutional adjudication "legalism" and "formalism" are effectively synonymous. Fifty years ago Judith Skhlar provided an eloquent explanation that remains informative today:

What is legalism? It is the ethical attitude that holds moral conduct to be a matter of rule following, and moral relationships to consist of duties and rights determined by rules ... The consequences for legal theory have not been altogether fortunate. The urge to draw a clear line between law and non-law has led to the constructing of ever more refined and rigid systems of formal definitions. This procedure has served to isolate law completely from the social context in which it exists. Law is endowed with its own discrete, integral history, its own "science," and its own values, which are all treated as a single "block" sealed off from general social history, from general social theory, from politics, and from morality.[45]

More recently, Richard Posner has similarly described "legalism" in terms of deductive reliance on formal rules. "The ideal legalist decision is the product of a syllogism in which a rule of law supplies the major premise, the facts of the case supply the minor one, and the decision is the conclusion."[46] In Antonin Scalia's words, legalism and legal formalism are both the intellectual effort to make the "rule of law" comport with "the law of rules."[47]

By the 1920s, a set of contrary approaches had come to be known under the general rubric of "legal realism." While legal realism encompasses a broad range

---

[41] Plessy v. Ferguson, 163 U.S. 537 (1896).

[42] Karen Orren, *Belated Feudalism: Labor, the Law, and Liberal Development in the United States* (New York: Cambridge University Press, 1992); William E. Forbath, *Law and the Shaping of the American Labor Movement* (Cambridge, MA: Harvard University Press, 1991).

[43] Charles H. Sheldon, *The Supreme Court: Politicians in Robes* (Beverly Hills, CA, 1970).

[44] Gillman, *The Constitution Besieged, supra.* n. 31.

[45] Judith N. Skhlar, *Legalism: Law, Morals, and Political Trials* (Cambridge, MA: Harvard University Press, 1964): 1–2. *See also* Lawrence Friedman, "On Legalistic Reasoning," *Wisc. L. Rev.* 1966 (1966).

[46] Richard Posner, *How Judges Think* (Cambridge, MA: Harvard University Press, 2008), 41. *See also* Lawrence B. Solum, The Supreme Court in Bondage: Constitutional Stare Decisis, Legal Formalism, and the Future of Unenumerated Rights, *U. Pa. J. Const. L.* 9 (2006), 155.

[47] Antonin Scalia, "The Rule of Law as a Law of Rules," *U. Chi. L. Rev.* 56 (1989), 1175.

of approaches, as a general term "realism" (or sometimes "antiformalism") meant a willingness or even eagerness to interpret rules in ways suitable to current conditions and concerns. Realists deliberately incorporated considerations of political and social judgment into their applications of legal rules, inspired by Oliver Wendell Holmes' dictum that "the life of the law has not been logic, it has been experience."[48]

It may be fairly said that no exercise of constitutional judgment can be completely divorced from the facts and circumstances in which it arises, nor can any attempt to achieve a just outcome in a particular case be divorced from the application of rules.[49] Nor did the judges of the time suggest otherwise. Justice Peckham's majority opinion in *Lochner* is littered with references to the politics of the day, and in particular his disapproval of what he saw a socialistic tendencies in some state legislatures. "It is impossible for us to shut our eyes to the fact that many of the laws of this character, while passed under what is claimed to be the police power for the purpose of protecting the public health or welfare, are, in reality, passed from other motives."[50]

Nevertheless, the judicial insistence on a combination of nonlegal substantive interpretation of "liberty" and the formalistic application of common law property rights created a constant tension with the democratic aspirations of legislatures, both state and federal. The conflict reached a stage of crisis with the Great Depression of 1929 and the Roosevelt administration's New Deal efforts to respond to the downturn. The Supreme Court and lower federal courts repeatedly struck down federal efforts at relief and state efforts at economic regulation. By the 1930s the political reaction was becoming extreme. The prevalent citizens' view of constitutional judging had become almost entirely negative, a combination of viewing judges as taking sides in economic conflicts (ironically enough) and as out-of-touch formalists unaware of the realities of modern life. The idea of judges and judging as the legitimate mechanisms of constitutional application were threatened. It is likely, although we have no empirical data, that the popular respect for courts in general and the Supreme Court in particular was lower at this point than at any other time in American history.

THE INTERPRETIVIST TURN: 1937–1980

There is a standard historical account that says that the US Supreme Court abruptly abandoned its opposition to government action, and with it the

---

[48] Oliver Wendell Holmes, Jr., *The Common Law* (Boston: Little, Brown, 1881), (Holmes Press, 2012), 1. On legal realism as a challenge to formalism in American legal interpretation, *see* Neil Duxbury, *Patterns of American Jurisprudence* (Oxford: Clarendon Press, 1995).

[49] Brian Z. Tamanaha, "Balanced Realism on Judging" *Valaparaiso Univ. L. Rev.* 44 (2010); Tamanaha, *Beyond the Formalist-Realist Divide: The Role of Politics in Judging* (Princeton, NJ: Princeton University Press, 2009).

[50] *Lochner*, 198 U.S. at 64.

Lochner era approach to constitutional judging, in one fell swoop in its 1937 term. The narrative is overstated, as earlier cases had indicated at least some willingness to permit legislatures to regulate economic affairs as an element of their police powers.[51] Through the 1930s chinks appeared in the armor of *Lochner*-style judging, at least partly in response to the economic crisis that was gripping the nation. For example, in *Blaisdell* in 1934 the Court upheld a Minnesota law suspending foreclosures. The opinion, by Chief Justice Hughes, was marked by formal legalistic distinctions (between "a contract" and "a remedy provided for breach of a contract") that were anathema to *Lochner*-era constitutional judgment and outraged the dissenting justices.[52]

But it is also true that a series of decisions in 1937 and 1938 announced a sharp departure in the nature of constitutional judging. Three examples stand out. In *West Coast Hotel* v. *Parrish* (1937), a majority of the Court reversed an earlier decision and upheld a minimum wage statute. The majority opinion, by Chief Justice Hughes, was remarkable for its explicit rebuke of the past practice of employing too broad a definition of economic "liberty." "The Constitution does not speak of freedom of contract. It speaks of liberty and prohibits the deprivation of liberty without due process of law. In prohibiting that deprivation, the Constitution does not recognize an absolute and uncontrollable liberty. Liberty in each of its phases has its history and connotation. But the liberty safeguarded is liberty in a social organization which requires the protection of law against the evils which menace the health, safety, morals and welfare of the people."[53] More broadly, the opinion stated under the Fourteenth Amendment legislatures, state and federal, would be perfectly within the scope of their police powers to determine that economic relations – and by extension a broad range of other relations – were matters affecting the public interest and thus a legitimate subject for regulation.

> The exploitation of a class of workers who are in an unequal position with respect to bargaining power, and are thus relatively defenseless against the denial of a living wage, is not only detrimental to their health and wellbeing, but casts a direct burden for their support upon the community. What these workers lose in wages, the taxpayers are called upon to pay ... The community is not bound to provide what is, in effect, a subsidy for unconscionable employers.[54]

Perhaps the most striking element in this passage is the phrase "the taxpayers are called upon to pay." Prior decisions of the legislature (poverty relief)

---

[51] Home Bldg. & Loan Ass'n. v. Blaisdell 290 U.S. 398 (1934, upholding a moratorium on mortgage foreclosures); Nebbia v. New York 291 U.S. 502 (1934, upholding state regulation of prices for dairy products).

[52] The distaste for formalistic technical interpretations did not extend to cases involving attempts to organize labor, in which as noted earlier courts consistently found grounds to use antitrust principles to prevent unionization. Orren, *Belated Feudalism, supra.* n. 40.

[53] West Coast Hotel v. Parrish, 300 U.S. 379, 391 (1937).

[54] *West Coast Hotel*, 300 U.S. at 398–99.

determined the subsequent scope of operation for police powers, a formulation that dramatically elevated the importance of legislation and democratic decision-making – that is, of common law police powers – over the protection of constitutionalized "liberties."

By itself, that was a dramatic reinterpretation of the police powers idea, but it was only the first step in redefining the activity of constitutional judging. In *Palko* v. *Connecticut* (1937), Justice Cardozo authored a majority opinion in which he explained that the meaning of the term "liberty" in the Fourteenth Amendment was that some but not all of the rights secured against actions of the federal government in the Bill of Rights would now apply also as limitations on actions by the states, a formulation that left almost no room for constitutional challenges to economic or social regulations based on an expansive conception of "liberty." This was called "partial incorporation," and the test for whether a particular textually secured right would apply against state governments was whether in the view of the justices the right in question was "essential to ordered liberty." If the answer to that question was "no," then even rights specifically listed in the Bill of Rights would not apply as against the states. As for other, non-enumerated rights, their status as constitutional guarantees was unclear.[55]

Parrish and *Palko* were cases involving challenges to state laws. In 1938, the Court heard a challenge to a federal law. The law in question was surely one of the less consequential and truthfully less defensible statutes in the Federal Register: a statute passed to protect Wisconsin dairy interests that prevented the interstate shipment of products that combined dairy and nondairy products (margarine mixed into butter) on the extremely dubious grounds of protecting public health. This was a law that a few years earlier would have looked ripe for rejection as blatant class legislation (because it benefited one group of producers over their economic competitors) as well as arbitrary (because the health claims were unlikely to withstand even the lightest scrutiny). In a unanimous opinion, Justice Stone wrote that the reference to public health in the statute itself was all that was needed to establish that the law served a public purpose. "The existence of facts supporting the legislative judgment is to be presumed, for regulatory legislation affecting ordinary commercial transactions is not to be pronounced unconstitutional unless, in the light of the facts made known or generally assumed, it is of such a character as to preclude the assumption that it rests upon some rational basis within the knowledge and experience of the legislators."[56]

As a statement of the principles of constitutional judging, these cases represented an outright retreat. Constitutional judgments would no longer be based on wide-ranging reexamination of empirical findings nor subjected to a test for unequal economic benefit. In general, judges would no longer be encouraged to apply broad philosophical notions of "liberty" or "arbitrariness"

[55] Palko v. Connecticut, 302 U.S. 19 (1937).
[56] United States v. Carolene Products, 304 U.S. 144, 152 (1938).

to constitutional questions. The new order of the day was deference to the democratic process on political grounds and a return to a more textually based, legalistic form of reasoning. The phrase "rational basis" identified the new approach. Perhaps the clearest statement of the new approach came a few years later in 1955, when a majority of the Court joined in an opinion by Justice Douglas that repeatedly found a basis for upholding a law on the basis of conclusions the legislature "may" have reached. "It is for the legislature, not the courts, to balance the advantages and disadvantages of the new requirement ... It is enough that there is an evil at hand for correction, and that it might be thought that the particular legislative measure was a rational way to correct it."[57]

In terms of the expectations of citizens, this deferential form of review constituted a return to the Marshallian language of purely legal judgment, emphasized by *Carolene Products'* declaration that "the existence of facts supporting the legislative judgment is to be presumed." And yet the *Carolene Products* opinion was addressed specifically to "legislation affecting ordinary commercial transactions." Justice Stone's deferential statement about presuming the existence of facts was hedged about with qualifiers. "Where the existence of a rational basis for legislation whose constitutionality is attacked depends upon facts beyond the sphere of judicial notice, such facts may properly be made the subject of judicial inquiry."[58] Most important, at the end of the section quoted previously, Stone added the most famous footnote in the history of American law:

There may be narrower scope for operation of the presumption of constitutionality when legislation appears on its face to be within a specific prohibition of the Constitution, such as those of the first ten amendments ... It is unnecessary to consider now whether legislation which restricts those political processes which can ordinarily be expected to bring about repeal of undesirable legislation is to be subjected to more exacting judicial scrutiny under the general prohibitions of the Fourteenth Amendment than are most other types of legislation ... Nor need we enquire whether similar considerations enter into the review of statutes directed at particular religious, or national, or racial minorities: whether prejudice against discrete and insular minorities may be a special condition, which tends seriously to curtail the operation of those political processes ordinarily to be relied upon to protect minorities, and which may call for a correspondingly more searching judicial inquiry.[59]

To a great extent, the logic of constitutional judging in cases involving the assertion of rights claims in the following decades (1940–1980) was driven by the three categories identified in footnote 4 of *Carolene Products*: protection of "discrete and insular minorities" under the Equal Protection Clause, protection and expansive interpretation of constitutionally guaranteed rights through the Due Process Clause, and intervention in situations where the ordinary processes of democratic process are deemed unreliable. The approach to constitutional

---

[57] Williamson v. Lee Optical, 348 U.S. 483, 488 (1955).
[58] *Carolene Products*, 304 U.S. at 153–54.   [59] *Carolene Products*, 304 U.S. at 152.

judgment may perhaps best be described as "legal hermeneutics." In essentially
every case, judges claimed to be basing their decisions on interpretations of the
constitutional text, usually with a focus on specific provisions. The language of
constitutional interpretation was consistently and self-consciously legalistic and
technical, marked by a proliferation of specific tests or standards applicable to
particular situations. The use of the old common law language of "police
powers" and "class legislation" was largely abandoned in favor of a
developing set of legal standards specific to constitutional judging. Judges
continued to serve in courts of general jurisdiction but came to view their
roles in constitutional cases as *sui generis*, conceptually distinct from both
ordinary law and political philosophy.

This shift in understanding represented a neo-Marshallian idea of
constitutional judging as adjudication of legal questions, with unexpected
result that limitations on political judging fall by the wayside when faced with
an articulable legal claim. The focus on textualism and specific language opened
up as many new rights claims as it foreclosed, as lawyers and judges applied
their creative energies to the interpretation of concepts as broad as "equal
protection" and "due process." These judges accepted the move of declaring
certain provisions of the Constitutions outside the bounds of judges'
competence because they were "political" rather than "legal." Judges also
continued to accept the limitations of the state action doctrine and displayed a
general acceptance of exclusive model of negative rights. But the legal
hermeneutics approach to constitutional interpretation permitted judges to
revisit standards to promote political equality, particularly where issues of
race and representation were concerned. In areas concerning the scope of
governmental authority over economic matters and other structural issues, the
justices continued the pattern of deference announced in 1938. But where civil
liberties were concerned, the period from the 1940s through 1980 saw an
unprecedented expansion in both constitutional guarantees and the scope of
federal authority under the Fourteenth Amendment.

None of these developments was noncontentious. Constitutional judges
continued to debate the question of whether the Bill of Rights applied against
the States in its entirely, only "selectively," and whether rights not mentioned in
the text at all could nonetheless be recognized as constitutionally guaranteed.[60]
Through the 1950s and 1960s, however, judges widely accepted the idea that
their mandate included the employment of legalistic reasoning to find both
broad individual rights protections and a broad grant of power to the federal
government. These "strong rights," however, were individually and specifically

---

[60] See, *e.g.*, Adamson v. California, 332 U.S. 946 (1947) and Duncan v. Louisiana, 391 U.S. 145
(1968) in which different justices variously proposed partial incorporation, total incorporation,
incorporation plus nontextual sources for rights, and complete reliance on nontextual sources
for rights.

defined.[61] There were few signs of a return to a broad and substantive understanding of "liberty" as the basis for constitutional judgment.

In many, even most, areas the legitimacy of this approach to constitutional judging was accepted even as specific decisions might be contested. Expansive protections for freedom of expression and religious practice, procedural protections for criminal suspects, complicated balancing tests applied to review empirical as well as legal judgments by government authorities, and permissive interpretations of the scope of governmental powers over economic activities were generally accepted as normal. But by the 1970s, certain areas of constitutional judging had become deeply controversial. Four in particular stand out for their political saliency and their consequences for expectations for constitutional judgment: racial integration, abortion and a general right of privacy, pornography, and restrictions on the actions of police and prosecutors.[62]

Racial integration provoked the most extreme reactions and did the most to reshape normative expectations about constitutional judging. In a series of cases beginning with *Brown* v. *Board of Education* (1954), the Supreme Court revisited the basic premise of *Plessy* v. *Ferguson* that separate treatment on the basis of race did not offend the Equal Protection Clause. The basic logic remained the same: the Constitution requires that laws be justified by non-arbitrary purposes that do not include the desire to "oppress or annoy" a minority group. What changed dramatically was the judges' willingness to defer to legislative descriptions of their purposes. The claim in *Plessy* that racial segregation was a neutral measure had never been persuasive, but the rejection of that claim entailed a major shift in the approach to constitutional judgment. Just as appeals to a generalized fear of political unrest were no longer accepted as the justification for restrictions on speech and appeals to long historical practice and social cohesion were no longer accepted to justify acts of religious establishment, claims of innate racial difference or fear of social discord were no longer accepted as justifications for racial discrimination.[63] In *Brown*, the Supreme Court ruled that racially segregated public schools violate the Equal Protection Clause. Widespread resistance to desegregation of schools led to a second opinion ordering implementation of desegregation with "all deliberate speed."[64] When that order, too, failed to secure cooperation from state and local officials, in the 1960s federal judges began to take control of school district operations, implementing busing and redistricting plans on the strength of their authority as constitutional arbiters. Judges in ordinary civil

---

[61] Nourse, *supra.* at n. 36.

[62] For an extensive description of the circumstances that gave rise to judicial efforts to restrain prosecutors and police, *see* William Stuntz, *The Collapse of American Criminal Justice* (Cambridge, MA: Belknap Press, 2013).

[63] Brown v. Board of Education of Topeka (Brown I), 347 U.S. 483 (1954).

[64] Brown v. Board of Education of Topeka (Brown II), 349 U.S. 294, 301 (1955).

cases had long been recognized to have the authority to take control over private businesses to enforce payment of debts or to command government officials to carry out specific duties. The assumption of this role by constitutional judges, however, appeared as something new: ironically, what federal judge were doing in the desegregation looked too much like ordinary law to citizens' accustomed to thinking of constitutional judging as an exercise in political philosophy.

The irony was not lost on critics of this approach to constitutional judgment. In a famous (or infamous) memorandum, then Supreme Court clerk William Rehnquist wrote that *Brown* should be decided in favor of state authority to segregate at risk of reviving the discredited style of judging that had been displayed in the *Lochner* era, stating, "I think that *Plessy* v. *Ferguson* was right and should be reaffirmed. If the Fourteenth Amendment did not enact Spencer's *Social Statistics* it just as surely did not enact Myrdahl's *American Dilemma.*"[65] Later as Justice and then Chief Justice of the Supreme Court, Rehnquist would continue to argue that his colleagues were exceeding the bounds of constitutional judgment and engaging in "judicial activism," by which he meant exceeding their authority to engage in the legalistic application of technical rules.

The same accusation of engaging in *Lochner*-style activism was leveled at judges who developed constitutional protections for privacy, including abortion, through the 1960s and 1970s. Initially, there were attempts to argue that a right to privacy could be derived directly from the Bill of Rights, either through the reserve clause of the Ninth Amendment or from the "penumbras and emanations" of rights secured by the First, Fourth, and Fifth Amendments.[66] The phrase "penumbras and emanations" was coined by Justice William Douglas. Literary merits aside, the phrase was unsatisfactory because of its attempt to simultaneously invoke a textual basis for the logic of the argument and an extratextual source for the particular right being asserted. Defenders of Douglas' opinion pointed to the fact that there are innumerable extratextual elements of American constitutionalism, including authorization for an Air Force, rights of association, and the principle of checks and balances. Douglas' right to privacy, however, suggested a revival of a broad and philosophical conception of "liberty," and in later cases the rights of privacy came to be explicitly grounded in that idea.[67]

As a political matter, racial segregation was an instance in which a regional majority found itself at odds with a national majority that consistently elected members of Congress committed to civil rights. Other issues were less

---

[65] William Rehnquist, "A Random Thought on the Segregation Cases," available at www.gpo.gov /fdsys/pkg/GPO-CHRG-REHNQUIST/pdf/GPO-CHRG-REHNQUIST-4–16-6.pdf (last visited September 14, 2015). Rehnquist later argued that the memo did not reflect his views, an assertion that has come to be viewed as unpersuasive. *See* Brad Snyder and John Q. Barrett, "Rehnquist's Missing Letter: A Former Law Clerk's 1955 Thoughts on Justice Jackson and *Brown*," *Boston College L. Rev.* 53 (2012), 631.

[66] Griswold v. Connecticut, 381 U.S. 479 (1965).

[67] *See, e.g.,* Roe v. Wade, 410 U.S. 113 (1970).

specifically regional. The protection of free speech went too far for some people when it extended to the protection of pornography; in 1968 Richard Nixon ran for President in a campaign that among other things promised to appoint federal judges who would crack down on "the pornos" and selected Warren Burger at least partly on that basis. Another element of Nixon's campaign was also directed at constitutional judging, as he promised to appoint judges who would side with the police rather than criminals. These were elements of a deliberate strategy to court disaffected voters, particularly in the South (the "Southern strategy"), by pointing to constitutional judges rather than the rest of the electorate as the threat to local traditions.[68] A central element of the politics of Southern resentment was an appeal to anger over federal judicial intervention in matters of school desegregation. The controversies were not unique to the South – Boston experienced a particularly ugly series of protests and counter-protests in the 1970s – but it was in the South, primarily, that rejection of court-mandated desegregation became a general rejection of "judicial activism."

Part of the reason constitutional judging became an element of national politics once again, as it had been in the 1930s, was that the federal courts were actively intervening in local and state affairs and granting Congress the authority to the same thing. Another change was the new presence of mass media. In 1943, Hollywood could produce a movie with the premise that a vacationing Supreme Court justice could become involved in local politics and make multiple public statements without being recognized.[69] That premise would have been dubious in the 1960s; it would have been nonsensical by 1980. Whether vilified or celebrated (and frequently both), Supreme Court justices and some federal judges were figures of national celebrity.

Among both critics and supporters of the actions of the courts in this period, citizens' came to expect a certain approach to constitutional judging and to feel aggrieved when it was perceived that judges departed from that approach. Constitutional law was normatively expected to highly technical, legalistic, and apolitical. It was also expected to be highly malleable, as regardless of ideology when a citizen's interests were threatened she was likely to think that a constitutional claim was at stake if only a sufficiently clever lawyer could be found to articulate it. The perception of constitutional judging constituted a positive encouragement to think of legal claims in constitutional terms. That perception only exacerbated the counter-majoritarian difficulty. Not only were judges perceived as activists imposing their personal preferences under the guise of "law," but even legitimate constitutional judging could result in empowering minorities or individuals against the majoritarian will of their community. In one sense, at least, the claim that the substantive due process and equal protection jurisprudence of the 1950s, 1960s, and 1970s represented a return

---

[68] The Southern strategy was described by Republican strategist Kevin Phillips as an appeal to "Negrophobe whites." James Boyd, "It's All in the Charts," *New York Times* May 17, 1970.
[69] *Stranger in Town* (MGM Studios, 1943).

to *Lochner* had some merit. Once again constitutional judging was being exercised against rather than in service of common law tradition. That point of similarity was likely too technical or subtle for most observers, however, to whom the question was whether proper constitutional judgment had been supplanted by politically motivated judicial activism. The idea that constitutional judges were constrained actors unable to do more than apply a body of law created elsewhere fell almost completely by the wayside among academics and the general public alike.

CONSTITUTIONAL JUDGMENT IN THE MODERN ERA: 1980–PRESENT

The election of Ronald Reagan in 1980 signaled changes in American politics in a number of ways. Reagan made issues of constitutionalism central to his campaign (along with economic and foreign policies). At a speech in August 1980 in Oxford, Mississippi, Reagan declared, "I believe in states' rights … I believe we have distorted the balance of our government today by giving powers that were never intended to be given in the Constitution to that federal establishment."[70] During Reagan's presidency, Attorney General Edwin Meese along with other prominent spokesmen such as Antonin Scalia and Robert Bork used dissatisfaction with the politically liberal outcomes of constitutional cases to promote a philosophy of originalism. To the public, the appeal was made in terms of restoring the strictly legal function of constitutional judges by preventing reference to current political thinking. Bork, a sitting federal judge, said, "Only by limiting themselves to the historic intentions underlying each clause of the Constitution can judges avoid becoming legislators." Meese's Justice Department issued guidelines for constitutional argument that said, "government attorneys should advance constitutional arguments based solely on this 'original meaning' … based solely on the ordinary use of the words at the time the provision at issue was ratified." The guidelines specifically called on all government attorneys to look for opportunities to challenge a series of earlier decisions, including decisions finding a right to sexual privacy and abortion, religious minorities' constitutional right to accommodation for their practices, procedural protections for criminal suspects, and the basic idea of "fundamental rights that invites courts to undertake a stricter scrutiny of the inherently legislative task of line drawing."[71]

On the Supreme Court, Reagan appointee Antonin Scalia became the most prominent proponent of a combination of originalism and clause-based textualism. Justice Scalia's version of originalism was not quite the same as Bork's. For Justice Scalia, the determinative question concerned the original

---

[70] http://web.archive.org/web/20110714165011/http://neshobademocrat.com/main.asp?SectionID=2&SubSectionID=297&ArticleID=15599&TM=60417.67.

[71] Gillman, Graber, and Whittington, *American Constitutionalism, supra* n. 1: vol. 2, 750.

"public meaning" of the text at the time of its adoption rather than the subjective "intent" of any particular individuals. "You will never hear me refer to original intent … If you are a textualist, you don't care about the intent, and I don't care if the Framers of the US Constitution had some secret meaning in mind when they adopted its words. I take the words as they were promulgated to the people of the United States, and what is the fairly understood meaning of those words."[72]

Apart from their differences, Meese, Scalia, Bork, and other originalists led a revival in formal legalism as an approach to constitutional judging, arguing that these were the limits of the legitimate role of a judge and that anything else – such as the substantive due process theories of the Warren and Burger Courts – would constitute "judicial activism." These arguments had immense purchase on the public imagination. The Republican Party platform in 1984 declared, "We commend the President for appointing federal judges committed to the rights of law-abiding citizens and traditional family values. We share the public's dissatisfaction with an elitist and unresponsive federal judiciary. If our legal institutions are to regain respect, they must respect the people's legitimate interest in a stable, orderly society. In his second term, President Reagan will continue to appoint Supreme Court and other federal judges who share our commitment to judicial restraint."[73]

Political liberals warned that accepting these norms for constitutional judging would result in a regression toward an earlier, less rights-protective role for the federal courts. When Bork was nominated for the Supreme Court in 1987, the result was a bruising confirmation fight. Senator Edward Kennedy described the consequences of originalism in dark terms: "Robert Bork's America is a land in which women would be forced into back-alley abortions, blacks would sit at segregated lunch counters, rogue police could break down citizens' doors in midnight raids, and schoolchildren could not be taught about evolution."[74] In response, Bork, Scalia, and other supporters of originalism insisted that they were not opposed to policies of equality and individual rights, only that in the cases at issue it was not the proper role of a constitutional judge to declare those policies to be constitutionally required.[75]

Despite the vehemence of these very public debates, it is important to recognize that as far as the proper role of a constitutional judge is concerned all the participants and the observing public took it for granted in the 1980s and 1990s that certain historically acceptable positions were no longer on the table.

[72] Antonin Scalia, "Judicial Adherence to the Text of Our Basic Law: A Theory of Constitutional Interpretation," *The Progressive Conservative* 5 (2003), www.proconservative.net /PCVol5Is225ScaliaTheoryConstlInterpretation.shtml (last visited July 3, 2016).

[73] Gillman, Graber, and Whittington, *American Constitutionalism, supra.*, n. 1: vol. vol. 2, 737.

[74] Available at www.npr.org/sections/itsallpolitics/2012/12/19/167645600/robert-borks-supreme -court-nomination-changed-everything-maybe-forever (last visited September 12, 2015).

[75] Antonin Scalia, "The Rule of Law as a Law of Rules," *University of Chicago Law Review* 56 (1989): 1175–81; Robert Bork, *The Tempting of America: The Political Seduction of the Law* (New York: Free Press, 1990).

On the one hand, there was no widespread support for a return to a style of constitutional judging that appeals to broad political principles without reference to legal precedents or the constitutional text in the manner of Chase's *Calder* opinion in 1793 or Peckham's *Lochner* ruling in 1905. On the other hand, particularly after Bork's nomination was rejected, judicial candidates took care to assert their allegiance to the body of constitutional precedents from earlier decades that had taken on sacrosanct status in American public consciousness. There was no widespread public support for allowing segregated schools or regulation of (heterosexual) adults' sex lives or doing away with constitutional restraints on police conduct, narrowing First Amendment protections, or prohibiting regulation of economic activities.

In the past two decades, disagreements over the nature of constitutional judgment have not diminished; if anything, they have become sharper. The different approaches of the justices who authored opinions in *Obergefell* v. *Hodges* in the summer of 2015 illustrate the point. The outcome of the case was simple: a majority of the justices found that the Constitution, through the Due Process Clause of the Fourteenth Amendment, guarantees the right of same-sex couples to marry under state laws on the same terms as mixed-sex couples. That outcome was controversial, to be sure. But what was more striking than the outcome was the range of approaches to constitutional judging that was displayed among the various opinions.

Writing for the majority, Justice Anthony Kennedy used language that seemed to reach back to the era of Chase, or at least to the tradition of reading "liberty" in broad and substantive terms that was seen in the *Lochner* era with respect to economic regulations. "The Constitution promises liberty to all within its reach, a liberty that includes certain specific rights that allow persons, within a lawful realm, to define and express their identity. The petitioners in these cases seek to find that liberty." In addition, Kennedy appealed to a core value of human dignity, a proposition that is central to the constitutional traditions of some European countries but that represents an innovation in American constitutional doctrine.[76]

Some observers, indeed, were surprised that the majority opinion did not focus on arguments from equal protection, which provides a body of precedent more obviously applicable to the case. Kennedy's focus on liberty and dignity, instead, articulated a mode of constitutional judging that eschews formal and legal argumentation in favor of broad philosophical propositions that the Constitution is found to embody. The move was not without precedent. In general, articulations of the "right to privacy" had already moved a considerable way toward an outright embrace of substantive rights ungrounded in textual provisions – that is, a move away from the interpretivist turn of the 1930s and toward a more philosophical, broadly political reading of "liberty." But Kennedy's language pushes still further in that direction.

---

[76] Obergefell v. Hodges, 576 U.S. ___, slip op. 1–2, 10 (2015).

In his dissenting opinion, Chief Justice Roberts mentions *Lochner* v. *New York* by name sixteen times. His basic complaint is that Kennedy's majority opinion is not "law" in the sense that Roberts thinks the Constitution ought to be. "The majority's decision is an act of will, not legal judgment. The right it announces has no basis in the Constitution or this Court's precedent. The majority expressly disclaims judicial 'caution' and omits even a pretense of humility ... Ultimately, only one precedent offers any support for the majority's methodology: *Lochner* v. *New York*." Roberts described the majority opinion in *Lochner* in harsh terms: "discredited," "unprincipled," and reflecting "naked policy preferences." As in his statement before Congress, Roberts here is careful to insist that the Constitution may be thought of as "law" either in the form of a statute (the written text) or common law reasoning ("this Court's precedent"). That is, Kennedy's approach is suspect because it treats the Constitution as a statement of political or philosophical principles rather than as a legal document.[77]

Justice Scalia dissented as well, but his focus was less on professional standards of constitutional judging than on what he saw as the broader problem of protecting democracy against an overreaching judiciary. "Today's decree says that my Ruler, and the Ruler of 320 million Americans coast-to-coast, is a majority of the nine lawyers on the Supreme Court ... This practice of constitutional revision by an unelected committee of nine, always accompanied (as it is today) by extravagant praise of liberty, robs the People of the most important liberty they asserted in the Declaration of Independence and won in the Revolution of 1776: the freedom to govern themselves."[78] Scalia insisted that his own preferred approach of originalist textualism defines the limits of the legitimate judicial role in constitutional cases.

Justice Thomas took a different tack. Like Kennedy he embraced the idea of relying on philosophical understandings of political principles, but political principles understood in originalist (and not textualist) terms. "Since well before 1787, liberty has been understood as freedom from government action, not entitlement to government benefits. The Framers created our Constitution to preserve that understanding of liberty. Yet the majority invokes our Constitution in the name of a 'liberty' that the Framers would not have recognized, to the detriment of the liberty they sought to protect ... This distortion of our Constitution not only ignores the text, it inverts the relationship between the individual and the state in our Republic. I cannot agree with it."[79] Justice Samuel Alito, finally, combined republican fears of corruption with an emphasis on legalism. "I do not doubt that my colleagues in the majority sincerely see in the Constitution a vision of liberty that happens to coincide with their own. But this sincerity is cause for concern, not comfort. What it evidences is the deep and

---

[77] *Obergefell*, slip op. at 10, 19–20 (Roberts, C.J., dissenting).

[78] *Obergefell*, slip op. at 2 (Scalia, J., dissenting).

[79] *Obergefell*, slip op. 1–2 (Thomas, J., dissenting).

perhaps irremediable corruption of our legal culture's conception of constitutional interpretation."[80]

What about the reactions of the American public observing this sharply worded exchange? The decision in *Obergefell* was announced on June 26, 2015. A poll conducted over the subsequent four weeks found that 51 percent of respondents approved of the decision against only 35 percent who disapproved. Yet in the same poll, when asked the question of what authority ought to decide the question of same-sex marriage in the abstract, only 37 percent chose the Supreme Court as against 27 percent who chose state referenda, 10 percent who chose state legislatures, a meager 6 percent who selected Congress, and 23 percent who said they did not know.[81]

The polling data do not tell us exactly why members of the American public hold different opinions about the case nor whether different philosophies of constitutional judging play a role in those opinions. But the data do suggest something about what Americans today expect of constitutional judges and whether they believe the courts are delivering on that expectation. Perhaps the most disturbing finding in this regard is Gallup's annual poll in which respondents are asked to express the degree to which they have confidence in various public institutions. From 1973 when the poll was initiated until 2006, the percentage of respondents expressing "a great deal" or "quite a lot" of confidence in the Supreme Court was consistently above 40 percent every year except one (1991, 39 percent): since 2007, the result has been below 40 percent every year, and in 2015 it was a dismal 32 percent.[82] On the other hand, one year earlier when the question was asked about "the judicial branch" in general, the resulting expression of "a great deal" or "quite a lot" of confidence was above 60 percent. And when asked in the same poll whether the Supreme Court was "too liberal," "too conservative," or "about right," respondents were evenly divided across the three categories of response, with the largest number (43 percent) choosing "about right."[83]

The public discussion of the proper role of constitutional judges took a dramatic turn with the passing of Justice Antonin Scalia in February 2016. President Obama nominated Judge Merrick Garland to be his successor, but the Senate declined to consider the nomination. In the subsequent presidential election, Donald Trump became President. President Trump nominated Neil Gorsuch to take over Scalia's seat, and Gorsuch was confirmed by the Senate in April 2017. The addition of Justice Gorsuch to the Court may have various effects on particular doctrinal issues. Gorsuch is considered more conservative than Scalia on a wide range of issues, especially the rights of criminal

---

[80] *Obergefell*, slip op. 7–8 (Alito, J., dissenting).
[81] Ipsos-Reuters poll conducted June 26–July 28, 2015, available at www.ipsos-na.com/download /pr.aspx?id=14683 (last visited September 14, 2015).
[82] Available at www.gallup.com/poll/1597/confidence-institutions.aspx (last visited September 14, 2015).
[83] Available at www.gallup.com/poll/4732/supreme-court.aspx (last visited September 14, 2015).

defendants, and has expressed strong views on the role of courts in reviewing the actions of administrative agencies.[84] The latter view, in particular, may turn out to be constitutionally significant given President Trump's early efforts to revise immigration policy and more generally because it speaks to Gorsuch's strong commitment to principles of separation of powers and the role of the judiciary in restraining executive action.

In terms of the Court's approach to constitutional judgment, however, the addition of Justice Gorsuch to replace Justice Scalia is unlikely to have a significant affect. Like Scalia, Gorsuch describes himself as an originalist and a textualist. In a speech describing the legacy of Justice Scalia, Gorsuch (not yet nominated for a seat on the Court) declared his allegiance to Scalia's approach to constitutional judgment.

[J]udges should ... strive (if humanly and so imperfectly) to apply the law as it is, focusing backward, not forward, and looking to the text, structure, and history to decide what a reasonable reader at the time of the events in question would have understood the law to be – not to decide cases based on their own moral convictions or the policy consequences they might believe might serve society best. As Justice Scalia put it, '[i]f you're going to be a good and faithful judge, you have to resign yourself to the fact that you're not always going to like the conclusions you reach. If you like them all the time, you're probably doing something wrong."[85]

As was discussed earlier, committing oneself to a historicist ("backward" looking) and textualist approach to constitutional interpretation leaves myriad questions unresolved. To say that Justice Gorsuch's approach to constitutional interpretation would be similar to that of Justice Scalia does not by any means imply that the outcomes of cases would be the same, that the extent to which other justices might be persuaded to share a view of a particular case might not be different, or that we can know with any certainty how Justice Scalia would have addressed the novel constitutional question with which the Court is currently faced. It is noteworthy, however, that to a great extent the discussion of Judge Gorsuch's nomination has focused on the role of constitutional judges. That question remains central to American constitutionalism independent of particular issues of law or doctrine.

---

[84] On the rights of criminal defendants, Justice Scalia's rulings were frequently more "liberal" – meaning protective of defendants' rights – than public observers acknowledged. *See The Unexpected Scalia: A Conservative Justice's Liberal Opinions* (New York: Cambridge University Press, 2017). On Gorsuch's view that courts should assume a significantly more active role in reviewing actions of federal agencies, *see* Guiterrez-Brizuela v. Lynch, Case No. No. 14-9585 (10th Cir. 2016), available at www.ca10.uscourts.gov/opinions/14/14-9585.pdf (last visited February 10, 2017).

[85] Neil Gorsuch, "2016 Sumner Canary Memorial Lecture: Of Lions and Bears, Judges and Legislators, and the Legacy of Justice Scalia," *Case Western L. Rev.* 66 (2016), 905, 921.

12

Suits against Officeholders

James E. Pfander

Among the more striking features of the law of remedies for harm inflicted by the federal government has been the relatively modest shift in the identity of the defendant. During the antebellum period, victims of government wrongs (wrongful tariffs and taxes, trespasses to person or property, groundless legal proceedings) often brought suit against individual officeholders in state court. Today, to be sure, Congress has authorized citizens to bring suit directly against the federal government as an entity and to do so in federal court. But the suit against the officeholder survives today as a mainstay of government accountability litigation. It operates in habeas litigation (the subject of Chapter 13), in litigation to secure injunctive and declaratory relief, often against unconstitutional action, and in suits for damages to redress past violations of constitutional rights. While we think of the Constitution as a cornerstone of limitations on the *government*, our remedial system continues to enforce the fundamental charter by acting on the individual *officers* who run the government.

This chapter will explore the nation's evolution from a remedial system primarily driven by common law suits against individual officers in state court to one now typified by suits brought against officers in federal court and on the basis of judge-made federal rights of action. It will do so by examining four case studies in government litigation, each involving somewhat similar alleged wrongs by the responsible government official. I have chosen these case studies from different historical eras: one from the antebellum period, when the reliance on common law suits against individual officials was at its height; one from the Gilded Age, when the federal courts began to oversee a body of administrative law alongside common law remedies and fashioned limits on individual liability; and one from the post–New Deal era, when the bureaucratization of ordinary remedies was complete but the Supreme Court struggled to preserve an independent action to address constitutional violations. A final case study explores the subtle ways in which suits against *state* government officials (often based on 42 U.S.C. § 1983) differ from those against their federal counterparts. Law grows more dense and complex, as time goes by, but does not necessarily offer the citizen a more sure-footed remedy for government-inflicted harm.

REPUTATION AND THE POSTAL SERVICE IN ANTEBELLUM AMERICA

Nathaniel Mitchell, the postmaster of Portland, Maine, had a problem. It was the summer of 1834, and someone was stealing letters from the postal service. Even worse, the thief was taking letters that contained money. Directed by his higher-ups to investigate, Mitchell sent a test or "decoy" package through the mail en route to Bath, Maine. When he checked the mail bag after it had passed through Camden, Maine, but before it was due to arrive in Bath, Mitchell found the decoy package missing and swore out a criminal complaint against the local deputy postmaster, one William Merriam. Merriam could not post bond, defaulted on several obligations, and suffered financial reversals. In the end, the package in question made its way to Bath after all, effectively exonerating Merriam of any wrongdoing.[1]

By the time of the Maine investigation, the US Postal Service was the nation's largest government employer. In 1831, the postal service employed some 8,700 postmasters, or roughly 75 percent of all civilian federal employees. (By way of contrast, the army consisted of only some 6,000 soldiers, mostly scattered in remote outposts.[2]) A vast network for spreading news throughout the nation, it was also the vehicle through which many Americans conducted interstate commercial transactions. Remittances, bonds, letters of credit, and banknotes all flowed through the mail. One estimate puts the value of all money transferred through the mail in 1850 at $100 million, more than double the federal budget for that year.[3] Theft of money from the mail was thus a serious concern, threatening to dampen confidence in the postal system as an instrumentality of interstate commerce.

Merriam brought suit against Mitchell in Maine state court, seeking recompense for the losses occasioned by his wrongful arrest and detention. (The claim against a federal official did not, as such, then qualify for adjudication in Maine's federal courts.) Mitchell argued by way of defense that he had inspected the mail bag that contained the "decoy," had found it missing, and thus had probable cause to suspect Merriam of theft. His attorney spun a tale of intrigue, suggesting that someone in cahoots with Merriam had smuggled the missing package back into the mail bag at a later time. But the jury opted for the most straightforward explanation: Mitchell had made a mistake, and the mistake had cost Merriam dearly. The jury returned a verdict of $1,666,

---

[1] See Merriam v. Mitchell, 13 Me. 439 (1836) (recounting the facts that gave rise to Merriam's suit). On the organization of the early postal service, see Richard R. John, Spreading the News (1998). On the use of decoys and special agents to investigate mail theft, see John, at 77.

[2] John, supra note 1, at 3–4.   [3] Id. at 53–55.

some ten to twenty times the annual compensation of the typical local postmaster. (For example, in 1835, one Abraham Lincoln earned $55.70 as the postmaster of New Salem, Illinois. Only 3 percent of postmasters, mainly in the big cities, earned in excess of $300 per year.)

On appeal to the Maine Supreme Court, Mitchell argued that he had not acted with the "malice" necessary to support a tort claim for malicious prosecution. He was simply doing his job as the agent of the postal service and had probable cause to suspect Merriam. The Maine court disagreed: the prosecution was based entirely on Mitchell's negligent search of the mail bag and the fact that he apparently overlooked the package in question. Such a negligent investigation could not supply the probable cause necessary to warrant the prosecution of "an innocent and unoffending man, who had given no color for suspicion against him." In such a case, "[r]eparation is demanded ... by the plainest dictates of common justice."[4] The Constitution itself could be said to demand as much, foreclosing unreasonable searches and seizures and limiting the issuance of warrants to circumstances in which there was probable cause.

Having exhausted the remedies available through the state courts in Maine, Mitchell turned to Congress for the adoption of a private bill of indemnity. Dating from the 1790s, the congressional practice of indemnification protected officers of the federal government from the financial losses associated with personal liability imposed on them for actions taken in the course and scope of their employment. By the time of Mitchell's petition, the indemnity practice was well established. Petitions for indemnity were referred for investigation to the Committee on Claims of the House of Representatives. If the committee found the petition meritorious, it would recommend the adoption of indemnifying legislation. Something on the order of two-thirds of official petitions resulted in the enactment of a bill of indemnity; Congress usually deferred to the Committee's findings.[5]

Mitchell's petition fared better before the committee on claims and before Congress than had his appeal to the Maine Supreme Court. Not only did the committee recommend and Congress adopt indemnifying legislation. Congressional records reveal that Mitchell successfully pursued indemnity on more than one occasion, first obtaining payment of the amount of the judgment and related costs ($2,600) and later securing compensation to cover additional costs and attorney's fees. In total, Mitchell was paid some $3,600 in indemnity as a result of petitions submitted to Congress in 1839 and 1842.[6]

The tale of *Merriam* v. *Mitchell* tells us much about the centrality of officer suits as a mode of ensuring government accountability. Merriam relied on local

---

[4] Merriam v. Mitchell, 13 Me. at 457.
[5] For an account of indemnity practice, see James E. Pfander and Jonathan L. Hunt, Public Wrongs and Private Bills: Indemnification and Government Accountability in the Early Republic, 85 *N.Y. U.L. Rev.* 1862 (2010).
[6] See Pfander and Hunt, supra note 5, at 1908–11.

institutions to secure recompense for harm inflicted by an agent of the federal government. His action in state court relied on common law theories of tort liability in characterizing the actions of Mitchell as wrongful. The state court responded by sending the case to the jury for a determination of the issue of malicious or wrongful prosecution. Even though one can probably best characterize Mitchell's actions as merely negligent (in apparently overlooking the presence of the decoy package), the Maine Supreme Court found that the absence of probable cause for the arrest of Merriam was sufficient to support a finding of malice. The court specifically declined to find that Mitchell deserved protection from liability as a government official, even though he appears to have acted in good faith to discharge his duties. In the end, then, Merriam was compensated for the financial reversals and reputational injury he suffered as a result of the wrongful institution of the criminal proceeding.

The apparent harshness of the system of personal liability was softened considerably by the decision of Congress to indemnify Mitchell. To be sure, Merriam could not sue the government directly; the doctrine of sovereign immunity barred unconsented suits against the federal government in either state or federal court. But the system of indemnity meant that while the federal government enjoyed a nominal immunity from suit in its own name, it nonetheless bore legal responsibility for the injuries that its officers inflicted in the course and scope of employment. While Merriam could not enforce that legal obligation directly, Mitchell did so through his petition for indemnity. By the 1830s, the system of indemnity through private bill had been in place for forty years and had given rise to a collection of relatively well-known precedents on the government's duty to indemnify. Indeed, in 1828, the clerk of Congress, Samuel Burch, published an index of legislation that included a special section devoted to indemnification through the use of private bills.[7] By 1850, the Supreme Court of the United States commented in passing that government officers like Mitchell who faced personal liability were not subject to any real inconvenience, given the Court's perception that this well-functioning system of private legislation protected the officer's "right" to indemnity.[8]

REPUTATION AND THE POSTAL SERVICE DURING THE GILDED AGE

By the latter half of the nineteenth century, the postal service had grown into a vastly more complex bureaucracy with thousands of employees, including several hundred in the main Washington, D.C., office alone. The nature of postal service employment had changed as well; local postmasters were no longer compensated on a fee-for-service basis but in legislation adopted in

---

[7] On Burch's Index and the institutionalization of indemnity practice in Congress, see Pfander and Hunt, supra note 5, at 1910–14.

[8] See Tracy v. Swartwout, 35 U.S. 80, 98–99 (1836) (referring to the government as "bound" to indemnify the officer for illegal actions in the line of duty).

1864 were transformed into salaried employees of the federal government. Alongside the growth of the federal bureaucracy came corresponding growth in the size of the Washington, D.C., bar, as lawyers came to specialize in administrative law at the seat of government. Even before the dramatic growth of the administrative state in the twentieth century, nineteenth-century administrative lawyers pursued such forms of practice as pension claims, land office claims, and money claims against the federal government before the federal Court of Claims. This court, established in 1855 and remodeled during and after the Civil War, operated under legislation that effectively waived the federal government's sovereign immunity from suit.[9] But while it handled money claims against the federal government in matters of property and contract, individuals seeking to impose liability in tort would continue to proceed against government officials (on the model of *Merriam* v. *Mitchell*) until the adoption of the Federal Tort Claims Act in 1946.[10]

Harvey Spalding, an attorney in Washington, D.C., during the last few decades of the nineteenth century, typified the new administrative lawyer. Although he handled pension and land claims, much of his work before the court of claims involved the assertion of money claims on behalf of former postmasters in the postal service. Spalding's postal work fell into two categories: he lobbied Congress for the adoption of legislation that would make back pay available to former postal workers and asserted claims on behalf of those who were entitled to the money. In these endeavors, he was fairly successful. Congress passed legislation in 1883, creating rules for the adjustment of postmaster salaries, apparently due in part to his efforts; Spalding initiated a raft of claims for adjusted salaries. On occasion, when the postal service rejected certain of the claims, Spalding brought suit in the court of claims. Some of his matters worked their way to the Supreme Court on appeal from the court of claims. Much of the Gilded Age law of postmaster salary adjustment bears his fingerprints.[11]

Over time, Spalding built up a client list that included several thousand former postmasters; he was, in short, an inventory lawyer before that term had taken root in the lexicon of American litigation. One can imagine that, as a repeat player in salary adjustment applications and litigation, he did not endear himself to the nation's postmaster generals.[12] Indeed, the Postmaster General

[9] See Floyd D. Shimomura, The History of Claims against the United States, 45 *La. L. Rev.* 625 (1985).

[10] On the origins of the Federal Tort Claims Act, see 1 Lester S. Jayson and Robert C. Longstreth, Handling Federal Tort Claims §§ 2.01–2.14 (2002). The act makes the federal government responsible for the torts of the officer, committed in the scope of employment, and enables the individual to sue the government directly.

[11] See United States v. Verdier, 164 U.S. 213 (1896) (noting Spalding's representation of post-master's estate in claim against the government before the court of claims).

[12] Apparently, the feelings were mutual. Consider the Court's reaction to Spalding's rhetoric as counsel for the postmaster-claimant in United States v. Ewing, 184 U.S. 140, 151 (1902): "We feel called upon to say that the charges of misconduct, maladministration, and fraud against the

responded to Spalding's petitions by sending any money due directly to the claimant, thereby bypassing Spalding and apparently seeking to undercut Spalding's attorney–client relationships.[13] Accompanying the payments was an official post office circular that read in part as follows:

congress directed that all checks or warrants should be made payable to the claimants, and transmitted direct to them, and that in the appropriation and enactment on this subject by congress, a copy of which is printed at the foot of this note, the direction was repeated. This was done because no attorney's services were necessary to the presentation of the claim before the department, and the congress desired all the proceeds to reach the person really entitled thereto. After a claim of this character is filed in the department, its examination, and the readjustment of the salary, if found proper, are made directly from the books and papers in the department, by its officers, and without further evidence.

You are further advised that by [federal law] any transfer of this claim or power of attorney for receiving payment of this warrant is null and void.

The practice of the postmaster general not only put the funds directly in the hands of clients, without affording Spalding an opportunity to subtract his fee, but also tended to suggest that it was the considered policy judgment of Congress that an attorney's services were unnecessary to the submission of a successful claim. To the extent that Spalding had filed powers of attorney along with the petitions, calling for payment of proceeds to himself in the first instance, the postmaster general was acting to override those agreements on the authority of Congress.[14]

Spalding felt aggrieved by the postmaster general's refusal to facilitate collection of his fees. Spalding could continue to collect his fees in accordance with his contracts. But one might suppose that the collection process grew far more cumbersome after his clients received their money and the circular. Instead of deducting and depositing his fee in Washington and forwarding the balance to his clients, Spalding would have to assert his right to the fee after the funds had reached his clients, possibly by bringing suit in the local courts. For impecunious clients, who might well have spent the money, collection of any judgment would be challenging. Accordingly, Spalding filed suit against the postmaster general, one Vilas, seeking $100,000 in damages for loss of fees and injury to his reputation and his business as an attorney. Indeed, Spalding alleged that the circular was "maliciously intended to cause the claimants to believe that

officers of the Post Office Department, so freely scattered through the pages of the briefs of counsel for appellee, are entirely unwarranted by anything contained in the record before us, and ought not to have been made."

[13] See Holt v. US, 29 Ct Claims 56 (1894) (postmaster general pays back salary adjustment directly to the widow of a deceased postmaster; Spalding successfully argues that payment should have been made to the estate's executor instead and forces government to pay a second time).

[14] See Spalding v. Vilas, 161 U.S. 483 (1896). The description of this and other features of the litigation has been drawn from the case reports and from a review of other cases in which Spalding appeared as counsel.

[Spalding's] claim for valuable services was false and fraudulent, and the same was inserted for no other purpose." As a result, several of Spalding's clients had apparently repudiated their contracts and had come to view Spalding as little more than a "common swindler."[15]

For the Court, the question was straightforward: was Spalding's claim for injury to his practice legally viable? Ultimately, the Court said no. All of the statements in the circular were literally true, as accurate descriptions of the relevant federal laws. To the extent that Vilas set them forth in circulars to those who were entitled to a salary adjustment, he was acting within the course and scope of his duties. To the extent that he expressed his opinion as to the value of an attorney's services, the opinion was protected speech that did not take the matter outside the scope of his official authority. To be sure, Spalding alleged that Vilas acted maliciously and with the intent to injure his business. But an allegation of malicious intent was not, alone, enough to make otherwise lawful official conduct actionable, at least where the official stayed within the scope of his official duty. In a unanimous opinion, the Court upheld the dismissal of Spalding's complaint, suggesting that Vilas enjoyed something akin to the common law immunity of superior court judges when acting within the scope of their jurisdiction.[16]

Two features of the *Spalding* litigation distinguish it from the dispute in *Merriam* v. *Mitchell*. For starters, Vilas did not cause any civil or criminal process to issue against Spalding and did not make any statements of fact about Spalding's practice that might be considered defamatory. Rather, as the Court found, Vilas spoke truthfully about the content of federal law, even though the context of the communication could be readily interpreted as casting doubt on the legitimacy and necessity of Spalding's work on behalf of his clients. Unlike Mitchell, in short, Vilas did not breach any common law duty owed to Spalding in the course of conducting the affairs of his office. Indeed, one might argue that Vilas's subtle message through the circular was in line with the policy underlying Congress's decision to disallow trafficking in the claims of former postmasters by requiring direct payment and by abrogating powers of attorney. But the Court neatly avoided these issues by concluding that so long as Vilas stayed within his line of duty, allegations that he acted maliciously to injure Spalding's reputation were not actionable.

One more factor may have influenced the Court's decision. In parallel litigation, one Mason had filed suit for an accounting, arguing that he was entitled to a share of Spalding's fees. The case appeared on the Court's docket as an appeal from the D.C. court system (the same lower court that had handled Spalding's claims against Vilas). While the Court agreed with Spalding in part and cut back on the size of the payments due to Mason, the more salient fact may have been the sheer size of Spalding's practice as revealed in the record of

---

[15] Id. at 486–88 (recounting allegations in complaint).
[16] See Spalding v. Vilas, 161 U.S. at 498–99.

his fee dispute. According to documents filed in the case, Spalding had earned something on the order of $165,000 in the course of representing thousands of postmasters in salary disputes.[17] Whatever impact Vilas's circulars may have had on Spalding's business, it must have been clear to the Court that Spalding had continued to earn significant fee income. As if to emphasize this point, the Court released both opinions on the very same day, March 2, 1896.

The two postal service cases reveal something about the curious operation of official malice in officer litigation. While Mitchell did not appear to have acted with any sort of personal malice toward Merriam, he was said to have committed an intentional tort by invading Merriam's common law interest in freedom from unwarranted criminal prosecutions. The Maine Supreme Court viewed tort law as establishing both the right of Merriam to sue and the outer limits of Mitchell's official discretion. Mitchell could conduct his investigation, acting within the scope of his office, and could take action based on his findings. But the common law tort of malicious prosecution set boundaries, framing Mitchell's work as a government employee. Congress might override the common law by statute, but until it did so, Merriam could invoke the common law as a source of rights against Mitchell (and, derivatively, against the government). Given the centrality of common law precepts to the decision in both cases, we might best understand the *Spalding* decision as one in which the Court refused to supplement the common law with a new right of action to protect the reputational and business interests of attorneys specializing in litigation against the government. Malicious conduct alone, even if presumed, did not give rise to a viable claim without an invasion of recognized rights of reputation, liberty, or property.[18]

Later decisions invoke *Spalding*, expanding the scope of government official immunity to encompass a broader range of activities. In *Barr* v. *Matteo*, a fractured Court upheld the claim of immunity put forward by an acting director of the federal rent stabilization board.[19] Barr, the new acting director, was under some pressure from a congressional investigation into the board's decision to allow employees take their annual leave in the form of cash payments. He issued a press release, expressing his own "violent" opposition to the practice but explaining that he had not previously been in a position to combat it. Now that he was, he announced that his first act in office would be to suspend the two employees responsible for the policy. Both officials sued, alleging defamation and arguing that Barr's duties did not include issuance of press releases. The Court nonetheless upheld Barr's claim of immunity, finding that the press release was

---

[17] See Spalding v. Mason, 161 U.S. 375 (1896) (recounting the thousands of postmaster clients Spalding had represented and the sizable fee income those clients had generated).

[18] The *Spalding* Court acknowledged that Vilas may have acted maliciously, observing that "the circumstances show that he is not disagreeably impressed by the fact that his action injuriously affects the claims of particular individuals." *Spalding*, 161 U.S. at 491.

[19] See Barr v. Matteo, 360 U.S. 564 (1959).

arguably within the bounds of his authority or at least not clearly prohibited.[20] A cogent dissent observed that the release was less clearly within the line of duty and more evidently false and misleading than the circular that Vilas sent to the recipients of back-pay awards. On the whole, then, the decision treats the director's claim of privilege or immunity as decisive and assigns less weight to the employees' interest in freedom from what could well have been defamation at common law. Notably, both of the employees had previously gained a measure of vindication when they were reinstated to their positions at the board.

REPUTATION AND COMMODITIES REGULATION
IN POST-WATERGATE AMERICA

If the bureaucracy that sought to cabin Harvey Spalding's fee income in the 1890s was more complex than the one that imprisoned the local postmaster William Merriam in 1834, then that confronting Arthur Economou in the 1970s was more variegated still. Economou and his firm were registered as commodity futures merchants with the Department of Agriculture. The department sought to revoke the registration, contending that Economou did not meet the minimum financial requirements. Economou chose to characterize the revocation as retaliation for his outspoken criticism of the department; his suits against Earl Butz, then secretary of the Department of Agriculture, and several other officials within the department eventually went to the Supreme Court.

Before explaining the Court's handling of the accountability and immunity issues in *Butz* v. *Economou*, we must take a brief detour into the law of administrative procedure, federal government tort liability, and constitutional tort litigation, all of which differed sharply from their precursors in the nineteenth century. As we will see, the simple common law model of government accountability invoked by Merriam and of Spalding had been virtually displaced by other federal remedies.

Administrative Procedure

A decisive shift away from reliance on common law officer suits as a mode of overseeing government compliance with law came in 1946 with the passage of the Administrative Procedure Act (APA).[21] The well-known terms of the APA establish a set of rules generally applicable to administrative process in the burgeoning federal bureaucracy, regulating such matters as agency rulemaking, agency adjudication, and judicial review. While judicial review was calibrated to occur after the completion of final agency action, the APA

---

[20] See *Barr*, 360 U.S. at 574–75.
[21] The Administrative Procedure Act, Pub. L. 79–404, 60 Stat. 237, codified at 5 U.S.C. §§ 501 et seq.

maintained a strong presumption in favor of the availability of such review. The presumption recognized the historical role of the federal courts in testing the legality of federal official action and reflected a perception that Article III of the Constitution imposed limits on the power of Congress to shift traditional objects of federal adjudication to agencies for final determination there.[22]

Two consequences flowed from the APA. First, the act represented a waiver of federal sovereign immunity, enabling litigants to name departments of the government as such in their federal judicial petitions for review of final agency action. While actions seeking to enjoin the government from violating constitutional rights might still proceed against the official in charge, challenges to agency action were now often brought against the agency rather than against its officialdom. Second, the act provided for litigation over federal agency action in the federal courts and implicitly foreclosed such litigation in the state courts. As a waiver of federal government sovereign immunity, the APA extends only to suits brought in the court "of the United States."[23] As a consequence, most observers have assumed that the state courts no longer enjoy concurrent jurisdiction over suits challenging federal agency action.

The APA's creation of exclusive federal jurisdiction over suits to review federal agency action further narrows access to state court. As for suits against federal *officials*, much state law has been displaced, as such, although it may still govern federal action by virtue of its incorporation into distinctively federal causes of action (such as those under the Federal Tort Claims Act and under the so-called *Bivens* right of action[24]). While the state courts for a time retained concurrent jurisdiction over certain claims against federal officials, based on state or federal law, Congress has extended federal removal jurisdiction to virtually any federal officer suit brought in state court, and the Department of Justice has an unyielding practice of removing all such claims to federal court.[25]

Federal Tort Claims

At about the same time it was adopting the APA, Congress enacted the Federal Tort Claims Act (FTCA), making the federal government responsible for the

[22] See, e.g., Crowell v. Benson, 285 U.S. 22 (1932).

[23] See Aminoil U.S.A., Inc. v. California State Water Resources Control Board, 674 F.2d 1227, 1235 (9th Cir. 1982) (state courts lack power to entertain suits against the federal government under the APA; waiver of government immunity applied only to suits brought in courts of the United States).

[24] See Bivens v. Six Unknown-Named Agents of the Federal Bureau of Narcotics, 403 U.S. 388 (1971).

[25] On the limits of federal officer removal, see Mesa v. California, 489 U.S. 121 (1989) (permitting removal only when the federal officers tenders a colorable federal defense to a state right of action). Today, Mitchell would likely invoke the officer removal provision in removing Merriam's suit from Maine state court. The Westfall Act, discussed later, considerably narrows the ambit of state law as a source of a right to sue federal officers.

torts of federal employees acting within the scope of their office or employment. Two factors appear to have moved Congress: a desire to shift the forum for the assessments of such claims from Congress itself (through petitions for private bill relief) to the federal courts and a concern with the potential injustice of the private bill process. As with the APA, the FTCA action proceeds not against the official but against the government as such. As with the APA, the FTCA authorized such suits to be brought only in federal court; state courts cannot hear such claims. But liability depends on state tort law to a large extent; the FTCA declares that the liability of the federal government shall be determined by the same standards applicable to a private person in "accordance with the (state) law of the place where the act or omission occurred."[26]

Several factors complicate the assertion of FTCA claims. First, the statute requires that the claimant file a notice of claim with the responsible administrative agency no later than two years after the claim accrues. Following the agency's reaction, the claimant may wish to settle or proceed to litigation within the relatively short six-month window that the law provides.[27] Second, the focus of the FTCA on paying claims arising from the negligence of government employees works better in some settings (such as liability for the negligent operation of government vehicles) than in other settings, where the official may inflict harm in the course of exercising a measure of discretion.[28] Third, the FTCA overlaps with other remedial schemes, creating problems of coordination that the courts have not handled well.[29]

Perhaps the biggest problem of coordination arose from the fact that, as originally enacted, the FTCA simply imposed vicarious liability on the federal government while leaving intact the state-law tort liability of the employee. That meant that a claimant could potentially pursue claims against both defendants, one against the government in federal court and one against the employee in state court. The FTCA attempted to coordinate in part, erecting a judgment bar when the claimant first sued the government, lost, and then attempted to sue the employee on the same tort claim.[30] But Congress eventually grew weary of duplicative litigation and, in the 1988 Westfall Act, provided that all such suits should proceed against the government in federal court rather than against the employees.[31]

---

[26] 28 U.S.C. § 1346.   [27] See 28 U.S.C. §§ 2401(b), 2675.

[28] See 28 U.S.C. § 2680 (creating exception from liability where employee performed a "discretionary function or duty"). See generally Dalehite v. United States, 346 U.S. 15 (1953).

[29] See, e.g., Manning v. United States, 546 U.S. 430 (7th Cir. 2008) (treating judge's own disposition of FTCA claim as a bar to enforcement of jury verdict favoring plaintiffs in a related *Bivens* action).

[30] For a summary of the judgment bar and its now outsized role in *Bivens* litigation, see James E. Pfander and Neil Aggarwal, *Bivens*, the Judgment Bar, and the Perils of Dynamic Textualism, 8 *U. St. Thomas L. Rev.* 417 (2011). For a decision modestly narrowing the judgment bar, see Simmons v. Himmelreich, 136 S. Ct. 1843 (2016).

[31] On the decision to switch away from suits against employees for ordinary tort-based liability, see James E. Pfander and David Baltmanis, Rethinking *Bivens*: Legitimacy and Constitutional

Bivens Claims

While these changes were unfolding in the ordinary law of government accountability, the Supreme Court made a simple but profound change in the way individuals enforce their constitutional rights against the federal government. By 1970, it was clear that an individual who faced the threat of an ongoing violation of his constitutional rights could sue the responsible official in federal court for injunctive and declaratory relief. The so-called *Ex parte Young* action, which the Court developed to secure the enforcement of constitutional rights against state actors, was extended to federal officials as well.[32] What was less clear in 1970 was how an individual litigant was to pursue damages for the unconstitutional conduct of federal officers. For state officials the answer was clear: individuals could sue under state law or could invoke a federal Reconstruction-era statute that provides for the recovery of damages for action taken under color of *state* law in violation of an individual's federal constitutional or statutory rights.[33] But the Reconstruction law, codified at 42 U.S.C. § 1983, did not apply to unconstitutional action under color of *federal* law, meaning that litigants would typically rely on state tort claims to vindicate their constitutional rights against federal officers (as had William Merriam in 1835).

Into this uncertain world stepped Webster Bivens. At the time he instituted his action against the officers of the Federal Bureau of Narcotics who had searched his home, he was serving time in federal prison on drug trafficking convictions. He sought damages against the officers, alleging that their warrantless search and subsequent actions violated his rights under the Fourth Amendment. He filed his pro se suit directly in federal court, apparently assuming that federal law offered a remedy. The government moved to dismiss, arguing that federal law created no right of action for constitutional claims for damages. On the government's theory, Bivens was obliged to refile his case in state court, asserting claims founded on state tort law. While the government would remove the action to federal court and litigate it there, state law would continue to provide the measure of the officers' liability, if any, for the constitutional torts of the officers.[34]

The Supreme Court responded by creating a judge-made federal law right of action, an analogue for the victims of federal official wrongdoing to the

---

Adjudication, 98 *Geo. L. J.* 117 (2009) (discussing the origins of the Westfall Act and the limited federal employee immunity it created).

[32] On the extension of *Ex parte Young*, 209 U.S. 123 (1908), to suits brought against federal officers, see Lane v. Hoglund, 244 U.S. 174 (1917) (issuing mandamus to compel federal official to issue patent for plot of land); Houston v. Ormes, 252 U.S. 469 (1920) (granting mandatory injunction to the secretary of the Treasury).

[33] See Monroe v. Pape, 365 U.S. 167 (1961).

[34] For an account, see James E. Pfander, *The Story of Bivens v. Six Unknown Named Agents of the Federal Narcotics Bureau* (invited chapter in Federal Courts Stories 275–99 (V. Jackson and J. Resnik eds. 2010)).

statutory section 1983 claim that applied to wrongdoing by state employees. But the right of action has a hit-or-miss quality; individuals must first persuade the federal court that the particular constitutional right in question will support a *Bivens* claims and they must overcome the doctrine of qualified immunity, which the Court has developed to protect officials from the threat of ruinous personal liability. Following the passage of the Westfall Act, moreover, individuals in the position of Bivens can no longer rely on state law tort claims as the basis for challenging government wrongdoing.[35] Most observers take the view that the state tort claims have been superseded by the Westfall Act immunity. But that gets us ahead of our story.

Understanding *Butz* v. *Economou*

At about the same time the Court was handing down its landmark decision in the *Bivens* case, Arthur Economou was seeking damages for retaliatory proceedings. Somewhat simplified, the story goes like this: the Department of Agriculture had audited Economou after concluding that certain of his required financial disclosures looked fishy. Following the audit, Department officials found that Economou was in willful violation of applicable regulations and initiated a disciplinary proceeding without first issuing any sort of warning letter. Although the hearing officer agreed with the department and issued a disciplinary order, the US Court of Appeals for the Second Circuit vacated the order for lack of notice. The department's failure to issue a warning letter was thought to have deprived Economou of his right to come into compliance and thereby to avoid a finding of willful violation. Following the appellate court's vacating the disciplinary order, Economou brought suit alleging that the department acted to punish him for his outspoken criticism of its practices. His complaint alleged both common law theories of liability (e.g., abuse of process, malicious prosecution, invasion of privacy, trespass) and constitutional tort claims for alleged violations of his due process rights under the Fifth Amendment and free speech rights under the First Amendment.[36]

Economou's action illustrates the complexity of government accountability litigation in a world grown thick with statutory remedies, a common law underpinning, and a constitutional overlay. Begin with the Administrative Procedure Act: it offered Economou a relatively straightforward framework for contesting the imposition of disciplinary sanctions. Final agency action is subject to review in a federal appellate court, and Economou successfully

---

[35] See Pfander and Baltmanis, supra note 31.

[36] For the decisions on which we have based this account of the Economou litigation, see Economou v. Butz, 370 F. Supp. 361 (S.D.N.Y. 1974); Economou v. Butz, 84 F.R.D. 678 (S.D.N.Y. 1979); Economou v. Butz, 466 F. Supp. 1351 (S.D.N.Y. 1979); Economou v. US Dep't of Agriculture, 494 F.2d 519 (2d Cir. 1974) (vacating sanction order); Economou v. US Dep't of Agriculture, 535 F.2d 688 (2d Cir. 1976) (overturning dismissal of Economou's claim for damages); Butz v. Economou, 438 U.S. 478 (1978) (reviewing Second Circuit decision).

pursued that avenue in securing the invalidation of the sanction. But to Economou, vindicated in his challenge to what he viewed as wrongful proceedings against him, simple exoneration did not make him whole (just as William Merriam was not made whole for his reputational and other losses by the dismissal of the criminal charges against him). He had suffered reputational injury, together with the disruption of his business, and the cost of mounting a defense. (Indeed, one can view the department's actions as designed to inflict just such an injury on a business that it viewed as out of compliance with federal standards.) Economou also sought to address what he saw as government overreaching, the more so given his perception that the proceeding was triggered by the desire of department officials to retaliate against him. The challenge of much government accountability litigation lies in determining what law governs the right of the individual to secure relief when the already fraught relationship between an agency and the target of its regulatory efforts grows more contentious and testy than usual.

Economou also relied on common law tort claims like those Merriam pursued against Mitchell. He contended that the department's officials had committed the torts of malicious prosecution and abuse of process. Such claims presuppose that the department's proceeding either was groundless (malicious prosecution) or was pursued for some ulterior purpose (abuse of process). (He also alleged invasion of privacy, negligence, and trespass.) Yet the common law erected some fences around such litigation, recognizing that the decision to prosecute deserves some protection from motive-based tort claims. Otherwise, every failed prosecution could result in a follow-on suit for damages. As a result, a common law privilege shields the prosecutor from liability, even as it subjects the complaining witness or charging party to possible liability. That means, in general, that the Merriams of the world can sue the Mitchells (as the complaining party) but cannot sue the presiding judge or the prosecutor who decides to go forward with the proceeding on the basis of the complaint. Mapping these common law forms of action onto the complexity of agency proceedings has proven quite difficult.

For starters, Economou faced the question of whom to sue. He could certainly name the agency itself and attempt to pursue common law claims against it. As we have seen, however, agencies act as arms of the federal government and enjoy immunity from suit in the absence of a federal statutory framework. The closest available framework, the FTCA, imposes liability on the government for common law torts committed by employees in the course of their employment. Still, the FTCA included a well-known exception for intentional torts, ruling out government liability for such claims as defamation, malicious prosecution, and abuse of process. (Congress amended the FTCA in 1974 to broaden the government's liability for intentional torts committed by law enforcement officers. But the Economou litigation was based on alleged misconduct that predated that law and few if any of the officials involved in the Economou case would qualify as law enforcement officers under the 1974 amendment.) In short, the Department of Agriculture may be a proper defendant in an action to review its work under the APA but not for purposes of intentional tort liability.

Economou could also sue the officials themselves, attempting to impose personal liability on them for their intentional torts in much the way that Merriam sued Mitchell. At the time of the Economou litigation, there was some uncertainty as to scope of federal officials' liability for common law tort claims. The FTCA assumed that the common law liability of the federal official survived the creation of *respondeat superior* liability in the federal government; as noted previously, special provisions were inserted into the law in an effort to coordinate the remedies against the government and its officials.[37] But those provisions were crafted to deal primarily with negligence liability; liability for intentional torts was added in 1974 with law enforcement officers in mind. The government long argued (and reiterated that argument in defense of Economou's claims) that officials enjoyed absolute immunity from personal liability suits based on state common law. While the Supreme Court ultimately rejected that view in 1988, Congress quickly adopted the Westfall Act to confer immunity from state law claims. Today, in short, Merriam could not sue Mitchell for malicious prosecution or false imprisonment. But Economou filed his action well before the Westfall Act, and he included common law official liability claims in his complaint.

Apart from common law claims, Economou included several *Bivens* claims. He argued that the government's action violated his rights in three respects: his First Amendment free speech rights were violated when the government retaliated against him for criticizing commodity regulation, and his Fifth Amendment due process rights were violated when the government failed to give him customary notice and invaded his privacy through the dissemination of the administrative complaint it filed against him. These claims were, as in *Bivens*, addressed to the responsible officials of the department; no action may be brought against the department itself for constitutional violations. The Court thus faced questions concerning the viability of such *Bivens* claims, the manner in which such claims interacted with common law theories of liability, and the degree to which the officials in question could claim immunity from suit either at common law or under *Bivens*.

After mixed success in the lower courts, Economou prevailed on a single issue at the Supreme Court. While the district court accepted the government's sweeping immunity claims, the court of appeals accorded government officials only a qualified immunity and reinstated Economou's lawsuit. At the Supreme Court, the government argued that high government officials, such as the Secretary of Agriculture, were entitled to absolute immunity from liability both at common law and under *Bivens*. Focusing on the constitutional claims,

---

[37] For an account of the coordination function, see Pfander and Aggrawal, supra note 30 (describing the FTCA's judgment bar as meant to block suit against the individual official after the official's conduct had been upheld in prior litigation against the federal government).

the Court chose to extend to the secretary and other department officials only a qualified immunity, an immunity that was available only where executive branch officials acted in good faith within the outer bounds of their duties. The Court deployed a variety of arguments in support of this conclusion: the importance of constitutional remediation, the perception that too broad a doctrine of immunity would undercut the principle of government account-ability articulated in *Marbury* v. *Madison,* the prior conclusion that executive officers of state governments enjoyed only a qualified immunity from suit, and the perception that officers at both levels of government should be treated the same way.[38]

While qualified immunity was thus the norm for both state and federal official actors, the Court did offer absolute immunity to department officials involved in the adjudication of the disciplinary claim against Economou. Under civil service rules and the APA, administrative law judges enjoy a measure of independence from the executive branch officials who appear before them: as the Court observed, hearing officers are insulated from at-will discharge and protected from retaliation at the hands of executive officers in the departments they serve. So long as these protections were in place, the Court viewed the work of the department hearing officer and prosecutor as similar to that of common law judges and prosecutors. Observing that such officials were entitled to absolute common law immunity for action taken within the scope of their jurisdiction or office, the Court extended a similar immunity to agency officials who play the same roles.[39]

Three Justices joined a dissent by Justice Rehnquist. For the dissent, the Economou claim was frivolous "in the extreme," and all of the federal officers in the case (not just the judges and prosecutors) were entitled to absolute immunity. As Justice Rehnquist saw things, prior decisions had established that executive officials acting within the scope of their duty enjoy absolute immunity from personal liability. While the Economou complaint couched certain of the claims in constitutional terms, Justice Rehnquist did not view that transformation as significantly altering the immunity calculus. To Justice Rehnquist's way of thinking, individuals can always dress their common law reputation and retaliation claims in constitutional garb; an immunity from suit offers little protection if it does not protect against such re-tailored claims. Justice Rehnquist's approach would have essentially foreclosed suits for damages against federal officials acting within the scope of their employment and remitted individuals in the position of Economou to whatever remedies federal statutes make available. That would not have left Economou entirely without a remedy: he could defend against government enforcement proceedings before the agency, petition the appellate court to overturn any sanctions (as he did), recover under the FTCA for losses resulting from

[38] See Butz v. Economou, 438 U.S. at 506 (quoting Marbury v. Madison, 1 Cranch 137 [1803]).
[39] Id. at 513–17.

common law negligence, and obtain injunctive and declaratory relief against ongoing violations of constitutional law, and seek damages for malicious official action outside the line of duty.

What to do, then, with the losses suffered by those who successfully challenge or fend off government enforcement proceedings? Innocent people may be harmed by well-meaning but flawed government investigations and enforcement proceedings; their right to seek recompense was the central lesson of *Merriam* v. *Mitchell*. The majority in *Butz* v. *Economou* sought to maintain the promise of recompense, at least when the government's action could be said to rise to the level of a constitutional violation. Writing five years after the Watergate hearings exposed a web of deliberate official wrongdoing emanating from the White House, the *Butz* Court was simply unwilling to foreclose all compensatory relief for overzealous enforcement and petty or unfeeling official action. In contrast, Justice Rehnquist and his fellow dissenters appear to have viewed official zealotry like taxation: as an inevitable by-product of government bureaucracy. Just as we accept taxes as the price of modern government, so too the dissent would have us accept a measure of callous or overzealous official behavior.[40]

Comparing *Merriam, Spalding,* and *Economou*

In comparing our three exemplary cases, we may usefully distinguish modes of litigation that seek to ascertain the simple legality of the government's claims from those that seek to remedy special injuries inflicted on individuals in the course of their interactions with the bureaucracy. Merriam successfully defended himself against the criminal prosecution, demonstrating that the decoy package arrived at its destination and disproving the government's claim of theft. But that exoneration did not address the collateral damage inflicted by the government's investigation. Similarly, Economou successfully petitioned to set aside the disciplinary order but did not obtain compensation for reputational injuries. Like Webster Bivens, against whom relevant criminal charges were dropped (because the search did not turn up any contraband), Economou was seeking compensation for the injuries occasioned by an arguably mistaken government proceeding.

Spalding's claim was of a different character. He had not been the target of a government investigation that went awry in some way. Instead, he was the victim, as he saw it, of government regulation. The postmaster general issued a piece of regulatory advice or guidance to its target population, postmasters with salary adjustment claims, informing them that any contracts assigning their interest or conferring powers of attorney were invalid under federal law, that

---

[40] *See, e.g.,* Wilkie v. Robbins, 551 U.S. 557 (2007) (declining to recognize a federal right of action to seek relief from a pattern of official retaliation that the Court described as "death by a thousand cuts").

they were entitled to the direct payment of their salary adjustment, and that the services of an attorney, though permissible, were not necessary to perfect their claims. Although this guidance complicated Spalding's life as an attorney, the Court viewed it as a permissible gloss on the action taken by Congress to protect the interests of the claimants.[41] In a sense, then, the Court's refusal to recognize a right in Spalding to sue Vilas can be seen as an early instance of deference to permissible agency interpretations of acts of Congress, not unlike the deference accorded agency interpretations today under the *Chevron* doctrine.[42]

To be sure, the Court subsequently devised a doctrine of regulatory takings under which individual property owners may contest regulatory action through which the government effectively appropriates or takes the value of the property in question.[43] But the property interest Spalding asserted in the efficient collection of his fees as an attorney would not likely qualify for protection under the doctrine and the government's regulation stopped well short of depriving Spalding of his stream of anticipated fee income. As a result, it appears that Spalding's losses were similar to those that any business will sustain when the executive branch adopts regulations to carry into effect legislation that Congress adopted for the public weal. Just as we do not compensate Economou for the burden of doing business in accordance with federal commodity regulations, we do not compensate Spalding for the cost of collecting his fees after Congress intervened to mandate direct payments to claimants rather than to attorneys.

It thus makes sense to distinguish Spalding's injury from those suffered by Merriam and Economou. Spalding suffered losses consequent to the exercise of permissible government regulatory authority; while he has the right to contest the regulation and argue that the government has gone too far, he cannot recover the costs incurred in complying with lawful regulations. In the Merriam and Economou cases, by contrast, the government arguably overstepped its bounds. While the government has the authority to investigate and prosecute, it does not necessarily enjoy immunity from suit for the losses that its wrongheaded or mistaken investigations impose on their targets. It may make sense to cast the burden of complying with otherwise proper government regulation on the Spaldings of the world; it makes less sense to require the Merriams and Economous and Bivenses of the world to bear the costs of government mistakes that result in injury to interests protected at common law.

---

[41] Congress has since essentially agreed with the result in *Spalding*, establishing a rule that the government owes no tort-based liability for acts of employees exercising "due care" in the execution of a statute or regulation. 28 U.S.C. § 2680(a).

[42] See Chevron USA Inc. v. Natural Resources Defense Council, Inc., 467 U.S. 837 (1984). *Chevron* holds that the federal courts must defer to an agency's interpretation of its own statute.

[43] Penn Cent. Transp. Co. v. New York City, 438 U.S. 104, 130–31 (1978); Tahoe-Sierra Pres. Council, Inc. v. Tahoe Reg'l Planning Agency, 535 U.S. 302, 342 (2002).

Post-*Economou* Developments

Since *Butz* v. *Economou*, the Court has further narrowed remedies for federal official misconduct. First, the Court has broadened qualified immunity to protect federal officers from suit except where they violate "clearly established" constitutional and statutory rights of which "a reasonable person would have known."[44] The avowed purpose of this switch from a focus on malice and good faith to a focus on the content of the law was to eliminate the need for an inquiry into the state of mind of the official defendant. At the time of the switch, pleading rules allowed plaintiffs to make general (rather than particularized) allegations of intentional or malicious conduct. Such allegations together with some evidence tending to establish a retaliatory motive could also prevent dismissal of the case on summary judgment and force a trial of the case before a jury. To address the perceived burden of such trials on well-meaning government officials, the Court sought a more objective standard. Immunity was to turn not on the state of mind of the official but on the clarity of the underlying norm. Only the violation of well-established federal norms will support a claim for damages.

Second, the Court has narrowed access to the *Bivens* right of action. While the Court in *Butz* assumed the viability of an action for retaliatory prosecution aimed at chilling government criticism (and the Second Circuit on remand expressly so ruled), later cases have refused to expand the *Bivens* remedy. To date, the Court has approved the recognition of suits to remedy Fourth Amendment violations, prison mistreatment that rises to the level of cruel and unusual punishment under the Eighth Amendment, and claims of race- or sex-based discrimination in violation of the equal protection component of the Fifth Amendment. But the Court has refused to recognize such claims when they arise in the context of the armed forces, has refused to extend the Eighth Amendment protection to privately run prison facilities, has refused to recognize an action for due process violations when other remedies have been provided, and has rejected the claim of a rancher who faced a pattern of harassment at the hands of Interior Department officials frustrated by his insistence on his property rights.[45] In many of these cases, the existence of alternative remedies perceived as adequate has persuaded the Court that no *Bivens* right of action was necessary.

Third, the Court has introduced a new "plausibility" feature into the pleading rules, enabling district courts to look behind allegations of malice in determining whether the claims against government officials may proceed.[46] Although in *Butz* the Court had refused to accord high government officials absolute immunity from suit, the subsequent change in the pleading rules broadened their qualified immunity

---

[44] Harlow v. Fitzgerald, 457 U.S. 800, 808 (1982).

[45] For a summary, see Pfander and Baltmanis, supra note 31 (discussing Wilkie v. Robbins, 551 U.S. 557 [2007]). See also Ziglar v. Abbasi, 137 S.Ct. 1843 (2017) (further narrowing access to new Bivens claims).

[46] See Ashcroft v. Iqbal, 556 U.S. 662 (2009). See generally, James E. Pfander, *Iqbal, Bivens*, and the Role of Judge-Made Law in Constitutional Litigation, 114 *Penn. State L. Rev.* 1387 (2010).

by inviting an assessment at the pleading stage of the "plausibility" of the complaint. It would no longer suffice to simply allege that an official took or authorized certain action with knowledge and malice; it was now necessary to set forth some facts that would support a plausible inference of knowledge and malice. As a practical matter, the change may shield some ambiguous government conduct from further scrutiny. Thus, the Court ruled in *Ashcroft* v. *Iqbal* that the Attorney General's approval of selective use of immigration law to round up Islamists in the wake of the September 11 attacks may be shielded from litigation unless the complaint alleges, plausibly, that the AG acted on racial or religious grounds rather than permissibly to protect the safety of American citizens.

On the other hand, Congress has acted to provide a measure of recompense for individuals who successfully defend themselves in litigation with the government. Under the Equal Access to Justice Act (EAJA), individuals who prevail in litigation against the federal government can recover both their costs and, in the discretion of the district judge, their attorney fees, at least where the government's position in the litigation was not substantially justified.[47] The EAJA thus affords a measure of compensation for the out-of-pocket costs incurred in fending off claims by the federal government that lack a reasonable basis in law and fact. But the EAJA does not offer compensation for the dignitary and reputational injuries that individuals may suffer in the course of defending against groundless claims and thus fails to address the injuries that moved both Merriam and Economou to sue.

OFFICER SUITS AT THE STATE AND LOCAL LEVEL AND SECTION 1983

So far, the chapter has focused on suits against federal officials, but state officials face a broad range of similar litigation in state and federal court. State law (including state tort and administrative law) certainly regulates the manner in which state and local officials interact with the public, and state courts frequently hear claims against state actors. In addition, the federal Constitution and federal statutes impose a variety of restrictions on state and local government activity. Surely the most important rights-conferring con-stitutional provision, the Fourteenth Amendment, declares that no state shall deny any person due process of law or equal protection of the laws.[48] Ratified as part of Reconstruction, the Fourteenth Amendment imposes direct limits on state action and has provided the vehicle through which the Supreme Court has

---

[47] EAJA, Act of October 21, 1980, Pub. L. 96–481, § 204, 94 Stat. 2327 et seq., codified as 5 U.S.C.A. § 504, and 28 U.S.C. § 2412. See generally Pierce v. Underwood, 487 U.S. 552 (1988) (finding that the government's position would qualify as substantially justified under the EAJA if it was "justified in the main – that is, justified to a degree that would satisfy a reasonable person").

[48] U.S. Const., am. 14.

made other federal constitutional guarantees applicable to the states. At roughly the same time, Congress adopted civil rights legislation aimed at enforcing the Fourteenth Amendment's protections for newly freed slaves and other vulnerable minorities. Section 1983 empowers individuals who suffer any deprivation of their federal constitutional or statutory rights *under color of state law* to sue for damages and injunctive relief. Anticipating the *Bivens* decision by a decade, the Supreme Court held that section 1983 claims may go forward in federal court even where state law and state courts promise remedies for the same misconduct.[49]

Section 1983 litigation exploded in the 1960s and 1970s, reflecting the rights consciousness of the civil rights revolution, the rise of public interest litigation, and the Court's willingness to recognize new constitutional limits on state action.[50] Congress supported these developments, at least initially. Legislation adopted in 1976 enabled successful civil rights' litigants to obtain an award of attorney's fees payable by state or local government defendants.[51] A period of retrenchment ensued, during which the Court narrowed the range of federal statutes that individuals can enforce through section 1983 claims,[52] limited the scope of certain constitutional protections,[53] and considerably expanded the scope of qualified immunity.[54] Congress joined the process of retrenchment in the mid-1990s, with the adoption of the Prison Litigation Reform Act (PLRA).[55] The PLRA requires prisoners to exhaust remedies before filing suit in federal court and imposes other restrictions on prisoner litigation. Much section 1983 litigation targets prison officials and street-level law enforcement officials. The focus on relief from individual officers reflects the Supreme Court's ruling that state-level agencies and departments are not proper parties to join as defendants in section 1983 litigation.[56]

---

[49] See Monroe v. Pape, 365 U.S. 167 (1961).

[50] See Eisenberg and Schwab, The Reality of Constitutional Tort Litigation, 72 *Cornell L. Rev.* 641 (1987) (reporting that filings grew from 200 cases per year in 1960 to more than 40,000 per year in the 1980s).

[51] See 42 U.S.C. § 1988.

[52] See, e.g., Gonzaga University v. Doe, 536 U.S. 273 (2002) (plaintiffs may use section 1983 to enforce only those federal statutes that specifically create a federal right in individuals).

[53] See, e.g., Daniels v. Williams, 474 U.S. 327 (1986) (merely negligent conduct on the part of state officials does not occasion a deprivation of liberty or property triggering Fourteenth Amendment scrutiny).

[54] See Pearson v. Callahan, 555 U.S. 223 (2009) (permitting lower courts to dismiss on qualified immunity grounds any time the claim fails to allege violation of a right "clearly established" in controlling federal law).

[55] See Prisoner Litigation Reform Act, 110 Stat. 1321 (1996). For evidence that the PLRA cut back significantly on the number of prison claims, both by imposing a filing fee requirement and by limiting the amount of attorney's fees, see Margo Schlanger, Inmate Litigation, 116 *Harv. L. Rev.* 1555 (2003).

[56] See Will v. Michigan Dep't of State Police, 491 U.S. 58 (1989) (a state agency or department is not a "person" subject to liability under the terms of section 1983). Cf. Monell v. Dep't of Social Servs., 436 U.S. 658 (1978) (local governmental bodies are "persons" subject to suit under section 1983).

In many contexts, section 1983 operates much like the *Bivens* remedy in enabling those injured by allegedly unconstitutional government conduct to seek an award of damages. Many of the same limitations apply, including the doctrine of qualified immunity.[57] The deliberate judicial expansion of immunity doctrine was initially justified as a way to protect the officers who would otherwise face the prospect of personal liability for the torts they commit within the scope of their employment. But the practice of indemnity (which continued into the twentieth century and remains in place today) means that relatively few (if any) state or federal officers bear the ultimate cost associated with liability imposed on them in *Bivens* and section 1983 litigation. Rather, in virtually all cases, the government supplies an attorney and covers the cost of any damages awarded in the litigation.[58] As a practical matter, qualified immunity creates an additional margin of appreciation that operates in favor of government action. Courts defer to executive action unless it violates "clearly established" law.

By creating a qualified immunity doctrine that turned on the clarity of the legal norm, the Court invited lower courts to dismiss on immunity grounds without ever addressing the merits of the constitutional claim. That meant that some questions of constitutional law could go undecided on the basis that the norm, if any, was not established with the clarity to sustain an action for damages. For a time, the Court attempted to address the resulting stagnation of the law by directing lower courts to address the merits first and only then to consider the clarity of the norm's articulation for immunity purposes.[59] But lower courts chafed under the obligation to address hypothetical constitutional claims in cases where they would have preferred to dismiss on the ground that the right in question did not meet the clearly established threshold necessary to overcome immunity.[60] The Court retreated in *Pearson* v. *Callahan*, restoring the lower courts' discretion to dismiss on immunity grounds without first clarifying the legal norm.[61] At the same time, the Court recognized that lower courts might sensibly continue to reach the merits first in some cases, especially in areas of law where the "development of constitutional precedent" can be beneficial.[62]

Referred to in the literature as the "order of battle" problem, the problem of how to sequence the decision of constitutional tort claims was nicely illustrated

---

[57] See Butz v. Economou, 438 U.S. 478 (1978) (indicating that the doctrine of qualified immunity should operate the same way in suits against both federal and state officials).

[58] See Cornelia T. L. Pillard, Taking Fiction Seriously: The Strange Results of Public Officials' Individual Liability under *Bivens*, 88 *Geo. L. J.* 65 (1999) (reporting that indemnity is routinely paid in Bivens actions); Joanna Schwartz, Police Indemnification, 89 *N. Y. U. L. Rev.* 885 (2014) (concluding on the basis of a survey that governments almost invariably indemnify police officers held liable in section 1983 litigation).

[59] See Saucier v. Katz, 533 U.S. 194 (2001) (mandating a merits-first order of decision to facilitate the process of expounding and clarifying legal norms).

[60] Pierre Leval, Judging under the Constitution: Dicta about Dicta, 81 *N. Y. U. L. Rev.* 1249, 1275 (2006) (summarizing from a lower-court judge's perspective the problems with *Saucier*).

[61] Pearson v. Callahan, 555 U.S. 223 (2009).   [62] Id. at 240.

in the case of Sarah Greene. Her section 1983 claim against Bob Camreta, an Oregon child welfare caseworker, sought damages for the violation of her family's constitutional rights. Camreta was assigned to investigate Greene's husband, Nimrod, on charges that he had inappropriately touched the "private parts" of a neighborhood child. In the course of the investigation, Camreta and a uniformed deputy sheriff went to the elementary school to conduct a two-hour interview of one of Nimrod's children, S. G., in an effort to determine if Nimrod had touched her inappropriately. Eventually Camreta had the two children removed from Sarah and Nimrod's home and brought before a child welfare agency for a sexual abuse examination that Sarah was not permitted to attend. Nimrod's criminal trial resulted in a hung jury, and he later accepted a plea to the abuse claim involving the neighbor child in exchange for dismissal of the abuse claims involving his own children.[63]

Sarah's complaint against Camreta highlighted three features of the investigation: the two-hour interview of her daughter, the removal of her two children from the home, and the sexual abuse examination. Although the district court dismissed all of the claims, citing the absence of clearly established law and invoking the officers' qualified immunity from suit, the Ninth Circuit reinstated Greene's claims relating to the removal of the children and her exclusion from the examination. As for the interview, the Ninth Circuit took a more cautious approach. It first found that Camreta's at-school interview constituted a seizure of S. G. within the meaning of the Fourth Amendment and further found that the seizure could be justified only through the issuance of a warrant or by securing parental consent. Because Camreta had obtained no such authorization, his interview was said to violate the Constitution.[64]

That did not end the court's analysis, however. Following the Supreme Court's lead,[65] the Ninth Circuit first reached the merits of the constitutional claim and only then turned to consider whether the law was established with the clarity needed to overcome Camreta's qualified immunity. The court found that it was not. Most of the prior cases involving the seizure of minors in sexual abuse investigations had taken place in connection with in-home interviews; the Ninth Circuit had not previously extended those precedents to interviews conducted at the school. As a result, despite the fact that Greene's rights were said to have been violated by the interview, no remedy in the form of an award of damages could be authorized against the official defendants.

Camreta and the Oregon state lawyers who were assisting with his defense thus faced a curious procedural predicament.[66] Although Camreta had

---

[63] See Greene v. Camreta, 588 F.3d 1011, 1016–20 (9th Cir. 2009) (recounting background).

[64] Id. at 1030.

[65] See Pearson v. Callahan, 555 U.S. 223 (2009) (permitting lower courts to address the merits first before deciding if the right was sufficiently well established to overcome qualified immunity).

[66] Camreta, an employee of the Oregon Department of Human Services, was represented in the Ninth Circuit by the Oregon state attorney general and solicitor general, among others. See Greene v. Camreta, 588 F.3d at 1015.

nominally won on the interview issue, in the sense that the claims for money damages against him had been dismissed, he was subject to a Ninth Circuit ruling that effectively prohibited him (and other Oregon child abuse caseworkers) from conducting in-school interviews without obtaining a warrant or the consent of the parents. The Ninth Circuit decision, in short, established a precedent that was meant to control assessments of the legality of caseworker interviews into the future. Yet, as a prevailing party on the issue, Camreta could not normally seek review of the decision in the Supreme Court. Parties can typically appeal only from adverse decisions.

Camreta (and Oregon) sought review nonetheless and persuaded the Supreme Court to hear the case. The challenge for the Court on appeal was how to square its body of qualified immunity law with the rules that govern appellate review. Camreta's only grievance with the Ninth Circuit's resolution lay in the decision's *future* impact on his ability to conduct in-school interviews. One supposes that Camreta himself may not have cared too much about the way the decision would structure investigations in the future; he could still either obtain a warrant or secure parental consent. More likely it was the state of Oregon, acting through lawyers in the offices of the attorney and solicitor general, that objected to the Ninth Circuit rule. In a world where constitutional protections limit the use of in-home interviews, the ability of caseworkers to conduct at-school interviews may have been seen as a valuable workaround. But as a non-party, the state could not well invoke its own interest in at-school interviews as a justification for seeking review.

Instead, the state pressed and the Court accepted the interests of Camreta as a justification for intervention. He remained a caseworker and could find the ruling below a potential hurdle to overcome in future child sexual abuse investigations. In this way, Oregon persuaded the Court that Camreta was an aggrieved party for purposes of appellate review. That means that the Court can continue to oversee the body of law that develops in connection with decisions, like that of the Ninth Circuit, that rule in favor of plaintiffs generally on the merits and in favor of the state official on the qualified immunity defense. As the Court explained, such decisions serve primarily to "have a significant future effect on the conduct of public officials."[67] They have scarcely anything to do with the provision of a remedy for the violation of a constitutional right, and they do not seem to fit well with other cases that foreswear judicial involvement except where the parties present concrete and immediate opposing interests.[68]

Camreta thus offers a window into the current model of constitutional tort litigation and reveals the vast changes that have occurred since the matter-of-fact award of damages in *Merriam v. Mitchell*. There, the jury was the institution of first resort, having been asked to evaluate the tort claims that grew out of

---

[67] Camreta v. Greene, 563 U.S. 692, 704 (2011).

[68] In Camreta, no such contest presented itself, thereby leading the Court to dismiss the case as moot. Id. at 710.

Merriam's eventual exoneration on criminal charges. In *Camreta*, and other constitutional tort claims today, by contrast, the jury serves as an institution of last resort, impaneled only in those rare cases in which, after the courts have clarified the law, the record reveals a disputed issue of material fact. The claims of the plaintiff, though motivated by a desire to secure recompense and a vindication of her rights, often serve as a vehicle to clarify applicable law. The Ninth Circuit opined on the at-school interview solely for the purpose of guiding future official conduct, and the Court was similarly motivated in agreeing to put in place a mechanism that would allow it to review such decisions.

CONCLUSION

Despite sweeping changes in the nature of litigation with the government, the suit to impose damages liability on government officers continues to play a role in the web of remedies available to citizens caught up in government regulation. When Merriam sued, common law provided the agreed-upon measure of legality. Immunity attached to only a modest slice of claims and, insofar as it applied to executive branch officials, only where it had been legislated into place. (Legislators and judges enjoyed common law immunity.) Litigation proceeded in state courts of general jurisdiction, eventually resulting in trial by jury. Indemnity was routinely available for defendants held personally liable for action taken in the course of their employment. Issues of mental state – the level of malice or intent underlying the official conduct in question – were for the jury to decide. For many trespassory torts, as was the case in *Merriam v. Mitchell*, even good faith errors in judgment could result in liability when the officer invaded a liberty interest.

By the end of the twentieth century, much of this had changed. Congress had absolutely immunized federal officers from liability based on common law tort claims; the federal government had accepted a portion of that liability instead, based on theories of respondeat superior. But the government did not agree to take responsibility for liability resulting from discretionary acts or from many of the intentional torts that had been the workhorses of government accountability litigation in the nineteenth century. Thus, the FTCA forecloses liability based on assault, battery, false imprisonment, false arrest, malicious prosecution, abuse of process, libel, slander, misrepresentation, deceit, or interference with contractual rights.[69] The modest restoration of liability for the acts or omissions of law enforcement officers extended only to assault, battery, false imprisonment, false arrest, malicious prosecution, and abuse of process.

The shift away from officer suits in tort as a tool of ensuring official compliance with law corresponded both with the rise of the administrative state and with the creation of alternative statutory remedies to address most claims of illegality. As we have seen, moreover, the *Bivens* action (for federal

[69] 28 U.S.C. 2680(h).

officials) and section 1983 (for state and local officials) provided a basis for constitutional tort liability that served in part to replace the nineteenth century's reliance on the common law tort liability system. Yet the *Bivens* claim has been hedged about by restrictions unknown at common law. Rather than offering litigants an absolute right to pursue violations, *Bivens* instituted a regime in which the federal courts exercise discretion in deciding whether to permit individuals to assert constitutional tort claims. By treating *Bivens* as a fallback remedy, federal courts refuse to permit damage claims in connection with a broad range of alleged constitutional violations. To the extent that *Bivens* has been read to bar claims that section 1983 would allow to proceed against state officials, moreover, government accountability law may turn on the identity of the defendant and the defendant's employer.[70]

Stepping back from the particular features of the *Bivens* and section 1983 remedies, one can raise significant questions about the wisdom of continuing to rely on suits against officers rather than suits against the governmental entity itself. Some scholars argue that the entity suit would perform more effectively in deterring government misconduct.[71] On this view, supervisory officials, facing the threat of departmental liability, would adopt a combination of incentives to shape the behavior of their subordinates so as to better ensure compliance with the law. Just as firms predictably take steps to reduce the expected cost of accidents when forced to internalize the costs of the torts their employees commit, so too one might expect that state and federal governments will take cost-effective steps to reduce expected liability for constitutional torts.

But two problems may undercut the effectiveness of what one might term the "internal check" on lawless government action. First, there may be a simple shortage of applicable law, a situation that the order of battle problem created by the doctrine of qualified immunity may exacerbate. To the extent that the absence of clear law leaves governmental actors in the dark about the legality of certain programs, one might argue that the federal courts should invigorate the *Bivens* doctrine to produce a broader range of guidance. They could achieve this result by broadening the right to sue and narrowing the scope of qualified immunity.[72] The internal check may fail for a second reason: excessive government zeal. Zeal can take many forms and can doubtless help to supply the "energy" for which the executive branch of government was lauded during the founding era. But excessive zeal can produce oppressive government action, as the homely case of *Merriam* v. *Mitchell* may illustrate. The imperfect quality

---

[70] See Pfander and Baltmanis, supra note 31 (highlighting the problems associated with disparate treatment of state and federal officials sued for constitutional torts).

[71] See Peter Schuck, *Suing Government: Citizen Remedies for Official Wrongs* (1984).

[72] I have suggested in earlier work that the federal courts might enhance their ability to expound the law by declaring the doctrine of qualified immunity inapplicable to claims for nominal damages. See James E. Pfander, *Resolving the Qualified Immunity Dilemma: Constitutional Tort Claims for Nominal Damages*, 111 *Colum. L. Rev.* 1601 (2011).

of the internal check suggests a continuing need for some form of external judicial test of the legality of government action.

How should one assess the wisdom of the current balance between official accountability and immunity? Officials within the executive branch genuinely believe that far too much frivolous litigation already makes its way into the federal judicial system. Indeed, some lower courts came to agree that Justice Rehnquist was right to characterize Arthur Economou's claim as frivolous in the extreme. His litigation with the Department of Agriculture and with other agencies (the Commodity Futures Trading Commission, the Securities Exchange Commission) continued well into the 1980s, and one court later imposed sanctions on him and characterized his business as little more than a Ponzi scheme.[73] But one cannot evaluate officer litigation by simply assessing the merits of two or three iconic cases. Many meritorious cases settle and many never give rise to the assertion of a claim. Those with meritorious claims may doubt the wisdom or efficacy of such litigation.

All in all, the complexity of modern government accountability litigation can make one yearn for the comparative simplicity of the early nineteenth century. Before being overtaken by entity suits under the FTCA, displaced by the Westfall Act, and subsumed in some forms of *Bivens* litigation, common law adjudication offered individuals like William Merriam a relatively simple remedy for government misconduct. His common law tort claim resulted in a jury verdict aimed at compensating him for mistreatment he received at the hands of his employer, the federal postal service. Just as the Maine courts trusted the jury to do right by Merriam, so might we trust the jury today to distinguish between frivolous and meritorious claims.[74] Rather than have our courts attempt to sniff out frivolous claims on the basis of the pleadings, we might do better simply to trust the jury to get it right. One suspects that a jury of their peers would have had little difficulty in rejecting the claims of Spalding and Economou.

---

[73] SEC v. American Board of Trade, Inc., 830 F.2d 431, 433 (2d Cir. 1987).

[74] On jury trial as protection against federal overreach, Essay of a Democratic Federalist, *Penn. Herald*, Oct. 12, 1787, reprinted in 3 *The Complete Antifederalist* 58, 61 (Herbert J. Storing ed., 1981).

13

Habeas Corpus

Amanda L. Tyler

> The Privilege of the Writ of Habeas Corpus shall not be suspended, unless when in Cases of Rebellion or Invasion the public Safety may require it.[1]

The habeas corpus provision in the US Constitution, known as the Suspension Clause, has long confounded courts and scholars as to its intended purpose. The wording of the clause seems to promise the availability of "[t]he Privilege of the Writ of Habeas Corpus" – or at least preclude Congress from undermining that privilege where it is otherwise available unless Congress takes the dramatic step of enacting suspension legislation. The very same clause, recognizing the extraordinary nature of suspension, precludes the legislature from adopting such a state of affairs except in the face of rare and dire circumstances – namely, in "Cases of Rebellion or Invasion." But beyond these apparent truths, numerous questions going to the nature and purpose of the habeas clause remain.

For example, what precisely does the "privilege of the writ of habeas corpus" protected in the Constitution actually embody? More specifically, does the "privilege" merely encompass a right of access to judicial review, or does it encompass an additional array of protections from government intrusions upon individual liberty? Further, may any person arrested and detained by the US government invoke the protections embodied in the Suspension Clause, or is its application more limited in scope? If the latter proposition controls, what is the critical distinction that triggers protection under the clause? Finally, does the Suspension Clause constrain the US government wherever it operates, or is its application limited by matters of geography? In the wake of the terrorist attacks of September 11, 2001, the Supreme Court has faced each of these questions in headline-grabbing cases, offering a range of answers.[2]

---

[1] U.S. Const. art. I, § 9, cl. 2.

[2] *See* Boumediene v. Bush, 553 U.S. 723 (2008) (holding that the Suspension Clause entitles noncitizen detainees held as enemy combatants at Guantánamo Bay to judicial review of their detentions); Hamdi v. Rumsfeld, 542 U.S. 507, 519 (2004) (plurality opinion) (concluding that

Tackling these and other questions going to the role of the Suspension Clause in the US constitutional framework requires careful study of the backdrop against which the founding generation adopted the clause. The writ of habeas corpus was, after all, an institution born of English legal origins, and it is imperative to understand those origins if one is to make sense of how they informed the early development of American law and ultimately the Suspension Clause. This chapter tells that story and carries it forward to chronicle how the Suspension Clause has been interpreted during pivotal episodes in American history. As will be seen, political and legal actors through Reconstruction consistently understood the constitutional privilege to prevent the government from detaining persons who could claim the protection of domestic law outside the criminal process. Suspension, in turn, served as the exclusive vehicle through which such detentions could be made legal. But as will also be seen, with the detention of Japanese Americans during World War II and the sanctioning of the concept of a citizen enemy combatant as part of the war on terrorism, the long-accepted suspension model broke down.

THE ENGLISH ORIGINS OF HABEAS CORPUS AND SUSPENSION

"The Privilege of the Writ of Habeas Corpus" and the concept of suspension both trace their origins to English judicial and parliamentary practice. Studying this English backdrop and how it influenced the development of early American law is therefore enormously important to understanding the backdrop against which the founding generation wrote the US Constitution.

The story begins with the common law writ of habeas corpus *ad subjiciendum*, a judicial creation that demanded cause for a prisoner's detention from his jailer.[3] As historian Paul Halliday's work shows, the common law writ came into regular use in the seventeenth century as a "prerogative writ" – namely, as the embodiment of royal power invoked by the Court of King's Bench in aid of the king's obligation to look after his subjects.[4] Over time, English judges came to employ the writ as a tool for inquiring into both the cause of the initial arrest and the continued detention of those who could claim the protection of domestic law.[5] Nonetheless, early in the seventeenth century, royal courts regularly countenanced

---

there is no constitutional bar on the detention without criminal charges of a citizen enemy combatant in the absence of a suspension); *see also* Rumsfeld v. Padilla, 542 U.S. 426, 451 (2004) (involving similar questions).

[3] This writ, also called "*ad subjiciendum et recipiendum*," translates as "to undergo and receive" the "corpus," or body, of the prisoner. The writ was directed to the relevant custodian, or jailor, who had custody of the prisoner.

[4] Paul D. Halliday, *Habeas Corpus: From England to Empire* 9 (2010). As Halliday recounts, in 1619, Chief Justice Sir Henry Montagu described "habeas corpus as a 'writ of the prerogative by which the king demands account for his subject who is restrained of his liberty.'" *Id.* at 65 (quoting (1619) Palmer 54, 81 Eng. Rep. 975 (K.B.)).

[5] Halliday, *supra* note 4, at 48–53.

returns (answers filed by a prisoner's jailor) to the writ citing the king's command to imprison as sufficient justification to detain (or at least sufficient to preclude judicial inquiry into detention), based on the contemporary understanding that the crown's directives themselves constituted the "law of the land."[6]

Over the course of the seventeenth century, judicial and legislative developments moved toward rejecting the idea that the royal command alone might constitute legitimate cause to arrest and detain. From an American standpoint, a critical moment in the story by which the English law of habeas corpus did so came with the passage of the English Habeas Corpus Act of 1679. Parliament's adoption of the Habeas Corpus Act coincided with the rise of parliamentary supremacy and a broader parliamentary effort to take control over matters of detention from the monarch and its courts. With the act, Parliament now controlled and defined what constituted legal cause to detain and royal fiat ceased to suffice. In short order, moreover, Parliament created a counterpart to the act's protections – namely, the concept of suspension, which Parliament designed as a tool it could invoke during wartime in order to legalize arrests made outside the criminal process, arrests that otherwise would have resulted in discharge of the prisoner under the terms of the Habeas Corpus Act.

The English Habeas Corpus Act of 1679 proved the culmination of a lengthy effort during the seventeenth century, spearheaded at its origins by John Selden and Sir Edward Coke, to secure strict limitations on what would constitute legitimate "cause" for detention of individuals by the crown.[7] The act, titled "An Act for the better secureing the Liberty of the Subject and for Prevention of Imprisonments beyond the Seas," declared that it was intended to address "great Delayes" by jailers "in makeing Returnes of Writts of Habeas Corpus to them directed" as well as other abuses undertaken "to avoid their yeilding Obedience to such Writts."[8] Toward that end, the act declared that it was "[f]or the prevention whereof and the more speedy Releife of all persons imprisoned for any such criminall or supposed criminall Matters." Accordingly, the Habeas Corpus Act's focus – cases involving persons imprisoned "for any Criminall or supposed Criminall Matter" – served to underscore its close connection to the criminal process. The act quickly came to be understood as embracing not just the cases of ordinary criminals but domestic enemies of the state as well.

---

[6] *See, e.g.*, Darnel's Case, (1627) 3 *Cobbett's Complete Collection of State Trials* 1, 59 (K.B.) (Eng.) (often called the "Case of the Five Knights").

[7] For an explication of the period leading up to enactment of the English Habeas Corpus Act, consult Amanda L. Tyler, A "Second Magna Carta": The English Habeas Corpus Act and the Statutory Origins of the Habeas Privilege, 91 *Notre Dame L. Rev.* 1949 (2016); *see also* Amanda L. Tyler, *Habeas Corpus in Wartime: From the Tower of London to Guantanamo Bay* 13–32 (2017) [hereinafter *Habeas Corpus in Wartime*]

[8] 1679, 31 Car. 2, c. 2, § 1 (Eng.), *reprinted in* 3 *The Founder's Constitution* 310 (Philip B. Kurland and Ralph Lerner eds. 1987). By its terms, the act sought to remedy the fact that "many of the King's subjects have beene and hereafter may be long detained in Prison in such Cases where by Law they are baylable." *Id.*

Many of the act's provisions codified preexisting, though not necessarily uniformly followed, judicial practices tied to the common law writ. It is therefore important to understand that in operation the act served to complement the common law writ, using it as a vehicle for enforcing its terms. (The common law writ, as Blackstone noted, also continued to serve as a method for redress available in "all ... cases of unjust imprisonment" that were not covered by the act.[9]) This being said, with the act , Parliament took control over a good deal of habeas law from the courts, and it did so with a statute that by its terms required courts to follow its mandates under threat of penalty.[10] The third section of the act set forth procedures for obtaining writs during court vacation periods, and later sections provided that the act would reach so-called "privileged places" and other areas previously beyond the range of habeas courts.[11] The seventh section of the act, in turn, made clear the connection between the writ of habeas corpus and the criminal process. It covered "any person or persons ... committed for High Treason or Fellony" and provided that where a prisoner committed on this basis was not indicted within two court terms (a period typically spanning only three to six months), the judges of King's Bench and other criminal courts were "*required* ... to sett at Liberty the Prisoner upon Baile."[12] Further, the section declared that "if any person or persons committed as aforesaid ... shall not be indicted and tryed the second Terme ... or upon his Tryall shall be acquitted, he shall be discharged from his Imprisonment."[13]

Thus, in its seventh section the English Habeas Corpus Act promised release to those held for criminal or "supposed" criminal matters, including even the most dangerous of suspects – those detained on accusations of treason – where they were not timely tried.[14] Indeed, those held for suspected treason during the Jacobite Wars of the late seventeenth and eighteenth centuries and later during the American Revolution routinely invoked the act's protections to their benefit,

---

[9] 3 *Blackstone's Commentaries* *137 (observing that "all other cases of unjust imprisonment" not covered by the act were "left to the *habeas corpus* at common law").

[10] 31 Car. 2, c. 2, § 10.

[11] Paul Halliday's work shows that vacation writs were sometimes issued before the act, *see* Halliday, *supra* note 4, at 55–56, but that the practice was far from uniform and courts denied such writs in several high-profile cases in the decade leading up to the English Act, *see id.* at 236–37, 239. Halliday's work documents a similar story with respect to the Privy Council's practice of sending prisoners to legal islands, detailing one case in which the passage of the act made all the difference. *See id.* at 240; *see also id.* at 231 (detailing additional cases).

[12] 31 Car. 2, c. 2, § 7 (emphasis added). Over time, the relevant language moved from section 7 to section 6 of the act.

[13] *Id.* Judges initially often evaded the act's protections by setting excessive bail; for that reason, the Declaration of Rights in 1689 declared that courts should not require excessive bail. *See* Declaration of Rights, 1688, 1 W. & M., sess. 2, c. 2, § 1 (Eng.).

[14] Chief Justice John Holt wrote shortly after passage of the English Act that its "design ... was to prevent a man's lying under an accusation for treason, &c. above two terms." Crosby's Case, (1694) 88 Eng. Rep. 1167 (K.B.) 1168 (Holt, C.J.).

either to force timely trial on criminal charges or to secure their discharge.[15] There was no such thing as detention for military purposes of those who could claim the protection of domestic law. Instead, the act promised such persons that they must be afforded the protections of the criminal process in a timely fashion or else be discharged. Nor did the act include any exceptions for times of war. It is for this very reason that Parliament invented the concept of suspension as a tool for displacing the protections associated with the Habeas Corpus Act.

As events unfolded, it took Parliament only ten years to invent the concept of suspension. Careful study of the historical episodes of suspension during the late seventeenth and eighteenth centuries demonstrates that the purpose consistently animating those suspensions was to empower the executive to arrest suspected traitors outside the formal criminal process. To take but one of many examples, the very first suspension, which came in the immediate wake of the Glorious Revolution, dramatically expanded the authority of the crown in the face of threats to the throne. William, having just been crowned in place of the dethroned James Stuart, asked Parliament in 1689 to suspend the Habeas Corpus Act in order to arrest solely on suspicion Jacobite supporters who sought to return the Stuart line to power. As his emissary conveyed the request to Parliament, the king sought the power to confine persons "committed on suspicion of Treason only," lest they be "deliver[ed]" by habeas corpus.[16] Parliament obliged, and in so doing, it created a dramatic emergency power.

Numerous attempts by the Jacobites to regain the British throne, combined with constant fighting with France, led to a host of suspensions in the decades that followed, with the last of these suspensions coming in response to the Jacobite Rebellion in Scotland in 1745. In each of these suspensions, Parliament empowered the crown to arrest those believed to pose a danger to the state on suspicion alone and detain them for the duration of the suspension without obligation to try them on criminal charges. Notably, in every one of these episodes, suspension was understood to set aside the protections set forth in the seventh section of the act as well as any complementary common law habeas role for the courts. Accordingly, as it came to be established in English law during the period leading up to the Revolutionary War, the suspension model contemplated that it was only by a suspension of the Habeas Corpus Act that detention outside the criminal process of persons

---

[15] For details on many such cases, consult generally Tyler, *Habeas Corpus in Wartime, supra* note 7, at 35–61; Amanda L. Tyler, Habeas Corpus and the American Revolution, 103 *Calif. L. Rev.* 635 (2015).

[16] 9 *Debates of the House of Commons, from the Year 1667 to the Year 1694,* at 129–30 (Anchitell Grey ed., London, n. pub. 1763) (remarks of Richard Hampden). For discussion of this suspension and its extensions, along with subsequent suspensions during the decades that followed, consult Amanda L. Tyler, The Forgotten Core Meaning of the Suspension Clause, 125 *Harv. L. Rev.* 901, 934–44 (2012).

who could claim the protection of domestic law could be made lawful –
even in wartime.[17]

CROSSING THE ATLANTIC

Although these principles were well settled by the middle of the eighteenth
century, the American Revolutionary War placed tremendous pressure on each
of them in turn. Further, the movement for independence proved an opportunity
for the Americans to embrace the Habeas Corpus Act as their own in structuring
their new legal frameworks. In time, the early American experience, which
understood all too well the role of suspension as an emergency power as well
as its potential for abuse, influenced the drafting of a Constitution that carefully
delineated the circumstances when suspension could be considered.

Part of understanding how the story played out requires recognizing how
deeply the colonists resented the fact that they had been consistently denied the
protections of the Habeas Corpus Act in America. Thus, to take but one of
many examples, in 1774, the Continental Congress decried the fact that
colonists were "the subjects of an arbitrary government, deprived of trial by
jury, and when imprisoned cannot claim the benefit of the habeas corpus Act,
that great bulwark and palladium of English liberty."[18] Such complaints
followed on the heels of several failed efforts by various colonies to adopt the
act for themselves. Why did the colonists care so much about the English act? A
big part of the answer lies not just in their collective experience in being denied
the act's protections but also in the fact that they were heavily steeped in
Blackstone, whose lectures published in 1765 glorified the Act as a "bulwark"
of "personal liberty" and a "second *magna carta*."[19] The Americans wanted to
enjoy the benefits of this second Magna Carta too.

As things unfolded, this patchwork legal framework – the act applying in
some areas but not in others – came to play a major role in how the British
treated American prisoners, so-called "Rebels," when captured during the war.
The stories of two prominent American prisoners detained in England during

---

[17] All this being said, during this same period, Parliament also often availed itself of its jealously
guarded power of attainder as a separate means to circumvent the protections of the Habeas
Corpus Act. For more details, consult Tyler, *Habeas Corpus in Wartime, supra* note 7, at 43–47.
Notably, suspension was not understood as necessary to detain for preventive purposes those
properly classified as prisoners of war. *See* Matthew Hale, 1 *Historia Placitorum Coronae: The
History of the Pleas of the Crown* 159 (Sollom Emlyn ed., Philadelphia, Robert H. Small 1847)
("[T]hose that raise war against the king may be of two kinds, subjects or foreigners: the former
are not properly enemies but rebels or traitors . . . ."). For elaboration of this important distinction, consult Halliday, *supra* note 4, at 170–73.
[18] [1774] 1 *Journals of the Continental Congress 1774–1789*, at 88 (Worthington Chauncey Ford
ed., 1904); *see also id.* at 107–8 (reiterating same complaints) (replicating Lettre Adressée aux
Habitans de la Province de Quebec (Oct. 26, 1774)).
[19] 1 Blackstone, at *126, *131, *133.

this period underscore the important role that the act, its geographic sweep, and its suspension played in the governing legal calculus during the war.

ETHAN ALLEN AND HIS GREEN MOUNTAIN BOYS

In September 1775, after having seized the important strategic post of Fort Ticonderoga in New York from the British, Captain Ethan Allen and his Green Mountain Boys headed north to Canada with the goal of capturing the city of Montreal. The poorly planned endeavor ended quickly with their capture. Once in the custody of British General Richard Prescott, Allen reported that he was treated badly and threatened with a traitor's execution. According to Allen's versions of the events, Prescott said: "I will not execute you now; but you shall grace a halter at Tyburn, God damn you."[20] In short order, British Lieutenant Governor Cramahé ordered Allen along with his cohort of "Rebel Prisoners" dispatched to England because he had "no proper Place to confine them in, or Troops to guard Them" in Canada.[21] After a weeks-long journey across the Atlantic Ocean, the prisoners landed in Falmouth, England, days before Christmas in December 1775.

Upon their arrival, Allen and his Boys were imprisoned by the British at Pendennis Castle in Cornwall. If Allen's personal *Narrative* (first published in 1779 and widely read in America[22]) is to be believed, people "came in great numbers out of curiosity, to see [him]."[23] But within only days of Allen's arrival, the British legal elite met and decided to send Allen and his fellow Rebels back to America as soon as possible. As Lord George Germain, Secretary of State for the Americas, wrote to the Lords of the Admiralty immediately after the meeting, it was "The King's Pleasure" that Allen and the other prisoners be removed to his Majesty's ship *Solebay*, which should "put to Sea with the first fair wind" and set course for Boston, where the prisoners were to be turned over to British General Howe.[24] After less than two weeks in England, Allen found himself headed back to America. Why?

The answer to this question reveals a great deal about the status of Anglo-American habeas law during this important period. In addition to political calculations stemming from apparent uncertainty on the part of the

---

[20] Ethan Allen, *A Narrative of Colonel Ethan Allen's Captivity, Written by Himself* 36 (Burlington, Vermont, H. Johnson & Co. 3d ed. 1838) [hereinafter Allen Narrative] (reporting Prescott's statement).

[21] Extract of Letter from Lieutenant Governor Cramahé to the Earl of Dartmouth (Nov. 9, 1775), The National Archives (Great Britain) [hereinafter TNA] SP 44/91/443.

[22] Initially, the book published in installments in, among other places, the *Pennsylvania Packet*. *See, e.g.*, Pa. Packet or Gen. Advertiser (Nov. 11, 1779) (publishing one portion discussing Allen's return to America).

[23] Allen Narrative, *supra* note 20, at 50; *see also id.* at 55–56.

[24] Letter from Lord George Germain to the Lords Commanders of the Admiralty (Dec. 27, 1775), TNA CO 5/122/398.

Administration as to whether it thought it could successfully prosecute the Rebels as traitors, there is extensive contemporary evidence to suggest that efforts were under way to invoke the protections of the English Habeas Corpus Act on behalf of Allen and his fellow Rebels in the British courts. For example, *The Annual Register* for 1775 reported of the prisoners: "[W]hilst their friends in London were preparing to bring them up by *habeas corpus*, to have the legality of their confinement discussed, they were sent back to North-America to be exchanged."[25] Similar stories ran in multiple other British papers during this time, including several that named prominent habeas counsel with ties to the American cause as having taken on the case. Further, one London newspaper specifically identified (and criticized) the administration's desire "to elude the Habeas Corpus Act" as the reason for sending Allen back to America.[26]

The internal documents of British officials confronting the question of what to do with Allen and the other Rebels also show a desire to make the problems posed by Allen's detention in England go away – and fast. As one admiralty lord wrote just days after Allen's arrival in England, the administration's "principal object" must be "to get the prisoners out of reach as soon as possible."[27] Out of reach of what? The answer, most likely, was the English courts, where a subject like Allen held on English soil had the right to invoke the protections of the Habeas Corpus Act and thereby force his trial or else secure his freedom.

As noted earlier, across the Atlantic, the Habeas Corpus Act was not in force, or at least that was the position to which the crown had subscribed for some time. Although several colonies had prominently attempted to adopt or invoke the protections of the Habeas Corpus Act as their own, they had met crown resistance at practically every turn. For example, in response to efforts in New York, Massachusetts, and North Carolina, the crown disclaimed operation of the English act in the colonies. In New York, for example, the colony's attempt to adopt the act met with James II's veto on the stated basis that "[t]his Priviledge is not granted to any of His Ma^{ts} Plantations where the Act of Habeas Corpus and all such other Bills do not take Place."[28]

---

[25] 18 *The Annual Register, or a View of the History, Politics, and Literature, for the Year 1775*, at 187 (London, J. Dodsley 1780). Allen wrote that once on board the *Solebay* his irons were removed and "[t]his remove was in consequence, as I have been since informed, of a writ of habeas corpus, which had been procured by some gentlemen in England, in order to obtain me my liberty." Allen Narrative, *supra* note 20, at 57–58.

[26] To the Printer of the Public Advertiser, *Pub. Advertiser*, Issue 14474 (Feb. 22, 1776) (referring to Allen's arrival in Corke as resulting from "a Violation of Law" and "criminal too, as it was notoriously done to elude the Habeas Corpus Act").

[27] Letter from Lord Hugh Palliser to the Earl of Sandwich (Dec. 29, 1775), *in* 1 *The Private Papers of John, Earl of Sandwich, First Lord of the Admiralty 1771–1782*, at 87 (G. R. Barnes and J. H. Owen eds., 1932).

[28] Observations upon the Charter of the Province of New-York, *in* 3 *Documents Relative to the Colonial History of the State of New-York* 357 (John Romeyn Brodhead ed., Albany, New York, Weed, Parsons & Co. 1853). For more details on this period, consult Tyler, *Habeas Corpus in Wartime*, *supra* note 7, at 63–98.

It followed that by sending Allen back across the Atlantic, the administration could avoid having to confront the Habeas Corpus Act's mandate that he be timely tried on criminal charges or else discharged. Also, in America, prisoner exchanges were up and running. It is important to note, however, that such exchanges did not follow under the king's formal sanction but instead by reason of "personal agreements" between Continental Army General George Washington and his British counterparts, first General Howe and then General Clinton. Indeed, Lord Germain took pains to remind General Howe that he was to effect exchanges "without the King's Dignity & Honor being committed, or His Majesty's Name used in any Negotiation for that purpose."[29] Entering a formal cartel with the Americans would have been tantamount to recognizing their American prisoners as being in the service of a foreign sovereign rather than traitors and rebels who needed to return to their proper allegiance.

THE AMERICAN REBELS LEARN ABOUT SUSPENSION

Ethan Allen was but a prelude to what was coming. Following the administration's decision to send him back to America, British ships arrived in a constant stream through 1776 to deposit American prisoners on British shores. These developments finally forced Parliament to address the legal status of American rebels held on English soil, where the Habeas Corpus Act was in full effect.

In early 1777, Lord North responded to these developments by invoking the same tool that earlier administrations had wielded during similar periods of unrest – he proposed a suspension. In introducing the measure to Parliament, Lord North explained:

[I]t had been customary upon similar occasions of rebellion, or danger of invasion, to enable the king to seize suspected persons ... But as the law stood ... it was not possible at present officially to apprehend the most suspected person ... It was necessary for the crown to have a power of confining them like other prisoners of war.[30]

In other words, the administration sought in the proposed legislation to legalize the detention of American Rebels without having to bring them to trial on criminal charges during the war.

---

[29] Letter from Lord George Germain to The Honorable Major General Howe (Feb. 1, 1776), TNA CO 5/93/16. In his own words, General Clinton refused to enter any formal cartel lest it "acknowledg[e] ... independency," and, like his predecessor, reached personal agreements with Washington to govern prisoner exchanges in America. *Massachusetts Historical Society, Report of Exchanges of Prisoners during the American Revolutionary War* 20 (Boston, 1861) (quoting Clinton).

[30] 19 *The Parliamentary History of England, from the Earliest Period to the Year 1803*, at 4 (London, T.C. Hansard 1814) [hereinafter Cobbett's Parliamentary History] (remarks of Lord Frederick North given to the House of Commons Feb. 6, 1777).

The bill, like the war that occasioned it, was controversial from the start. Those who opposed the bill doubted that it was needed. As one member of Parliament (who reportedly had earlier taken up Ethan Allen's case as counsel) argued, there was no active "rebellion within the kingdom," a fact that, in his view, eliminated any reason for a suspension. "Are we," he asked, "afraid that the people American will pass the Atlantic on a bridge, and come over and conquer us?"[31]

Despite the misgivings raised by several members who spoke during the debates, Parliament ultimately passed Lord North's measure by a substantial margin. As enacted, the suspension legislation applied only to persons suspected of the crimes of high treason or piracy committed in America or on the high seas and authorized their detention without bail or mainprize. In other words, Parliament was careful to target only Americans, and it did so for the purpose of addressing "a Rebellion and War [that] ha[s] been openly and traiterously levied and carried on in certain of his Majesty's Colonies and Plantations in *America*, and Acts of Treason and Piracy [that] have been committed on the High Seas." Acknowledging that many American prisoners "have been, or may be brought into this Kingdom, and into other Parts of his Majesty's Dominions," Parliament justified legislation modeled upon earlier suspension acts by the fact that "it may be inconvenient in many such Cases to proceed forthwith to the Trial of such Criminals, and at the same Time of evil Example to suffer them to go at large."[32]

Parliament subsequently extended the legislation multiple times to last through much of the war. Popularly known as North's Act, it quickly earned the ire of Americans, with George Washington complaining in his *Manifesto* that the British now sanctioned "arbitrary imprisonment" by reason of the "suspension of the Habeas Corpus Act."[33] On the ground, the act rendered lawful the indefinite detention without trial of almost 3,000 captured Americans brought to England during the war.

It was only once independence became a foregone conclusion that Parliament finally permitted the suspension to lapse, recognizing the law as no longer necessary to hold the remaining American prisoners on English soil without trial. This followed from the fact that as peace negotiations unfolded, Parliament declared that its government's relationship with the American

---

[31] *Id.* at 7 (remarks of John Dunning).

[32] An Act to Impower his Majesty to Secure and Detain Persons Charged with, or Suspected of, the Crime of High Treason, Committed in any of his Majesty's Colonies or Plantations in *America*, or on the High Seas, or the Crime of Piracy, 17 Geo. 3, c. 9 (1777) (Gr. Brit.); *see* 35 *H. L. Jour.* (1777) 78, 82–83 (Gr. Brit.) (noting royal assent given Mar. 3, 1777).

[33] George Washington, Manifesto of General Washington, Commander in Chief of the Forces of the United States of America, in Answer to General Burgoyne's Proclamation (July 19, 1777), *in* 47 *The Gentleman's Magazine, and Historical Chronicle for the Year 1777*, at 456–57 (Sylvanus Urban ed., London, D. Henry Sept. 1777), *reprinted in* Continental J. & Wkly. Advertiser (Boston) (Mar. 5, 1778), at 3.

prisoners – now viewed as in the service of a newly acknowledged (if not yet formally recognized) independent country – was no longer governed by domestic law but instead by the Law of Nations, which permitted the detention of prisoners of war without criminal trial for the purpose of preventing their return to the battlefield.[34]

TO THE TOWER FOR HENRY LAURENS

During the war, one prominent American who came to understand all too well the dramatic nature of suspension was Henry Laurens. The British captured Laurens, who had served as President of the Continental Congress earlier in the war, off the coast of Newfoundland in 1780 while he was en route aboard the *Mercury* to secure the support of the Netherlands for the American war effort. While under chase from the twenty-eight-gun British ship *Vestal*, Laurens burned or dumped overboard most of his papers in a desperate effort to destroy evidence of the purpose of his voyage. As Laurens soon learned, however, paper floats. Thus, his captors were able to recover a sufficient number of what he had dumped, including a draft treaty, to discern his charge and condemn him as a traitor.[35]

Laurens's captors transported him to England where, upon his arrival, he protested to no avail that he was an American ambassador and therefore his imprisonment violated international law. Of course, the British did not view him as an ambassador – he purported to be in the service of a country that did not exist in the eyes of the British – and instead they consistently treated him as a traitor.[36] In short order, the North Administration issued a warrant to commit Laurens to the Tower of London for high treason.[37] To the Tower Laurens went

[34] *See* An Act for the Better Detaining, and More Easy Exchange, of *American* Prisoners Brought into *Great Britain*, 1782, 22 Geo. 3, c. 10 (Gr. Brit.); *see also* 36 H. L. Jour. (1782) 425–26 (Gr. Brit.) (noting royal assent given Mar. 25, 1782). The statute declared that "it may and shall be lawful for his Majesty, during the Continuance of the present Hostilities, to hold and detain . . . as *Prisoners of War*, all Natives or other Inhabitants of the Thirteen revolted Colonies not at His Majesty's Peace." *Id.* The act likewise authorized the discharge or exchange of such prisoners "according to the Custom and Usage of War, and the Law of Nations . . . any Warrant of Commitment, or Cause therein expressed, or any Law, Custom, or Usage, to the contrary notwithstanding." *Id.*

[35] *See* Jack Rakove, *Revolutionaries: A New History of the Invention of America* 236–38 (2010) (detailing events); Henry Laurens, *Journal and Narrative of Capture and Confinement in the Tower of London* [hereinafter Laurens, *Narrative*], *in* 15 *The Papers of Henry Laurens: December 11, 1778–August 31, 1782*, at 332–35 (David R. Chestnut et al. eds., 2000). Based in part on this discovery, within months the British declared war on the Netherlands.

[36] *See* 15 *The Papers of Henry Laurens*, *supra* note 35, at 436 (replicating *Examination of Henry Laurens*, printed in *London Evening Post*, Oct. 5–7, 1780 ["When he was told that he was to be committed to the Tower, he told them it was violating the law of nations to detain an Ambassador . . . ."]); *see also* David Duncan Wallace, *The Life of Henry Laurens* 358–63 (1915).

[37] *See* Warrant for the Commitment of Henry Laurens to the Tower of London, TNA WO 94/10/518; SP 44/96/91; CO 5/43/485.

and remained – at his own expense, no less – for some fifteen months. (If you ask the yeoman warders at the Tower today, they will cheerfully point out where Laurens lived.) During this time, his family learned a powerful lesson in the importance of geography to the British legal framework. In England, Henry Laurens languished in the Tower as a state prisoner charged with treason. Meanwhile, British troops captured his son John after the fall of Charleston, South Carolina, where the Habeas Corpus Act did not apply, at least according to formal British policy. With there being no Habeas Corpus Act to "suspend," the British could theoretically detain American Rebels without charges on American soil. That said, because the British lacked any large prisons, they entered into a series of informal prisoner exchanges with the Americans. John Laurens was one of the beneficiaries, winning his parole through an exchange while his father remained a prisoner in the Tower.[38]

The British finally released the senior Laurens, but only after Edmund Burke interceded on his behalf and Laurens, promising to return to stand trial for high treason, secured approval by the Privy Council and posted bond before the Chief Justice of King's Bench, Lord Mansfield.[39] By the spring of 1782, with the North Administration having fallen and peace negotiations having begun, the British finally dropped any pretense of trying Laurens, discharging his obligation to appear for trial. The British then agreed to his exchange for General Cornwallis, who had surrendered at Yorktown in a defeat that turned the tide of the war in favor of the Americans. (Interestingly, Cornwallis also held the title of constable of the very Tower in which Laurens had been detained, and John Laurens had participated in the negotiations over the terms of Cornwallis's surrender at Yorktown.)

In what can only be deemed an ironic conclusion to Laurens's story, he reports in his *Narrative* that during his peace negotiations with Lord Shelburne in the spring of 1782, Shelburne told him:

Well Mr Laurens if we must acknowledge your Independence I shall be grieved as I have already said for your own sakes, you will lose the benefit of the Habeas Corpus Act.[40]

Never mind that the Laurens had never known those benefits, having been denied by the crown operation of the act in the colonies and subsequently confined without trial in England during the act's suspension.

---

[38] For discussion of John Laurens, consult Rakove, *supra* note 35, at 212–41, 276.

[39] *See* Laurens, *Narrative, supra* note 35, at 395–97; *see also* Wallace, *supra* note 36, at 388; Daniel J. McDonough, Christopher Gadsden, and Henry Laurens, *The Parallel Lives of Two American Patriots* 259 (2000). A copy of the Record of Bail taken may be found at 10 B.F. *Stevens's Facsimiles of Manuscripts in European Archives Relating to America* 295 (No. 988) (London, Malby & Sons 1890), and a copy of the entry of the Order of Discharge of Laurens's recognizance may be found at *id.* at 303 (No. 990).

[40] Laurens, *Narrative, supra* note 35, at 400 (reporting Shelburne's remarks). For greater details on habeas corpus during the Revolutionary War period, consult Tyler, *supra* note 15, at 648–93.

SUSPENSION AND THE HABEAS CORPUS ACT
IN REVOLUTIONARY AMERICA

Meanwhile, on the other side of the Atlantic, the newly declared independent States were embracing the English Habeas Corpus Act as their own and also, in some cases, the concept of suspension. In studying these early legal frameworks, one finds extensive evidence that the idea of the habeas privilege was linked inextricably to the English act, and a number of states adopted formally the act's terms as part of their new constitutions and codes. Other states introduced the protections of the act through common law judicial processes that were later codified in statutory law.

It bears emphasis that many states embraced the Habeas Corpus Act through specific legislation as opposed to by implication as part of general statutes that adopted British statutory law wholesale. The prominence of the act in early American political and legal discourse is demonstrated by, for example, South Carolina's newly declared General Assembly taking up confirmation of the act's operation as one its very first matters in March 1776.[41] Another prominent example may be found in Georgia's inclusion in its constitution of 1777 of express provision that "the principles of the Habeas Corpus Act, shall be part of this Constitution."[42] As though to drive home the point, Georgia attached verbatim copies of the English Habeas Corpus Act to its original public distribution.[43]

Nor was the British Parliament the only body to suspend the protections associated with the English act during the American Revolutionary War. When threatened with invasion, at least six of the newly declared independent states passed their own suspension acts modeled on the English precedents from the late seventeenth and eighteenth centuries. They did so in order to legalize the detention of the disaffected outside the criminal process. These states included Massachusetts, Pennsylvania, Maryland, South Carolina, Virginia, and New Jersey.[44] One case during the war illustrates well the influence of the English suspension model on early American law. Pennsylvania's Chief Justice Thomas McKean – the first person to sign the Declaration of Independence – presided over the closely followed wartime case of twenty Quakers who had been taken into custody and held based on the suspicion that they were aiding the British. The Quakers petitioned for relief to McKean's court, invoking the English Habeas Corpus Act to argue that they were entitled to a timely criminal trial or else their freedom. As McKean later explained in a letter to his friend John Adams, in the absence of a suspension, he felt obligated to grant their discharge

---

[41] *Journal of the General Assembly of South Carolina, March 26, 1776–April 11, 1776*, at 21, 24, 26 (A. S. Salley, Jr. ed., 1906).

[42] Ga. Const. of 1777, art. LX.

[43] Charles Francis Jenkins, *Button Gwinnett: Signer of the Declaration of Independence* 109 (1926).

[44] For details of these suspensions, consult Tyler, *supra* note 16, at 958–68.

by reason of the act, which he recognized as in force in Pennsylvania.[45] Before he could do so, however, the Pennsylvania legislature intervened and enacted a suspension that rendered lawful the detention without trial of those suspected of treason. The legislation purported by its terms "to restrain for some limited Time the Operation of the Habeas Corpus Act."[46] The act thereby stripped McKean of any authority to discharge the Quakers.

In the years following the war, a wave of additional states adopted (or, in some cases, reaffirmed) statutes embracing the core terms of the English act, including particularly its seventh section, as part of their codified laws. This list includes Pennsylvania, Massachusetts, New York, New Jersey, Delaware, Maryland, South Carolina, Georgia, and North Carolina.[47] Some states also constitutionalized its terms, either explicitly, as in the case of Georgia, or by connecting the habeas privilege to the concept of suspension and embracing the understanding that without a suspension, one held on suspicion of criminal activity must be tried in due course, as in Massachusetts.[48] One of the most significant of the statutory adoptions of the English act's terms occurred just three months before the Constitutional Convention convened in Philadelphia in 1787, when New York passed a statute almost identical to the 1679 act. The legislation, tracking the seventh section of its English predecessor, made explicit the requirement that any person "committed for treason or felony" who is not "indicted and tried [by] the second term [of the] sessions" of the relevant court "after his commitment shall be discharged from his imprisonment."[49] Underscoring the pervasive influence of the English Habeas Corpus Act on the development of early American law, the great New York jurist and legal commentator Chancellor James Kent observed in 1827 that "the statute of 31 Charles II. c. 2 is the basis of all the American statutes on the subject."[50]

---

[45] Letter from Thomas McKean to John Adams, Sept. 19, 1777, *in* 5 The Papers of John Adams No. PJA05d178 (Massachusetts Historical Society Digital Edition) (observing that "[t]he habeas corpus Act forms a part of the Code of the Pennsylvania laws, and has been always justly esteemed the palladium of liberty").

[46] *Journal and Proceedings of the General Assembly of the Common-wealth of Pennsylvania* 88 (John Dunlap, ed. 1777).

[47] For extensive details on this period, consult Tyler, *Habeas Corpus in Wartime, supra* note 7, at 101–121.

[48] Mass. Const. of 1780, pt. 2, ch. VI, art. VII ("The privilege and benefit of the writ of Habeas Corpus shall be enjoyed in this Commonwealth in the most free, easy, cheap, expeditious and ample manner; and shall not be suspended by the Legislature, except upon the most urgent and pressing occasions, and for a limited time not exceeding twelve months."). The debates leading up to adoption of this provision, which demonstrate its linking with the English Habeas Corpus Act, are discussed in Tyler, *supra* note 16, at 963–64.

[49] An Act for the Better Securing the Liberty of the Citizens of this State, and for Prevention of Imprisonments (Feb. 21, 1787), *in* 1 *Laws of the State of New York* 369, 369 (New York, Thomas Greenleaf 1792).

[50] James Kent, 2 *Commentaries on American Law* 24 (New York O. Halsted 1827).

CONSTITUTIONALIZING THE PRIVILEGE – A "GOOD START"
TO A BILL OF RIGHTS

Such proved the backdrop against which the founding generation wrote the Suspension Clause. It should therefore come as no surprise that when one takes the story forward to the Constitutional Convention and Ratification Debates, there is widespread evidence of the continuing influence of the English Habeas Corpus Act and suspension framework on early American habeas jurisprudence, and particularly the Suspension Clause.

When the delegates to the Constitutional Convention met in Philadelphia in 1787, they set to work on a new federal structure that would replace the Articles of Confederation. As an initial matter, the delegates resolved that the new federal government would be empowered to act directly upon the people rather than exclusively through member states, as had been the case under the Articles.[51] Next, the delegates turned to a formal separation of powers for the design of the federal government – a marked departure from the British model – as well as to a Supreme Court and authorization for the creation of inferior national courts that would operate independently of the political branches. It was within the larger conversation about the judicial branch that the delegates discussed those protections that British rule had denied the colonists: namely the rights associated with the English Habeas Corpus Act and the right to trial by jury.

As things unfolded, there was only very limited discussion at the convention of what ultimately became the Suspension Clause in the US Constitution. Four days after the convention came to order, Charles Pinckney introduced a draft plan to the convention that received no reported discussion. But one of his proposals laid the groundwork for the Suspension Clause and introduced a concept that would survive in the clause's final form – namely, the restriction on suspensions "except in case of rebellion or invasion."[52] Pinckney may have been influenced by the recent adoption in Ireland of the English Habeas Corpus Act, which copied much of the language of the 1679 act verbatim, with the notable addition of limiting the Irish Council from suspending the act except "during such time only as there shall be an actual invasion or rebellion in this kingdom or Great Britain."[53]

Months later, Pinckney moved again for recognition of the habeas privilege along with constraints on when it could be suspended. *Farrand's Records of the Federal Convention of 1787* reports that the proposal read:

The privileges and benefit of the Writ of Habeas corpus shall be enjoyed in this Government in the most expeditious and ample manner; and shall not be suspended

---

[51] Rakove, *supra* note 35, at 55.
[52] 1 *The Debates in the Several State Conventions, on the Adoption of the Federal Constitution* 148 (Jonathan Elliot ed., 2nd ed., Philadelphia, J.B. Lippincott & Co. 1881) [hereinafter Elliot's Debates] (replicating Charles Pinckney's draft plan, Article VI).
[53] An Act for Better Securing the Liberty of the Subject, 1781, 21 & 22 Geo. 3, c. 11, § XVI (Ir.).

by the Legislature except upon the most urgent and pressing occasions, and for a time period not exceeding [—] months.[54]

In the limited debates that followed, the delegates instead came to adopt wording proposed by Gouverneur Morris that read: "The privilege of the writ of Habeas Corpus shall not be suspended, unless where in cases of Rebellion or invasion the public safety may require it."[55]

At this point, Madison's notes recount that the delegates took a vote on Morris's proposal. All agreed on the first part that standing alone prohibited suspension under any circumstances: "The privilege of the writ of Habeas Corpus shall not be suspended ... ." It was the second part of the proposed clause, which recognized a power to suspend, that elicited dissent. Specifically, North Carolina, South Carolina, and Georgia voted against including such language in the draft clause.[56]

Several important lessons may be taken from the convention. First, the delegates clearly recognized an important connection between habeas corpus, suspension, and requiring criminal prosecution of those taken into custody who could claim the protection of domestic law. For example, the delegates initially placed the Suspension Clause in the judiciary article (then Article XI) right alongside the guarantee that "[t]he trial of all crimes (except in cases of impeachment) shall be by jury."[57] The jury-trial right had also been the subject of discussion just before the drafters took up discussion of the habeas clause.[58] Further, in promoting the draft Constitution in the *Federalist Papers*, Alexander Hamilton lauded the fact that the Constitution provided for "trial by jury in criminal cases, aided by the *habeas corpus act*."[59] Second, as Hamilton's remarks exemplify, there was widespread association of the proposed Suspension Clause's protection of the privilege with the English Habeas Corpus Act. Indeed, participants throughout the ratification debates connected the two directly; others simply took for granted the fact that the clause's limitations on suspension were intended to safeguard the same

---

[54] James Madison, Notes on the Constitutional Convention (Aug. 20, 1787), *in* 2 *The Records of the Federal Convention of 1787*, at 340, 341 (Max Farrand ed., 1911) [hereinafter Farrand's Records].

[55] *Id.* at 438 (internal quotation marks omitted). The Committee on Style later changed the wording of the clause by substituting "when" for "where." *See* Report of Committee of Style (Sept. 12, 1787), *in* 2 Farrand's Records, *supra* note 54, at 596.

[56] Madison, *in* 2 Farrand's Records, *supra* note 54, at 438; *see also* I Elliot's Debates, *supra* note 52, at 270 (reporting the approval of Morris's proposed wording).

[57] Madison, *in* 2 Farrand's Records, *supra* note 54, at 438 (internal quotation mark omitted). At this point, the draft put the jury-trial guarantee in Article XI, Section 4, and the habeas clause in Article XI, Section 5. *See id.* The Committee of Style reorganized the articles and separated the two clauses, moving the habeas clause to Article I and leaving the guarantee of a jury trial in criminal cases in the judiciary article, which became Article III. *See* Report of Committee of Style (Sept. 12, 1787), *in id.* at 590, 596, 601; *see also* U.S. Const. art. III, § 2, cl. 3 (Jury Clause).

[58] Madison, *in* 2 Farrand's Records, *supra* note 54, at 438.

[59] The Federalist No. 83, at 499 (Alexander Hamilton) (Clinton Rossiter ed., 2003) (emphasis added).

protections that Parliament had invented suspension to displace – namely, those associated with the seventh section of the English Habeas Corpus Act.[60]

This backdrop helps put in context many of the comments made during the Constitutional Convention and Ratification Debates about the Suspension Clause. In particular, it helps explain why Alexander Hamilton took the position in support of ratification that a Bill of Rights was unnecessary. Hamilton believed that securing protection of the privilege in the Constitution and with it many of the constitutional protections that had long been linked to the English Habeas Corpus Act – such as the right to presentment or indictment, speedy trial, and protection from excessive bail – rendered express provision for these rights unnecessary. Indeed, even the Antifederalist *Federal Farmer* pointed to the Suspension Clause and its neighboring provisions as "a partial bill of rights."[61] A few decades later, Chief Justice John Marshall highlighted the profound influence of the English act on the Constitution's habeas clause when he referenced the English statute as the basis of the constitutional privilege. As he wrote in Ex parte *Watkins*, when interpreting the Suspension Clause, one must look to "that law which is in a considerable degree incorporated into our own" – specifically, "the celebrated *habeas corpus* act" of 1679.[62]

WITH CIVIL WAR, SUSPENSION

It was not until the Confederate attack on Fort Sumter on April 12, 1861, launching the Civil War that the United States witnessed its first suspension at the federal level. President Lincoln viewed the secession of the Confederate States as illegal and considered those who supported the Confederacy to be traitors who needed to return to their proper allegiance.[63] In this regard, the

---

[60] Another prominent contemporary example that associated the act with the clause was Luther Martin's *Genuine Information*. Luther Martin, *The Genuine Information Delivered to the Legislature of the State of Maryland Relative to the Proceedings of the General Convention Lately Held at Philadelphia* (1788), *reprinted in* 2 *The Complete Anti-Federalist* 19, ¶ 2.4.72, at 62 (Herbert J. Storing ed., 1981) (opposing the Suspension Clause for bestowing the power on the federal government to "suspend[] the habeas corpus act"). For greater discussion of this point, consult Tyler, *Habeas Corpus in Wartime, supra* note 7, at 123–140; and Tyler, *supra* note 16, at 969–75.

[61] Letter IV from the Federal Farmer to the Republican (Oct. 12, 1787), *in Observations Leading to a Fair Examination of the System of Government Proposed by the Late Convention; and to Several Essential and Necessary Alterations to It* (1787), *reprinted in* 2 *The Complete Anti-Federalist, supra* note 60, at 214, ¶ 2.8.51, at 248; *see also id.* ¶¶ 2.8.51–.52, at 248–49. This backdrop also explains why Thomas Jefferson, when arguing against the recognition of any suspension power, pointed to the treason clause as the appropriate basis by which the government should proceed against persons owing allegiance who sided with the enemy in times of war. For details, consult Tyler, *supra* note 16, at 974–75.

[62] *Ex parte* Watkins, 28 U.S. (3 Pet.) 193, 201–2 (1830) (Marshall, C.J.) (observing that it was to remedy detention on "suspicions which could not be sustained by evidence" that the "celebrated *habeas corpus* act of the 31st of Charles II. was enacted").

[63] Abraham Lincoln, First Inaugural Address (Mar. 4, 1861), *in Abraham Lincoln: Speeches and Writings, 1859–1865*, at 215, 218 (Don E. Fehrenbacher ed., 1989) (arguing that secession was illegal and that "the Union [was] unbroken"). Later in the war, Lincoln offered those who had

Union view of the secessionists mirrored that held by the British with respect to the American Rebels years earlier. This view of allegiance would also shape how the Union treated Confederates when held as prisoners.

Within days of the attack on Fort Sumter, Lincoln authorized Union military leaders to suspend habeas wherever they believed it necessary to protect key geographic areas.[64] Lincoln did so famously on his own and without congressional approval. To be sure, initially Congress was unable to meet to grant him this authority, but well after the body reconvened and for the next two years until Congress finally enacted suspension legislation, Lincoln kept right on authorizing suspensions throughout the country.[65] Lincoln's unilateral assumption of what had always been a legislative power – suspension, after all, owed its very creation to Parliament – came under criticism almost immediately and soon sparked a widespread public debate.[66]

"THE GREAT SUSPENDER" AND THE CASE OF JOHN MERRYMAN

From the outset of the war, Lincoln recognized Maryland as situated in a critically important location. Union troops needed to pass through the state to reach Washington, DC, and just seven days after the Confederate assault on Fort Sumter, mobs had attacked a Massachusetts regiment traveling through Baltimore heading south, killing four members. Although the Maryland legislature had voted against secession, it also took numerous steps to frustrate Union efforts, such as refusing to reopen rail lines to the north and pushing for the withdrawal of federal troops from the state. Matters escalated to the point that the governor deployed the state militia and reportedly approved of orders that several key bridges be destroyed to thwart Union troop movements through the state. One of those believed to play a role in destroying bridges was a Maryland farmer by the name of John Merryman.

---

supported the Confederacy the opportunity to proclaim their allegiance to the Union and, in many cases, earn a presidential pardon. *See* Proclamation No. 11, 13 Stat. 737 (Dec. 8, 1863) (excepting certain persons from its scope).

[64] *See, e.g.*, Letter from Abraham Lincoln to Winfield Scott (Apr. 25, 1861), *in* 4 *The Collected Works of Abraham Lincoln* 344 (Roy P. Basler et al. eds., 1953) [hereinafter Collected Works] (authorizing suspension of the privilege in Maryland in situations of the "extremest necessity"); Letter from Abraham Lincoln to Winfield Scott (Apr. 27, 1861), *in* 4 Collected Works, *supra*, at 347 (authorizing suspension of the privilege in the face of "resistance" encountered between Philadelphia and Washington).

[65] For details and citations, consult Tyler, *Habeas Corpus in Wartime, supra* note 7, at 159–171.

[66] Numerous pamphlets on this subject were published during this period. For a list of citations, consult William F. Duker, *A Constitutional History of Habeas Corpus* 178 n. 189 (1980); and Sydney G. Fisher, The Suspension of Habeas Corpus during the War of the Rebellion, 3 *Pol. Sci. Q.* 454, 485–88 (1888). I borrow the phrase "the Great Suspender" from Saikrishna Bangalore Prakash, The Great Suspender's Unconstitutional Suspension of the Great Writ, 3 *Alb. Gov't L. Rev.* 575 (2010).

Union troops arrested Merryman, believed to be an officer of a secessionist group called the Baltimore County Horse Guards, at his home in Baltimore on a Saturday. Labeling him a traitor, the military took him to Fort McHenry for imprisonment. It does not appear that the government ever drew up a warrant for Merryman's arrest. This likely followed because George Cadwalader, the Union military commander in Maryland, did not believe that he needed one to detain Merryman. President Lincoln had given his military commanders in Maryland full discretion to suspend habeas corpus as needed to protect key military areas and, having exercised that authority, Cadwalader held the view that it was therefore legal for him to detain persons suspected of treasonous acts without charges. The very same day of Merryman's arrest, however, a lawyer prepared a habeas petition on his behalf, swearing to it before the US Commissioner in Baltimore and then arranging for its presentation in Washington to the Chief Justice of the Supreme Court, Roger B. Taney. On Sunday, Taney ordered General Cadwalader to appear and produce the body of John Merryman and demonstrate legal justification for his detention at hearing the next day. For the hearing, Taney traveled to Baltimore, doing so, in his words, so as not to "withdraw General Cadwalader ... from the limits of his military command."[67] But Cadwalader declined to appear, instead sending a deputy to explain the general's position that a suspension legalized Merryman's detention and rendered any judicial inquiry improper.

Taney made quick work of Cadwalader's arguments, writing in his opinion on the matter:

I understand that the president not only claims the right to suspend the writ of habeas corpus himself, at his discretion, but to delegate that discretionary power to a military officer ... I certainly listened to it with some surprise, for I had supposed it to be one of those points of constitutional law upon which there was no difference of opinion, and that it was admitted on all hands, that the privilege of the writ could not be suspended, except by act of congress.[68]

Taney knew his history, relating the developments leading up to adoption of what he called "the great habeas corpus act" during the reign of Charles II and analogizing the general accusations leveled at Merryman to those advanced by the crown as the basis for locking up John Selden – whose detention without criminal charges in the Tower of London had both laid the groundwork and highlighted the need for habeas legislation in the seventeenth century.[69] Taney emphasized that "[t]he great and inestimable value of the habeas corpus act of the 31 Car. II. is, that it contains provisions which compel courts and judges, and all parties concerned, to perform their duties promptly, in the manner specified in the statute."

[67] *Ex parte* Merryman, 17 F. Cas. 144 (C.C.D. Md. 1861) (No. 9487). [68] *Id.* at 148.
[69] For details on Selden's important role in the development of Anglo-American habeas law, consult Tyler, *Habeas Corpus in Wartime, supra* note 7, at 14–21.

That "manner" or tradition, Taney explained, formed the basis of American habeas law and specifically established two important benchmarks of constitutional law. The first such principle, Taney wrote, was that only the legislative body possessed the power to suspend habeas, for "[i]f the president of the United States may suspend the writ, then the constitution of the United States has conferred upon him more regal and absolute power over the liberty of the citizen, than the people of England have thought it safe to entrust to the crown . . . ."[70] Second, Taney wrote, the entire history of the English act and its incorporation into American law required that one be charged and tried in due course in the absence of a valid suspension or else be discharged. It followed that Taney held that Merryman's detention was unconstitutional.

Almost as though smarting for confrontation, Taney concluded by noting that he had arranged for his opinion to be delivered to President Lincoln directly, who, Taney wrote, would then be left "to determine what measures he will take to cause the civil process of the United States to be respected and enforced." The administration responded by eventually indicting Merryman on various charges, including treason, although for various reasons the government never did try him.[71] Notwithstanding the change of course in Merryman's particular case, however, Lincoln openly rejected Taney's opinion as wrong, proclaiming numerous additional suspensions in the absence of suspension legislation and defending the President's unilateral power to suspend before Congress, asserting that "[i]t was not believed that any law was violated."[72]

Chief Justice Taney's tenure on the Supreme Court is not the subject of much celebration (he authored the *Dred Scott* decision, after all), but he was most assuredly right in *Merryman* as to the question of which branch possesses the authority to suspend habeas. It bears noting, moreover, that his conclusion was the same as that reached in *dicta* by Chief Justice Marshall years earlier.[73] As Taney observed, the drafters of the Constitution placed the Suspension Clause in Article I – the legislative article – and suspension was, at its origins, a legislative creation born out of a movement to take control over matters of

---

[70] *Id.* at 151 (quoting 1 Blackstone *136); *see also id.* (citing 3 Story, Commentaries on the Constitution § 1336).

[71] For a defense of some of Lincoln's actions, consult Richard H. Fallon, Jr., Executive Power and the Political Constitution, 2007 *Utah L. Rev.* 1, 21. Other decisions from the war were consistent with *Merryman. See, e.g., In re* Kemp, 16 Wis. 384 (1863).

[72] *See* Abraham Lincoln, Message to Congress (July 4, 1861), *in* 4 Collected Works, *supra* note 64, at 430. The original version of Lincoln's statement here read: "I violated no law." *Id.* at 430 n.53. Lincoln's Attorney General also prepared a written defense of his position. *See* Letter from the Attorney General to the Speaker of the House of Representatives (July 5, 1861) *in* H.R. Exec. Doc. No. 37-5, at 12 (1st Sess. 1861).

[73] *See Ex parte* Bollman, 8 U.S. (4 Cranch) 75, 101 (1807) (Marshall, C.J.) ("If at any time the public safety should require the suspension of the powers vested by [Judiciary Act] in the courts of the United States, it is for the legislature to say so.").

detention from the executive.[74] The idea that the executive could suspend habeas without legislative involvement – at least when the legislature is able to meet and consider the matter – is entirely at odds both with this history and the founding generation's deep suspicion of concentrated executive authority.[75]

THE SWEEP OF SUSPENSION

Lincoln may have been mistaken about which branch possessed the authority to suspend, but he certainly appreciated the dramatic nature of suspension and understood its necessity as a means of legalizing arrests that otherwise would be unconstitutional in the ordinary course. Referring to the Suspension Clause, Lincoln wrote that the "provision plainly attests to the understanding of those who made the constitution that . . . the purpose" of suspension was so that "men may be held in custody whom the courts acting on ordinary rules, would discharge."[76] The "ordinary rules" to which Lincoln was referring comprised the protections inherent in the criminal process. Thus, as Lincoln explained the operation of the clause: "Habeas Corpus, does not discharge men who are proved to be guilty of defined crime; and its suspension is allowed by the constitution on purpose that, men may be arrested and held, who can not be proved to be guilty of defined crime, 'when in cases of Rebellion or Invasion the public Safety may require it.'"[77] In these dire circumstances, Lincoln wrote, "arrests are made, not so much for what has been done, as for what probably would be done [-] for the preventive . . . ."[78]

In the period before Congress's passage of legislation in 1863 that formally authorized the President to suspend the writ as necessary to defend the Union, military officials arrested thousands of civilians under Lincoln's orders.[79] As

[74] Further, the first proposed language that launched the discussions over the Suspension Clause, introduced by Charles Pinckney, specifically referenced the legislature. *See* Madison (Aug. 20, 1787), *in* 2 Farrand's Records, *supra* note 54, at 340, 341.

[75] To borrow from Justice Jackson, "emergency powers are consistent with free government only when their control is lodged elsewhere than in the Executive who exercises them." Youngstown Sheet & Tube Co. v. Sawyer, 343 U.S. 579, 652 (1952) (Jackson, J., concurring). For an outstanding explication of the position that suspension is a congressional power, *see* Prakash, *supra* note 66, at 591–613.

[76] Letter from Abraham Lincoln to Erastus Corning and Others (June 12, 1863), *in* 6 *The Collected Works of Abraham Lincoln* 260, 264 (Roy P. Basler et al. eds., 1953) (internal citation omitted). Similarly, Lincoln wrote that the Suspension Clause distinguishes between "arrests by process of courts, and arrests in cases of rebellion." *Id.* at 264–65.

[77] *Id.* It followed, in Lincoln's view, that suspension allows even for "instances of arresting innocent persons," something "always likely to occur in such cases." *Id.* at 263.

[78] *Id.* at 265. Lincoln further explained that suspension was necessary to "arrest, and detain, without resort to the ordinary processes and forms of law, such individuals as he might deem dangerous to the public safety." Abraham Lincoln, Message to Congress (July 4, 1861), *in* 4 Collected Works, *supra* note 64, at 421, 429.

[79] In trying to ascertain the precise number, Civil War historian Mark Neely found numerous recordkeeping failures yet concluded from his extensive research that "far more than" the often-

Lincoln historian James G. Randall has written: "The arrests were made on suspicion. Prisoners were not told why they were seized ... [T]he purpose of the whole process was *temporary military detention*."[80] As noted, Lincoln firmly believed that the Confederate states could not legally secede from the Union, and it followed that he held the view that southerners retained their duty of allegiance to the Union. Accordingly, Lincoln also subscribed to the position that the detention of Confederate soldiers and their civilian supporters outside the criminal process required a suspension. This explains why on September 24, 1862, Lincoln proclaimed a sweeping suspension, the terms of which reached virtually every prisoner who might be captured in the war. Specifically, he ordered:

That the writ of habeas corpus is suspended in respect to all persons arrested, or who are now, or hereafter during the rebellion shall be, imprisoned in any fort, camp, arsenal, military prison, or other place of confinement by any military authority or by the sentence of any court-martial or military commission.[81]

After actively debating suspension for two years, Congress eventually put to rest the controversy over whether the President could suspend ahead of it. In 1863, Congress passed legislation titled "An Act relating to Habeas Corpus, and regulating Judicial Proceedings in Certain Cases." The first section of the act provided:

That, during the present rebellion, the President of the United States, whenever, in his judgment, the public safety may require it, is authorized to suspend the privilege of the writ of habeas corpus in any case throughout the United States, or any part thereof. And whenever and wherever the said privilege shall be suspended, as aforesaid, no military or other officer shall be compelled, in answer to any writ of habeas corpus, to return the body of any person or persons detained by him by authority of the President ... so long as said suspension by the President shall remain in force, and said rebellion continue.[82]

---

invoked number of "13,535 civilians were arrested." Mark E. Neely, Jr., *The Fate of Liberty: Abraham Lincoln and Civil Liberties* 130 (1991); *see also id.* at 44, 136, 233–34.

[80] James G. Randall, *Constitutional Problems under Lincoln* 150 (1926) (emphasis added); *see also id.* (labeling these detentions "precautionary"); *id.* at 149 (noting that during the early days of the war "hundreds of prisoners were apprehended"). Randall further observed: "That all this procedure was arbitrary, that it involved the withholding of constitutional guarantees normally available, is of course evident." *Id.* at 152.

[81] Proclamation No. 1, 13 Stat. 730 (1862). This proclamation followed an earlier sweeping proclamation suspending the privilege with respect to all draft evaders and "all persons arrested for disloyal practices." Executive Order (Aug. 8, 1862), *in* 7 *A Compilation of the Messages and Papers of the Presidents* 3322 (James D. Richardson ed., New York, Bureau of National Literature, Inc. 1897).

[82] Act of Mar. 3, 1863, ch. 81, § 1, 12 Stat. 755, 755. The act provided that officers need not file returns in habeas proceedings while a presidential order of suspension remained in force and the rebellion "continued." *Id.* For more details, consult Amanda L. Tyler, Suspension as an Emergency Power, 118 *Yale L. J.* 600, 637–55 (2009).

Congress intended its chosen wording (stating that the President "is authorized" rather than "is hereby authorized") to be ambiguous on the question of whether the bill was an investiture of the power in the President or a validation of the President's prior acts.[83]

Now unquestionably armed with the authority to address the "clear, flagrant, and gigantic case of Rebellion" tearing apart the Union,[84] Lincoln issued an even more sweeping suspension in September 1863. (Notably, Lincoln cited the 1863 act as the basis of his authority, almost conceding the questionable constitutionality of his earlier proclamations.) In it, he declared:

[T]he public safety does require that the privilege of the said writ shall now be suspended throughout the United States in the cases where, by the authority of the President of the United States, military, naval, and civil officers of the United States, or any of them, hold persons under their command or in their custody, either as prisoners of war, spies, or aiders or abettors of the enemy ....[85]

Lincoln's proclamation specifically encompassed persons held in military custody as "prisoners of war" – a category surely intended to encompass Confederate soldiers captured on the battlefield. Even Lincoln did not believe that the President had inherent authority to detain such persons in the absence of a suspension, a position that was consistent with his view that Confederates and their sympathizers still owed a duty of allegiance to the Union. In the wake of this proclaimed suspension, Union military officials detained thousands of individuals across the country, including scores captured in battle.[86] The government tried only a portion of those detained during the war for criminal conduct, and in most cases, those trials occurred before military tribunals, a practice that implicates a host of additional constitutional issues.[87] Suspension remained the law in some states as late as a full year after Confederate General Robert E. Lee surrendered to Union General Ulysses S. Grant at the Appomattox Court House, when President Andrew Johnson, Lincoln's successor, finally lifted the last of the suspension's applications.[88]

---

[83] *See* Cong. Globe, 37th Cong., 3d Sess. 1186 (1863) (statement of Sen. Trumbull) (observing that both those who believed the power to suspend resides in Congress and those who thought it resides with the President could vote for a bill worded in this fashion); Cong. Globe, 37th Cong., 3d Sess. 1094 (1863) (statement of Sen. Bayard) (referring to the measure as "intentionally ambiguous ... [and] intended to be so framed that it may be read two ways").

[84] Letter from Abraham Lincoln to Erastus Corning and Others, *supra* note 76, at 264.

[85] Proclamation No. 7, 13 Stat. 734, 734 (1863). Lincoln's proclamation also encompassed those in the US military, military deserters, and draft dodgers. *See id.*

[86] For extensive details on prisoners detained during the war, consult generally Neely, *supra* note 79.

[87] For details, consult Daniel Farber, *Lincoln's Constitution* 20 (2003).

[88] Specifically, Johnson lifted the suspension's application to a number of states in December 1865, to several more in April 1866, and finally to the last remaining state in August 1866. *See, e.g.,* Andrew Johnson, A Proclamation (Dec. 1, 1865), *in* 8 *A Compilation of the Messages and Papers of the Presidents* 3531 (James D. Richardson ed., New York, Bureau of Nat'l Literature, Inc.

MILITARY TRIALS AND HABEAS CORPUS

The use of military tribunals during the war proved another controversial aspect of Lincoln's agenda and earned the postwar rebuke of the Supreme Court in its 1866 decision in Ex parte *Milligan*. In areas in which the regular civilian courts were "open and their process unobstructed," five members of the Court held, civilians must be tried by civilian courts and given the full panoply of constitutional rights relating to criminal procedure, including a jury trial – even in the face of ongoing civil war. As the Court phrased it, "[t]he Constitution of the United States is a law for rulers and people, equally in war and in peace, and covers with the shield of its protection all classes of men, at all times, and under all circumstances."[89]

Lambdin Milligan had been tried by a military tribunal in Indiana for various charges relating to supporting the Confederacy (including a charge of "violat[ing] the laws of war"[90]), convicted, and sentenced to death. When Milligan sought habeas corpus relief challenging the legitimacy of his conviction, the Supreme Court sided with him, based in part on its view that "in Indiana the Federal authority was always unopposed, and its courts always open to hear criminal accusations and redress grievances." (Interestingly, the Court contrasted Virginia, "where the national authority was overturned and the courts driven out," an observation that suggests that the Justices joining the majority opinion were quite comfortable issuing an opinion regarding whether wartime conditions in certain areas warranted emergency measures.[91]) It was of no significance to the majority that Milligan had been charged with violations of the laws of war. Such laws, the Court concluded, "can never be applied to citizens in states which have upheld the authority of the government, and where the courts are open and their process unobstructed."[92] (The Supreme Court later called this aspect of the *Milligan* opinion into question in the hastily decided World War II case of Ex parte *Quirin*.[93])

The *Milligan* Court also rejected the argument that the existence of a nationwide suspension sanctioned Milligan's trial before a military commission. Suspension, the Court held, only authorizes *detention* during its operation; it says nothing about the propriety of employing a military versus civilian court to try civilians, nor does it legitimate the denial of standard constitutional protections. Put another way, as Justice Davis phrased it, "[t]he Constitution goes no further. It does not say after a writ of *habeas corpus* is denied a citizen, that he shall be tried otherwise than by the course of the common law ... [The founding generation] limited the suspension to one great right, and left the rest to remain forever inviolable."[94]

1897). For additional citations, consult Tyler, *Habeas Corpus in Wartime, supra* note 7, at 171 and accompanying notes.

[89] *Ex parte* Milligan, 71 U.S. (4 Wall.) 2, 120–21 (1866).   [90] *Id.* at 6.   [91] *Id.* at 127.

[92] *Id.* at 121.   [93] 317 U.S. 1 (1942).

[94] Milligan, 71 U.S. (4 Wall.) at 126; *see also id.* at 125–26 (observing that "in a great crisis," it is "essential" that "there should be a power somewhere of suspending the writ of *habeas corpus*"

RECONSTRUCTION AND SUSPENSION TO PROMOTE
THE ADVANCEMENT OF CIVIL RIGHTS

As the battlefields of the Civil War smoldered, the job of reconstructing the Union began. As part of that effort, lessons hard learned during the preceding period called upon the Constitution to play a new role. And so, ratification of the Reconstruction Amendments – specifically, the Thirteenth, Fourteenth, and Fifteenth – extended rights to liberty, equality, and the vote to persons regardless of race. These profound alterations to the original compact, however, met dramatic resistance in many portions of the country that had once comprised the Confederacy.

Specifically, during this period, in many parts of the South, the Ku Klux Klan became a domestic terrorist organization of tremendous consequence. Klan violence in certain areas, including particularly the northern counties of South Carolina, was shocking in its scope and brutality. Night riders inflicted horrific violence on African Americans and more generally anyone who opposed the Klan, and these routine occurrences met little if any resistance or prosecution from local authorities.[95] The Klan also targeted anyone who dared to testify against its members while also controlling many arms of local government and rendering some Southern states "unable to provide even the semblance of criminal law enforcement."[96]

This state of affairs led the victorious Union general-turned-President Ulysses S. Grant in March 1871 to "urgently recommend" legislation in light of the fact that "the power to correct these evils is beyond the control of the State authorities." As he also observed, it was "not clear" whether "the power of the Executive of the United States, acting within the limits of existing laws, is sufficient for present emergencies . . . ."[97] Congress responded with what came to be known as the Ku Klux Klan Act of 1871, which in its third and fourth sections authorized the President to declare martial law and suspend habeas

---

because "[i]n the emergency of the times, an immediate public investigation according to law may not be possible; and yet, the peril to the country may be too imminent to suffer such persons to go at large").

[95] For details, consult Lou Falkner Williams, *The Great South Carolina Ku Klux Klan Trials: 1871–1872*, at 19–39 (1996) [hereinafter Williams, *Ku Klux Klan Trials*]; Lou Falkner Williams, The Constitution and the Ku Klux Klan on Trial: Federal Enforcement and Local Resistance in South Carolina, 1871–72, 2 *Ga. J. S. Legal Hist.* 41, 50 (1993).

[96] Robert J. Kaczorowski, *The Politics of Judicial Interpretation: The Federal Courts, Department of Justice and Civil Rights, 1866–1876*, at 81 (1985); Kermit L. Hall, Political Power and Constitutional Legitimacy: The South Carolina Ku Klux Klan Trials, 1871–1872, 33 *Emory L. J.* 921, 925 (1984) (noting that local law enforcement undermined federal efforts to restore order to the region).

[97] Letter from Ulysses S. Grant to the Senate and House of Representatives (Mar. 23, 1871), *in* 9 A Compilation of the Messages and Papers of the Presidents 4081 (James D. Richardson ed., New York, Bureau of National Literature, Inc. 1897).

corpus in districts where "the conviction of . . . offenders and the preservation of the public safety shall become . . . impracticable."[98]

President Grant referred to these sections of the act as conferring upon him "extraordinary powers" that he would invoke only "reluctant[ly]" and "in cases of imperative necessity. . . for the purpose of securing to all citizens. . . the peaceful enjoyment of the rights guaranteed to them by the Constitution and laws."[99] Invoke them he did, soon suspending habeas in the South Carolina upcountry, a key Klan stronghold.[100] In the events that followed, military officials, led by Major Lewis Merrill, arrested scores of suspected Klan members. As Merrill's aide in South Carolina, Louis Post, wrote, these arrests were "without warrant or specific accusation" of criminal conduct; persons were targeted based on their presumed membership in the Klan.[101] The objectives of the arrests included uncovering the identity of key Klansmen and preventing witness intimidation.

Two important aspects of this episode warrant highlighting. First, when the suspension lapsed, everyone understood that suspects could no longer be detained without charges, and accordingly, many of those in custody were referred for prosecution on federal criminal law charges, while others were released.[102] Second, in evaluating the suspension immediately after it lapsed, Congress concluded "that where the membership, mysteries, and power of the organization have been kept concealed [suspension] is the most and perhaps only effective remedy for its suppression."[103] The example therefore is one in which suspension served as a potent tool for infiltrating a highly secretive organization to uncover its structure and membership.

A NEW ROLE FOR HABEAS CORPUS AND THE FEDERAL COURTS

During Reconstruction, Congress also dramatically expanded the concept of habeas corpus in American law, taking an old writ and fashioning a new role for it. Up until this time, federal courts did not review state criminal cases except through direct appeal to the Supreme Court. In 1867, Congress for the first time vested the lower federal courts with jurisdiction to review habeas corpus petitions

---

[98] Ch. 22, 17 Stat. 13.

[99] Ulysses S. Grant, A Proclamation (May 3, 1871), *in* 9 Messages and Papers, *supra* note 97, at 4088.

[100] *See* Ulysses S. Grant, A Proclamation (Oct. 17, 1871), *in* 9 Messages and Papers, *supra* note 97, at 4090, 4091; Ulysses S. Grant, A Proclamation (Nov. 10, 1871), *in* 9 Messages and Papers, *supra*, at 4093, 4095.

[101] Louis F. Post, A "Carpetbagger" in South Carolina, 10 *J. Negro Hist.* 10, 41 (1925).

[102] For more details on this suspension and its aftermath, *see* Tyler, *supra* note 82, at 655–62; *see also* Williams, *Ku Klux Klan Trials, supra* note 95, at 122–25 (noting that the Department of Justice subsequently launched a policy of appeasement, culminating in President Grant's 1873 offer of clemency and pardons to Klan members caught in Merrill's sweeps).

[103] S. Rep. No. 42-41, pt. 1, at 99 (1872).

from prisoners held in state custody under state criminal convictions. That legislation specifically conferred on federal courts the power "to grant writs of habeas corpus in all cases where any person may be restrained of his or her liberty in violation of the constitution, or of any treaty or law of the United States."[104]

Over time, the Supreme Court expanded this "collateral" avenue of review to encompass not only claims attacking the jurisdiction of a convicting court but constitutional claims more generally. In this regard, the Court's 1953 decision in *Brown* v. *Allen* stands as the high-water mark of the exercise of this kind of habeas jurisdiction.[105] As Justice Frankfurter explained in his opinion in the case, "[b]y giving the federal courts [this] jurisdiction [in 1867], Congress has imbedded into federal legislation the historic function of habeas corpus adapted to reaching an enlarged area of claims."[106] Under the *Brown* regime, both federal and state prisoners committed by criminal convictions could now use habeas corpus to secure a second round of judicial review of the many constitutional claims typically implicated by the criminal process. As Justice Frankfurter explained in *Brown*, such review was to be undertaken on a *de novo* basis, for "the prior State determination of a claim under the United States Constitution cannot foreclose consideration of such a claim, else the State court would have the final say which the Congress, by the Act of 1867, provided it should not have."[107]

In 1996, however, Congress dramatically scaled back the scope of review of state court criminal convictions in federal court collateral habeas proceedings in the Antiterrorism and Effective Death Penalty Act (AEDPA).[108] AEDPA introduced for the first time a statute of limitations for federal court collateral habeas petitions, dramatically limited the filing of successive petitions, severely curtailed the opportunity for factual hearings in such proceedings, and required federal courts to defer to "reasonable," even if "incorrect," holdings of state courts with respect to federal constitutional claims. As the Supreme Court recently explained, AEDPA's deferential standard requires a prisoner to show that a state court's ruling on his or her claims "was so lacking in justification that there was an error well understood and comprehended in existing law beyond any possibility for fairminded disagreement."[109]

---

[104] *See* Act of Feb. 5, 1867, 14 Stat. 385.   [105] 344 U.S. 443 (1953).

[106] *Id.* at 500 (Opinion of Frankfurter, J.). Subsequent cases treated Justice Frankfurter's opinion, one of eight written in the case, to be the controlling opinion in *Brown*.

[107] *Id.* Over time, the Supreme Court precluded certain constitution claims from habeas review, *see* Stone v. Powell, 428 U.S. 465 (1976) (Fourth Amendment claims); required that claims be timely presented to state courts in order to preserve them for federal habeas review, *see* Wainwright v. Sykes, 433 U.S. 72 (1977); and barring limited exceptions, precluded federal habeas relief for newly recognized legal claims, *see* Teague v. Lane, 489 U.S. 288 (1989).

[108] 110 Stat. 1214 (1996).

[109] Harrington v. Richter, 562 U.S. 86, 103 (2011); *see also* Williams v. Taylor, 529 U.S. 362, 410-12 (2000) (O'Connor, J.) (setting forth the controlling interpretation of AEDPA standard of review provision, 28 U.S.C. § 2254(d)(1)).

Today, it is a rare occasion when a state prisoner satisfies AEDPA's standard and secures relief from a federal habeas court. For this reason, some have argued that many aspects of AEDPA transgress constitutional boundaries. In particular, in one early case interpreting the statute, Justice John Paul Stevens argued that AEDPA's provision requiring deference to state court decisions on constitutional claims that are "reasonable," yet contrary to the conclusion a federal court would reach in its independent judgment, violates the separation of powers.[110] In that case, however, Justice Stevens found himself on the losing end of the argument. To date, the Supreme Court has broadly interpreted and routinely upheld AEDPA's provisions.[111]

WORLD WAR II AND THE FORGOTTEN SUSPENSION CLAUSE

In the immediate wake of the Japanese attack on Pearl Harbor that ushered the United States into World War II, there was a suspension of habeas corpus, but it was limited to what was then the Hawaiian Territory and it followed under special procedures set forth in the Hawaiian Organic Act of 1900.[112] With respect to the mainland United States, Congress never debated, much less passed, any suspension legislation. Instead, it was largely the military orders carrying out President Franklin Delano Roosevelt's Executive Order 9066 that governed the treatment of those suspected of potential disloyalty. The President's order gave the Secretary of War the authority to designate military zones "from which any or all persons may be excluded" and provide for the regulation of the terms on which persons could enter, remain in, or be forced to leave such areas.[113] Under the auspices of 9066, the military imposed curfews, designated large swaths of the western United States as military areas of exclusion, and ultimately created "relocation centers" across the West – all

---

[110] *See id.* at 378–79 (Stevens, J.) (relying upon *Marbury* v. *Madison* to contend that "[w]hen federal judges exercise . . . the 'judicial Power' of Article III of the Constitution . . . [a]t the core of this power is the federal courts independent responsibility . . . to interpret federal law").

[111] *See, e.g.,* Cullen v. Pinholster, 563 U.S. 170 (2011) (reading AEDPA's provisions governing deference to state court findings of fact to preclude most hearings); Felker v. Turpin, 518 U.S. 651 (1996) (declining to reach the claim that AEDPA's limitations on successive petitions violate the Suspension Clause). Although the Court observed in United States v. Hayman, 342 U.S. 205 (1952), that "at common law a judgment of conviction rendered by a court of general criminal jurisdiction was conclusive proof that confinement was legal," *id.* at 211, it recently held that state court collateral review proceedings must give retroactive application to new substantive constitutional rules "that place certain criminal laws and punishments altogether beyond the State's power to impose," Montgomery v. Louisiana, 136 S.Ct. 718, 723 (2016). Given the constitutional premises of *Montgomery*, it likely extends to federal habeas proceedings and calls into question any provisions of AEDPA that would preclude such application.

[112] Ch. 339, 31 Stat. 141; *id.* § 67, 31 Stat. at 153 (authorizing territorial governor to suspend "in case of rebellion or invasion, or imminent danger thereof, when the public safety requires it"). For details, consult Duncan v. Kahanamoku, 327 U.S. 304, 307–8 (1946).

[113] 3 C.F.R. 1092 (1942) (repealed 1976).

aimed at controlling the movements of, and ultimately detaining against their will, persons of Japanese ancestry during the war.[114]

The result was unlike anything that had ever occurred in American history. More than 120,000 Japanese Americans – including more than 70,000 US citizens of Japanese ancestry – were forced from their homes and incarcerated in camps scattered across the west. Before these policies were put into place, many prominent government officials expressed great skepticism over the need for such measures. The skeptics included Federal Bureau of Investigation Director J. Edgar Hoover, who reportedly told Attorney General Francis Biddle that the push for such policies was "based primarily upon public and political pressure rather than on factual data."[115] There were also enormous constitutional problems with the policies. Beyond the fact that the policies were born of insidious racial and ethnic discrimination, the internment stands as the largest single violation of the Suspension Clause ever witnessed in history.

In four cases, Japanese Americans challenged the constitutionality of the military policies all the way to the Supreme Court. One of the first cases decided by the Court set the tone for those that followed. Gordon Hirabayashi, a student at the University of Washington and US citizen whose parents had immigrated from Japan, refused to register with military authorities as part of a process that was likely to result in his relocation to a camp. He also violated the curfew order in place where he lived. After being prosecuted and convicted in a civilian court based on this conduct, Hirabayashi challenged the governing military regulations as violating the nondelegation doctrine and the Fifth Amendment. When his case reached the Supreme Court, it rejected both arguments, opining with respect to the latter:

The adoption by Government, in the crisis of war and of threatened invasion, of measures for the public safety, based upon the recognition of facts and circumstances which indicate that a group of one national extraction may menace that safety more than others, is not wholly beyond the limits of the Constitution and is not to be condemned merely because in other and in most circumstances racial distinctions are irrelevant.[116]

---

[114] *See, e.g.*, Public Proclamation No. 3, 7 Fed. Reg. 2543 (Mar. 24, 1942) (establishing curfew within designated military areas, limiting travel, and regulating other activities); Public Proclamation No. 8, 7 Fed. Reg. 8346 (June 27, 1942) (compelling "persons of Japanese ancestry" evacuated from Military Areas to report to "Relocation Centers for their relocation, maintenance and supervision"); Civilian Restrictive Order 1, 8 Fed. Reg. 982 (May 19, 1942) (prohibiting "all persons of Japanese ancestry, both alien and non-alien," within "Assembly Centers, Reception Centers or Relocation Centers pursuant to exclusion orders" from leaving such areas without prior written authorization). For additional details, consult *Ex parte* Endo, 323 U.S. 283, 289 (1944). Congress ratified portions of President Roosevelt's Executive Order 9066, making it a criminal offense to remain in designated military zones. *See* Act of Mar. 21, 1942, Pub. L. No. 77-503, 56 Stat. 173 (repealed 1976).

[115] Francis Biddle, *In Brief Authority* 224 (1962) (quoting from a memo sent by Hoover to Attorney General Biddle) (internal quotation marks omitted).

[116] Hirabayashi v. United States, 320 U.S. 81, 101 (1943).

The Supreme Court reached a similar outcome the next year in Fred Korematsu's case. Korematsu, born and raised in Oakland, California, was also the son of Japanese immigrants and also a US citizen. The government prosecuted Korematsu for remaining in a designated military zone when he refused to comply with the military's exclusion restrictions. As in *Hirabayashi*, however, Korematsu's challenge to his conviction failed to move the Supreme Court, which declined to "reject as unfounded the judgment of the military authorities and of Congress that there were disloyal members of that population, whose number and strength could not be precisely and quickly ascertained."[117]

Unlike in *Hirabayashi*, however, this time the majority's position met with dissent. Specifically, one dissenter, Justice Owen Roberts, summarized the case as involving "convicting a citizen as a punishment for not submitting to imprisonment in a concentration camp, based on his ancestry, and solely because of his ancestry, without evidence or inquiry concerning his loyalty and good disposition towards the United States."[118] Another dissenter, Justice Frank Murphy, labeled the military framework operating in the western US as "fall[ing] into the ugly abyss of racism."[119] The final dissenter, Justice Robert Jackson, reduced the case to the following: "Now, if any fundamental assumption underlies our system, it is that guilt is personal and not inheritable."[120]

On the same day that the Court decided *Korematsu*, it also handed down its decision in Ex parte *Endo*. Mitsuye Endo was a US citizen who had been fired from her job working for the State of California based on her Japanese ancestry. Soon thereafter, under the military regulations, she had been forced to evacuate the military area encompassing where she lived in Sacramento, California, report to an assembly center, and then report for detention with her family at Tule Lake Camp. Meanwhile, her brother was serving in the US Army. In a petition for a writ of habeas corpus, Endo argued that the wartime internment of Japanese Americans was unconstitutional, citing *Milligan* and a host of additional historical precedents as establishing that the government had no general authority to detain citizens without criminal charges. Endo's case posed the only direct challenge to the detention of Japanese Americans that reached the Supreme Court.

In an attempt to moot Endo's case, the government offered her release on the condition that she be relocated outside the evacuation zones. She refused, aware that her release would moot her case. Ultimately, the Supreme Court decided the case on narrow grounds – namely, by concluding that governing regulations required the release of concededly loyal citizens, like Endo, from relocation centers. In so doing, the Court never reached the important Suspension Clause issues weighing in the balance.[121] Internal Court documents suggest that Chief Justice Harlan Fiske Stone, fully aware that the Court would decide the case unanimously in Endo's favor, held up the decision to give President Roosevelt

---

[117] Korematsu v. United States, 323 U.S. 214, 218 (1944).
[118] *Id.* at 226 (Roberts, J., dissenting).   [119] *Id.* at 234 (Murphy, J., dissenting).
[120] *Id.* at 243 (Jackson, J., dissenting).   [121] *See Ex parte* Endo, 323 U.S. 283 (1944).

time to act ahead of the Court and suspend 9066. Once the military announced that it would begin lifting the evacuation orders and closing the camps, the Court handed down its decision in the case the very next day. The closing of the camps commenced within weeks.

Assessment of these cases, along with the treatment of Japanese Americans during World War II more generally, has focused predominantly on the discriminatory components of the government's actions. It is easy to see why. After all, as countless scholars have documented, discrimination played a huge role in the debates leading up to the adoption of the policies put in place by US Army Lieutenant General John L. DeWitt, Military Commander of the Western Defense Command. This fact, moreover, implicates a host of enormously troubling constitutional considerations under equal protection jurisprudence.

But what seems to have escaped notice is the fact that the internment policy – at least as applied to citizens – ran categorically afoul of the Suspension Clause. Indeed, history had long dictated that the core purpose of the Suspension Clause was to prohibit the detention of citizens outside the criminal process in the absence of a valid suspension. This is the lesson of earlier wartime episodes, including the American Revolutionary War and the Civil War. Specifically, where those suspected of disloyalty enjoyed the habeas privilege under either the Habeas Corpus Act or the Suspension Clause, Anglo-American habeas jurisprudence had always required a valid suspension to authorize detention for national security purposes outside the criminal process – *even in wartime*. The regrettable legacy of the World War II detention of Japanese Americans is the creation of a precedent that gave constitutional sanction to "a policy of mass incarceration under military auspices,"[122] all in the absence of a suspension.

HABEAS CORPUS TODAY: CONFRONTING THE AGE OF TERRORISM

The terrorist attacks of September 11, 2001, and the Supreme Court cases that followed have led to renewed interest in the Suspension Clause and its role in our Constitution. Within days of the attacks, Congress enacted the Authorization for Use of Military Force (AUMF).[123] That law empowered the executive to "use all necessary and appropriate force against those nations, organizations, or persons he determines planned, authorized, committed, or aided the terrorist attacks that occurred on September 11, 2001 ... in order to prevent any future acts of international terrorism against the United States by such nations, organizations, or persons."[124]

In carrying out the mandate of the AUMF, the executive branch has pursued a lengthy and evolving war on terrorism. In prosecuting the war, the US military has taken numerous suspected terrorists and others believed to possess ties to al Qaeda

---

[122] Morton Grodzins, *Americans Betrayed: Politics and the Japanese Evacuation* 374 (1949).
[123] Pub. L. No. 107-40, 115 Stat. 224 (2001) (codified at 50 U.S.C. § 1541 note (2006)).
[124] *Id.* § 2, 115 Stat. at 224.

and other terrorist organizations into custody, including American citizens. On occasion, the government has initiated criminal charges against captured individuals.[125] The government has also labeled numerous prisoners as "enemy combatants" and held them without criminal charges in military confinement. In the years since 2001, the government has detained hundreds of persons in this posture at the US Naval Base at Guantánamo Bay, Cuba. It has also held two US citizens as enemy combatants in military custody on US soil: José Padilla and Yaser Hamdi.

The government arrested Padilla in 2002 upon his arrival at Chicago's O'Hare International Airport, to which he had traveled, via Europe, from Pakistan. The government initially detained Padilla on a material witness warrant stemming from the ongoing grand jury investigation into the attacks of September 11.[126] Days later, the President declared him an "enemy combatant" and ordered his transfer to the custody of the Department of Defense. Following this, the government detained Padilla in military custody without criminal charges for over three years before finally transferring him to civilian authorities and charging him with various crimes. In the meantime, Padilla protested consistently – but ultimately unsuccessfully – that his military detention violated the Suspension Clause.[127]

Afghan Northern Alliance fighters captured Yaser Hamdi, who had been born in the United States but grew up in Saudi Arabia, in Afghanistan in 2001. When turning him over to the US military, the Northern Alliance reported that it had captured Hamdi fighting with the enemy Taliban. In time, the military transferred Hamdi to a naval brig in South Carolina where it labeled him an "enemy combatant" and claimed the power to detain him indefinitely for the duration of the war on terrorism. Hamdi's father challenged the lawfulness of Hamdi's detention in a habeas petition that ultimately made its way to the Supreme Court and produced an important decision on the meaning of the Suspension Clause.

In the case, *Hamdi* v. *Rumsfeld*, a fractured Court rejected the government's assertion that the executive could detain a citizen indefinitely without affording the detainee some opportunity to challenge his classification as an enemy combatant.[128] At the same time, however, the Court held that the Suspension Clause does not preclude the detention of a citizen in a posture akin to a prisoner

---

[125] One example is John Walker Lindh's case. The government proceeded criminally against Lindh, a US citizen captured in Afghanistan while fighting with the Taliban against American forces, and he eventually pleaded guilty to two charges. *See* Katharine Q. Seelye, Regretful Lindh Gets 20 Years in Taliban Case, *N.Y. Times*, Oct. 5, 2002, at A1.

[126] *See* Rumsfeld v. Padilla, 542 U.S. 426, 430-31 (2004).

[127] The Supreme Court reviewed Padilla's case in 2004 but declined to reach the merits of his claims on jurisdictional grounds. *See id.* at 430, 451. In subsequent litigation, Padilla again sought Supreme Court review. At that point, the government transferred Padilla to civilian custody, a fact that all but mooted his second petition to the Supreme Court. *See* Padilla v. Hanft, 547 U.S. 1062, 1063 (2006) (Kennedy, J., concurring in denial of certiorari).

[128] Hamdi v. Rumsfeld, 542 U.S. 507, 510, 533 (2004) (plurality opinion).

of war, even in the absence of a suspension. In Justice O'Connor's words: "There is no bar to this Nation's holding one of its own citizens as an enemy combatant."[129]

Thus, Justice O'Connor's opinion in *Hamdi* sanctioned the idea that citizens could be detained in military custody without charges and held that the government did not need the authorization of a valid suspension to do so. It would seem that the holding applies to Padilla's case as well, unless Padilla's domestic point of capture is significant to the analysis, something unclear under Justice O'Connor's opinion. Either way, the *Hamdi* opinion on this score is deeply problematic in light of the long history of a habeas privilege tethered to the English Habeas Corpus Act and the suspension model that controlled during the American Revolution, founding era, and Civil War periods. Studying those periods reveals that the entire purpose of the Suspension Clause was to present the government with a decision either to bring criminal charges against citizens who may claim the protection of domestic law and provide them with a timely trial or else suspend the privilege in order to legalize detention outside the criminal process. Put another way, the so-called "citizen-enemy combatant" was a concept unknown to the law at the founding and well through the Civil War.[130]

This being said, more difficult cases wait in the wings. They include questions going to the application of the Suspension Clause to US military installations in Guantanamo Bay, Cuba, and other foreign locations as well as questions about who may claim the clause's protections and broader questions regarding how domestic constitutional law interacts with the international laws of war. The Supreme Court took up some of these questions in the 2008 case of *Boumediene* v. *Bush* and held that noncitizen detainees in the war on terrorism imprisoned at Guantanamo Bay, Cuba, could invoke the Suspension Clause to force judicial review of their classification as enemy combatants in the federal courts.[131] In this respect, the opinion built on *Hamdi* and extended its reasoning both geographically and in terms of who may claim the protection of the Suspension Clause. As in *Hamdi*, in *Boumediene*, the Court did not understand the Suspension Clause to preclude detention without charges but instead to promise a general right to review of one's detention, assuming all along that persons may be detained as enemy combatants. In this respect, also like *Hamdi*, the *Boumediene* decision represents a departure from the longstanding link between the Suspension Clause and the historical office of the privilege, which

---

[129] *Id.* at 519 (plurality opinion).

[130] Justice Scalia's dissent, joined by Justice Stevens, embraced and followed the historical narrative that had defined the constitutional habeas privilege and suspension model. *See id.* at 554–79 (Scalia, J., dissenting).

[131] 553 U.S. 723 (2008). Whether the holding in *Boumediene* should be extended beyond Guantanamo Bay has been the subject of considerable debate. *See, e.g.*, Al Maqaleh v. Gates, 605 F.3d 84, 92-99 (D.C. Cir. 2010) (concluding that *Boumediene* does not extend to the American military base in Bagram, Afghanistan).

prohibited detention outside the criminal process in the absence of a declared suspension.[132]

CONCLUSION

Oliver Wendell Holmes once famously warned that "[w]e must beware of the pitfall of antiquarianism, and must remember that for our purposes our only interest in the past is for the light it throws upon the present."[133] Notwithstanding this cautionary instruction, when construing the Suspension Clause, "antiquarianism" is almost unavoidable. This is because, to borrow from Chief Justice John Marshall, the term "habeas corpus" was "used in the [C]onstitution, as one which was well understood."[134] As the stories told here convey, the founding generation embraced in the Suspension Clause a conception of the "Privilege of the Writ of Habeas Corpus" derived from the seventh section of the English Habeas Corpus Act along with the suspension model created by Parliament to set aside the protections associated with the English Act. In so doing, the founding generation constitutionalized a well-entrenched framework for addressing the emergencies that inevitably would arise in the future – namely, a suspension model derived from the English practice that leaves it to the political branches to balance the needs of national security against individual liberty in times of crisis. But the Constitution only permits such balancing in truly extraordinary times – namely, in "Cases of Rebellion or Invasion [when] the public Safety may require it." Thus, by its very design, the Suspension Clause provides for a specific lever by which the Constitution can adapt in times of emergency to give the executive expanded powers to detain outside the criminal process those who may claim the protection of domestic law. In striking this balance, the Suspension Clause functions both as an "express provision for exercise of extraordinary authority because of a crisis"[135] and as one of the single most important protections of individual liberty found in the Constitution.

The twentieth and twenty-first centuries have witnessed the breakdown of this framework, most notably with the mass detention of Japanese American citizens during World War II and also with the recognition of the idea that US citizens may be detained as enemy combatants. In this respect, revisiting the historical backdrop of the Suspension Clause is arguably more important than ever – for it has, to return to Holmes, a great deal of light to shed on not only how we should evaluate these modern episodes but also more generally how we should understand the Suspension Clause to function in our constitutional framework going forward.

---

[132] For more on the historical relationship between the laws of war and domestic habeas law as well as the *Boumediene* decision and how that relationship might impact the issues raised therein, consult Tyler, *Habeas Corpus in Wartime, supra* note 7, at 245–276.

[133] O. W. Holmes, The Path of the Law, 10 *Harv. L. Rev.* 457, 474 (1897).

[134] *Ex parte* Watkins, 28 U.S. 193, 201 (1830).

[135] Youngstown Sheet & Tube Co. v. Sawyer, 343 U.S. 579, 650 (1952) (Jackson, J., concurring).

14

The Supreme Court, the Constitution, and American Public Policy

John I. Hanley and Gordon Silverstein

There is no longer any debate that members of the US Supreme Court are politicians in robes.[1] But the robes matter. Law is different, and judicial actors pursue their policy and ideological preferences in different ways than do elected officials and bureaucrats. To understand the Court's role in public policy, its promise as well as its pathologies, we need to understand that the Court is different – that it speaks in a different voice, operates with different time horizons, and is driven by different incentives. Only then can we hope to make real progress in understanding the Court's role in public policy.

In 1803, the US Supreme Court declared that it had an obligation "to say what the law is":[2] to rule on what state and national governments *may* do, what they may *not* do, and, less frequently, what they *must* do.

This simple menu would seem to lend itself to a rigorous and parsimonious quantitative analysis of Court power and impact. The Court says may, may not, or must. Individual litigants and government officials abide by that decision or they do not. If they comply, the Court can be said to have exercised power. If they do not, the Court can be said to have failed. It seems a simple proposition – did the litigants and the government comply with the ruling or not?

It's not that simple. The Court is a political institution, to be sure. But it functions in very different ways than do the elected branches or the bureaucracy. And understanding the Court's role, its valuable interventions as well as the unintended consequences it has had in shaping public policy, requires a holistic approach rather than a simple aggregation of court rulings where there has been compliance versus those where there has not.

---

[1] Charles Sheldon, *The Supreme Court: Politicians in Robes* (Beverly Hills, CA: Glencoe Press, 1970).
[2] Marbury v. Madison, 5 U.S. 137 (1803).

THE DISTINCTIVE FEATURES OF THE JUDICIAL ROLE
IN PUBLIC POLICY

In 1957 the noted political scientist Robert Dahl published two extraordinarily influential articles. One was a consideration of the "concept of power."[3] The other tried to contextualize the role of the Supreme Court at a time of dramatic rulings under the leadership of Chief Justice Earl Warren.[4] Far from a threat to majoritarian democracy, Dahl argued, the Supreme Court usually ends up in alignment with the dominant political regime, neither far in front nor far behind public opinion.[5]

Of course, this work built on the premise that power could be defined, measured, and tested. While Dahl acknowledged that there were important differences between and among various aspects of power (influence, control, and authority, for example), he noted that he would "use these terms interchangeably," though he added that in many instances, "distinctions are necessary and useful."[6] In "The Concept of Power," Dahl offered a now classic definition: "A has power over B," Dahl wrote, "to the extent that he can get B to do something that B would not otherwise do."[7]

This is a compelling definition of power for elected officials, executive agents, and even authority figures in business. But when we turn to the US Supreme Court, it is far too limited and fails to fully account for the variety of ways in which judicial rulings influence even where they do not control.

Dahl himself famously argued that "by itself, the Court is almost powerless to affect the course of national policy."[8] And if we use Dahl's "concept of power" definition, then he is absolutely right. But to explore how judicial practice affects the course of national policy even when it cannot control, we must move away from the false clarity of a simple measure of power, even though doing so "must inevitably result in a formal definition that is not easy to apply in concrete research problems."[9]

The Court does not simply declare which side wins and which loses. The Court gives reasons.[10] There are opinions, concurrences, and dissents.[11] Reasons are necessary because our judicial system is rooted in the common law tradition, a tradition of judge-made law in which justifications are knit together to create a tapestry, with each decision building on, extending, favoring, or disfavoring previous rulings in areas of the law that may not appear directly related.

---

[3] Robert Dahl. "The Concept of Power," *Behaviorial Science* 2(3) (1957): 202.
[4] Robert Dahl, "Decision-Making in a Democracy: The Supreme Court as National Policy-Maker," *Journal of Public Law* 6 (1957): 279.
[5] Ibid.   [6] Dahl, "The Concept of Power."   [7] Ibid.
[8] Dahl, "Decision-Making in a Democracy," 293.   [9] Dahl, "The Concept of Power."
[10] Martin Shapiro, "The Giving Reasons Requirement," *University of Chicago Legal Forum* (1992): 179.
[11] Martin Shapiro, "The Impact of Supreme Court Decisions," *J. Legal Educ.* 23 (1970–71): 77, 86.

Unlike elected officials, judges must consider how doctrinal changes in one area of the law inevitably constrain (even if they do not control) their options in other areas of law. For example: Is a case concerning the mandatory provision of contraceptive funding as part of a national health insurance program a case concerning the Equal Protection Clause? Is it a case concerning the guarantee of liberty through the Due Process Clause? Or is it a case about the First Amendment's Free Exercise, Establishment, or Free Speech clause? It might be one, two, or all of the above. And a decision built on one of those provisions may spill over and influence (and constrain) judicial choices in a myriad of cases built on that same constitutional provision.

The interrelationship of judicial rulings is just one example of how dissimilar are the incentives and constraints faced by judicial actors as opposed to elected officials. Another critical difference is that the Court's time horizons are very much longer than are those of elected officials: US senators have six-year horizons, Presidents see the world in two four-year blocks or less, while members of the House work in two-year cycles. But federal judges are appointed for life. With a recent trend of appointing Justices at a younger age combined with an ever-expanding life expectancy, a Supreme Court Justice operates in a time frame that can easily reach thirty years or more.[12]

A third vital difference is that elected officials can start with a blank page and Anglo-American judges nearly never do. While elected officials certainly can elect to build on existing laws and regulations (repairing Obamacare), they can just as easily attempt to start all over without regard to existing practice (repealing or replacing Obamacare), as Donald Trump amply demonstrated in the early weeks of his administration. Lower federal courts do not have this luxury. Even the Justices of the US Supreme Court, who are theoretically free to reverse their own rulings, are typically reluctant to do so because of the common law tradition of deference to precedent, as well as the practical consequences that might follow a quick or poorly reasoned reversal.[13] A radical shift in the Court's approach to one area of law (such as contraceptive funding) can cause ripple effects through a host of other areas in ways that legislation, regulations, and executive orders typically do not.

A fourth difference grows out of the third. One response to the Court's complex tapestry of decisions is to seek refuge in a notion of the Court as a

---

[12] Justice Scalia served for thirty years and Justice Rehnquist for thirty-three years, while Justice Kennedy has already served for twenty-eight years.

[13] A related concern came into sharp relief in the first weeks of the Trump administration. The 1996 Congressional Review Act (5 U.S.C. § Part I/chapter 8) authorizes Congress to overrule regulations put into effect by the executive by passage of a joint resolution. But this provision is limited to the first sixty days after the regulation is promulgated. The idea is that if a regulation has been in effect for more than sixty days, interested parties have already adjusted their behavior to the rule, and to drop it at that point would be deeply dislocating to those involved. This offers another way to think about precedent and the ways in which it influences, while it does not control, decision making.

simple applier of rules. This was the image Chief Justice John Roberts offered in his 2005 confirmation hearing, when he declared that it was not the Court's job to promote any political agenda. Instead, he said, our legal system assumes that the Court will act as "a fair and unbiased umpire, one who calls the game according to the existing rules and does so competently and honestly every day."[14] Judges, Roberts added, "are like umpires. Umpires don't make the rules, they apply them."[15]

But here is the problem: the Court's most fundamental set of rules – the Constitution – is a very short one, with precious few amendments (just seventeen since 1791). And that set of rules is anything but a comprehensive code book. As Chief Justice John Marshall explained it in *McCulloch* v. *Maryland* in 1819, a constitution, unlike a legal code, is merely an outline, one that marks out and identifies "its important objects" while "the minor ingredients which compose those objects" are to be "deduced from the nature of the objects themselves."[16] Even the most determined Justice could not possibly approach the job as a rule-bound umpire might.[17]

Consider a more practical demonstration of the problem: Professor Peter Edelman noted in his testimony at the Roberts confirmation hearing that if the Justices were merely umpires enforcing the rule book, we would not expect to see so many 5–4 Court decisions (or 7–2 decisions, for that matter).[18] Any set of rules so prone to divergent conclusions by experts would soon be replaced: it is impossible to imagine a baseball game in which a large number of decisions were decided by a "swing" umpire deciding the call on a 5–4 vote.

The Constitution, as noted previously, is not the only set of rules structuring the Court's role in public policy. The First Amendment guarantees each citizen the right to speak and to petition the government for a redress of grievances. The Constitution gives no such easy access to the Supreme Court, instead limiting the judicial power to a specified set of "cases" and "controversies." Building on that, the Court itself has developed a complex set of rules, often referred to as "threshold requirements," to determine who can bring a case, when, and under what conditions. These are critical in the Court's ability to control its docket. Many important judicial decisions, having profound effects on politics and public policy, actually turn on legal issues such as who can bring a case, when, and under what circumstances. Determining who gets to bring a case to the Court – and who is shut out – can fundamentally determine policy results without the Court even considering the policy question itself.

---

[14] Confirmation Hearing on the Nomination of John G. Roberts to Be Chief Justice. Committee of the Judiciary, United States Senate. 109th Congress, 1st Session. Sept. 12–15, 2005, p. 31.
[15] Ibid., p. 55.   [16] McCulloch v. Maryland, 17 U.S. 316, 407 (1819).
[17] Major League Baseball's 2016 official rule book has more than 58,000 words. The US Constitution, by contrast, has just 7,620 words.
[18] Testimony of Peter Edelman. Confirmation Hearing on the Nomination of John G. Roberts to Be Chief Justice. Committee of the Judiciary, United States Senate. 109th Congress, 1st Session. Sept. 12–15, 2005, p. 513.

Consider, for instance, the heated struggle over Donald Trump's executive order, issued just days into his presidency, halting immigration from and denying valid visas to residents of seven predominantly Muslim countries. The states of Washington and Minnesota went to federal court to seek a temporary injunction blocking the order. The Trump administration argued that the case should not even be heard, since neither of the states had suffered the sort of tangible injury that would give them standing to sue. A federal district court judge disagreed, as did a unanimous three-judge panel of the Ninth Circuit Court of appeals. They ruled that the states had standing to file their case, and that there was therefore no reason to lift the restraining order. These court rulings undoubtedly had a significant (though perhaps only temporary) impact on public policy – and also on the lives of thousands of citizens and potential immigrants. But neither the district court nor the appeals court considered the case on its merits, nor did they inquire into the efficacy of the policy embodied in the executive order. Instead, the lower courts and even the Supreme Court focused on the question of "standing" – do the parties challenging the order have the right to bring their cases in the first place?

Standing is just one of a number of critical threshold requirements litigants must meet before a court will even hear the case. But since refusing to hear a case can, in fact, determine the policy outcome, this is often as important as a vote on the merits. In the immigration example, had the court refused to entertain the claims made by Washington and Minnesota, the travel ban would never have been lifted, with huge domestic and international policy ramifications.

This is not a practice that necessarily favors one side of the political spectrum over the other. The Court's 2014 decision in *Burwell* v. *Hobby Lobby Stores* opened the courts to profit-making corporations that wanted to assert a corporate claim for religious liberty – a right heretofore limited exclusively to individuals and non-profit entities. *Hobby Lobby* was only indirectly concerned with the scope of religious liberty; more fundamentally, it was about who had the right to make religious liberty claims in court.

Here then are clear examples of the ways in which courts approach and influence public policy quite differently than do the elected branches. They overlap in their tools and practices, to be sure, but there are important distinctions as well. Finally, and perhaps most significant, is the observation Alexander Hamilton made in the *Federalist Papers*: that the Supreme Court "has no influence over either the sword or the purse; no direction either of the strength or of the wealth of the society; and can take no active resolution whatever." It is, he said, entirely dependent on the other branches: Congress for funds and the executive for force where force might be needed to ensure compliance.[19] This suggests that the Court's power declines when applied in situations that require the cooperation of the other branches or the use of tools and practices foreign to the judicial tradition. And, as a rule, the more the

---

[19] Alexander Hamilton, *Federalist 78*.

Court's rulings concern the direction and scope of public policy, the more they will depend on other branches and tools to implement that policy. In short, policies "point to a chain of causation between initial conditions and future consequences ... Implementation, then, is the ability to forge subsequent links in the causal chain so as to obtain the desired results."[20] The weak administrative power of the judiciary means that it must rely on others to forge policy links, and to the degree that it attempts to forge links itself, the choice of *how* and *at what level* to intervene matters a great deal, since a court cannot expand the scope of its actions or modify its behavior as easily as a bureaucracy. Successful implementation, in short, requires an understanding of institutions and policy that is not simply analogized to legislative- or executive-focused models.

THE COURT'S POWER TO SAY WHAT THE GOVERNMENT MAY AND MAY NOT DO

Because the Court is a reactive institution, it is typically asked to decide if government action is permitted or precluded: to rule whether the government *may* or *may not* act. This seems like a simple binary choice. But whereas umpires typically operate in the binary world – out or safe, ball or strike, foul or fair – Supreme Court Justices do not.

Consider the Affordable Care Act. In *NFIB* v. *Sebelius*, the Supreme Court was asked if the Constitution permitted the government to impose a penalty on those who failed to secure adequate health insurance through either private or government plans. The Court ruled, 5–4, that the government *could* impose this penalty. For those counting cases, this is where the story ends. But to fully understand the Court's role in public policy, we need to pay close attention to not only the outcome of the case but the reasons given.

The Affordable Care Act ultimately hinges on a mandate: unless healthy people are obliged or incentivized to sign up for the program, it cannot work. The mandate in the ACA imposes a fee on those who do not have adequate insurance. But where in the Constitution does the government find the authority to impose this requirement or the power to punish those who do not? The Obama administration and most liberal legal scholars assumed the mandate was grounded in the government's authority to regulate interstate and foreign commerce.[21] Health care is a huge business, after all, and any changes in the cost of health care or its quality would have significant effects on commerce "among the several states."

[20] Jeffrey L. Pressman and Aaron B. Wildavsky, *Implementation: How Great Expectations in Washington Are Dashed in Oakland; Or, Why It's Amazing That Federal Programs Work at All* (Berkeley, CA: University of California Press, 1973), xxi.

[21] U.S. Constitution, Article I, Section 8, paragraph 3: "The Congress shall have power ... to regulate commerce with foreign nations, and among the several states and with the Indian Tribes ...."

The Court upheld the mandate, but the swing vote came from Chief Justice Roberts, who was heavily concerned with preserving the Court's authority and legitimacy and therefore reluctant to strike down such a complex and consequential piece of legislation. But Roberts was also deeply concerned that the case not fundamentally derail his larger political, jurisprudential, and policy objective, which was to prevent constitutionally dubious expansions of federal power. The solution turned not on his vote to uphold the ACA but rather on the rationale for that vote. Roberts rejected the government's Commerce Clause claim and instead labeled the penalty attached to the mandate to be a tax whose constitutional justification came not from the Commerce Clause but, instead, from Congress's Article I authority to lay and collect taxes.[22]

To have accepted the government's assertion that this power was grounded in the Commerce Clause would have set back Roberts's broader goal of narrowing the scope of national power. Since the Commerce Clause has been the primary superhighway of national power since the late 1930s, any decision further fortifying this route to power would be deeply threatening to that larger agenda. In the end, Chief Justice Roberts was willing to concede the battle (and allow the ACA to be built on the taxing power) in an effort to win the war (rolling back the ever-expanding Commerce Clause).

Why does this matter? Because there is almost no exercise of national power that doesn't affect "commerce with foreign nations and among the states," whereas the taxing power is far narrower and – at least in theory – containable. Expanding the Commerce Clause to allow the ACA penalty would have undermined future judicial efforts to narrow and contain national power. In contrast, saying that the government *may* impose a penalty through the taxing power (a clear, explicit, and more limited constitutional power) allowed Roberts to continue his larger project of taming the Commerce Clause. To have ruled the other way would have imperiled that effort and handed any future progressive majority in American politics an even more robust constitutional foundation on which to build the case for an expansive regulatory state. But note that this longer, larger struggle would not turn up in a simple Dahlian count of the Court's vote.

The question at issue in *NFIB* v. *Sibelius* has a long and storied past. From 1895 until 1937, when Franklin Delano Roosevelt obtained his first opportunity to appoint a Supreme Court Justice, the Court's majority held that the Constitution provided few mechanisms for the regulation of economic policy. The Court used the Commerce and Contract Clauses as well as protections for liberty and property in the Due Process Clause of the Fifth and Fourteenth Amendments to constrain government – state and national – from using legislative or regulatory remedies to respond to economic crises such as

---

[22] U.S. Constitution, Article I, Section 8, paragraph 1: "The Congress shall have power to lay and collect taxes, duties, imposts and excises, to pay the debts and provide for the common defense and general welfare of the United States . . . ."

the Great Depression.[23] In 1937, Justice Harlan F. Stone would note in a letter to his sister that by forbidding Congress and the states to act, the Supreme Court has "tied Uncle Sam up in a hard knot."

Though FDR's infamous "Court-packing" plan failed, time and age did what legislation could not: by the end of his presidency, FDR had appointed eight justices to the US Supreme Court, and in 1938, the Court essentially declared itself out of the business of containing the Commerce Clause or patrolling the regulation of the economy.[24] The Commerce Clause soon became the most important vehicle for the assertion of national power. The 1964 Civil Rights Act, for example, which banned racial discrimination in public accommodations, rested squarely on the Commerce Clause. This had the benefit of securing a great number of civil rights (those that could be tied to commerce). But it also skewed future legislative and regulatory efforts, in the sense that civil rights that could not be tied to commerce often went unprotected.

In short, the Court's vote is sometimes only one part of a larger story, and not necessarily the most important part. As the Justices do, we must take a longer view and consider the implications of the reasons given, not only for the case at hand but also for later cases raising similar jurisprudential issues.

WHEN THE COURT TELLS THE GOVERNMENT WHAT IT MUST DO

Though less common, the Court also may consider a ruling that the Government "*must* act," and not simply that it "may or may not." One could crudely argue that the Court's heyday with "must" came in the Warren and Burger Court era. In some instances, the Court has been backed into this command function: a lack of compliance with the Court's "may" or "may not" rulings can press the Court to assert itself and insist not only that government act but that it do so in a particular way.

In other instances, the Court has embraced this role, insisting that the Constitution itself mandates government action, as happened with the implementation of the Court's doctrine of "one-man-one-vote," which mandated major legislative redistricting initiatives across the country, as well as with the Court's rulings on criminal procedure. These two examples – redistricting and criminal procedure – make clear that the Court's ability to control policy outcomes turns heavily on the degree to which it is employing the traditional tools of judicial authority. This finding sits well with Matthew Hall's study showing that the "probability of the Court successfully exercising power

---

[23] Just as a sample: Hammer v. Dagenhart, 247 U.S. 251 (1918); Railroad Retirement Board v. Alton, 295 U.S. 330 (1935); A.L.A. Schechter Poultry Corporation v. U.S., 295 U.S. 495 (1935); Carter v. Carter Coal, 298 U.S. 238 (1936).
[24] United States v. Carolene Products Co., 304 U.S. 144 (1938).

increases" when "its ruling can be directly implemented by lower state or federal courts."²⁵

When "Must" Requires Only Court Intervention

The rulings that the Court can have greatest confidence will be implemented are those that concern policies over which lower courts have exclusive jurisdiction to enforce compliance. In such cases the implementation and enforcement of judicial commands requires little or no cooperation or coordination with the other branches of government. Indeed, the lower courts can largely force compliance using only the judicial tools they have at hand.

Here, one might think of the Court's 1961 ruling in *Mapp* v. *Ohio*, which held that evidence obtained without a proper warrant must be excluded from trial. This "exclusionary" rule essentially said to the government, "If you want to offer evidence in court, you *must* follow court-mandated procedures."²⁶ While this logically flows from broader principles of due process, it is not something clearly and explicitly commanded by the Constitution's criminal procedure–related clauses.²⁷

A second example is the mandate to provide state-funded legal counsel for those facing trial who cannot otherwise afford to hire counsel (*Gideon* v. *Wainwright*). In 1963, a man named Clarence Earl Gideon was arrested and charged with breaking and entering. When he appeared in court, Gideon told the judge that he could not afford to hire a lawyer and asked that one be provided for him. Florida law only allowed for state-funded counsel in capital cases, and so the request was denied. After being convicted and sentenced to five years in prison, Gideon lost an appeal to the Florida Supreme Court. He then sent a petition to the US Supreme Court. The Court accepted the case, sided with Gideon, and held that those facing criminal charges had a right to a fair trial and that a fair trial required legal counsel. The government, the Court ruled, *must* provide counsel for those who could not otherwise afford it.

Who would decide whether an accused person had been provided adequate counsel? Judges and courts. Who would pay for this? Not the Court. So how could the Court be confident of compliance? Because the courts would ultimately decide appeals based on the *Gideon* ruling. And if the Court simply ordered the release of any defendant not represented by counsel, the states would have a powerful, possibly irresistible incentive to comply with its order.

Similarly, consider a 1966 ruling, a portion of which literally millions of people across the globe can recite. They know that prior to police interrogation,

²⁵ Matthew E. K. Hall, *The Nature of Supreme Court Power* (New York: Cambridge University Press, 2011).

²⁶ Mapp v. Ohio, 367 U.S. 643 (1961).

²⁷ Akil Reed Amar, *The Constitution and Criminal Procedure* (New Haven, CT: Yale University Press, 1998).

a suspect must be read a list of his or her rights. And while the Court did not explicitly dictate the precise words that would be read, the Court's "suggested" language in *Miranda* v. *Arizona* was almost exactly what every police officer – in real life or in the movies – recites to this day. The Court ruled that a suspect "must be warned prior to any questioning that he has the right to remain silent, that anything he says can be used against him in a court of law, that he has the right to the presence of an attorney, and that, if he cannot afford an attorney one will be appointed for him prior to any questioning if he so desires."[28]

How would this be implemented? And by whom? Chief Justice Warren answered that as well. "[U]nless and until such warnings and waiver are demonstrated by the prosecution at trial, no evidence obtained as a result of interrogation can be used against him." The evidence that had been gained from the interrogation would be excluded from trial. Trials, of course, are under the exclusive jurisdiction of judges. Police (government) were free to violate the Court's mandate, but the courts were then instructed to exclude that same evidence. There wasn't a great deal of nuance or ongoing cooperation needed for implementation. As Chief Justice Rehnquist wrote in a decision reaffirming the holding in *Miranda* in 2000: "The law in this area is clear. This Court has supervisory authority over the federal courts, and we may use that authority to prescribe rules of evidence and procedure that are binding in those tribunals."[29]

When Judicial Tools Don't Fit the Policy Problem

In *Mapp, Miranda,* and *Gideon* the Court used judicial tools in a policy arena that the Judges understood and over which they had firm control. We can "score" these as instances of important Court interventions in public policy. But consider what happens when the Court confronts policy problems that are only exacerbated by the use of judicial tools, for example, the case Chief Justice Earl Warren referred to as "[t]he most important case of my tenure on the Court."[30] *Baker* v. *Carr*[31] set in motion a series of rulings that forced the states to redraw their electoral districts, thereby drastically reshaping political power in America. Like many other predominantly rural and agricultural states, Tennessee underwent a process of urbanization in the 1940s and 1950s. Prior to this, less than 10 percent of the state's population had lived in the three urban counties that were the focus of the case; but by 1960 those same counties accounted for nearly 40 percent of the state's population. But despite this population shift, the state legislature still reflected the earlier population distribution. This devalued the votes of urban dwellers and inflated rural political power. The Tennessee courts saw this as a "political question" to be

---

[28] Miranda v. Arizona, 384 U.S. 436, 479 (1966).
[29] Dickerson v. United States, 530 U.S. 428 (2000).
[30] Earl Warren, *The Memoirs of Earl Warren* (Garden City: Doubleday, 1977), 306.
[31] Baker v. Carr, 369 U.S. 186 (1962).

resolved by the elected branches – a position in line with that of Supreme Court Justice Felix Frankfurter.[32] The problem with leaving it to the political process was that those currently in office – who would have to approve any change – had overwhelming incentives to retain the status quo. Any change would diminish the power of the rural legislators then in office and enhance the power of those in the minority. To rely on the political process was futile.

We can skip ahead and simply code the case: the Supreme Court voted 6–2 in favor of requiring Tennessee to redraw its legislative districts. One might even end the story here, noting simply that the Court stood by its decision in subsequent cases, forcing state after state to undergo redistricting. But to approach this line of cases in such a narrow and formal manner would miss entirely the consequences of the *reasoning* that underpinned the Court's original decision.

To get anything done in the Supreme Court requires a majority. In *Baker*, there was a clear majority in favor of redistricting but there was no agreement on the underlying rationale. There were a number of plausible constitutional foundations on which to build; the most obvious were the "Guarantee" Clause of Article IV and the Equal Protection Clause of the Fourteenth Amendment. The Guarantee Clause provides that "[t]he United States shall guarantee to every State in the Union a Republican Form of Government." Using the Guarantee Clause might have allowed the Justices to think about what is required to meet this threshold. That, in turn, might have left room for variation and adaptation to a diverse set of states. The Equal Protection Clause, on the other hand, leads us to think about voting as an individual right in the nature of a property right. Instead of considering the nature of *effective* representation, we focus instead on *equal* representation. Building on the Equal Protection Clause led the Court to ever more fine-grained examinations of the precise distribution of political power.

In a 1963 case, Justice Douglas wrote that the conception of political equality in the US Constitution "can mean only one thing – one person, one vote."[33] And in *Wesberry* v. *Sanders* in 1966, the Court ruled that "as nearly as practicable, one man's vote in a congressional election is to be worth as much as another's."[34] By 1969 the Court would reject a Missouri plan where the largest district was just 3 percent more populous than "the mathematical ideal" and the smallest was not even 3 percent under that ideal.[35] Thirteen years later, the Court would reject a New Jersey plan where the difference between largest and smallest district would have been less than seven-tenths of 1 percent.[36]

One can then ask: Did the Court's intervention in policy here lead to fair representation? Did it lead to equal representation? Or did it open the door to

---

[32] Colegrove v. Green, 328 U.S. 549 (1946)   [33] Gray v. Sanders, 372 U.S. 368, 381 (1963).
[34] Wesberry v. Sanders, 376 U.S. 1, 8 (1964).
[35] Kirkpatrick v. Preisler, 394 U.S. 526, 528–529 (1969).
[36] Karcher v. Daggett, 462 U.S. 725 (1983).

sophisticated computer modeling that has produced the districts (and partisanship) we grapple with today?[37]

This is not to say that the Court was wrong in its result in *Baker,* but it is to say that the rationale it chose may have been more important. And why did it choose that rationale? The majority made that choice because at least three Justices likely would have voted the other way had the decision been based on the Guarantee Clause.[38] And it chose this option because the Court (and lower courts) is far more comfortable measuring against an objective numerical standard than it is weighing the ambiguity of what constitutes a "Republican form of government." It is not, in short, enough to know the vote in a case and the ideological alignment of the Court to understand the Court's role in public policy.

Working at Cross-Purposes: Abortion

The choice of constitutional foundation can also profoundly affect the Court's efficacy in implementing its rulings. The Supreme Court's struggle with abortion rights provides a clear example. Apart from being perhaps the most controversial decision of recent decades, *Roe* v. *Wade* has focused a great deal of scholarly attention on the social and political impact of Court decisions as well as the relationship between public opinion and judicial choices.[39] The abortion cases also demonstrate how the Court's reasoning – and the response by the other branches (and the public) to its reasoning – can shape subsequent cases, legislation, and litigation long into the future.

In *Roe,* the Court took a dramatic step – ruling that the states had virtually no role to play in any decisions about terminating pregnancy during the first trimester. And yet the Court left much to the state legislatures, state judges, and lower federal court judges – all of whom would profoundly shape this policy as it moved from judicial opinion to implementation. Most prominently: What regulations might be permitted in the second and third trimesters? Once again, the constitutional foundation on which the decision was built would be profoundly important. Then-Circuit Court Judge Ruth Bader Ginsburg would

---

[37] For contrasting recent views on the relationship between partisan control of redistricting and election outcomes, see Jowei Chen and David Cottrell, "Evaluating Partisan Gains from Congressional Gerrymandering: Using Computer Simulations to Estimate the Effect of Gerrymandering in the U.S. House." 44 *Electoral Studies* 329–40 (2016); Anthony McGann, Charles Smith, Michael Latner, and Alex Keena, *Gerrymandering in America: The House of Representatives, the Supreme Court, and the Future of Popular Sovereignty* (New York: Cambridge University Press, 2016).

[38] A more detailed discussion of the judicial imperatives driving this decision can be found in Gordon Silverstein, *Law's Allure: How Law Shapes, Constrains, Saves, and Kills Politics* (New York: Cambridge University Press, 2009), Chapter 3.

[39] Lee Epstein and Joseph F. Kobylka, *The Supreme Court and Legal Change: Abortion and the Death Penalty* (Chapel Hill, NC: University of North Carolina Press, 1992); Linda Greenhouse and Reva Siegel, "Before Roe v. Wade: Voices That Shaped the Abortion Debate before the Supreme Court's Ruling," *SSRN* (2012).

later argue in a law review article that the Court, instead of relying on a right to privacy derived from the Fourteenth Amendment's Due Process Clause, should have built its abortion jurisprudence on the Equal Protection Clause. This would have allowed the Court to move more incrementally rather than taking the sweeping position that there was a fundamental, constitutional, individual right to choose to terminate pregnancy.[40] Alternatively, the Court could have taken its fundamental rights argument to its logical conclusion: that a woman's right to choose could not be interfered with at least to viability, if not all the way to live birth. But it did neither. Instead the Court chose to build on a fundamental rights platform that included a complex balancing of competing interests.

To say that there is a fundamental right to choose to terminate a pregnancy in the first trimester also raised another profound problem. If there is a fundamental right in play, would it be enough to simply say the government *may not* interfere with a woman's choice? Or does the fact that a fundamental right is in play mean that the Court, logically, would have to tell the government that it *must* provide that service for women who could not afford it? What sort of a right might this be if it was a right available only to those with means? This issue took focus as states moved to exclude abortions from being covered under state-paid programs for the poor. Meanwhile, federal funding for abortions in the Medicaid program was blocked by the 1976 Hyde amendment. And these restrictions, both state[41] and federal,[42] were upheld by the Supreme Court. In so doing, the Court declined to apply the logic of its own opinion, in which (at least in the first trimester) it was asserted that a woman had a fundamental right to make this choice.

And so the Court was in the awkward position of having asserted a right (which implied a *must*) and yet having neither the means to implement the logical implications of that decision nor the capacity to insist that the other branches do so. As the Court withdrew from asserting a strong, affirmative right to an abortion, it also laid the groundwork for a diminution of that right in a pair of 1976 rulings, *Planned Parenthood v. Danforth* and *Bellotti v. Baird I.*[43] In *Bellotti* and *Danforth*, the Court started to articulate what would come to be known as the "undue burden" standard – the rule that regulations of abortion (parental consent in *Bellotti* and recordkeeping and reporting provisions in *Danforth*) could not impose undue burdens on the right to choose. The following year, in *Maher v. Roe* (1977), Justice Powell expanded the application of the "undue burden" criteria from the specific state regulations in *Bellotti* and *Danforth*, holding that "a state-created obstacle need not be absolute to be impermissible ...." Instead, the Court now held, a state

---

[40] Ruth Bader Ginsburg, "Speaking in a Judicial Voice," *NYU Law Review* 67 (1992): 1185–1209.
[41] Beal v. Doe, 432 U.S. 438 (1977); Maher v. Roe, 432 U.S. 464 (1977).
[42] Harris v. McRae (1980). 448 U.S. 297 (1980).
[43] Bellotti v. Baird I, 443 U.S. 622 (1979) and Planned Parenthood v. Danforth 428 U.S. 52, 132 (1976). See Epstein and Kobylka, *The Supreme Court and Legal Change*, for a comprehensive review.

imposed regulation or restriction was "not unconstitutional unless it unduly burdens the right to seek an abortion."

Twelve years later, Justice Sandra Day O'Connor cast the pivotal vote in *Webster* v. *Reproductive Services* (1989) to substitute the "undue burden" standard, with all of its ambiguity and subjectivity, for *Roe*'s trimester framework.[44] This deeply subjective term provided states with great latitude to impose limits on abortion. And they took up this invitation with vigor. As a result, the Court was forced to address the question of what the states *must* do – but now from a new angle. If an abortion decision had the effect of closing abortion clinics, would the Court rule on how many abortion providers were required? Would the Court use data on the number of abortions performed to determine when a burden had become "undue"?

In 2016, in *Whole Women's Health* v. *Hellerstedt*, the Court confronted a Texas statute requiring all physicians performing abortions to have admitting privileges at a hospital within thirty miles and establishing a strict set of building codes, safety requirements, and staffing standards for clinics. The practical effect of these rules would have been the closing of four-fifths of the clinics performing abortions in Texas, forcing those seeking these services to travel more than 150 miles to obtain them. A 5–3 majority struck down the Texas regulations. By striking down the entire statute, the Court avoided the burden of having to evaluate each of these burdens in isolation. Here the Court seemed to entertain a return to the other side of "must" – that is to say, a return to "robust judicial protection" for abortion rights.[45]

And yet the ambiguous boundary between acceptable burdens and "undue" ones remains. Indeed, an often overlooked part of this story is an institutional factor that allowed the Court in its abortion rulings to float between *may/may not* and *must*. This was the existence of a significant network of nonhospital clinics that became the primary providers of abortion services as hospitals increasingly distanced themselves from this procedure. This reality had two primary effects: It largely removed hospitals and most of the mainstream medical profession as potential sources of community support for a more robust right to choose. It also meant that abortion opponents were not facing down well-established community institutions and instead could focus on smaller institutions outside of the medical (and community) mainstream.

Another critical factor was public opinion. This is not typically the Court's central (or explicit) concern. But it was Robert Dahl who assured his readers that the Court was unlikely to long be out of step with public opinion. And, indeed, the 1960s saw a rising trend in support for some degree of liberalization of abortion laws, particularly those concerning the health of the pregnant woman and those resulting from rape and incest. But public support for

---

[44] Webster v. Reproductive Health Services, 492 U.S. 490 (1989).
[45] Linda Greenhouse and Reva B. Siegel, "The Difference a Whole Woman Makes: Protection for the Abortion Right After Whole Woman's Health," 126 *Yale L. J. F.* (2016): 126.

abortion in cases where a woman wanted to terminate a pregnancy for economic or family planning reasons was never strong.[46] An initial uptick in support for abortion rights in the immediate aftermath of the *Roe* decision proved ephemeral.[47] And as it became increasingly clear that the American public was sharply divided over the question of abortion rights, the Court, following Dahl, moderated its stance, tolerating more and more restrictions.

So what do we conclude about abortion? For forty-three years, the Court has stood by its holding that a woman has a fundamental right to access abortion services (provided she can pay for them), but that right has been significantly restricted by Court rulings handed down during this same period. *Roe* (and the cases that followed) offer a harsh lesson in the challenges of implementation in arenas that require more than simple judicial compliance. Implementation requires the support and constructive engagement of other government and nongovernmental institutions alike. In this environment, even a *may/may not* approach faces considerable obstacles. If the Court's judgment is unpopular or flawed, other actors may force it into increasingly awkward, uncomfortable, unpopular positions that well may undermine any possibility of successful implementation: the Court's attempts to navigate a specific set of state restrictions created precedents that would eventually be exploited to permit a much wider set of constraints on abortion rights.

Secondly, while *stare decisis* – the tradition that previous decisions govern current cases – is not formally binding on the Supreme Court, the Justices are nonetheless loath to reverse major and contentious decisions of a previous Court. Indeed, it was a commitment to *stare decisis* and the need to abide by settled expectations that generated the deciding votes in *Planned Parenthood* v. *Casey (1992)*. There, Justices David Souter and Anthony Kennedy joined Justice O'Connor in declaring that "after considering the fundamental constitutional questions resolved by *Roe*, principles of institutional integrity, and the rule of *stare decisis*, we are led to conclude this: the essential holding of *Roe* v. *Wade* should be retained and once again reaffirmed." The stronger argument, they insisted, "is for affirming *Roe*'s central holding, with whatever degree or personal reluctance any of us may have, not for overruling it."[48]

---

[46] Surveys between 1962 and 1972 show that there was growing support for some liberalization of abortion laws – even by Catholics. Epstein and Kobylka, *The Supreme Court and Legal Change*, 147–48, 152, 187–88. The December 1965 study for the National Opinion Research Council showed 64 percent of Catholics favoring liberalized abortion rules where the health of the mother was in danger. But when abortion was sought for economic reasons (a woman felt she could not afford to raise the child), support dropped to just 21 percent, and when the reason was simply that a woman did not want an additional child, the support fell to 15 percent. David J. Garrow, *Liberty and Sexuality: The Right to Privacy and the Making of Roe v. Wade* (Berkeley: University of California Press, 1998), 303.

[47] John Hanley, Michael Salamone, and Matthew Wright, "Reviving the Schoolmaster: Reevaluating Public Opinion in the Wake of Roe v. Wade," *Political Research Quarterly* 65 (2012): 408–21.

[48] Planned Parenthood v. Casey, 505 U.S. 833, 846, 861 (1992).

It is hard if not impossible to imagine that a commitment to maintaining past reasoning or to protecting settled expectations would have constrained the elected branches for long. In the nineteen years between *Roe* and *Casey*, there were ten rounds of congressional elections and five occupants of the Oval Office. Policies would ebb and flow, reverse and reappear. But the Court is different: three of the Justices on the Court for *Roe* were still on the Court for *Casey*. And while *stare decisis*, settled expectations, and precedent are by no means binding, they do matter for the Court, and they are largely responsible for keeping the last vestiges of *Roe* in place.

Gay Rights, the Court, and Public Policy: Lead, Follow, or Get Out of the Way?

Though constructed from virtually identical constitutional reasoning as the Court's conclusion that there was a right to choose a first-trimester abortion, the right to same-sex intimacy presents a dramatically different narrative and suggests (at present) a very different view of the Court as a participant in the construction of controversial public policies. The progress of gay rights in the courts shows that the Supreme Court need not be at the forefront of major policy change in order to play an important role. The Court can lead, to be sure – but it can also have a significant impact when it follows and ratifies decisions handed down by state and lower federal courts.

In contrast to its abortion rulings, the Court acted on same-sex marriage only after a complex political process had been playing out for decades, mostly at the state level. Policy had been developed and challenged. State courts had weighed in on specific concerns. When the Supreme Court ruled that same-sex couples could not be denied a marriage license from the state, compliance would largely require that court officers and sworn government employees issue the appropriate paperwork. It would not require an executive's force of arms or any sort of legislative appropriations. Avenues for opposition or backlash had, over the preceding years, been blocked off. One can of course criticize the Court for not entering the fray earlier; perhaps many lives would have been profoundly enriched had the Court taken the lead in the 1970s – or 1990s or at the turn of the century – rather than waiting until 2015 to endorse same-sex marriage rights.[49] But one could also praise the Court, arguing that had the Court tried to lead, implementation might well have worked out much as it did in the abortion controversy.

"Liberty," Justice Kennedy states in the opening of his opinion in *Lawrence* v. *Texas* in 2003, "protects the person from unwarranted government intrusions into a dwelling or other private places." Weighing the alleged interests of the state against "freedom of . . . certain intimate conduct," the Court struck down Texas's ban on homosexual sodomy while avoiding creating a formula or test that could be applied to disputes over other types of discrimination, and particularly to

---

[49] Obergefell v. Hodges, 576 U.S. ___ (2015).

same-sex marriage. The majority opinion declined to treat sexuality as a class akin to race or gender for purposes of the Fourteenth Amendment's Equal Protection Clause. Thus, the Court took an incremental step – one broadly consistent with public opinion[50] – *without* elaborating a broader theory of when and how laws targeting a particular type of "intimate conduct" run afoul of the Constitution.

At the time, some described *Lawrence* as a false promise. Gerald Rosenberg argued that gay rights groups were falling into the same trap that had ensnared abortion rights advocates before them – relying on the courts and expansive, judicially defined rights to achieve what politics could not do as easily or as fast. The subtitle of Rosenberg's chapter on the gay rights cases – "When Will They Ever Learn?" – sums up his concern. Another prominent view attacked the *Lawrence* majority's false modesty – that is, its steadfast refusal to consider that its reasoning seemed destined to extend to same-sex marriage. Justice Antonin Scalia's dissent stressed this point, arguing that the Court's rejection of sodomy laws compelled it to invalidate all other forms of morals legislation. Of the majority's claim that its logic stopped short of same-sex marriage, Justice Scalia wrote, "Do not believe it."

In the end, Scalia's forecast came to be. But fears in the gay rights community that backlash would set back the gay rights movement did not come to pass. Thomas Keck surveyed the terrain of LGBT rights in the years after *Lawrence* and found an overall expansion of state antidiscrimination provisions, hate crimes statutes, and other legal protections for same-sex couples, even as several states enacted statutory or constitutional provisions forbidding same-sex marriage or civil partnerships.[51] Conceding that some public employee benefits or local antidiscrimination provisions were obliterated in the post-*Lawrence* rush to codify opposition to same-sex marriage, Keck argues that these policy reversals were greatly outweighed by pro-LGBT action elsewhere.

In *Romer* v. *Evans* (1996), the Court relied on the Equal Protection Clause to strike down an amendment to Colorado's state constitution prohibiting the state and localities from granting "protected status" to gay, lesbian, or bisexual persons. According to Justice Kennedy's opinion, the breadth of the Colorado amendment undermined claims that the measure achieved "any identifiable legitimate purpose or discrete objective." After *Lawrence* was decided, *Romer* served as a barrier against attempts to pass far-reaching legislation bearing on sexual minorities. And

---

[50] In the Gallup Poll, the portion of respondents saying that "gay or lesbian relations between consenting adults" should be legal attained 59 and 60 percent in two May 2003 polls before *Lawrence* was announced. In the first three post-*Lawrence* polls, this figure dropped to 46–50 percent. "Gay and Lesbian Rights – Gallup Historical Trends," www.gallup.com/poll/1651/gay-lesbian-rights.aspx. See also Patrick J. Egan, Nathaniel Persily, and Kevin Wallsten, "Gay Rights," in Persily et al., *Public Opinion and Constitutional Controversy* (New York: Oxford University Press, 2008), 234–66.

[51] Thomas Keck, "Beyond Backlash: Assessing the Impact of Judicial Decisions on LGBT Rights," *L. & Soc. Rev.* 43 (2009): 151.

when *state* courts asserted a right to same-sex marriage (as the California Supreme Court did in 2008), the deck became stacked against countermeasures. Thus, when California voters in November 2008 narrowly approved a state constitutional amendment banning gay marriage, a federal judge could examine the motivations and arguments of the ballot proposition's advocates to conclude that the amendment had "most likely" passed due to "a desire to advance the belief that opposite-sex couples are morally superior to same-sex couples."[52]

While marriage quickly emerged as a central focus for activists and the public, it was not the only issue of concern to gay rights advocates. Alison Gash notes that in the years after *Lawrence*, same-sex adoption and parental rights emerged mostly unscathed from state legislative and constitutional initiatives. Concerning adoption, Gash argues that advocates made important advances through the deliberate use of "low-visibility" tactics. Often court-centered, these were incremental efforts that did not require or make use of a blockbuster Supreme Court ruling to break through political barriers.[53] This strategy avoided the all-or-nothing sort of Court ruling that might well have derailed the movement. Imagine the impact a definitive ruling on a right to same-sex marriage might have had in the 1980s or early 1990s. Indeed, the movement's success in areas such as adoption suggests that a strategy built through legislation and regulatory challenges in individual states and localities followed by state and lower federal court review may well be a pattern other social policy advocates should consider.[54]

This is not to suggest that the pattern in these cases is ideal or fully satisfying to those involved. The struggle over gay rights was certainly not put to rest by *Obergefell*. The combination of the Religious Freedom Restoration Act and an increasingly conservative Court suggest another route by which opponents of gay rights may pursue their agenda. Here we can see important potential spillover effects: building on cases like *Hobby Lobby*, the Court seems increasingly willing to entertain claims that the RFRA and the First Amendment itself provide protection to private businesses and nonprofit organizations who engage in religiously-motivated discrimination against customers and employees. This development could flip the story: instead of the Court saying that government *may not* prohibit same-sex couples from marrying – and prohibiting state-sanctioned discrimination on the basis of sexual orientation – the Court's rulings could shift the discrimination to the private sector and hold that the government *may not* force private businesses to serve customers on the basis of sexual orientation.

[52] Perry v. Schwarzenegger, 704 F. Supp. 2d 921 (2012).
[53] Alison Gash, *Below the Radar: How Silence Can Save Civil Rights* (New York: Oxford University Press, 2015).
[54] The question of whether lower courts pushed the Supreme Court or whether the Supreme Court waited for this pressure to develop is an interesting one that is much deserving of research attention.

CONCLUSION

Recognizing that courts and judges are political is not the end of an inquiry but the beginning of one. Surely judges have an impact on public policy. Just as surely, their impact is not determined by a simple majority vote. As Martin Shapiro noted in 1970, the question of impact raises three challenges. There is, he notes, "the impact study based on a single Supreme Court decision": a command is issued, and we measure whether it is obeyed. At the "opposite extreme" is impact on American political life – the far broader ways in which society is changed by a pattern of court decisions. And in between is a study of the impact of Supreme Court opinions "in terms of the words it has spoken rather than the commands it has issued."

A Court ruling will produce a rush to the TV cameras on the steps of the Supreme Court, instant analysis, and instant condemnation or applause. But the real measure of the impact of a court ruling will emerge far more slowly, as interested parties, other judges, lawyers, and the public digest the opinion and game out its implications. And while the Court hands down fewer than ninety decisions a year, those opinions cover a huge swath of legal, political, and policy terrain. And those opinions interact with each other in ways a Justice considering the development of doctrine across a lifetime must consider (while a member of Congress facing reelection every two years may not). This is not a plea to return to hide-bound doctrinalism. Instead, it is an insistence that language – whether aimed primarily at the other Justices, the bar, the legal academy, or the public itself – is important for influencing the behavior necessary for policy implementation.[55]

If judges hope to see their rulings fully implemented, they too must pay careful attention to capacity – is it possible to put their rulings into effect? Are the requirements and standards "workable"? *Can* they be implemented? This concern led Justice Blackmun to reverse his own position in an important set of cases concerning the boundary between state sovereignty and national authority in the 1980s, arguing that the Court's effort to define a limit on national authority by creating a category of what the Court called "traditional state functions" was simply "unworkable."[56] Unworkablity doesn't matter if you are simply voting an ideological preference, nor does it register if you are simply counting wins and losses. But if you are interested in policy and its implementation, then workability matters a great deal.

---

[55] The middle category – the analysis of how and when and why judicial rulings shape and constrain political choices and outcomes – is at the root of Silverstein, *Law's Allure*, particularly chapter 3: "Law Is Different."

[56] In Garcia v. San Antonio Metro Transit, 469 U.S. 528 (1985), Justice Blackmun abandoned the court-fashioned concept of "traditional state functions" as arenas free from federal regulation, which he had endorsed just nine years earlier in National League of Cities v. Usery, 426 U.S. 833 (1976).

Structure, role, and resources weigh heavily on the Court's prospects for having its rulings implemented. Justices may be "politicians in robes," but it is incorrect to make assertions about their behavior and motives with the same firmness that we might for members of Congress or Presidents. Aside from meeting a standard of "good behavior," federal judges do not need to satisfy the demands of an external constituency. Justices' utilization of recent law school graduates as clerks rather than relying exclusively on a professional bureaucracy increases the distance between the Supreme Court and the legislative and executive branches. While the Court's personnel has doubled since 1974,[57] more people actually work for the Congressional Research Service than for the US Supreme Court. The Court could lobby to hire an army of policy experts[58] – but that is not its institutional function nor its comparative advantage. As long as this is the case, the style, objectives, and political awareness of justices will be consequential for policy outcomes. Despite the tendency of today's judicial appointees to reflect very strong ideological commitments, judgment and reason-giving remain central to the judiciary's role in the public policy process.

[57] Lee Epstein et al., *The Supreme Court Compendium*, 5th ed. (Los Angeles: Sage Press, 2012).
[58] This approach was actually recommended in James P. Levine and Theodore L. Becker. "Toward and Beyond a Theory of Supreme Court Impact," *American Behavioral Scientist* 13 (1970): 561–73.

15

The Constitution, the Law, and Social Change: Mapping Pathways of Influence

Tomiko Brown-Nagin

Justice Oliver Wendell Holmes, the father of legal realism, famously wrote: "The life of the law has not been logic; it has been experience."[1] This essay considers the idea of experience – or events external to legal doctrine – affecting the law. In Holmes's formulation, the experiences capable of shaping the law included moral and political theories, public policy preferences, commonly held prejudices, and the "felt necessities of the time." This essay considers a different category of experiences that may be relevant to the law: the power of social movements – groups of citizens mobilized in support of a cause – to shape and be shaped by the law and, thus, to influence social change.

The essay rests on the premise that social movements deploy the Constitution and other types of rights talk to "frame" disputes[2] and move forward their agendas.[3] It

---

[1] Oliver Wendell Holmes, *The Common Law* (Cambridge, MA: Harvard University Press, 2009 [1881]).

[2] On framing as a social movement tactic, see David A. Snow, "Framing Processes, Ideology, and Discursive Fields," in David A. Snow and Sarah A. Soule, eds., *The Blackwell Companion to Social Movements* (Malden, MA: Wiley-Blackwell, 2007), 380–412.

[3] Until recently, scholars of social movements dismissed law as a subject for analysis and scholars of constitutional law dismissed social movements as an object of scholarly inquiry. Social movement scholars focused on how citizens used participatory tactics such as demonstrations and boycotts to influence public policy. In the past decade, movement scholars recognized law as a site of struggle and an appropriate subject of analysis. See, e.g., Michael W. McCann's discussion of the symbolic and substantive effects of comparable worth litigation in *Rights at Work: Pay Equity Reform and the Politics of Legal Mobilization* (Chicago: University of Chicago Press, 1994), 48. Scholars of constitutional law and social change typically approached the subject as students of the US Supreme Court and of its precedents. These scholars examined whether the Court – an institution whose power of judicial review is constrained by politics and a lack of enforcement power – could induce change in socially divisive cases. Court-centric scholars concluded that the Court almost never affected fundamental societal change. In the school desegregation context and others, change occurred through the executive or legislative branches. See Gerald N. Rosenberg, *The Hollow Hope: Can Courts Bring About Social Change?* 2nd ed. (Chicago: University of Chicago Press, 2008), 1–26; cf. Michael J. Klarman, *From Jim Crow to Civil Rights* (New York: Oxford University Press, 2004), 468; see also Lee Epstein and Joseph F. Kobylka, *The Supreme*

describes how movements crystallize grievances, mobilize supporters, demobilize antagonists, and attract bystander support by referencing constitutional rights and other ideas about law.[4] Employing a "thick" conception of law, the work not only references the Constitution – the "paramount law" – but also examines other iterations of law. This approach follows the lead of the movements themselves. More often than not, social movement activists have found the Constitution's negative (rather than affirmative) formulation of rights deficient; consequently, they have turned to other legal texts to supplement Constitutional arguments. For example, reformers have frequently deployed the aspirational language of the Declaration of Independence and the Preamble to the Constitution to augment precepts found in the Constitution's text.[5] Consequently, this essay's discussion of how social movements leverage law also analyzes the Declaration and Preamble, as well as US Supreme Court decisions and popular understandings of law, which are also important resources for activists.[6]

In addition to employing a thicker conception of law, this essay regards law as just one lever – a single resource – among others available to change agents. Constitutional argumentation is not the only element in a movement's tactical repertoire; movements deploy rights talk in concert with other tactics as a protest strategy unfolds over time.[7] Like human capital, time, money, and social networks, constitutional argumentation is just one tool in the arsenal of activists.[8]

Court and Legal Change: Abortion and the Death Penalty (Chapel Hill, NC: University of North Carolina Press, 1992). Court-centric scholars' skepticism of the Court's power is but a variation on Alexander Hamilton's centuries-old observation about the judicial branch. Without the sword or the purse at its disposal, the Court lacks the power to enforce its own rulings. Consequently, the judiciary was destined, Hamilton claimed, to be the "least dangerous branch." *The Federalist*, No. 78.

[4] Snow, "Framing Processes, Ideology, and Discursive Fields," 384 (discussing "politics of significcation" of "collective action frames").

[5] The significance of the Declaration and the Preamble are contested, but generally the texts are viewed as aspirational rather than authoritative documents. See Lee J. Strang, "Originalism, the Declaration of Independence, and the Constitution: A Unique Role in Constitutional Interpretation?" *Penn State Law Review* 111 (2006): 413, 414–15 (noting argument that the Declaration of Independence has no standing in constitutional interpretation); but see Scott Douglas Gerber, *To Secure These Rights: The Declaration of Independence and Constitutional Interpretation* (New York: New York University Press, 1996) (arguing that the Declaration is a key to constitutional interpretation).

[6] For a meditation on the multiple meanings of law, see Catherine Fiske and Robert W. Gordon, "'Law As' …: Theory and Method in Legal History," *UC Irvine Law Review* 1 (2012): 519–41; Hendrik Hartog, "Pigs and Posivitism," *Wisconsin Law Rev* (1985): 899–936, 900.

[7] On the various forms of law that protest movements deploy over their life spans, see Tomiko Brown-Nagin, *Courage to Dissent: Atlanta and the Long History of the Civil Rights Movement* (New York: Oxford University Press, 2011) (discussing use of participatory tactics, negotiation, lobbying, and constitutional litigation in the civil rights movement).

[8] See Bob Edwards and John D. McCarthy, "Resources and Social Movement Mobilization," in Snow et al., eds., *The Blackwell Companion to Social Movements*, 116–52.

The remainder of this essay examines signature episodes in law and history from the perspective outlined earlier. First, it defines four ways in which protest movements leverage the Constitution and rights talk. Next, it describes and analyzes the ways in which lawyers and non-lawyers in the twentieth-century civil rights movement invoked constitutional and legal precepts to advance racial justice. Finally, it examines how other reform movements – including advocates of abolitionism, woman suffrage, and women's liberation – have deployed rights talk to push forward their agendas.

MODES OF INFLUENCE

Protest movements promote their causes by leveraging the Constitution and rights talk.[9] But how, precisely, do movements utilize the law to gain advantage? Four modes of influence are critical. Movements rely on the law: to make legal claims, for moral suasion, for cultural identification, and for political mobilization.

The Juri-centric Perspective on Rights and Social Change

Claims Making

The first mode of influence is the most familiar. Change movements sometimes deploy the Constitution and rights talk conventionally – to make legal claims in court. In the textbook example, supporters of a movement come together because of a shared grievance; they then convert the grievance, or complaint, into a constitutional claim. In most cases, movements transform a grievance into a claim in collaboration with an attorney; the lawyer serves as a translator for the movement.[10] She is the movement's representative in court, interacting

---

[9] For other explorations of this idea, see William N. Eskridge, Jr., "Some Effects of Identity-Based Social Movements on Constitutional Law in the Twentieth Century," *Michigan Law Review* 100 (2002): 2062–2407, 2353 (discussing impact of "identity-based social movements" on the articulation of rights); Reva B. Siegel, "Text in Contest: Gender and the Constitution from a Social Movement Perspective," *University of Pennsylvania Law Review* 150 (2001): 297–351 (discussing feminist movement's impact on equal protection jurisprudence); William E. Forbath, *Law and the Shaping of the American Labor Movement* (Cambridge, MA: Harvard University Press, 1991); William E. Forbath, "Caste, Class, and Equal Citizenship," *Michigan Law Review* 98 (1999): 1–91; James Gray Pope, "Labor's Constitution of Freedom," *Yale Law Journal* 106 (1997): 941–1031; Scott L. Cummings and Douglas NeJaime, "Lawyering for Marriage Equality," *UCLA Law Review* 57 (2010): 1235; Douglas NeJaime, "Constitutional Change, Courts and Social Movements," *Michigan L. Rev.* 113 (2013): 877–902; Jack Balkin and Reva B. Siegel, "Principles, Practices and Social Movements," *University of Pennsylvania Law Review* 154 (2006): 927–50.

[10] For discussion of this process and how lawyers do and do not adequately represent the aggrieved, see Derrick A. Bell, "Serving Two Masters: Integration Ideals and Client Interests in School Desegregation Litigation," *Yale Law Journal* 85 (1976): 470–516, 512 (arguing that civil rights lawyers who litigated school desegregation cases balanced clients' and constituents' interests); Risa L. Goluboff, *The Lost Promise of Civil Rights* (Cambridge, MA: Harvard University Press,

with the adjudicator of the grievance. The lawyer also functions as the movement's mediator; she is a broker of conflict between opposing sides during negotiations about remedies for the grievance.[11]

Consistent with the textbook example, many scholars have recounted efforts by protest groups to vindicate constitutional claims in the US Supreme Court.[12] In these traditional scholarly accounts, constitutional litigation is a win-or-lose, do-or-die proposition. Such court-centric scholarship focuses on landmark Supreme Court cases such as *Brown* v. *Board of Education*[13] and *Roe* v. *Wade*[14] and the lawyers who conceived and executed the winning legal strategies in these cases.[15]

This court-centric model of protest movements' interaction with law is insightful but incomplete. Movements do much more with the law than turn to courts to adjudicate constitutional cases.

Movement-Centered Perspectives on Rights and Social Change

Courtroom-based tactics typically are secondary elements of social movements' protest strategies. Participatory activities such as sit-ins, boycotts, and demonstrations are primary elements. Social movement activists prioritize participatory approaches because these tactics facilitate political engagement by and for all, particularly political and social outsiders with little sway in courtrooms and formal politics.[16] Deploying participatory activities along with constitutional and legal argumentation, activists seek to persuade the

---

2007) (arguing that NAACP's desegregation litigation displaced other pressing civil rights concerns, including economic inequality); cf. Lucie White, "Subordination, Rhetorical Survival Skills and Sunday Shoes: Notes on the Hearing of Mrs. G.," *Buffalo Law Review* 38 (1990): 1–58 (discussing the importance of an attorney listening to an indigent client's story).

[11] For a classic example, see Bell, "Serving Two Masters"; see also Brown-Nagin, *Courage to Dissent*, 83–114, 175–212, 253–305. For modern examples, see Scott L. Cummings, "Community Economic Development as Progressive Politics: Towards a Grassroots Movement for Economic Justice," *Stanford Law Review* 54 (2001): 399–493.

[12] See, e.g., Rosenberg, *The Hollow Hope* (asking, in the context of civil rights, women's rights, and the environment, whether courts can produce significant social reform and concluding that fundamental change through law rarely occurs); cf. Klarman, *From Jim Crow to Civil Rights* (concluding that Supreme Court decisions alone did not fundamentally alter race relations).

[13] See Rosenburg, *Hollow Hope*, 1–36.

[14] See Mary Zeigler, "The Price of Privacy, 1973 to the Present," *Harvard Journal of Law and Gender* 37 (2014): 285–330, 286.

[15] More recent scholarship about landmark cases such as Brown v. Board of Education and Roe v. Wade contains a more movement-focused, less juri-centric understanding of how social movements leverage the law. See, e.g., Brown-Nagin, *Courage to Dissent*, Chp. 7–8; Reva B. Siegel, "Constitutional Culture, Social Movement Conflict and Constitutional Change: The Case of the De Facto ERA," *California Law Review* 94 (2006): 1323–1419.

[16] Kay Lehman Schlozman et al., "The People with No Lobby in Washington," *Boston Globe*, Aug. 26, 2012, p. 1 (data shows that business-oriented groups dominate lobbying). The study concluded that "the interests of the haves" dominate politics.

public and policymakers to support the movement's moral, cultural, and political imperatives.[17]

Law as a Moral Resource

Social movements frequently deploy constitutional and legal rhetoric for moral reinforcement.[18] Activists seek to influence public morality or to shape community standards by drawing upon commonly recognized, oft-invoked legal texts. Change agents most frequently tether their causes to the natural law concepts embedded in the US Constitution and in the Declaration of Independence. These texts' allusions to concepts such as "liberty" and "equality" are thought to articulate the nation's foundational and aspirational moral principles.[19]

Movements can gain tremendous advantage by employing constitutional and legal constructs for moral suasion. When a constitutional principle is cited for moral force, it can be used creatively and flexibly. Protest movements can employ the rhetoric without the constraints imposed during litigation.[20] In courts of law, attorneys who want to win must craft persuasive arguments that fit preexisting legal frameworks. A lawyer who claims that the Fourteenth Amendment's reference to "equal protection" supports his client's right to marry a same-sex partner must persuade a judge that his claim is cognizable and credible under the law developed by courts. It would not be enough to claim that "equal protection" means "fairness" and that the concept of "fairness" supports his claim. Outside of the courtroom, in contrast, advocates can invoke constitutional concepts without hewing closely to legal precedents. The judiciary's interpretation of the meaning of phrases such as "equal protection" or "liberty" may be instructive,

---

[17] The more fluid, movement-centered conception of law and its role in protest efforts make sense in light of reform movements' relationship to the state and formal politics. Protest movements usually are formed by outsiders bent on bringing pressure to bear on insiders. The disaffected typically choose forms of protest that are not creatures of or controlled by the state. Their protest tactics are disruptive and contentious. See Bert Klandermans, *The Social Psychology of Protest* (Cambridge: Blackwell Publishers, 1997).

[18] For discussion of how moral evaluations affect political action and protest movements, see James Jasper, *The Art of Moral Protest* (Chicago: University of Chicago Press, 1997), 12–13, 19–42, 29–33, 107, 154.

[19] The literature on the relationship between law and morality is immense. Much of the literature distinguishes between legal and moral rules; other literature follows natural law theory, which posits a close relationship between moral and legal precepts. *Compare* H. L. A. Hart, *The Concept of Law* (Oxford: Oxford University Press, 1961) *with* Ronald Dworkin, *Freedom's Law: The Moral Reading of the American Constitution* (Oxford: Oxford University Press, 1996) *and with* Randy E. Barnett, *Restoring the Lost Constitution: The Presumption of Liberty* (Princeton: Princeton University Press, rev. ed. 2014).

[20] See, e.g., Tomiko Brown-Nagin, "Elites, Social Movements, and the Law: The Case of Affirmative Action," *Columbia Law Review* 105 (2005): 1436–1528 (distinguishing definitional and aspirational uses of law).

but it is not necessarily authoritative.[21] The public, rather than a court, determines whether advocates' grievances are credible and whether they deserve a remedy.

Constitutional rhetoric, like other forms of legal rhetoric, is sufficiently malleable that social movements on opposing sides of an issue often have deployed the same or similar rights-based language to claim moral standing. Both abolitionists and slaveholders supported their causes by invoking Enlightenment ideals of inalienable, God-given rights to life, liberty, and property. Similarly, pro-life as well as pro-choice proponents in the abortion debate seek moral standing by citing the Constitution's references to "persons," "life," "due process," and "equal protection."[22] Pro-life activists claim that it is immoral to "murder" a "person," even if the personhood is inchoate.[23] Meanwhile, pro-choice activists view the pregnant woman as the "person" whose rights are violated if her choice to terminate is denied.[24] In a battle for moral standing, the flexibility of legal rhetoric is at once an asset and a detriment. Unmoored from context and devoid of an authoritative interpreter, legal concepts cannot settle disputes. Instead, legal constructs are one among several other tools that mobilized groups use to move public opinion and engage politics.

Law as a Cultural Resource

Historian Edwin S. Corwin once proclaimed that a "cult of the Constitution" exists in the United States.[25] The public venerates the US Constitution – together with the Declaration of Independence, US constitutional law, and the US court system – because these texts and institutions are thought to encompass America's highest ideals.[26] Americans also revere the rule of law, democracy, liberty, and equality – all concepts fundamental to America's constitutional system. These concepts, along with the Constitution's text and legal institutions, define American culture. Because of their centrality to American

---

[21] See Alan Brownstein and Paul Dau, "The Constitutional Morality of Abortion," *Boston College Law Review* 33 (1992): 689–762, 691 (noting the struggle of opponents and proponents of abortion rights to fit their moral arguments into an appropriate constitutional context).

[22] See Brownstein and Dau, "The Constitutional Morality of Abortion," 700–6.

[23] See Lyle Denniston, "The Defining Moments of Jayne Bray," in Epstein et al., eds., *A Year in the Life of the Supreme Court* (Durham, NC: Duke University Press, 1995), 61–98, 63.

[24] Brownstein and Dau, "The Constitutional Morality of Abortion," 727.

[25] See Edward S. Corwin, "The Constitution as an Instrument and as Symbol," *American Political Science Review* 30 (1936): 1071–85, 1078 (1936).

[26] Michael Kammen, *A Machine That Would Go of Itself: The Constitution in American Culture* (New York: Alfred A. Knopf, 1986) (describing dominance of US Constitution); Richard P. Cole, "Orthodoxy and Heresy: The Nineteenth Century History of the Rule of Law Reconsidered," *Indiana Law Review* 32 (1999): 1335–82, 1340 (discussing cultural ascendency of American law, including recitations from Constitution in nineteenth-century US schools); Berndt Ostendorf, "Why Is American Popular Culture So Popular," *Amerikastudien/American Studies* 46 (2001): 339–66 (noting that "utopia" has many "American-designed engines," including rule of law and republicanism).

identity, movements invoke the Constitution and related constructs as cultural resources, or as markers of a society's customs and beliefs.[27]

America's origin story makes clear the association between legal institutions, ideals, and texts and American culture. In the familiar narrative, storytellers contrast the United States and its system of "laws not men" to the tyranny and abuses of authority of England's King George III. The reconstruction of the constitutional order during both the Civil War and the civil rights eras is thought to have reinforced the nation's commitment to liberty and equal protection. These ideals – taught in public schools,[28] touted by governmental officials in public addresses,[29] and even recognized by foreigners[30] – make America unique and special.

Even if advocates do not fully subscribe to the national origin story, social reform movements deploy the cultural totems associated with it. That is, movements invoke the narrative and its cultural accoutrements not only to praise it but also to critique it and often to show that, in certain contexts, America's sense of itself is a myth. Rights are illusory.[31]

Americans who have been deprived of equal rights figure prominently among the activists who have remarked upon the wide gap between the country's cultural tenants and its daily practices. In recent years, opponents of excessive force by police officers have been especially likely to invoke America's legal and cultural touchstones to point out the chasm between official malfeasance and the society's cardinal tenants. When critiquing police misbehavior and harassment, both the Black Power Movement of the 1960s and the more recent Black Lives Matter movement have invoked the national commitment to the rule of law and to equal protection.[32] How, they asked, can a social

---

[27] See Jasper, *The Art of Moral Protest*, 69; Robert C. Post, "The Supreme Court, 2002 Term–Foreword: Fashioning the Legal Constitution: Culture, Courts, and Law," *Harvard Law Review* 117 (2003): 4, 8. See generally Paul W. Kahn, *The Cultural Study of Law: Reconstructing Legal Scholarship* (Chicago: University of Chicago Press, 1999), 27–30 (arguing that "legal order ... is a constructed social world" whose constitutive elements should be analyzed for what they reveal about citizens' understandings of time, space, community, and authority).

[28] See Cole, "Orthodoxy and Heresy," 1335, 1340.

[29] See, e.g., President Barack Obama, Remarks by the President at Fourth of July Celebration, July 5, 2014 (essence of America is "revolutionary idea" of equality, self-government, human freedom embodied in Declaration); President George W. Bush, Remarks at an Independence Day Celebration in Philadelphia, July 4, 2001 ("A wonderful country was born and a revolutionary idea sent forth to all mankind: Freedom, not by the good graces of government but as the birthright of every individual; equality, not as a theory of philosophers but by the design of our Creator; natural rights, not for the few, not even for a fortunate many but for all people, in all places, in all times. The world still echoes with the ideals of America's Declaration. ... From the ideals of the Declaration came the laws and the Constitution.").

[30] See Alexis de Tocqueville, *Democracy in America* (1835).

[31] For an overview, see David Papke, *Heretics in the Temple: Americans Who Reject the Nation's Legal Faith* (New York: New York University Press, 1998).

[32] See Blake Simons, "A New Constitution or the Bullet," Sept. 17, 2015 available at http://afrikanblackcoalition.org/2015/09/a-new-constitution-or-the-bullet/ (last accessed on Oct. 24,

system premised on the evenhanded rule of law, instead of rule by might, condone unwarranted violence and bias by police forces? To the extent that social movements are able to demonstrate hypocrisy by the state or its agents by referencing law as culture, they can gain significant advantage in bids for public recognition and credibility.

Law as a Political Resource

Protest groups draw on constitutional and legal precepts to make claims, to gain moral standing, to mark cultural boundaries, and, this essay now argues, to build political support. The law can be used, that is, to popularize a cause and its grievances and thus to push forward a movement's socio-political agenda.[33] Theorists of social movements view mobilized groups as an "important source of countervailing power" within elite-dominated political structures.[34] When appealing to the public for members, moral support, or financial resources, a movement might allude to a miscarriage of justice perpetrated by a court, a jury, or another authority figure. By alleging such systemic injustice, the mobilized group might convince its target audience that the legal system is captured, unfair, and unreliable; therefore, political support for the cause is critical.[35] Moreover, by leveraging the law for political purposes, a movement can gain concessions – even without an official legal decree that validates it cause.[36] Numerous historical examples illustrate these points, as the essay next demonstrates.[37]

THE CIVIL RIGHTS MOVEMENT AND THE LAW

For many years, scholars debated whether developments in constitutional law or in politics caused the profound changes in race relations that occurred during the mid-twentieth century in the United States. Some argued that the US Supreme Court's decision in *Brown* v. *Board of Education* laid the groundwork for the civil rights movement and the country's subsequent embrace of formal racial equality. In this account, the strategic genius of lawyers and heroic actions of

---

2015); Paul Butler, "Racially Based Jury Nullification: Black Power in the Criminal Justice System," *Yale Law Journal* 105 (1995): 677–725; Zach Newman, "'Hands Up, Don't Shoot': Policing, Fatal Force, and Equal Protection in the Age of Colorblindness," *Hastings Constitutional Law Quarterly* 43 (2015): 117–62.

[33] See Andrew S. McFarland, "Social Movements and Theories of American Politics," in Doug McAdam, Anne N. Costain, and Andrew S. McFarland, eds., *Social Movements and American Political Institutions* (Lanham, MD: Rowman & Littlefield, 1998), 7–19, 8, 11.

[34] Ibid.   [35] Ibid.

[36] See Michael McCann, "Social Movements and the Mobilization of Law," in *Social Movements and American Political Institutions*, 201–15, 208–9.

[37] Collective actors in all the nation's cataclysmic social change movements pushed their agendas through appeals to rights talk and legal institutions. See Eskridge, "Some Effects of Identity-Based Social Movements" ("[N]o theory of constitutional law can be adequate or successful which does not centrally involve [identity-based social movements] and their jurisprudence."); Siegel, "Text in Contest" (discussing feminist movement's effect on equal protection jurisprudence).

courts explained the revolutionary changes in race relations that occurred during the mid-twentieth century.[38] Others argued that political activists who took stands against Jim Crow in the Armed Forces, on railways, and in other public accommodations set in motion the changes that resulted in the Court's and Congress's mandates of formal racial equality in 1954 and 1964.[39]

The debate over whether constitutional or political activism caused the civil rights revolution misses the overarching point made in the previous section: the choice between court-based and political, moral, or cultural uses of the law is a false one. Both lawyers and non-lawyers deployed constitutional and legal concepts to great advantage. Working inside and outside of the courtroom, activists pushed the racial equality agenda forward.

The civil rights movement constitutes perhaps the best modern example of a social reform campaign's effective appropriation of constitutional constructs in varied ways: to claim rights, for moral suasion, to demarcate culture, and for political advantage. The movement – composed of many different types of organizations and people – deployed law in ways befitting each group. The NAACP Legal Defense Fund (Inc. Fund), led by lawyers, made text- and history-based constitutional arguments to claim rights. The Southern Christian Leadership Conference (SCLC), led by ministers, deployed the Declaration of Independence and constitutional rhetoric to make moral arguments. The Student Non-Violent Coordinating Committee (SNCC), anchored by student activists and supported by lawyer-collaborators, referred to the hortatory precepts of the Declaration and the text of the Constitution for political and cultural purposes and to claim rights. Together all these groups effectively used law as an analytical frame and pushed the public, the courts, and Congress to end racial segregation and institute a legal regime premised on racial equality.

Law for Claims Making

During the 1940s, when Thurgood Marshall and the Inc. Fund turned to the US Constitution as a tool to fight racial oppression, other racial justice activists doubted the strategy. The Constitution – the same document that justified

---

[38] See, e.g., Richard Kluger, *Simple Justice: The History of Brown v. Board of Education* (New York: Alfred A. Knopf, 1976), ix (arguing that the US Supreme Court singularly corrected the "grave injustice" of racial inequality, which deviated from America's foundational principles); Charles V. Hamilton, "Federal Law and Courts in the Civil Rights Movement," in Charles W. Eagles, ed., *The Civil Rights Movement in America: Essays* (Oxford, MS: University Press of Mississippi, 1986), 97–117.

[39] See, e.g., John Dittmer, "The Politics of the Mississippi Movement," in Eagles, ed., *The Civil Rights Movement in America*, 65–93 (arguing that postwar political developments and indigenous institutions account for later activism in Mississippi); Clayborne Carson, Civil Rights Reform and the Black Freedom Struggle, in Eagles, ed., *The Civil Rights Movement in America*, 19–32 (analyzing and according significance to the goals and tactics of local participants in "black freedom struggle").

slavery and segregation – seemed unlikely to dismantle discrimination in education, voting, employment, public accommodations, or any of the numerous other contexts where blacks faced discrimination. A. Phillip Randolph, the labor leader, and Ralph Bunche, the political scientist, called the Inc. Fund naïve. Both men acknowledged that the Constitution's open-ended language could support many interpretations of the law. Nevertheless, they doubted that the federal courts would mandate racial equality. In all likelihood, the all-white judiciary would share the racist beliefs of the legislators who had enacted segregation laws. And, in the unlikely event that a court did rule in blacks' favor, whites charged with implementing favorable decisions might well undermine the rule of law. The Inc. Fund's misguided allegiance to the Constitution and the courts, Randolph and Bunche feared, would weaken black demands for justice.[40]

However, Thurgood Marshall and his colleagues did not rely on the Constitution out of blind faith. They invoked the nation's foundational document out of necessity and with full awareness that judges and lawyers, politicos, and property holders had often used constitutional constructs to justify racial oppression. Marshall personified the critical consciousness with which civil rights lawyers made constitutional arguments. Years later, after he had been appointed to the US Supreme Court, Marshall acknowledged that the "government [the framers] devised was defective from the start."[41] The original, un-amended Constitution of 1787 had sanctioned slavery and had relegated women to an inferior legal status.[42] Fortunately, the founding fathers had not fixed the Constitution's meaning in Philadelphia in 1787, Marshall noted. The Constitution had been changed by "several amendments, a civil war, and momentous social transformation."[43]

In the Inc. Fund's litigation campaign against segregation, Marshall laid claim to the US Constitution as amended during Reconstruction – African Americans' "brief moment in the sun."[44] Charles Hamilton Houston, Marshall's mentor, taught that injustice could be challenged under the US Constitution if students deployed the principles in the document "creatively"

---

[40] See A. Phillip Randolph and Chandler Owen, "A Socialist Critique in the Messenger," in August Meier, Elliott M. Rudwick, and Francis L. Broderick, eds., *Black Protest Thought in the Twentieth Century* (Indianapolis: Bobbs-Merrill, 1971), 81–100; Ralphe Bunche, "A Critical Analysis of the Tactics and Programs of Minority Groups," *Journal of Negro Education* (1935): 308–20.

[41] Thurgood Marshall, Remarks at the Annual Seminar of the San Francisco Patent and Trademark Law Association (May 6, 1987), www.thurgoodmarshall.com/speeches/constitu tional_speech.htm.

[42] Ibid.

[43] See Thurgood Marshall, Reflections on the Bicentennial of the United States Constitution, *Harvard Law Review* 101 (1987): 1–5, 4–5.

[44] W. E. B. DuBois, *Black Reconstruction in America: Toward a History of the Part Which Black Folk Played in the Attempt to Reconstruct Democracy in America, 1860–1880* (New Brunswick, NJ: Transaction Publishers, 2013), 26.

and "innovative[ly]."[45] Following his mentor's suggestion, Marshall sought to realize the promise of the Thirteenth, Fourteenth, and Fifteenth Amendments through litigation in the federal courts.[46] Together with his legal team, he attacked segregation in schools and other race-based distinctions through lawsuits predicated on the Fourteenth Amendment's guarantees of and due process.[47] In five school segregation cases, the Inc. Fund exposed stark racial disparities in publicly supported secondary education.[48] The facts demonstrated that states had not complied with *Plessy* v. *Ferguson*'s "separate but equal" rule.[49] Later, the lawyers directly challenged *Plessy* by contending that separate could never be made equal.[50] The expansive language of the Constitution – "no state" shall deprive citizens of "equal protection of the laws" – controlled the outcomes in the school segregation cases, Marshall argued.[51]

Even the reconstructed Constitution, however, fell short of the aspirations that Marshall ascribed to it. At the time the Fourteenth Amendment was ratified, only the most ardent proponents of Reconstruction argued that the amendment banned segregation in schools or other forms of racial distinctions.[52] In fact, Congress's imposition of segregation in the District of Columbia's schools suggested just the opposite. If the Inc. Fund prevailed, it would *not* be because the terms of the Fourteenth Amendment plainly dictated that result.

Fortunately for Marshall, recent judicial interpretations of the Equal Protection and Due Process clauses buttressed the Inc. Fund's challenge to segregation in public education.[53] The Supreme Court's holding in the Japanese internment cases – that distinctions based solely on race or ancestry must be subjected to strict judicial scrutiny – suggested that the Court might

---

[45] See Darlene Clark Hine, "Black Lawyers and the Twentieth-Century Struggle for Constitutional Change," in John Hope Franklin and Genna Ree McNeil, eds., *African Americans and the Living Constitution* (Washington, DC: Smithsonian, 1995): 33–55; see also Genna Rae McNeil, *Groundwork: Charles Hamilton Houston and the Struggle for Civil Rights* (Philadelphia: University of Pennsylvania Press, 1984) 4–5, 84–85.

[46] On Marshall's faith in the American order, see Charles Zelden, *Thurgood Marshall: Race, Rights, and the Struggle for a More Perfect Union* (New York: Routledge, 2013), 2.

[47] Ibid.; Tushnet, *The NAACP's Legal Strategy against Segregated Education, 1925–1950* (Chapel Hill, NC: University of North Carolina Press, 1987), 105–37.

[48] The five cases consolidated in Brown originated in Kansas, South Carolina, the District of Columbia, Delaware, and Virginia. Kluger, *Simple Justice*.

[49] Plessy v Ferguson, 163 U.S. 537 (1896); see also Cumming v. Board of Education, 175 U. S. 528; Gong Lum v. Rice, 275 U. S. 78.

[50] See Brown v. Board of Education, 347 U.S. 483, 488 (1954).

[51] Brief for Appellants, Brown v. Board of Education, U.S. 483 (1954) (No. 1), 5.

[52] Brown v. Board of Education, 347 U.S. 483, 489–90.

[53] See Hirabayashi v. United States, 320 U. S. 81, 100 (1943) ("Distinctions between citizens solely because of their ancestry are by their very nature odious to a free people whose institutions are founded upon the doctrine of equality. For that reason, legislative classification or discrimination based on race alone has often been held to be a denial of equal protection ....").

take a dim view of laws mandating race-based segregation. The Inc. Fund's victories in cases challenging inequality in higher education also boded well for its frontal assault on Jim Crow in elementary and secondary education.[54]

In the end, Marshall's gamble on constitutional litigation paid off. Working in a favorable post–World War II geopolitical context,[55] the lawyers persuaded the US Supreme Court that separate could never be truly equal under law in the area of public education. The Justices reached a unanimous decision in favor of the Inc. Fund notwithstanding inconclusive evidence as to whether the Fourteenth Amendment's framers had intended to ban school segregation.[56] Ultimately, the Constitution's equality rhetoric – when juxtaposed to the harms of segregation[57] – carried the day, just as Marshall had hoped. In an age when blacks had achieved "outstanding success in the arts and sciences as well as in the business and professional world,"[58] the Court at last condemned Jim Crow as a relic of a bygone era.

The Inc. Fund's landmark victory in *Brown* v. *Board of Education* enhanced Marshall's faith in the rule of law and increased his distrust of alternative reform strategies. When other leaders in the black freedom movement challenged the Inc. Fund's lawyers' tactical dominance, Marshall pushed back. "The way to change America," he insisted, was "through the courts."[59] In the wake of his victory in *Brown*, Marshall's faith in the courts made sense. But he failed to acknowledge a critical fact: litigators had no monopoly on change or on the Constitution. Practitioners of direct action – another favored tool in the repertoire of protest movements – also laid claim to the Constitution, often with great success.

Law as Moral Resource

Dr. Martin Luther King, Jr. – the famed leader of epic nonviolent direct action campaigns against segregation under the aegis of the SCLC – frequently invoked

---

[54] Missouri ex rel. Gaines v. Canada, 305 U. S. 337; Sipuel v. Board of Regents of the University of Oklahoma, 332 U. S. 631; Sweatt v. Painter, 339 U. S. 629.

[55] See Mary Dudziak, *Cold War Civil Rights: Race and the Image of American Democracy* (Princeton: Princeton University Press, 2011).

[56] Brown v. Board of Education, 347 U.S. 483, 492–93 ("In approaching this problem, we cannot turn the clock back to 1868 when the Amendment was adopted, or even to 1896 when *Plessy* v. *Ferguson* was written. We must consider public education in the light of its full development and its present place in American life throughout the Nation.").

[57] The Court concluded: "Segregation of white and colored children in public schools has a detrimental effect upon the colored children. The impact is greater when it has the sanction of the law; for the policy of separating the races is usually interpreted as denoting the inferiority of the negro group." Ibid. at 494.

[58] Ibid. at 490.

[59] See Brown-Nagin, *Courage to Dissent*, 4; see also Mark V. Tushnet, *Making Civil Rights Law: Thurgood Marshall and the Supreme Court, 1936–1961* (New York: Oxford University Press, 1994), 309–10 (describing NAACP's initial "ambivalen[ce] about the sit-in tactic").

the Constitution, the Declaration of Independence, and Supreme Court precedents for moral authority. King argued that the rights conferred in the Constitution, the principles articulated in the Declaration of Independence, and the Supreme Court's stand against school segregation all demonstrated that Jim Crow violated both the laws of man and the laws of God.[60] He articulated this view in an important speech during the Montgomery Bus Boycott. At the very first meeting of the Montgomery Improvement Association, the local group that spearheaded the boycott, King justified the protest against undignified treatment (and, ultimately, segregation) on city buses by invoking the constitutional rights of American citizens. As King exhorted the standing-room only crowd, the audience affirmed his words in the call and response style common in Black Baptist churches. King said:

We are here ... because first and foremost – we are American citizens (*That's right*) and we are determined to apply our citizenship – to the fullness of its means. (*Yeah, That's right*) We are here also because of our love for democracy, (*Yes*) because of our deep-seated belief that democracy transformed from thin paper to thick action (*Yes*) is the greatest form of government on earth. (*That's right*) ...

[T]his is the glory of America, with all of its faults (Yeah) This is the glory of our democracy. [T]he great glory of American democracy is the right to protest for right.[61]

In addition to citing these legal constructs, King referenced the US Supreme Court's decision in *Brown* v. *Board of Education*, decided a year prior to the boycott. King reasoned that if segregation in schools violated the Equal Protection Clause of the Constitution, then so, too, must segregation on city buses violate the Constitution.

If we are wrong, the Supreme Court of this nation is wrong. (*Yes sir*) [*Applause*] If we are wrong, the Constitution of the United States is wrong. (*Yes*) [*Applause*] If we are wrong, God Almighty is wrong. (*That's right*) [*Applause*][62]

The "speech that launched the boycott," as it is called, masterfully used constitutional rights talk to rally the community and place nonviolent direct action on a moral high ground.

In his August 29, 1963, address at the March on Washington, Dr. King once again called upon America to redeem its promises. King and the other speakers that day sought an omnibus federal antidiscrimination law, which they hoped would put America on the path to realizing the dream of racial equality.

---

[60] See Randall Kennedy, "Martin Luther King's Constitution: A Legal History of the Montgomery Bus Boycott," *Yale Law Journal* 98 (1989): 999–1067, 1021–22; see also Carlton Waterhouse, "Dr. King's Speech: Surveying the Landscape of Law and Justice in the Speeches, Sermons, and Writings of Dr. Martin Luther King, Jr.," *Law and Inequality* 30 (2012): 91–124, 108–9.

[61] Martin Luther King Jr., MIA Mass Meeting at Holt Street Baptist Church, 1955, available at http://mlk-kpp01.stanford.edu/kingweb/publications/papers/vol3/551205.004-MIA_Mass_Meeting_at_Holt_Street_Baptist_Church.htm (last accessed Jan. 7, 2016).

[62] Ibid.

Throughout his "I Have a Dream" speech, King made reference to the rule of law and to rights-based notions of morality and equality. He juxtaposed the words of the Emancipation Proclamation with those of the Declaration of Independence and the US Constitution – to powerful effect. The speech posited that, despite the proclamation, black Americans still had not achieved freedom. "One hundred years later," King said, "the life of the Negro is still sadly crippled by the manacles of segregation and the chains of discrimination." Blacks had therefore come to the nation's capital in 1963 seeking redress, or the opportunity to redeem a "promissory note." By virtue of the nation's founding documents, King argued, African Americans deserved true freedom. "Now is the time to make real the promises of democracy," he intoned, for the dream of black redemption was "deeply rooted in the American dream."

I have a dream that one day this nation will rise up and live out the true meaning of its creed: "We hold these truths to be self-evident, that all men are created equal."[63]

Over the course of his short life, King invoked the nation's foundational legal texts on numerous other occasions to justify the movement's demonstrations, picketing, and boycotts and its demands for federal antidiscrimination, voting rights, and antipoverty legislation. He summarized the relationship between the movement and these legal texts in his final public address, which took place in Memphis on April 3, 1968 – the night before he was assassinated.

The civil rights leader had journeyed to Memphis to dramatize the plight of the working poor. In joining a march by striking sanitation workers, King tethered the legacies of the civil rights and labor rights movements.[64] City leaders disapproved of King's intervention in the strike; their complaints grew louder after black protesters broke windows and looted at a King-led march. This was the context in which King delivered his "I've Been to the Mountaintop" address. Citing the First Amendment, he defended the striking workers on the grounds that they, like other Americans, were simply seeking freedom. "When the movement petitioned for redress," he said, it did so with the goal of persuading authorities to "[b]e true to what you said on paper."[65]

---

[63] Martin Luther King Jr., "I Have a Dream," available at www.americanrhetoric.com/speeches /mlkihaveadream.htm (last accessed Jan. 7, 2016).

[64] See Thomas Jackson, *From Civil Rights to Human Rights: Martin Luther King, Jr., and the Struggle for Economic Justice* (Philadelphia: University of Pennsylvania Press, 2009), 351.

[65] King eloquently summarized the relationship between these documents and the movement's goals in his final public address, which took place in Memphis in 1968: All we say to America is, "Be true to what you said on paper." If I lived in China or even Russia, or any totalitarian country, maybe I could understand the denial of certain basic First Amendment privileges, because they hadn't committed themselves to that over there. But somewhere I read of the freedom of assembly. Somewhere I read of the freedom of speech. Somewhere I read of the freedom of the press. Somewhere I read that the greatness of America is the right to protest for right. Martin Luther King Jr., "I've Been to the Mountaintop," in Amy A. Kass, ed., *Giving Well, Doing Good: Readings for Thoughtful Philanthropists* (Bloomington, IN: University of Indiana Press, 2008), 441–48, 444. The lawyers of the NAACP, too, cited the right to assemble and petition for redress

He continued: "Somewhere I read of the freedom of assembly. Somewhere I read of the freedom of the press. Somewhere I read the greatest of America is the right to protest for right."[66] Although King never argued cases in a courtroom, in his final address – and in numerous other speeches – he brilliantly deployed the Constitution to advance black freedom.

Law as Cultural and Political Resource

The Student Nonviolent Coordinating Committee – a college student-led group called the "shock troops" of the civil rights movement – also deployed rights talk. SNCC invoked the Constitution, the Declaration of Independence, and court cases to identify dominant cultural constructs and to inspire political mobilization. The organization gained political traction by exposing the hypocrisy of American institutions and American leaders. After SNCC identified America's cultural touchstones, as encapsulated in sacred constitutional and legal texts, the group argued that America had deviated from its stated principles.

SNCC flawlessly executed this political method during the sit-ins. The group referenced the words of familiar legal texts to show that the rights were not real but fictive. The students who launched the Atlanta sit-ins against segregation in public accommodations argued: "We are striving for the freedom that should be ours under the Constitution."[67] And, using phrasing characteristic of the Declaration of Independence, the protesters said: "We hold that" segregation is "not in keeping with the ideals of Democracy."[68] On this occasion and others, SNCC exposed fissures in the cultural fabric. The group relied on well-known American legal texts – the "master's own tools" – to dismantle the master's house.

SNCC also cited judicial interpretations of the Constitution to reveal deficiencies in the constitutional order. Striking a contrast to Dr. King, who had praised *Brown* v. *Board of Education*, SNCC argued that the US Supreme Court's actions in the landmark case illustrated how American institutions had failed African Americans. The problem was not the Court's interpretation of the Fourteenth Amendment. SNCC took issue with how easily the Justices backed away from the decision in the face of white resistance.

John Lewis, a chairman of SNCC who later became a member of Congress, explained the students' viewpoint. "[W]e thought [after *Brown*] we would be going to better schools, and it just didn't happen." "Nothing" changed.[69] Lonnie King, leader of the Atlanta student movement, agreed: "We have left the Supreme Court decision to the courts, and in six years, barely one per cent of

---

when it sought to protect its members from retaliation in Southern states hostile to the association's very existence and bent on destroying its activism. See NAACP v. Button, 371 U.S. 415 (1963); NAACP v. Alabama, 357 U.S. 449 (1958).

[66] King, "I've Been to the Mountaintop."
[67] Quoted in Brown-Nagin, *Courage to Dissent*, 137.   [68] Ibid.   [69] Ibid.

the school districts in the South have been integrated."[70] Even *Cooper* v. *Aaron*, the Court's September 1958 decision asserting its supremacy in the face of the Little Rock, Arkansas, school desegregation crisis, provided short-lived inspiration. The Court undercut *Cooper* the next year when it refused to strike down pupil placement laws that required black applicants to white schools to undergo burdensome application procedures, including psychological and intelligence tests.[71] As a result of these decisions, the students viewed the Court as a symbol of white officials' indifference to equal rights.

Citing a loss of faith in the Court and its interpretation of the law, students mobilized politically. They spurned constitutional litigation and turned to participatory forms of protest. SNCC favored the sit-in, a form of nonviolent direct action and the same kind of tactic that activists had used with success during the Montgomery Bus Boycott. SNCC's communications director, Julian Bond, explained the relationship between the group's tactical choices and its disappointment with the courts. Prior to the sit-ins and the boycott, Bond explained, the movement had been all about "filing a suit."[72] The new tactics – boycotts, demonstrations, pickets, rallies, and sit-ins – afforded every citizen – not just legal experts – the opportunity to contribute to the struggle for equality. SNCC's stinging critique of the constitutional order redounded to its – and the civil rights movement's – political advantage.[73]

AN ARRAY OF SOCIAL MOVEMENTS DEPLOY RIGHTS TALK

The civil rights struggle is just one of many protest movements that have deployed law as a resource in reform campaigns. Well before the 1960s and well after that tumultuous decade, activists found ways to leverage the Constitution, other legal texts, and rule of law constructs to push forward their agendas.

The Long Resistance

Dr. Martin Luther King Jr. once observed that the "arc of the moral universe is long but it bends toward justice."[74] The concept of the "long resistance" embeds in scholarship about social change the expanded temporal element that King referenced. Scholars who argue for a "long" conception of the civil

---

[70] Ibid.

[71] See, e.g., Shuttlesworth v. Birmingham Board of Education, 162 F. Supp. 372, (N.D. Ala.), affirmed 358 U.S. 101 (1958), which involved the family of nationally prominent civil rights activists Rev. Fred and Mrs. Ruby Shuttlesworth; see also Brown-Nagin, *Courage to Dissent*, 137.

[72] Ibid.   [73] Ibid.

[74] In fact, the original quote is credited by some to Rev. Theodore Parker, an abolitionist. See http://quoteinvestigator.com/2012/11/15/arc-of-universe/ (accessed on Jan. 15, 2016).

rights movement locate the roots of the struggle for racial equality in the labor conflicts of the 1930s.[75] Other scholars advocate an even longer conception of the movement's temporal arc: the struggle's heritage stretches back to the nineteenth-century fight against slavery – the defining struggle over labor in US history.[76]

Consistent with the long resistance concept, this section connects antislavery and civil rights activism and joins both to its discussion of how protest movements leverage the law. Thurgood Marshall, Martin Luther King Jr., and SNCC's legal, moral, cultural, and political battles against racial injustice borrowed tactics from abolitionists.[77] A long campaign against oppression by abolitionists, sustained by civil rights activists, resulted in epochal racial changes during the 1960s.

Abolitionism

If *Plessy* v. *Ferguson* (1896) framed twentieth-century disputes over racial inequality, *Dred Scott* v. *Sandford* (1857) stirred nineteenth-century antiracist activism. In *Dred Scott*, the US Supreme Court held that, as matter of original intent of the Constitution, no person of African descent could be a citizen of the United States.[78] The US Supreme Court's most notorious decision, *Dred Scott* inspired fervent abolitionist resistance.[79] The case joined the Fugitive Slave Act of 1850, which required authorities to assist in the recovery of escaped slaves, as flashpoints that propelled the most profound opposition yet to human bondage.[80]

Abolitionists responded to federal and state laws that supported slave holders' rights to property in men by making the case for freedom. The activists attacked slavery with moral, political, and constitutional arguments. Frederick Douglass, the former slave turned internationally known abolitionist, rejected the *Dred Scott* Court's claim that the US Constitution condoned and protected slavery. In his 1860 speech "The Constitution of the United States: Is It Pro-Slavery or Anti-Slavery?" Douglass argued that the original Constitution of 1787, as written by the framers in Philadelphia, did not, in fact, support a

---

[75] Jacqueline Dowd Hall, "The Long Civil Rights Movement and the Political Uses of the Past," *Journal of American History* 91 (2005): 1233–63.

[76] See Aaron Sheehan-Dean, "The Long Civil War: A Historiography of the Consequences of the Civil War," *Virginia Magazine of History and Biography* 119 (2011): 106–53.

[77] See Zoe Frances Trodd, *The Reusable Past: Abolitionist Aesthetics in the Protest Literature of the Long Civil Rights Movement* (Ph.D. Dissertation, Harvard University, 2009); see also Susan Carle, *Defining the Struggle: National Organizing for Racial Justice, 1880–1915* (New York: Oxford University Press, 2015) (discussing post-Reconstruction activism).

[78] 60 U.S. 393 (1857).

[79] See Don E. Fehrenbacher, *The Dred Scott Case: Its Significance in American Law and Politics* (New York: Oxford University Press, 2001), 160–62, 278–79, 287, 341–42 (discussing attempts to abolish Fugitive Slave Law through both legislation and litigation).

[80] Ibid.

pro-slavery position. "I ... deny that the Constitution guarantees the right to hold property in man."[81]

Douglass reached this conclusion through an ingenious textual interpretation of the Constitution. When Douglass examined the "simple text of the paper itself" apart from the political context (or "the secret motives" and "dishonest intentions") in which the framers drafted the document, he could find no support for slavery. Douglass' textual approach must prevail, he argued, for "[t]*hey [the framers] were for a generation, but the Constitution is for ages."* Far from sanctioning slavery, the Constitution went to great lengths to avoid doing so. Douglass's reading of the Constitution privileged linguistic ambiguities in – and non-intuitive interpretations of – the three-fifths clause[82] and the slave trade clause.[83] His antislavery interpretation of the Constitution also rested on his reading of the Preamble. "The Constitution['s]" language is "we the people," he noted, "not we the white people."[84] In sum, Douglass argued that slavery violated the principles of the American Revolution. Douglass's laying claim to the Constitution buoyed abolitionists, even if few agreed with his aspirational interpretation of it.[85]

William Lloyd Garrison, publisher of the *Liberator* and leader of the Massachusetts Anti-Slavery Society, shared Douglass' antislavery purpose but not his constitutional interpretation. Garrison made a moral case for abolition by taking the opposite tack of Douglass. Garrison lambasted the Constitution – a "bloody" and "wicked" compact[86] – *because* it condoned un-freedom.[87] Just as Douglass popularized his antislavery interpretation of the Constitution in his public addresses, Garrison cited law's complicity in slavery in rousing speeches. In 1854, at a Fourth of July rally where he stood on a stage decorated with an inverted US flag, Garrison told stories about the terrible impact of the 1850

---

[81] Frederick Douglass, "The Constitution of the United States: Is It Pro-Slavery or Anti-Slavery?," Glasgow, Scotland, Mar. 26, 1860.

[82] Of the three-fifths clause, Douglass said: "It is a downright disability laid upon the slaveholding States; one which deprives those States of two-fifths of their natural basis of representation. A black man in a free State is worth just two-fifths more than a black man in a slave State, as a basis of political power under the Constitution. Therefore, instead of encouraging slavery, the Constitution encourages freedom by giving an increase of 'two-fifths' of political power to free over slave States."

[83] Douglass read the slave trade clause as antislavery. "[T]his part of the Constitution, so far as the slave trade is concerned, became a dead letter more than 50 years ago, and now binds no man's conscience for the continuance of any slave trade whatsoever ... The abolition of the slave trade was supposed to be the certain death of slavery."

[84] Douglass, "The Constitution of the United States."

[85] See Brown-Nagin, "Elites, Social Movements, and the Law," 1528 (defining aspirational versus definitional uses of the law). The article argues that "[s]ocial movements may profitably use rights talk to inspire political mobilization, although with less success than legal mobilization theorists assume. But social movements that make law definitional risk undermining their insurgent role in the political process and thus losing their agenda-setting ability."

[86] William Lloyd Garrison, "On the Constitution and the Union," *Liberator*, Dec. 29, 1832.

[87] See ibid.

Fugitive Slave Act. Because of the law, Garrison explained, authorities seized people – human beings – bound them with iron chains, and held them for re-enslavement. The law turned people into things and made a lie of the Declaration of the Independence. Garrison then dramatized his condemnation of the pro-slavery Constitution and the Fugitive Slave Law: he lit a match to both texts.[88]

Garrison's dramatic display of contempt for the Constitution and the Fugitive Slave Law reflected and shaped the times. By the 1850s many abolitionists sought to force a permanent solution to the sectional conflict over slavery. John Brown's 1859 raid on the federal arsenal at Harper's Ferry, Virginia, epitomized abolitionists' resolve. Before long, the unyielding abolitionists, pitted against equally resolute proponents of slavery, pushed the divided nation toward a civil war. The Union's victory led to Reconstruction and to constitutional amendments that reversed *Dred Scott* and conferred citizenship upon black Americans.[89] One hundred years later, during the "Second Reconstruction," King, Marshall, and student activists continued a process abolitionists had begun – reckoning with slavery.

Suffrage

The long resistance, which stretched from the era of abolition to the age of civil rights, also shaped reform movements by and for women. Female leaders' experiences in the antislavery movement inspired them to fight for woman suffrage and equal rights. Much as the US Supreme Court's hypocrisy in *Brown*'s wake inspired civil rights activism, abolitionists' missteps during a signature event generated pro-woman activism.

The 1840 world antislavery conference in London set the stage for women's activism. Organizers barred abolitionists Elizabeth Cady Stanton and Lucretia Mott – and all women – from the convention floor, humiliating female activists.[90] Stanton could hardly believe that "abolitionists, who felt so keenly the wrongs of the slave, should be so oblivious to the equal wrongs of their own mothers, wives, and sisters."[91] As a result of their disappointment with the abolitionists, women mobilized. Stanton and Mott resolved to begin a society to

---

[88] See Paul Finkelman, "Garrison's Constitution: The Covenant with Death and How It Was Made," *Prologue: Quarterly of the National Archives* 32 (2000): 231–45; Henry Mayer, *All on Fire: William Lloyd Garrison and the Abolition of Slavery* (New York: St. Martin's Press, 1998).

[89] Of course Brown subsequently was executed for treason and murder. See Steven Lubet, "John Brown's Trial," *Alabama Law Review* 52 (2001): 425–66, 425–27 (describing John Brown's raid and trial as a critical event in history of abolitionism).

[90] See Jean H. Baker, *Sisters: The Lives of America's Suffragists* (New York: Hill & Wang, 2005), 103.

[91] Geoffrey C. Ward and Ken Burns, *Not for Ourselves Alone: The Story of Elizabeth Cady Stanton and Susan B. Anthony* (New York: Knopf, 1999), 30.

advance women's rights.[92] Mott called the first Woman's Rights Convention at Seneca Falls, New York, in 1848; that meeting launched the woman suffrage movement.[93]

Once the suffrage movement got under way, women deployed many abolitionist tactics to seek equality for themselves.[94] Proponents of woman suffrage invoked rhetoric from the Declaration and the Constitution's Preamble to advocate for women's equality, after concluding, like racial justice activists, that the Constitution itself did not fully address their plights. Delegates to the 1848 Woman's Rights Convention, for example, modeled their "Declaration of Sentiments" on the Declaration of Independence. If the natural rights philosophy justified the colonists' revolt against King George III, it also legitimized women's revolt against male oppression. The suffragists' statement began: "We hold these truths to be self-evident: that all men and women are created equal."[95] The Declaration then detailed men's injuries to women and wives, just as the Declaration of Independence contained a bill of particulars listing King George's tyrannical injuries against the colonies.[96] The Declaration of Sentiments listed the following deviations from democratic principles, among other male crimes:

> He has never permitted her to exercise her alienable right to the elective franchise.
> He has compelled her to submit to laws, in the formation of which she had no voice.

The long list detailed numerous other injuries, including denial of education, property rights, and taxation without representation.[97] The Declaration categorically rejected the idea of a separate woman's "sphere," long embodied in the doctrine of coverture – the English common law concept that a married woman's rights were subsumed within her husband's.[98] The concept of "consent of governed" applied to women, no less than others, the suffragists concluded.

Whereas the Reconstruction Constitution provided plausible – if not certain – support to advocates of racial equality, the new constitutional order proved a daunting challenge for proponents of women's rights. For women, the Fourteenth and Fifteenth Amendments changed the face of the Constitution in ways both welcome and unwelcome. That is to say, the text simultaneously

---

[92] Baker, *Sisters*, 104.

[93] Aileen S. Kraditor, *The Ideas of the Woman Suffrage Movement, 1890–1920* (New York: Norton, 1981), 1.

[94] In fact, prominent male abolitionists – including Frederick Douglass and William Lloyd Garrison – supported the women's cause and offered strategic and political support. See ibid. at 1; Baker, *Sisters*, 103; see also William Lloyd Garrison, "Women's Rights," *Liberator*, Oct. 28, 1853; Frederick Douglass, "On Women's Suffrage," *Woman's Journal*, Apr. 14, 1888.

[95] Kraditor, *The Ideas of the Woman Suffrage Movement*, 49; Ward and Burns, *Not for Ourselves Alone*, 58.

[96] Baker, *Sisters*, 114.   [97] Ward and Burns, *Not for Ourselves Alone*, 59.

[98] See William Blackstone, *Commentaries on the Laws of England*, Vol. 1 (1765), 442–45.

advanced the abolitionist cause and undermined the struggle for woman suffrage.[99] The Fourteenth Amendment's citizenship clause overturned *Dred Scott* but, at the same time, indicated that males, only, were entitled to equal voting rights.[100] Moreover, the Fifteenth Amendment banned discrimination on the basis of "race, color, or previous condition of servitude"[101] alone. For the first time, the Constitution explicitly condoned sex-based discrimination.[102] Outraged proponents of woman suffrage found political inspiration in the Constitution's discriminatory text.

Under the aegis of the National Woman Suffrage Association, Susan B. Anthony and Elizabeth Cady Stanton organized a multi-faceted suffrage strategy. The group's tactics included lobbying, civil disobedience, and litigation. Anthony waged a clever effort to dramatize the injustice of denying women the vote in 1872 that, at turns, involved all three tactics. Contrary to law and custom, Anthony managed to cast a ballot in the presidential election of 1872. Charged with voting illegally, she stood trial in New York and was convicted and fined. As a woman, she could not testify in her own defense at trial. But in an 1873 address, "On Women's Right to Vote," she nevertheless managed to state her case against the unjust laws.[103] Like Frederick Douglass before her, Anthony cited the Preamble to the Constitution in the speech, arguing that the original meaning of citizenship did not exclude women. The Preamble to the Constitution says: "[W]e, the people; not we, the white male citizens; nor yet we, the male citizens; but we, the whole people, who formed the Union."[104]

And we formed it, not to not to give the blessings of liberty, but to secure them; not to the half of ourselves and the half of our posterity, but to the whole people – women as well as men. And it is a downright mockery to talk to women of their enjoyment of the blessings of liberty while they are denied the use of the only means of securing them provided by this democratic-republican government – the ballot.[105]

Unless commentators denied the personhood of women, Anthony argued, females could not be denied the vote. "Every discrimination against women in the constitutions and laws of the several states is today null and void," Anthony argued, "precisely as is every one against Negroes."[106] By according the Declaration and the Preamble to the Constitution authoritative weight, the

---

[99] See Joan Hoff, *Law, Gender, and Injustice: A Legal History of U.S. Women* (New York: New York University Press, 1991), 145–50; Linda Kerber, *No Constitutional Right to Be Ladies: Women and the Obligations of Citizenship* (New York: Macmillan, 1999).

[100] See Kerber, *No Constitutional Right*, 99.

[101] Ibid. The amendment divided the coalition that favored both woman suffrage and freedman's rights. Frederick Douglass rejected criticism by famously proclaiming, "This is the Negro's hour." Baker, *Sisters*, 37.

[102] See Kerber, *No Constitutional Right*, 87.

[103] Susan B. Anthony, "On Women's Right to Vote" (The History Place – Great Speeches Collection). http://www.historyplace.com/speeches/anthony.htm.

[104] Ibid.   [105] Ibid.   [106] Ibid.

suffrage movement – like the abolitionist movement before it and the civil rights movement after it – contested the legal status of women. The movements also contested what counted as authoritative and binding legal principles.

Despite the elegance of Anthony's speech, the hortatory language of the Preamble and the Declaration did not establish legal rules that bound legislators and courts. Indeed, in *Minor* v. *Happersett*, decided three years after Anthony's speech, the US Supreme Court denied that woman suffrage followed the concession that the Fourteenth Amendment conferred citizenship upon women.[107] Women could be members of the political community, the Court held, but nevertheless denied voting rights.[108] The US Constitution did not confer the right to vote upon anyone; it merely banned certain restrictions on the exercise of the franchise, held the Court. Pursuant to this interpretation of the Constitution, the states retained the power to establish qualifications for voting. "If the law is wrong, it ought to be changed," the Justices noted. "[B]ut," the Court said, "the power for that is not with us." Thus, the battle for woman suffrage continued into the next century.

Women only gained suffrage after the face of the Constitution changed. In 1919, after decades of political agitation, Congress enacted the Nineteenth Amendment to the Constitution. The amendment banned discrimination in voting "on account of sex."[109] The damage done to women's rights by the exclusionary language of the Fourteenth and Fifteenth Amendments had proved an encumbrance but had not been fatal to women's struggle for equality. Nevertheless, law continued to play a contradictory role in the equality struggles of women. Despite the Nineteenth Amendment, women remained subject to gender bias in the workplace, in politics, and even in the home.[110] Therefore, women's resistance to inequality continued, notwithstanding the enactment of the Nineteenth Amendment, much the same as the black struggle for equality persisted despite the advent of the Reconstruction Amendments.

Women's Liberation

During the late twentieth century, a new generation of activists – proponents of "women's liberation" – attacked the sex discrimination that persisted in American society despite the Nineteenth Amendment. The struggle for civil rights helped to inspire the woman's liberation movement, just as abolitionism had inspired the woman suffrage movement.[111] When males relegated females to support roles and excluded them from leadership positions in the civil rights movement, disillusioned women mobilized.[112]

---

[107] 88 U.S. 162, 178.   [108] Ibid.   [109] US Constitution, Nineteenth Amendment.
[110] See Hoff, *Law Gender and Injustice*, 192–315.
[111] See Serena Mayeri, *Reasoning from Race: Feminism, Law and the Civil Rights Revolution* (Cambridge, MA; Harvard University Press, 2014), 3–6.
[112] See, e.g., Sara Evans, *Personal Politics: The Roots of Women's Liberation in the Civil Rights Movement and the New Left* (New York: Vintage, 1979).

Women's liberation organizations unified around the goals of expanding women's civic and political participation and increasing women's educational and employment opportunities. The National Organization for Women (NOW) took the lead in advancing these objectives.[113] Leaders of NOW made constitutional arguments to advance the organization's agenda. Betty Freidan, a NOW cofounder, called the women's movement a "Second American Revolution." Like Susan B. Anthony, Freidan tethered the woman's liberation movement to the ideas articulated in the Declaration of Independence.[114] In court, lawyers for women's causes drew analogies to race discrimination, now constitutionally and statutorily proscribed.[115] The strategy proved successful. Arguing that equal protection demanded the same treatment of women and men, just as it did of blacks and whites, the women's liberation movement prevailed in numerous Fourteenth Amendment cases.[116]

Some advocates of women's equality criticized these analogical arguments, however. The Fourteenth Amendment demanded that women conform to the male norm, they said, a version of equality that fell far short of liberation. Such arguments would never destroy patriarchy. True liberation demanded critiques of economic structures, cultural norms, and biological differences that caused or justified the oppression of women. These arguments could not be made within the Fourteenth Amendment's narrow, antidiscrimination framework.[117]

Such constitutional and cultural critiques generated a demand for a new amendment to the Constitution, the Equal Rights Amendment (ERA). The ERA had first been proposed during the nineteenth century by woman suffragists.[118] The proposed addition to the Constitution stated: "Equality of rights under the law shall not be denied or abridged by the United States or by any state on account of sex." The amendment also conferred upon Congress authority to enact legislation to enforce it. The constitutional change did not come to pass, however: the ERA passed Congress, yet fell three states short of ratification. Women's ambitions for more direct constitutional protection went unfulfilled.[119]

---

[113] See Zillah R. Eisenstein, *The Radical Future of Liberal Feminism* (New York: Longman, 1981), 177–79.

[114] Betty Friedan, *It Changed My Life: Writings on the Women's Movement* (Cambridge, MA: Harvard University Press, 1976), 229.

[115] See Mayeri, *Reasoning from Race*, 1–40.

[116] See Reed v. Reed, 404 U.S. 71 (1971) (sex-based discrimination in appointment of estate administrators unconstitutional); Frontiero v. Richardson, 411 U.S. 677 (1973) (finding statute that discriminated against men for purposes of awarding spousal dependency benefits unconstitutional); Craig v. Boren, 429 U.S. 1990 (1976) (holding state law that discriminated on basis of sex for purposes of non-intoxicating beer purchases unconstitutional).

[117] See Eisenstein, *The Radical Future of Liberal Feminism*, 177–79.

[118] Janet K. Boles, *The Politics of the Equal Rights Amendment* (New York: Longman, 1979).

[119] Ibid.

CONCLUSION

Protest movements have frequently turned to the Constitution and rights talk to gain leverage. Movements have deployed the law conventionally, litigating claims in courts that established landmark Supreme Court decisions. However, movements have also deployed rights talk successfully without ever attaining victory in a courtroom.[120] At different points in American history, abolitionists and woman suffragists, civil rights leaders, and women's liberation advocates have invoked a thick conception of law to achieve their moral, cultural, and political aims.[121] Leaders of these movements advanced their causes in numerous, creative ways. They made space for change by citing constitutional and legal constructs during public addresses, by criticizing unfavorable judicial decisions during sit-ins, and by alleging violations of "rights" during demonstrations. Abolitionists and civil rights activists cited legal rhetoric for moral authority. Student activists relied on culturally resonant legal texts to expose society's hypocrisy. Constitutional and legal constructs proved powerful tools for social movements in all these contexts and many others not discussed in this essay.

Nevertheless, protest movements can lose ground when they rely on rights talk, and, as this essay shows, many have suffered setbacks when deploying constitutional and legal constructs. The Fourteenth Amendment to the Constitution undermined woman suffrage because of what it said; the same amendment disappointed proponents of women's liberation because of what it left unsaid. In *Plessy*, the Supreme Court interpreted equal protection in ways that frustrated advocates of racial equality. In *Brown*, the Court reversed course, imbuing the amendment with the opposite meaning. Reversals of fortune occurred with frequency, and advocates could never be sure of long-lasting victory. Movements can deploy the constitutional and legal argumentation for leverage but cannot expect it to definitively resolve a dispute.

Thus, this essay concludes, rights talk is an essential – but unreliable – resource for change movements. When movements engage the Constitution, the law, and legal constructs, they must be prepared to reap risks as well as rewards. Stated differently, "freedom is a constant struggle."[122]

---

[120] McCann, *Rights at Work* (arguing that equal pay litigation had important symbolic effect on comparable worth movement and made pay scales more equitable to women); Kevin J. McMahon and Michael Paris, "The Politics of Rights Revisited: Rosenberg, McCann, and the New Institutionalism," in David A. Schultz, ed., *Leveraging the Law: Using the Courts to Achieve Social Change* (New York: Peter Lang, 1998), 63–82 (arguing that Professor Rosenberg undervalues direct and indirect positive effects of *Brown* on Montgomery bus boycott).

[121] On social movements' repertoires, see Jeff Goodwin and James M. Jasper, *The Social Movements Reader* (Hoboken, NJ: Wiley-Blackwell, 2003), 221.

[122] Lyrics by Barbara Dane and the Chambers Brothers, "Freedom Is a Constant Struggle." *Songs of the Civil Rights Movement*. Susie Erenrich and the Cultural Center for Social Change: Washington, D.C., 1994. CD.

16

Balancing Privacy and National Security: A Rule of Lenity for National Security Surveillance Law

Orin S. Kerr

In the summer of 2013, Edward Snowden began an astonishing series of national security leaks that shed new light on the classified work of the Foreign Intelligence Surveillance Court (FISC).[1] Created in 1978, the FISC was designed to introduce a judicial role into the US regime of foreign intelligence surveillance.[2] The Snowden leaks revealed that the FISC operated differently than outsiders had assumed. Although the FISC had been created primarily as a court to review warrant applications, it had morphed into a regulatory body that issued long opinions secretly approving surveillance programs that Congress had never considered – and likely would not have approved.

The Snowden disclosures led Congress to enact reforms to the FISC as part of the USA Freedom Act of 2015.[3] The new law tries to make the FISC more like a regular lawmaking court. It aims to improve the FISC by blending the characteristics of an ex parte court that merely reviews court order applications with those of a traditional adversarial lawmaking court. By helping the FISC act more like an adversarial lawmaking court, the thinking runs, the reforms can improve the decision making of the FISC and ensure more reliable interpretations of the foreign intelligence surveillance laws.

This essay will take a different approach. It will argue that Congress should go in the opposite direction: instead of helping the FISC act more like a regular lawmaking court, Congress should improve the surveillance laws by making sure the FISC will not act as a lawmaking court. Congress should enact an interpretive rule requiring that government powers granted under the Foreign

---

[1] See Luke Harding, *The Snowden Files: The Inside Story of the World's Most Wanted Man* 5, 9–11 (2014). The disclosures began on June 5, 2013. See Dustin Volz, Everything We Learned from Edward Snowden in 2013, *Nat'l J.* (Dec. 31, 2013), www.nationaljournal.com/defense/every thing-we-learned-from-edward-snowden-in-2013-20131231.

[2] For a history and overview of the Foreign Intelligence Surveillance Act (FISA), see David S. Kris and J. Douglas Wilson, *National Security & Prosecutions* 2d chs. 1–4 (2012).

[3] Pub. L. No. 114-23 (2015).

Intelligence Surveillance Act (FISA) be narrowly construed. I will call this rule of narrow construction a "rule of lenity," borrowing a term often used to advocate a narrow interpretation of criminal statutes. When the government's power under existing law is ambiguous, the FISC should adopt the narrower construction that favors the individual instead of the State. If the executive wants new surveillance powers, it should go to Congress for those powers instead of to the courts. Within constitutional boundaries, the power to define national security law will rest with the elected branches and, in turn, with the people.

Adopting a rule of narrow interpretation for national security surveillance law would have two important benefits. First, it would promote democratic accountability and transparency. It would limit the decision-making authority of the secret FISC and give that power to the open and public legislature. It would enable a feedback loop that allows the public to control the scope of government powers through the elected branches.

Second, a narrow interpretive approach would shift power to the branch of government best suited to balance privacy and security in changing technologies. FISC judges are poorly equipped to choose surveillance rules, as they are merely trial judges acting in secret without the benefit of adversarial briefing and public commentary. Congress is much better able to draw the appropriate lines of power. Congress can draw on experts, legislate comprehensively, and account for the latest technological developments.

Of course, adopting a rule of interpretation would not be a panacea. It would be helpful only to the extent courts follow it, and it would facilitate process rather than guarantee any particular surveillance rule. At the same time, a rule of lenity would provide a simple mechanism to encourage more transparent and effective surveillance laws. It would not solve everything. But it is an easy first step.

This essay will proceed in three parts. The first part will explain the basic dynamic of ex parte regulation in surveillance law as well as the special challenges of using that model to regulate national security surveillance law. The second part will explain how Edward Snowden's disclosures have revealed the FISC's failed efforts to act as a lawmaking court in its ex parte role. It will then survey how the USA Freedom Act helps make the FISC more of an adversarial court. The third part will propose that Congress should instead adopt a rule of lenity. It will explain the benefits of a rule of lenity, and it will consider how the rule would act in practice to further more accountable and balanced surveillance laws.

EX PARTE REGULATION OF SURVEILLANCE PRACTICES

In 1978, Congress enacted the first comprehensive statute to regulate national security surveillance law, the Foreign Intelligence Surveillance Act.[4] The core mechanism of FISA is the process of regulation by ex parte court orders. To

---

[4] See 1 Kris and Wilson, supra note 2, §4:1, at 116.

understand FISA and the case for a rule of narrow interpretation, it is necessary to understand both the theory behind regulating surveillance practices using ex parte court orders and the challenges of doing so in the specific context of national security. This part begins by explaining the basic theory of ex parte regulation. It then turns to the conditions of successful use of that approach, and it concludes with a discussion of how national security surveillance creates an ongoing need for reform of surveillance rules.

Ex Parte Court Orders and the Privacy/Security Balance

When lawyers envision the judicial function, they ordinarily imagine decision makers ruling in adversarial disputes.[5] One side brings a claim. The other side denies liability. The judge rules for one side and against the other. The losing side can appeal, and the case can proceed all the way to the Supreme Court. The appellate courts settle the law, adopting legal interpretations that govern future disputes.[6] We can call this the adversarial model of a lawmaking court. It features two adversarial sides, and it places the judiciary in the role of decision maker between them.

Although this is the common understanding of the judicial function, there is a second role for courts that is used widely in surveillance law. The second role is that of an ex parte court that reviews court order applications. When the law regulates using ex parte court orders, no surveillance or government investigation is permitted unless the government first obtains preapproval from a judge (often referred to in this context as a "magistrate"). The government must go to the magistrate and apply for an order allowing surveillance. If the legal requirements of the court order have been satisfied, the magistrate signs the order and the surveillance can occur. If the legal requirements of the court order have not been satisfied, the magistrate must refuse to sign the order and the surveillance cannot occur. We can call this method ex parte regulation. It features only one side, and it places the reviewing judge in a largely ministerial role of determining if the legal requirements of an application have been satisfied.[7]

Modern surveillance statutes make frequent use of ex parte regulation to try to strike an optimal balance between privacy and security.[8] On one hand, surveillance protects the public by informing the government of threats and

---

[5] This is the traditional role described in Abram Chayes, The Role of the Judge in Public Law Litigation, 89 *Harv. L. Rev.* 1281, 1285–86 (1976).

[6] See id.

[7] See Orin S. Kerr, Ex Ante Regulation of Computer Search and Seizure, 96 *Va. L. Rev.* 1241, 1260–77 (2010) (discussing the usual procedures for ruling on warrants).

[8] For statutory examples, see 18 U.S.C. §2703(a) (2012) (requiring a warrant to obtain email); id. §3121 (requiring a court order to obtain a pen register). The primary constitutional example is found in the text of the Fourth Amendment: "[N]o Warrants shall issue, but upon probable cause, supported by Oath or affirmation, and particularly describing the place to be searched, and the persons or things to be seized." U.S. Const. amend. IV.

dangers. On the other hand, surveillance invades privacy and threatens civil liberties.[9] Ex parte regulation attempts to optimize the privacy/security balance by allowing surveillance when the expected benefit to security outweighs its harm to privacy. The conditions of surveillance are set by some legal decision maker, which in the case of statutory regulation is the legislature. The decision maker tries to set the conditions of surveillance so that the more severe the privacy invasion, the higher the showing required by the law. Ideally, if the threshold for obtaining a court order has been set properly, reviewing magistrates should allow surveillance when the security benefits outweigh the privacy harms but prohibit surveillance otherwise.

Consider how this works with the well-known example of a probable cause search warrant under the Fourth Amendment.[10] When the Fourth Amendment requires a warrant, a government agent must come to the judge with an application. The government must establish the constitutional requirements of probable cause and particularity.[11] Probable cause establishes the government's interest in the search by showing good reasons to think the search will be successful.[12] The particularity requirement shows that the search will be relatively narrow, as it will be limited to a specific place and specific evidence.[13] When probable cause and particularity have been satisfied, the resulting search should, on average, result in a benefit to the government that outweighs the privacy invasion. In the argot of Fourth Amendment law, the search will be constitutionally reasonable.

Importantly, the imposition of an ex parte court order requirement envisions a narrow role for the magistrate tasked with reviewing the application. In the case of a constitutional requirement such as a traditional Fourth Amendment warrant, the text of the Fourth Amendment defines the required showing.[14] The reviewing magistrate's job is only to say if the standard has been met.[15] In the case of a statutory regime, the legislature drafts the statute with specific thresholds for the government to satisfy that reflect the legislature's weighing of the privacy and security values implicated by the surveillance. The role of the reviewing magistrate is limited; the magistrate only determines if the threshold facts have been shown.[16] The policymaking task of setting that threshold is up to the rule maker, not the reviewing magistrate. The magistrate serves an

---

[9] See Neil M. Richards, The Dangers of Surveillance, 126 *Harv. L. Rev.* 1934, 1939–52 (2013).

[10] See U.S. Const. amend. IV.

[11] See id.; see also Fed. R. Crim. P. 41(a) (permitting a federal judge to issue a warrant based on probable cause and particularity).

[12] See Illinois v. Gates, 462 U.S. 213, 238 (1983) (defining probable cause in the case of a search warrant as "a fair probability that contraband or evidence of a crime will be found in a particular place").

[13] See Maryland v. Garrison, 480 U.S. 79, 84 (1987).   [14] See U.S. Const. amend. IV.

[15] See Abraham S. Goldstein, The Search Warrant, the Magistrate, and Judicial Review, 62 *N. Y. U. L. Rev.* 1173, 1196 (1987) ("The few cases . . . hold that a judge has a 'ministerial' duty to issue a warrant after 'probable cause' has been established.").

[16] See id.

essentially ministerial role of making sure that no orders will issue unless the rule maker's standards have been satisfied.

Conditions of Successful Ex Parte Regulation

Ex parte court orders can provide a stable and effective way to balance privacy and security when two related criteria are met. The first condition of successful ex parte regulation is the existence of a feedback mechanism. In any surveillance system, there must be some way of knowing how the rules are working in practice. In general, however, ex parte regulation generates no feedback.[17] Reviewing magistrates decide to grant the applications or reject them. When they reject applications, they do not write opinions explaining why. If a judge denies a warrant application, the denial is not an appealable final order.[18] There is no case to appeal. And when magistrates grant applications, they merely sign the orders. With the order issued, the magistrate's task is done.

Because the ex parte process does not itself generate feedback, the functioning of an ex parte regulatory system requires an alternative method of oversight. Consider the Fourth Amendment's exclusionary rule, which can provide for suppression of evidence when the government obtains evidence in violation of the prohibition on unreasonable searches and seizures.[19] Ex ante, judges review warrant applications and sign them to approve searches. But the primary feedback mechanism is ex post review. After a warrant is issued, leads to a successful search, and then results in criminal charges, the defendant can move to suppress the evidence and ask the reviewing court to assess ex post whether investigators violated the Fourth Amendment.[20]

Under an exclusionary rule, ex post review shifts the judicial function from that of ex parte regulation to the classic adversarial model of a lawmaking court. The defendant will claim that the law was violated, and the government will disagree. The court will author an opinion explaining the facts and reaching a decision, and the loser can later appeal that ruling up through the appellate courts. Published decisions on how the investigators acted provide courts and legislators with feedback about how the law is working in practice.

---

[17] There are some narrow exceptions. For example, under Federal Rule of Criminal Procedure 41, the agents must file a return on the warrant with the issuing magistrate that informs the magistrate what property was seized pursuant to the warrant. Fed. R. Crim. P. 41(f)(1)(D) ("The officer executing the warrant must promptly return it – together with a copy of the inventory – to the magistrate judge designated on the warrant.").

[18] See United States v. Savides, 658 F.Supp. 1399, 1404 (N.D. Ill. 1987), aff'd sub nom. United States v. Pace, 898 F.2d 1218 (7th Cir. 1990). But see In re Application of the United States for Historical Cell Site Data, 724 F.3d 600, 605 (5th Cir. 2013) (concluding that the government may appeal the denial of an ex parte court order for historical cell site information sought under 18 U.S.C. §2703[d]).

[19] See generally 3 Wayne R. LaFave et al., *Criminal Procedure* §9.4(b) (3d ed. 2007) (describing the exclusionary rule).

[20] See id.

The second condition of stable ex parte regulation is technological stability. The basic thinking behind ex parte regulation is that a specific kind of surveillance will generally be worthwhile when a specific factual predicate has been satisfied. When technology remains stable, the kind of surveillance and the nature of the factual predicate will remain constant and relatively clear. The balance implicit in the statute stays steady over time. Again, consider a warrant to search a home based on probable cause. What it means to search a home has remained fairly constant over time. The act of searching a home for evidence in the eighteenth century was basically the same as it is in the twenty-first century.[21] And the kinds of facts that constitute probable cause today are essentially the same as in earlier generations. As a result, the ancient rule that the government needs probable cause and a warrant to search a home remains a viable and clear rule.

That balance becomes unstable, however, if technology is in flux. If the technological facts of surveillance change, the invasiveness of surveillance changes along with it. On paper, the legal rule will look the same. But in practice, changing technology can dramatically alter the significance of the rule. Two related problems emerge. First, as the technological facts change, the rule may end up allowing a vastly different amount of surveillance than was assumed when the rule was initially created. Second, the meaning of the law itself can become uncertain. Existing language that defines the government's burden in one technological era may become quite fuzzy in another technological era. New facts will create significant ambiguities as to how the old legal standard applies.

The second problem is particularly troubling for the problem of national security surveillance law, and an example may be helpful to demonstrate the point. Consider the scope of the Pen Register statute in the dawn of the Internet era. In 1986, Congress enacted the Pen Register statute as part of the Electronic Communications Privacy Act to create privacy protection that limits the real-time acquisition of communications network metadata.[22] At the time, Congress was focused on the telephone network. The US Supreme Court had held in *Smith* v. *Maryland* that the government could install a pen register to learn the numbers dialed from a telephone without triggering the Fourth Amendment.[23] The Pen Register statute stepped into the space Smith left unregulated by requiring a court order before investigators could order the phone company to collect the numbers dialed from a telephone.[24]

---

[21] See Orin S. Kerr, An Equilibrium-Adjustment Theory of the Fourth Amendment, 125 *Harv. L. Rev.* 476, 517–18 (2011).

[22] See 18 U.S.C. §§3121–27 (2012). The Pen Register statute was passed as part of the Electronic Communications Privacy Act of 1986, Pub. L. No. 99-508, §301(a), 100 Stat. 1848, 1868–72 (codified as amended at 18 U.S.C. §§3121–24, 3126–27 [2012]).

[23] 442 U.S. 735, 745–46 (1979).

[24] From 1986 to 2001, the definition of "pen register" in the statute was telephone-specific: the law defined a pen register as "a device which records or decodes electronic or other impulses which identify the numbers dialed or otherwise transmitted on the telephone line to which such device is attached." 18 U.S.C. §3126(3) (Supp. V 1986) (amended 2001); cf. United States v. Guglielmo,

Starting in the 1990s, however, the question arose whether the Pen Register statute also applied to the Internet.[25] As a policy matter, it made eminent sense that it would. Otherwise there was no privacy law at all that limited government access to Internet metadata collected in real time. But the 1986 language was not drafted with the Internet in mind and contained at least some apparently telephone-specific text.[26] As a result, it was a close call, purely as a matter of statutory interpretation, as to whether the privacy law applied beyond the telephone context.[27] Congress eventually stepped in to resolve the ambiguity and extended the statute to the Internet,[28] in part due to an unpublished magistrate judge's opinion, unknown outside the government, holding that the statute did not apply to the Internet.[29] But before the law was amended, the old text left the application of the law to an important new technology surprisingly unclear. And despite the obvious importance of the question, few outside the small circle of surveillance law nerds even knew the question existed until Congress publicly amended the statute in 2001.

FISA and the Conditions of National Security Surveillance

Now let's turn to the Foreign Intelligence Surveillance Act.[30] As enacted in 1978, its purpose was to replace the prior regime of surveillance regulated only by the Fourth Amendment with a new system of ex parte court order regulation adapted from the law of criminal investigations.[31] In its original form, it required a wiretapping order, modeled on the Wiretap Act, a criminal law, before the government could wiretap agents of foreign powers in the United States.[32] Over time, FISA expanded its use of ex parte orders. It added an ex parte order requirement for the national security equivalent of physical searches pursuant to warrants in 1994[33] and for the national security equivalent of grand jury subpoenas and pen registers in 1998.[34] In 2007 and 2008 amendments, it

---

245 F.Supp. 534, 535 (N.D. Ill. 1965) ("The pen register is a mechanical device attached on occasion to a given telephone line, usually at central telephone offices. A pulsation of the dial on a line to which the pen register is attached records on a paper tape dashes equal to the number dialed.").

[25] Orin S. Kerr, Internet Surveillance Law after the USA PATRIOT Act: The Big Brother That Isn't, 97 *Nw. U. L. Rev.* 607, 632–36 (2003).

[26] The competing arguments are explained in detail in id.   [27] See id. at 632–33.

[28] See id. at 636–38.

[29] See id. at 635 (citing In re United States, Cr.-00-6091 [N.D. Cal. Nov. 17, 2000] [Trumbull, Mag. J.] [unpublished opinion]).

[30] 50 U.S.C. §§1801–71 (2012).   [31] See 1 Kris and Wilson, supra note 2, §§3.6–3.7, at 102–8.

[32] See Foreign Intelligence Surveillance Act of 1978, Pub. L. No. 95-511, 92 Stat. 1783 (codified as amended at 50 U.S.C. §§1801–11 [2012]).

[33] See Intelligence Authorization Act for Fiscal Year 1995, Pub. L. No. 103-359, §807, 108 Stat. 3423, 3443–53 (1994) (codified as amended at 50 U.S.C. §§1821–29 [2012]).

[34] See Intelligence Authorization Act for Fiscal Year 1999, Pub. L. No. 105-272, §§601–2, 112 Stat. 2396, 2404–12 (1998) (codified as amended at 50 U.S.C. §§1841–46, 1861–62 [2012]).

added blanket court orders of individuals believed to be located outside the United States.[35] For all of these court orders, the executive branch must apply for an order before a special court of appointed federal district judges, meeting as part-time members of the FISC, to obtain approval.

In light of the prior discussion, we can see that the conditions of foreign intelligence surveillance pose significant problems for ex parte regulation. The first problem is technological. Communications network technology changes rapidly, and the national security agencies are at the leading edge of technological change. The second problem is the absence of a strong, democratically accountable feedback loop to monitor how the laws are working in practice.

For agencies like the National Security Agency (NSA), technological advantage is critical. The country's national security apparatus has an extraordinarily large budget, and it uses the most advanced technology to conduct surveillance and analysis of foreign intelligence.[36] The NSA follows wherever communications technology goes, seeking to acquire that information, store it, and analyze it with an efficiency and capability unknown in the private sector. And the advent of computers and the Internet have made technological change a constant. For most users, the changes are imperceptible. The telephone and the Internet just work, as if by magic. But for the computer geeks who help run national security surveillance, it is what happens behind the scenes that matters. Surveillance experts focus on how the network actually works and what powers the government has to monitor the traffic over it. The internal perception of users is irrelevant. And from the expert perspective, both the Internet and technological surveillance tools are constantly morphing and relentlessly dynamic.[37]

Second, national security surveillance lacks a natural alternative feedback loop to inform Congress of how its surveillance rules are working. The goal of national security surveillance is the collection of information that can be used inside the government but ordinarily will not be publicly disclosed. Unlike the criminal process, there is no obvious end of the road when the case is over, the evidence comes out, and ex post review can occur. When the government collects information for national security purposes, it is a one-way street. The government gets the information, and it is never seen again.[38]

---

[35] See Protect America Act of 2007, Pub. L. No. 110-55, §§2–3, 121 Stat. 552, 552–55; FISA Amendments Act of 2008, Pub. L. No. 110-261, §101, 122 Stat. 2436, 2437–58 (2008) (codified at 50 U.S.C. §§1881a–g [2012]).

[36] According to the classified budget documents released by Edward Snowden, the NSA was scheduled to receive $10.5 billion in 2013. See Barton Gellman and Greg Miller, "Black Budget" Revealed: Top-Secret Summary Details U.S. Spy Network's Successes, Failures and Objectives, *Wash. Post*, Aug. 29, 2013, at A1.

[37] I documented some of the changes in Orin S. Kerr, The Next Generation Communications Privacy Act, 162 *U. Pa. L. Rev.* 373, 390–410 (2014).

[38] Even if court challenges are brought, they rarely succeed. In many cases, the state secrets doctrine will block civil suits designed to obtain rulings on surveillance practices. See Laura K. Donohue,

Congress has addressed the absence of a natural feedback loop by requiring the executive to provide classified briefings about intelligence efforts to members of the House and Senate Intelligence and Judiciary Committees. Specifically, 50 U.S.C. § 1871(a) requires the Attorney General to provide semiannual reports to these committees that provide members information, including "a summary of significant legal interpretations of this chapter involving matters before the Foreign Intelligence Surveillance Court or the Foreign Intelligence Surveillance Court of Review"[39] as well as "copies of all decisions ... or opinions of the Foreign Intelligence Surveillance Court or Foreign Intelligence Surveillance Court of Review that include significant construction or interpretation of the provisions of this chapter."[40] The basic idea is to strike a balance between protecting vital secrets and democratic accountability by informing members of the major committees but not the Congress as a whole nor the public.[41]

Although well-intentioned, these limited disclosures fail to generate the necessary feedback about what the law authorizes. That is true for two reasons. First, elected representatives are poorly equipped to represent majority preference when the public is intentionally left in the dark. Elected representatives briefed on classified programs may not understand the programs themselves. Even if they understand the programs, they will not know how the public would react. It is particularly challenging to predict responses to secret surveillance programs the public cannot readily imagine based on technologies few even know exist. Plus, elected officials will not know if the public will ever learn of the programs to make predicted public reaction particularly salient. Awareness of eventual disclosure focuses attention on the likely public response. Its absence directs attention elsewhere.

Further, even if disclosure to Congress as a whole were sufficient, disclosure to specific committees raises special problems. The membership of the Judiciary and Intelligence Committees are not picked at random.[42] Over time, the committee membership may develop a close relationship with the agencies

---

The Shadow of State Secrets, 159 *U. Pa. L. Rev.* 77, 84–88 (2010). Under the state secrets privilege, courts can reject civil suits if the litigation would reveal valuable intelligence information. See id. at 82. In effect, the common path of civil litigation is closed in order to keep the government's secrets confidential. Once again, there is no feedback loop: The design of national security surveillance is to avoid published opinions explaining surveillance practices and how they work. See id. at 84–85.

[39] 50 U.S.C. §1871(a)(4) (2012).   [40] Id. §1871(a)(5).

[41] See L. Elaine Halcin and Frederick M. Kaiser, Cong. Research Serv., RL32525, Congressional Oversight of Intelligence: Current Structure and Alternatives (2012), available at http://assets .opencrs.com/rpts/RL32525_20120314.pdf.

[42] See id. at 6–7; see also Frequently Asked Questions about Committees, U.S. Senate, www.senate .gov/general/common/generic/committee_faq.htm#committee_assignment (last visited May 5, 2014) ("Each party assigns, by resolution, its own members to committees, and each committee distributes its members among subcommittees.").

they oversee.[43] And it may be difficult for members of the relevant committees to persuade the Congress as a whole of the need for reform. None of this denigrates the hard work and careful attention that these committees provide to oversight of national security surveillance. Such oversight can be particularly effective when focused on compliance with the law. At the same time, disclosure limited to specific committees does not create feedback necessary to ensure the democratic accountability of surveillance law itself.

Ex parte regulation works best with transparent practices and stable technology. National security surveillance offers the worst of both worlds, with secret practices and rapid technological change. Obsolete and uncertain legal restrictions are inevitable. The key question is how the law will deal with the ambiguities and obsolescence.

THE FISC AND THE FAILURE OF THE HYBRID APPROACH

The leaks beginning in the summer of 2013 revealed the operation of the FISC for the first time. Edward Snowden leaked several documents, and the public reaction pushed the Obama administration to release redacted versions of FISC opinions. The unearthed decisions revealed that the FISC had assumed a new role. Although designed as an ex parte court tasked primarily with reviewing court order applications, the FISC had secretly taken on an additional important role of a lawmaking court. The resulting hybrid placed the FISC in a position akin to an executive agency with broad powers to regulate national security law.

Equally importantly, the released FISC opinions revealed that the FISC had interpreted the surveillance laws in surprising and perhaps shocking ways. Technological change had destabilized key aspects of FISA and created ambiguities that the FISC then tried to resolve.[44] Because no public feedback loop existed, the FISC's interpretations had remained secret. And acting in secret, the FISC had issued opinions approving programs far removed from the statutory text that astonished the public when the Snowden disclosures made them public.

This part of the discussion explains the new hybrid role of the FISC revealed by Snowden's disclosures. Acting in secret, the FISC transformed itself into a novel mixture of an ex parte court and an adversarial court that effectively created the legal standards for national security surveillance law. The result has been a body of secret law that seems removed from what a majority of the public would approve.[45] That novel role for the FISC triggered the USA Freedom Act,

---

[43] See, e.g., Lauren Fox, Spy Game: Why Congress Is Limited in Its CIA Oversight, *U.S. News & World Rep.* (Mar. 12, 2014), www.usnews.com/news/articles/?2014/03/12/spy-game-why-congress-is-lim ited-in-its-cia-oversight ("In the years since the Sept. 11 terrorist attacks, the intelligence community has maintained a cozy relationship with the Senate Intelligence Committee tasked with overseeing its activities.").

[44] See infra Section II.B.

[45] Confident conclusions about public opinion are difficult because relatively few members of the public understand the details of individual surveillance programs and polling questions are often

which among other things tries to make the FISC a better-functioning hybrid court.

The Hybrid Role of the FISC Exposed

Until the summer of 2013, almost all of the FISC's work product remained highly classified. Every year, the Justice Department (DOJ) released a one- to two-page summary reporting the number of FISC orders that the government had applied for and the court had granted.[46] But these summaries shed almost no light on the work of the FISC. Even the fact that almost every FISC application recorded was granted was a source of mystery, as the published figures do not indicate whether the FISC judges work with the DOJ lawyers informally to consider possible applications before formal applications are made.[47]

Most importantly, it was not public what (if anything) the FISC did beyond approve or disapprove the government's applications to conduct surveillance. Did the FISC issue opinions? Did it conduct substantive review of surveillance practices? No one in the general public knew the answers. The traditional role of ex parte and ex ante review is merely to review applications and either sign or refuse to sign orders. Ex parte review normally does not generate case law or lead to opinions. But until the summer of 2013, the work of the FISC remained secret – both as to whether the FISC had exceeded the traditional role of an ex parte court and, if so, as to how the FISC had regulated the executive branch and what legal interpretations it had adopted.

The flurry of Snowden documents changed that. Starting in the summer of 2013, several documents from the FISC were disclosed.[48] And in response to Snowden's leaks, the federal government released additional troves of FISC

---

imprecise. Nonetheless, public opinion on NSA surveillance practices generally has tended to poll slightly negative in the wake of Snowden's disclosures. When asked in a January 2014 Pew Research Center/*USA Today* survey, "Overall, do you approve or disapprove of the government's collection of telephone and internet data as part of anti-terrorism efforts?," 53 percent disapproved and 40 percent approved. See Pew Research Ctr., Obama's NSA Speech Has Little Impact on Skeptical Public: Most Say U.S. Should Pursue Criminal Case against Snowden 12 (Jan. 20, 2014), available at www.people-press.org/files/legacy-pdf/1-20-14%20NSA%20Release.pdf; see also Letter from Senators Ron Wyden and Mark Udall to Attorney Gen. Eric Holder 1 (Mar. 15, 2012), available at www.fas.org/irp/congress/?2012_cr/wydeno31512.pdf ("We believe most Americans would be stunned to learn the details of how these secret court opinions have interpreted section 215 of the Patriot Act.").

[46] The reports are available at FISA Annual Reports to Congress, Fed'n of Am. Scientists, www.fas.org/irp/agency/doj/fisa/#rept (last visited May 12, 2014).

[47] In 2012, 1,789 applications to conduct electronic surveillance were made before the FISC. One application was withdrawn, and 1,788 were approved, forty with modifications. See Letter from Peter J. Kadzik, Principal Deputy Assistant Attorney Gen., to Harry Reid, Senate Majority Leader, 2012 FISA Annual Report to Congress (Apr. 30, 2013), available at www.fas.org/irp/agency/doj/fisa/2012rept.pdf.

[48] See Harding, supra note 1. The disclosures began on June 5, 2013. Volz, supra note 1.

materials.[49] The documents revealed that the FISC had indeed issued legal opinions on its surveillance powers. When faced with an application for surveillance based on a questionable reading of its powers, the FISC had issued opinions interpreting its authorities. FISC opinions also engaged in extensive oversight of the NSA's compliance with its earlier orders.[50]

The FISC's opinions that regulated the FISC were striking in their content and form. First, the quality of the FISC's legal analysis was surprisingly poor. The FISC had authorized vastly more surveillance than outside observers could have imagined based on the public text of the statute. In the hands of the FISC judges, acting in secret, the text of FISA was no longer a reliable guide to executive branch authority.

The FISC's Work Product Revealed

The most important example of the FISC's weak decision making is the FISC's approval of the bulk telephony metadata program under Section 215 of the USA PATRIOT Act.[51] Section 215 is a national security analog to the traditional grand jury subpoena power in criminal investigations. In criminal cases, grand juries (generally controlled by prosecutors) can order third parties to hand over documents as long as compliance is not overly burdensome and the materials sought are relevant to a criminal investigation.[52] Grand jury subpoenas are not self-executing, however. Although issued by prosecutors in the name of the grand jury, the recipient of a subpoena can challenge a subpoena before a judge prior to compliance.[53]

On its face, Section 215 contemplates a similar power for national security investigators. It allows the government to obtain a court order from third parties for any tangible things under the traditional standards for subpoenas.[54] Section 215 employs one significant modification of the usual process for grand jury subpoenas: the judicial review occurs automatically at the outset so that the court must sign off on the request at the beginning instead of waiting for a later challenge.[55] Despite this difference, the Section 215 authority is expressly limited to that which any federal prosecutor would have in a criminal case.

---

[49] David S. Kris, On the Bulk Collection of Tangible Things 6–8 (Lawfare Research Paper Series, 2013), www.lawfareblog.com/wp-content/uploads/2013/09/?Lawfare-Research-Paper-Series -No.-4-2.pdf.

[50] See, e.g., In re Application of the FBI for an Order Requiring the Prod. of Tangible Things from [Redacted], No. BR 13-109, 2013 WL 5741573, at *7, *9–10 (FISA Ct. Aug. 29, 2013) (hereinafter In re FBI Application).

[51] USA PATRIOT Act, Pub. L. No. 107-56, §215, 115 Stat. 272, 287 (2001) (codified as amended at 50 U.S.C. §1861 [2012]); see also In re FBI Application, supra note 50, at *7–10 (approving the bulk telephony metadata program).

[52] See 3 LaFave et al., supra note 19, §8.7, at 151–77.

[53] See In re Horowitz, 482 F.2d 72, 75–80 (2d Cir. 1973).

[54] 50 U.S.C. §1861(c) (2012); see 3 LaFave et al., supra note 19, §8.7, at 151–77.

[55] Id. §1861(c)(2)(D).

According to the statute, a court may issue a Section 215 order only if the tangible thing obtained could "be obtained with a subpoena duces tecum issued by a court of the United States in aid of a grand jury investigation."[56] In other words, if a federal prosecutor in Topeka or San Antonio could not issue a lawful grand jury subpoena for the records, the FISC could not enter an order requiring a third party to hand over those records under Section 215.

Despite this limitation, the FISC ruled that Section 215 authorized an astonishing program: it enabled the government to obtain individual orders requiring telephone providers to hand over certain non-content records of all telephone calls of all of their customers in real time.[57] Telephone companies with tens of millions of customers had been secretly handing over telephone records of all of their customers for years, all pursuant to bulk Section 215 court orders that covered tens of millions of customers – and with all of the calls they made, presumably billions of telephone call records – at once.[58] The government then queried the database when it had reasonable suspicion to believe that a particular number was involved in terrorist activity, obtaining the records of that number, the records of any number in contact with that number, and the records of any number in contact with the numbers in contact with the original number.[59]

As a practical matter, the FISC had created its own surveillance authority. On its face, Section 215 simply authorized a national security subpoena power.[60] But by blending the roles of ex parte court and adversarial court, the FISC had interpreted FISA to authorize a new kind of program: a collect-it-all-and-query-with-suspicion model that bore no particular resemblance to the statute that purported to justify it. The FISC's interpretation obviated the need for the executive branch to seek express legislative approval for new programs. And it did this entirely in secret, leading to a massive surveillance program the very nature of which was unknown and unknowable to the public.

How had this come to pass? The key difficulty was that technology had outpaced the law. The limits of the subpoena power are well established except in one important respect: their application to computerized records. Subpoenas must seek relevant information, but sometimes that relevant information can be hidden in a database. Lower courts have entered divided opinions on whether and when a subpoena can be used to obtain a database to be searched later on for the relevant information. On one hand, courts have held that, in principle, the subpoena power can be used in that way.[61] At the same time, courts have indicated that there are limits on how far this power

---

[56] Id. §1861(c)(2)(D).

[57] See Administration White Paper, Bulk Collection of Telephony Metadata under Section 215 of the USA PATRIOT Act 2–5 (2013), archived at http://perma.cc/8RJN-EDB7; Kris, supra note 54, at 2–3.

[58] See Kris, supra note 49, at 2–6.　　[59] See id. at 10–12.　　[60] 50 U.S.C. §1861(c).

[61] See, e.g., Carrillo Huettel, LLP v. SEC, No. 11cv65-WQH (CAB), 2011 WL 601369, at *2 (S.D. Cal. Feb. 11, 2011).

can go.[62] For example, the power can only be used when necessary, based on whether it is possible to obtain the relevant records some other way.[63]

The FISC opinions harnessed this ambiguity to approve a program far removed from the statutory text. As summarized in an opinion by Judge Eagan,[64] the FISC reasoned that the government could subpoena every phone record all at once because it appeared necessary to do so. Why did it appear necessary? Here, the FISC simply recited the statements offered by the executive branch.[65] The Justice Department informed the FISC that, in its view, it was necessary to have all telephony metadata in order to do effective analysis of that metadata and identify terrorist suspects.[66] The FISC accepted this assertion as true,[67] effectively assuming the key fact based on the government's say-so.

At bottom, the FISC's argument was largely circular. It was legal to subpoena every phone record because it was necessary to do so to achieve the legitimate aim of the statute, and it was necessary to do so because the government claimed that the program was the only way to identify terrorists effectively. In other words, the program was legal because the government claimed it was effective. As construed in secret by the FISC, the government could obtain any database as long as the government secretly claimed that it needed the database. Because Section 215 incorporates the subpoena standard,[68] and the FISC had interpreted the subpoena standard to allow bulk collection, the FISC interpreted Section 215 to authorize the bulk collection program.

Whatever the merits of the bulk telephony metadata program as policy, the text of Section 215 does not authorize it. For the FISC to be correct, any federal prosecutor anywhere in the country could have compelled every phone company to hand over all of its telephony metadata on an ongoing basis so long as the prosecutor claimed that it was necessary to help solve a case. It is hard to imagine a federal judge allowing such a subpoena in a criminal case, which would cover the records of hundreds of millions of people on an ongoing basis. And because the Section 215 authority is expressly limited based on what a federal prosecutor could subpoena, it is difficult to read Section 215 as allowing that authority in the national security surveillance context.

---

[62] In re Grand Jury Subpoena Duces Tecum Dated Nov. 15, 1993, 846 F.Supp. 11, 13-14 (S.D.N.Y. 1994).

[63] Id. at 13.   [64] In re FBI Application, supra note 50, at *7, *9.   [65] See id. at *7.   [66] See id.

[67] After reciting the government's claim, Judge Eagan writes: "The fact that international terrorist operatives are using telephone communications, and that it is necessary to obtain the bulk collection of a telephone company's metadata to determine those connections between known and unknown international terrorist operatives as part of authorized investigations, is sufficient to meet the low statutory hurdle set out in Section 215 to obtain a production of records." Id. Judge Eagan provides no further analysis, effectively accepting the government's assertion of necessity on its face.

[68] 50 U.S.C. §1861(c)(2)(D) (2012).

The FISC's allowance of bulk collection under Section 215 is just one of several examples of the weak reasoning found in the FISC opinions.[69] Taken together, the poor quality of the FISC's work product demonstrates the failure of the FISC's hybrid approach to surveillance regulation. By combining ex parte procedures with the rulemaking power of an adversarial court, the FISC created a secret body of law that bore only a weak resemblance to the public statutes that Congress enacted. The role of Congress became an afterthought.

The USA Freedom Act

The USA Freedom Act was designed, in part, to correct the structure of FISC lawmaking. Its procedural reforms share a common theme: they aim to make the FISC more like a regular adversarial court. That is, the USA Freedom Act assumes that the FISC's problem is that it is an ex parte court and that the best solution is to introduce the procedures common to an adversarial lawmaking court. With the FISC's procedures reformed, the thinking goes, the FISC will adopt more persuasive interpretations of FISA. National security surveillance law will then develop in a more predictable and accountable way.

Consider three significant changes the USA Freedom Act introduced. First, the law adds a provision permitting the FISC to appoint an amicus curiae – a friend of the court – to appear before the FISC when an application "presents a novel or significant interpretation of the law."[70] The amicus must "possess expertise in privacy and civil liberties, intelligence collection, communications technology, or any other area that may lend legal or technical expertise."[71] Second, the FISC can certify "any question of law that may affect resolution of the matter in controversy"[72] to the Foreign Intelligence Court of Review when the FISC determines review is warranted "because of a need for uniformity or because consideration by the [Court of Review] would serve the interests of justice."[73] Third, the Foreign Intelligence Court of Review can certify questions to the US Supreme Court.[74]

These changes share the assumption that the FISC should continue to serve as a lawmaking court. On one hand, the USA Freedom Act maintains the FISC as an ex parte court in structure: The government continues to go to the FISC to seek approvals of court orders. On the other hand, the law tries to introduce adversarial mechanisms that are thought to generate reliable decision making. Underlying these mechanisms is the assumption that the FISC should be making law in its decisions.

---

[69] For another example, see Orin Kerr, Problems with the FISC's Newly-Declassified Opinion on Bulk Collection of Internet Metadata, Lawfare Blog (Nov. 19, 2013), www.lawfareblog.com /2013/11/problems-with-the-fiscs-newly-declassified-opinion-on-bulk-collection-of-internet -metadata/.

[70] See 50 U.S.C. 1803(i).   [71] 50 U.S.C. 1803(i)(3)(A).   [72] 50 U.S.C. 1803(j).   [73] Id.
[74] 50 U.S.C. 1803(k).

Of course, not every application will raise difficult interpretive issues. But when the government does come to the FISC with an application based on a controversial reading of the law, the assumption goes, the FISC should enter a ruling. The reforms simply try to improve the environment in which this occurs. At the very least, the thinking goes, there should be some sort of briefing on the other side in some cases. At the very least, there should be some kind of appeal, at least in some cases. And at the very least, there should be some sort of public notice of the interpretation that the FISC has adopted. The reforms accept the FISC as a hybrid between an ex parte court and a lawmaking court, and they try to create better conditions for lawmaking.

A RULE OF LENITY FOR NATIONAL SECURITY SURVEILLANCE LAW

This part introduces a different way to improve national security surveillance law. The better solution is to adopt a rule of lenity for judicial interpretations of the national security surveillance statutes. When courts interpret those laws, ambiguity should be construed in favor of the citizen and against the State. This rule would allow Congress to revisit the national security laws and decide whether to give the executive branch specific powers that it may seek. But that task properly belongs to Congress rather than the courts. Updating the surveillance laws should occur in public view with public feedback. Narrow judicial construction will encourage that dynamic by revising the role of the different branches in national security surveillance law. The Snowden disclosures revealed that the FISC has placed itself in charge. A rule of lenity would limit the role of the FISC and place the primary responsibility for rulemaking where it belongs: with the people, acting through their elected representatives.

This part makes the case for a rule of lenity in four steps. First, it introduces the rule of lenity from criminal law as an example of an interpretive rule that construes executive power narrowly. Second, it argues that Congress should borrow the basic approach of a rule of lenity from criminal law and apply it to national security surveillance law by enacting a new statute that provides interpretive guidance to the courts. Third, it explains the three major benefits of such an approach: it would encourage transparency and accountability, it places decision-making authority in the branch best suited to balance privacy and security, and it avoids the constitutional and practical difficulties with existing reform proposals. The discussion concludes by considering how the proposal would work in practice. In particular, it responds to the objection that such a proposal would make no difference because courts could simply ignore it.

The Rule of Lenity in Criminal Law

The rule of lenity is a principle of interpretation used for construing ambiguous criminal statutes. Under the rule, "ambiguity concerning the ambit of criminal statutes should be resolved in favor of lenity."[75] When the legislature has not spoken clearly as to what is punished, the rule of lenity breaks the tie in favor of the individual instead of the State.[76] Of course, where the meaning of a statute can be determined from the usual legal materials, that meaning must be adopted. But when language in criminal statutes is subject to several fair interpretations, the rule of lenity directs courts to adopt the narrow interpretation.

The rule of lenity is rooted in the separation of powers. It reflects the fundamental directive that legislatures, not courts, should have the primary role in determining what is a crime. Crimes reflect the judgment of the public as expressed through its legislature: criminal offenses are charged in the name of "The People." The rule of lenity helps ensure democratic accountability by directing courts not to engage in common law decision making about the scope of criminal conduct.[77] Of course, legislatures can revisit statutes and broaden them through the legislative process.[78] But the rule of lenity aims to ensure that the broadening reflects the public input of the legislature, not the decisions of unaccountable judges. In so doing, it limits the scope of government power to what an ordinary citizen might understand upon following the work of the legislature and reading the rules it enacts.[79]

Consider a classic example of the rule of lenity, *McBoyle* v. *United States*.[80] The defendant had transported an airplane across state lines that he knew had been stolen.[81] The government charged the defendant with interstate transportation of a "motor vehicle," a term defined by statute as "an automobile, automobile truck, automobile wagon, motor cycle, or any other self-propelled vehicle not designed for running on rails."[82] The question before the Court was whether an airplane counted as a "self-propelled vehicle not designed for running on rails" and specifically whether an airplane was a "vehicle."[83]

Writing for a unanimous Court, Justice Holmes concluded that an airplane was not a vehicle for purposes of the statute and therefore ruled in favor of the defendant.[84] As a matter of policy, Justice Holmes noted, it would be sensible to include airplanes within the statute's prohibition. Indeed, "if the legislature had thought of it," Holmes speculated, "very likely broader words would have been used."[85] But the judicial role was narrower:

Although it is not likely that a criminal will carefully consider the text of the law before he murders or steals, it is reasonable that a fair warning should be given to the world in

---

[75] Rewis v. United States, 401 U.S. 808, 812 (1971).

[76] See, e.g., United States v. Canal Barge Co., 631 F.3d 347, 353 (6th Cir. 2011).

[77] See Zachary Price, The Rule of Lenity as a Rule of Structure, 72 *Fordham L. Rev.* 885, 886 (2004).

[78] Subject to the void for vagueness doctrine, of course. See, e.g., City of Chicago v. Morales, 527 U.S. 41, 56–64 (1999).

[79] See Price, supra note 77, at 886–88.   [80] 283 U.S. 25 (1931).   [81] Id.   [82] Id. at 26.

[83] Id. at 25–26.   [84] Id. at 27.   [85] Id.

language that the common world will understand, of what the law intends to do if a certain line is passed. To make the warning fair, so far as possible the line should be clear.[86]

Justice Holmes therefore read the term "vehicle" in its more natural and common way to mean mode of transportation on land.[87] The policy question of whether airplanes should be included was left to a future Congress.

Adopting a Lenity Rule for Surveillance Law

The principle of the rule of lenity should be adapted to apply in the context of national security surveillance law. Congress should adopt a rule of narrow judicial interpretation when courts are called on to interpret the scope of government power those laws grant. Ambiguity in the scope of the national security surveillance statutes should be construed against the government. The tiebreaker should go to the individual, not the State. Under this approach, courts would be unable to engage in common law decision making designed to make policy or resolve difficult legislative questions. The hybrid FISC role would be rejected. Instead, the FISC would stay out of lawmaking and defer to Congress. If the executive concluded that the laws were out of date, it would be up to the executive to go to Congress, rather than the FISC, to seek an amendment.

A rule of lenity for national security surveillance law would distribute power properly among the branches of government, much as it does in the context of criminal law. It would reflect the fundamental directive that legislatures, not courts, should have the primary role in determining what executive branch action complies with the law. National security surveillance statutes reflect the judgment of the public as expressed through its legislature. An appropriate interpretive rule can help ensure this distribution of power by directing courts not to engage in common law decision making about the scope of surveillance powers conduct. Of course, Congress would be free to revisit statutes and broaden them through the legislative process. The President's role in proposing and approving legislation, and the recognition of his Article II authority as Commander in Chief,[88] would ensure significant influence on congressional output. But the rule of lenity would ensure that the broadening reflects the public input of the legislature, not the decisions of unaccountable judges.

The interpretive rule would be created by express statutory enactment. It could be fairly simple to draft and enact. Congress could simply pass a new

---

[86] Id.   [87] See id.

[88] U.S. Const. art. II, §2, cl. 1 ("The President shall be Commander in Chief of the Army and Navy of the United States, and of the Militia of the several States, when called into the actual Service of the United States ....").

section of Chapter 36 of Title 50, the chapter reserved for national security surveillance, along these lines:

50 U.S.C. § 1886: Rule of Lenity

The scope of government powers permitted by this chapter shall be construed narrowly.

Congress has the constitutional authority to enact such an interpretive rule. Scholars have debated whether Congress could enact principles of judicial interpretation that would apply to the entire US Code all at once.[89] Professor Tribe argues that Congress has no such authority, at least as applied prospectively, as it would allow one Congress to improperly bind future Congresses.[90] Professor Rosenkranz disagrees and argues that Congress has such power.[91] But the rule of lenity offered here avoids this debate with its specific focus. The proposed rule of lenity would govern only a single chapter of a single title of the US Code, Chapter 36 of Title 50, governing national security surveillance. Such a statute-specific provision is generally thought to be within Congress's power.[92]

Congress's interpretive rule for the Racketeer Influenced and Corrupt Organizations Act (RICO)[93] provides a helpful example. When Congress enacted RICO, it included a rule to govern its judicial interpretation: "The provisions of this title shall be liberally construed to effectuate its remedial purpose."[94] The Supreme Court has referred to this rule as RICO's "liberal-construction requirement,"[95] and it has relied on Congress's directive to dictate that RICO "is to be read broadly."[96] The Supreme Court's RICO case law has not questioned Congress's power to adopt this interpretive rule, and its cases have taken the rule seriously as a guide to judicial construction.[97]

The Criminal Appeals Act, 18 U.S.C. § 3731, contains a similar interpretive rule. The statute governs when the Justice Department can appeal an adverse ruling from a federal district court, and it includes a directive that "[t]he provisions of this section shall be liberally construed to effectuate its

---

[89] See Nicholas Quinn Rosenkranz, Federal Rules of Statutory Interpretation, 115 *Harv. L. Rev.* 2085, 2086–88 (2002) (discussing legislative power to modify canons of interpretation). An example of such a questionable interpretive rule is 15 U.S.C. §2403(c) (2012), which states that "[t]he laws, rules, regulations, and policies of the United States shall be . . . interpreted as to give full force and effect" to federal policy encouraging high productivity growth in the economy.

[90] See 1 Laurence H. Tribe, *American Constitutional Law* §2–3, at 126 n.1 (3d ed. 2000).

[91] See Rosenkranz, supra note 89, at 2115–20.

[92] See id. at 2119 n.146; see also Kent Greenawalt, *Statutory and Common Law Interpretation* 128 (2013) (concluding that such guidance should be constitutional).

[93] 18 U.S.C. §§1961–68 (2012).

[94] Organized Crime Control Act of 1970, Pub. L. No. 91-452, §904(a), 84 Stat. 922, 947 (codified as note to 18 U.S.C. §1961 [2012]).

[95] Sedima, S.P.R.L. v. Imrex Co., 473 U.S. 479, 491 n.10 (1985).　　[96] Id. at 497–98.

[97] See id.; see also Reves v. Ernst & Young, 507 U.S. 170, 183 (1993) (discussing the rule); Russello v. United States, 464 U.S. 16, 26–27 (1983) (same).

purposes."[98] As with RICO's liberal-construction requirement, the Supreme Court and lower courts have relied on this language in adopting a broad interpretation of the executive branch's power to appeal adverse rulings.[99]

Although not enacted to govern the scope of federal executive power, the statutory clear-statement rule for preemption of state laws that regulate insurance provides another example of a congressionally mandated interpretive rule that the courts have taken seriously.[100] 15 U.S.C. § 1011 states that:

Congress hereby declares that the continued regulation and taxation by the several States of the business of insurance is in the public interest, and that silence on the part of the Congress shall not be construed to impose any barrier to the regulation or taxation of such business by the several States.[101]

As interpreted by the Supreme Court, the provision directs courts not to hold state laws regulating the business of insurance to be preempted "unless a federal statute specifically requires otherwise."[102]

The liberal-construction requirements of RICO and the Criminal Appeals Act, as well as the clear-statement rule for the state preemption of insurance, provide significant precedents in favor of the lawfulness of an interpretive rule for FISA. That is especially so for the examples of RICO and the Criminal Appeals Act. If Congress can adopt interpretive rules broadening executive power, Congress should have the same power to adopt an interpretive rule that narrows executive power.

Three Benefits of a Rule of Lenity

The proposed rule of lenity offers three significant benefits. The first is democracy reinforcement. National security surveillance practices constantly change as technology advances. Technological change creates ambiguities as to the scope of government power. Some branch of government must respond to those ambiguities: either the courts or Congress or a combination of both. A rule of narrow interpretation would force the elected legislature to play the primary role of responding to technological change. It would force decisions to be made in public by legislators who are accountable to voters instead of in secret by judges with life tenure. A rule of lenity would therefore ensure more accountable and more democratic decision making in the field of national security surveillance.

---

[98] 18 U.S.C. §3731 (2012).
[99] See, e.g., Serfass v. United States, 420 U.S. 377, 387 (1975); United States v. Wolk, 466 F.2d 1143, 1146 n.2 (8th Cir. 1972).
[100] See 15 U.S.C. §1011 (2012).   [101] Id.
[102] U.S. Dep't of Treasury v. Fabe, 508 U.S. 491, 507 (1993).

The democracy-reinforcing benefit of lenity operates in large part through transparency. Under such a rule, ambiguity created by technological change would require the executive to obtain statutory approval from Congress for new powers. The request and consideration must occur in public, as the statutory surveillance laws are public laws published in the US Code.[103] Congress can then debate the executive branch's proposal, and members of the public can weigh in about how much power the executive should have. In this way, the rule of lenity fuels transparency. It enables the public to know the basic grants of authority to the executive branch, permitting a feedback loop that allows public opinion to help drive reform.

A second benefit of the proposed interpretive approach is that it would empower the branch of government best suited to balance privacy and security as technology changes.[104] As already suggested, judges are poorly suited to strike the proper balance because they struggle to understand technology.[105] Because judges also can only see issues that litigants ask them to review, they lack an institutional capacity to understand the broad contours of technological change.[106] In contrast, legislatures can hold hearings about technological change and can consult and hear from experts; they can regulate comprehensively and can readily revisit prior judgments when old technological assumptions have become outdated.[107] For these reasons, surveillance law involving new and evolving technology generally works best when Congress takes the leading role. A rule of lenity would push Congress to assume that role by directing ambiguities to be resolved legislatively instead of by judges.

The institutional advantage of Congress in the surveillance field is particularly pressing in the context of national security law. The FISC is an ex parte court staffed by trial judges.[108] The trial judges of the FISC hear only from one side, the government, and they must decide cases in secret without the advantage of amicus briefs or public commentary. Only the government can appeal. If the government makes a representation as to what rules are needed,

---

[103] The laws passed by Congress are published as the "Public Laws" of the United States. See Federal Register: About Public Law Listings, Nat'l Archives, www.archives.gov/federal-register/laws /about.html ("When a bill is signed into law by the President it is sent to the Office of the Federal Register to be assigned a law number and paginated for the *United States Statutes at Large*. Afterwards, a list of Public Laws is created, posted online, and then published in the Federal Register.").

[104] See Orin S. Kerr, The Fourth Amendment and New Technologies: Constitutional Myths and the Case for Caution, 102 *Mich. L. Rev.* 801, 805, 857–87 (2004) (discussing the "institutional limitations of judicial rulemaking" and the "significant institutional advantage" of legislatures with respect to the regulation of "criminal investigations involving new technologies").

[105] Id. at 875–82.   [106] Id. at 875–76.   [107] Id. at 875, 881–82.

[108] 50 U.S.C. §1803(a)(1) (2012) ("The Chief Justice of the United States shall publicly designate 11 district court judges from at least seven of the United States judicial circuits of whom no fewer than 3 shall reside within 20 miles of the District of Columbia who shall constitute a court which shall have jurisdiction to hear applications for and grant orders approving electronic surveillance . . . .").

the judges have no way to determine if the government's claims are true or false. This is an extraordinarily poor environment for policymaking. The FISC judges lack an effective way to determine what rules are optimal or how FISC-imposed rules work or fail to work. A rule of lenity recognizes this institutional disadvantage and ensures that the FISC does not play a significant role in making the policy choices required to determine how to balance privacy and security in new technology.

Instead of trying to improve the FISC by creating a better hybrid between an ex parte court and a regular court, a rule of lenity would limit the lawmaking power of the FISC and eliminate the need for a hybrid at all. Without substantial lawmaking powers, the FISC would not make the kinds of momentous decisions that require adversarial briefing, appellate review, and publication. By rejecting the rulemaking power of the FISC, a rule of lenity would eliminate the need for the adversarial apparatus necessary for reliable decision making based on an assumption of a hybrid court.

Predicting the Effect of a Rule of Lenity

An important counterargument to my proposal is that it might not actually work. In the criminal context, the rule of lenity often receives only lip service.[109] It is often honored only in the breach. More broadly, interpretive rules are effective only to the extent courts actually pay attention to them: Courts may simply ignore such interpretive rules or read them so narrowly as to make them irrelevant. Given these difficulties, why would we think that a rule of lenity would make a difference in the context of national security surveillance?

These are fair concerns. At the same time, I think there are three reasons to think that the statutory enactment of a rule of lenity would have a substantial effect. First, courts have relied on analogous statutory interpretive rules in the context of RICO, the Criminal Appeals Act, and federal/state preemption.[110] Indications that courts take Congress's interpretive directives seriously in those contexts suggest that they would also take such a directive seriously here. To be sure, the rule of lenity in criminal law is often ignored. But criminal law's rule of lenity is a product of judicial interpretation and background principles, not express statutory text. A statutory rule of narrow interpretation would likely have more force.

---

[109] Price, supra note 77, at 886. ("Nowadays [the rule of lenity] appears occasionally as a supplemental justification for interpretations favored on other grounds; it never stands alone to compel narrow readings."); Note, The New Rule of Lenity, 119 *Harv. L. Rev.* 2420, 2420 (2006) ("[C]ritics may explain the routine invocations of the rule of lenity as mere lip service; courts may nominally acknowledge the rule, but they find statutes to be unambiguous and therefore decline to apply it unless they would have found for the defendant on other grounds anyway.").

[110] See the section of this chapter titled "Adopting a Lenity Rule for Surveillance Law."

Second, congressional enactment of an interpretive rule would be a rebuke to the FISC. Adoption of such a rule would put FISC judges on notice that Congress had rejected its self-assumed role as a decision-making court. Some FISC judges might resist the rule of lenity to defend the court's prior decisions. But new appointments to the FISC would know that they were joining a court that Congress had directed to stay out of the policymaking sphere. The rule of lenity would stand as a congressional directive to the FISC. It would not be impossible to ignore. But it would not be easy to ignore, either.

Third, the potential significance of a rule of narrow interpretation is suggested by the FISC's apparent adoption of a contrary rule of interpretation in the first FISC opinion to allow bulk collection of metadata. In November 2013, the Office of the Director of National Intelligence published a declassified and heavily redacted FISC opinion from 2004, authored by Judge Kollar-Kotelly, that had allowed bulk collection under a part of FISA known as the pen register provisions.[111] As I have detailed elsewhere, Judge Kollar-Kotelly's opinion offered a highly implausible reading of the relevant statutory text.[112] But overlooked in the commentary on the opinion was the rule of interpretation she invented to construe FISA broadly.

In interpreting FISA, Judge Kollar-Kotelly announced that "any ambiguity" in the statutory text should be resolved in favor of the government. This was necessary, she reasoned, because a broad interpretation would "promote the purpose of Congress"[113] in enacting the USA PATRIOT Act. Several provisions of the PATRIOT Act had been designed to loosen standards of government monitoring of non-content information. Reading the pen register provisions of FISA broadly to allow bulk collection was consistent with this general purpose, leading the court to resolve ambiguity in the government's favor.

Judge Kollar-Kotelly's interpretive method tried to help Congress achieve goals that Congress had never actually considered. It used specific statutory amendments that broadened a statute in some ways to read the statute as having been broadened in other ways. But the significance of Kollar-Kotelly's rule is that she used it to support a broad reading of the statute in light of the ambiguities triggered by technological change. The appearance of such a presumption to resolve ambiguity helps emphasize the extent to which the FISC's interpretive work is based on such resolutions. Just as a broad theory

---

[111] The case name and docket number are redacted. See FISC Opinion and Order, No. PR/TT [redacted] (FISA Ct. [date redacted]) (Kollar-Kotelly, J.), available at www.dni.gov/?files/docu ments/1118/CLEANEDPRTT%201.pdf; see also Press Release, Office of the Dir. of Nat'l Intelligence, DNI Clapper Declassifies Additional Intelligence Community Documents Regarding Collection Under Section 501 of the Foreign Intelligence Surveillance Act (Nov. 18, 2013), available at www.dni.gov/?index.php/?newsroom/press-releases/191-press-releases-2013/964-dni-clapper -declassifies-additional-intelligence-community-documents-regarding-collection-under-section -501-of-the-foreign-intelligence-surveillance-act-nov (providing links to declassified intelligence community documents including FISC opinions).

[112] See Kerr, supra note 69.   [113] See FISC Opinion and Order, supra note 111, at 18.

could assist the FISC in adopting a broad interpretation, a message from Congress directing the FISC to resolve ambiguities in favor of the individual instead of the State could assist the FISC in adopting narrow interpretations in the future.

CONCLUSION

Edward Snowden's disclosures revealed the flaws in the FISC's experiment with ex parte regulation. The FISC has taken on a hybrid role, both reviewing applications and handing down long opinions interpreting the scope of executive power as technology creates ambiguity. The USA Freedom Act embraces that hybrid role. It tries to work within the role that the FISC has given itself and to improve the context of legal decision making on the assumption that the courts must interpret what the law means.

This essay has argued for a different approach. The best path is to reject the hybrid role of the FISC, not to try to improve it. Instead of encouraging the FISC to assume lawmaking powers, Congress should discourage that role by requiring the FISC to follow a rule of lenity. A rule of lenity would push lawmaking authority back to Congress where it belongs, encouraging public rule making by the body best situated to balance privacy and security. The FISC should be restored to its original role, that of an ex parte court. Such a change would not single-handedly solve the problems with national security surveillance law. But it would be a simple start that should be among the options Congress considers when it next amends the Foreign Intelligence Surveillance Act.

Index